Hebrews

THE NIV APPLICATION COMMENTARY

From biblical text . . . to contemporary life

HEBREWS

THE NIV APPLICATION COMMENTARY

From biblical text . . . to contemporary life

GEORGE H. GUTHRIE

ZONDERVAN®

GRAND RAPIDS, MICHIGAN 49530 USA

ZONDERVAN.COM/
AUTHOR**TRACKER**

ZONDERVAN®

The NIV Application Commentary: Hebrews
Copyright © 1998 by George H. Guthrie

Requests for information should be addressed to:

Zondervan, *Grand Rapids, Michigan 49530*

Library of Congress Cataloging-in-Publication Data

Guthrie, George H.
    Hebrews / George H. Guthrie.
       p. cm.—(NIV application commentary)
    Includes bibliographical references and index.
    ISBN-10: 0-310-49390-0
    ISBN-13: 978-0-310-49390-7
    1. Bible. N.T. Hebrews—Commentaries. I. Title. II. Series.
  BS 2775.3.G865 1998
  227'.87077–dc21   98–29708

This edition printed on acid-free paper.

Printed in the United States of America

07 08 09 10 11 12 • 16 15 14 13 12 11

DEDICATION

To my parents
Howard and Ida Guthrie
who taught me to love God's Word
and church from my earliest memories

Contents

7
Series Introduction

11
General Editor's Preface

13
Author's Preface

16
Abbreviations

17
Introduction

39
Outline of Hebrews

41
Annotated Bibliography

45
Text and Commentary on Hebrews

453
Scripture Index

463
Subject Index

The NIV Application Commentary Series

When complete, the NIV Application Commentary
will include the following volumes:

Old Testament Volumes

Genesis, John H. Walton
Exodus, Peter Enns
Leviticus/Numbers, Roy Gane
Deuteronomy, Daniel I. Block
Joshua, Robert L. Hubbard Jr.
Judges/Ruth, K. Lawson Younger
1-2 Samuel, Bill T. Arnold
1-2 Kings, Gus Konkel
1-2 Chronicles, Andrew E. Hill
Ezra/Nehemiah, Douglas J. Green
Esther, Karen H. Jobes
Job, Dennis R. Magary
Psalms Volume 1, Gerald H. Wilson
Psalms Volume 2, Jamie A. Grant
Proverbs, Paul Koptak
Ecclesiastes/Song of Songs, Iain Provan
Isaiah, John N. Oswalt
Jeremiah/Lamentations, J. Andrew Dearman
Ezekiel, Iain M. Duguid
Daniel, Tremper Longman III
Hosea/Amos/Micah, Gary V. Smith
Jonah/Nahum/Habakkuk/Zephaniah,
    James Bruckner
Joel/Obadiah/Malachi, David W. Baker
Haggai/Zechariah, Mark J. Boda

New Testament Volumes

Matthew, Michael J. Wilkins
Mark, David E. Garland
Luke, Darrell L. Bock
John, Gary M. Burge
Acts, Ajith Fernando
Romans, Douglas J. Moo
1 Corinthians, Craig Blomberg
2 Corinthians, Scott Hafemann
Galatians, Scot McKnight
Ephesians, Klyne Snodgrass
Philippians, Frank Thielman
Colossians/Philemon, David E. Garland
1-2 Thessalonians, Michael W. Holmes
1-2 Timothy/Titus, Walter L. Liefeld
Hebrews, George H. Guthrie
James, David P. Nystrom
1 Peter, Scot McKnight
2 Peter/Jude, Douglas J. Moo
Letters of John, Gary M. Burge
Revelation, Craig S. Keener

To see which titles are available,
visit our web site at http://www.zondervan.com

NIV Application Commentary
Series Introduction

THE NIV APPLICATION COMMENTARY SERIES is unique. Most commentaries help us make the journey from the twentieth century back to the first century. They enable us to cross the barriers of time, culture, language, and geography that separate us from the biblical world. Yet they only offer a one-way ticket to the past and assume that we can somehow make the return journey on our own. Once they have explained the *original meaning* of a book or passage, these commentaries give us little or no help in exploring its *contemporary significance*. The information they offer is valuable, but the job is only half done.

Recently, a few commentaries have included some contemporary application as *one* of their goals. Yet that application is often sketchy or moralistic, and some volumes sound more like printed sermons than commentaries.

The primary goal of the NIV Application Commentary Series is to help you with the difficult but vital task of bringing an ancient message into a modern context. The series not only focuses on application as a finished product but also helps you think through the *process* of moving from the original meaning of a passage to its contemporary significance. These are commentaries, not popular expositions. They are works of reference, not devotional literature.

The format of the series is designed to achieve the goals of the series. Each passage is treated in three sections: *Original Meaning*, *Bridging Contexts*, and *Contemporary Significance*.

THIS SECTION HELPS you understand the meaning of the biblical text in its first-century context. All of the elements of traditional exegesis—in concise form—are discussed here. These include the historical, literary, and cultural context of the passage. The authors discuss matters related to grammar and syntax, and the meaning of biblical words. They also seek to explore the main ideas of the passage and how the biblical author develops those ideas.[1]

---

1. Please note that when the authors discuss words in the original biblical languages, the series uses the general rather than the scholarly method of transliteration.

After reading this section, you will understand the problems, questions, and concerns of the *original audience* and how the biblical author addressed those issues. This understanding is foundational to any legitimate application of the text today.

THIS SECTION BUILDS a bridge between the world of the Bible and the world of today, between the original context and the contemporary context, by focusing on both the timely and timeless aspects of the text.

God's Word is *timely*. The authors of Scripture spoke to specific situations, problems, and questions. Paul warned the Galatians about the consequences of circumcision and the dangers of trying to be justified by law (Gal. 5:2–5). The author of Hebrews tried to convince his readers that Christ is superior to Moses, the Aaronic priests, and the Old Testament sacrifices. John urged his readers to "test the spirits" of those who taught a form of incipient Gnosticism (1 John 4:1–6). In each of these cases, the timely nature of Scripture enables us to hear God's Word in situations that were *concrete* rather than abstract.

Yet the timely nature of Scripture also creates problems. Our situations, difficulties, and questions are not always directly related to those faced by the people in the Bible. Therefore, God's word to them does not always seem relevant to us. For example, when was the last time someone urged you to be circumcised, claiming that it was a necessary part of justification? How many people today care whether Christ is superior to the Aaronic priests? And how can a "test" designed to expose incipient Gnosticism be of any value in a modern culture?

Fortunately, Scripture is not only timely but *timeless*. Just as God spoke to the original audience, so he still speaks to us through the pages of Scripture. Because we share a common humanity with the people of the Bible, we discover a *universal dimension* in the problems they faced and the solutions God gave them. The timeless nature of Scripture enables it to speak with power in every time and in every culture.

Those who fail to recognize that Scripture is both timely and timeless run into a host of problems. For example, those who are intimidated by timely books such as Hebrews or Galatians might avoid reading them because they seem meaningless today. At the other extreme, those who are convinced of the timeless nature of Scripture, but who fail to discern its timely element, may "wax eloquent" about the Melchizedekian priesthood to a sleeping congregation.

The purpose of this section, therefore, is to help you discern what is time-less in the timely pages of the New Testament—and what is not. For exam-ple, if Paul's primary concern is not circumcision (as he tells us in Gal. 5:6), what *is* he concerned about? If discussions about the Aaronic priesthood or Melchizedek seem irrelevant today, what is of abiding value in these passages? If people try to "test the spirits" today with a test designed for a specific first-century heresy, what other biblical test might be more appropriate?

Yet this section does not merely uncover that which is timeless in a pas-sage but also helps you to see *how* it is uncovered. The author of the com-mentary seeks to take what is implicit in the text and make it explicit, to take a process that normally is intuitive and explain it in a logical, orderly fash-ion. How do we know that circumcision is not Paul's primary concern? What clues in the text or its context help us realize that Paul's real concern is at a deeper level?

Of course, those passages in which the historical distance between us and the original readers is greatest require a longer treatment. Conversely, those passages in which the historical distance is smaller or seemingly nonex-istent require less attention.

One final clarification. Because this section prepares the way for dis-cussing the contemporary significance of the passage, there is not always a sharp distinction or a clear break between this section and the one that fol-lows. Yet when both sections are read together, you should have a strong sense of moving from the world of the Bible to the world of today.

THIS SECTION ALLOWS the biblical message to speak with as much power today as it did when it was first written. How can you apply what you learned about Jerusalem, Ephesus, or Corinth to our present-day needs in Chicago, Los Angeles, or London? How can you take a message originally spoken in Greek and Aramaic and communicate it clearly in our own language? How can you take the eternal truths originally spoken in a different time and culture and apply them to the similar-yet-dif-ferent needs of our culture?

In order to achieve these goals, this section gives you help in several key areas.

First, it helps you identify contemporary situations, problems, or questions that are truly comparable to those faced by the original audience. Because contemporary situations are seldom identical to those faced in the first cen-tury, you must seek situations that are analogous if your applications are to be relevant.

Second, this section explores a variety of contexts in which the passage might be applied today. You will look at personal applications, but you will also be encouraged to think beyond private concerns to the society and culture at large.

Third, this section will alert you to any problems or difficulties you might encounter in seeking to apply the passage. And if there are several legitimate ways to apply a passage (areas in which Christians disagree), the author will bring these to your attention and help you think through the issues involved.

In seeking to achieve these goals, the contributors to this series attempt to avoid two extremes. They avoid making such specific applications that the commentary might quickly become dated. They also avoid discussing the significance of the passage in such a general way that it fails to engage contemporary life and culture.

Above all, contributors to this series have made a diligent effort not to sound moralistic or preachy. The NIV Application Commentary Series does not seek to provide ready-made sermon materials but rather tools, ideas, and insights that will help you communicate God's Word with power. If we help you to achieve that goal, then we have fulfilled the purpose for this series.

—The Editors

General Editor's Preface

PERHAPS NO ISSUE PERPLEXES the modern church more than why baby boomers don't go to church. Even if you factor in the return of many such families when children arrive and parents decide to get them "churched," the baby boomers qualify as the modern church's lost generation.

A popular way to analyze this problem is to bring all the power of the social sciences to bear. Mailed surveys, demographic analyses, and personal interviews have provided researchers with a wealth of information. The result has been user-friendly services complete with new formats, positive messages, and relevant preaching styles. Much of this is useful.

But it is just possible that the best thing to do would be for every church member to read and study the message of Hebrews. As George Guthrie shows in the pages that follow, Hebrews was written to immature Christians who were tempted to fall away from church attendance and returned to their pre-Christian lifestyle. It was written to "encourage discouraged believers drifting away from real Christianity by bolstering commitment to draw near to God and to endure in commitment to Christ," and it was "especially relevant for those tempted to turn from Christianity or Christian fellowship to preconversion patterns of life." Sounds like the baby-boomer church attendance problem may not be as unique as we sometimes think.

The real issue, of course, is to take a close look at what the unknown author of Hebrews prescribes to the early church to deal with this situation. No social science here! In fact, the prescription is almost pure theology. The message of Hebrews can be summed up in a single phrase: "God speaks effectively to us through Jesus." If we can just unpack those seven words of all their theological meaning, we have a way to approach baby boomers (and Generation Xers, and whoever else) with the message of the gospel that will demand a hearing.

God speaks. First-century people had trouble with the idea that only one God spoke to them. Twenty-first century people have trouble with the idea that any God would speak to them. The secularizing of the twentieth century has done its work. This thinking is not the work of spiritual skepticism so much as the work of distributing any spirituality that is not generated by our human desires and abilities. We want to do it our way, and in the process we forget to listen for the voice of God. God speaks.

Effectively. God's voice is not a crying in the wilderness, a spitting in the wind. It is effective. First-century people believed the gods made a difference;

twenty-first century people cannot believe it. When George Gallup asks Americans if they think their religion can help solve the world's problems, most say no. The author of Hebrews says yes.

To us. As self-centered as twenty-first century people are, there is still a doubt that a God (if one exists) would speak (if we could hear) in such a way that makes a difference in solving the world's problems. God speaks to me? But that is part of Hebrews' message: We are the target audience of God's effective speaking.

Through Jesus. The key to understanding the message of Hebrews is to recognize that in Jesus, God's unique Son, we have the ultimate solution to the world's problems. Jesus is how God has chosen to act once and for all. Jesus is superior to the priests, the prophets, the law. A Jesus-less gospel is a gospel deserving rejection. Without Jesus we should sleep in on Sunday morning. With Jesus, nothing should keep us from our Sunday morning pew.

These seven words and four ideas are what the author of Hebrews used to communicate gospel truth to a generation on the verge of throwing it all away. These seven words and four ideas have the same power to heal today— the power to save us from our sins (even baby boomers).

—Terry C. Muck

Author's Preface

SEVERAL YEARS AGO, while traveling on a rainy day to speak at a youth conference in the Northeast, I had a brief layover in a small airport. I struck up a conversation with a middle-aged man who told me about his family, occupation, and the purpose of his trip. Then, between sips of coffee, I informed him about the conference at which I would be speaking over the next two days and my work as a graduate student in seminary. Since he was a committed Christian layman, he was delighted to hear about my ministry and studies. We even found that we shared a common background as members of Baptist churches.

When I mentioned that I was working on a master's thesis, the gentleman inquired about my topic. My response—that I was working on the book of Hebrews—brought a pained expression to his face. He somewhat apologetically told me he had never really studied that book and, in fact, was quite intimidated by it. He had always gotten lost in the twists and turns of Hebrews' theology, in obscure people (like Melchizedek) and figures of speech, and in the seeming lack of a clear development in the argument. Furthermore, whatever preaching he had heard on Hebrews had been limited to no more than a smattering of sermons on some of its more familiar texts.

Here was an educated, committed Christian who had never had any meaningful interaction with one of the most meaning-*full* books of the New Testament. That bothered me a great deal. My own study of Hebrews had revealed a discourse of immense power, beauty, and challenge. The fruits of that study had already had a profound impact on both my mind and my heart and had convinced me that the message of the book is greatly needed by today's church.

Since that encounter over a decade ago, an approximation of this conversation has recurred from time to time. People delight in asking what my wife and I have come to call *the question*: "Who do you think wrote Hebrews?" Yet dialogue too often ends there. When in my classes on "Hebrews and the General Epistles" I ask my students how many of them have ever heard a series of exegetical messages from the book, few hands go up. Yet, here is a book with so much to offer the modern church!

In fairness to all of us who have struggled with the complex orchestration of ideas in Hebrews, the book, while resonating with power, beauty, and theological depth, appears enigmatic upon a surface reading. William Barclay once wrote, "When we come to read the *Letter to the Hebrews* we come to read what is, for the person of today, the most difficult book in the whole New Testament."[1] To enter emotionally and intellectually into the author's discourse is like encountering a conversation in a foreign language of which you have only partial knowledge, or like entering a game without knowing all the rules. However, we can receive great help in studying the author's own conventions used in crafting the work. Once his methods and patterns of thinking are clarified, we will begin to feel more at home in Hebrews' thought-world and can benefit from its message.

In recent years I considered writing a commentary that would attempt to clarify the message of Hebrews for pastors and laypeople and, therefore, facilitate the preaching and teaching of this "word of exhortation." So it is with great gratitude to the editors of the NIV Application Commentary Series that I have taken up this task. I believe in the importance of exegetical study and preaching for the health of God's church, and, therefore, I believe in the intention of this commentary series. Not only is it a singular honor to join the enterprise, but I have been enriched by the time spent in reflection and writing, stretching as I have attempted to move responsibly from the ancient context to our own.

I must say a special word of thanks to Scot McKnight, who suggested my participation to Zondervan and whose other volumes in this series have provided challenging and stimulating examples to follow. Dr. Louise Bentley, teacher par excellence and a master editor, dealt with large sections of material in the initial manuscript before it ever reached the editors at Zondervan. In addition to mundane matters such as sentence structure and organization, Dr. Bentley provided gracious encouragement and meaningful comments on content. The general editor, Terry Muck, and Marianne Meye Thompson, a consulting editor for the New Testament volumes, both performed their work admirably, keeping me on track at numerous points by asking penetrating questions. Jack Kuhatschek and Verlyn Verbrugge, editors at Zondervan, also provided welcomed encouragement at key moments in the work, and both have become good friends in the process. I also appreciate the encouragement from Carol Kragt, an unofficial "editor" who has been enthusiastic about the book in its prepublication form.

As always, my colleagues at Union University, including the Christian Studies faculty, members of the broader faculty, the librarians, and the university's administration, have provided encouragement each in their own ways. Kathi Glidewell specifically rendered service by typing the subject index. It is a joy to work in an environment that is both rigorously academic

---

1. William Barclay, *The Letter to the Hebrews* (Philadelphia: Westminster, 1957), ix.

and unashamedly committed to Christ and his "unshakable kingdom" (Heb. 12:28–29). I have also asked for prayer for this project time and again from friends around the world but especially those at Northbrook Church, to which my family and I have belonged since that community's establishment in 1993. For the sincerity and effectiveness of those prayers I am deeply grateful.

As always, my dear wife has encouraged me beyond the call of duty, ministering to me in the midst of our joint ministry to others. In the process of writing we remodeled a house, had a lovely second child, Anna, and saw our number one, Joshua, outgrow several series of clothing. Through it all Pat has maintained a beautiful spirit of vision and fun. She is my dearest friend and my most cherished partner in life. I especially enjoyed our tea-time conversations on the "Bridging Contexts" and "Contemporary Significance" sections of this volume.

—George H. Guthrie
Christmas, 1997

Abbreviations

AB	Anchor Bible
AJBA	*Australian Journal of Biblical Archaeology*
BDF	Blass-Debrunner-Funk, *A Greek Grammar of the New Testament and Other Early Christian Literature*
Bib	*Biblica*
BibSac	*Bibliotheca Sacra*
BJRL	*Bulletin of the John Rylands Library*
BZ	*Biblische Zeitschrift*
CJT	*Canadian Journal of Theology*
DLNT	*Dictionary of the Later New Testament and Its Developments*
EBC	*Expositor's Bible Commentary*
EDNT	*Exegetical Dictionary of the New Testament*
EDT	*Evangelical Dictionary of Theology*
IBS	*Irish Biblical Studies*
ICC	International Critical Commentary
KEKNT	Kritisch-exegetischer Kommentar über das Neue Testament
NIV	New International Version
NICNT	New International Commentary on the New Testament
NIGTC	New International Greek Testament Commentary
NovT	*Novum Testamentum*
NovTSup	Supplements to Novum Testamentum
NTS	*New Testament Studies*
SB	Sources bibliques
SBLDS	Society of Biblical Literature Dissertation Series
SBLMS	Society of Biblical Literature Monograph Series
ScrHier	Scripta hierasolymitana
SNTU	*Studien für die Neue Testament Umwelt*
SJT	*Scottish Journal of Theology*
SwJT	*Southwestern Journal of Theology*
TNTC	Tyndale New Testament Commentaries
TrinJ	*Trinity Journal*
TynBul	*Tyndale Bulletin*
WBC	Word Biblical Commentary
WTJ	*Westminster Journal of Theology*
ZNW	*Zeitschrift für die neutestamentliche Wissenschaft*

Introduction

Antonius sat alone in a deteriorating second-story apartment located in a slum on the slope of Esquiline hill in Rome. As rain pelted the age-worn wall outside, a plate of bread and vegetables and a cup of sour wine rested on the make-shift table. The room had turned dark with the coming of this storm, and Antonius lit a small oil lamp against the gloom. With the light, hungry roaches materialized, scampering to the dark safety of cracks in the wall. In the apartment next door a baby cried, and the infant's father screamed obscenities at the infant's mother. An urgent conversation rose and then faded as an unseen pair of business partners walked down the stairs. Somewhere in the muddy street below a unit of Roman soldiers marched past, driven under sharp orders from its commander. Antonius sat alone, thinking.

That morning his employer, a rough, burly fellow named Brutus, once again turned from the task of pricing fruits and vegetables to ridicule this young Christian. The verbal jabs had become as annoying as gnats darting to and fro in the shop's pungent air. Brutus was big, obnoxious, and cruel. Antonius cringed against the man's emotional blows, wishing he could strike back out of his hurt and embarrassment. Each time he "turned the other cheek" it received a slap in kind. Yet, he bit his lip, nursed his wounded pride, and again asked the Lord's forgiveness for his thoughts.

Persecution of the church in Rome had yet to result in martyrdom, but since the expulsion of Jews under the Emperor Claudius, Christians had continued to be harassed to various degrees by both Jews and pagans. Upon the expulsion some had suffered imprisonment, beatings, and the seizure of their properties. That was almost fifteen years ago now. Antonius had not been part of the Christian church at that time but had heard about the conflict. In fact his own grandfather, ruler of the Synagogue of the Augustenses, had been one of the most outspoken opponents of the Christians. When at seventeen Antonius converted to Christianity, the old man almost died, declaring Antonius dead in a shouting match that ended in tears and a tattered relationship.

In recent months abuse of the church had escalated with the amused approval of the emperor himself, and now emotional fatigue was taking its toll. Footsteps in the hall; a scream in the night; meaningless events that, nevertheless, set Antonius's heart racing. He had been told the cost of following the Messiah, but somehow his experience was different than he expected. In the beginning he thought his joy would never be broken, that he would always feel the presence of God. He had been taught that the Lord, the righteous Judge, would vindicate his new covenant people. Did not the Scriptures, speaking of the Messiah, say that God had put "all things in subjection under his feet"? But the church had taken a great beating lately, and members of its various house-groups had become discouraged and were questioning whether Christ was really in control. In their hearts they wondered if God had closed his ears against their cries for relief. Some, in their disillusionment, doubted and left the church altogether.

Antonius Bardavid remembered the traditions of the synagogue and the support of the Jewish community, the joy of the festivals, and the solemn celebrations of the Jewish calendar. He appreciated the fellowship of Christ's community, but genuinely missed the traditions of his ancestors—and he missed members of his family. He watched them from a distance as they walked together to market by the Tiber River. Some of them still would not speak to him and passed him on the street as they would a Gentile. That was difficult, and today his loneliness closed in around him like a dark, damp blanket.

To make matters worse he was one of the poorer members of the church. When Antonius became a Christian, he lost his job as a tailor's apprentice in the Jewish quarter. He now spent his days sorting rotting produce, sweeping the floor, swatting flies, and receiving orders from obnoxious Roman slaves shopping for rich mistresses. He stooped so low as to take pieces of rotten fruit home to supplement his meager food supply. Even rich men's slaves fared better. Earlier in the week, Gaius, the kitchen slave of an equestrian who lived in the area, tossed him a handful of over-ripe figs saying, "Here, Christian! Change your cannibalistic diet by taking a bit of good fruit." Laughter hung with the gnats in the air. To be poor and a Christian invited double portions of ridicule.

Antonius had missed the weekly meal and worship for the past two weeks, and his heart had cooled somewhat toward the little house-group. A spiritual itch in the back of his spirit warned him, cautioning him concerning his loss of perspective; yet, in recent days he had begun to snuff such thoughts from his mind as quickly as they came. Antonius's bitterness over his current circumstances was growing and slowly obscuring the Truth.

That night the believers were to meet for worship and encouragement. Rumor had it the leaders had received a document from back east somewhere. Although discouraged and tempted to skip the meeting again, Antonius's curiosity was aroused, and he decided to travel the short distance to the neighborhood house at which the fellowship was to meet. Entering the gathering room, he spoke greetings to several friends, who also looked tired from the day's work. The hostess offered something to drink and friendly banter, but dejection hung like a cloud over the room. When the meal was finished, the group's leader, a good and godly man of almost seventy years, finally arrived. Joseph was a bit out of breath, having come from a meeting with the other leaders half way across the city. He was visibly moved as he stood smiling before the group of about twenty, his hands shaking slightly from advancing age. After a few words of introduction Joseph took a deep breath and explained he had talked the other leaders into allowing his group the first reading of the scroll. With a twinkle in his eye the elder said, "I believe you will find this quite relevant." He unrolled the first part of the parchment and began reading with vigor: "In the past God spoke to our forefathers through the prophets at many times and in various ways, but in these last days he has spoken to us by his Son. . . ."

Discouragement. What believer through the ages, at one time or another, has not felt its numbing grip pulling him or her toward the mire of self-pity and despair? Life, and thus the Christian life, is fraught with trials that suck the emotional winds from our sails. When discouragement comes—the kind of discouragement that screams questions at the faith—we need encouragement and perspective; we need the community of faith; we need help to stay the course of commitment. Hebrews was written to offer such help.

Commentators have had to write tentatively concerning issues of background when it comes to this wonderfully complex document. As William L. Lane notes, "Hebrews is a delight for the person who enjoys puzzles."[1] The author simply left us little in the way of overt remarks on his own context and the context of the recipients. Yet, like a Sherlock Holmes mystery, clues in the text lead the interested investigator to feasible conclusions. Although fictitious, the account of our young man Antonius may not be far from the actual setting behind the book of Hebrews.

The Setting, Purpose, and Date of Hebrews

THE ORIGINAL HEARERS. The original recipients of this New Testament book had a rich background in Jewish worship and thought. Several dynamics in the text point to the conclusion that the first audience came out of a setting oriented to Jewish thought and worship. (1) The author assumes his audience has an extensive knowledge of the Old Testament. Of all the writings of the New Testament, none is more saturated with overt references to the Old Testament.[2] The author so filled his discourse with Old Testament thoughts and passages that they permeate every chapter. Thirty-five quotations from a Greek[3] translation of the Old Testament and thirty-four allusions work to support the development of Hebrews' argument. In addition, the writer offers nineteen summaries of Old Testament material, and thirteen times he mentions an Old Testament name or topic, often without reference to a specific context.

(2) The author uses theological concepts that were popular in the Greek-speaking synagogues of the first century. These include a veneration of Moses as one having special access to God (3:1–6), angels as the mediators of the

---

1. William L. Lane, *Hebrews 1–8*, WBC (Dallas: Word, 1991), xlvii.

2. Revelation rivals Hebrews on the extent to which the Old Testament is used, but the material is packaged quite differently than in Hebrews, the author primarily alluding to Old Testament material in his statements and imagery. On the uses of the Old Testament in Hebrews see George H. Guthrie, "The Old Testament in Hebrews," *DLNT*, 841–50; George B. Caird, "The Exegetical Method of the Epistle to the Hebrews," *CJT* 5 (1959): 44–51; J. C. McCullough, "The Old Testament Quotations in Hebrews," *NTS* 26 (1979–80): 363–79.

3. The author's Old Testament text was the Greek translation commonly referred to as the Septuagint. In Palestine and the East, synagogues often used the Hebrew text with an oral translation in Aramaic, although Hellenistic synagogues of the area certainly used the Greek. Use of the Greek translation predominated in the synagogues of Diaspora Judaism. See F. F. Bruce, *New Testament History* (Garden City: Anchor Books, 1972), 144.

older covenant revelation (2:1–4), and references to the divine Wisdom's role in creation (1:1–4).[4]

(3) A potential danger to this community seems to lie in the temptation to reject Christianity and return to Judaism proper. Although some scholars have taken these insights to indicate a thoroughly Jewish audience for Hebrews, one must remember that many Gentiles affiliated themselves with first-century synagogues, either as proselytes or God-fearers. Consequently, some Gentiles came to Christ with a rich background in Jewish worship and extensive knowledge of the Jewish Scriptures. Therefore, the exact mix of Jews and Gentiles in this church group must remain a mystery. However, prior to accepting Christ the worship orientation of these believers had been to the synagogue.

The believers addressed by Hebrews probably constituted a house church, or group of house churches, in or near the city of Rome. Tradition has it that in 753 B.C., about the same time the Hebrew visionary Amos hurled his sermons against the northern kingdom of Israel, a man named Romulus established a small settlement on the banks of the Tiber River. This event could not have had more far-reaching historical significance. By the mid-first century A.D. the city of Rome would boast a population of over one million and lead an empire spanning continents. Living among its citizens were between forty and sixty thousand Jews, whose community had formed a significant segment of Roman society for over one hundred years.[5] Many were Roman citizens, spoke Greek, and had Greek names, although, as with our fictitious friend Antonius, they often gave Latin names to their offspring.[6] Acts 2:10 reports that among those at the first preaching of the gospel were Jews from Rome; it is likely that some of these converted to Christianity and returned to the empire's capital, establishing the church there.

Although a number of destinations for the book of Hebrews have been suggested,[7] Rome seems the most likely, based on available evidence. (1) In Hebrews 13:24 the author addresses the audience with these words: "Those from Italy send you their greetings." This phrase is ambiguous in Greek. However, in the New Testament the phrase "from Italy" occurs in Acts 18:2, referring to Aquila and Priscilla. This husband and wife team was residing in Corinth,

---

4. Lane, *Hebrews 1–8*, liv–lv.

5. The Jewish community in Rome had largely been established when, in 62 B.C., Pompey brought Jewish captives back to the city after taking Jerusalem. Many of these were subsequently freed and made Roman citizens. See James D. G. Dunn, *Romans 1–8*, WBC (Dallas: Word, 1988), xlv–xlvi.

6. Bruce, *New Testament History*, 137.

7. For a wide variety of reasons scholars have set forth Jerusalem, Samaria, Caesarea, Colosse, Cyprus, Alexandria, or even Spain. See Bruce, *The Epistle to the Hebrews*, 10–14.

Luke tells us, and, with other Jews, had been expelled "from Italy" (i.e., Rome) at the decree of Claudius.[8] Therefore, a likely interpretation of Hebrews 13:24 is that people from Rome, now residing elsewhere, were sending greetings back to the believers in Rome via the document we know as Hebrews.

(2) Whereas pastors in the Christian communities were normally referred to as "elders" or "overseers," in Hebrews alone among the New Testament documents they are called "leaders" (*hegoumenoi*) (13:7, 17, 24). Outside the New Testament this designation for church leadership occurs in two early Christian documents, *1 Clement* and *The Shepherd of Hermas*, both of which we know to have been associated with the church at Rome.

(3) *First Clement*, a pastoral letter written from Clement of Rome to the church at Corinth sometime around the end of the first century, demonstrates extensive use of Hebrews. One section in particular (36:1–6) shows direct literary dependence on the book, and the rest of the document bears the marks of Hebrews' influence. Therefore, the earliest evidence of Hebrews' use in the ancient church locates the document in Rome.

Members of this church were becoming discouraged about Christian commitment. Especially from the exhortation sections,[9] we see reflected in Hebrews a community of believers who were struggling against spiritual lethargy, which, if not addressed, could lead them to abandoning their Christian confession. In 2:1–4 the preacher warns them against drifting from the Christian message, reminding them of the consequences of disobedience. He challenges them to faithfulness with the positive example of Jesus in 3:1–6 and with the negative example of those who fell in the desert in 3:7–4:2. In 4:3–11 the hearers are encouraged to consider the promise of eschatological rest, and, in 4:12–13, they are warned of the penetrating, powerful, judging word of God.

The writer to the Hebrews then challenges his readers to hold fast their Christian confession (4:14; 10:23) and describes his audience as spiritually immature, even though their Christian experience should have borne more fruit, given the length of their experience (5:11–6:3). In 6:4–8 he again offers warning through a negative example—in this case those who have already fallen away from the community of Christian faith. He then offers encouragement via his confidence in them and the confidence they should have in the promises of God (6:9–20).

These believers should not abandon their constant fellowship with one another but should be mutual sources of encouragement and stimulation to

---

8. On the edict of Claudius see Lane, *Hebrews 1–8*, lxiii–lxvi.

9. For a discussion of the interplay between exhortation and exposition in Hebrews see below, pp. 27–30 .

Christian commitment (10:24–25). The writer gives harsh warning of the judgment awaiting those who turn away from God (10:26–31), then holds before them the positive example of their own past commitment (10:32–39). The theme of endurance holds together the exhortation from 10:32 through 12:17. He offers an "example list" in Hebrews 11, demonstrating the effectiveness of a life of faith through Old Testament persons who found pleasure with God. Jesus again plays the role of positive example in 12:1–2, and the hearers are encouraged to bear up under God's discipline as that offered by a father to his children (12:3–13). A negative example is Esau, who sold his birthright to satisfy an earthly appetite (12:14–17).

These exhortations to persevere in Christian faith climax with the highly stylized contrast between two mountains—Sinai, a place of terror, and Zion, a place of promise (12:18–24). The preacher presents, in 12:26–29, a final harsh warning against neglecting divine revelation. Finally, with the last chapter of Hebrews, he offers numerous practical considerations for the community, including the exhortations not to "be carried away by all kinds of strange teachings" (13:9), to bear "the disgrace he bore" (13:13), and to "not forget to do good and to share with others" (13:16).

The exhortation sections of Hebrews, therefore, reveal a community of Christian believers, some of whom were wavering in their devotion to Christ. Their experience of persecution and an increasingly blurred picture of Jesus and the Christian faith had led to a further drifting from right thinking and right living. They were in need of perseverance in the things of God so that they might experience the full measure of his promises. This is our author's challenge: *to encourage a group of discouraged believers drifting from real Christianity by bolstering their commitment to draw near to God and to endure in commitment to Christ.*

Date of writing. If a Roman destination accurately interprets the evidence concerning the provenance of Hebrews, several points concerning the present circumstance of the audience help to narrow the date of writing. (1) They had been Christians for a while. In Hebrews 5:11–6:3 the preacher rebukes the hearers' immaturity, an immaturity unreasonably prolonged considering the amount of time since their entrance to the Christian community. (2) According to 10:32–34 these believers had faced and persevered in a time of serious persecution in the past. (3) They had yet to suffer martyrdom for the faith (12:4) but were now facing a more severe time of trial (11:35–12:3; 12:7; 13:3, 12–13), in which some of their number were defecting.

Although dating most of the New Testament literature is a difficult endeavor, with any propositions considered tentative, the situation indicated by the data above suggests Hebrews was written in the mid-60s A.D., just prior to the extreme persecution of the Roman church under Nero. At this point the Roman church had been in existence for about three decades. The conflict with Jews and the government in A.D. 49, which led to the expulsion by Claudius, would account for the earlier time of testing experienced by this community (10:32–39). Also, Nero's rising threat to the church accounts for the fear of death and the waning of commitment indicated in Hebrews.[10]

Authorship

WHO, THEN, WAS the Christian minister called on by God to meet this exacting challenge? Few questions concerning the New Testament have fostered more curiosity and fewer firm answers than the query, "Who wrote the book of Hebrews?" This popular question has raised speculation since the second century, because Hebrews provides no personal introduction of the author to his audience. Earliest suggestions included such noteworthy people as Paul, Luke, Clement of Rome, and Barnabas. More recent proposals set forth Priscilla,[11] Jude, Apollos, Philip, and Silvanus.[12] As with other matters of background we are almost entirely dependent on evidence internal to the book. So, what does the work reveal of its maker?

---

10. Lane, *Hebrews 1–8*, lxvi.

11. Adolph von Harnack made the interesting suggestion that Priscilla may have penned Hebrews. However, referring to himself, the author uses a masculine singular pronoun at 11:32, which seems to rule out the possibility. The position has been taken up more recently by Ruth Hoppin, *Priscilla: Author of the Epistle to the Hebrews, and Other Essays* (New York: Exposition, 1969).

12. The question of Pauline authorship has been answered with a resounding "no" from virtually all modern scholars, regardless of theological orientation. In the first centuries of the Christian church the fathers were of mixed opinion on the matter. In the Eastern branch of the church, focused in Alexandria, several early thinkers associated Hebrews with the Pauline corpus, an opinion that dominated the East following the second century. Yet, even Clement of Alexandria (c. A.D. 150–215) and Origen (A.D. 185–215), leaders of the Alexandrian school, acknowledged that the style of this book differs sharply from Paul. In the West, focused in Rome, the church fathers felt the book did not originate with Paul. Several dynamics in the text mitigate strongly against seeing Paul as the author of Hebrews. Foreign to Paul's literature are many of the images (e.g., the nautical pictures of a ship in 2:1 and an anchor in 6:19), theological motifs (especially the high priest theme), and vocabulary of Hebrews (169 terms found in Hebrews occur nowhere else in the New Testament). In addition, the author uses different formulae to introduce quotes from the Old Testament. Perhaps most telling, the author of Hebrews describes himself as one who received the gospel tradition from the original witnesses (2:3), a perspective uncharacteristic of Paul (cf. Rom. 1:1; 1 Cor. 15:8; Gal. 1:11–16).

For general overviews of the authorship question see Lane, *Hebrews 1–8*, xlix–li; Harold Attridge *The Epistle to the Hebrews*, Hermeneia (Philadelphia: Fortress, 1989), 1–6; Paul Ellingworth *The Epistle to the Hebrews: A Commentary on the Greek Text*, NIGTC (Grand Rapids: Eerdmans 1993), 3–21; F. F. Bruce, *The Epistle to the Hebrews*, NICNT, rev. ed. (Grand Rapids: Eerdmans, 1990), 14–20.

The author of Hebrews was a dynamic preacher. By the first century the synagogue had become the center of Jewish social and religious culture throughout the Mediterranean world; the climax of synagogue worship was exposition of the Scriptures.[13] Homilies focused on the interpretation of Old Testament texts, the preacher quoting or alluding to a passage and then commenting on its various words or phrases. Often other passages were brought to the discussion, based on a common word or phrase.[14] The preacher also interspersed his message with exhortations to the congregation.

It is widely recognized that Hebrews begins like a sermon rather than a letter. In addition to its introduction, this New Testament book has numerous affinities with ancient sermons associated with the Greek-speaking synagogues of the day.[15] At 13:22 the author himself calls the document a "word [or message] of exhortation" (*tou logou tes parakleseos*), a designation used elsewhere to refer to a sermon. For example, Paul and Barnabas were offered an opportunity to preach at a synagogue in Pisidian Antioch: "On the Sabbath they entered the synagogue and sat down. After the reading from the Law and the Prophets, the synagogue rulers sent word to them, saying 'Brothers, if you have a message of encouragement (*logos parakleseos*) for the people, please speak'" (Acts 13:14–15). The phrase is the same as in Hebrews 13:22, with the exception that the Acts passage omits the articles.[16] Therefore, the author of Hebrews crafted his work in the form of a first-century sermon. In fact, it may be our earliest and most complete sermon addressed to an established Christian community. By any informed estimation, Hebrews, with its striking rhetorical power and elegance, ranks among the greatest homiletical achievements of all time.

The author of Hebrews was knowledgeable of the Old Testament and its interpretation. We have already noted the author's extensive use of the Old Testament in our treatment of his audience.[17] As mentioned there, he fills his sermon with a mixture of allusions to and quotations of Old Testament

---

13. F. F. Bruce, *New Testament History*, 143–44. Here Bruce notes the general pattern of synagogue services in the New Testament era. The service started with the call to worship and the recitation of both the *Shema*, with associated benedictions, and the Decalogue. Prayers and benedictions followed, along with the reading of the Law and the Prophets. The service culminated with an exposition of Old Testament texts and concluded with a blessing.

14. For an example of this in Hebrews see below, pp. 149, 152, 159.

15. In a 1955 study Hartwig Thyen demonstrated numerous characteristics Hebrews shares with synagogue sermons of the same era. See *Der Stil des jüdisch-hellenistischen Homilie* (Göttingen: Vandenhoeck & Ruprecht, 1955). For a more accessible treatment see William L. Lane, "Hebrews: A Sermon in Search of a Setting," *SWJT* 28 (1985): 13–18.

16. In Hebrews 13 the author refers to a specific message (the book he has just written), which calls for use of the definite article. The statement by the synagogue leaders mentioned in Acts 13 is indefinite since a specific message is not in view.

17. See above, p. 19.

texts. We must remember that the "Bible" our author had in hand was a collection of scrolls. He did not have the benefit of chapter and verse demarcation or of a cross-referencing system. What he did have was a cultural heritage that emphasized the memorization of the Scriptures. His copious use of the Old Testament reveals a mind saturated with the Word of God and a heart committed to that Word as bearing the utmost authority. With other teachers of first-century, Greek-speaking synagogues, the author of Hebrews most often presents the Scriptures as falling from the lips of God.

Just as modern preachers are taught methods of interpretation, rabbis of the first century used commonly held perspectives on how a text should be interpreted. As the author of Hebrews expounds the Scriptures, he does so utilizing a number of these hermeneutical techniques. Especially two principles, *verbal analogy* and *an argument from lesser to greater*, play significant roles in the development of Hebrews. The former refers to an interpreter's utilization of one passage to explain another in light of a term or phrase the two have in common. The latter principle is based on the assumption that what applies in a lesser situation certainly applies in a more important situation.[18] Our author uses these and other techniques with deftness and acumen.

Therefore, the author of Hebrews may be said to have been a gifted expositor, thoroughly versed in the Old Testament and trained in the homiletical skills of the synagogue of his day. Communicating the Word of God to his audience, he was passionate about the authority and relevance of the Old Testament and convinced of its central role in exhorting his fellow believers to remain faithful to Christ.

The author of Hebrews was highly educated. In the ancient world when students went for advanced education, they studied rhetoric, and it seems clear this author had extensive academic training in the subject.

> What he learned—the sign, in his culture, of an educated man—was a formal and highly stylized means of self-expression and argumentation. What his peers would look for as the mark of his attainment was his ability to handle extremely traditional forms of speech and thought in a manner that formally adhered to the rules [of rhetoric] but, within these boundaries, found something interesting to say. These are indeed the traits of an "Alexandrian" art; our own age, in the grip of a very different set of artistic canons, finds them almost impossible to appreciate.[19]

---

18. See especially Richard Longenecker, *Biblical Exegesis in the Apostolic Period* (Grand Rapids: Eerdmans, 1975), 158–85; E. Earle Ellis, *Paul's Use of the Old Testament* (Grand Rapids: Baker, 1981). For examples of the uses of these techniques in Hebrews see below, pp. 67–68, 84–85.

19. Michael Grant and Rachel Kitzinger, eds., *Civilization of the Ancient Mediterranean Greece and Rome* (New York: Charles Scribner's Sons, 1988), 2:1099–1100.

For example, in the book's first four verses, which one commentator has called the most perfect Greek sentence in the New Testament,[20] the author of Hebrews uses periodic style (a crafted configuration of clauses and phrases that concludes with a majestic ending), effectiveness, compactness, contrast, poetic structure, omissions, figures, repetition (alliteration), and rhythm—all features extolled in the rhetorical handbooks of the day.[21] His use of the Greek language ranks at the top of New Testament authors; his rich vocabulary reveals the background of one widely read.

Some have associated the author with the intellectual culture of Alexandria, a focal point for rhetorical education in the Roman world, because of his use of terminology also found in the works of Philo of Alexandria and *Wisdom of Solomon*. However, these works probably enjoyed great exposure throughout Greek-speaking Judaism and may not indicate a specific geographical location.[22] What is certain is that our writer brought numerous skills gained through advanced education to his task.

The author of Hebrews was a committed minister of Jesus Christ and deeply concerned about the spiritual state of the group of believers he addressed. Drawing on his tremendous training in Old Testament thought, homiletics, and rhetoric, the author joins these to his understanding of the Christian tradition[23] to carry out the pastoral ministry of encouraging a group of believers to stay the course of Christian commitment. He seems to have a detailed knowledge of the congregation's past and present situations (e.g., 10:32–34; 13:7–24) and, through the urgency of his message, communicates a deep concern for them.[24]

The discussion above offers a basic portrait of the preacher-minister-rhetor who wrote the book of Hebrews. The question of his exact identity is unanswerable; any suggestion remains a "best guess." However, a reasonable suggestion is found in the New Testament figure Apollos, so believed by Martin Luther to be the author of Hebrews. In Acts 18:24–28 Luke describes Apollos as a Jew from Alexandria, who was "eloquent" (a term used

---

20. Ceslas Spicq, *L'Épître aux Hébreux*, SB (Paris: J. Gabalda, 1977), 56.

21. David A. Black, "Hebrews 1:1–4: A Study in Discourse Analysis," *WTJ* 49 (1987): 181–92.

22. See especially L. D. Hurst, *The Epistle to the Hebrews: Its Background of Thought* (Cambridge: Cambridge Univ. Press, 1990), 12.

23. L. D. Hurst has demonstrated the book's theological points of contact with Paul's writings, 1 Peter, and the so-called "Stephen tradition" of Acts 7 (ibid., 87–130). This is hardly surprising, given the interaction between Christian communities of the time. The author himself tells us that he draws on the Christian teaching handed down by the first witnesses of the Lord's life and ministry (Heb. 2:3).

24. Lane, *Hebrews 1–8*, 1–2.

of those with rhetorical training) and thoroughly versed in the Scriptures. Furthermore, he was a pastor who had received the gospel from eyewitnesses of Jesus' ministry (Heb. 2:3), was at home in the Greek-speaking synagogues of the Mediterranean, and had close acquaintances from Italy (see Heb. 13:24). With Origen we confess our ignorance: "Who wrote the epistle, God knows the truth."[25] Whoever he was, we owe him respect for his rhetorical craftsmanship, admiration for the depth of his theological reflection, and gratitude for this enduring word of exhortation.

The Structure and Argument of Hebrews

ALTHOUGH THE AUTHOR chooses to address the pressing problem facing this community in the form of a sermon, the development and structure of this sermon's argument have baffled commentators through the centuries.[26] A quick look at the introductions to several commentaries demonstrates the lack of consensus on this matter among those who have attempted to outline the book. The most popular approach is to understand the sermon as built around the important "superiority" motif: "Christ Superior to the Prophets" (1:1–3), "Christ Superior to the Angels" (1:4–2:18), "Christ Superior to Moses" (3:1–4:13), etc.[27] However, this approach fails to take seriously the two distinct types of literature found in Hebrews, namely, *exposition*, in which the author expounds the person and work of Christ, and *exhortation*, in which he seeks to motivate the congregation to a positive response.[28] Hebrews does not develop in a neat outline from point A to point Z. Rather, the author switches back and forth between exposition and exhortation. Although the two work

---

25. Eusebius, *Hist. Eccl.* 6.25.14.

26. For a detailed look at the history of the discussion and a proposed solution, see George H. Guthrie, *The Structure of Hebrews: A Text-Linguistic Analysis*, NovtSup (Leiden: E. J. Brill, 1994).

27. P. E. Hughes, *A Commentary on the Epistle to the Hebrews* (Grand Rapids: Eerdmans, 1977), ix–x.

28. For example, Hughes (ibid.) labels the first unit of the book "Christ Superior to the Prophets" (1:1–3). However, that this is the main import of the passage is questionable. Certainly 1:4–2:18 presents the Son in relation to the angels, depicting his superiority to them in 1:4–14. Yet, in 2:10–18 the author stresses the positional subordination of the Son, that is, that he became "lower than the angels" to suffer for humanity. The material of 3:1–4:13 Hughes designates "Christ Superior to Moses," but a close look at that section reveals that comparison to Moses is accomplished in 3:1–6. The rest of the section covers the negative example of those who fell in the desert (3:7–19), a transition (4:1–2), and the promise of rest for the people of God (4:3–11). Thus, building an outline of Hebrews around the "better than" theme, although highlighting an important aspect of the discourse, must be judged too simplistic.

together powerfully, weaving a tapestry of concepts toward the accomplishment of his purpose, they contribute to that purpose in different manners.

Imagine that I came to your church this past Sunday and preached on the subject of faith, using, as my text, the story of Abraham in Genesis 12. The three points of my exegetical sermon were the "Call to Faith" (Gen. 12:1–3), the "Commitment of Faith" (12:4–5), and the "Confirmation of Faith" (12:6–7). With each of these points I *explained* several verses of the text, commenting on background, terms, and stylistic features. The development of the message moved from point to point in a logical manner, each point building on the one before it.

However, following each point I interjected a strong exhortation to the congregation, turning momentarily from expounding the text to challenging them to take action. With each of these challenges I addressed them directly and reiterated the same basic theme: "My fellow believers, you are called by God today to live as people of faith!" I used different examples each time I returned to the exhortation and connected the exhortation to the exegetical point I had just finished, but hammered home again and again the same challenge to live by faith. Thus the sermon developed both by a point-by-point exposition of the text and the reiteration of the action needed to live out the text today. Hebrews develops in much the same manner.

Exposition. The expositional material in Hebrews addresses the person and work of the Son of God, and does so with a logically developing argument.[29]

Introduction: God Has Spoken to Us in a Son (1:1–4)
  I. The Position of the Son in Relation to the Angels (1:5–2:18)
    A. The Son Superior to the Angels (1:5–14)
    ab. The Superior Son for a Time Became Positionally Lower than the Angels (2:5–9)
    B. The Son Lower than the Angels (i.e., among humans) to Suffer for the "Sons" (i.e., heirs) (2:10–18)
  II. The Position of the Son, Our High Priest, in Relation to the Earthly Sacrificial System (4:14–10:25)
    Opening: We Have a Sinless High Priest Who Has Gone Into Heaven (4:14–16)
    A. The Appointment of the Son as a Superior High Priest (5:1–10; 7:1–28)
      1. Introduction: The Son Taken from Among Humans and Appointed According to the Order of Melchizedek (5:1–10)

---

29. Guthrie, *The Structure of Hebrews*, 121–27.

2. The Superiority of Melchizedek (7:1–10)
3. The Superiority of Our Eternal, Melchizedekan
   High Priest (7:11–28)
ab. We Have Such a High Priest Who is a Minister in
    Heaven (8:1–2)
B. The Superior Offering of the Appointed High Priest
   (8:3–10:18)
   1. Introduction: The More Excellent Ministry of the
      Heavenly High Priest (8:3–6)
   2. The Superiority of the New Covenant (8:7–13)
   3. The Superior New Covenant Offering (9:1–10:18)
Closing: We Have a Great Priest Who Takes Us Into
   Heaven (10:19–25)

Following the introduction of 1:1–4, the preacher presents his material on Christ in two main movements, each with several subsections: "The Position of the Son in Relation to the Angels" (1:5–2:18), and "The Position of the Son, Our High Priest, in Relation to the Earthly Sacrificial System." The first subsection of the material on Christ's relation to the angels communicates "The Son Superior to the Angels" (1:5–14). This is followed by the second subsection, "The Son Lower Than the Angels (i.e., among humans) to Suffer for the 'Sons' (i.e., heirs)" (2:10–18). These first two units are bridged by a brief transition in 2:5–9. The first section of the second movement, the high-priestly ministry of Christ, occurs at 5:1–10; 7:1–28, where the author presents "The Appointment of the Son as a Superior High Priest." Following a short transition at 8:1–2, the preacher moves from the appointment to the offering of the heavenly high priest (8:3–10:18).

Notice the logical and spatial development of the steps in the writer's sermon. The Son begins at the highest point in the universe, exalted above the angels (1:5–14). He comes down among humanity ("lower than the angels") in order to deliver us from sin (2:10–18). On the basis of his solidarity with humankind the Son is taken from among us and appointed high priest (5:1–10; 7:1–28). Finally, by virtue of this appointment he is able to move into the heavenly sphere once again and offer a superior, heavenly offering for sin. See diagram 1 on the following page.

Exhortation. Regarding the hortatory material of Hebrews, we find a much different approach. Whereas the exposition on the Son focuses on different main themes section by section, the units of exhortation return again and again to the same key motifs: falling away, sin, punishment, promise, the need to receive the message of God, the voice of God, Jesus/the Son, faith, obedience, endurance, entering in, and the use of examples. In the various themes of his

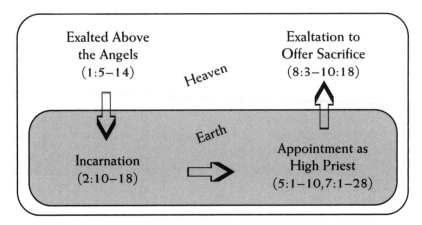

Diagram 1

exhortations, the preacher turns from a focus on the Son to focus the white-hot truth of God's Word on his congregation. These subjects are woven together in a complex of warnings, encouragement, and the portrayal of both positive and negative examples, all of which offer the hearers a dichotomy of decision.

The preacher asserts that God's Word to this community is either a word of promise or a word of punishment. If they endure through faith, they can lay hold of the promised inheritance. However, if they fall away, rejecting the Word of God, they fall into severe judgment. Therefore, with his appeals, the author repeatedly returns to the same themes, reemphasizing both the positive possibilities and the potential dangers of the hearers' next step. Here he does much more than instruct—he seeks to motivate, to challenge the audience to action. See diagram 2.

The main message of Hebrews. How, then, does this preacher's use of exposition and exhortation work together to challenge these lethargic believers to endure in their commitment to Christ? In the hortatory sections he offers powerful warnings, challenges, examples, and reminders of God's faithfulness to his promises, all based on God's Word. He lays a solid foundation for his exhortation with a thorough exposition on the Son of God. The expository and hortatory sections in Hebrews overlap in the relationship of the hearers, to whom God has spoken his powerful word, with the Son, of whom and to whom God has also made proclamations. The ultimate bases for endurance, therefore, are their new-covenant relationship with God's superior Son and an ongoing openness to God's Word. In other words, one's endurance ultimately will depend on the health of one's relationship to Christ and faithful obedience to the Word.[30]

---

30. For a complete outline of Hebrews, see pp. 39–40, below.

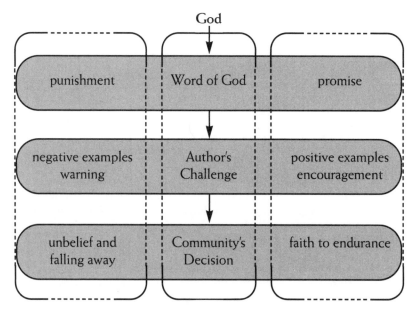

God

punishment	Word of God	promise
negative examples warning	Author's Challenge	positive examples encouragement
unbelief and falling away	Community's Decision	faith to endurance

Diagram 2: Exhortation in Hebrews

From His World to Ours:
Thoughts on Interpreting Hebrews

WITH A FAIRLY CLEAR PICTURE of Hebrews' original setting, we have high-lighted clues in the text that indicate a faltering community in need of strengthening their commitment by drawing near to God. Hebrews also offers us a partial portrait of the author, an educated preacher who loved the Old Testament and the people to whom he preached. Thus we have moved back in time to see some aspects of the "why," "who," and "how" surrounding this dynamic discourse. Yet, we must not stay there. You and I live in a modern world and need a fresh word of encouragement. Can Hebrews speak to us? Can it reach across the centuries and breathe strength into our "feeble arms and weak knees" (12:12)? The conviction reflected in this commentary is that it not only can but must. We too are under obligation to hear the voice of God today (3:7–19). Yet, to hear that voice clearly and apply the Word responsibly presents us with an exciting and demanding challenge.

Back in the summer of 1981 a friend from college and I traveled to seminary in Texas. Danny and I grew up in the same part of the country, and with only a few words between us, we normally understood each other perfectly. To us "barbecue" meant shredded pork, Paris was a town in West Tennessee, and to "carry" someone to church meant giving them a lift in your car. Of course, such expressions were executed with more syllables than needed since we each spoke with a southern accent! At seminary, however, I found communication could be more challenging. To my friends from Texas, "barbecue" was beef brisket and Paris was a town in northeast Texas. To my surprise, a "tank" was a small body of water used for fishing or watering the cows.

During this time I was also privileged to know several close friends from around the world. One of the first was a man from Korea, who went on to be a leader in church development in Seoul. To understand my Korean friend took a great deal more effort than discourse with any of my U.S. friends, regardless of what part of the country they called home. As we ate *pulgoki* (Korean "barbecue") and fermented cabbage, we struggled for the right words to communicate our thoughts. We often found that cultural differences and the definitions of specific terms had to be understood before meaningful discourse could occur. The effort was always worth it; with time we forged a deep friendship.

In each of these situations, cultural and linguistic "distance" affected the communication process. Such distance exists even in the closest of family relationships (as any parent of teenagers knows quite well!), but as I ventured into communication encounters with those far removed from my immediate culture of West Tennessee, I found more effort was needed for understanding to take place. The fewer commonalties between my culture and that of the person with whom I was trying to communicate, the more resources I needed to bridge the cultural and linguistic distance.

Consider this analogy. The Forked Deer, a small river approximately thirty feet wide, flows near my home. As I travel to work each day, I pass over this river, and, thankfully, the highway department in my area built a sturdy bridge there long ago. The financial and human resources needed to build the bridge were extensive, but that bridge certainly makes travel to work much easier. Some fifty miles away, near Dyersburg, Tennessee, a huge bridge reaches one mile across the Mississippi River. Because of the great distance, the financial resources, people resources, and time needed to build that structure were many, many times those needed for the little bridge near my home. The effort and expense has paid off in ease of travel for those who formerly had to travel across the mighty Mississippi by ferry—a dangerous and time-consuming mode of transportation. Far, far to the south, near the mouth of the Mississippi, in southern Louisiana, lies the Atchafalaya Swamp. As my family and I traveled recently from Houston, Texas, to New Orleans, we passed right through this swamp on a bridge seventeen miles long! Those who built the bridge had a much greater distance to span than those who built the bridge over the Mississippi River, and they had to do it in an area filled with alligators and snakes! The greater the distance, the greater the resources needed to span that distance.

Understanding the communication of another person, whether in written, spoken, or visual form, presents a singularly exciting challenge, and the challenge grows as language and cultural factors are added to the equation. The greater the cultural and linguistic distance, the more resources are needed. Yet with the help of the proper resources we can understand the communication of others as bridges are built across these divides.

The message of Hebrews was written almost two millennia ago, in the Greek language, by an educated person of Jewish descent, in the form of a synagogue sermon, and for a church located in Greco-Roman culture. To say the least, this message is packaged in strange wrappings and lies on the far side of a wide cultural and linguistic divide. It might be called the Atchafalaya Swamp of the New Testament (complete with "hermeneutical alligators" swimming around a few key passages!). Hebrews can seem terribly enigmatic and foreign with its uses of rabbinic interpretive methodologies, strange characters like Melchizedek, rhetorical arguments, and obscure theological concepts. Yet, there are resources available to help us bridge the distance and understand what Hebrews would say to us today.

(1) The intent of this commentary is really two-directional. We not only want to move across the bridge of time to Hebrews' ancient context, seeking to understand what the book meant to the original audience, but we also want to ask, "What does it mean to us today?" and "How do we come back across the bridge, moving responsibly from the ancient context to our own?" Therefore we must consider the principles that will guide our trek across the hermeneutical bridge to Hebrews and back again to the contemporary church.

Our discussion of the historical background of Hebrews, although leading to some conclusions that must be considered tentative, is an important one.[31] God originally chose to reveal truth through Hebrews at a specific time in history and in specific cultural contexts. To understand what this book speaks to us today, we must first understand what it communicated to the original audience, keeping in mind both the correspondences and the differences between our situation and theirs. For example, the trials this ancient congregation faced seem to have stemmed from their association with the Christian movement. Hebrews 10:36 reads, "You need to persevere so that when you have done the will of God, you will receive what he has promised." The author encourages this house church to continue to confess the name

---

31. See G. H. Guthrie, "New Testament Exegesis and the Catholic Epistles," in *Handbook for New Testament Exegesis*, ed. Stanley Porter (Leiden: E. J. Brill, 1998), 591–606.

of Christ, even though that confession may cost them socially and physically. He assures them that God has a reward for them at the end of their current path of tears.

The modern Christian who applies this passage to a broken-down car— reasoning, for example, "If I just persevere God will meet my need for a new auto"—is in danger hermeneutically of "coloring outside the lines." Based on the background of this passage, its message is much more directly applicable to the woman facing harassment at her job because of her Christian confession, or to Christians in the underground church of China, many of whom have been imprisoned or left destitute because of their association with the body of Christ. Nevertheless, the book of Hebrews as a whole does speak to anyone struggling with the sin of unbelief or spiritual laziness (3:13; 6:12) and addresses a wide variety of difficult situations that demand faith and perseverance (11:1–40). The book is especially relevant for those tempted to turn from Christianity, or Christian fellowship, in order to return to pre-conversion patterns of life.

(2) We must be ever mindful of the genre in which this document was crafted—a sermon. This means the author probably intended the writing to be *heard* by the audience in one sitting.[32] Once this is understood, much of the repetition in the book makes sense. When I teach a class on Hebrews, I often begin the first day of lecture by dressing up in the garb of the ancient Mediterranean world and reading a large portion of the book. When finished I ask the class to tell me what they noticed from the reading that they had not noticed in Hebrews before. Of course many of the stylistic details are lost in the English translation. Nevertheless, they begin to get the feel of Hebrews as a piece of homiletical craftsmanship and sense the flow of the book's messages.

In the Bridging Contexts sections of the commentary, therefore, we will constantly refer to the big picture in this sermon. I want to address how each section plays its specific role in the message and answer the question concerning the preacher's intended impact on his listeners. This, of course, bleeds into the important area of literary context as a key for the interpretive process. A discourse is not merely the sum of its parts. Each part has a specific role with others in accomplishing the author's intended goal. In understanding the intended impact at various points in the book, we can ask the impact Hebrews might have on us, that is, what the bases are for our motivation to persevere in following Christ.

(3) Finally, we must attempt to do justice to the author's use of language and style. We especially want to be careful of certain exegetical fallacies

---

32. The same can be said for the letters of the New Testament. Documents in the ancient world were very expensive and few people owned personal copies.

related to word meanings.[33] Many a faulty application of the Scriptures rests on poor exegesis of terms and phrases in the text.

The Contemporary Significance of Hebrews: The Problem and Promise of Perseverance— A Tale of Two Couples

ONCE WE HAVE HEARD the ancient word, remaining sensitive to historical and literary context, genre, and language, we will begin our adventure back across the bridge of interpretation to the needs of our own time. Once understood, no New Testament document speaks more relevantly or powerfully to a crying need in the modern church, as illustrated in the following story.[34]

Betty Johnson had grown up a Presbyterian but quit attending when she went to college. Her husband, Fred, had never been involved in church, and the couple stayed busy in the first years of marriage building their respective careers as an accountant and doctor. After the birth of their first child, Betty felt a need to expose her daughter to the things of God. So she visited Community Church one Sunday morning and was pleasantly surprised by the warmth of the people. The next Sunday evening, she convinced Fred to go with her to a potluck supper. Fred genuinely enjoyed the people he met, and, being a guitar player, was impressed by the young man playing the guitar for the fellowship. This couple gradually became more and more involved until Betty joined the church and Fred made a commitment to Christ. Betty did volunteer service on the church newsletter, Fred joined in the worship team as a guitar player, and their kids were involved in the children's program. Both Fred and Betty were seen as key leaders in Community Church.

One of Betty's best friends in the coming years was Amanda. A leader in the church's women's ministry, Amanda had become a Christian at the age of six. She grew up in a loving home in the Midwest with two parents deeply committed to Christ and the church. Amanda was president of the youth group in high school, sang in the choir, and was involved in the Young People for Christ organization. When she went to college, she attended a small Christian university near her hometown and became deeply involved with Campus Crusade.

At her university was a young man named Tom Smith, who was working on a master's degree in business. He was not a Christian but was charming,

---

33. See D. A. Carson, *Exegetical Fallacies* (Grand Rapids: Baker, 1984); Grant R. Osborne, *The Hermeneutical Spiral* (Downers Grove, Ill.: InterVarsity Press, 1991), 65–75.

34. The illustration that follows is based on a composite of situations I have encountered in my ministry. The names have been changed to protect the privacy of those described.

handsome, and intelligent, and he did agree to go to church with her from time to time. Against the counsel of her parents, pastor, and some close friends, Amanda started dating Tom seriously and eventually said "yes" to his proposal of marriage. After marriage, the rigors of his graduate program gave Tom less and less time to attend church. When he finished grad school, the Smiths moved to Texas and bought a home right down the street from Fred and Betty Johnson. Amanda became involved in Community Church almost immediately; Tom did not.

About two years later Betty went through a crisis of faith. When her children reached school age, she had decided to go back to work part-time at a large accounting firm in the area. She became close to several of the young professional women at the office. Betty was refreshed by their winsome attitudes and zest for life. With her heavy responsibilities at church and home Betty had begun to feel a bit burned out. Knowing she should be witnessing to her new friends at work, she felt she had neither the gifts nor emotional energy. Her friends' occasional jabs at Christianity stung and motivated her to keep her faith to herself. These women seemed fulfilled and, for the most part, had decent relationships at home. They read the latest books on parenting and marriage and seemed to be doing well with life. They enjoyed themselves, attending parties and going on weekend trips with their husbands. Her church life began to seem dull. Who was she to tell them they needed to accept Christ to have a "full and meaningful life." She shared her concerns with her husband and Amanda, but it didn't seem to help.

Just before Betty Johnson's reentry to the workplace, Tom Smith, the husband for whom Amanda had prayed faithfully for six years, became a believer. Pastor David had been playing golf with Tom for two years, when one day on the golf course Tom saw his need for Jesus. Amanda was ecstatic and wept openly the night Tom was baptized. In the months to come Tom devoured the Scriptures and became involved with numerous ministry opportunities at church. He was "on fire" for the Lord, attending men's meetings and inviting non-Christian friends to worship services. Tom, although busy in his blossoming business, became even more committed to his family, and life was good at the Smith end of the street.

At the other end of the street Fred and Betty Johnson maintained a degree of equilibrium in their marriage, but Betty eventually dropped out of church completely. Nevertheless, Fred stayed the course of church involvement, taking their daughter with him occasionally and continuing his ministry in Community Church's worship team. Yet, after two years Fred began missing worship periodically. A weekend trip to Betty's parents. Summer vacation. Two weeks of illness, during which he stayed at home and watched a megachurch service on television. These "excused absences" were joined by

Sunday mornings that found Fred tired and just wanting to spend more time with his family. Unfortunately, these became more and more frequent until Fred had dropped out of church almost completely.

Pastor David, whose heart broke over this family, received an even greater shock about a year later. Tom Smith, the most energetic young convert with whom the pastor had ever worked, the faithful follower of Christ who had "burned all his candles at both ends" in the Lord's service, renounced the Christian faith. No explanation. No conversation. Nothing. He did not even tell Amanda what had happened to bring about his apostasy. He simply quit coming, quit confessing, and quit caring. The pastor could not believe it. These defections affected him deeply. He cried, and prayed, and wondered what he could have done for these friends who, seemingly, had walked closely to Christ. Moreover, he wondered what he could say or do in the future to keep other members of his church from falling away.

A theological and pastoral issue. Christians through the centuries have discussed, debated, and despaired over the references to "falling away" in Hebrews. With his harsh warnings against falling, is the author simply speaking of a "back-slidden" condition experienced by believers who have drifted away from God; or can genuine followers of Christ lose their salvation? On the other hand, perhaps those "who have once been enlightened, who have tasted the heavenly gift" (6:4), never were Christians at all. Perhaps they had been exposed to the gospel, almost crossing the threshold of commitment, only to turn away from God prior to being transformed by the power of God. Such questions are the stuff of theological debates—and these are vitally important questions.

At appropriate points in this commentary we will deal seriously with the theological issue of apostasy. However, I would like for us to begin by focusing on Hebrews as a pastoral appeal; this may offer a common starting point for us no matter where we fall on the Calvinist-Arminian theological spectrum. If you have been involved in church for some time, you have witnessed the same types of situations occurring in Community Church. If you have been or are a pastor, Sunday school teacher, Bible study leader, or concerned church member, you can probably empathize with the broken heart of pastor David as you have watched good friends or family members drift away from God.

The writer of Hebrews is a biblical theologian of the first order. Yet, he brings his theology to bear in service of a critical pastoral need, struggling to help friends in danger of defecting from Christian commitment. In writing Hebrews his first concern is to present a dynamic, motivational, relational appeal, not a cold theological treatise. Again, I intend no dichotomy here. His pastoral ministry is anchored deeply in the waters of his Christian doctrine. However, he confronts an issue encountered by church leaders—whatever their interpretation of Hebrews 6:4–8—throughout the centuries: How do I help my people maintain their commitment to Christ in the face of rigorous opposition to their perseverance? This was the question facing our fictitious church leader in Rome and the question facing pastor David, both struggling to deal with the people for whom they cared deeply; this is the question facing many of us today.

The author of Hebrews takes the question seriously indeed, for he was certain that to fall away from God is a terribly serious and dangerous business, for "'the Lord will judge his people.' It is a dreadful thing to fall into the hands of the living God" (10:30–31). This is the point upon which we can agree. For even one member of the Christian community (however we interpret his or her status) to drift away from God is a horrifying tragedy. It should disturb us greatly that thousands each year jettison their church involvement, too many denying the faith altogether. To be sure, the question of whether many of these were really true Christians to begin with is valid. They certainly have quit attending for a wide variety of reasons and represent a broad spectrum of continuing relationships or nonrelationships with the church. Yet, it should alarm us that the attrition rate is so high and challenge us to consider what can be done about it.

Elsewhere around the world our brothers and sisters face intense persecution, some experiencing beatings, rape, theft, and even death. How should the body of Christ respond to these believers? How can their pastors preach effectively words of hope and encouragement in light of such devastating opposition? In this commentary we will deal with how the author of Hebrews seeks to answer these dilemmas, and we will seek to bring his answers responsibly across the hermeneutical bridge to points of application in our contemporary contexts.

Outline of Hebrews

Note: Exposition is in plain text, exhortation is italicized and indented, and bold material indicates the unit consititutes an overlap between exposition and exhortation.

Introduction: God Has Spoken to Us in a Son (1:1–4)

I. The Position of the Son in Relation to the Angels (1:5–2:18)

A. The Son Superior to the Angels (1:5–14)

WARNING: Do Not Reject the Word Spoken Through God's Son! (2:1–4)

ab. The Superior Son for a Time Became Positionally Lower Than the Angels (2:5–9)

B. The Son Lower Than the Angels (i.e., among humans) to Suffer for the "Sons" (i.e., heirs) (2:10–18)

Jesus, the Supreme Example of a Faithful Son (3:1–6)

The Negative Example of Those Who Fell Through Faithlessness (3:7–19)

Transition (4:1–2)

The Promise of Rest for Those Who Are Faithful (4:3–11)

WARNING: Consider the Power of God's Word (4:12–13)

II. The Position of the Son, Our High Priest, in Relation to the Earthly Sacrificial System (4:14–10:25)

Overlap: We Have a Sinless HIgh Priest Who Has Gone Into Heaven (4:14–16)

A. The Appointment of the Son as a Superior High Priest (5:1–10; 7:1–28)

1. Introduction: The Son Taken From Among Humans and Appointed According to the Order of Melchizedek (5:1–10)

The Present Problem With the Hearers (5:11–6:3)

WARNING: The Danger of Falling Away from the Christian Faith (6:4–8)

Mitigation: The Author's Confidence in and Desire for the Hearers (6:9–12)

God's Promise Our Basis of Hope (6:13–20)

2. The Superiority of Melchizedek (7:1–10)

3. The Superiority of Our Eternal, Melchizedekan High Priest (7:11–28)

ab. We Have Such a High Priest Who Is a Minister in Heaven (8:1–2)

B. The Superior Offering of the Appointed High Priest (8:3–10:18)

  1. Introduction: The More Excellent Ministry of the Heavenly High Priest (8:3–6)

  2. The Superiority of the New Covenant (8:7–13)

  3. The Superior New Covenant Offering (9:1–10:18)

  Introduction: The Pattern of Old Covenant Worship: Place, With Blood, Effect (9:1–10)

  a. Christ's Superior Blood (9:13–22)

  b. A Sacrifice in Heaven (9:23–24)

  c. An Eternal Sacrifice (10:1–18)

Overlap: We Have a Great Priest Who Takes Us Into Heaven (10:19–25)

WARNING: The Danger of Rejecting God's Truth and God's Son (10:26–31)

The Positive Example of the Hearers' Past and an Admonition to Endure to Receive the Promise (10:32–39)

The Positive Example of the Old Testament Faithful (11:1–40)

Reject Sin and Fix Your Eyes on Jesus, Surpreme Example of Endurance (12:1–2)

Endure Discipline as Sons (12:3–17)

The Blessings of the New Covenant (12:18–24)

WARNING: Do Not Reject God's Word! (12:25–29)

Practical Exhortations (13:1–19)

Benediction (13:20–21)

Conclusion (13:22–25)

Annotated Bibliography

Commentaries

Attridge, Harold. *The Epistle to the Hebrews*. Hermeneia. Philadelphia: Fortress, 1989. A technical commentary that offers a wealth of information and a balanced treatment of the text at most points. This commentary has a strong orientation to issues related to background. After the two-volume work by Lane, this is the best technical commentary on Hebrews.

Bruce, F. F. *The Epistle to the Hebrews*, rev. ed. NICNT. Grand Rapids: Eerdmans, 1990. Prior to the publication of the technical commentaries by Lane and Attridge, this volume, originally published in 1963, was the best English-language work available, with that by P. E. Hughes running a close second. The commentary follows Bruce's pattern of outstanding evangelical scholarship in the task of elucidating the New Testament.

Buchanan, George W. *To the Hebrews*. AB. Garden City, N.Y.: Doubleday, 1972. Sometimes peculiar in his interpretations, Buchanan understands Hebrews to be a sermon on Psalm 110. Not one of the more helpful commentaries to the average layperson.

Calvin, John. *Commentaries on the Epistle of Paul the Apostle to the Hebrews*. Trans. by John Owen. Grand Rapids: Eerdmans, 1949. Reprint Grand Rapids: Baker, 1984. Consistently sound theological reflection from the great Reformer.

Delitzsch, Franz. *Commentary on the Epistle to the Hebrews*. Trans. Thomas L. Kingsbury. 2 vols. Grand Rapids: Eerdmans, 1952. Originally published in German in 1857, this work has stood the test of time. The translation of a line toward the end of the author's preface reads, "How far, indeed, does every human exposition fall short of the fulness of the unsearchable word!" How true! Yet, Delitzsch's two-volume work has much to offer.

Ellingworth, Paul. *Commentary on Hebrews*. NIGTC. Grand Rapids: Eerdmans, 1993. This is an outstanding source of information that, with the technical commentaries of Lane and Attridge, should be consulted. However, Ellingworth's treatment often misses important contextual concerns and shows too little sensitivity to the overall structure of Hebrews.

Guthrie, Donald. *The Epistle to the Hebrews*. TNTC. Grand Rapids: Eerdmans, 1983. Another stalwart of modern evangelical scholarship, Guthrie offers a nontechnical commentary providing consistent insights into the text.

Hagner, Donald A. *Hebrews*. New International Biblical Commentary. Peabody, Mass.: Hendrickson, 1990. This is a solid evangelical commentary that, although brief, offers consistently helpful insights to the book.

Hughes, P. E. *A Commentary on the Epistle to the Hebrews*. Grand Rapids: Eerdmans, 1977. Not as detailed as Bruce in some respects but more inclined to deal with wide-ranging theological issues in the course of commentary. Prior to Lane and Attridge, with the exception of Bruce, Hughes offers the most helpful English-language commentary on the text of Hebrews.

Jewett, Robert. *Letter to Pilgrims: A Commentary on the Epistle to the Hebrews*. New York: Pilgrim, 1981. As the title suggests, Jewett reads Hebrews in light of the "journey" motif inherent in the book.

Kistemaker, Simon. *Hebrews*. Grand Rapids: Baker, 1984. With a scholarly underpinning, this commentary is readable and more expositional than exegetical.

Lane, William L. *Hebrews: Call to Commitment*. Hendrickson, 1985. A popular treatment from one of the foremost scholars on Hebrews. Volume 1: *Hebrews 1–8*. WBC. Dallas: Word, 1991. Volume 2: *Hebrews 9–13*. WBC. Dallas: Word, 1991. These two volumes offer the best technical exegetical commentary available today. Lane presents an extensive and helpful introduction on the book, is consistently rigorous in his discussion of exegetical matters, and excels at theological reflection.

Moffatt, J. *A Critical and Exegetical Commentary on the Epistle to the Hebrews*. ICC. Edinburgh: T. & T. Clark, 1924. An older technical commentary on the book that has now been eclipsed by the more recent works of Lane and Attridge.

Montefiore, Hugh. *A Commentary on the Epistle to the Hebrews*. Black's New Testament Commentaries. London: Adam & Charles Black, 1964. Clearly written and accessible to the nonspecialist.

Morris, Leon. "Hebrews." *Expositor's Bible Commentary* (Grand Rapids: Zondervan, 1981), 12:1–158. Part of the *Expositor's Bible Commentary*, this volume offers sound, straightforward exegesis of most points. Bruce and Hughes provide greater depth with the same intention.

Westcott, Brooke Foss. *The Epistle to the Hebrews: The Greek Text with Notes and Essays*. London: MacMillan, 1929. An older work from the later nineteenth century that is rich in insight and worthy of consistent use in study.

Expositions of Hebrews

Barclay, William. *The Letter to the Hebrews*. The Daily Study Bible. Philadelphia: Westminster, 1957. A helpful little tool, especially in providing thought-provoking ideas on the application of the text.

Brown, Raymond. *Christ Above All: The Message of Hebrews.* The Bible Speaks Today. Downers Grove, Ill.: InterVarsity, 1982. A readable, nontechnical treatment of Hebrews.

Studies Related to the Book of Hebrews

Berkouwer, G. C. *Faith and Perseverance.* Grand Rapids: Eerdmans, 1958. An important theological treatment on perseverance.

Caird, G. B. "The Exegetical Method of the Epistle to the Hebrews." *CJT* 5 (1959): 44–51. Caird joined those suggesting that Hebrews, rather than a Christian treatment of platonic philosophy, expresses thoroughly Jewish-Christian concerns.

Filson, Floyd. *"Yesterday": A Study of Hebrews in Light of Chapter 13.* Studies in Biblical Theology. Naperville, Ill.: Alec R. Allenson, 1967. Filson demonstrates that chapter 13, rather than an appendage, as some scholars suggest, is integral to Hebrews and provides helpful insights to the rest of the book.

Gundry Volf, Judith M. *Paul and Perseverance: Staying in and Falling Away.* Louisville: Westminster/John Knox, 1990. Perhaps the most important recent work defending the idea of perseverance from a Reformed, evangelical perspective.

Guthrie, George H. *The Structure of Hebrews: A Text-Linguistic Analysis.* NovTSup 73. Leiden: Brill, 1994; reprint: Grand Rapids: Baker, 1998. My attempt to update the discussion on the structure of Hebrews, this book outlines the basis for the structural understanding of Hebrews given in this commentary. The work is technical and most suited to those with an understanding of Greek.

Hay, David M. *Glory at the Right Hand: Psalm 110 in Early Christianity.* SBLMS. Cambridge: Cambridge Univ. Press, 1980. An outstanding work on the Old Testament passage most quoted in the New Testament.

Hughes, Graham. *Hebrews and Hermeneutics: The Epistle to the Hebrews As a New Testament Example of Biblical Interpretation.* Cambridge: Cambridge Univ. Press, 1979. A stimulating treatment of the hermeneutical principles inherent in Hebrews.

Hurst, L. D. *The Epistle to the Hebrews: Its Background of Thought.* SNTSMS. Cambridge: Cambridge Univ. Press, 1990. The best recent discussion of the background for Hebrews' thought. Hurst understands the author of Hebrews to be influenced by a number of communities, including Jewish apocalyptic.

Lane, William L. "Hebrews: A Sermon in Search of a Setting." *SwJT* 28 (1985): 13–18. A helpful summary of the case for Hebrews as a sermon.

Lincoln, Andrew T. *Paradise Now and Not Yet: Studies in the Role of the Heavenly Dimension in Paul's Thought with Special Reference to His Eschatology*. Grand Rapids: Baker, 1981. Lincoln's monograph addresses the tension between salvation as already inaugurated in the Christian community and a promised reality of the age to come.

Lindars, Barnabas. *The Theology of the Letter to the Hebrews*. New Testament Theology. Cambridge: Cambridge Univ. Press, 1991. A summary of the main theological motifs in Hebrews, this little volume is well executed and helpful as a supplement to commentaries.

Longenecker, Richard N. *Biblical Exegesis in the Apostolic Period*. Grand Rapids: Eerdmans, 1975. A treatment of the methods used by the rabbis and New Testament authors in the first century.

McCullough, J. C. "Some Recent Developments in Research on the Epistle to the Hebrews." *IBS* 2 (1980): 141–65. This and the three sister articles that follow provide an excellent summary of research on Hebrews in the last four decades.

_____. "Some Recent Developments in Research on the Epistle to the Hebrews: II." *IBS* 3 (1981): 28–43.

_____. "Hebrews in Recent Scholarship." *IBS* 16 (1994): 66–86.

_____. "Hebrews in Recent Scholarship (Part 2)." *IBS* 16 (1994): 108–20.

Hebrews 1:1-4

IN THE PAST God spoke to our forefathers through the prophets at many times and in various ways, ²but in these last days he has spoken to us by his Son, whom he appointed heir of all things, and through whom he made the universe. ³The Son is the radiance of God's glory and the exact representation of his being, sustaining all things by his powerful word. After he had provided purification for sins, he sat down at the right hand of the Majesty in heaven. ⁴So he became as much superior to the angels as the name he has inherited is superior to theirs.

Original Meaning

BECAUSE HEBREWS BEGINS like a sermon,¹ without any mention of sender, addressees, or words of greeting, the author opens with a majestic overture, rhetorically eloquent and theologically packed. This beautifully constructed opening statement begins by contrasting the revelation given under the older testament economy with that given under the new. This contrast focuses on and climaxes in the person of God's Son—heir, agent of creation, sustainer of the universe, Savior, and sovereign—who now sits at the right hand of God.

Although most translations, including the NIV, present this introduction in several sentences, Hebrews 1:1–4 in Greek forms a single, multiclause sentence, built around the main clause "God . . . has spoken."² Thus God and his communication to humanity through the Son engage the author's attention from the first. These beautifully crafted verses fall into two main subdivisions, the first addressing divine revelation (1:1–2a) and the second the person, work, and status of God's Son (1:2b–4).

The Climax of Divine Communication (1:1–2a)

THE AUTHOR BEGINS by presenting divine revelation in parallel contrasts between the "older" communication during the time of the prophets and the

---

1. See above, p. 24.

2. This clause is made of the main subject, "God" (*theos*), in v. 1 and the main verb, "he has spoken" (*elalesen*), in v. 2. The word translated "spoke" in the NIV's v. 1 is actually a participle dependent on the main verb.

"newer" communication through the Son. He contrasts four areas: the era of the revelation, the recipients, the agents, and the ways in which the revelation was manifested.

	Older Communication	Newer Communication
Era	in the past	in these last days
Recipients	to our forefathers	to us
Agents	through the prophets	by his Son
Ways	in various ways	in one way (implied)

The eras mentioned contrast two time frames. The time "in the past" (or "formerly") refers to the time prior to the coming of Messiah, and correspondingly, the coming time was seen as initiating "the last days." The author uses the adjective "these" (*touton*) in verse 2, expressing the Christian conviction that the last days have been initiated already.[3]

Divine revelation came "to our forefathers [i.e., those under the older covenants] through the prophets." The latter phrase should not be understood as narrowly referring to those designated as the "major" and "minor" writing prophets of our Old Testament. Rather, the author considers all through whom God manifested his will as owning the prophetic mantle, although the manner of these prophesies varied considerably. As to the manner of the divine revelation, it was "at many times" (*polymeros*)—that is, it was temporally fragmented rather than in a complete package—and "in various ways" (*polytropos*), a word that suggests the diversity of forms of that revelation. The suggestion brings to mind Old Testament commands, exhortations, stories, visions, dreams, mighty acts, breathtaking theophanies, and a still small voice, to name a few.[4]

This older revelation was expansive but incomplete. By contrast, the revelation of these last days has come "to us," the receptors of the Christian message. It constitutes God's climactic communication to humanity and has been brought via God's Son; that is, rather than being fragmentary and varied, it may be considered whole, focused in the person and work of Christ. The author included no article prior to the word "Son" (*huio*). Whereas in many languages this may suggest that Jesus is merely one son in a crowd of sons, the emphasis here is on the unique relationship of Jesus with the

---

3. Lane, *Hebrews 1–8*, 10. Early Christian doctrine corresponded to Jewish thought of the day in understanding the history of God's working as divided into two successive ages. Christian thought, however, understood the final age, that of the "last days," to have been ushered in with the coming of Jesus.

4. Harold Attridge, *The Epistle to the Hebrews*, Hermeneia (Philadelphia: Fortress, 1989), 37.

Father—*one who relates to him as son.*[5] Whereas the prophets of old were many, the bearer of God's word for the last days was uniquely qualified for the responsibility. The author's statement should not be understood as concentrating only on the teachings of Jesus, although the words of Christ are vitally important to him (2:3–4). Rather, the whole of the incarnation—person, words, and acts—should be understood as communicating God's ultimate word to his new covenant people.

The Person, Work, and Status of the Son (1:2b–4)

FOLLOWING THE TERM "Son" the author of Hebrews provides seven affirmations describing the Son's person, work, and current status. (1) "Whom he appointed heir of all things" probably alludes to Psalm 2:8: "Ask of me, and I will make the nations your inheritance, the ends of the earth your possession." At Hebrews 1:5, a verse in the immediate context of 1:1–4, the author quotes Psalm 2:7, again affirming the unique relation of this Son with God the Father. If this psalm indeed lies behind the author's thought in Hebrews 1:2, the inheritance of "all things" expands the idea to include the whole of the created order (2:5). In our author's thought, this royal inheritance of Christ has only been inaugurated but will be consummated at the end of the age (1:13; 2:8–9). Thus this initial proposition both affirms the present and anticipates the future rule of Christ.

(2) The next affirmation, "through whom he made the universe," takes a backward look at another of the Son's roles. With other writers of the New Testament, Hebrews proclaims the Son as the Father's agent in the creation of the universe (see 1:10; cf. John 1:3; Col. 1:16). Note Paul's expression of this conviction in 1 Corinthians 8:6: "Yet for us there is but one God, the Father, from whom all things came and for whom we live; and there is but one Lord, Jesus Christ, through whom all things came and through whom we live." Paul here makes a distinction between the role of the Father and that of the Son; yet, both are included in the work of creation. He affirms the Father as the source of the created order and the Son as the Father's agent in the creative process.[6] The Son, to whom all of creation will be subjected in the end (cf. 1 Cor. 15:28; Heb. 1:13; 2:5, 8), is he through whom it originated in the beginning.

(3) Four participial clauses flank and support the author's next main statement concerning the Son's exaltation to the right hand of God (1:4). The first of these deals with the Son's divine nature: He "is the radiance of God's glory

---

5. Paul Ellingworth, *The Epistle to the Hebrews: A Commentary on the Greek Text*, NIGTC (Grand Rapids: Eerdmans, 1993), 93–94.

6. Millard Erickson, *Christian Theology* (Grand Rapids: Baker, 1985), 372.

and the exact representation of his being." The two parts of this statement affirm the same truth. In biblical literature the "glory" often refers to the luminous manifestation of God's person.[7] The word translated "radiance" (*apaugasma*), used only here in the New Testament, carries the sense of "splendor" or "intense brightness."[8] One cannot separate the experience of looking at the brightness of a light from seeing the light itself because they are too closely associated. By analogy, to see the Son is to view God's glory or manifest presence. So as the "radiance of his glory" the Son is the manifestation of the person and presence of God (e.g., Luke 9:32; John 1:14; 2:11; 17:5; Rom. 8:17; 1 Cor. 2:8; Phil. 3:21; 2 Thess. 2:14).

Similarly, the Son is "the exact representation of his being." The word rendered "representation" (*charakter*), also used only here in the New Testament, originally denoted an instrument used for engraving, and later the impression made by such an instrument. For example, it could refer to the impression made on coins.[9] The word thus speaks of the features of an object or person by which we are able to recognize it for what it is.[10] The imagery may also call to mind the "representation" of a parent one often sees in the face of his or her children. To see the face of the child immediately exhibits the close family relationship. What the Son represents is the "being" of the Father, that is, his essential nature. The phrase "representation of his being," therefore, closely parallels other New Testament passages that speak of Jesus as the "form," "likeness," or "image" of God (e.g., John 1:2; Phil. 2:6; Col. 1:15). So the Son provides a true and trustworthy picture of the person of the Father.

(4) The Son is also the one "sustaining all things by his powerful word." The background of the Son's "sustaining [bearing] all things" should probably be understood in a managerial sense. The action speaks of the continual organization and carrying forward of the created order to a designed end, an activity ascribed to God in Jewish writings. This is not the idea of the Son holding up the weight of the world as the mighty Atlas of Greek mythology, but rather the dynamic progression of creation through his governmental power.[11] He carries out this government "by his powerful word." So, as the world was created by the word of God through the Son (1:2; 11:3), it is sustained by the Son's powerful word.

---

7. E.g., Ex. 16:7; 33:18; Isa. 40:5.

8. Donald Hagner, *Hebrews*, New International Biblical Commentary (Peabody, Mass.: Hendrickson, 1990), 23.

9. Leon Morris, "Hebrews," *EBC* (Grand Rapids: Zondervan, 1981), 12:14.

10. B. F. Westcott, *The Epistle to the Hebrews: The Greek Text with Notes and Essays* (London: MacMillan and Co., 1889), 12.

11. Ibid., 13–14.

(5) "Purification for sins" constitutes one of the author's major concerns (see esp. 9:1–10:18, which addresses the superior offering for sin under the new covenant). Behind his treatment of the subject stand the Old Testament concepts of the Day of Atonement (Lev. 16) and the blood of the covenant (Ex. 24), along with a number of other subtopics.[12] Here, in the statement of Hebrews 1:3, is the introduction's reference to Christ's sacrificial death on the cross. What the Son "had provided" was a forgiveness that would be permanent and lead into the very presence of God.

(6) At the heart of the introduction, the author centers on the Son's present status as the one at God's right hand (1:3). This allusion to Psalm 110:1, the Old Testament passage to which authors of the New Testament refer most often, presents the exaltation of Christ. The concept of "the right hand" represents either superior power or ultimate honor, though it also carries the derivative meanings of "greatness" or "favor."[13] As adapted in the New Testament, Psalm 110:1 supported Jesus' messiahship, vindication (through resurrection and exaltation), role as judge, lordship, and his intercession on behalf of believers.[14]

The references to "the Majesty" here and at 8:1 are unique among allusions to Psalm 110:1 in the New Testament. The word originally described God's power, greatness, or strength (e.g., Deut. 32:3; 1 Chron. 29:11; Ps. 145:3, 6). As used in Hebrews 1:3 it constitutes a reverential periphrasis for "God" commonly used in Jewish circles of the day.[15] "In heaven" is God's locale and particularly his privileged position.[16] Thus, the Son, creator of the universe and heir of all things, has been exalted to an exceptional position of authority and honor.

(7) The result of the exaltation is that the Son "became as much superior to the angels as the name he has inherited is superior to theirs." Many commentators have noted this book returns again and again to contrast Christ and Christianity with the persons and institutions of the older

---

12. E.g., the ashes of the red heifer (Num. 19:9; cf. Heb. 9:13); a variety of sacrifices, such as the whole burnt offering and the sin offering (Heb. 10:5–11). It seems from 10:11 that the daily sacrifices were also in view.

13. Walter Grundmann, "δεξιός," in *TDNT*, 2:38.

14. This psalm is quoted or alluded to twenty-two times in the New Testament. See W. R. G. Loader, "Christ at the Right Hand: Psalm 110:1 in the New Testament," *NTS* 24 (1978): 199–217; David M. Hay, *Glory at the Right Hand: Psalm 110 in Early Christianity*, SBLMS (Cambridge: Cambridge Univ. Press, 1980). For a discussion of the treatment of this psalm in Hebrews, see George H. Guthrie, *The Structure of Hebrews: A Text-Linguistic Analysis*, NovTSup 73 (Leiden: E. J. Brill, 1994), 123–24.

15. Attridge, *The Epistle to the Hebrews*, 46.

16. Otto Michel, *Der Brief an die Hebräer*, KEKNT (Göttingen: Vandenhoeck & Ruprecht, 1966), 102.

covenant. Here, in his comparison of the exalted Son with the angels, the author has moved from Jesus' nature and work to his status. The Son has moved to a position of authority and governance above the status of the angels.

How much greater is his position? "As much superior ... as the name he inherited is superior to theirs." The first word translated "superior" in 1:4 (*kreitton*) is the author's favorite when drawing attention to the preeminence of Christ and the new covenant religion. Christ is a superior priest (7:7); Christ's followers have a superior hope (7:19) because they are involved in the Son's superior covenant (7:22; 8:6), which is based on superior promises (8:6); Christ made a superior sacrifice (9:23; 12:24); therefore, believers have a superior possession (10:34), a superior country (11:16), a superior resurrection (11:35), and a superior privilege (11:40). A comparative, the other term translated "superior" (*diaphoroteron*), can also be rendered "more excellent" and is used again at 8:6 to describe Christ's ministry in comparison with the old covenant system.

Based on the previous reference to "Son" in verse 2 and the Old Testament texts that immediately follow in verses 5–14, most scholars have understood "name" in verse 4 to refer to the title "Son."[17] However, "Son" in verse 2 is not titular; in the collection of quotations that follow, the title "Son" is joined by the titles "God" (v. 8) and "Lord" (v. 10). Although it cannot be denied that the concept of "sonship" is prominent in this section of the book, it seems that uppermost in the author's mind in the collection of Old Testament texts of 1:5–14 is the preeminence of the exalted Son. He is the one who deserves worship (v. 6), has a throne and a scepter (v. 8), has been anointed (as a king?) (v. 9), has made the earth and heavens (v. 10), and has been exalted to the right hand of God (v. 13).

The word translated here as "name" has a broad range of meanings, including "name," "status," "title," "rank," "reputation," or even "person." Richard Longenecker has pointed out "the name," initially used as a pious reference to God, came to be employed among early Jewish Christians as a designation for Jesus.[18] Both Ephesians 1:21 and Philippians 2:9, for example, speak of the exaltation of Christ over powers of the universe, as does the author of Hebrews. In each of those texts Jesus' "name" is said to be above every other. This designation connoted the Messiah's power and divinity. In Hebrews 1:4 what the Son inherited was the title "the name," a designation or rank formerly reserved for God.

---

17. See Héring, *L'Épître aux Hébreux*, 24; Michel, *Der Brief an die Hebräer*, 106.
18. Richard Longenecker, *The Christology of Early Jewish Christianity* (Grand Rapids: Baker, 1981), 41–46 (see Acts 3:16; 4:7, 10; 16:18; 19:13–17; Eph. 1:21; Phil. 2:9).

Summary. Through his brief but tightly packed introduction, the preacher eloquently proclaims in two movements a rich, full overture to the "symphony" of ideas in Hebrews. In the first (1:1–2a) he declares to his first hearers that God, a communicator of expansive, foundational revelations through the older testament, has offered his ultimate revelation in one related to him as son. Then, in the second movement, the introduction climaxes in the Son's sacrificial work and resultant exaltation to the "right hand" of God. Through graphic imagery the purification for sins and exaltation are related dynamically to the close relationship of the Son to the Father, attributing to Christ a nature (the "radiance of God's glory" and "the exact representation of his being"), works (the creation and sustaining of the universe), and status (the inheritance of a "name") that point to his deity and the uniqueness of his relationship with the Father. With this well-spoken word the author begins his sermon and lays a potent theological foundation for the rest of the sermon.

WHAT, THEN, ARE the vehicles on which the meaning of this beautiful passage can be brought to our context today? In the process of bridging the contexts between the author's message and contemporary culture we are confronted with a number of challenging dynamics. The passage is complex in the original language since the author presents us with one extended sentence in these four verses. How, then, are we to understand the organization of his ideas? Which ideas are focal for the author? What is he trying to accomplish through the introduction?

These questions raise a second important issue. In 1:1–4 we find no fewer than ten weighty topics, which span from heaven to earth and from eternity past to eternity future. The list of themes reads like part of the table of contents in a systematic theology textbook! How can we focus our application when we are confronted with so much substance in such a short space?

Finally, terminology used of the Son in this introduction, such as "radiance," "representation," and "having become superior," is somewhat vague and carefully nuanced. It is, therefore, open to theological abuse by those who would do a surface reading without further probing the significance of the author's language. How can we discern what the author is trying to say about Christ?

When presented with a complex passage, one finds help in returning to basic principles of interpretation. These provide stability and direction in sorting through the complexities confronting us. In "Bridging Contexts," therefore, we need to consider how genre (i.e., the kind of literature with which we are dealing) impacts our understanding, and therefore our application, of the text. The grammatical structure of the text offers further assistance. Moreover, certain terminological and theological clarification may be found by considering the broader context of the book of Hebrews itself.

Focusing on the author's central concerns. In the introduction, we reflected the critical judgment that Hebrews presents us with an early Christian sermon, crafted by a person whose experience of worship was oriented to the Greek-speaking synagogue and whose rhetorical abilities had been honed in the Greco-Roman educational institutions of the day. Both ancient Jewish homiletics and Greco-Roman oratory placed great emphasis on a work having an appropriate beginning, otherwise known as the *exordium* or *proem*.[19] In that introduction the speaker presented the main topic(s) or text of his speech or sermon and sought to rivet the attention of the audience. Our author accomplishes both with admirable skill.

We need to recognize that this approach to crafting a sermon's introduction has both similarities with and differences from sermon preparation today. The student in a seminary homiletics class will likely be taught to "grab the audience's attention" through several means, including the reading of the passage to be preached and the use of a graphic illustration or a clear statement of the sermon's main thesis. In this way the intention of a contemporary sermon's introduction is the same as that of an introduction in an ancient speech or sermon—we want to make sure our listeners are tuned in before we get to the body of the message. However, most preachers today have not been taught to include stylistic devices and a tightly woven overview of the sermon's main theological assertions, two dynamics evident in Hebrews 1:1–4. Therefore, we must alert ourselves to these aspects of this passage to catch the full impact the author intends for his introduction.

True to the form of well-executed oral presentations in his culture, the preacher of Hebrews weaves together a series of topics in his introduction that forms the core of his sermon. His purpose is to alert the reader to the foundational propositions of the book. When read in light of the rest of Hebrews, we find at least nine themes in the introduction that exercise con-

---

19. For example, Jewish sermons were often introduced by referring to the text to be expounded. On this aspect of Jewish homiletics see Peder Borgen, *Bread From Heaven: An Exegetical Study of the Concept of Manna in the Gospel of John and the Writings of Philo*, NovTSup (Leiden: E. J. Brill, 1965), 59–98; E. Earle Ellis, "Isaiah in the New Testament," *SwJT* 34 (1991): 31–32. For the form of speeches in the rhetorical schools see Duane F. Watson, *Invention, Arrangement, and Style: Rhetorical Criticism of Jude and 2 Peter*, SBLDS (Atlanta: Scholars Press, 1988), 21; Donald L. Clark, *Rhetoric in Greco-Roman Education* (Morningside Heights, N.Y.: Columbia Univ. Press, 1957), 112–13; D. A. Russell and M. Winterbottom, eds., *Ancient Literary Criticism: The Principal Texts in New Translations* (Oxford: Clarendon, 1972), 170.

---

siderable influence in the rest of the book. Four of these constitute overarching concerns for the whole sermon, and the five others are main topics for certain sections of this discourse. The four main concepts that govern the whole of Hebrews are:

- the term for "God" (*theos*), along with pronouns referring to God
- various designations and pronominal references to God's Son, Jesus, along with his exaltation to the right hand of God
- terms related to "the word of God"
- references to the Christian community being addressed, used either of the book's author or hearers, or both

(1) The main term used for God (*theos*) occurs sixty-eight times in Hebrews, being found in almost every unit. The uses of *theos* are flanked by numerous pronouns referring to God. Thus, we are on safe ground in asserting that Hebrews is "God-centered" from beginning to end.

(2) The author accesses a variety of designations to refer to Jesus, including "Son," "firstborn," "God," "Jesus," "high priest," "Lord," "Christ," "Jesus Christ," and "shepherd." With these and supporting pronouns throughout Hebrews, the author keeps his hearers' attention focused on the one first introduced in the book as "Son" (1:2). Critical to his Christological reflections is his quotation of, or allusions to, Psalm 110:1, the text he uses to spotlight the exaltation of Christ at key turning points in the book.[20]

(3) Another concept introduced in Hebrews 1:1–4 is "the word of God." Often God is said to have "spoken" his "word." This spoken word of God addresses either the Son or the hearers, who are to listen to his "voice."

(4) The speaker constantly refers to himself, his hearers, or the community as a whole, especially in his exhortation sections.

In other words, the preacher may be said to weave the following threads through the entire sermon: God is communicator, his word is effective, his now exalted Son (both in his person and work) is the ultimate means of his communication, and the church group is the immediate recipient of that communication.[21] So the opening statement in Hebrews introduces us to the heart of the book as a whole: God has something to say to the church, and that message focuses preeminently in the person and work of the exalted Son. These propositions must be central as we apply Hebrews 1:1–4.

Several other important elements in the introduction have a powerful impact on certain sections by supporting the four central themes explained

---

20. Guthrie, *The Structure of Hebrews*, 123.
21. See above, p. 30.

above. They are topics related to the heavenly realm,[22] "inheritance,"[23] the "better than" motif,[24] "sin"[25] (either the act or purification), and "angels."[26] That these topics play a supporting role in the rest of the book, highlights both their importance to the book (thus the author's inclusion of them in the introduction) and their subordination to the four main topics mentioned above. Thus, we must read these supporting topics within the larger framework of Hebrews, recognizing the role of each in the author's overarching scheme.

At the same time, these must not be elevated to first place among the author's concerns. For example, an outline of the book built around the "better than" motif, although communicating an important aspect of Hebrews, may obscure the author's primary concern of God's communication to the church through the Son. Even to focus on the purification of sin, one of the most important themes of Hebrews, as the central theme is misguided and misses the bigger picture. Therefore, in seeking to apply 1:1–4 we must focus on the heart of this passage and consider how we might apply these supporting themes at the points the author himself highlights in subsections of the sermon.

A well-crafted introduction was designed not only to show the main topics of a sermon, but also to capture the attention of the hearers. Our author accomplishes this objective by artistically presenting basic Christian belief. For example, in the first verse of the book this gifted preacher uses alliteration, employing five words which begin with the Greek letter "p": *polymeros kai polytropos palai ho theos lalesas tois patrasin en tois prophetais*. As noted in the "Original Meaning" section, the first two verses also exhibit an effective use of parallelism, contrasting the older revelation with the newer given through the Son.[27] The statements in verses 2–3 concerning the Son's inheritance, his role in creation, and his exaltation all begin with relative pronouns: "who . . . through whom . . . who." Some scholars have pointed to literary elements in the introduction as indicating the presence of an ancient Christian hymn, although others have attempted to refute this assertion.[28] Whether the author

---

22. See 1:3, 10; 3:1; 4:14; 6:4; 7:26; 8:1, 5; 9:23–24; 11:12, 16; 12:22–26.
23. See 1:2, 4, 14; 6:12, 17; 9:15; 11:7–8; 12:17.
24. See 1:4; 3:3; 6:9; 7:7, 19, 22; 8:6; 9:23; 10:34; 11:16, 35, 40; 12:24.
25. Found twenty-five times throughout the sermon.
26. See 1:4, 5, 6, 7, 13; 2:2, 5, 7, 9, 16; 12:22; 13:2.
27. See above p. 46.
28. The hymnic character of Heb. 1:2–3 has been called into question by D. W. B. Robinson, "The Literary Structure of Hebrews 1:1–4," *AJBA* 2 (1972): 178–86, who does so on the basis of the balanced structure of ideas in Heb. 1:1–4; J. Frankowski, "Early Christian Hymns Recorded in the New Testament: A Reconsideration of the Question in Light

melded into these verses a Christian hymn with which he was familiar or crafted a passage of eloquent prose himself, these verses are highly artistic and obviously have a specific purpose.

The author does not use his ability with stylistic flair to impress but to rivet the hearers' attention and center it on God's act of communication, especially heard in the person, works, and status of the Son. He accomplishes this objective by presenting a theological framework he shares with other early Christian writers.[29] This framework presents Christ in his preexistence, incarnation, and exaltation. Here the author presents this theology in a chiastic structure[30] (one built around distant parallels):

A God has appointed Christ as heir	*enthronement*
B Through him he created the world	*cosmic action*
C He is the radiance of God's glory	*relation to God*
C' He bears God's stamp	*relation to God*
B' He governs the universe	*cosmic action*
(having made purification for sins)	*(incarnation)*
A' He sat down at God's right hand	*enthronement*

As we attempt to apply Hebrews 1:1–4 to the contemporary church, we must come to grips with the Christology of early Christian doctrine as well as how to respond to that Christology and those who challenge it. The author's crafting of this text challenges us to consider how theology might be communicated artistically and effectively to those in need of hearing "the Word of God through the Son" today.

The structure of Hebrews 1:1–4. A second interpretive guideline that aids in unraveling this complex text is the grammatical structure of the passage. We have already noted that these verses may be divided into two main movements, the first (1:1–2a) addressing the "Climax of Divine Communication," and the second (1:2b–4) the "Person, Work, and Status of the Son."

---

of Heb 1,3," *BZ* 27 (1983): 183–94. Yet, parts of Heb. 1:2–3 (scholars disagree on the exact beginning and ending of the "fragment") as a hymn fragment have been supported by several scholars on the bases of form and content. See, for example, Ralph P. Martin, *Carmen Christi: Philippians ii.5–11 in Recent Interpretation and in the Setting of Early Christian Worship* (Cambridge: Cambridge Univ. Press, 1967), 18–19; Jack T. Sanders, *The New Testament Christological Hymns: Their Historical Religious Background* (Cambridge: Cambridge Univ. Press, 1971), 92–94.

29. The pattern of God's Son leaving heaven, coming to earth to suffer and die for humanity, and then being exalted back to heaven finds expression at various places in the New Testament; of special interest is Phil. 2:5–11. See Attridge, *The Epistle to the Hebrews*, 78–81; Martin Hengel, *The Son of God* (Philadelphia: Fortress, 1976), 87.

30. Adapted from Ellingworth, *The Epistle to the Hebrews*, 95.

As demonstrated in the Original Meaning section, the first of these movements sets God's revelation in the premessianic age over against the revelation of "these last days" and does so by presenting the eras, recipients, agents, and manner of each.

Parallelism is a style through which the author communicates correspondences and contrasts between the two eras. This does not mean, however, that the two eras are merely successive periods in which God's word was given to his people. Nor does it mean that revelation of the past era has been rendered insignificant by the present Christian era. The grammatical relationships in this passage suggest a dynamic relationship between the two periods of time. It is important to note the word translated "spoke" in verse 1 is a participle dependent on the main verb translated "he has spoken" in verse 2. The sense communicated by these words is "having spoken in the past . . . God spoke to us by his Son." The participle may be interpreted as "circumstantial," that is, providing circumstances surrounding the action of the main verb. Thus there exists a connection between the older revelation and the newer.

This relationship suggests a continuity alongside the discontinuity in God's communication as we move from one age to the next. God is still the one speaking (continuity), but he now has communicated to us climactically by the agent of his Son (discontinuity). This revelation of the new age builds on, rather than does away with, the revelation of the old, as seen by the author's extensive use of the Old Testament in the rest of the book as a witness to the Messiah.[31] It would be a hermeneutical mistake to use this passage as a basis for rejecting the Old Testament.

As we have already suggested, the second movement of 1:1–4 highlights seven affirmations concerning the Son (1:2b–4). The first two—that the Son has been appointed heir and was the agent of creation—are expressed in relative clauses introduced by "whom" and "through whom" (*hon* and *di' hou* respectively). At the heart of the third relative clause (introduced by *hos*) is the proclamation that the Son has sat down at the right hand of God, and the rest of the affirmations are subordinate to this clause, supporting the idea of the Son's exaltation (lit. trans. follows).

> *Son*
> v. 2b * *whom he appointed heir of all things*
>   *and*
>   * *through whom he made the universe*

---

31. F. F. Bruce, *The Epistle to the Hebrews*, NICNT (Grand Rapids: Eerdmans, 1990), 45.

v. 3   * who ...

> being the radiance of God's glory
> and
> > the exact representation of his being
> sustaining all things by his powerful word
> having provided purification for sins
> ... sat down at the right hand of the Majesty

v. 4   having become as much superior to the angels ...

Thus, the grammatical structure of the passage highlights what we have already suggested as a key theme governing the entire discourse: the exaltation of the Son to the right hand of God.[32] This constitutes a launching point as the author moves to his discussion of Christ's superiority to the angels in 1:5–14 and plays a vital role at key turning points in Hebrews (1:13; 8:1; 10:12; 12:2).[33] The one seated at the right hand is the one who is the reflection of God's glory and the representation of his being, the one bearing all things by his powerful word, the one who made purification of sins, and the one who is now preeminent over the angels. In moving the message of the passage to contemporary contexts, therefore, we must allow our focus in this second part of the book's introduction to be drawn to the exaltation of Christ and ask what implications it has for us today.

Theological terminology and the broader context of Hebrews. Although the language used of God's Son in 1:1–4 is powerfully figurative, it may seem vague to modern minds. This fact opens the way for theological missteps if the introduction is not read in light of its broader context. For example, someone might suggest that, since the Son is the "radiance" or "reflection" (a common translation of the term) of God's glory and the "representation" of his being, he is inferior to God. Yet, as we noted in the Original Meaning section, the author consistently ascribes to the Son actions and a nature that identified him with God. The Son's identification with God is further supported by the broader context. In 1:6 he receives worship from the angels and in 1:8 the Son is addressed with the designation "God" (*theos*): "Your throne, O God, will last for ever and ever, and righteousness will be the scepter of your kingdom."[34]

However, the erroneous proposition that the Son is indistinct from the Father might be drawn from the same statements. Since the "radiance" and the "glory" may be seen as the same, one might reason that no distinction can be

---

32. See above, pp. 53–54.

33. Guthrie, *The Structure of Hebrews*, 123.

34. See A. W. Wainwright, "The Confession 'Jesus is God' in the New Testament," *SJT* 10 (1959): 286–87; M. J. Harris, "The Translation and Significance of θεός in Hebrews 1:8–9," *TynBul* 36 (1985): 129–62.

made between the two. A heresy beginning in the second century and known as "modalistic monarchianism" made such a suggestion. The modalists submitted that there is one Godhead, which can be called by three different names, depending on the situation. The Father, Son, and Spirit, therefore, are merely successive revelations of the same person.[35] Yet, both in the introduction and throughout Hebrews we find the Father and the Son referred to as distinct persons of the Godhead. The Father speaks to the Son (1:5); the Son has been made lower than the angels for a time (2:5–9); the Son proclaims the Father's name (2:12); the Son was faithful in obedience to the Father (3:1–6); and so on.

Another part of 1:1–4 that can be misunderstood is the statement, "So he became as much superior to the angels. . . ." Does this mean that the Son was, by nature, inferior to the angels prior to the exaltation? Some forms of another early heresy, "dynamic monarchianism," held that Jesus became divine only after the resurrection.[36] Yet this position cannot be affirmed in light of both the introduction and the rest of the book of Hebrews. This passage is spatially oriented. That Jesus "became much superior" means that he went from earth back to heaven.[37] As already noted, the book affirms the deity of the Son in his preexistence. No mere mortal, Jesus was there at the beginning of time to lay the foundations of the world (1:10–11).

Summary of "Bridging Contexts." In our attempt to think through principles by which the message of Hebrews 1:1–4 might be applied accurately today, two central truths in this passage have risen to the surface. (1) The introduction to Hebrews boldly and artistically states that God is a communicator who has spoken to the church. This communication has progressed beyond, but has continuity with, the older covenant revelation in that God is still the one speaking and the Old Testament bears witness to the new era. (2) God has communicated ultimately in the person of his Son. This Son is proclaimed as one with, but distinct from, God the Father, having a nature, activity, and position that identify him with God. The person and work of the Son is brought to climax and focus in his exaltation to God's right hand, a position of ultimate authority and honor in the universe.

THEOLOGY AS THE **foundation for Christian practice.** Some branches of the church have always placed great emphasis on practical, experiential Christianity. In recent decades groups such as the Navigators and Campus Crusade for Christ rightly have stressed "discipleship"

---

35. Millard Erickson, *Christian Theology*, 334.
36. Ibid., 333.
37. Guthrie, *The Structure of Hebrews*, 121–24.

and the need for application in the daily life of the believer. Since the early 1970s many mainline churches have joined this emphasis, teaching classes on such topics as "How to Have a Quiet Time," "Scripture Memory," "Marriage and the Family," and "Sharing Christ in the Marketplace." Too many of these groups, with nonmainline churches as well, have dropped offering "Basic Christian Doctrine" classes altogether. We want to know how Christianity affects our lives today and how it can help us make it though tomorrow.

In their devotional times, many Christians find themselves returning again and again to the "practical" sections of Scripture, like the book of James or those sections of Paul's writings in which he deals with "real life" issues, such as marriage or money. This material can be applied readily to the nitty-gritty issues of living in contemporary culture. On the shelves of any Christian bookstore, one finds hundreds of Christian self-help books on a plethora of topics and only a handful dealing with theological issues.

At times we drift dangerously close to the backwaters of our culture's pragmatism, going so far as to judge sermons on the basis of whether we were offered anything practical or relevant. If the truth taught in a Bible study, devotional time, or sermon does not have immediate implications, we do not embrace it. With our society we glorify "doers" above "thinkers." Thus, the rock star or the football hero who may be immature and shallow theo-logically is elevated as a star witness to Christianity.

Warm-hearted, devotional, application-oriented Christianity should be encouraged. The Scriptures were written to change, mold, and direct the lives of God's people. Yet grave danger lies in focusing on the so-called "practical" teachings of Christianity *to the neglect of the "theological."* Theology and practice are both vitally important aspects of following Christ. Notice that in his intro-duction to the book, the author of Hebrews lays a foundation for his entire sermon with basic Christian doctrine. He uses dogma as a precursor to praxis.

At the same time, the author hints of his practical concerns by remind-ing his audience that the word of God is "to us," a foreshadowing of his hor-tatory sections. He later follows with such exhortations as "encourage one another" (3:13; 10:25), "lay aside sin" (12:1–2), and get busy with relation-ships and right attitudes (e.g., 13:1–6). Therefore, the introduction to Hebrews challenges us at the point of seeing the powerful life and ministry tool offered in sound theology. Right theology lays an important foundation for a Christian life robustly lived. A neglect of theology, on the other hand, has detrimental effects on the church and individual Christian lives. In the mid-part of this century Dorothy Sayers wrote:

> Official Christianity, of late years, has been having what is known
> as bad press. We are constantly assured that the churches are empty

because preachers insist too much upon doctrine—dull dogma as people call it. The fact is the precise opposite. It is the neglect of dogma that makes for dullness. The Christian faith is the most exciting drama that ever staggered the imagination of man—and the dogma is the drama. . . .

Christ, in His divine innocence, said to the woman of Samaria, "Ye worship ye know not what"—being apparently under the impression that it might be desirable, on the whole, to know what one was worshipping. He thus showed himself sadly out of touch with the twentieth-century mind, for the cry today is: "Away with the tedious complexities of dogma—let us have the simple spirit of worship; just worship, no matter of what!" The only drawback to this demand for a generalized and undirected worship is the practical difficulty of arousing any sort of enthusiasm for the worship of nothing in particular.[38]

Those who neglect theology may live a shallow, insipid form of Christianity that, in the end, neither affects life nor endures the test of time.

Another pitfall accompanying the neglect of theology consists of a drift into aberrations of orthodox Christianity. One watches in horror as sincere Christians express infatuation with books like *Embraced by the Light*, supposedly the account of a near-death experience, which is full of wrong-headed propositions about God and reality.[39] Others base their prayer lives and "spiritual warfare" on "principles" learned in the fiction of Frank Peretti, or build material hopes around promises made by the vendors of the health-and-wealth gospel. These bear witness to Hebrews' insistence on right thinking as essential for right living. Thus the task of theology is to keep us "on track" in the Christian life. The author of Hebrews presents it as foundational to perseverance in that life. Theology "is an act of repentant humility," wrote Karl Barth, in which "the Church seeks again and again to examine itself critically. . . . It has to be a watchman so as to carefully observe that constant threatening and invasive error to which the life of the Church is in danger, because it is composed of fallible, erring, sinful people."[40]

However, the demand for the right teaching and learning of theology cuts two ways. Remember that the author of Hebrews presents his opening thesis *artistically*. When members of our churches or students in our schools are

---

38. Dorothy L. Sayers, *The Whimsical Christian: Eighteen Essays by Dorothy L. Sayers* (New York: Macmillan, 1978), 11, 23.

39. Betty J. Eadie, *Embraced by the Light* (Placerville, Calif.: Gold Leaf, 1992). For a critique of such near-death experiences, see William M. Arnor, *Heaven Can't Wait: A Survey of Alleged Trips to the Other Side* (Grand Rapids: Baker, 1996).

40. Karl Barth, "Theology," in *God in Action* (Edinburgh: T. & T. Clark, 1936), 39–57.

intimidated by massive systematic theologies or are bored to tears over dry doctrinal lectures, we tend to write them off as "intellectually deficient" or "lacking theological depth." Yet, some of the responsibility falls to those of us behind the pulpit and in front of the classroom. We must ask whether we are helping matters by our manner of presentation. Perhaps we erect barriers to the content through poor patterns of communication. The author of Hebrews has shown great skill and care in packaging his doctrine to get the attention of his hearers.

Perhaps to our lectures we could add poetry, drama, or music to communicate orthodox teachings of the faith. In the church I attend we sing a chorus, partially based on Hebrews 6:19–20, through which we praise our Lord with the words:

My hope is not in this life, nor this passing world's reward
But my hope is in a life that will never fade
My hope is in You Jesus, risen King, ascended Lord
Even death itself could not hold you in the grave

And Jesus you've gone before us, and your faithfulness never fails
In the darkness you reassure us, you're the anchor beyond the veil.

As we sing, we meditate on profound truths of the faith. One also thinks of majestic hymns such as "A Mighty Fortress" or "Great Is Thy Faithfulness." Also, a great deal of theology, exclaimed C. S. Lewis, may be "sneaked in" via a good story, which he proved with the *Chronicles of Narnia* and other works. Some theologians may see these as trite or simplistic expressions of profound truths. Yet passages such as Hebrews 1:1–4 and Philippians 2:5–11 suggest the New Testament writers offered their readers basic theological truths, simply presented, but which presupposed a larger body of theology.

Biblical preaching. The topic of divine communication in the introduction of Hebrews also focuses attention on the issue of preaching—that is, preaching skillfully executed. The presupposition most basic to the activity of preaching is "God has spoken," for ultimately it is the word of God, not our words, that has the power to change peoples' lives.[41] The author of Hebrews displays a conviction concerning the importance of preaching; for it is through this "word of exhortation" we call Hebrews that he asserts God's climactic word through his Son.

---

41. Of preaching Dr. D. Martyn Lloyd-Jones states, "Any true definition of preaching must say that man is there to deliver the message of God, a message from God to those people. If you prefer the language of Paul, he is 'an ambassador for Christ.' That is what he is, he is a commissioned person, and he is standing there as the mouthpiece of God and of Christ to address these people." See his *Preaching and Preachers* (Grand Rapids: Zondervan, 1972), 53.

Yet in some circles today, preaching is being challenged as an outdated mode of communication, and this challenge must be answered. Speaking of the importance of preaching to Christianity, John Stott writes:

Preaching is indispensable to Christianity. Without preaching a necessary part of its authenticity has been lost. For Christianity is, in its very essence, a religion of the Word of God. No attempt to understand Christianity can succeed which overlooks or denies the truth that the living God has taken the initiative to reveal himself savingly to fallen humanity; or that his self-revelation has been given by the most straightforward means of communication known to us, namely by a word and words; or that he calls upon those who have heard his Word to speak it to others.[42]

And of its relevance for our contemporary context Karl Barth states:

It is simply a truism, that there is nothing more important, more urgent, more helpful, more redemptive and more salutary, there is nothing, from the viewpoint of heaven and earth, more relevant to the real situation than the speaking and the hearing of the Word of God in the originative and regulative power of its truth.[43]

Therefore, the church of this or any century must give attention to the preached word as a primary instrument of change and spiritual development. Although the world may reject the activity as vain babbling, it is the preached word, as far as it is true to the revealed word, through which God manifests his power (1 Cor. 1:17–29). Thus God calls preachers to study in such a way that they accurately reflect the message of Scripture (2 Tim. 2:15–16).

The challenge of naturalism and relativism. Another area in which the introduction to Hebrews speaks to our contemporary context concerns certain philosophies that permeate Western culture and have made great inroads to the church itself. A fundamental aspect of modernity, and an aspect that still holds profound influence even as our culture is shifting to a postmodern orientation, is *naturalism*. Naturalism holds that nature constitutes the totality of reality. There is no "supernature" that stands outside the cause-and-effect natural processes of the universe. Therefore, all of your thoughts, all of your feelings, every event you ever experienced (including what you would classify as "religious experiences"), can all be attributed to nature.[44]

---

42. John Stott, *Between Two Worlds: The Art of Preaching in the Twentieth Century* (Grand Rapids: Eerdmans, 1982), 15.

43. Karl Barth, *The Word of God and the Word of Man* (New York: Peter Smith, 1958), 123–24.

44. See C. S. Lewis, *Miracles: A Preliminary Study* (New York: MacMillan, 1947), 15–22; M. H. MacDonald, "Naturalism," *EDT*, 750–51.

Thus, religion becomes a process "from the bottom up," consisting of human reflections on a concept called "god." That is, religion originates in the minds of people. There is no such thing as revelation, since there is no God standing above or outside of nature to act upon it. For some modern theologians and biblical critics, this philosophy is a basic assumption.

However, Hebrews boldly proclaims a perspective diametrically opposed to naturalism. God stands above the natural processes of this world (since he created them) and speaks to humanity. For Hebrews religion works "from the top down"; that is, God reveals his truth and his will. His revelation is coherent, consistent, and authoritative, and we are obliged both to listen to it and to obey it.

This brings us to the problem of *relativism* for the modern church. This "ism" is much more inherent to postmodernism, the philosophical climate that dominates Western culture as we move into the twenty-first century. Modernism, committed to the absence of anything supernatural, proposed that individual minds, guided by scientific investigation, were the means to arrive at truth and thus to obtain instruction for life.[45] Postmodernism, on the other hand, suggests that "truth" and "reality" are merely perceptions dictated by one's particular worldview. Since truth is merely a social construct, everyone's "truth" (scientific or otherwise) becomes equally valid.[46] Thus, acceptance (i.e., reckoning all views as equally valid) becomes the most important social norm. A letter to the editor in the local paper to which I subscribe clearly expressed this perspective. Speaking of his rejection of Christianity he wrote:

> This does not condemn my soul. There are hundreds of millions of non-Christians in the world, and their gods are just as real and valid as Christianity's. Perhaps those who cannot understand that simple truth are the ones in need of guidance and sympathy.

This perspective rests on the basic assumption that religion only has value as a social expression and that therefore, all religions are equally *invalid* as means of arriving at an ultimate, universal, normative Truth. Some currents in postmodernism, especially as expressed at the popular level, are more open to the supernatural than is thoroughgoing modernism. However, the "god" to which some postmodernists are open is a god both ill-defined and tolerant of all expressions of religion. S/he is the mother/father-god of the universe, who welcomes all her/his world children regardless of their belief systems. Since relativism offers no specific god, however, it also offers no specific help personally or socially.

---

45. John Dewey, *Reconstruction in Philosophy* (New York: Henry Holt, 1929), 47–49.

46. J. Richard Middleton and Brian J. Walsh, *Truth Is Stranger Than It Used to Be: Biblical Faith in a Postmodern Age* (Downers Grove, Ill.: InterVarsity, 1995), 32–33.

Postmodernism leads, therefore, to devastating moral confusion.[47] As the culture around us, and many within the church, bow to the relativism of postmodernity and as the culture plummets to deeper and deeper levels of social bewilderment and crisis, those who take seriously the biblical witness to the Son as the ultimate Word of God must stand with Hebrews in stating categorically, "God has spoken." This proposition not only lays the foundation for Christian preaching but also offers hope for all modern people, providing them with a stable point of reference for life.

Modern views of Jesus. As we have seen, the Son of God, as a focal subject in Hebrews 1:1—4, is that Son who was preexistent, became incarnate, and was then exalted to the right hand of God. We might say that the contemporary Jesus has come a long way since Hebrews was written—a long way down to earth. This exaltation, according to some modern Jesus scholars, only occurred in the minds and theologizing of the early church. Thus, the exalted Jesus of the New Testament is being recast variously today as cynic philosopher, charismatic man of the spirit, an eschatological prophet, a prophet of social change, and a sage.[48]

The modern studies of Jesus have been popularized most by the "Jesus Seminar," a group of seventy-four scholars who meet regularly to vote on the authenticity of the Gospels' accounts concerning Jesus. Among their "findings": Only eighteen percent of sayings ascribed to Jesus in the Gospels are authentic, and Jesus did not really rise from the dead. The latter, not surprising (given the Seminar's commitment to philosophical naturalism), directly contradicts a basic tenet inherent in the exaltation proclamation of Hebrews 1:3. Although the Seminar has been harshly criticized for poor methodology, outdated presuppositions, and neglect of work done among New Testament scholars outside their group,[49] their media machine has given them a broad hearing in popular culture.

Earlier in this century G. Campbell Morgan suggested that when the church ceases to lift Christ to the height where all people can see him, it becomes useless and a fraud.[50] The modern views of Jesus that attempt to

---

47. Ibid., 61.

48. See Ben Witherington III, *The Jesus Quest: The Third Search for the Jew of Nazareth* (Downers Grove, Ill.: InterVarsity, 1995); Scot McKnight, "Who Is Jesus: An Introduction to Jesus Studies," 51—72 in *Jesus Under Fire: Modern Scholarship Reinvents the Historical Jesus*, ed. Michael J. Wilkins and J. P. Moreland (Grand Rapids: Zondervan, 1995); Luke Timothy Johnson, *The Real Jesus: The Mistaken Quest for the Historical Jesus and the Truth of the Traditional Gospels* (San Francisco: HarperSanFrancisco, 1996).

49. In addition to the works in the previous footnote, see D. A. Carson, "Five Gospels, No Christ," *Christianity Today* (April 25, 1994), 30—33; Craig Blomberg, "Where Do We Start Studying Jesus," 17—50 in *Jesus Under Fire*.

50. As quoted in "Reflections," *Christianity Today* (May 20, 1996), 54.

---

make Christianity "fit" for modern perspectives actually undermine the heart of Christianity—that Jesus was vindicated as the Messiah, God's Son, by his resurrection from the dead, and that he was exalted to the right hand of God as Lord of the universe—and the church's ministry.

It is only the exalted Jesus who can make purification of sins, according to Hebrews (1:3; 8:1—2; 9:1—10:18), and provide us a way to draw near to God (4:14—16; 10:19—25). It is only the exalted Jesus who can offer help to us in our time of need (4:15—16), deliver us from death (2:14—15), and lead us to glory (2:10; 12:22—24). In short, it is only the exalted Jesus who is fit for our worship and attention and who can help us persevere in the Christian life. The problem with the insipid Jesus of the Jesus Seminar consists not in his humanity, but in that he is no more than human. As such he is unable to offer anything to modern people beyond the inspiration of his words and ideas—and precious few of these survive the Seminar's "analysis."

In his book *Evangelicanism and the Future of Christianity*, Alistar McGrath, formerly a theological liberal and now one of Evangelicalism's strongest spokesmen, writes concerning his disillusionment with liberalism:

> Yet the more I thought about the liberal project, and the more I wrestled with its agenda and approaches, the more I felt that it was academically vulnerable and spiritually inadequate. Its pastoral weaknesses became especially evident to me during a three-year period as a pastor in Nottingham (1980—1983), in which I came to realize that liberalism had little to offer in the midst of the harsh pastoral realities of unemployment, illness and death.[51]

By contrast, the Son of Hebrews 1:1—4 has much to offer humanity in general and the church in particular. As the preexistent One, who has paid for our sins and been exalted to the right hand of God, he is our true, present source of hope and help.

---

51. Alistar McGrath, *Evangelicanism and the Future of Christianity* (Downers Grove, Ill.: Inter-Varsity, 1995), 13.

Hebrews 1:5-14

F OR TO WHICH of the angels did God ever say,

> "You are my Son;
>   today I have become your Father"?

Or again,

> "I will be his Father,
>   and he will be my Son"?

⁶And again, when God brings his firstborn into the world, he says,

> "Let all God's angels worship him."

⁷In speaking of the angels he says,

> "He makes his angels winds,
>   his servants flames of fire."

⁸But about the Son he says,

> "Your throne, O God, will last for ever and ever,
>   and righteousness will be the scepter of your kingdom.
> ⁹You have loved righteousness and hated wickedness;
>   therefore God, your God, has set you above
>   your companions
>   by anointing you with the oil of joy."

¹⁰He also says,

> "In the beginning, O Lord, you laid the foundations
>   of the earth,
>   and the heavens are the work of your hands.
> ¹¹They will perish, but you remain;
>   they will all wear out like a garment.
> ¹²You will roll them up like a robe;
>   like a garment they will be changed.
> But you remain the same,
>   and your years will never end."

¹³To which of the angels did God ever say,

> "Sit at my right hand
> until I make your enemies
>   a footstool for your feet"?

¹⁴Are not all angels ministering spirits sent to serve those who will inherit salvation?

Original Meaning — AT LEAST TWO points become clear in Hebrews 1:5–14. (1) The author continues a number of vitally important themes he had introduced in the first four verses. These include God's speaking, Christ as "Son" of God, the Son's role in creation, and his enthronement at the exaltation. Moreover, included at every hand are implicit and explicit references to the Son's deity and to his place "above" the angels. These topics provide important threads tying together the chain of quotations in this passage.

(2) The enthronement of the Son as Messiah, God's anointed king, is focal; the climactic quote of Psalm 110:1 at verse 13 is most fitting as a summary of this chain of Old Testament texts. An important proclamation of this messianic psalm, the subjection of the Son's enemies, also lies behind the author's use of Psalm 2:7 (in v. 5) and 45:6–7 (in vv. 8–9).

During the era in which Hebrews was written, teachers of Scripture (e.g., the rabbis, teachers associated with Qumran, and some New Testament writers) built support for a theological position by stringing together various Old Testament texts. Such "chain quotations" offered defense of the position being taught through the quantity of support given. One finds this approach, for example, in Paul's letter to the Romans at 9:25–29; 10:18–21; and 11:8–10. The desired effect was to offer so much evidence that your listeners shook their heads in agreement with you by the end of these quotations.[1]

This method the author of Hebrews uses in 1:5–14. He presents three pairs of Old Testament passages, followed by the final quotation of Psalm 110:1, in support of the Son's superiority to the angels. The first pair (Ps. 2:7; 2 Sam. 7:14) proclaims the Son's superiority by virtue of his unique relationship to the Father (Heb. 1:5). The second (Ps. 97:7;[2] 104:4) focuses attention on the angels' positive, but inferior, position and ministry (Heb. 1:6–7). The Son's eternality constitutes the topic of the third pair of texts (Ps. 45:6–7; 102:25–27).

The two passages in each duo are joined by "catchwords" held in common. Psalm 2:7 and 2 Samuel 7:14 share the term "Son" (*huios*) and the pronouns "I" (*ego*) and "my/to me" (*mou/moi*). The second pair (Ps. 97:7; 104:4) are brought together through their common reference to "angels" (*angeloi*). Finally, various forms of the pronoun "you" and the attestations to the Son's eternality draw together Psalm 45:6–7 and 102:25–27.

---

1. E. Earle Ellis, *Paul's Use of the Old Testament* (Grand Rapids: Baker, 1981), 49–50; Markus Barth, "The Old Testament in Hebrews," in *Issues in New Testament Interpretation*, ed. W. Klassen and G. F. Snyder (New York: Harper and Row, 1962), 64.

2. This quotation also bears resemblance to the Septuagint form of Deut. 32:43. See Bruce, *The Epistle to the Hebrews*, 56–58.

With Hebrews 1:13 this chain's climax appears—the quotation of Psalm 110:1 (the messianic exaltation passage alluded to in Heb. 1:3). The last verse of this section (1:14) effects a transition to 2:1–4 by restating the content of Psalm 104:4 (quoted in Heb. 1:7).

The Son's Unique Relationship to the Father (1:5)

THE AUTHOR BEGINS with a question: "For to which of the angels did God ever say. . .?" Rather than a request for information, this query is rhetorical, a way of making an assertion. The writer is, in fact, proclaiming, "There is no angel to whom God has said . . . !" The two quotations in verse 5 continue a focus on the sonship of Jesus started in 1:2.

It seems clear from the Dead Sea Scrolls that the concept of the Messiah as God's Son was an aspect of Jewish thinking even prior to the Christian era.[3] Also, numerous passages in the Gospels focus on Jesus' unique relationship to God as Father.[4] Our Lord adopts the designation "Son" in both overt statements and inferences (e.g., referring to God as "my Father"), and the title itself, as used by other characters in the divine drama, is often closely associated with the title "Christ" (i.e., Messiah; see Matt. 16:16; 26:63; Mark 8:29; Luke 4:41; John 11:27; 20:31). As the Christian movement expanded, the appellation "Son" formed an important aspect of early Christian preaching about Jesus (e.g., Acts 9:20–22).

Both Psalm 2:7 and 2 Samuel 7:14 had been adopted in earliest Christianity as pointing to the enthronement of Messiah. In its original context, Psalm 2 speaks of the concerted rebellion of the nations and their rulers against God and his Anointed One. The psalmist asserts that this rebellion will be smashed by the awesome, overwhelming power of the King whom God has enthroned in Mount Zion. Early Christ-followers applied this psalm to Jesus as Messiah and saw in it the promise of victory over those earthly forces opposed to the church (e.g., Acts 4:23–31; 13:33–34). Second Samuel 7:14 communicates the words of the prophet Nathan to David, promising that great king that one of his offspring will have an eternal kingdom. The author of Hebrews sees the fulfillment of this prophesy in the person of the exalted Son.[5]

But what of the temporal imagery in these two texts? What does it mean that God has "become" the Son's Father "today" and that he "will be" his

---

3. In 4Q Florilegium, 2 Sam. 7:14 is given explicit messianic application. See Longenecker, *The Christology of Early Jewish Christianity*, 95.

4. See such focal pericopes as those regarding Jesus' birth, his time in the temple at age twelve, his baptism, and his temptation in the desert (Mark 1:9–11; Luke 1:32; 2:41–50; 3:21–22; 4:1–13).

5. Hughes, *The Epistle to the Hebrews*, 56–57.

Father? These, of course, are not references to a bringing into existence, nor what some in the church would later call "the eternal generation of the Son," speaking of the eternal nature of the relationship between God and his Messiah. We have already seen that Jesus was considered the Son prior to creation itself and is later referred to as "Son" in the Incarnation (e.g., Heb. 5:8). Rather, the early church understood these passages to refer to Jesus' induction into his royal position as King of the universe at the resurrection and exaltation. With these events God vindicated Jesus as Messiah and established his eternal kingdom (see Acts 13:32–34; Rom. 1:4). God's becoming the Son's Father, then, refers to God's open expression of their relationship upon Christ's enthronement, an interpretation that fits both Old Testament contexts in question.[6]

The Inferior Position of the Angels (1:6–7)

THE TERM FIRSTBORN (*prototokon*) continues the idea of sonship established thus far in Hebrews. In the ancient world this term most often referred to the (human or animal) child first born to a mother. Furthermore, it had strong religious overtones in the consecration of the firstborn to Yahweh (e.g., Ex. 13:2, 15; 22:29; Lev. 27:26; Num. 3:13). A firstborn son had a special place in the heart of his father (e.g., 2 Sam. 13:36–37; 1 Chron. 3:1), shared the father's authority, and inherited the lion's share of his property.[7] In most of the eight New Testament occurrences of the word, it serves as a title for Christ, expressing his preeminence in the church and the cosmos, and is especially associated with the resurrection (Rom. 8:29; Col. 1:15, 18; Heb. 11:23; Rev. 1:5).

"World" (*oikoumenen*) refers not to planet earth, but rather to the heavenly realm.[8] This interpretation finds support in the author's use of the same word speaking of the heavenly realm at 2:5 and well fits the immediate context, which magnifies the exaltation of the Son to the right hand of God. The occasion used to introduce 1:6 is the same highlighted in 1:5.

Verses 6–7 present the angels in two activities that imply their subordination to the Son. (1) With the quote of Psalm 97:7 they are exhorted to "worship" the Son, an act that implies the Son's deity. (2) Psalm 104:4 expresses their role as servants of God—a theme made more clear by the author's recapitulation of, and further comment on, this passage later at Hebrews 1:14: "Are not all angels ministering spirits sent to serve those who

---

6. Ibid., 54–55; and especially Delitzsch, *Commentary on the Epistle to the Hebrews*, 64–65.

7. Ceslas Spicq, *Theological Lexicon of the New Testament*, trans. James D. Ernest, 3 vols. (Peabody, Mass.: Hendrickson, 1994), 3:210.

8. Bruce, *The Epistle to the Hebrews*, 58; Lane, *Hebrews 1–8*, 26–27.

will inherit salvation?" In the Scriptures angels are created, heavenly beings, who primarily function as messengers for God, revealing his will or announcing key events (e.g., Gen. 19:1–22; Ex. 3:2–6; Judg. 2:1–5; Matt. 1:20–24). They also serve to protect God's people (e.g., Ex. 14:19–20; 1 Kings 19:1–8; Acts 12:7–11). In contexts accentuating God's power and majesty, angels worship him or attend his throne.[9] It is therefore of no small significance that they here are said to worship the Son, an implicit acclamation of his deity.

The Eternality of the Son's Reign and Relationship to the Cosmos (1:8–12)

THE PREACHER'S THIRD pair of Old Testament texts returns full attention to the Son, celebrating both his status as the divine, eternal, anointed King (1:8–9) and his role as builder and terminator of the cosmos (1:10–12). These two passages focus on three overarching themes. (1) They speak of the Son's authority. The Son sits on a "throne," has a "scepter," and has a "kingdom" (1:8). Furthermore, he has been anointed "above [his] companions" as king (1:9). He is also the one with the authority to lay "the foundations of the earth" and to mold "the heavens" with his "hands" (1:10).

(2) The author's use of these texts draws attention to the Son's eternal nature. As promised to his ancestor in the flesh, David, the Messiah's kingdom is one that "will last forever and ever" (1:8). The Lord was there "in the beginning" (1:10), and his "years will never end" (1:12). By contrast, the created order changes, becoming old and perishable. Like long-worn clothing the Son will fold it up at the end of the age (1:11–12), but he remains "the same" (1:12).

(3) In addition to the affirmation of the Son's deity implied in these creation statements, Hebrews 1:8 has one of the most explicit references to Jesus as God found in the New Testament: "Your throne, O God, will last forever and ever."[10]

The Son's Position at the Right Hand in Contrast with the Position of the Angels (1:13–14)

THE AUTHOR'S STRING of Old Testament quotations comes to its zenith with his quote of Psalm 110:1: "Sit at my right hand until I make your enemies a

---

9. Mike Martin, "Angel," *Holman Bible Dictionary*, ed. Trent C. Butler (Nashville, Tenn: Holman, 1991), 51–52.

10. Most scholars take the use of *ho theos* in 1:8 as vocative. See R. E. Brown, *Jesus, God and Man* (Milwaukee: Bruce, 1967), 25; esp. Murray Harris, *Jesus As God: The New Testament Use of Theos in Reference to Jesus* (Grand Rapids: Baker, 1992), 205–27.

footstool for your feet."[11] He introduces the excerpt with a rhetorical question similar to the one found in 1:5. This repetition effects a stylistic device known as an *inclusio*. Writers and speakers of the ancient world did not use subheadings, as we do, to mark off sections of their work. The *inclusio*, a device used for that purpose, involved the bracketing of a unit of text through the same or similar statements at the beginning and end.[12] Thus the reappearance of the rhetorical question at this point signals that the author is about to conclude this portion on the superiority of the Son to the angels.

The difference between the allusion to Psalm 110:1 found at Hebrews 1:3 and the direct quote of this text at 1:13 is that the quotation here includes the duration of the "sitting": "until I make your enemies a footstool for your feet." As with the references to Psalm 2:7 (in v. 5) and Psalm 45:6–7 (in vv. 8–9), the enthronement of the Son has a corresponding implication— defeat for the enemies of God and his Anointed. The recitation of Psalm 110:1 here, moreover, anticipates the author's use of Psalm 8:4–6 in Hebrews 2:5–9, which also speaks of the subjection of all things under the feet of the Messiah.

Summary. The preacher marshals these Old Testament quotations to provide a clear picture of the status of the angels relative to the Son. The Son sits at the preeminent position in the universe, with the angels in an inferior position as the servants who worship him. The Son has an eternal throne, from which the angels are sent out to minister. God has never spoken such proclamations as found in 1:5, 8–13 to the angels. Rather, his proclamations concerning them (1:6–7) show the angels' inferiority. The Son alone is the favored object of divine decrees expressing royalty. By the end of this string of texts, no one in the author's audience can doubt the superiority of the Son over the angels.

BEFORE WE CONSIDER interpretive issues surrounding the author's main points in this passage, it is important to identify a number of procedural dynamics and assumptions that form the backdrop for Hebrews 1:5–14. (1) Why does the author focus such attention on the angels? Were the listeners allured by the worship of angels or tempted to interpret Christ as an angel, as suggested by some scholars? (2) We must then consider four scriptural and four theological assumptions that lie behind

---

11. For a discussion of this psalm see above, p. 49.
12. Guthrie, *The Structure of Hebrews*, 15, 76–89. This device is used throughout Hebrews.

his uses of the Old Testament in this passage. With this groundwork in place, we can center attention on the main propositions the author wishes to communicate through this chain of Old Testament quotations.

Why the angels? Some scholars have understood the comparison of Christ with the angels in Hebrews 1 to indicate the readers were toying with the worship of angels[13] or, perhaps, a form of errant Christology in which Christ was considered subordinate to an angel.[14] Although speculation concerning angels seemed to present a problem in some New Testament communities (e.g., the church at Colosse) and was known in various Jewish and Gnostic circles,[15] this interpretation misunderstands the author's intention for the comparison.

The author establishes the unquestionable superiority of the Son to execute his first exhortation, found in 2:1—4, which consists of an "argument from lesser to greater." This method of argumentation, often used by the rabbis, held if something is true in a lesser situation, it certainly is true in a greater, or more important, situation. Having established Christ's superiority to the angels, the preacher proceeds to argue in 2:1—4: Those who rejected the revelation given through the angels were severely punished; since the Son is greater than the angels, it follows that those who reject the revelation given through him deserve even greater punishment.

In 2:1—4, in other words, the author casts the angels in a positive, though inferior, role.[16] This positive role is basic to the rhetorical argument that the hearers need to take seriously the revelation delivered through the Son. So the answer to our question "Why the angels?" has nothing to do with the worship of them and everything to do with the execution of a skillful argument on the part of our author. To be sure, the listeners had a high regard for and interest in angels, as did others from a worship orientation in Greek-speaking Judaism. At this time Jews placed great emphasis on angels as intermediaries between God and people. They were seen as exalted beings who functioned as heavenly emissaries. This fact makes the rhetorical argument all the more powerful. The audience's respect for the role of angels provided a reference point from which to speak of the much higher position (and, therefore, authority) of the Son of God. In this insight one finds the author's purpose for 1:5—14: *The preacher wishes to impress on his listeners the Son's supreme, unequivocal authority.*

---

13. T. W. Manson, "The Problem of the Epistle to the Hebrews," *BJRL* 32 (1949–1950): 1–17.

14. Y. Yadin, "The Dead Sea Scrolls and the Epistle to the Hebrews," ScrHier 4 (1958): 36–55.

15. Ellingworth, *The Epistle to the Hebrews*, 103.

16. Lane, *Hebrews 1–8*, 17.

Assumptions concerning the Old Testament. Hebrews presents us with the best example of thoroughgoing early Christian exegesis of the Old Testament;[17] behind this exegesis lie several assumptions clearly illustrated in the "chain" of 1:5–14. (1) *The Old Testament consists of the words of God.* Hebrews never mentions an Old Testament author, nor does the preacher use "it is written," Paul's favorite way to introduce an Old Testament quotation. Rather, such quotations are almost always framed as coming directly from the mouth of God, being introduced with forms of the verb "to say" (*lego*). The author, therefore, understands God as the speaker of these passages.

(2) *The Old Testament presents truth.* Our writer of Hebrews assumes that since the Old Testament presents the words of God, those words are true in what they communicate. His arguments would make no sense if this were not the case. Notice that in the chain quotation, with the exception of the introductory formulae, he feels no compulsion to explain the texts. He simply states them as offering facts concerning the Son and the angels.

(3) *The Old Testament presents a unified revelation.* This assumption is especially seen in the author's uses of verbal analogy, the rabbinic technique of considering two passages together on the basis of a word or words they had in common. [18] Inherent to this methodology is the presupposition that God speaks consistently and systematically through Scripture. This approach is similar to what modern interpreters do in cross-referencing a text under examination.

(4) *The Old Testament bears witness to Christ.* Speaking of the early church's Christological interpretation of the Old Testament, Klyne Snodgrass states:

> Texts that may have been general statements about the nation, prophets, priests, or kings were often *idealized* in anticipation of God's end-time deliverer who would fill the categories as no one else had. David had been the king *par excellence*, but one day there would be a king like him, only better. The early church applied such texts to Jesus because of their conviction about his identity. The conviction about his identity did *not* derive from the Old Testament. They did not find texts and then find Jesus. They found Jesus and then saw how the Scriptures fit with him. They were not *proving* his identity in the technical sense so much as they were demonstrating how the Scriptures fit with him. Often they were merely following his lead in pointing to texts that summarized his ministry.[19]

---

17. See esp. G. B. Caird, "The Exegetical Method of the Epistle to the Hebrews," *CJT* 5 (1959): 44–51.

18. See above, p. 67.

19. Klyne Snodgrass, "The Use of the Old Testament in the New," in *New Testament Criticism and Interpretation*, ed. David Alan Black and David S. Dockery (Grand Rapids: Zondervan, 1991), 418.

Christological interpretation could not be more forcefully illustrated than it is in the chain quotation of Hebrews 1. The author reads the Old Testament through the glasses of a Christian, with Christ at the center of interpretation. Moreover, he draws most of his material concerning Christ from the Psalms. These four assumptions form the bases for the manner in which he handles the Old Testament here and throughout the book.

Theological assumptions. To these assumptions concerning the Old Testament may be added several theological assumptions behind Hebrews 1:5–14. (1) *The author understands the Son to be equal with God.* This is unmistakable from his act of addressing the Son (via the Old Testament quotation) with the vocative "O God" in 1:8, as well as his application of Old Testament creation passages to the Son.

(2) As seen especially in his quotation of Psalm 102:25–27, *the author believes the Son to be Lord over the cosmos.* With other early Christian writers, he proclaims the Son as both originator and terminator of the universe; thus, all reality has its unity in him (e.g., Eph. 3:9; Col. 1:16–17; Rev. 4:11; 10:6).

(3) From the author's emphasis on the angels, we can conclude *he believes in a spiritual realm inhabited by spiritual beings called angels.* These beings have specific functions in the mind of this preacher, especially the worship of God and ministry to his people.

(4) *The author assumes that Christ has his enemies and that all of these enemies have yet to be placed under his feet* (1:13). This final assumption addresses their dilemma of persecution, as we shall see in the following chapters. The listeners were overwhelmed with the sense that forces around them were out of their control. Therefore, they questioned God's control of their circumstances (e.g., 2:8–9).

These assumptions concerning the Old Testament and reality as the readers were experiencing it provide a theological framework from which the author approaches his material in 1:5–14. He presents his message with the conviction and vigor of one convinced that his worldview reflects reality. The author's enthusiasm and confidence challenge us concerning the theological frameworks with which we approach the task of applying this text. Do we have a clearly articulated theology of the Scriptures? Do we have a studied and reasoned Christology? Have we continued to explore and read theological works to sharpen our minds in these areas?[20] If we have a "soft" theological foundation, our application, at the end of the day, will be weakened. Application must have its reasons and impetuses, and these are theological in nature. With this in mind, we turn to certain interpretive issues surrounding the author's main points.

---

20. A good place to start is Millard Erickson's *Christian Theology* (Grand Rapids: Baker, 1985), used in many seminaries as an introductory systematic theology.

Three main points. As demonstrated in the Original Meaning section, this preacher of Old Testament texts supports his main theme of the Son's superiority to the angels with three main points. We must consider several interpretive questions and quagmires surrounding each of these. (1) Hebrews 1:5 teaches that the Son is superior to the angels by virtue of his unique relationship to the Father. One can fall into the proverbial ditch with this passage on one of two sides of the hermeneutical road. On the one hand, an "Arian" interpretation of the begetting of the Son by the Father in Psalm 2 must be flatly denied. Arius, a fourth-century heretic, insisted that the Son had a point of beginning, saying of him: "And before he was begotten or created or appointed or established, he did not exist; for he was not unbegotten. We are persecuted because we say: 'the Son has a beginning, but God is without beginning.'"[21] The council of Nicea, which met in A.D. 325, answered Arianism by interpreting the "begetting" to mean that he was "of the same essence of the Father, God of God, Light of Light, very God of very God, begotten, not made, being of one substance [*homoousios*] with the Father. . . ." This creed follows the pattern seen in Hebrews 1 of stressing the Son's nature as divine.

On the other hand, to interpret Hebrews 1:5 as asserting the "eternal begetting" of the Son by the Father is also misdirected. For example, Augustine and Thomas Aquinas understood the "today" in this verse to be the day of God's unchangeable eternity. P. E. Hughes follows Westcott in pointing out that this interpretation is foreign to the context.[22] What is important is the Old Testament background of these passages, supporting a royal enthronement interpretation of the "begetting," and their use elsewhere in early Christian teaching points to the resurrection/exaltation as the fulfillment.[23] The idea communicated is that the Son came into inheritance of all the rights and authority of his filial relationship to the Father when he was enthroned at God's right hand.[24] This is the author's first building block in asserting the supremacy of the Son over the angels.

(2) The next point (cf. 1:6–7) focuses attention on the inferiority of the angels. One might be tempted, based on the command "when God brings his firstborn into the world . . . 'Let all God's angels worship him'" in verse 6, to think of the birth of Jesus and the Yuletide singing of the heavenly host

---

21. Alister E. McGrath, ed. *The Christian Theology Reader* (Cambridge, Mass.: Blackwell, 1995), 140. For a fuller treatment of Arianism and the answer given in the church councils, see Millard J. Erickson, *The Word Became Flesh* (Grand Rapids: Baker, 1991), 47–58.

22. Hughes, *The Epistle to the Hebrews*, 54.

23. See above, pp. 68–69.

24. See Bruce, *The Epistle to the Hebrews*, 54.

(Luke 2:8–14). Yet, as shown in our Original Meaning discussion, the term "world" in verse 6 almost certainly speaks of the heavenly realm, an interpretation fitting to the immediate context, which focuses on the enthronement.[25] The key for understanding the author's intention in verses 6–7 is to note that Psalm 104:4 (and possibly 97:7) features activities performed by the angels. They worship the Son (Heb. 1:6) and are ministers for God (v. 7), the latter being further emphasized in 1:14. By these activities they are shown to be inferior to the Son, whom they worship and serve.

We must hasten to reemphasize that the angels play a positive role in the first two chapters of Hebrews. The first level of our application at this point should not focus on "bad things" that threaten to redirect our commitment to, and the veneration due, Christ. We could rush to an application that pinpointed money, fame, or pleasure as supplanting our affections for the Lord. However, the sense of the author's comparison with the angels in 1:6–7 is more like this: "Even when compared to beings as high as the angels, the Son is of an infinitely higher status. As great as other people or institutions are, look at the surpassing greatness of Christ by comparison. He is the point of reference by which all others must be evaluated."

(3) The final building block in the author's treatment of the Son's superiority to the angels (1:8–12) contains two main topics. (a) The preacher, through the vocative "O God" (v. 8) and the proclamation of the Son's role in the cosmos (vv. 10–12), unmistakably ascribes deity to the Son. (b) Closely associated with this, the author focuses on the Son's eternal rule and nature (1:8, 11–12). At this point it is appropriate to mention the formulation of Trinitarian doctrine worked out in the council of Constantinople (A.D. 381) and expressed well a few years later by Augustine: "We believe that the Father, Son and Holy Spirit are one God, maker and ruler of every creature, and that 'Father' is not 'Son,' nor 'Holy Spirit' 'Father' or 'Son'; but a Trinity of mutually related persons, and a unity of equal essence."[26]

In other words, God is one essence (the one God), but there are three distinct persons in the Godhead. It may seem strange to introduce a discussion of the Trinity to our discussion of Christology, but the early Christological debates over heresies such as Arianism gave rise to the Trinitarian discussions later. The statements concerning the Son in Hebrews 1:8–12 fit well this orthodox formula, "distinct persons and one essence." In that passage we have the Son directly addressed as God (v. 8), and in the next breath the declaration that God has anointed him, setting him above his companions (v. 9). These proclamations express no contradiction but rather a mystery,

---

25. See above, p. 69.
26. *De Trinitate,* 9.1.1–9.5.8.

which to our finite minds is incomprehensible.[27] Theological blunders occur when we emphasize the "unity" of the Godhead to the neglect of the distinctness of persons, or visa versa.

Hebrews 1:5–14 climaxes with the quotation of Psalm 110:1, which presents clearly the exaltation of Christ to the right hand of God. This Old Testament text further demonstrates that the preacher's main interest at this point lies in impressing on the listeners the supreme position and authority of the Son. This impression he uses to good effect in the next chapter.

IT IS NO exaggeration to suggest that Western culture in general and the church in particular are in the midst of an authority crisis. In the wake of Watergate, the moral demise of religious leaders, and the 60s' rejection of moral and cultural norms, we live with the ever-present, nagging question: "To whom or what should we listen in order to find out what to believe and how to order our lives?"[28]

Some answer the question by turning to the occult. Psychic hotlines, a joke just a few years ago in comedy routines, now rake in hundreds of thousands of dollars from those who call the appropriate 900 numbers. Most bookstores have extensive sections on "New Age" and "Eastern Religion." Spirituality is marketable, running sales to one-half billion dollars annually. To many, however, this spirituality abandons any notion of authority or accountability, the spiritual experience being gauged by its achievement of self-authentication.[29] Others look to science as the savior of humanity. Science will save us from cancer and AIDS, we pray, and eventually will unlock the mysteries of the universe. Still others look to religious leaders or gurus who interpret God and reality for them. Even within the Christian church, confusion exists over the nature and authority of Scripture[30] and the nature of authority held by church leadership.

As we have seen in this section, the author uses a chain of Old Testament quotations to a specific end. He focuses the listeners' attention on the preeminent position of Jesus in order to draw them to the preeminent authority of Jesus. Therefore, these verses speak volumes to an age grappling with

---

27. See especially Erickson, *Christian Theology*, 339–40.

28. For a secular sociological analysis, see Robert Nisbet, *Twilight of Authority* (New York: Oxford Univ. Press, 1979).

29. For example, James Redfield's *The Celestine Prophecy*, which to date has sold five million copies.

30. David S. Dockery, *Christian Scripture: An Evangelical Perspective on Inspiration, Authority and Interpretation* (Nashville: Broadman & Holman, 1995), 1.

issues of authority—to whom should we listen; whom can we trust; who has the right answers to our life questions?

Spiritual reference points. One problem in a relativistic culture is the confusion over where to look for truth and meaning in life. The "spiritual reference points" keep shifting as we try great books, great speakers, great churches, and great experiences, hoping that these will produce answers and provide points of reference by which to navigate the difficulties of modern life. A parallel between Hebrews' audience and many modern people is a fascination with and high respect for angels. My wife and I frequent a local bookstore and café where, *sans bambinos,* we can browse the books after enjoying a fine meal, tea, and pastries. On a recent visit, knowing I would soon be writing on this section of Hebrews, I decided to count the works in their religion section addressing the topic of angels. In this "secular" store making no claim to specialize in religious books were *eighty-five* different works! They had intriguing titles, such as *Angels A to Z, Know Your Angels, Ask Your Angels, Angelic Healing, Angelic Voices, Angel Magi, Angels: An Endangered Species, Meditating with the Angels,* and (my personal favorite) *Big George: The Autobiography of an Angel.* They ranged from those attempting to present a biblical explication, like Billy Graham's *Angels,* to *Angels and Aliens*—clearly of a different stripe.

This fascination with angels is also evident from the popularity of the television drama *Touched by an Angel,* a show about heavenly beings who help people in a variety of difficult circumstances. There are magazines, such as *Angel Times,* dedicated to recounting the contacts numerous moderns have had with angelic beings. My wife recently talked to a lady who, since a professed encounter with an angel during a near-death experience, has been collecting angel figurines.

Angels are clearly both popular and big business in Western societies. The question is, how should the church respond to this cultural trend? Keeping in mind that the author of Hebrews uses his first audience's respect for angels to speak to their need for a higher opinion of the Son, I believe there are at least two applications we can draw from his contrast of Christ and the angels. (1) We must build on a biblical understanding of angels. Christians need to know what the Scriptures reveal about angels; thus, the topic should be addressed from pulpit to classroom podium.[31]

Much contemporary angelology has strong New Age overtones. Based on dubious metaphysical and psychological experiences, it often is divorced from biblical revelation. Many see any spiritual encounter, regardless of its nature or message, as communicating truth, and even some professing to be

---

31. See, for example, the recent volume by Duane Garrett, *Angels and the New Spirituality* (Nashville: Broadman & Holman, 1995).

followers of Christ are buying into the broader culture's infatuation with angels. Yet, as 1 John 4:1 warns, we are not to believe every spirit, but should test the spirits to see whether they are from God. Paul also reminds us that even Satan himself masquerades as an angel of light (2 Cor. 11:14).

Notice that the author of Hebrews draws on the Old Testament witness to angels. That witness does not present angels as independent vendors of ecstatic spiritual experience but as servants of the living God. Moreover, by their activity of worship they point to the Son (1:6-7), and rather than criss-crossing the planet for any and every human encounter, they are sent out specifically "to serve those who will inherit salvation" (1:14).

(2) We can use a biblically based discussion of angels as a launching point from which to speak about the supremacy of the Son of God. The author of Hebrews uses his audience's respect for angels as a reference point from which to zero in on the greater authority of Christ. When was the last time you heard a message detailing the power and glory of angels that then proceeded to magnify God's Son by comparison? What if we invited people to come hear a lecture on angels? This passage would be appropriate to use evangelistically[32] with those who do not know Christ (but are interested in angels) and educationally with those who do. Thus, we could use the topic of "angels" as a means of explaining, by contrast, the exalted status and person of Christ, as does the author of Hebrews. We could call people to rivet their attention on the word of God as delivered by the Son and challenge them to obedience to that delivered word.

Jesus' enthronement and unique relationship to the Father. During my years in seminary two young men came to my door seeking to share their "faith" with me. Shortly into the conversation I said, "Tell me what you believe about Jesus." Taking out their version of the New Testament and turning to John 1:1, they explained, "The Greek here shows that Jesus was *a god* (or lesser being), not *the* one true God." I asked them to wait a minute while I went inside to get my Greek New Testament. Upon returning I handed the speaker my Greek text and asked him to translate the passage, which he could not do. It turns out that their interpretation was based on a faulty understanding of the use of the article in the Greek language. They reasoned that since the word for God (*theos*) has no article in front of it, the word used of the *logos* in John 1:1 is indefinite, that is, "a god." The problem with

---

32. One might think of Paul's sermon at Mars Hill, where he used that culture's general belief in "the unknown god" as a starting point for a sermon on the one, true God (Acts 17:22-31). The author's argument in 1:5-14 will eventually reach the question of the "rejection of salvation" in 2:1-4. Therefore, although the passage addresses Christians, an evangelistic application is not inappropriate.

this interpretation is that a Greek term needs no article to be definite, especially if there is only one of the subject under consideration.

Several years later in a New Testament survey class, while I was using this experience to speak to the role of grammar in interpretation, a Mormon lady in the back of the room blurted out, "But Dr. Guthrie, you can't say they were wrong. They were just sharing what they sincerely believed!" I responded, "If you believe that Jesus is not God, and I believe that Jesus is God, one of us is wrong. There are only so many options."

From cults to traditional religions, from critical scholars to the culturally sensitive, the deity of Jesus—his unique relationship with the Father shown in his exaltation—has presented a stumbling block through the ages. Unable to deny his phenomenal impact and the impressiveness of his teaching, many deny his nature by presenting him as less than God. Yet, as C. S. Lewis noted in his classic *Mere Christianity*, we do not enjoy the option of casting Jesus as a good teacher but not God. From what he himself taught, Jesus was Lord, liar, or lunatic. The answer in Hebrews is unambiguous: The Son's deity is vindicated by his exaltation to the right hand of the Majesty (1:5, 13) and confessed in the traditional material of earliest Christianity. The cults and critics who deny this truth deny the authority of Jesus for their lives.

This doctrine of the deity of Christ must be recognized as a key to perseverance in the Christian life. The erosion of confidence in this orthodox tenet of the faith inevitably undermines one's relationship with the living, enthroned Jesus. We will see in the chapters ahead that Hebrews challenges its readers to "consider Jesus" (3:1; 12:1–2), the exalted author and finisher of the faith, as a means of staying the course of commitment. Our Lord is the Eternal One (1:8–12; 13:8), and we need not fear that our changing circumstances or the passing of time will diminish his abilities on our behalf. With a clear picture of Jesus as God, we also are impressed with our accountability to him as the One who will judge the living and the dead (2:1–4).

The agent of creation. In the beginning of scientific investigation, many pursued scientific knowledge from the conviction that God had ordered the universe. However, with the advent of the Enlightenment, old theological moorings were abandoned, and science became for many not only a philosophical orientation but also a means of pursuing truth. Science, in other words, became the supreme epistemological authority of the universe. There was no creation, they suggested, but just a cosmic accident that resulted in an evolutionary process ending in what we know as physical reality. Some fundamentalist Christians have reacted by rejecting science altogether, putting it in a dichotomous relationship over against revelation and focusing on the age of the earth as the issue central to the creation debate. Other Christians, however, stress that science can play a positive role of participating with the heavens in declaring the glory of God (Ps. 19:1—6) for those who will listen.[33]

Hugh Ross is one of the latter. In his book *Creation and Time*, Ross suggests that recent findings in astrophysics present believers with an unprecedented opportunity to proclaim the biblical picture of God as creator to the scientific community. Among the facts about the universe agreed upon by virtually all astronomers, Ross presents the following:

(1) The universe is only billions of years old, not quadrillions or a near infinite number of years.

(2) The universe can be traced back to a single, ultimate origin of matter, energy, time, and space as we know them, and, therefore, the Cause of the event must have an existence independent of the universe.

(3) The universe, our galaxy, and our solar system demonstrate more than sixty characteristics that require exquisite fine-tuning for their very existence and for the existence of any kind of physical life. Three of the characteristics must be fine-tuned to a precision of one part in 10^{37} or better.[34]

Even secular scientists are acknowledging the profound theological implications of such findings. Among the evidence, none has greater implications than that which supports the so-called Big Bang. In April 1992, George Smoot, project leader for the satellite dubbed Cosmic Background Explorer, proclaimed that the ripples in the radiation left over from the Big Bang had been observed. He commented, "What we found is evidence for the birth of the universe,"[35] and "It's like looking at God."[36] Speaking of the recent findings in astronomy, agnostic Robert Jastrow writes that scientists have been "scaling the mountains of ignorance . . . conquering the highest peak . . . pulling [themselves] over the final rock . . . [to be] greeted by a band of theologians who have been sitting there for centuries."[37]

Moderns are confronted with overwhelming evidence for an "Entity," a Creator, who exists outside the reach of their exploratory means. The

---

33. See Hugh Ross, *Creation and Time: A Biblical and Scientific Perspective on the Creation-Date Controversy* (Colorado Springs, Col.: NavPress, 1994); Howard J. Van Till et al., *Science Held Hostage: What's Wrong With Creation Science and Evolutionism* (Downers Grove, Ill.: InterVarsity, 1988). Both volumes present scathing evaluations of the Creation Science Movement.

34. Ross, *Creation and Time*, 126—27, 132.

35. Associated Press, "U.S. Scientists Find a 'Holy Grail': Ripples at Edge of the Universe," *London International Herald Tribune* (April 24, 1992), 1.

36. Thomas H. Maugh, "Relics of 'Big Bang' Seen for the First Time," *Los Angeles Times* (April 24, 1992), A1, A30.

37. As quoted in Ross, *Creation and Time*, 128.

scientific system of "authority" has found its limitations, encountering an aspect of what theologians call "general revelation." The "specific revelation" of Hebrews is that the Son of God is the One who has "laid the foundations of the earth" and woven the heavens with his hands (1:10). Of course, science cannot prove that Jesus is that Agent of creation. What it does do, however, is to confirm the picture of the creation that the Bible (and Hebrews specifically) has presented all along—that what we know as physical reality has not always existed and that God, an all-powerful and transcendent Being, created the universe in an orderly fashion and governs that universe still.

For Christ's followers a glimpse at the awesome dimensions and physical dynamics of the universe should remind us of the phenomenal and incomprehensible authority, power, and creativity of the Son of God and bring us to our knees in worship. We should be reminded that as the One who stands outside of time, our eternal Lord provides a stability to our existence that can only be had through a relationship with him. The world around us is becoming old, like worn-out clothes ready to be folded and put away, but he remains the same (1:11–12).

We can say to our friends in the broader society, "This God, about whom scientists are uncovering so much evidence, has done more than create; he has entered our physical realm in the person of Jesus Christ, in order to communicate truth to us that is beyond scientific investigation. Part of that truth is that God's Son, as the Agent of creation, is also our ultimate authority, to whom we all must give account."[38]

---

38. Cf. Paul's sermon at Mars Hill in Acts 17:22–31, where he moves from a general understanding of God as creator to humanity's accountability to God.

Hebrews 2:1-4

W̲E̲ ̲M̲U̲S̲T̲ ̲P̲A̲Y̲ more careful attention, therefore, to what we have heard, so that we do not drift away. ²For if the message spoken by angels was binding, and every violation and disobedience received its just punishment, ³how shall we escape if we ignore such a great salvation? This salvation, which was first announced by the Lord, was confirmed to us by those who heard him. ⁴God also testified to it by signs, wonders and various miracles, and gifts of the Holy Spirit distributed according to his will.

Original Meaning

HAVING ESTABLISHED THE supreme authority of the Son of God in 1:5–14, the preacher builds on that truth by turning momentarily from his exposition of Christ and confronting the listeners with their responsibility. The exhortation falls in three parts. It opens with a statement concerning the danger of drifting and the safeguard against it by paying attention to traditional Christian teaching (2:1). The author continues his discussion with a rationale for this caution against drifting (2:2–3a): If those who were disobedient to the older revelation given through angels were strictly punished, certainly those who turn away from salvation will not escape penalty. The third part (2:3b–4) describes salvation as first proclaimed by the Lord and confirmed both by the original witnesses and by God's acts of wonders, miracles, and gifts of the Spirit.

A Caution Against Drifting (2:1)

THE FIRST PHRASE of 2:1–4 (*dia touto*, "therefore" in NIV) connects 2:1–4 to the string of Old Testament texts in 1:5–14. This phrase can also be rendered "for this reason" and suggests that the supremacy of the Son, as established in the previous unit, is the grounds for this word of exhortation. The author shifts to the first person plural pronoun, "we," giving direct exhortation to the Christian community: "We must pay more careful attention." The word "must" (*dei*) shows the logical necessity of following the preacher's instructions. We must not only pay attention in the sense of acknowledging the presence of something, but should pay "more careful" (*perissoteros*) attention, concentrating to a greater extent than we have been. The object of our attention is "what we have heard," that is, the word spoken via the Son (1:2). The author clarifies the content of this word, left ambiguous for the moment, in verses 3–4, where he defines it as the message of salvation.

The image of "drifting" is an especially potent one. The word used here (*pararuomai*) could signify objects that slip away, such as a ring that slips off the finger, or objects that go in the wrong direction, such as a piece of food that goes into the windpipe.[1] Perhaps the image closer to our author's intention in this passage is that of a ship drifting, missing a harbor it intended to enter because of strong currents or winds.[2] The author does not define the "currents" with which the audience struggles, but it is clear they are in danger of moving from a spiritual vantage point where the gospel is the focus.

Motivation for Heeding This Admonition (2:2–3a)

IN VERSES 2–3A the author utilizes a tool from rabbinic homiletics—an "argument from lesser to greater"—to motivate the congregation to action.[3] Punishment received for rejecting what God spoke through angels under the old covenant constitutes the "lesser" situation in this case.[4] The idea of the angels as mediators of the divine revelation on Mount Sinai had gained special attraction to Judaism in the Greek-speaking synagogues of the Mediterranean world.[5] Josephus wrote, "And for ourselves, we have learned from God the most excellent of our teachings, and the most holy part of our law by angels."[6]

The author appeals to his listeners' understanding of the Torah, reminding them that the older covenant message delivered through angels was "binding"; to neglect that word brought about sure, severe punishment. Dealing with sin was never taken lightly by God, but "every" violation received a just punishment. The words translated in the NIV as "violation" and "disobedience" speak of a conscious rejection of God's will. In 2:1–4 and more broadly in Hebrews, the author often associates disobedience with an unwillingness to listen to God's voice (e.g., 2:1; 3:7–19; 12:25).

---

1. Westcott, *The Epistle to the Hebrews*, 36–37; as in Aristotle, *De partibus animalium*, 3.3. In the Greek text of Prov. 3:21 the word is used of not letting right teachings slip away from one's attention. Notice, however, that in Heb. 2:1 it is the person who is drifting.

2. Ibid.; see also Lenski, *The Interpretation of the Epistle to the Hebrews*, 64.

3. Also referred to as a fortiori or קל והומר (*qal wahomer*).

4. The "if" at the beginning of verse 2 initiates the front end of a "real case" conditional clause. This type of clause assumes the reality of what is being stated and could almost be translated with "since" (BDF, 187).

5. Lane, *Hebrews 1–8*, 37. See Acts 7:38; Gal. 3:19.

6. *Antiquities*, 15.36.

The preacher continues by presenting the "greater" situation in the form of a rhetorical question, focusing on rejection of the word of salvation given through the Lord. This rhetorical question expects a negative answer if the condition is met: We will have no escape "if we neglect such a great salvation." That one finds scriptural precedent in God's punishment of the disobedient in the lesser situation provides a basis for the assumption that even more severe punishment will be forthcoming in the greater.

Amelesantes, the word rendered "ignore," is a participle appropriately translated with conditional force in the NIV. It means to neglect through apathy or not to care enough about something (1 Tim. 4:14). The word could be used of a doctor or government official who, having made a public commitment, defaulted on that commitment.[7] Thus, those who care so little about the word of salvation that they neglect it will find no escape from the punishment they deserve.

The Message of Salvation (2:3b–4)

THE AUTHOR OF Hebrews continues with an encapsulated history of salvation's proclamation. The focus remains on speaking and hearing the divine message. "This salvation," he asserts, "was first announced by the Lord." Although it had been prophesied in the Old Testament, the beginning of the gospel's proclamation in clarity and fulfillment came with the Messiah, who announced, "The time has come. . . . The kingdom of God is near. Repent and believe the good news!" (Mark 1:15).[8] His preaching of the good news of salvation characterized Jesus' ministry (Matt. 9:35).

Neither the author nor the recipients of Hebrews had directly heard Jesus preach the message of salvation; they were "second generation" Christians, having received that word from "those who heard him." The word "confirm" carries the sense of firm assurance or guarantee.[9] Thus, although the author and his hearers had not heard the message of salvation from the mouth of Jesus himself, it was something they could count on absolutely.

Yet an even greater witness came alongside, assuring the validity of the original eyewitnesses' testimony of salvation: "God testified to it by signs, wonders and various miracles, and gifts of the Holy Spirit distributed according to his will" (2:4). The language used here is legal, suggesting that God has entered the "courtroom" of history to corroborate the testimony of those who followed the Lord by proclaiming salvation. God has not simply spoken

---

7. Spicq, *Theological Lexicon of the New Testament*, 1:87–89.
8. Bruce, *The Epistle to the Hebrews*, 68.
9. Spicq, *Theological Lexicon of the New Testament*, 1:280.

a word of confirmation, however, but has acted in "signs, wonders and various miracles." The triple expression "signs, wonders and miracles" was used in early Christianity to speak of God's activity among his people, accompanying the preaching of the gospel (e.g., Acts 2:22; Rom. 15:19; 2 Cor. 12:12). God's working of such powerful acts played a significant role in the apologetics of early Christian preachers (e.g., Acts 3:1–10; 14:3–11).[10]

IN DEALING WITH 1:1–4 we noted the importance of understanding its parallel structure in contrasting the older covenant revelation with that of the newer covenant.[11] In 2:1–4 this contrast again forms the backdrop, but angels have replaced the prophets as agents of revelation. Moreover, the author utilizes the contrast in a different way. In Hebrews 2 he builds on the theme of the "supremacy of the Son" (1:5–14) to execute an argument from the lesser to the greater.

Theological presuppositions. This argument presupposes several theological foundation stones that should be identified as we bridge the gap between the ancient horizon and our own. (1) As in 1:1–2, *the preacher presupposes the validity of the older media of divine revelation.* He offers no hint that the word of God given through angels has been invalidated. Divine revelation is progressive, moving not from false to true, but from a lesser to a greater revelation. This revelation is both complementary, in that the new covenant fulfills the old, and supplementary, in that there are dimensions in the new covenant not found in the old. The capstone of revelation is Jesus Christ and his work and word of salvation.[12]

(2) The present passage assumes *a continuity in the character and activity of God between the old and new covenant eras.* This presupposition understands God to be a just God who punishes sin. Whether holding his people accountable under the law of Sinai or holding them accountable to the word delivered through the Son, transgressions are confronted and punished.

(3) Corresponding to our previous point, *the character of the older and newer recipients of God's message of salvation has continuity.* For people of both new and old covenants, the possibility of violations exist; therefore, a need to warn against drifting emerges. These last two related assertions—that God's character is consistent when we move from the Old to the New Testament and that the moral needs and obligations of people under both covenants remains the

---

10. Attridge, *The Epistle to the Hebrews,* 67.
11. See above, pp. 45–46.
12. Dockery, *Christian Scripture,* 21.

same—form the core bases for the ethical use of the Old Testament in Hebrews and other New Testament literature. Our God is the same God, and we struggle with sin as did our Old Testament counterparts.

Therefore, in order to bring this text to our contemporary contexts with power and effectiveness, we must address, and must help those to whom we speak address, the twin issues of authority and accountability. If our listeners do not have a clear concept of God's right to rule their lives, if they have no sense of accountability to the divine Word, then our teaching or preaching of this passage loses its rhetorical power. This text cannot "speak" to them if they rest comfortably in a self-centered authority that judges all of life in light of one's own self-actualization rather than according to the will and ways of God. Furthermore, those of us who have preached "once-saved, always-saved" to the neglect of teachings on accountability have done a disservice to the body of Christ and her members, offering an unbalanced view of a right relationship to God. We must never maximize the grace of God to the neglect of the holiness of God and God's desire for the holiness of his people.[13]

Limitations on our study. Beyond recognition of the principles underlying the preacher's a fortiori argument, to apply this passage appropriately we must acknowledge the limitations of our research, refusing to go beyond them with our applications. At times the author speaks in more general terms rather than specific theological or ethical propositions. In such cases we are tempted to rush to applications supplied more from our theological preunderstandings than from the actual content in the passage in question.

For example, what does it mean to "drift away" from what we have heard (2:1) and to "ignore such a great salvation" (2:3)? A surface reading might lead one to assume the passage speaks of a non-Christian who drifts by an opportunity for salvation. Yet the author uses the pronoun "we" (v. 1), which he consistently employs to address the Christian community. Moreover, the imagery of the "message spoken by angels" that was "binding" points to those of old who were in covenant with God. This raises the likelihood that their counterparts in this passage see themselves as new covenant people (cf. 10:30).

But if the author is speaking to the Christian community in this text, what does it mean for one to drift from the message of salvation? Does it mean to fall out of fellowship with God, or, more seriously, to lose salvation? It would seem the action involves at least a moving away from the message of salvation. Notice in this passage that it is the *message* rather than God himself from which they are drifting. Can one drift from the message without drifting from God? From the broader context of Hebrews, the answer to this question is a resounding "no!"

---

13. See below, pp. 141–43.

This raises another set of issues: What is the nature of the "punishment" implied in verse 3? What would be "just" (v. 2) for one who is drifting? Does this mean punishment in the sense of discipline for a person who still belongs to God, or is it the punishment of excommunication, or is it punishment for an unbeliever who has never known Christ? As we consider the other warning passages in Hebrews later in this commentary, we find that the author is notoriously ambiguous in dealing with certain issues.[14] My point for now, however, is to suggest that we be careful not to press our applications beyond the principles clearly revealed in the passage. In our process of application, it is tempting to say more, or less, than a given passage warrants.

The main points of the passage. What, then, are the principles clearly indicated by Hebrews 2:1–4? (1) *The author calls his audience to personal commitment and responsibility.* From the author's use of the first person plural pronoun and his employment of covenant imagery, it seems certain he is addressing Christians, or at least those who consider themselves so. Therefore, the "drifting" and "ignoring of salvation" must mean that those who have professed Christ in the past are in danger of losing sight of the gospel (cf. Gal. 1:6–10).

Some of the Christians the author addresses were living on the edge of the community, slowly slipping away from a firm commitment to the message of salvation. Although he does not define the "currents" causing them to drift—perhaps there were several—it is likely, from our composite of this church,[15] that persecution played a part in obscuring the gospel and distancing them from the fellowship of faith.

The author's concern, however, could not be more clear. In the face of dangerous drifting, Hebrews 2:1–4 calls believers to personal commitment and responsibility. Two solutions to the problem, one negative and the other positive, accompany this exhortation against drifting.

(2) In verses 2–3a, *the preacher motivates his listeners through threat of punishment.* Rather than highlighting a specific penalty for disobedience, the author provides a generalized statement concerning older covenant punishment: "Every violation and disobedience" received a punishment appropriate to the act. Correspondingly, no definition or details accompany the punishment implied in the rhetorical question of verse 3. What can be said for certain at this point, therefore, is that those who "drift" and "ignore" are in deep trouble in relation to God. Punishment is certain and will be executed justly and according to the offense.

---

14. See below, p. 225. We could do a broader context study of the warning passages in Hebrews at this point, but I have chosen to delay that study until we get to 6:4–8, which is perhaps the most-discussed apostasy passage in the book and the passage I consider to be at the structural center of the book's exhortation material.

15. See above, p. 22.

(3) *The positive answer to the problem of drifting lies in the traditional word of salvation to which they are to "pay more careful attention" (v. 1).* The author considers historical events and testimonies as validating this message as a stabilizing factor in the Christian life. That the message was "announced by the Lord," "confirmed to us by those who heard him," and "testified" to by God, all refer to what the author considers historical occurrences within the experience of Christ-followers, pointing to the validity of their Christian belief. He includes the experience of the Christian community ("to us") in that history. Therefore, Christians who hold onto the message of salvation stand in historical continuity of relationship and mission with Jesus, the apostles, and even God himself.[16]

A CALL TO commitment and responsibility. The American critic and author Louis Kronenberger is credited with the saying, "The trouble with our age is that it is all signpost and no destination." From every vantage point we hear calls of the culture to turn down different roads from the one we are traveling as we cruise chaotically, bereft of specific ideas about where we should be headed. Today's people have become more and more migratory and less and less stable in relation to extended families, home, place of residence, workplace, politics, and church.

Studies identify a disenchantment with tradition as one primary characteristic of the so-called "baby boom" generation; those of Generation X give no indication of changing the trend. We have become a society of consumers who are constantly "shopping" for everything from new material goods to new philosophies and experiences. We maintain commitment to values and institutions only as long as they fulfill our needs of the moment. Sadly, the church has not been immune to these trends. Many professed Christians float from congregation to congregation in search of the right worship service, Bible study, children's care, or teen ministry, sometimes partaking of different programs at different churches at a given point in time. We in the Christian community too often mirror the broader society, living as spiritual consumer-drifters within the broader culture of consumer-drifters.

Those of us involved in church leadership should step back and search the faces in our congregation. This may be difficult if you minister in a large church. What faces present a year ago are missing from the crowd? Where have they gone? Why have they gone? What can be done to close the back door? These questions constitute one of the greatest practical areas of concern in modern church life.

---

16. Cf. Luke 1:1–4; Acts 2:22–36; 26:24–29; 1 Cor. 15:1–8.

It is likely that few Americans pass through our back doors because of overt persecution from the society around them. Persecution is much more a fact of life in the underground church in China or the world's Muslim countries, such as Malaysia. Some drift from the church because of disillusionment with church leaders or other institutional dynamics. However, many drift because they lack a solid grasp on commitment and personal responsibility. This problem is exacerbated in Western culture by the concurrent, contradictory longings for both autonomy and status as victim. J. Richard Middleton and Brian J. Walsh write:

> If the modern autonomous self sought to dominate the world (and other human beings) in the name of what we now recognize to be a fictitious and ideological ideal (universal, rational human progress), the postmodern (or hypermodern) self fluctuates between the quest for a new form of autonomy and the experience of victimization. Compulsively seeking personal advancement (ungrounded in a grandiose ideal) via aggressive control of one's situation and refashioning of one's image, fueled all the while by an insatiable desire for unlimited experience of the carnivalesque smorgasbord of life, the postmodern/hypermodern self is nevertheless overcome by a sense of meaninglessness, powerlessness, rootlessness, homelessness, and fragmentation, where the self is incapacitated before its infinite possibilities, reduced to an effect of its plural contexts and consequently haunted by a deep-rooted sense of anomie. The "I want it all" attitude is easily transmuted into "I'm paralyzed in the face of it all." The postmodern self thus exists in a perpetual state of dialectical self-contradiction.[17]

The drive for autonomous living—to control my own life and destiny—runs counter to Christian commitment. For the autonomous self the premier question is not "What do I owe to God or this community?" but "What can this God and community do to help me in my pursuit of self-actualization?" In other words, as long as God and the community are useful in helping me "get and keep it all together," I will participate. When that ceases to happen or my autonomy is threatened by these relationships, I will drift elsewhere.

As victims we refuse to take personal responsibility for ourselves or our actions. If we kill or hurt someone, it is due to the society, our parents, our bosses, or some other aspect of our circumstances. In the context of church, if we drift away, it must be due to the church, the pastor, the Sunday school teacher, the music minister, or difficulties at home or work. Surely, we reason, it cannot be our fault. We only see ourselves dysfunctional by birth,

---

17. Middleton and Walsh, *Truth is Stranger Than It Used to Be*, 109–10.

upbringing, or current relationships, but never by our own actions. Phyllis McGinley writes, "[Sin] has been made not only ugly but passé. People are no longer sinful, they are only immature or underprivileged or frightened or, more particularly, sick."[18] To be sure, many true victims exist, languishing under a myriad of difficult circumstances, and the church must minister to them. Yet, when we inappropriately embrace the "victim mentality" of the culture, we step away from taking personal responsibility to which we are called as Christians.

Consequently, we must regain a "sense of sin," taking our personal, moral accountability before God seriously. The only way this can be accomplished is by paying more careful attention to the word of salvation delivered through God's Son. It is wonderfully good news, but presupposes the bad news of sin's devastating power and dominion. If we skew the bad news, neglecting the concept of personal sinfulness, the good news ceases to be wonderfully "good," for there is nothing from which we need to be delivered.

The place of punishment in Christian teaching. This brings us to a second area of application. As recognized by Stanley Grenz, the *Star Trek* television series and movies provide interesting mirrors to our culture's belief systems.[19] In *Star Trek V: The Final Frontier*, Spock's brother, a renegade Vulcan very much in touch with his inner feelings (and determined to help everyone else get in touch with their inner feelings) hijacks the *Enterprise* and leads the crew in a search for the ultimate frontier—the place where God lives. Passing through the great barrier that stands between known space and "heaven," the searchers find the world for which they have been seeking; and they find "god." This god manifests himself as "one god, many faces" (he is the god of the Klingons, the Vulcans, humans, etc.), and then, being doubted by Captain Kirk, proceeds to zap everyone in sight. One of the last standing, crusty old "Bones," the ship's doctor, is confronted by the deity: "Do you doubt me too?" Bones replies, "I don't believe in any god who inflicts pain for his pleasure."

This theologically loaded statement, made in context with regard to an evil, alien being, reflects a common misconception of the God of the Bible. For God to be a God of punishment, the thought goes, must mean that he gets joy from administering pain. Contemporary cultural wisdom suggests that we must do away with any conception of divine punishment. Speaking at a gay rights demonstration in the mid-1980s, a New York bishop stated triumphantly that the conception of a god who punishes for such "so-called sins" as homosexuality stems from "primitive, barbaric passages of the Old

---

18. Phyllis McGinley, *The Province of the Heart* (New York: Viking, 1959), 35–36.
19. Stanley J. Grenz, *A Primer on Postmodernism* (Grand Rapids: Eerdmans, 1996), ch. 1.

Testament."[20] Thus, the concept of punishment, in the minds of some, must be written off as outdated.

Yet, the theme of just punishment for disobedience to God's will looms large in both Testaments of the Bible. Under the old covenant, punishment was meted out for sins such as murder (Gen. 9:5–6; Num. 35:16–21), adultery (Lev. 20:10; Deut. 22:24), incest (Lev. 20:11–14), bestiality (Ex. 22:19), sodomy (Lev. 18:22; 20:13), and perjury (Zech. 5:4). A person received from God according to his or her deeds (Job 34:11; Ps. 62:12; Prov. 24:12; Ezek. 7:3, 27), and as in Hebrews 2:1–4, there was no escape for those who turned away from God (Job 11:20; Prov. 1:24–31; Jer. 11:11).

Jesus likewise emphasized the reality of judgment (Matt. 5:22; 16:27; 23:14; 25:41–46), as do the writers of the New Testament (Rom. 2:3; Col. 3:25; Rev. 14:10–11). Thus the author of Hebrews fits well within the traditional teaching of earliest Christianity (Heb. 6:2; 10:28–31), holding up the reality of punishment as a motivation for those who would drift carelessly away from God. The foundation for God's punishment resides in his holy character and his divine love, for the Scriptures depict sin as a power that moves people away from the holiness of God and warps their existence as God's creations.

In addition to my teaching and administrative duties at the university, I serve as one of several copastors in a local church. This church might be described as "seeker sensitive," a phrase that has come to be associated with various approaches to church growth. Although the intentions and methodology of some seeker-sensitive churches have been misunderstood at times, they try to address the problem of communicating the gospel in our culture. Without compromising doctrine, we should seek to build bridges of communication with seekers under the sound of our preaching. It is valid to analyze the cultural trappings (e.g., pews, style of music, art, etc.) of our contexts that stand in the way of moderns really hearing our message.

However, we must be careful to keep a sharp demarcation between the mode and context of communication and the message itself. If we are lax in this regard, we can easily begin to adapt not only the mode of communication but also the message to the comfort level of both seekers and believers. To preach the Scriptures faithfully means that we address all the topics Scripture addresses, including the topic of punishment. That topic, although uncomfortable to communicate and hear, is nonnegotiable for those who would preach biblically. For believers it needs to form an aspect of motivation to obedience and perseverance in the Christian life.

---

20. Charles Colson, *Who Speaks for God: Confronting the World With Real Christianity* (Westchester, Ill.: Crossway, 1985), 20.

The word of salvation and historicity of the faith. Thankfully, we have more than a word of punishment to motivate us; we have the positive, emancipating word of salvation. It is important to recognize that the author of Hebrews points to this word as a stabilizing factor for Christian discipleship. The message of salvation as traditionally preached by Jesus and the first eyewitnesses, that gospel to which God bore witness through mighty acts, provides an authoritative point of reference from which to assess relationship to God and the world. It affords a perspective higher than ourselves and our circumstances, embodying the essence of God's will for humankind as revealed in Christ.

It is significant that the author of Hebrews points us specifically to the salvation of which he speaks, connecting it to the history of early Christianity. Many modern biblical critics and theologians suggest faith has nothing to do with "real" events in history. On a recent PBS special Harold Kushner, a popular Jewish author and theologian, was asked whether Abraham, Isaac, and Jacob were real persons. He responded that it does not make any difference. The impact of their stories on us is real; they have molded our histories, and that is all that matters.

But is that really the case? Most modern New Testament scholars are still strongly influenced by Rudolph Bultmann, who made a sharp distinction between "the Jesus of history" and "the Christ of faith." They reason that the early Christian documents are so overwhelmed with the theological perspective of the early church that they cannot be trusted to report the real historical facts. What does it matter, they reason, whether Jesus did or said anything recorded in the New Testament; we can experience Christianity by taking a "leap of faith." Yet, the early Christians themselves pointed time and again to what they considered real events in history that validated the gospel message (e.g., Luke 1:1–4; 1 Cor. 15:1–6). They also assumed that the gospel would not be valid if the key event—the Resurrection—had not taken place. As Paul states in 1 Corinthians 15:14–15, 17:

> And if Christ has not been raised, our preaching is useless and so is your faith. More than that, we are then found to be false witnesses about God, for we have testified about God that he raised Christ from the dead.... And if Christ has not been raised, your faith is futile; you are still in your sins.

So too the author of Hebrews looks to the confirmation of the gospel by the first witnesses and by God himself as significant. Faith in the message is not a "leap in the dark" but a decision to commit oneself to God through Christ, based on reliable testimony of the apostles. The apostolic tradition helps Christians stay true to the salvation preached by Jesus. Toward the end of the second century, Irenaeus, in his work *Against All Heresies*, had this to say about those who deny the apostolic tradition in favor of their own philosophies:

> When [the heretics] are refuted out of the Scriptures, they turn to accusing the Scriptures themselves, as if they were not right or did not possess authority, because the Scriptures contain a variety of statements, and because it is not possible for those who do not know the tradition to find the truth in them. For this has not been handed down by means of writings, but by the "living voice." ... Yet, when we appeal once more to that tradition which is from the apostles, safeguarded in the churches by successions of presbyters, we provoke them into becoming the enemies of traditions, claiming to be wiser than those presbyters, and even the apostles themselves, and to have discovered the undefiled truth.... Thus they end up agreeing with neither the Scriptures nor with tradition.... Everyone who wishes to perceive the truth should consider the apostolic tradition, which has been made known in every church in the entire world....
>
> Therefore, as there are so many demonstrations of this fact, there is no need to look anywhere else for the truth which we can easily obtain from the church. The apostles have, as it were, deposited this truth in all its fullness in this depository, so that whoever wants to may draw from this water of life. This is the gate of life; all others are thieves and robbers.[21]

To this the church father Tertullian adds:

> What they preached—that is, what Christ revealed to them—ought, by this ruling, to be established only by those churches which those apostles founded by their preaching and, as they say, by the living voice, and subsequently through their letters. If this is true, all doctrine which is in agreement with those apostolic churches, the sources and originals of the faith, must be accounted as the truth, since it indubitably preserves what the churches received from the apostles, the apostles from Christ, and Christ from God....[22]

Thus, the traditional teaching of orthodox doctrine, including the word of salvation, was seen as vital to Christian life and thought in the earliest centuries of the church—and it should be seen as such for us as well, for we

---

21. *Adversus haereses*, 2.2.1–2.4.1, as quoted in McGrath, *The Christian Theology Reader*, 43–44.

22. *De praescriptione haereticorum*, 20.4–21.4; 32.1, in McGrath, *The Christian Theology Reader*, 46.

and those around us need God's supernatural deliverance. Ultimately, we do not need a human solution to the sin-instigated dilemmas, in which we find ourselves incarcerated. We need salvation, as revealed by Jesus, confirmed by the first witnesses, and borne witness to by God himself. To drift away from this message, to treat it carelessly, invites spiritual ruin. On the other hand, to pay close attention to the word of salvation provides stability in our trek as followers of Christ, for that word of deliverance constitutes a foundation stone in one's relationship to God.

Hebrews 2:5–9

I T IS NOT to angels that he has subjected the world to
come, about which we are speaking. ⁶But there is a place
where someone has testified:

> "What is man that you are mindful of him,
>   the son of man that you care for him?
> ⁷You made him a little lower than the angels;
>   you crowned him with glory and honor
> ⁸   and put everything under his feet."

In putting everything under him, God left nothing that is not
subject to him. Yet at present we do not see everything subject to him. ⁹But we see Jesus, who was made a little lower
than the angels, now crowned with glory and honor because
he suffered death, so that by the grace of God he might taste
death for everyone.

THUS FAR IN Hebrews the author has maintained
a persistent focus on the exalted status of the Son
of God. In 2:5–9, however, that focus shifts to
his incarnation, a passage crafted specifically to
move the discussion from the Son's heavenly position to his earthly ministry. In their outlines of Hebrews, a number of scholars have arranged this
passage with 2:10–18,[1] but the key to understanding this text lies in its role
as a transition. The author resumes his exposition on Christ, from which he
briefly departed following 1:14, by introducing Psalm 8:4–6 to his discussion.
This Old Testament quotation, interpreted Christologically in 2:8–9,[2] contains both elements of exaltation and incarnation, and, therefore, provides
the perfect vehicle for moving to a discussion in 2:10–18 about the Son's solidarity with humanity.

---

1. E.g., Robert Jewett, *Letter to Pilgrims: A Commentary on the Epistle to the Hebrews* (New York:
Pilgrim, 1981), 41–42; Ellingworth, *The Epistle to the Hebrews*, 143–44.

2. Although some have insisted on interpreting the author's use of Psalm 8 here as referring to humanity in general, the author clearly interprets the passage Christologically. See
Attridge, *The Epistle to the Hebrews*, 70–72; Hagner, *Hebrews*, 44–47; Hughes, *The Epistle to the
Hebrews*, 84. For other places in the New Testament where the psalm is used Christologically, see Matt. 21:16; 1 Cor. 15:27; Eph. 1:22.

Hebrews 2:5–9, which we title "The Superior Son for a Time Became Positionally Lower Than the Angels," may be divided roughly into two parts: (1) an introduction followed by the quotation of Psalm 8:4–6 (vv. 5–8a), and (2) an interpretation of the psalm's meaning (vv. 8b–9).

Submission of All Things to Christ (2:5–8a)

ANCIENT JUDAISM HELD to the belief that angels had been placed by God over the nations of the world. The basis for this belief went back to an interpretation of Deuteronomy 32:8 (cf. NIV note), which referred to the boundaries of the nations as set according to the number of God's angels. Later, in Daniel 10:20–21; 12:1, angels are designated as the "prince of Persia" and "prince of Greece," and Michael is referred to as "the great prince" who watches over God's people, Israel. As in the New Testament (e.g., Eph. 6:12), some of the principalities in Daniel are depicted as evil, opposing the will and work of God (Dan. 10:20–21).[3] Yet angels, whether good or bad, will hold no position of government in the coming age (see Heb. 2:5–9).

The quote of Psalm 110:1 in Hebrews 1:13, rather than the exhortation of 2:1–4, gives rise to the statement, "It is not to angels that he has subjected the world to come, about which we are speaking."[4] The author has in mind the part of Psalm 110 that reads, "until I make your enemies a footstool for your feet." This is the subjugation of "the world to come" to which the author refers in 2:5.

In the New Testament the word translated "subjected" in the NIV (*hypotasso*) is widely used. Christians are to submit to God (1 Cor. 15:28; Heb. 12:9) and to God's law (Rom. 8:7). On the human level they are to subject themselves to one another (1 Cor. 16:16; Eph. 5:21); wives submit to husbands (Eph. 5:24; Col. 3:18; Titus 2:5; 1 Peter 3:1, 5), the young to the old (1 Peter 5:5), slaves to masters (Eph. 6:5; Titus 2:9; 1 Peter 2:18), and believers in general to governing authorities (Rom. 13:1). Thus submission, that act of yielding to the perspective or position of another, constitutes a fundamental element of Christian practice.[5] More broadly, however, all the powers of the universe—even those that do not do so willingly—must submit to Christ (1 Cor. 15:27–28; Eph. 1:22; Phil. 2:10–11; 3:21; 1 Peter 3:22).

---

3. On the subjection of earthly nations to the angels, see Bruce, *Epistle to the Hebrews*, 71.

4. Remember that each point in the author's exposition on Christ builds on the one before it. In this sense the author, following the intervening exhortations that separate expositional blocks, makes a transition from the end of the previous expositional unit. See discussion of the book's structure above (pp. 27–30) and my discussion of "distant hookwords" in *The Structure of Hebrews*, 96–100. To get the effect of how smoothly the author resumes his discussion of 1:5–14 with 2:5, read the former passage and then immediately read 2:5–9.

5. Spicq, *Theological Lexicon of the New Testament*, 424–26; R. Bergmeier, "ὑποτάσσω," *EDNT*, 3:408.

The author understands both Psalm 8:4–6 and 110:1 to contain a reference to those placed under Christ's feet.[6] As seen in the diagram below, the preacher employs Psalm 8 because, in addition to its references to the Son's supremacy by virtue of exaltation, it mentions a time during which the Son came down to earth, taking on a "status" or position (as a human being) that was lower than that of the angels; the author then turns to the Incarnation in 2:10–18.[7]

The Son Higher Than the Angels
(1:5–14)

"What is man that you are mindful of him,
the son of man that you care for him?
[7]You made him a little lower than the angels;
you crowned him with glory and honor
[8]and put everything under his feet."

The Son Lower Than the Angels
to Suffer for the Sons
(2:10–18)

The statement about the Incarnation in Psalm 8, as interpreted by our author, reads, "You made him a little lower than the angels." The word *brachy* (lit., "little") in this phrase can be understood in two ways: a small measure of distance or substance ("just a little lower"), or a small amount of time ("for a little while"). This latter meaning seems to fit the context better since the author is not interested in the degree to which the Son was of a lower status than the angels. Moreover, the author is expressing the thought that Christ walked the earth as a human being for a brief time before being exalted back to heaven.[8] The psalm moves from this statement of humiliation to a statement of glorification, in which the Son of Man is said to have been "crowned with glory and honor" and to have had "everything" placed "under his feet."

What We Do and Do Not See at Present (2:8b–9)

UPON CLOSE CONSIDERATION, Psalm 110:1 and 8:4–6 seem to contradict at a crucial point. Both psalms speak of the subjugation of all things to Christ but appear to address different time frames. Psalm 110:1 looks to the future

---

6. On the use of the rabbinic technique "verbal analogy" see above, p. 67; 1 Cor. 15:25–27 also juxtaposes these two messianic psalms.

7. On the use of "intermediary transitions" see Guthrie, *The Structure of Hebrews*, 105–11.

8. See Hagner, *Hebrews*, 45–46; Attridge, *The Epistle to the Hebrews*, 76.

("until I make your enemies a footstool for your feet") while 8:6 speaks of the subjugation as an accomplished fact ("You . . . put everything under his feet"). Given the potential puzzlement arising from the two passages, our author employs a rabbinic technique called "dispelling confusion," which involved discussing the conundrum in a way so as to clarify the passages in question.

The author, in effect, answers the question, "Which is it? Have all things been subjugated to the Son, or does his universal dominance lie in the future?" with "Both!" He first makes clear that God indeed has placed everything under the Son's feet already, as suggested by Psalm 8 (having "left nothing that is not subject to him"). The authority of Christ is already all-encompassing. Psalm 110:1, on the other hand, means "at present we do not see everything subject to him."

At various points early Christian teachers present Christ's exaltation over the powers as a *fait accompli* (Eph. 1:20–22; 1 Peter 3:22). This accomplished fact, however, might seem confusing at best and tacitly absurd at worst to someone looking at a church ravished by the forces of darkness. Persecuted Christians in Rome may have been asking, "Why are we being hurt by powers already placed under the feet of Christ? Has God not subjected all things to the Son?" The author, referring to Psalm 8, answers this question in the affirmative, but, based on Psalm 110:1, goes on to explain we have yet to see the *full* impact of his authority. This latter point aligns with other exaltation passages in the New Testament, which, also based on Psalm 110:1, speak of the subjugation of all things as a future event (e.g., 1 Cor. 15:25–26).

This tension between the "now" and the "not yet," between what is present reality but not yet seen, expresses what may be referred to as "the inaugurated rule of Christ." That is, the reign of Christ and the reality of Christian experience have begun, but will not be fully actualized until a final consummation at the end of the age. The Son's rule is already a reality; that reality, however, must be confessed by faith until we see its full impact at the end of the age.[9]

Nevertheless, the One whom we see now is much more important than the realized subjugation of all things to the Son. "We see Jesus," the incarnate sufferer who has been crowned with glory and honor. When the author says we "see" Jesus, he anticipates exhortations to "consider" him later in the book (3:1; 12:1–2). These exhortations focus both on Jesus' earthly obedience to the Father and his subsequent exaltation. To "see Jesus," therefore, does not mean a physical perception, but rather a spiritual perception, recognizing both the witness of his earthly endurance and his present exalted position.

---

9. See especially Andrew T. Lincoln, *Paradise Now and Not Yet: Studies in the Role of the Heavenly Dimension in Paul's Thought with Special Reference to His Eschatology* (Grand Rapids: Baker, 1991).

This statement the author presents artistically in the Greek text, framing "we see Jesus" with two parts of the psalm (i.e., "lower than the angels," and "crowned with glory and honor").[10] The "him" who was made for a while lower than the angels (2:7a) is now clearly identified as Jesus. The preacher then specifies the means by which Jesus was crowned with glory and honor: "because he suffered death." The final phrase of the passage, "so that by the grace of God he might taste death for everyone," makes a transition to the next unit (2:10–18), which deals with the Son's suffering on behalf of the heirs.

AS WE BEGIN to move toward application of Hebrews 2:5–9, two points are crucial if we are to avoid serious missteps in bringing the text into our modern contexts. (1) The author's use of Psalm 8 must be understood as Christological rather than anthropological. In addition to this psalm being used Christologically elsewhere in the New Testament, the author himself clearly interprets it in light of Christ. He understands that Jesus is the one made lower than the angels for a time and the one whom, speaking of the exaltation, God "has crowned . . . with glory and honor and put everything under his feet" (v. 5, 9). Barclay, for example, completely misses the point of the passage by focusing on humanity's plight rather than on the Son's exaltation and incarnation.[11] The Christological interpretation of Psalm 8 affirms Christ's identification with humanity, or perhaps his role as representative of humanity, but the focus is on his experience and position, not ours.

(2) The author's use of Psalm 8 must be seen as transitional. The opening statement, which speaks of the subjugation of the world to come, clearly points back to the quotation of Psalm 110:1 in Hebrews 1:13. As already stated, the author uses Psalm 110 in conjunction with Psalm 8 because of their common reference to all things being put under the feet of the Son. The clarifying comments of 2:8–9 make sense in light of the two psalms being considered together. Furthermore, Psalm 8, with its emphasis both on humiliation as well as exaltation, effects a smooth transition to the next unit which highlights Christ's suffering.

---

10. Attridge, *The Epistle to the Hebrews*, 72–73.

11. William Barclay, *The Letter to the Hebrews: Revised Edition*, The Daily Study Bible Series (Philadelphia: Westminster, 1976), 24–25. Barclay presents the following as the main points of the passage: (1) The Son shows us the ideal of what humanity should be; (2) he shows us the actual state of humanity; (3) he shows us how the actual can be changed into the ideal through Christ.

As a transition between two major blocks of the sermon, therefore, our application should not be weighted toward either exaltation or incarnation but rather the connection between the two. This connection is both *spatial* and *temporal*. It is *spatial* in that the experience of the Son has spanned the distance from heaven to earth. The all-powerful Son exalted above the principalities of the universe—the Lord of heaven—is the same one who has lived among us, identified with us, and died for us. Jesus is both the one who has authority over all the forces of the universe (including the evil angels in charge of the evil, church-opposing nations) and the one who, having been for a time lower than the angels, can identify with us and has suffered for us. This is intended as a basis of hope and will constitute a key theme in the rest of Hebrews.

This connection between heaven and earth, however, seems ironic for those experiencing persecution. If Christ, even though he can identify with us in our suffering, now has power over those making us suffer, why does he remain silent? This poses a specifically Christian form of the theological query known as the "problem of evil,"[12] which brings us to a second crucial connection between the exaltation and incarnation: the *temporal* connection between the present time and the time to come. Herein lies the answer to the seeming contradiction presented by an exalted Christ and a persecuted church—God's timing. In his incarnation the Son of God offered himself as a sacrifice for the forgiveness of sins. Thus he opened the way for God's new covenant to be established with those who respond to the preaching of the Gospel.

The intervening time between the exaltation and consummation of Christ's rule allows for God's mission of reconciliation as the church proclaims forgiveness in Christ. However, this in-between time also involves suffering for the church since Christ's domination of the powers, while being real (i.e., an accomplished fact), has yet to be fully realized. There exists, therefore,

> a tension between the "already" and the "not yet" of the Christian hope, but each is essential to the other. In the language of the seer of Patmos, the Lamb that was slain has by his death won the decisive victory (Rev. 5:5), but its final outworking, in reward and judgment, lies in the future (Rev. 22:12). The fact that we now "see Jesus crowned with glory and honor" is guarantee enough that God "has put all things under his feet" (Heb. 2:8–9). His people already share his risen life, and those who

---

12. See Alister McGrath, *Christian Theology: An Introduction* (Cambridge, Mass.: Blackwell, 1994), 228–33.

reject him are "condemned already" (John 3:18). For the Fourth Evangelist, the judgment of the world coincided with the passion of the incarnate Word (John 12:31); yet a future resurrection to judgment is contemplated as well as a resurrection to life (John 5:29).[13]

The New Testament fosters the position that the kingdom has been established and its effects set in motion, but its full realization is postponed until the second coming of Christ (Heb. 9:28).

BASED ON OUR study and discussion of 2:5–9, three themes should occupy our attention as we apply this text to the church today. (1) All things have already been submitted to Christ at his exaltation at the right hand of God. (2) The subjection of all things to Christ, although a present reality, will not be fully perceptible until the end of the age. (3) Christians should focus on both Jesus' example of endurance and his present position as regent of the universe, which serve as twin bases for endurance in the midst of our difficulties.

Grappling with the silence of God. Several years ago my family and I lived just down Sanders Bluff Road from Barry and Brenda with their three young boys, John, Drew, and Wade—a wonderful family. Barry was fun, a man of deep faith who talked openly of his love for Christ; Pat and Brenda enjoyed having tea together (a picture of one of their outings is still magnetized to our refrigerator), and the boys were great with our Joshua, who trailed them in age. We were excited about our new-found friends.

In 1993 Brenda contracted liver cancer. In the months that followed, family, friends, and churches in our area prayed, fasted, and believed in God for a miracle. I have never seen such consistency or fervency of prayer. Barry, a great man of faith, was a spiritual rock, ministering to his family and waiting on the Lord. Nevertheless, the answer for which we prayed—Brenda's healing from cancer—did not come this side of the grave. At the end of this unrelenting illness her emaciated body, only a shadow of the lovely young mother we loved, finally succumbed to the disease. The funeral heralded the victory we as Christians have in death; yet I believe an emotional undercurrent ran through the auditorium that day as sincere, saddened believers asked the question, "God, why did you not answer our prayers?"

To this example could be added countless thousands: the child born with a deformity in spite of prayers for a healthy baby; the missionary who loses

---

13. F. F. Bruce, "Eschatology," *EDT*, 365.

a spouse in an auto accident on the field of calling; a homosexual entangled in lust, desperately asking for deliverance from his obsessions; the unanswered prayer for a job; or the request for financial help that seems to get no higher than the ceiling. In times of God's silence Jesus' promise of "whatever you ask in prayer" (Mark 11:24) seems mocking, and we cry out with the psalmist in Psalm 44:23—26:

> Awake, O Lord! Why do you sleep?
>> Rouse yourself! Do not reject us forever.
> Why do you hide your face
>> and forget our misery and oppression?
> We are brought down to the dust;
>> our bodies cling to the ground.
> Rise up and help us;
>> redeem us because of your unfailing love.

"Unfailing love?" we ask. What exactly does that mean? If God loves us, why does he not intervene on our behalf?[14]

The persecuted church. To persecuted Christians around the world this question must seem especially relevant. As reported in a 1996 *Christianity Today* article, Christians are a minority in 87 of the world's countries and territories. In many of these, believers are interrogated, imprisoned, harassed, fined, and killed because of the faith. For example, Islamic countries such as Sudan, Kuwait, Pakistan, Iran, and Saudi Arabia restrict or prohibit the practice of Christianity. Five Christian women in Sudan were given the death penalty in August 1995 for their confession of Christ, and other believers in that country have been raped and tortured by government forces. Three months earlier in Cuba, Pastor Orson Vila was arrested and imprisoned for holding church meetings at his home.

In Vietnam, both Protestant and Catholic leaders also have been imprisoned for leading religious activities. Just over the border in northern provinces of Laos, Christians have been forced to sign affidavits renouncing their faith, and officials have initiated a campaign to close all churches. Xiao Biguang, a Chinese intellectual who came to Christ after the Tiananmen Square massacre, has spent the past two years in prison for "creating a negative atmosphere among students" in China. His wife, Gou Qinghui, has lost her teaching job and been detained by authorities on four occasions. She has not seen her husband since his arrest.[15] This couple is part of a persecuted, underground

---

14. See esp. Philip Yancey, *Disappointment with God: Three Questions No One Asks Aloud* (Grand Rapids: Zondervan, 1988).

15. Kim A. Lawton, "The Suffering Church," *Christianity Today* 40 (July 15, 1996): 54–61, 64.

church in China that may number as many as fifty million members. To these dramatic examples could be added less dramatic, but painful, situations around the world in which believers are tormented by bosses or family members unsympathetic to Christian belief and practice.

God's answers. So why, at times, does God not answer the cries of these persecuted believers as they are beaten, raped, imprisoned, or killed? Why does he not always answer the prayer for healing, staying the hand of death? Why does he sometimes refuse to respond to our desperate call for help?

The question here is not *whether* God answers prayer. He most certainly does! The people of God through faith have "conquered kingdoms, administered justice ... gained what was promised; ... shut the mouths of lions, quenched the fury of the flames, and escaped the edge of the sword ..." (Heb. 11:33–34). The question is how should we respond when "we do not see everything submitted to him." This too has been the experience of God's faithful through the ages: "Some faced jeers and flogging, while still others were chained and put in prison. They were stoned; they were sawed in two; they were put to death by the sword. They went about in sheepskins and goat-skins, destitute, persecuted and mistreated" (11:36–37). Although these people, like those earlier mentioned, were commended for their faith, these did not receive what was promised (11:39). So, what is going on when, in our immediate situations, Christ does not seem to be in control?

The answer to our dilemma lies in our perception of reality and, specifically, the nature of the Christian faith. In Western Christianity especially, "we have become committed to relieving the pain behind our problems rather than using our pain to wrestle more passionately with the character and purposes of God. *Feeling better has become more important than finding God.* And worse, we assume that people who find God always feel better."[16] To focus on our situations, our problems, our pains as primary (rather than the purposes of God) is to move away from important aspects of following Christ. We must follow Christ in the way of suffering. God's people have always been persecuted as counter to the power systems of this world; the enemy death still walks the highways of the globe, having yet to be put completely out of commission (1 Cor. 15:25–27); this "in-between time" is a time of tears and pain (Rev. 21:4).

Yet, in these experiences we walk in the way of Christ, who was persecuted, wept, and died. "To this you were called, because Christ suffered for you, leaving you an example, that you should follow in his steps" (1 Peter 2:21). Persecution has always been the *normal* Christian experience (e.g., Matt. 24:8–10; Mark 13:9–13; Acts 5:29–42; Rom. 8:35–37; 2 Cor. 4:8–12;

---

16. Larry Crabb, *Finding God* (Grand Rapids: Zondervan, 1993), 18.

Phil. 1:29; Col. 1:24). As we look to the example of Jesus in his earthly experiences of persecution, we gain strength for endurance. We see that sometimes what looks to be the darkest hour in this world's perspective is actually the brightest; the feeling of being forsaken by God may even occur at the pinnacle of our mission for him (Matt. 27:45–46). When we see Jesus in his incarnation, we are reminded of the price attached to living as God's person for God's purposes in a fallen world. He often brings glory to himself and "works for the good" (Rom. 8:28) through our pain. Jesus shows us a trust-God-and-hold-to-it-at-all-costs kind of faith.[17]

Moreover, as we consider Jesus, the now exalted Lord of the universe, we perceive that the last chapters of our stories have yet to be written. The exaltation heralds the ultimate demise of all powers of persecution, the burial of death, and the wiping away of all tears from our eyes, reunion with loved ones, and the supply of every need. We will not always live in the "in-between time." The age of hope looms on the horizon, dwarfing the pains of the present.

The problem of evil for the Christian lies not in God's abilities, nor even in our perception of his will and timing (cf. Job 42:3–4), but in our perception of Jesus. As a pilot in a dense fog keeps on course by looking to the instruments, Jesus provides a reference point from which to assess the greater realities of any given situation. What we need is to "see Jesus" (2:8–9), to take a "double look" at him in his incarnation and exaltation.

---

17. Yancey, *Disappointment with God*, 206.

Hebrews 2:10–18

I N BRINGING MANY sons to glory, it was fitting that God, for whom and through whom everything exists, should make the author of their salvation perfect through suffering. [11]Both the one who makes men holy and those who are made holy are of the same family. So Jesus is not ashamed to call them brothers. [12]He says,

> "I will declare your name to my brothers;
> in the presence of the congregation I will sing
> your praises."

[13]And again,

> "I will put my trust in him."

And again he says,

> "Here am I, and the children God has given me."

[14]Since the children have flesh and blood, he too shared in their humanity so that by his death he might destroy him who holds the power of death—that is, the devil [15]and free those who all their lives were held in slavery by their fear of death. [16]For surely it is not angels he helps, but Abraham's descendants. [17]For this reason he had to be made like his brothers in every way, in order that he might become a merciful and faithful high priest in service to God, and that he might make atonement for the sins of the people. [18]Because he himself suffered when he was tempted, he is able to help those who are being tempted.

WE COME NOW to the final section on the position of the Son relative to the angels (1:5–2:18). In 1:5–14 the preacher covered the Son's superiority to the angels, followed immediately by an exhortation to heed the Superior One's word of salvation (2:1–4). In 2:5–9, he made a transition by focusing on Psalm 8:4–6 with the title, "The Superior Son for a Time Became Positionally Lower Than the Angels." Having made the transition, the writer now brings his discussion fully "down to earth," addressing the Incarnation in a section titled "The Son Lower Than the Angels (i.e., among human beings) to Suffer for the 'Sons.'" Here he presents the Incarnation as prerequisite for the Son's identification with and suffering for humanity. Hebrews 2:10–18 may be divided into an introduction (v. 10), the Son's solidarity with humanity (vv. 11–13), presentation of the reason for the Incarnation (vv. 14–16), and a conclusion (vv. 17–18).

The Appropriateness of the Son's Suffering (2:10)

THE SHIFT FROM such a robust treatment of the Son's exaltation, supremacy, and power to the Son's suffering in death must have seemed abrupt to the first listeners. This theme of "the crucified Lord" scandalized the first-century world. Note how Paul spoke of the cross as "a stumbling block to Jews and foolishness to Gentiles, but to those whom God has called . . . the power of God and the wisdom of God" (1 Cor. 1:23–24). Agreeing with Paul, our author shows that Jesus' death on the cross was "fitting" (*eprepen*); he places this word first in his sentence for emphasis. Writers and speakers of the ancient world utilized this word to communicate that which was "appropriate" or "suitable" (e.g., Eph. 5:3; 1 Tim. 2:10; Titus 2:1).

In 2:10 the author proclaims that what God has done in the suffering of Jesus is in line with what we know of his character and purposes.[1] It is in accord both with his holiness and love and has accomplished God's plan to redeem people. The Son's affliction was ordered by the One "for whom and through whom everything exists," God thus being both the great Cause and the Director who brings the salvation of his new covenant people to reality.

As shown by the context, "suffering" refers not to pain in general but specifically to the suffering of death (2:9, 14–15), a recurring theme in Hebrews (5:7–10; 9:26–28; 12:1–3). God uses Jesus' death in "bringing many sons to glory"; the term *sons* constitutes a reference to the people of God rather than to humanity in general.[2] Those fellow heirs with Christ (cf. 1:14) are brought to "glory," the heavenly realm in which people experience the presence of God.[3] Thus, through the death of Jesus God's people join with the Son, moving from earth to heaven.

As the One who makes the heavenly pilgrimage of believers possible, Jesus is considered "the author of their salvation." *Archegon* (rendered "author" by the NIV) can be translated "trailblazer" or "guide," emphasizing the Son's role in bringing the new covenant people to glory. However, the word might be translated better by "champion"—the preacher using the idea of the divine

---

1. Lane, *Hebrews 1–8*, 55.

2. See Ellingworth, *The Epistle to the Hebrews*, 159–60.

3. Rom. 8:17; 1 Cor. 15:43; Phil. 3:21; Col. 1:27. On eschatological glory in Jewish literature, see Dan. 12:3; 1 Enoch 39:4–6; 45:3; 2 Enoch 22:8–18; 4 Ezra 7:91, 98.

hero common in the ancient Greek world. For example, Hercules was called "champion" (*archegos*) and "savior" (*soter*). If this is the author's intention, it is comparable to a modern preacher saying Jesus is "the real superman," as crass as that might sound. It was simply a way of expressing a meaningful analogy that Jesus has come to our rescue.

In what sense has he been made "perfect" through his suffering of death? As in 5:9, the author does not mean that Christ had been "imperfect," in the sense of being flawed or errant. Generally the word means "complete, whole, or adequate." In Jewish literature the idea of perfection is applied at times to death as the completion or seal of life.[4] Perfection in Hebrews has to do with fully completing a course, making it to the end of God's plan. That Jesus was made "perfect through suffering," therefore, connotes his full obedience to his mission of death on the cross and, perhaps, the adequacy of that act for bringing the children of God to glory.

The Son's Solidarity with the "Sons" (2:11–13)

THE NEXT MOVEMENT of the passage focuses on the fraternal relationship of Jesus with the people of God. Translated by the NIV with "of the same family," the phrase *ex henos pantes* ("all out of one") is ambiguous; its meaning has been debated since the first centuries of the church. The word "one" (*henos*) is an adjective that, in form, can be either masculine or neuter. If understood as a masculine, the word could refer to God as the Father of both the Son and Christians ("out of one God"), or perhaps even Abraham, stressing the heritage of God's people ("out of one ancestor") (see 2:16). On the other hand, if taken as a neuter, it would refer to the human nature shared by Jesus and the people of God ("out of one nature").

Most commentators, both ancient and modern, have opted for *henos* as a reference to God the Father; the emphasis in the context on sonship in relation to God supports this choice.[5] However, the main point of the passage has to do with Jesus' participation in the experience of being human, and, therefore, the understanding of *henos* as "physical human existence" cannot be ruled out. Both "the One who makes people holy" and "those who are made holy" translate timeless present participles of the verb "sanctify" (*hagiazo*), used here for the first time in Hebrews; elsewhere the verb is associated with the purification made possible by the sacrificial spilling of Jesus' blood (10:10, 14, 29).

The solidarity between the Son of God and the heirs of God results in a graciousness on the part of Christ: He is not ashamed to call us "brothers" (i.e.,

---

4. Attridge, *The Epistle to the Hebrews*, 85–86.
5. See the discussion in Ellingworth, *The Epistle to the Hebrews*, 164–65.

"family"). In verses 12–13 the author sets forth two texts, Psalm 22:22 and Isaiah 8:17b–18, as Old Testament support for Christ's solidarity with believers. At first glance the text from Psalms might seem to provide poor support for the author's discussion. However, the preacher did not choose these verses from the Scriptures arbitrarily; rather, he tapped a well of messianic teaching with which his audience would have been readily familiar.

Psalm 22:22 stems from a portion of Scripture that the early church perceived as containing significant prophesies of Christ's suffering.[6] The psalm begins with the words of anguish used by Jesus from the cross, "My God, my God, why have you forsaken me?" (Ps. 22:1; cf. Matt. 27:46). In Psalm 22:7–8 one finds the righteous one being taunted with such phrases as "He trusts in the LORD; let the LORD rescue him"—words that mirror the ridicule of the religious leaders around the cross (Matt. 27:43). Psalm 22:16–18 speaks specifically of the piercing of the righteous one's hands and feet, the wholeness of his bones, and the parceling out his garments through casting lots (Matt. 27:35; John 19:23, 31–36). The first twenty-one verses of Psalm 22, which afford graphic parallels to events surrounding Christ's crucifixion, are a righteous man's plea for deliverance. Thus the psalm as a whole fits well into the author's broader concern with Jesus' suffering of death on the cross.

With Psalm 22:22 (the verse quoted in Heb. 2:12) the psalm turns to a declaration of trust, in which the righteous one expresses joy and praise for God's attention to his cry for help. This quote supports the author's proclamation of solidarity between Jesus and the people of God in two ways. (1) He sees in its reference to "brothers" the establishment of a spiritual family relationship by the Son's sacrificial death. (2) The phrase "in the presence of the congregation" places emphasis on Jesus' location in our midst on earth, where we are "lower than the angels." It thus constitutes a reference to his incarnation. Psalm 22, therefore, offers a rich backdrop for a discussion on the Son's incarnation, suffering, and the familial relationships.

The next Old Testament passage to which the author of Hebrews turns (Isa. 8:17b–18) is also in proximity to a text having messianic import for the early church. In Isaiah 8:14 one finds the Lord described as "a stone that causes men to stumble and a rock that makes them fall," words applied to Christ by New Testament authors (Rom. 9:33; 1 Peter 2:8). Paul points to the crucifixion as that part of Jesus' experience that causes stumbling (1 Cor. 1:23). The broader context of the quotation in Hebrews 2:14, therefore, also fits the discussion of Christ's death.

The preacher in Hebrews presents Isaiah 8:17b–18 in a two-step process in order to make three distinct points. (1) He emphasizes verse

---

6. Hughes, *A Commentary on the Epistle to the Hebrews,* 107.

17b: "I will put my trust in him." In its original context this confession of reverential faith was given by the prophet in the face of the Assyrian crisis when, in the eighth century B.C., that powerful nation threatened the Israelites with devastation. Here the author of Hebrews understands the prophesy to express Jesus' trust toward the Father. (2) He then offers the next portion of the Isaiah passage—"Here am I, and the children God has given me"—to demonstrate that the Truster is in a familial relationship with other "children." (3) The clause "Here am I" points again to his living with God's children.

The author of Hebrews uses these two messianic passages (Ps. 22:22 and Isa. 8:17b–18) for at least three specific ends. (1) With their emphases on the Messiah's "brothers" and believers' designation as "children," these texts support the close family relationship established between the Son and the people of God. (2) Both passages refer to the Son's living with God's people. (3) In their broader contexts both speak to the Son's suffering as well as his posture of trust toward the Father. Consequently, they are appropriate for the author's purposes, especially when understood against a fertile backdrop of early Christian messianic interpretation.

The Reasons for the Incarnation (2:14–16)

THE AUTHOR NOW turns to address the necessity of the Incarnation. It might help to work our way backwards through the logic of his argument in verse 14. The goal of the Incarnation was twofold. (1) By becoming human the Son sought to "destroy him who holds the power of death—that is, the devil." The word "destroy" (*katargeo*) means "to render inoperative or ineffective." That the devil holds the power of death was not a uniquely Christian thought in the first century.[7] As the purveyor of sin and all that is opposed to God's will, the devil may be considered in league with the enemy death, both of whom will face their final end in "the lake of fire" (Rev. 20:14). Thus, Jesus took on our flesh and blood to nullify the devil's work. Since Christians still experience death (although they have nothing to fear from it), the proposition in 2:14 is another aspect of the preacher's perspective on the inaugurated rule of the Son.[8]

How, then, did the Son destroy the one having the power of death? The answer is "by his death." From our broader Christian theology it would be natural to think of the resurrection as destroying the devil's work, but that is not what the author has in mind here. The context suggests that the devil was

---

7. E.g., Wisdom of Solomon 2:23–24. See the discussion in Lane, *Hebrews 1–8*, 61.
8. See above, p. 99.

undone and death's bite rendered insipid by Christ's death, specifically his sac-rifice for sin (cf. 1 Cor. 15:56). Since death was the prescription for victory in this case, the only way the Son could accomplish the needed task was to die, and the only way to die was to become human. This is, for our author, the logic of the Incarnation.

(2) In 2:15 the preacher considers the second happy outcome of the Incar-nation: "Those who all their lives were held in slavery by their fear of death" have been liberated. A believer's fear of death no longer paralyzes and enslaves because Jesus has disabled death's master. As our champion he has stormed the very gates of the enemy and laid hold of his stronghold, opening wide the doors of our captivity and pointing us to the path of freedom.[9]

In 2:16 the author follows this statement of proclamation with an expla-nation. The Son helps "Abraham's descendants"—not angels. This verse begins with "for surely" (*gar depou*), meaning something to the effect "for as we well know." The congregation, having been exposed to early Christian doctrine (6:1–3), would have understood that Jesus' sacrifice on the cross was not for angels, but for those who inherit the promises of Abraham (6:13–17).

Conclusion (2:17–18)

WITH THE FINAL two verses of this passage the author sets up an effective tran-sition to the great central section of Hebrews on Jesus' high priesthood, beginning with 4:14 and running through 10:25.[10] Hebrews 2:17–18 shares no fewer than eight words or phrases with 4:14–5:3: "high priest" (2:17; 4:14; 5:1), "sin" (2:17; 4:15; 5:1,3), "merciful/mercy" (2:17; 4:16), "tempted" (2:18; 4:15), "help" (2:18; 4:16), "in service (matters related) to God" (2:17; 5:1), "the people" (2:17; 5:3), and the obligation to do something (2:17; 5:3).[11] Through these concepts the preacher introduces an expansion on his reasons for the Incarnation built around the high priest motif, which he expounds in 4:14–10:25. The Son had to become human because high priests are taken from among human beings (see 5:1), and he had to become a high priest in order to offer the ultimate sacrifice for sins (2:17). Finally, verse 18 presents a practical ramification of his suffering—that he is able to help us in our temptation.[12]

---

9. In the Old Testament, Greek mythology, and Jewish apocalyptic literature, the "divine deliverer" theme was expressed. See Lane, *Hebrews 1–8*, 61–62.

10. On the author's use of "distant hookwords" to effect transitions, see Guthrie, *The Struc-ture of Hebrews*, 96–100.

11. Ibid., 97–99.

12. For a discussion on Jesus' high priesthood and temptation, see below, p. 174.

Bridging Contexts

IN THESE VERSES the interpreter confronts a fairly complex passage, with unfamiliar terminology, Old Testament quotations the uses of which are not readily apparent, and logical constructs that must be dissected for clarity. The Original Meaning section has begun the spade work necessary for proper application of the passage. However, we must focus on the author's main concerns and several interpretive pitfalls.

Dealing with transitions. The extensive use of transitions in Hebrews presents the modern preacher or commentator with a dilemma: How do we treat these transitional elements as we move to the process of application? Specifically, since the topic of high priesthood is raised at the end of this passage, should we go ahead and speak of possible applications for the topic at this point?

We have already pointed out that verses 17–18 serve a primary role of setting up a transition to the great central section of Hebrews. Commentators variously present the section on Christ's high priesthood as beginning at 3:1; 4:14; 5:1; and 7:1.[13] Several of these analyses fail to distinguish between passages in which the high priest theme is a focal motif and those in which the theme is used to effect transition. Since the author of Hebrews begins to deal in earnest with Jesus' high priesthood at 4:14, we will reserve our treatment of high priesthood until we get to the central section of Hebrews. The critical decision reflected in this commentary is to focus on key, repeated topics in the book when the author of Hebrews himself brings those subjects into focus. Therefore, when, as in 2:17–18, the author raises a topic in anticipation of a greater treatment of the topic later in the book, that theme will be considered "transitional" and not a main focus of the section currently under consideration. This gives due weight to the author's intention in introducing the topic at a given point in the book.

Certainly, the high priest and sacrifice themes serve well the main topics of 2:10–16; they would not be effective elements for transition if they did not. However, they have a specific role to play, and they play that role elegantly. Rather than constituting the heart of the author's concerns in 2:10–18, these two topics play off those concerns and point to a later section.

What, then, are the author's intended foci for 2:10–18? Identification of the characteristic terms or themes used throughout a passage helps to form

---

13. E.g., at 3:1: Albert Vanhoye, "Literarische Struktur und theologische Botschaft des Hebräerbriefs (1. Teil)," *SNTU* 4 (1979): 119–47 ; at 4:14: Bruce, *The Epistle to the Hebrews,* 114; at 5:1: George W. Buchanan, *To the Hebrews,* AB (Garden City, N.Y.: Doubleday, 1972), xxxi; and at 7:1: James Swetnam, "Form and Content in Hebrews 7–13," *Bib* 55 (1974): 333–48.

threads of meaning that connect the various elements of the passage. In 2:10–18 two main topics tie the whole together: the Incarnation and the Son's suffering.

The Incarnation. A main topic threading its way through the entire passage is that of the Son's close relationship to the children of God through his incarnation. The Son brings believers to glory (2:10) and is not ashamed to call them family since he and they share a common experience (2:11–12, 14). He is in their midst (2:12–13), having become like them by taking on flesh and blood (2:14, 17), and, therefore, he can give them help (2:14–15, 18). Thus, the solidarity of Christ with God's people forms a central theme for 2:10–18. He is depicted as fully human and, therefore, can relate fully to people.

We should pause to address the gender-specific language of "sons" and "brothers" used in this passage, which some in our modern culture will label as "politically incorrect." Out of their conviction that such language denigrates the female sex or impedes females' identification with the text, branches within biblical scholarship are working to use more inclusive language in their translations. This sensitivity is warranted—women of the new covenant, just as much as their male counterparts, have ownership of the promises and proclamations of 2:10–18.

Nevertheless, a caution also is in order. One must think through the analogical nature of theological language.[14] Divine revelation makes use of images and concepts from human experience to draw analogies to God's activities or personality. When the Scriptures use masculine imagery concerning God, such as "Father," it does not mean that God has a sexual orientation. Moreover, when we call God "Father," we do not mean that he has fathered us biologically; that is a pagan concept. We have not been born of flesh and blood by the Father (John 1:13), but of the Spirit.

The images communicated through analogous language, however, do communicate specific truths about God. When the writers of Scripture speak of God as "Father," they mean that God has characteristics and activities analogous to what we know as fatherhood, especially fatherhood as known in the ancient world when the Scriptures were written. For example, in the ancient world God as Father communicated his provision for, protection over, and loving guidance of his children. In the present context the image of God as Father especially communicates God's granting of an inheritance to his people. It is a mistake simply to change the language to "Mother" or even "Father/Mother" since what the author intended to communicate through the specific image of fatherhood is thereby changed. What we should ask is, "How can we make clear the truth that this image intends to communicate?"

---

14. McGrath, *Christian Theology*, 135–36, 205–7.

When in 2:10–18 the author speaks of us as "sons" or "brothers," he has specific reasons for doing so. The concept of sonship flows from the author's treatment of Jesus as *the* Son and closely relates to the idea of inheritance in the ancient world. The use also effects a pleasing literary device with the juxtaposition of the "Son" with the "sons." Jesus as the firstborn Son is inheritor of the universe. This must not be taken to mean that God gave birth to Jesus as a physical father would procreate and have a son. The image speaks of dynamics in the relationship that exists between the first and second persons of the Trinity.

This relationship involves honor, unique position, and responsibility, as well as subordination. Sons in the ancient world held a position of honor and responsibility not held by daughters in the ancient world. The author of Hebrews uses "sons" to refer to all the people of God, male and female, as God's honored children and receptors of his inheritance. So when a female Christian reads that Jesus brings "many sons to glory," she should interpret the statement as meaning "Jesus brings me to glory as an honored child for whom there awaits an inheritance."

The writer takes the term "brothers," on the other hand, directly from the Old Testament text of Psalm 22:22. In ancient culture the image of brotherhood spoke of the intimacy of relationship, shared experience, and loyalty. Thus, the image communicates a close association, such as in a fraternal relationship. Hebrews 2:12 does not mean Jesus only proclaims God's name to males, but as the parallel in the next line suggests, he announces God's name to all those in "the congregation," that is, the people of God with whom he enjoys an intimate relationship.

There are at least two important presuppositions to note concerning this relationship between the Son and the people of God. (1) The emphasis of Jesus' being "in the midst" forms an important contrast with the focus on exaltation in 1:5–14. Emphasis lies with the Son's being below the angels and with his brothers rather than his being "above" his companions (1:9), superior to the angels, and over his enemies (1:13). (2) The movement from above to below—the purposeful appropriation of human existence—presupposes the Son's preexistence and subsequent incarnation.

What does it mean to say that the Son of God became human, or as 2:14 puts it, "shared in [the sons'] humanity"? The authors of the New Testament present the Incarnation straightforwardly. John 1:14 states, "The Word became flesh and made his dwelling among us. We have seen his glory, the glory of the One and Only, who came from the Father, full of grace and truth." Similarly, in Philippians 2:6–7 Paul writes, "Who, being in very nature God, did not consider equality with God something to be grasped, but made himself nothing, taking the very nature of a servant, being made in human likeness." Note too 1 Timothy 3:16b: "He appeared in a body, was vindicated by the Spirit, was seen by angels, was preached among the nations, was believed on in the world, was taken up in glory." These passages present simply the fact of the Incarnation without an analysis of the relationship between the divine and human in Christ.

However, as the Christian movement developed in the first centuries, heresies arose, which skewed certain biblical data and denied the full humanity of Christ. Docetism (from the Greek word *dokeo*, meaning "to seem"), for example, held that Jesus just seemed to be human. This aberration of early Christianity is probably the problem addressed by 1 John. Some forms of Docetism were associated with a broader philosophical-theological system of belief known as Gnosticism, which held in part that all physical matter is evil. It followed, then, that the divine would not take on real human flesh and thus be corrupted by evil.[15] In addressing this heresy Ignatius of Antioch, who was martyred about A.D. 107, wrote:

> So do not pay attention when anyone speaks to you apart from Jesus Christ, who was of the family of David, the child of Mary, who was truly born, who ate and drank, who was truly persecuted under Pontius Pilate, was truly crucified and truly died, in full view of heaven, earth, and hell, and who was truly raised from the dead. . . . But if, as some godless people, that is, unbelievers, say, he suffered in mere appearance—being themselves mere appearances—why am I in bonds?[16]

Another theological perspective, condemned in the fourth century, was Apollinarianism. Apollinarius held that in Jesus the Word had taken the place of a normal human mind and spirit. Thus, Jesus was not fully human because he did not share these aspects of human existence with the rest of humanity. Apollinarius even understood Jesus' flesh to be fused with his divinity and therefore "glorified," or "divine flesh." His teachings were condemned at a series of meetings held in the eighth and ninth decades of the fourth century.[17]

Because of such heresies church leaders of the first four centuries A.D. saw the need to articulate more clearly what Scripture implies concerning the Incarnation. In the fourth century, for example, Athanasius emphasized elements in Scripture that point to the deity of Christ, and others that point to his humanity, such as his thirst, tiredness, or pain; both need to be affirmed.

---

15. Erickson, *The Word Became Flesh*, 44–46.

16. *Letter to the Trallians*, 9–10 in Sources Chrétiennes, 2d ed., ed. P. Th. Camelot (Paris: Cerf, 1951), 10:118–20.

17. Erickson, *The Word Became Flesh*, 58–61.

A century after Athanasius the Chalcedonian formulation of Christology stressed that Jesus was one person with two distinct natures, at the same time fully divine and fully human. His deity was not changed by his humanity, and in the person of Jesus deity could not be separated from his humanity. He was not made less than God by becoming human but could be said to have added complete humanity to his deity. Thus the church fathers who influenced and crafted the Chalcedonian expression of Christology affirmed the following reflected in Hebrews 2:10–18: That Jesus suffered and partook of flesh and blood, becoming like his brothers and sisters, means that Jesus really did become human. He drank deeply of the human experience.

The Son's suffering. The preacher first mentions the sufferings (in death) experienced by the Son at 2:10. As noted earlier, the quotations of Psalm 22:22 and Isaiah 8:17–18 in Hebrews 2:12–13 show the hermeneutical importance of considering the broader Old Testament context when seeking to understand an author's use of a specific quotation. In their broader contexts both of these Old Testament passages carry connotations of righteous suffering. They were read specifically by the early Christian community as messianic prophecies of the Crucifixion. Furthermore, the Son's death is again mentioned in 2:14 and his suffering in 2:18. Thus the topic of suffering permeates 2:10–18 from beginning to end.

The author has a specific suffering in mind—that of the Son's death on the cross. He later draws an overt connection between Christ's suffering and that of the Christian community (e.g., 12:1–3), but the primary point in 2:10–18 is that the Son has worked great accomplishments on behalf of God's people through his death. The author may have the sufferings of the Christian community and specifically their fear of death under persecution in mind,[18] but to draw a general application to the suffering of believers at this point is unwarranted. Furthermore, the concept of perfection speaks of the completion of the Son's mission through his death.

Some in the church's history have magnified suffering as a means of accomplishing a state of spiritual perfection. At times martyrs were venerated and seen as having special status before God. Ascetics such as Simeon Stylites, who spent the last part of his life on top of a pillar, and others who denied themselves normal physical provisions such as food, shelter, and social contact, sought to drown their carnal desires in a steady stream of rigorous spiritual disciplines. Yet the New Testament cautions against asceticism as a means of spiritual enrichment (e.g., Col. 2:20–23). Asceticism of any age is wrong-headed when seen in light of the gospel's truth.

---

18. See Lane, *Hebrews: A Call to Commitment*, 52.

If one takes an ascetic interpretation of Hebrews 2:10, reasoning, "If Jesus was perfected through suffering, then I will also get rid of my sinfulness through my suffering," one is seriously misinterpreting the verse on several counts. The "perfection" of Jesus in this verse does not speak to an eradication of imperfection or sinfulness (as in the ascetic's buffeting his body to overcome sinfulness), but of the suffering Christ did on the cross. Also, the ascetic interpretation turns the intention of Hebrews' words on its head. The point of the passage is that we need a champion who has accomplished for us something we could not do for ourselves. By Jesus' completing his course in suffering for our sins we have the victory, not by our self-flagellation.

Moreover, 2:10–18 places great emphasis on the purposefulness of the Incarnation and the sufferings of Jesus. The Son took on humanity for specific reasons: to give us help, to destroy the devil, to liberate us from the fear of death, and to make us holy through the forgiveness of sins. The Incarnation, therefore, far from being a topic relegated to a theological ivory tower, has vast practical ramifications for life in this world, the living Christ being our source of help, deliverance, and holiness.

NEOAPOLLINARIANISM. DURING THE winter term of 1980, as a part of my college education, I served as a chaplain intern at Fort Pillow, a medium-maximum security prison in Tennessee. Along with my two colleagues from the university I was given little supervision in my attempt to minister to a wide range of inmates. The food was terrible, pornography was everywhere, and the culture, as is often the case in prison, was one of deception and "special insider rules." Even the assistant chaplain informed me he no longer believed in God.

Since I was at Fort Pillow as a religion student, I had the assignment to observe various types of religious meetings conducted on the prison grounds. Among these was my first exposure to Islam. Following one worship service a young, energetic preacher of the Koran and I had a lively conversation; of course, I wanted to talk about Jesus. My friend was quite willing to speak of Jesus as a prophet, but the thought of him as God was completely outrageous in his view. How could a holy God take on corruptible human flesh? Did we mean that God had physical intercourse with Mary? Of course not, I assured him. Nevertheless, he was scandalized by the idea of the Incarnation, as are many devotees of other religions and philosophies.

Even many Christians who claim to be "orthodox" or "biblical" struggle to imagine Jesus as *fully* human, as sinlessly sharing a broad gamut of our fleshly existence (Heb. 4:15). As Max Lucado writes in his down-to-earth style, we get a bit uncomfortable imagining the "exalted Lord of glory" as truly one of us:

> Angels watched as Mary changed God's diaper. The universe watched with wonder as The Almighty learned to walk. Children played in the street with him. And had the synagogue leader in Nazareth known who was listening to his sermons. . . .
>
> Jesus may have had pimples. He may have been tone-deaf. Perhaps a girl down the street had a crush on him or vice-versa. It could be that his knees were bony. One thing's for sure: He was, while completely divine, completely human.
>
> For thirty-three years he would feel everything you and I have ever felt. He felt weak. He grew weary. He was afraid of failure. He was susceptible to wooing women. He got colds, burped, and had body odor. His feelings got hurt. His feet got tired. And his head ached.
>
> To think of Jesus in such a light is—well, it seems almost irreverent, doesn't it? It's not something we like to do; it's uncomfortable. It is much easier to keep the humanity out of the incarnation. Clean the manure from around the manger. Wipe the sweat out of his eyes. Pretend he never snored or blew his nose or hit his thumb with a hammer.[19]

Thus if we are careless in our thinking about Jesus, we can slip into a form of Neoapollinarianism, embracing his divinity but holding his full humanity at arm's length. Yet, it is important that we understand the extent to which God went to win our redemption. Through the Incarnation God became an "insider," not merely acting on our human predicament from without, but transforming it from within. In a famous answer to Apollinarianism in the fourth century, Gregory of Nazianzus stated, "What has not been assumed cannot be restored," meaning that for redemption to reach into every darkened corner of human existence, Jesus had to take on that existence in its entirety. He was not merely God encased in flesh, but was truly human; as human he was vulnerable.

He who was the all-powerful Lord, who cast the stars to their appointed rounds, who sat above the globe spinning it through his powerful word, became vulnerable as he walked on the sod he himself had created. In mind and body he was truly human. Nowhere is that vulnerability seen more starkly than in the Son's suffering of death. In 2:10—18 the author of Hebrews focuses on this suffering as a main purpose of the Incarnation—he had to be fully human in order to die. Henry Hart Milman writes of this paradox of the vulnerable God:

---

19. Max Lucado, *God Came Near: Chronicles of the Christ* (Portland, Ore.: Multnomah, 1987), 26.

When God went back to Heaven—the living God—
    Rode he the heavens upon a fiery car?
Waved seraph-wings along His glorious road?
    Stood still to wonder each bright wandering star?

Upon the cross he hung, and bowed the head,
    And prayed for them that smote, and them that cursed;
And, drop by drop, His slow life-blood was shed,
    And His last hour of suffering was His worst.[20]

The limitations of human ability. What is missed both by those who deny the divinity of Jesus and those who reject his full humanity is that we as human beings needed a bridge between deity and humanity that could be built only by one who had experienced fully both sides of the gulf separating us from God. This is the biblical picture.

Of course a true humanist would deny that human beings have needs that can only be met outside themselves, and modern cultures have been permeated with elements of this thinking. We want to be "self-made," to "pull ourselves up by our own bootstraps." We do not need any primitive notion of "God" to assuage our fears and feelings of inadequacy or to eliminate our limitations. We as humans can forge our own truth, discern our own perspectives on beauty, and liberate ourselves from the psychological, physical, and social ills by which we are plagued. John Dewey wrote, "Man is capable, if he will but exercise the required courage, intelligence and effort, of shaping his own fate."[21]

Although much can be said for self-initiative, hard work, and self-confidence—and humanity has chalked up a plethora of impressive accomplishments—a true humanist is out of touch with the massiveness of human limitation. "Humanism," wrote French philosopher Simone Weil, "was not wrong in thinking that truth, beauty, liberty, and equality are of infinite value, but in thinking that man can get them for himself without grace."[22] We need someone greater than ourselves to come into our experience from the outside and lead us, teach us, and rescue us. In short, we need a champion to storm the gates of our prisons and liberate us, ripping the keys to enslavement from the devil's grip and setting our feet on the path of true life.

What is surprising is the form our champion took and the means of our liberation. The one of all power took the position of the powerless. The Lord of life drank deeply of death. The way he brought us up to God was

---

20. "God with Us," *The Jesus of the Poets, An Anthology*, ed. Leonard R. Gribble (New York: Richard R. Smith, 1930), 94.

21. John Dewey, *Reconstruction in Philosophy* (New York: Henry Holt, 1929), 47–49.

22. "The Romanesque Renaissance," in *Cahiers du Sud* (Marseilles, 1941; repr. in *Selected Essays*, ed. by Richard Rees, 1962).

by coming completely down to, even below our level, taking the form of a servant. Since we could not save ourselves, he did not save himself from the worst of human experiences. The limitless Lord of the universe took on limitations in order to free us from ours, and nowhere are our limitations more clearly recognized than in face of death.

Angst over death. American filmmaker Woody Allen summed up humanity's uneasiness with death when he said, "It's not that I'm afraid to die, I just don't want to be there when it happens." This death angst is expressed well in Somerset Maughm's "Appointment in Samarra," an old tale about a servant who had gone to the market in Baghdad and come back to his master shaken over an encounter there.

> "Master, just now when I was in the marketplace I was jostled by a woman in the crowd, and when I turned I saw that it was Death that jostled me. She looked at me and made a threatening gesture. Now lend me your horse and I will ride away from this city and avoid my fate. I will go to Samarra and there Death will not find me." The merchant lent him his horse, and the servant mounted it, and he dug his spurs in its flanks and as fast as the horse could gallop he went. When the merchant went down to the marketplace he saw Death standing in the crowd and he came to Death and said, "Why did you make a threatening gesture to my servant when you saw him this morning?" "That was not a threatening gesture," Death said. "It was only a start of surprise. I was astonished to see him in Baghdad, for I have an appointment with him tonight in Samarra."

No matter how confident one may be over human ability, our limitation concerning death is undeniable and our meeting with it inevitable.[23]

We must point out that Hebrews does not say we have been delivered from death itself, but from slavery to the *fear* of death—a fear that might encompass both the process of dying and the state of being dead. In his book *The Art of Dying* Robert Neale lists three aspects of this fear. (1) We fear *the loss of mastery*.

> I guess I fear dying because it involves a real loss of control. When you are dying, you have almost no control. There is an incredible vulnerability—and that's scary. It is almost as if one's last few minutes of life involve a vulnerability akin to one's first few minutes of life. Losing control over a body and environment which were at one time your servants must be a frightening experience.[24]

---

23. As told in Robert E. Neale, *The Art of Dying* (New York: Harper & Row, 1973), 22–23.
24. Ibid., 34.

So, as Job's tormentor Bildad the Shuhite called it, death is the "king of terrors" (Job 18:14).

(2) We fear *incompleteness and failure*. Especially for those who have enjoyed life and sought certain achievements, whether personal or professional, life can hold a great deal of joy and fulfillment. There exists a stark finality to death. We are confronted with an end, a door shut never to be reopened, the final page of a book, now put down and never to be picked up again. Things left undone will never be brought to completion once we have crossed this finish line.

(3) We fear *separation from our loved ones*. For those of us who have meaningful relationships with family, the pain of that separation cuts deeply.

(4) To these three can be added a fourth from psychiatrist Elisabeth Kübler-Ross in her book *Death: The Final Stage of Growth*. In chapter 2 Kübler-Ross suggests it is difficult for us to accept death because it *leads us to a realm of unfamiliarity*. Although it is all around us, we never really see it from the inside until we experience it. Especially for those who are not religious and for whom death cannot be viewed as natural, it is an obscene mystery.[25] Death therefore becomes a specter to be avoided, a master to which we are enslaved, and an enemy at which we rage. "Do not go gentle into that good night," wrote Welsh poet Dylan Thomas in his poem; "old age should burn and rave at close of day; rage, rage, against the dying of the light."

Christians too experience apprehension over death, still an enemy and one yet to experience our Master's full judgment (1 Cor. 15:26). So in what way have we been delivered from slavery to this fear? (1) For the believer there is a sense of the known mixed with the unknown of death—or rather the Known One. Christian hope is based on the fact that because of the forgiveness of our sins through Christ's suffering of death, we know one who has gone before us. Thus, although the dark mystery of death has not been fully exposed to the light, we have the comfort of one who has experience in dealing with it.

Author, speaker, and former missionary Elisabeth Elliot tells of an occasion in the jungles of South America when, as she and her Indian guide were traveling a primitive path, her trail suddenly dropped into a ravine. The only means across was a fallen tree. The Indian guide nimbly jumped onto the tree and started across. Elliot, who confesses she was mortified at the prospect of falling, hesitated. Her guide, perceiving her apprehension, came back across, held out his hand, grasped hers, and led her across safely. The stability of one who had obvious mastery of the situation gave her the needed confidence. Paul tells us that Christ is "the firstfruits of those who have fallen asleep"

---

25. Susan Sontag, *Illness As Metaphor* (New York: Farrer, Straus and Giroux, 1978), ch. 7.

(1 Cor. 15:20), an agricultural image that speaks of the initial produce of a crop to ripen. As the first to come through death, Jesus gives us confidence and stability as we face our own.

(2) Our sense of incompleteness and failure is counterbalanced with hope of an eternal future—a future bought by Jesus' sacrificial death. When I preached at my grandfather's funeral, I closed with the final page from *The Last Battle*, the final volume of C. S. Lewis's Chronicles of Narnia. Aslan—the Christ-figure in the series—that great, untamed Lion from over the sea, has brought the children to his country, the *real*, eternal Narnia. The children are afraid that Aslan will once again send them back to England, but the Great Lion assures them that they no longer have to leave him:

> "There was a real railway accident," said Aslan softly. "Your father and mother and all of you are—as you used to call it in the Shadow-Lands—dead. The term is over: the holidays have begun. The dream is ended: this is the morning."
>
> And as he spoke He no longer looked to them like a lion; but the things that began to happen after that were so great and beautiful that I cannot write them. And for us this is the end of all the stories, and we can most truly say that they all lived happily ever after. But for them it was only the beginning of the real story. All their life in this world and all their adventures in Narnia had only been the cover and the title page: now at last they were beginning Chapter One of the Great Story, which no one on earth has read: which goes on for ever: in which every chapter is better than the one before.

The cities and lands of planet earth are not the end of the road for the believer but mere terminals, visited for a while as we pass through (11:15–16; 13:14). Since we have been made ultimately for his pleasure, ultimate completeness and success will be found in the Eternal One's presence when he says, "Well done!"

(3) Our fear of separation has been turned inside out. In the heavenly kingdom we will enjoy relationships with those from whom we have been separated by death. Paul writes, "Brothers we do not want you to be ignorant about those who fall asleep, or to grieve like the rest of men, who have no hope. We believe that Jesus died and rose again and so we believe that God will bring with Jesus those who have fallen asleep in him" (1 Thess. 4:13–14). In Hebrews our final destination is the heavenly Jerusalem, where all believers live eternally (Heb. 12:22–24).

(4) As followers of Christ, we have already surrendered mastery of our lives, realizing that control of our destinies was an illusion all along. As we surrender to the lordship of Christ, we relinquish self-legislation, submit-

ting ourselves to his higher authority and power. It is in that submission—that pre-death dying to self—that we find true life and freedom (Gal. 2:20). It is in the surrender of our earthly hopes that we find eternal hope. Fear of a loss of control dissipates in giving control to One who cares for us deeply and has the power to handle any situation.

In recent years a friend of mine had the privilege of visiting an old Chinese pastor who had spent twenty-five years in prison because of his faith in Christ. This pastor and other Christian leaders in China were brought before Chairman Mao and commanded to join the government's official church. They informed the chairman that they would not compromise the gospel. The pastor whom my friend visited was the only one to leave prison alive; he continues to lead many believers in the study of Scripture. During that visit the suggestion was made that the two of them go out for a meal. Being concerned for the church leader's safety, my friend asked if he would get in trouble for talking openly with a Westerner. The old man replied with a smile, "What can they do to me?" In other words, you cannot kill a man who has already died to himself. This peaceful, joyous, persecuted Christian statesman embodies that truth.

Hebrews 2:14–16 plays a part in a larger theological construct in the New Testament called the promise of Christian hope. Death has no sting or victory for believers because sin, which gives death its sting, has been paid for by the death of Christ, our champion. This has afforded us a relationship with the One who has conquered death, entering its mysterious halls before us, and it assures us that life after life shines brightly both relationally and purposefully in the eternal kingdom. He is in control of all situations, including our dying.

We may still experience some trepidation at the idea of our own death, but we are no longer enslaved to those fears. This passage speaks of the great Christian hope—that of eternal life.[26] So instead of cowering from death, we can proclaim with Paul: "'Death has been swallowed up in victory.' 'Where, O death, is your victory? Where, O death, is your sting?' ... But thanks be to God! He gives us the victory through our Lord Jesus Christ" (1 Cor. 15:54–55, 57).

---

26. See Acts 2:26; 23:6; 26:7; Rom. 5:2; 8:25; 1 Cor. 15:19; Gal. 5:5; Col. 1:5; 1 Thess. 4:13; Titus 1:2.

Hebrews 3:1–19

THEREFORE, HOLY BROTHERS, who share in the heavenly calling, fix your thoughts on Jesus, the apostle and high priest whom we confess. ²He was faithful to the one who appointed him, just as Moses was faithful in all God's house. ³Jesus has been found worthy of greater honor than Moses, just as the builder of a house has greater honor than the house itself. ⁴For every house is built by someone, but God is the builder of everything. ⁵Moses was faithful as a servant in all God's house, testifying to what would be said in the future. ⁶But Christ is faithful as a son over God's house. And we are his house, if we hold on to our courage and the hope of which we boast.

⁷So, as the Holy Spirit says:

"Today, if you hear his voice,
⁸   do not harden your hearts
   as you did in the rebellion,
      during the time of testing in the desert,
⁹ where your fathers tested and tried me
      and for forty years saw what I did.
¹⁰ That is why I was angry with that generation,
      and I said, 'Their hearts are always going astray,
      and they have not known my ways.'
¹¹ So I declared on oath in my anger,
      'They shall never enter my rest.'"

¹²See to it, brothers, that none of you has a sinful, unbelieving heart that turns away from the living God. ¹³But encourage one another daily, as long as it is called Today, so that none of you may be hardened by sin's deceitfulness. ¹⁴We have come to share in Christ if we hold firmly till the end the confidence we had at first. ¹⁵As has just been said:

"Today, if you hear his voice,
   do not harden your hearts
   as you did in the rebellion."

¹⁶Who were they who heard and rebelled? Were they not all those Moses led out of Egypt? ¹⁷And with whom was he

angry for forty years? Was it not with those who sinned, whose bodies fell in the desert? ¹⁸And to whom did God swear that they would never enter his rest if not to those who disobeyed? ¹⁹So we see that they were not able to enter, because of their unbelief.

HEBREWS MAKES A POWERFUL, motivational impact on its readers in part by moving strategically back and forth between expositional material concerning Jesus and exhortations that confront the audience with the need for decisive action. With the exception of 2:1–4, the section running from 1:5 to 2:18 explains the status of the Son of God vis-à-vis the angels. As the exalted Lord, maker and ruler of the cosmos, Christ is "above" the angels (1:5–14). This fact forms the basis for an argument from lesser to greater in 2:1–4.[1] Having been above the angels, the Son made a transition (2:5–9), coming to a status "below the angels," joining ranks with us as humans in order to suffer death for the people of God (2:10–18).

Hebrews 3:1–4:16 forms the first major block in which the preacher maintains an extended and varied exhortation. The first half of this exhortation (3:1–19) has two primary divisions. (1) Verses 1–6 draw a comparison between Moses' faithfulness as a servant and the filial faithfulness of Jesus. The author presents Jesus as the supreme example of faithfulness while building on his audience's respect for Moses, whom they revere as a great religious figure. (2) Verses 7–19 consist of a quotation of Psalm 95:7–11 and a commentary on that passage. In this section the author presents the people led out of Egypt by Moses as a paradigmatic picture of unfaithfulness. With chapter 3, therefore, the author aims to confront his hearers with a challenge to be faithful in their Christian commitment.

A Positive Example: Jesus' Faithfulness as a Son (3:1–6)

THE AUTHOR OF Hebrews often follows a distinct pattern in his exhortations—setting forth the *exhortation* itself and then its *basis* or *grounds*. This pattern provides the framework for 3:1–6 in the following manner. (1) In verses 1–2 we are challenged to consider Jesus as the paradigmatic image of faithfulness. In this exhortation the writer compares the Son of God with Moses. Jesus was faithful to the appointment God had given him, just as Moses was faithful to his appointed tasks. (2) In verses 3–6 the author

---

1. See above, pp. 84–85.

then provides the basis for the exhortation of verses 1–2. He highlights two contrasts between Jesus and Moses and demonstrates why Jesus, not Moses, should merit our ultimate attention. To be sure, Moses plays an important role but only as his faithfulness sheds light on the greater role of the Son of God.

In verse 1 the word "therefore" effects a smooth transition from the previous statement concerning the high-priestly help offered believers by Jesus (2:17–18). As he usually does in his exhortation sections, the preacher addresses his audience directly, calling them "holy brothers, who share in the heavenly calling" (3:1). That they are "holy" (*hagioi*) refers to the "purification of sins" in 1:3 and to Jesus as "the one who makes men holy" in 2:11. This leaves no doubt concerning the audience being addressed. The author's challenge confronts those whom he considers part of the community of faith.

As those who are being brought to glory (2:10), the readers "share in the heavenly calling." The verbal form "share" in the NIV actually translates a plural noun meaning "partakers" or "sharers" (*metochoi*), the same word used at 1:9 ("companions"). In the ancient world this word sometimes meant a companion to whom one related closely, such as a house mate or an associate in a business endeavor (e.g., Luke 5:7).[2] In Hebrews 3:1 the term connotes an intimate relationship forged in a common spiritual reality. These believers share a "heavenly calling" because Hebrews depicts the Christian life as a pilgrimage of following our great high priest, Jesus, into the presence of God in the heavenly Most Holy Place (e.g., 4:14–16; 6:19–20; 10:19–25; 11:14–16; 12:22–24). Rather than living with an earthbound perspective, the Christ-follower, responding to God's call, lives in light of a heavenly orientation.

The command to "fix your thoughts on Jesus, the apostle and high priest whom we confess" forms the core of the author's exhortation. "Fix your thoughts" renders the verb *katanoeo*, which can mean "consider, think about, notice, observe." When Luke translates Jesus' teaching that a person should "pay ... attention to" the beam in one's own eye (Luke 6:41) or "consider" the lilies of the field (12:27), he uses this word. From the context, the challenge of Hebrews 3:1 seems to be to consider carefully the example of Jesus as "the apostle and high priest whom we confess."

Hebrews 3:1 is the only place in the New Testament where Jesus is called an "apostle." This unusual designation for God's Son probably concerns his role as the one sent to proclaim God's name (2:12) and message (cf. Matt. 10:40; 15:24; Mark 9:37; Luke 10:16; Gal. 4:4).[3] In the two key passages

---

2. Spicq, *Theological Lexicon of the New Testament*, 2:478–80.
3. Attridge, *The Epistle to the Hebrews*, 107.

that frame the great central section of Hebrews, the author refers to "the confession" (*homologia*) of the Christian community (Heb. 4:14; 10:23).[4] The believers, in following the example of the Old Testament faithful (11:13), are to be "confessors" (13:15); that is, they are to make a formal, public profession of faith in Christ. In the original context of Hebrews this may refer to a confession made at baptism. The preacher, therefore, calls his readers back to a serious focus on the one whom they had claimed in the past as the great center of their lives.

Furthermore, we are to fix our thoughts on Jesus' being "faithful to the one who appointed him" (i.e., to God). The focus of our attention, therefore, rests not only on the exalted Lord at the right hand, but on the supreme example of the Incarnate One, who remained true to God's appointment in the midst of adverse circumstances while here on earth (12:1–3).

Jesus' faithfulness is comparable to that of Moses. They both were true to the calling they had received from God. Moses held a special place in the hearts of the Jews of the first century. He was considered to be the greatest person in history in certain strands of Jewish tradition, and in some, the Messiah was expected to be a "new Moses" (cf. Deut. 18:15–18: "The LORD your God will raise up for you a prophet like me from among your own brothers ...").[5] Other evidence suggests that Moses held an even higher status than the angels because of his special intimacy with God.[6] Therefore, the author of Hebrews moves naturally from his discussion of the angels as Old Testament messengers (2:1–2) to the preeminent messenger of the old covenant—Moses himself.

Flowing from this introduction of Moses, the author in the following chapters will maintain a focused contrast between Jesus as founder of the new covenant and "the Mosaic era, the Mosaic covenant, and the Mosaic cult."[7] That Moses was faithful over a "house" (3:2) alludes specifically to Numbers 12:7 and means that his ministry involved establishment of and responsibility for a defined group of people in special relationship to God.

Whereas verse 2 draws a comparison between Jesus and Moses, verse 3 begins a treatment of the contrast between the two great figures—a contrast meant to highlight the superiority of Jesus' example. This proclamation of Jesus' superior worthiness expands in two directions. (1) In verses 3–4 the author draws an analogy using architectural imagery, probably playing off the

---

4. On the important role of 4:14–16 and 10:19–25 in the structure of Hebrews see above, pp. 28–29.

5. Ellingworth, *The Epistle to the Hebrews*, 194.

6. Mary Rose D'Angelo, *Moses in the Letter to the Hebrews*, SBLDS (Missoula, Mont.: Scholars, 1979), 91–131.

7. Lane, *Hebrews 1–8*, 73.

reference to "house" in verse 2. To look at a beautiful, artfully crafted building may inspire appreciation or wonder, but praise belongs to the craftsman rather than the craft. In this case the author of Hebrews considers Moses as part of the house that Jesus built. The inference to which the analogy points is that Jesus, as God, has made Moses, a member of the people of Israel, and as Creator is worthy of more honor and glory than one of his creatures. Thus, the author continues to point to Jesus as God.

(2) Verses 5–6 proclaim Jesus as worthy of more glory than Moses by comparing their respective earthly roles, executed in faithfulness to God the Father. Moses was faithful "as a servant" (*ōs therapon*), whereas Christ was faithful "as a son" (*ōs huios*). The sphere of Moses' ministry was "*in all of God's house*," meaning that his authority and leadership extended over all God's people at that time. He, however, was a part of that house as a servant rather than an heir. The purpose of his role was to point to later revelation, anticipating the fullness of God's revelation in the Son. Christ, on the other hand, was "*over God's house*," not in it. Servants have an obligation to faithfulness, but sons have a special, vested interest in and authority over the house. Jesus displayed a filial kind of faithfulness as the Lord and founder of his house, the new covenant people of God.

The author now shifts from the examples of Moses, and especially Jesus, to confronting the listeners with the question of their own faithfulness or lack thereof. We are part of the Son's house (i.e., the new covenant people of God) "if we hold on to our courage and the hope of which we boast." The word rendered "hold on" (*katecho*) could be used by ancient authors to mean "hold to, keep, detain, contain, occupy, or possess." In secular sources students could be said to "retain" a body of teaching, which roughly parallels the Christian admonition to hold to the traditions of the faith (e.g., 1 Cor. 11:2; 15:2).[8] In Hebrews the word is used to speak of keeping a tight grip on the Christian faith, keeping it from slipping away (4:14; 10:23). This "holding fast," therefore, constitutes a main objective of the author for his congregation.

We are to "hold on to our courage and the hope of which we boast." "Courage" (*paressia*) connotes public boldness and confidence, the opposite of shrinking from an open stand with the community of faith. Believers boast of the "hope" found in our new covenant relationship with Christ, through which our sins are forgiven and we draw near to God (6:11, 18; 7:19; 10:23).

The entire clause is, of course, conditional: We may be considered part of the people of God *if* we hold fast to the Christian faith.[9]

---

8. Spicq, *Theological Lexicon of the New Testament*, 2:288.
9. See below, pp. 134–36.

A Negative Example:
The Faithless of the Desert (3:7–19)

WITH VERSE 7 the preacher moves quite naturally from the positive examples of Moses and Jesus to the negative example of those unfaithful wanderers who because of their disobedience failed and fell in the desert. To change the direction of the discussion, the author employs Psalm 95:7c–11 as a catalyst. This Old Testament quotation begins with its own exhortation: "Today, if you hear his voice, do not harden your hearts. . . ." The "so" (*dio*) of Hebrews 3:7 builds on the implicit warning of the previous verse. In essence the author is saying, "since we cannot be considered Christ's house if we do not hold fast, therefore" we must heed the admonition of this Old Testament passage. The phrase "as the Holy Spirit says" demonstrates the author's view that this admonition provides a direct, fresh, contemporary word to his listeners. He understands Psalm 95:7c–11 as an important warning for those who are in danger of drifting.

The psalm quotation itself may be divided into three parts. (1) The exhortation "do not harden your hearts" lies at the center of the first part. This warning follows a temporal frame of reference ("today") and a conditional clause ("if you hear his voice"). (2) The next portion (beginning with "as you did in the rebellion" and running through the end of verse 9) offers an example or illustration. In neither the Old Testament text nor the presentation of the psalm here in Hebrews does one find the phrase "you did" in "as . . . in the rebellion." That is, the psalm's author does not include his listeners in the negative example. Rather, the example is that of a former generation—"their fathers," who had "tested and tried" the Lord in spite of his miraculous works on their behalf. Therefore, "do not harden your hearts as *those people did* in the rebellion" offers a better translation at this point. (3) The final segment of the psalm confronts the hearers with the judgment experienced by that rebellious generation. God "was angry" with them because of their wandering hearts and their lack of understanding his ways (Ps. 95:10). Therefore, he swore that they would not enter his rest (95:11).

In 3:12–19 the author of Hebrews takes the concepts "heart," "day," "today," "hear," "enter," "test," "rest," "unbelief," and "swear" from the psalm, weaving them into a potent commentary and exhortation. The unit begins with the twin exhortations to "see to it . . . that" (lit., "take care lest") and "encourage one another" (vv. 12–13). The first of these confronts the listeners with a general warning directed at the community. The believers should "take care" or "beware" (*blepo*, "see," used metaphorically) because within any Christian community there may be those whose outward association does not reflect the inward condition of the heart. The danger lies in anyone who might possess "a sinful, unbelieving heart that turns away from the living God."

The second exhortation comes in the form of a positive admonition. The hearers are to "encourage one another daily" so that none of them will experience a spiritual hardening brought on by sin's deceitfulness. Taken from the psalm, the word "today" speaks of the present time of opportunity for a right relationship with God. The author's conviction that this psalm directly addresses this Christian congregation may be seen in the phrase "as long as it is called Today," suggesting the contemporary relevance of the passage as the Word of God. For this community struggling with the problem of spiritual drifting, hardening of the heart was both a real danger and avoidable. If it was to be avoided, however, the recipients of Hebrews had to relate to one another in an atmosphere of encouragement.

Continuing with another sober word of warning, in 3:14 the author writes: "We have come to share in Christ if we hold firmly till the end the confidence we had at first." At 3:1 the author addresses the community as "sharers of the heavenly calling,"[10] but in 3:14 he places a condition on that designation. The proposition "we have come to share in Christ" in the NIV translates a Greek clause more literally rendered with "we have become sharers [or companions, *metochoi*] of Christ" (cf. 3:1). The verb translated "have come" (*gegonamen*) is a perfect tense form and may be interpreted as focusing on a present state of being; that is, "we have become in the past and, therefore, are sharers. . . ." As in 3:1, to "share in" means simply to experience a relationship with a companion, namely, Christ—to be part of "his house" (3:6).

What then of the condition? The word for "if" is *eanper*, and in the New Testament literature only Hebrews uses this word. The condition placed on being companions of Christ has to do with holding "firmly . . . the confidence we had at first." The word translated "hold" in 3:14 is the same as that used in 3:6, but here "firmly" is added. This word was used to refer to what was solid, durable, valid, confirmed, or guaranteed. In a legal or business sense it connoted the stability of a contractual relationship.[11] It was something on which one could depend, and it speaks here of the dependability or firmness of the Christian's commitment, a commitment that had been expressed with assurance at the inception of each believer's relationship with the Lord. Thus, real Christian experience contains the quality of durability, lasting "till the end"—a reference to the death of the one holding the confidence or to the time when Christ returns (9:28).

In 3:15 the preacher ends a long Greek sentence started in verse 12 by quoting again the "exhortation" portion of the psalm (Ps. 95:7b–8a). This

---

10. See above, p. 126.
11. Spicq, *Theological Lexicon of the New Testament*, 1:280.

section of the psalm serves as a summary for verses 12–14, emphasizing again the warning against a hardened heart and the need to listen to God's voice "today." The quotation of verse 15 also leads into the final segment of this unit.

In 3:16–19 the author follows a stylistic pattern of asking a question and then providing an answer. The questions at the beginning of each verse are taken directly from the quote of Psalm 95:7c–11. The answers provided, however, derive from other Old Testament passages that have to do with the desert wanderings. That those who came out of Egypt with Moses were the same as those who rebelled against the Lord (Heb. 3:16) may be concluded from Deuteronomy 9; Numbers 14:1–38; or Psalm 106. That "those who sinned, whose bodies fell in the desert," were the same as those with whom God was upset (Heb. 3:17) also derives from either Numbers 14:1–38 or Psalm 106. The concept of the disobedient ones as those to whom God swore they would not enter his rest (Heb. 3:18) finds expression in Deuteronomy 9:7, 24.

The unit concludes with a summary statement in 3:19, explaining that at its core the wanderers' inability to enter God's rest stemmed from their unbelief, thus linking the concepts of unbelief and disobedience (cf. Num. 14:11; Deut. 9:23; Ps. 78:22, 32).

Summary. Hebrews 3 builds a series of exhortations, based on positive and negative examples, and revolves around two types of Old Testament material. Forming a foundation for a more fervent consideration of Christ, verses 1–6 rests on a treatment of the great leader Moses, highly esteemed by the Jews of the first century. The audience's admiration for Moses assures the rhetorical impact of demonstrating Jesus' greater status. Verses 7–19, on the other hand, presents an extensive Old Testament quotation and a commentary/exhortation derived from it. The details of this text offer the preacher the substance of his exhortations. In short, the hearers are not to follow the example of those who fell in the desert but are to hold firmly to their Christian confidence, keeping a soft heart and a vigilance against sin. They accomplish this in part by encouraging one another during this present age in which they have opportunity ("today") to respond obediently to God's voice.

AS WE SEEK to interpret this passage for our contemporary contexts, we confront a number of dynamics in this rich text that must be addressed. We must ask, for example, the significance of the shift in genre—the kind of literature—as we move from 2:18 to 3:1. Within that discussion we must ask the specific purpose of both the positive and negative examples used. What does the author wish to accomplish by the use of these examples? What presuppositions lie behind their use? What are the limitations of these examples, and how can we guard against reading more into them than the author intended? The interesting "conditional warnings" of 3:6, 14 and, especially, their mix of seemingly present and future time frames pose other issues of interpretation. Finally, we must attempt to discern the principles inherent in the author's exhortation to faithfulness; does he give any direction in how one can maintain a life of faithful obedience?

A shift to exhortation. We have already marked several points of continuity between 2:10–18 and the unit under consideration. The author continues to speak of Jesus in terms of "son," and 3:1 contains a reference to him as "high priest" (a transitional element that echoes 2:17). That there are those being brought to "glory" in 2:10 reflects a similar sentiment as expressed in the hearers' being sharers in the "heavenly calling" of 3:1. The author knows how to lead his hearers from one thought to the next with smooth transitions. However, it is also important for us to note aspects of discontinuity as we move from one section of the discourse to another. We must ask: "What new dynamics or information does this portion of the book add to the discussion thus far?" and "What specific role does the author intend this passage to play?"

With 3:1 the author makes a decisive shift to exhortation as marked by his change in addressing the listeners directly as "holy brothers." The function here, while closely intermeshed with and building on the expositional material on Christ, is distinct from it. The preacher uses conventional means of motivating his audience to action. This is the purpose of exhortation; we, however, must ascertain the nature of that motivation.

Examples as a means of motivation. In the ancient world preachers of the synagogue and Greco-Roman orators used positive examples to challenge their audiences to desired actions and negative examples to highlight those actions from which one should refrain. At its most basic level, the employment of an example assumes some analogy between the situation of the person(s) used as the example and the person(s) being addressed. To what end does the author of Hebrews introduce the great Old Testament figure, Moses?

The primary aspect of Moses' life to which the author points is his faithfulness, the overarching theme of 3:1–19. The picture of Moses as a faithful servant in all God's house (3:2, 5) proves useful to the author because the old covenant lawgiver provides a stark picture of fidelity in a position of leadership. With 2:10–18 the sermon has moved from a heavenly to an earthly focus, and Moses depicts a person of this world who has lived faithfully for God.

However, Moses does not serve as a direct example in 3:1–6 but rather as an indirect one. The author does not challenge the hearers to follow his example in this passage (that will come later in ch. 11). Rather, he uses Moses as a reference point from which to highlight the greater faithfulness of Christ. The preacher challenges his companions in the heavenly calling to "fix [their] thoughts on Jesus" (3:1). Since believers are "children," we especially need an example of someone who has lived out a filial faithfulness. Thus Jesus, as the Son of God, provides an example superior to that of even the greatest of Old Testament figures. Furthermore, as the Creator he has a greater inherent authority than Moses, who was a part of his creation. Thus, the author builds on the greatness of Moses and asserts that as great as this religious figure might be, Jesus must be the object of a Christian's ultimate focus.

The use of Moses in the exhortation of 3:1–6, therefore, affirms both the usefulness and the limitations of a human example. Such an example may be foundational for a discussion of devotion to God because it provides a picture of how others have responded positively to God in challenges somewhat analogous to our own. It also shows us that God has used imperfect human beings in his purposes in the past. Such examples, therefore, can be encouraging as we witness God's use of those who struggle with sin as we do. We might point out that Moses is a *scriptural example;* the telling of Moses' example was inspired by God for the benefit of the people of God. There must, therefore, be a distinction made between various levels of examples for a Christian.

Yet, Moses' example primarily serves to emphasize the greater example of Christ. No sinful human example—even a scriptural one—suffices as the ultimate model for a Christian. Christ's example eclipses all true examples for the community of faith. It is Jesus who provides the perfect picture of faithful commitment to God, for he alone lived apart from the taint of sin.

If Moses serves the author's purpose in 3:1–6 by providing a positive portrayal of commitment, the desert wanderers of 3:7–19 offer a negative example of those who failed to take the desired action. Their use in Hebrews parallels Paul's admonition in 1 Corinthians 10:1–11 to avoid Israel's mistakes. Having itemized their various sins to be shunned, Paul writes, "These things happened to them as examples and were written down as warnings for us, on whom the fulfillment of the ages has come" (10:11). In Hebrews 3 the author focuses on the wanderers' sin of turning away from God in a time of testing; it may be that he uses this psalm in part because of the severe test being experienced by his hearers. As with the Israelite wanderers, if those who had confessed Christ turn their backs on him in their time of testing and discouragement, it will constitute disobedience.

Moreover, the preacher's employment of the desert wanderers as paradigmatic affirms the danger to which his hearers are subject, since the example would be useless if there were no real parallel. No one would suggest that the readers of Hebrews should eschew disobedience because God might take them out to a literal desert to die. We also must be careful of assuming that the image directly corresponds to being cut off from a relationship with God by loss of salvation, although that possibility must be addressed. Jewish scholars debated whether those who fell in the desert had any part in the life to come; the author of Hebrews does not say specifically. The picture of those who fell provides a stark picture of judgment and the terrible possibility of falling away from God because of a hardened, sinful heart. Although the exact nature of that judgment has yet to be brought into focus, the danger depicted is severe. Their example shows that anyone who provokes God through unbelief and disobedience faces his wrath.

Interpreting the conditional clauses of 3:6 and 3:14. In analyzing the details of 3:1–19 the student encounters certain tensions in the author's perspective on his audience. He addresses them as sharers "in the heavenly calling" in verse 1 only to put a condition on that designation in verse 14: "We have come to share in Christ if we hold firmly till the end the confidence we had at first." He refers to the community as Jesus' "house" in verse 6, but then immediately qualifies that affirmation with "if we hold on to our courage and the hope of which we boast."

How, then, should we interpret these conditional statements in verses 6 and 14? At least two insights give guidance for dealing with these complex passages. (1) *In the main clauses of these conditional sentences* (the part that grammarians refer to as the "apodosis"),[12] *the author seems to address the hearers corporately as Christians.* This may seem obvious to many who read the English "we are his house" (v. 6) and "we have come" (v. 14), but Greek tense forms (e.g., the present used in v. 6 and the perfect in v. 14) may be used in conjunction with various time frames—including past, present, and future—or without reference to a time frame at all. We largely depend on the context to discern whether a specific time frame is in mind.

In 3:14 the writer states: "We have become sharers of Christ" (pers. trans.). In virtually every one of the thirty times the author uses the verb "to become" (*ginomai*) in the book, he speaks of a state of existence or status to which there has been a change from a former state of existence or status. For example, Christ has become better than the angels (1:4), a high priest (2:17; 5:5), and the source of eternal salvation (5:9). The hearers have become dull of hearing (5:11) and, in the past, had become sharers with those who had been persecuted (10:33). Noah became an heir of righteousness (11:7), Moses became grown (11:24), and heroes of the faith became mighty (11:34). Therefore, if we judge from the use of the term in the rest of Hebrews, "to

---

12. Daniel B. Wallace, *Greek Grammar Beyond the Basics: An Exegetical Syntax of the New Testament* (Grand Rapids: Zondervan, 1996), 684.

become" in 3:14 probably refers to a new state of existence, namely, participation in this community.

Further, we have demonstrated that to be part of Jesus' "house" and to be a "sharer" of him are references to the hearers as Christians. That the author understands this to be their state of existence finds support in his various references to them. He speaks of them as "holy brothers" (3:1), those who "share in the heavenly calling" (3:1), "dear friends" who manifest things accompanying salvation (6:9), and those who had made a Christian confession (3:1; 4:14; 10:23). He also indicates that they are those who have suffered for the Christian faith in the past (10:32), who are "sons" of God (12:5–13), who have come to Mount Zion (12:22–24), and who are part of the community of "saints" (13:24). These are a few of his designations for the people in the community to which he is writing. Thus, based on the broader context, when the author refers to them as Jesus' house in 3:6 and as those who "share in Christ" in 3:14, he seems to affirm a present reality; he is addressing a group of Christ-followers.

(2) *The reference to the congregation corporately as Christians is followed by a qualification.* In effect the author says, "Point A is true, if point B is true"; that is, we are Christ's house, providing that we hold on to . . . ; we have come to be sharers with Christ, if we hold firmly till the end. . . . The closest parallels to these constructions as used in Hebrews are found in Paul's writings. Notice how each statement of fact is followed by a qualification:

> *Romans 8:9:* You, however, are controlled not by the sinful nature but by the Spirit, if the Spirit of God lives in you.
>
> *Romans 8:17:* Now if we are children, then we are heirs—heirs of God and co-heirs with Christ, if indeed we share in his sufferings in order that we may also share in his glory.
>
> *Romans 11:22:* Consider therefore the kindness and sternness of God: sternness to those who fell, but kindness to you, provided that [lit., if] you continue in his kindness.
>
> *2 Corinthians 13:5b:* Do you not realize that Christ Jesus is in you— unless, of course, you fail the test?
>
> *Colossians 1:22–23:* But now he has reconciled you by Christ's physical body through death to present you holy in his sight, without blemish and free from accusation—if you continue in your faith, established and firm, not moved from the hope held out in the gospel.

Each of these Pauline examples, along with our passages from Hebrews, has to do with a person's relationship to God! What interpretation offers an explanation?

The tensions inherent in these conditional constructions indicate a fundamental principle for dealing with matters related to a person's relationship with Christ: Human perspective on the status of another person before God is limited. The author of Hebrews, Paul, you, and I—every human being— have limitations on what we can know about the spiritual condition of another person, and to some degree, we are dependent on an outward manifestation of spiritual realities (cf. Matt. 7:15–23; James 2:14–26). Thus, in Hebrews 4:1 the preacher encourages his readers' caution lest, while the promised rest is available, any of them should *seem* (*dokeo*) to have fallen short of it. He has been *persuaded* of better things concerning them than the travesty described in 6:4–8 by their actions (6:9); it is through their perseverance that they will realize the *full certainty* of their hope (6:11).

These passages, in other words, speak of the limitations on human perspective when it comes to matters of salvation and fit well a larger theological vein in the New Testament. In 2 Corinthians 13:5a Paul exhorts his readers, "Examine yourselves to see whether you are in the faith; test yourselves." First John offers similar admonitions: "We know that we have come to know him if we obey his commands" (1 John 2:3); "This is how we know we are in him: Whoever claims to live in him must walk as Jesus did" (2:5b– 6); "Dear children, let us not love with words or tongue but with actions and in truth. This then is how we know that we belong to the truth, and how we set our hearts at rest in his presence . . ." (3:18–19). The inner reality of one's relationship with God is manifested in outward action and gives assurance.

The author of Hebrews cannot give unqualified assurance to those drifting away from God that they indeed have a part in God's house or are sharers in Christ. He addresses them collectively as believers, but realizes that some in the group may manifest a different reality as time goes on (cf. 1 John 2:19). Perseverance does not gain salvation but demonstrates the reality that true salvation indeed has been inaugurated.[13] If the end comes and a person is not in relationship with Christ, it means that the person had never truly become Christ's companion.

---

13. I use the term *inaugurated* of salvation to mean that salvation begins when a person confesses Christ but will be consummated upon Christ's return (Heb. 9:28). Salvation involves a continuity of past, present, and future (Rom. 8:29–30; 1 Thess. 5:9; 2 Thess. 2:13– 14). God's Spirit has been given as a down payment (Rom. 8:23; 2 Cor. 1:22; 5:5), and he will complete the work he has started in us (Phil. 1:6). See Judith M. Gundry Volf, *Paul and Perseverance: Staying in and Falling Away* (Louisville, Ky.: Westminster/John Knox, 1990), 9– 47. I use the term *inaugurated* differently than Scot McKnight in his article "The Warning Passages of Hebrews: A Formal Analysis and Theological Conclusions," *TrinJ* 13 (1992): 57– 58. McKnight holds that one can have true salvation and then lose it. My position is that true salvation has a continuity from conversion to glorification.

Five principles of faithfulness inherent in these examples. Hebrews 3:1–19 presents two units, one focusing on the positive example of Jesus and the other on the negative example of the fallen desert wanderers; both cohere around the theme of faithfulness. As we move to application of this text, the author's underlying assumptions concerning the nature of faithfulness should be brought into focus. In other words, how would his hearers respond to his exhortation? How should one think about devotion in the Christian life?

(1) *A healthy focus on Christ encourages one to faithfulness.* We are to fix our thoughts on the One who is the supreme example of faithfulness (3:1–2). This is more than mental gymnastics or mere assent to a creed, for we are Christ's house, his companions (3:6, 14). Therefore, the author continues to spotlight Jesus as the key to the problem facing his listeners and suggests that the health of one's relationship to him will determine perseverance.

(2) *Faithfulness is volitional as well as emotional or intellectual.* Inherent in the exhortations and examples of Hebrews 3 is the assumption that the hearers should *choose* to remain faithful to God. They may be challenged emotionally by his examples and stimulated by the logic of his exposition, but these dynamics are in service to the motivational import of his discussion. He wants his audience to act on his challenge. The "Today" of Psalm 95:7 shows that the time of opportunity is now (Heb. 3:13).

(3) *The twin failings of sinfulness and unbelief can hinder faithfulness.* The sinful, disobedient heart turns away from God because it does not truly believe in him (3:12, 18–19). By deceit sin hardens the heart, bringing about rebellion and the judgment of God (3:13, 16–17). These failings characterize those who fell in the desert, their devastation providing a stark reminder that the unfaithful must face consequences.

(4) *The faithful persevere in commitment until the end.* If we are to be considered faithful, we must "hold on to our courage and the hope of which we boast" (3:6), a statement that suggests public identification with Christ and the church. Faithfulness, therefore, must be lived out in the public arena in consistent Christ-following until the end. In this way the confidence we expressed at the beginning of our commitment will be validated as we hold firmly to it (3:14).

(5) *Faithfulness is communal,* each believer depending on others in the body of Christ for encouragement. We are part of a spiritual family and fellow travelers in a heavenly calling (3:1). We share a common experience in God's household (3:6) and as Christ's companions (3:14); therefore, we should offer one another daily encouragement (3:13).

Summary. In Hebrews 3:1–19 the genre of exhortation suggests that the author intends to motivate the listeners to take a desired course of action. He builds his challenge by use of powerful examples, both positive and negative.

The author presents Christ himself as the ultimate, positive example of faithfulness, while utilizing the religious hero Moses as a reference point from which to focus on the greater example of Jesus.

Carrying out an exposition of Psalm 95 the preacher paints a stark portrait of unfaithfulness by using those faltering, faithless wanderers of the desert. The conditional sentences of 3:6 and 3:14 offer a special hermeneutical challenge with their qualifications on the hearers' status as true Christians. These qualifications indicate the limitations on human perspective when it comes to matters of personal salvation and fit a larger theological viewpoint evidenced by other New Testament writers. Holding fast to one's confidence in Christ, therefore, manifests the reality of one's relationship to him. The whole of Hebrews 3 teaches that faithfulness is encouraged by a healthy focus on Christ. As a volitional dynamic, faithfulness may be affected adversely by sinfulness and unbelief and positively by others in the body of Christ. Finally, true faithfulness manifests itself most clearly in an endurance all the way to the end of the path that God has laid for us.

OF HEROES AND SUPERSTARS. Some time ago a group of young children were asked whom they saw as heroes. Among the recipients of honor were Michael Jackson, Madonna, sports figures, and a United States president. The majority were what previous generations called "celebrities," who reserved the term *hero* for those known for special courage, nobility, achievement, and sacrifice. Our age of high tech has transformed the movie actor, the singer, and the football star into larger-than-life figures, blurring the lines between superstar status and true heroism. Political leaders garner admiration for ingenuity rather than moral fortitude. In his 1995 review of the book *Churchill* by Norman Rose, Henry Kissinger offered insightful demarcations between true political heroes and mere superstars:

> Our age finds it difficult to come to grips with figures like Winston Churchill. The political leaders with whom we are familiar generally aspire to be superstars rather than heroes. The distinction is crucial. Superstars strive for approbation; heroes walk alone. Superstars crave consensus; heroes define themselves by the judgment of a future they see it as their task to bring about. Superstars seek success in a technique for eliciting support; heroes pursue success as the outgrowth of inner values.
>
> The modern political leader rarely ventures to comment in public without having tested his views on focus groups, if indeed he does

not derive them from a focus group. To a man like Churchill, the very concept of focus groups would have been unimaginable.

Thus in the space of a generation, Churchill, the quintessential hero, has been transformed from the mythic to the nearly incomprehensible.[14]

Walking alone, inner values producing outward action—these are the materials of true heroism. In a *U. S. News* editorial of August 12, 1996, writer David Gergen, reflecting on the 1996 summer Olympics in Atlanta, affirms that athletes like Kerri Strug, who, after spraining her ankle, completed a final vault to help her U.S. gymnastics team win the gold, deserve the designation *hero*. But Gergen laments the fact that "we reserve hero status these days for young men and women who can flip, sprint and swim their way into our hearts." The editorialist suggests that even expanding our view of heroism to military generals and astronauts draws the parameters too narrowly. Heroes are often unsung, giving their lives quietly in a variety of walks in life. We as a culture have confused true heroism with fame.

The church has bought into this fuzzy thinking and the exaltation of superstardom. When a sports figure or rock star becomes a Christian, we see it as a special coup for the faith. We seem to think that their acceptance of Christianity gives special validity to the kingdom of God or that their fame will greatly advance the cause. The writer, the singer, or the athlete is interviewed for her special wisdom in life. The gilded image of the familiar face has obscured the truly heroic, who give their lives in the trenches of daily Christian sacrifice.

We need genuine heroes who can be held up as examples of devotion to Christ. Commenting on this need, Elisabeth Elliot writes, "How else shall we grasp the meaning of courage or strength or holiness? We need to see such truth made visible in the lives of human beings. . . ."[15] In Hebrews 3:1–6 the author does not disparage the community's attribution of honor to Moses; he builds on it. The use of a heroic example in this passage (although Moses' example is used only indirectly) calls the preacher of today to consider how he or she uses examples in preaching and challenges modern church persons to reflect on whether they are distinguishing between superstars and true heroes.

At least five levels of examples can be demarcated, the first three with which the author of Hebrews does not deal but which serve to clarify his uses of examples. (1) Fictional heroes can include the allegory, fable, myth, or parable. Of allegory Dorothy Sayers writes:

---

14. *New York Times* (July 16, 1995).
15. Elisabeth Elliot, *The Mark of a Man* (Old Tappan, N.J.: Revell, 1981), 128.

Allegory is a distinct literary form, whose aim and method are to dramatize a psychological experience so as to make it more vivid and more comprehensible. Parable and fable are two other literary forms that do much the same thing. Each of them tells a literal story that is complete in itself, but which also presents a likeness to some spiritual or psychological experience so that it can be used to signify and interpret that experience; and the story is told, not for its own sake, but for the sake of what it signifies. At the bottom of all such stories there lies this perception of a likeness between two experiences, the one familiar and the other unfamiliar, so that the one can be used to shed light on the other.[16]

In allegories such as *The Chronicles of Narnia, The Pilgrim's Progress, The Faerie Queene*, or *The Divine Comedy* writers express their feelings and perceptions of life, touching abstract qualities by presenting stories with which we can identify in some way. I have never gone sword in hand into battle against an evil oppressor, but I have taken joy in knowing some evil has been defeated. I have never taken a literal journey through a land inhabited by dangerous animals or other perils, but I am on a journey in which I need encouragement to have courage. The heroes of fiction may be accessed as potent illustrations of character; used well they stretch the imagination of how we might live more effectively.

(2) We can point to true heroes from the arenas of sports, the military, politics, personal achievement, or humanitarianism to draw analogies to spiritual truths. Churchill's leadership, an athlete's determination, the man who gives his life to save others—these can provide useful, parallel pictures of certain character qualities lauded in biblical literature. We must be careful, however, to keep in mind that these are not the spiritual realities themselves, but only illustrations that help to clarify certain greater spiritual truths.

(3) We need to do more in our preaching with great heroes of Christian history, from ancient times to modern. Think of figures such as the martyr Polycarp, who, in response to the governor's offer of release if he would revile Christ, replied, "Eighty-six years I have been his servant, and he has never done wrong to me. How then can I blaspheme my King, who saved me?" (Martyrdom of Polycarp 9). William Tyndale, that great scholar of the 1500s, gave his life to translate parts of the Scriptures into English. He was strangled and burned in October 1536. Hudson Taylor, a missionary of the nineteenth century, brought numerous innovations to the modern missions movement and, at great personal cost, paved the way for millions in inland China to hear the gospel.

---

16. Sayers, *The Whimsical Christian*, 207.

Contemporary figures such as Billy Graham, who has maintained a ministry of integrity for decades, also serve as appropriate models for the faithful.

(4) Now we come to the most important examples and those used by the author of Hebrews: Followers of God in Scripture should be held up as examples of faithfulness, their examples being affirmed by God himself through the inspired Word. Some of my earliest memories are of a large, red Bible storybook, which my parents read to me as a preschooler. I learned of David, Daniel, and Paul from an early age. My son has just turned four years old, and I am teaching him of these heroes of the faith. We should preach David to show devotion and courage, Daniel to show trust, and Paul to demonstrate sacrifice in the face of an antagonistic culture. As Christian parents we should ask ourselves the identity of those whom our children are embracing as heroes and heroines. Are they more enamored with sports or cartoon figures than biblical examples of devotion to God?

(5) Finally, the author of Hebrews uses Jesus as the ultimate example of faithfulness. Spiritual examples of devotion are validated to the degree they are eclipsed by Christ himself. Great religious heroes like Moses serve as spiritual telescopes, tools used by God to magnify Someone greater than themselves. For it is to Jesus, the One who stands at the heart of the faith, that we must look if we are to endure in our Christian commitment. We must preach sound doctrine, but are we also utilizing the example of Jesus' endurance in our teaching on daily Christian devotion? We must preach him as the cosmic Christ, who set the stars on their appointed paths, but are we employing his treading of the path to Calvary as an example of commitment and sacrifice? Are we helping our children, our congregations, and ourselves "fix [our] thoughts on Jesus" (3:1)? All other examples must be judged in light of this question, for he is not only the preeminent Lord of the universe but also our supreme example of a hero.

True and false assurances. Biblical theology provides a rich spectrum of truths about humanity and our relationship to God. From God's sovereignty to human responsibility, from grace to judgment, from the deity of Christ to his humanity, from conversion to salvation consummated (i.e., glorification), many doctrinal truths must be held in balance with related, equally important truths.[17] To focus on parts of Scripture to the exclusion of other parts proves damaging to the church and individual Christians, and we often get things out of balance. This tendency suggests one reason why systematic, exegetical study of the Bible is so important. Through such study we confront the whole counsel of God and, hopefully, adjust our perspectives accordingly.

---

17. See Klyne Snodgrass, *Between Two Truths: Living With Biblical Tensions* (Grand Rapids: Zondervan, 1990).

The qualifications in 3:6, 14 highlight at least two areas in which many modern evangelicals have lost balance doctrinally and end up giving converts to Christianity false assurances in relation to salvation. The problem stems not from heresy per se, but from an emphasis on certain biblical teachings to the practical exclusion of others. Hebrews calls us to consider how we must adjust our thinking and practice.

(1) In some circles we emphasize the vital doctrine of grace to the point of minimizing personal responsibility and accountability in the Christian life. In effect we communicate, "If you have made a Christian confession, your relationship with God is secured—no matter how you live from this point on."[18] I actually hear people who are living blatantly sinful lifestyles and are disconnected from the church speak of their "conversion experience" as insurance against God's judgment. They reason, "I'm OK with God because I have accepted Jesus as my Savior," or "I joined the church years ago."

Such people understand grace to mean that they are afforded an insider relationship with God that renders their present lifestyles meaningless. Similarly, in my New Testament survey classes I have had students who reject the notion of church discipline in the name of grace—and do so vehemently! "To love the sinner," they say, "is what Jesus would do. Who are we to judge another person?" Thus they leave out the hard side of love that would bring an errant person back to spiritual health and relationship with the church (see 1 Cor. 5).

Both groups abuse the grace of God and garner it as a tool for promoting moral laxity. Paul addresses those who pervert his grace doctrine by suggesting it encourages a libertine lifestyle free from moral restraints (e.g., Rom. 6:1–4). He unequivocally asserts that nothing is further from the truth. Relationship with Christ involves the reckoning of oneself as dead to sin, denying sin's mastery over the mortal body (6:8–14). Grace provides a means for freedom from sin, not freedom to sin.

For the author of Hebrews, those drifting away from God with hearts callused by sin are in serious trouble. The conditional clauses of Hebrews 3:6, 14 suggest that assurance of salvation—assurance that we have partaken of the grace of God—in part depends on the vitality of one's ongoing relationship with Christ and the church. This is not to suggest that one earns salvation through faithfulness but that faithfulness is evidence of one's salvation. It may be that a "drifter" truly has a relationship with Christ and will come around again to Christian commitment. Yet, the drifter in a state of drifting

---

18. In the current "lordship theology" debate, this has been a concern, for example, with those holding the so-called "lordship salvation" view as they have countered those holding the "free grace" view. For an overview and assessment of the discussion see Millard J. Erickson, "Lordship Theology: The Current Controversy," *SwJT* 33 (Spring 1991): 5–15.

has no assurance of his or her right standing before God since God's grace is not being manifested in that person's life.

I grew up in a tradition that places such emphasis on the initial conversion experience that assurance of salvation is almost entirely related to that experience. If one struggles with assurance he or she is told, "Do you remember when you prayed to receive Christ? Do you believe you were sincere when you asked for salvation? If so, you can be sure you are a Christian. God does not lie, and in Romans 10:9–10 he says if you confess Jesus as Lord with your mouth and believe in your heart that God resurrected him, you will be saved." It may well be that the one doubting salvation needs to be reminded of God's faithfulness. However, grave danger lies in a focus on an experience—often in the distant past—and in an encouragement to put trust in a past prayer rather than in the God of salvation.

This same danger exists for those traditions in which a public confession of Christ is made following participation in a confirmation class of some sort. If we encourage individuals to anchor their assurance in any past event, we give them an uncertain foundation and may give false assurance to those who should really be doubting the reality of their relationship with God! Remember that the author of Hebrews is warning those who have made a confession of Christ in the past and suggests that some of their number may have fallen short (3:1). Jesus himself says that at the judgment some who called him "Lord" will be turned away for lack of a relationship with him (Matt. 7:22–23).

Therefore, we have no right to give assurance to those who have turned their backs on God—in fact, we should affirm their lack of assurance! We must never say, "I remember when you accepted Christ," or "You went through confirmation when you were twelve," using those experiences as a basis for giving them assurance of God's acceptance. We cannot look into a person's heart and see his or her spiritual condition. It would be better to say, "Since you have turned your back on God, the validity of your relationship with Christ has been called into question. You need to repent and examine yourself to see if you are in the faith." The author of Hebrews does challenge his hearers to remember their past confession of Christ (4:14; 10:23)—but as a basis for faithfulness rather than a basis for assurance.

Cultivating faithfulness. We live in an age of sound bytes constantly luring us to new and better products or experiences with instant access to services, information, and opportunities. In this fast-paced age we sprint from one life experience to the next; to some, Hebrews' emphasis on a "long-distance," well-paced faith may seem out of step. Yet, obedience to God must be lived in the daily, often mundane experiences of life over a long period of time, often without immediate gratification for our effort. Hebrews 3 challenges believers of all ages to take seriously their commitment to Christ and remain faithful to him as a life pattern. How then can we cultivate lives of faithfulness, which will endure over the long haul?

(1) *Faithfulness flows from a clear and healthy view of Jesus*. In the author's exhortation to consider Jesus, one finds the reminder that true, unflagging Christ-followers focus their purpose and perspective on the apostle and high priest whom we confess—Jesus himself. If Jesus is our ultimate example of faithfulness, we must have a clear picture of him. The author of Hebrews intends to help us in this matter by offering a lucid exposition of Scripture and Christian teaching concerning the person of Christ.

How, then, do we keep the Son of God in focus? Let me suggest at least two interlocking means. (a) We must have a doctrinally sound understanding of the Son. The author's extensive treatment of early Christian doctrine concerning Jesus emphasizes this need. As believers we must, therefore, study Scripture and meditate on it. Further, reading great theological discussions that have taken place in the church's history can help clarify our understanding of Jesus and guard against aberrant christologies. In our churches we should expound New Testament passages on Jesus (Hebrews would be a great place to start!) and offer basic theology classes for our members. Our private lives should include daily reading and study of the Bible, as well as times for reading and reflecting on theological works of both ancient and contemporary writers. If we are to be people sound in our thinking, these activities should constitute a normal aspect of Christian living.

(b) Another dimension of keeping Jesus in focus exists in cultivating intimacy with the Savior through prayer and obedience. Doctrine constitutes not an end in itself, but rather points us to the living Lord whom we serve. At its heart Hebrews concerns a powerful relational dimension. After all, we are his "companions" and on an adventure with him (3:14); we are part of Christ's household (3:6) and are in process of learning faithfulness from him. In effect, his high priesthood wins us entrance into the presence of God, providing us a way to draw near (4:14–16). Yet, being a faithful companion of Christ in prayer and living a devoted life must be nurtured—a process for which our modern culture of haste is not always conducive.

> One barrier to full intimacy with the Savior is hurriedness. Intimacy may not be rushed. To meet with the Son of God takes time. We cannot dash into his presence and choke down spiritual inwardness before we hurry to our one o'clock appointment. Inwardness is time-consuming, open only to minds willing to sample spirituality in small bites, savoring each one.
>
> Intimacy with Christ comes from entering his presence with inner peace rather than bursting into his presence from the hassles of life. A

relaxed contemplation of the indwelling Christ allows for an inner communion impossible to achieve while oppressed by busyness and care.

Holy living is not abrupt living. No one who hurries into the presence of God is content to remain for long. Those who hurry in, hurry out.[19]

Therefore, along with public confession we must attend to the health of our inner life. As Gordon MacDonald notes, when we neglect the inner life, we risk a "sinkhole" type of collapse in our lives and ministries since we do not have the spiritual and emotional resources to hold up under the external pressures we face.[20] On the other hand, when we cultivate closeness with Jesus, meeting with him in prayer and allowing him through God's Word to "speak with [us] face to face, as a man speaks with his friend" (Ex. 33:11), we gain inner strength for endurance on the path by which we follow him. If we are struggling with faithfulness, we can begin to assess our situation by considering how clearly we see Jesus at present—both doctrinally and relationally. If the incessant crashes and explosions of personal challenges—be they persecution, sin problems, or other difficulties—threaten to drown out the voice of God, we can turn our trek back to spiritual health by seeking Jesus. He is experienced in making a way out of seemingly unconquerable situations.

(2) *Faithfulness involves choosing obedience based on trust in God.* Inherent in the author's exhortations—"fix your thoughts on Jesus" (3:1), "do not harden your hearts" (3:8), "see to it ... that none of you has a sinful, unbelieving heart" (3:12), and "encourage one another daily" (3:13)—lies an understanding that faithfulness is volitional rather than merely emotional or even intellectual. Thus we cultivate faithfulness by listening to God's voice and choosing life patterns of obedience. Correspondingly we must reject sin, which hardens the heart toward God.

Practically speaking we must, therefore, expose our lives meaningfully to God's Word and adjust our thoughts and lifestyles accordingly. This means hearing the Word preached and asking honestly, "What do I need to confess and from what do I need to repent?" and "How should my life be lived this week based on what I have heard?" Through times of reading and reflecting on Scripture we expose our inner lives to the voice of God for change, encouragement, and maturation. Once exposed, however, we must then act on the Word. This pattern of openness and of change takes faith in God and challenges us strenuously.

Modern Western culture has associated faith, to a great extent, with the miraculous, an association that is appropriate biblically. Yet we must hold up

---

19. Calvin Miller, "No Hurry," in *Couples' NIV Devotional Bible*, ed. staff of *Marriage Partnership Magazine* (Grand Rapids: Zondervan, 1994), 935.
20. Gordon MacDonald, *Ordering Your Private World* (Chicago: Moody, 1984), 13–14.

the association of faith with *faithfulness* if we are to be true to the broader picture of faith in Scripture. The author of Hebrews associates belief in God so closely with obedience to him that the two are practically indistinguishable. This association grows out of the author's use of the desert wanderers as an example. They were disobedient to the voice of God in the desert because they did not trust him to win them entrance to the land of promise. In one sense, we can say that all sin originates from thinking that God has less than our best interests at heart (e.g., Gen. 3:1–7). The thief doubts God's provision, the sexually immoral person denies the sufficiency of God's design for sexual fulfillment, the religiously proud does not trust God's priority on humility. On the relationship between faith and obedience George Mac-Donald writes:

> Faith is that which, knowing the Lord's will, goes and does it; or, not knowing it, stands and waits.... But to put God to the question in any other way than by saying, "What wilt thou have me to do?" is an attempt to compel God to declare Himself, or to hasten His work.... The man is therein dissociating himself from God so far that, instead of acting by the divine will from within, he acts in God's face, as it were, to see what He will do. Man's first business is, "What does God want me to do?"—not "What will God do if I do so and so?"[21]

(3) *Faithfulness grows from an encouraging association with the community of faith.* In 3:13 the author prompts us to "encourage one another daily." In other words, the give and take of positive encouragement from others in the body of Christ provides a safeguard against heart-hardening sin and spiritual bankruptcy. If I am counseling someone struggling with faithfulness, I issue the challenge to renew commitment to a group of believers. We learn faith and deepen faith by exercising it, reading Scripture, and meditating on the great acts of God, but life lived with the people of faith is an indispensible ingredient in a faithful walk.

Those of us in church leadership must ask ourselves how we can foster meaningful subgroups in our churches into which believers can be assimilated and where they may find encouragement to face life's challenges. As noted by Philip Yancey in his book *Church: Why Bother?*[22] in the intimacy of small church groups we are forced to rub shoulders with others in the body, many of whom are not like us. We grow from exposure to their walks with Christ and are encouraged in our own walks.

---

21. As quoted in *God's Treasury of Virtues: An Inspirational Collection of Stories, Quotes, Hymns, Scriptures and Poems* (Tulsa, Okla.: Honor Books, 1995), 299.
22. Philip Yancey, *Church: Why Bother?* (Grand Rapids: Zondervan, 1997), 27–31.

On March 10, 1904, the great escape artist Houdini was challenged to a contest by *The Illustrated Mirror* of London. The paper dared the showman to escape from a complex form of handcuffs with six locks on each cuff and nine tumblers on each lock. The performer took the challenge with thousands gathered at the London Hippodrome to see if he could escape these new bonds. Having been handcuffed securely, Houdini ducked down into a box to struggle out of sight of the crowd. After about twenty minutes the entertainer popped up out of the box; the gathering roared their approval but suddenly quieted as they realized the cuffs were still in place. Houdini smiled, asked for more light, and went back into the box. Fifteen minutes passed, and once again the escape artist appeared. Again the crowd cheered enthusiastically. Houdini smiled, saying that he just needed to flex his knees. Down he went. After about twenty minutes he came up again, taking a pocketknife from his vest and holding it in his teeth. Houdini slashed his coat to ribbons, freeing himself of the hot and heavy garment, and then jumped back into the box. The crowd cheered him on. This time he only stayed in the box for ten minutes and then emerged a free man holding the cuffs in his hands. The crowd gave an extended ovation for the master of escape. Later a reporter asked Houdini why he kept popping up out of the box when he was not yet free. He replied that he needed to hear the encouragement of the crowd.[23]

Those of us who live in Christian community struggle, often in dark solitude, against discouragement as a result of sin, conflict with culture, physical fatigue, relational discord, and other dynamics that close in around us. When we come out of our solitude into the light of Christian fellowship, we need to experience applause and encouragement from others in the body of Christ. This gives us the courage to go back to our struggles with new energy and hope. From a human point of view such affirmation can make all the difference in holding "firmly till the end" the confidence that began our Christian commitment.

---

23. For this episode from the life of Houdini, see Charles R. Swindoll, *Come Before Winter and Share My Hope* (Portland, Ore.: Multnomah, 1985), 283.

Hebrews 4:1–13

THEREFORE, SINCE THE promise of entering his rest still stands, let us be careful that none of you be found to have fallen short of it. ²For we also have had the gospel preached to us, just as they did; but the message they heard was of no value to them, because those who heard did not combine it with faith. ³Now we who have believed enter that rest, just as God has said,

"So I declared on oath in my anger,
'They shall never enter my rest.'"

And yet his work has been finished since the creation of the world. ⁴For somewhere he has spoken about the seventh day in these words: "And on the seventh day God rested from all his work." ⁵And again in the passage above he says, "They shall never enter my rest."

⁶It still remains that some will enter that rest, and those who formerly had the gospel preached to them did not go in, because of their disobedience. ⁷Therefore God again set a certain day, calling it Today, when a long time later he spoke through David, as was said before:

"Today, if you hear his voice,
do not harden your hearts."

⁸For if Joshua had given them rest, God would not have spoken later about another day. ⁹There remains, then, a Sabbath-rest for the people of God; ¹⁰for anyone who enters God's rest also rests from his own work, just as God did from his. ¹¹Let us, therefore, make every effort to enter that rest, so that no one will fall by following their example of disobedience.

¹²For the word of God is living and active. Sharper than any double-edged sword, it penetrates even to dividing soul and spirit, joints and marrow; it judges the thoughts and attitudes of the heart. ¹³Nothing in all creation is hidden from God's sight. Everything is uncovered and laid bare before the eyes of him to whom we must give account.

ONE OF THE most fascinating, enigmatic, and tightly argued sections of Hebrews runs from 4:1 through 4:13. Verses 1–2 effect an "intermediary transition,"[1] which moves the discussion from consideration of those who failed to enter God's rest (3:7–19) to an explication of the continuing promise of rest for the new people of God (4:3–11). This discussion uses verbal analogy to associate Psalm 95 with another passage that speaks of "rest," Genesis 2:2 (Heb. 4:3–5).[2] For our author, the fact that God through David—long after the desert fiasco—mentions a specific time frame for entering the rest (i.e., "Today"), demonstrates that the "rest" was not limited to the physical entrance into Canaan by the people of Israel (4:6–9). In fact, the author reasons, God's rest must be defined as a spiritual reality in which one ceases from one's own work (4:10). We must, however, choose to enter that rest and keep from falling short of it (4:11).

Having presented his exegetical work on the relationship between Psalm 95 and Genesis 2:2, the preacher then closes the section with a stark warning concerning the power of God's inescapable word (4:12–13). This final warning reaches back and accesses Psalm 95's challenge to "hear [God's] voice," providing an effective conclusion to the material on the contrast between "falling short of" or "entering" God's rest.

Transition: From the Problem of the Wanderers to the Promise of Rest "Today" (4:1–2)

THE AUTHOR OF Hebrews was a master of effective transitions. He begins chapter 4 by weaving his concern that the hearers not "fall short" (the emphasis in his commentary on Ps. 95 in Heb. 3) with an introduction to the promised rest that still exists for God's people. Hebrews 4:1 offers an exhortation to spiritual caution, and 4:2 provides a basis for this exhortation: Hearing God's word is not enough; it must be combined with faith. These two verses, therefore, serve as a transition and summarize the content of both 3:7–19 and 4:3–13, by which they are sandwiched. Further, 4:1–2 exhorts the hearers to take action on the basis of the author's discussion.

The old interpretation adage goes, "When you see a 'therefore,' ask what it is there for." The grammar may be poor, but the hermeneutical reminder remains appropriate. The author of Hebrews frequently uses the Greek word *oun* ("therefore") to introduce a given action that has been or should be undertaken, and it is especially prevalent in chapter 4 (vv. 1, 6, 11, 14, 16). The

---

1. For discussion of "intermediary transitions" see above, p. 98.
2. On the author's uses of verbal analogy see above, p. 67.

previous negative example of the desert wanderers gives rise to an exhortation to "be careful" (*phobeomai*). The NIV at this point fails to communicate the seriousness of the situation and would have been more true to the context by staying with a more common rendering of this Greek verb—"let us fear." In the New Testament this word often expresses an appropriate reverence and awe that stem from mighty acts of God and accompany faith.[3] More than mere caution, it communicates an emotional state in which one reflects upon the awesome dimensions of God's power. Therefore, the preacher here exhorts his hearers to adjust their attitude concerning their present spiritual situation and to bring it in line with a reverent reflection on the gravity of being out of step with God's will.

In the Greek text, the clause translated by the NIV "since the promise of entering his rest still stands" follows this exhortation to "fear." The word "since" interprets the participle *kataleipomenes* as causal, that is, "because the promise still stands." However, the entire section from 3:7 to 4:11 is temporally charged, as can be seen from the author's emphasis on the word "Today." It would be better, therefore, to understand the participle as temporal, communicating duration: "while the promise of entering his rest still stands." This clause anticipates a fuller argument in 4:6–10 concerning the present opportunity indicated by the word "Today."

What gives rise to fear is the possibility that any of the community's number should appear to have fallen short of or should lack the promised rest. The word translated "be found" means "to seem" when used with an impersonal subject (as it is here). It suggests the ambiguity attached to an assessment of individual members' spiritual states. The author does not say unequivocally that any particular person has fallen short, but that appropriate caution is in order since that possibility exists. The perfect infinitive "to have fallen short" suggests that this spiritual state consists of one never truly having entered the rest of God.

> Our author is intent on demonstrating the possibility, with the hope that in doing so he will prevent its becoming a reality, that within the community of faith there may be hypocrites or defectors whose position is one of unbelief rather than faith. Any such, of course, do not truly belong to the church, except in a formal and external sense, and the *rest* that is promised does not pertain to them.[4]

This supposition finds further support in verse 2, which capitalizes on the negative example of the Old Testament fallen. Both the old covenant com-

---

3. Balz and Schneider, *Exegetical Dictionary of the New Testament*, 3:429.
4. Hughes, *The Epistle to the Hebrews*, 158.

munity and those of the new era have had God's word preached to them. For the author's audience the "gospel" means the word of salvation proclaimed first through the Lord (2:3–4); for the community in the desert the good news was the promise of entrance into the land of Canaan. The difference between the "hearers" of the desert and of the true Christian community lies not in the word preached, which for both was a word of promise, but in the type of listening performed by each group. The Israelite community physically may have heard the words but their hearing was "faith-less"—true spiritual hearing involves active faith as a component. The caution in 4:1–2 pertains to those of the community whose response to the gospel parallels the faith-vacant response of those who fell in the desert when offered entrance into the land of Canaan.

Identification of the "Rest" (4:3–5)

IT IS, THEREFORE, those who "have believed" who are in the process of entering God's rest. What then is this "rest" of which the preacher speaks and which should be an object of concern for the community? Although in verse 10 the author defines the "rest" minimally as ceasing from one's own works, he offers no specific points of reference as to where or when this takes place. Is the "rest" a present spiritual state or an eschatological destination (i.e., heaven)?

Scholars have spilled much ink over this question, with mixed results. One of the most significant works on the subject is by O. Hofius, who, based on his study of Jewish apocalyptic, argues that "rest" must be understood as oriented to the end of the Christian's journey—the entrance into the heavenly Most Holy Place at the end of the age. This interpretation of the "rest" as having a future orientation has also been adopted, for example, by P. E. Hughes and finds support in the pilgrimage motif of the book, with its emphasis on persevering to the end.

G. Theissen, on the other hand, has responded to Hofius by pointing out the association of "rest" with God's rest on the seventh day. Commentators have noted that in Genesis 1–2 the first six days of creation have an end, or evening; the seventh day, however, is an "open-ended day," which has no end. This, for Theissen, suggests that the rest must not be limited to a location and a point in time.[5] God's "rest" must be seen as a present reality. The present context, with its emphasis on "Today" as a present time of opportunity, seems to support this position.

---

5. See O. Hofius, Katapausis: *Die Vorstellung vom endzeitlichen Ruheort im Hebräerbrief* (Tübingen: Mohr, 1970); G. Theissen, *Untersuchungen zum Hebräerbrief* (Gütersloh: Mohn, 1969); Lane, *Hebrews 1–8.* See especially the overview of various positions in Attridge, *Epistle to the Hebrews,* 127–28.

Furthermore, how could those of the community seem to have fallen short *now* if the rest lies entirely in the future? If the concept of rest as discussed in Hebrews 4 has an entirely future orientation, all of the members of the community are short of achieving it at present. Although elements in Hebrews point to attainment of God's promises in the future, the present appropriation of God's "rest" must be considered an aspect of our author's concern.

The problem lies in the ambiguity of the discussion at this juncture in Hebrews and may be stated simply:

> The promise of rest may be accepted today; but whether entry into that rest is accomplished now through faith, at death (12:23, "the spirits of just men *made perfect*"—i.e., "at rest"?), or at the final consummation (i.e., "rest" = "the city to come" of 13:14?) is nearly impossible to say. It probably includes all three.[6]

This final assertion fits well the author's theological orientation evidenced elsewhere in Hebrews—that Christian realities have been inaugurated but have yet to be consummated. Therefore, the "rest" is something a believer enters (and thus experiences) now, but this rest in its fullness remains a promised destination for the future.[7] Harold Attridge articulates this position well:

> Thus the imagery of rest is best understood as a complex symbol for the whole soteriological process that Hebrews never fully articulates, but which involves both personal and corporate dimensions. It is the process of entry into God's presence, the heavenly homeland (11:16), the unshakeable kingdom (12:28), begun at baptism (10:22) and consummated as a whole eschatologically.[8]

The author associates the "rest" into which the desert wanderers failed to enter with the "rest" of God in Genesis 2:2. Psalm 95 and Genesis 2 are brought together by the rabbinic technique of "verbal analogy": the association of two passages on the basis of a word or words used in common. Psalm 95:11 states, "They shall never enter my rest [*katapausin*]," and Genesis 2:2 reads, "And on the seventh day God rested [*katepausen*] from all his work." The author of Hebrews wishes to emphasize two things by this association: The

---

6. Hurst, *The Epistle to the Hebrews*, 71.

7. This view is also supported by Dale F. Leschert, *Hermeneutical Foundations of Hebrews: A Study in the Validity of the Epistle's Interpretation of Some Core Citations from the Psalms* (Lewiston, N.Y.: Edwin Mellen, 1995), 168–70, who concludes that for both the writer of Psalm 95 and the author of Hebrews "rest is a personal experience that may be entered into in the present, but the writer of Hebrews adds an eschatological dimension which is not found in the psalm, unless it is there seminally."

8. Attridge, *Epistle to the Hebrews*, 128.

"rest" of God is not something of the past (4:6–9), and by its nature it involves the cessation of work (4:10). The author hints at the first of these propositions in verse 3 when he states, "And yet his work has been finished since the creation of the world." He offers this statement as a comment on his reiteration of Psalm 95:11, which shows that the "rest" of God, mentioned in Genesis 2, was an ongoing reality when the psalmist wrote. This understanding is developed in verses 6–11.

The Promise of Rest Still Stands (4:6–11)

IN VERSE 6 the preacher proclaims, "It still remains that some will enter that rest." The Greek text includes the phrase *epei oun* ("since therefore"), indicating that the author is building on his previous discussion and now moving to an implication. That a rest "remains" for some means that the issue of rest was not closed with those disobedient ones to whom God had originally promised rest in the land. For the author of Hebrews the psalmist clearly bears witness to this fact through Psalm 95. As the psalm indicates, God again determined or appointed a specific day, namely, "Today."

Now the author's logic and the specificity with which he reads the Old Testament text comes into view again. This ancient expositor's reasoning goes as follows.

- David lived long after the original receptors of God's promise of rest (v. 7).
- God, through David, again issued an implied promise through Psalm 95 that the people of God may enter his rest by not following the pattern of disobedience found in the desert story (v. 7).
- God gave this promise of rest through the psalmist because the physical entrance into the land under the leadership of Joshua did not fulfill the original promise (v. 8).[9]
- The universally relevant Word of God, issued in the form of Psalm 95, shows that a Sabbath rest still exists for the people of God, who are under obligation to "hear his voice" in the time frame of "Today" (v. 9).
- Verse 10 concludes this portion of the author's exposition by reflecting on the interpretive relevance of Genesis 2 for the Psalm 95 text: The essence of entering God's rest means resting from one's own work just as God did on the seventh day.[10]

---

9. Hagner points out that since the Greek names for Joshua and Jesus are both *Iesous*, the hearers would have been struck with the contrast between the "Jesus" of the Old Testament, who did not give rest, and the Jesus of the New Testament, who brings real rest to the people of God. See Hagner, *Hebrews*, 71.

10. For the possible theological interpretations here see below, pp. 154–55, 164–65.

Up to this point in the discussion the author has used the term *katapausis* ("rest") to communicate the concept of rest. In verse 9, however, he strategically introduces the word *sabbatismos* (the earliest known use of the word in Greek literature). He appears to have coined the word from the verb form *sabbatizein*, which means "to celebrate the Sabbath with praise." *Sabbatismos*, therefore, may suggest the festive joy surrounding a celebration of the Sabbath, in which one joins in praise and adoration of God.[11] Thus, the author joins the concept of "rest" to the concept of "Sabbath," based upon his exegesis of the Old Testament.

An important clue to the specific Sabbath the author has in mind may be found in the book of Leviticus, where the Pentateuch also joins the concepts of "ceasing work" and "Sabbath." Consider the following passages from chapters 16 and 23:

> This is to be a lasting ordinance for you: On the tenth day of the seventh month you must deny yourselves and not do any work—whether native-born or an alien living among you—because on this day atonement will be made for you, to cleanse you. Then, before the LORD, you will be clean from all your sins. It is a sabbath of rest, and you must deny yourselves; it is a lasting ordinance. (Lev. 16:29–31)
>
> The LORD said to Moses, "The tenth day of this seventh month is the Day of Atonement. Hold a sacred assembly and deny yourselves, and present an offering made to the LORD by fire. Do no work on that day, because it is the Day of Atonement, when atonement is made for you before the LORD your God. ... It is a sabbath of rest for you, and you must deny yourselves." (Lev. 23:26–28, 32)

Here the Sabbath ordinance is associated directly with the high-priestly offering on the Day of Atonement, an offering vital to the author's discussion in the following chapters (Heb. 8:3–10:18). By this lasting ordinance the people of God were not to "do any work," and God would cleanse them from their sins.

It must be admitted, of course, that the author does not make an overt reference to these texts in Leviticus. However, the broader context in which he mentions the preaching of the gospel (4:1–2)—a message that included the forgiveness of sins being received by faith—and the passage of our great high priest, Jesus, "through the heavens" into the heavenly Most Holy Place[12] (4:14), can be said to support such a tie. In this interpretation the Sabbath

---

11. Lane, *Hebrews 1–8*, 101–2.

12. The parallel to "gone through the heavens" in 4:14 is found in 10:19–20 and clearly refers to Jesus' passing into the heavenly Most Holy Place.

that remains for God's people is a new covenant Day of Atonement Sabbath, in which they are cleansed from their sins.

In 4:11 the author follows with an exhortation and a rationale: "Let us, therefore, make every effort to enter that rest, so that no one will fall by following their example of disobedience." The verb *spoudazo* means "work hard," "apply oneself diligently," or "do one's best."[13] It speaks of focused attention toward the accomplishment of a given task. Those of the author's community who have yet to combine faith with hearing the gospel must rivet their attention on responding in both celebration and obedience to the call of God to enter his rest. They demonstrate their faith by active obedience rather than by passive repose.

Here, then, the reader confronts a paradox—the true, spiritual rest of God, in which one is cleansed from sin, may be entered not by cessation of effort but by its application. Rather than contradicting himself, the author has a specific theological framework in mind. Those of the desert wanderings failed to enter God's promised rest (i.e., the land of promise) because they stopped short of obedience to God's command to enter. Thus by disobeying, by distrusting God, and by taking their own counsel as to what would be best in the situation, they failed to enter God's rest. Correspondingly, the hearers of Hebrews must not stop short of obedience to God's call to enter the promised Sabbath rest of atonement. To stop short—that is, failing to combine hearing of the gospel with faith (i.e., trusting obedience; 4:1–2)—results in spiritual devastation. Therefore, the listeners should be obedient to the "voice" of God (3:7) that they have heard.[14] This is imperative since that voice is one that issues both promises and words of punishment, as detailed in verses 12–13.

Warning: Consider the Power of God's Word (4:12–13)

HEBREWS 4:12–13, WHICH one scholar has referred to as "a rhapsody on God's penetrating word,"[15] evinces masterful literary craftsmanship and has captivated the attention of Christians through the ages. What should be pointed out from the beginning is that this description of God's word echoes the author's treatment of Psalm 95, with its emphasis on the "voice" of God that we should "hear" (95:7). Psalm 95, therefore, forms the basis for the author's comments on "the word" in Hebrews 4:12–13.

The matrix of thought around which first-century Judaism and earliest Christianity reflected on the Old Testament held the word of God to be a

---

13. Spicq, *Theological Lexicon of the New Testament*, 3:276–78.
14. Cf. Heb. 2:1–4.
15. Attridge, *The Epistle to the Hebrews*, 133.

creative, administrating, and judging force, which at times was personi-fied.[16] Elsewhere in the New Testament, authors associate the sword imagery with the word of God. For example, in Ephesians 6:17 the word of God is referred to as "the sword of the spirit"; in Revelation 1:16; 2:12; and 19:15 the "sharp sword" proceeds from the mouth of the Son of Man, a symbol of the dynamic, spoken word of judgment. In Hebrews 4:12–13 the word is a sharp word of discernment, which penetrates the darkest corners of human existence.

The author describes God's word first of all as "living and active." The for-mer adjective stands at the head of the verse, perhaps for emphasis, and asserts that that word, rather than being outdated, a "dead" speech-act of a bygone era, still exists as a dynamic force with which one must reckon. "Active" pro-claims the word as effective in carrying out God's intentions. The same word that at creation set the elements of the cosmos to their appointed tasks and still governs the universe toward God's desired intentions (1:2–3), has the ability to effect change in people. It is not static and passive but dynamic, inter-active, and transforming as it interfaces with the people of God.

The sword imagery emphasizes that while God's word is a word of promise to those who would enter God's rest, it is also a discerning word of judgment. Verse 12 asserts that like a sword that cuts and thrusts, the word penetrates and divides, being able to reach into the depths of a person's inner life. In listing the parts of a person on which the word acts—"soul and spirit, joints and marrow"—the preacher simply proclaims the word's ability to break past a surface religion to an inner, spiritual reality. Rather than dealing with externals such as religious observance, the penetrating word "judges the thoughts and attitudes of the heart."

Lest one think carelessly about the extent of God's discernment, the author assures us through verse 13 that "nothing in all creation is hidden from God's sight. Everything is uncovered and laid bare before the eyes of him to whom we must give account." The word translated "uncovered" (*gymnos*), which nor-mally communicates nakedness or having a lack of adequate clothing, was also used figuratively of being helpless or unprotected. In the context of God's penetrating word, the concept calls to mind a complete inability to hide any-thing from God's gaze. Those who have not responded to God's word in obe-dience are spiritually naked, vulnerable before his awesome gaze. A similar imagery is evoked by the participle translated "laid bare," which means "exposed." This theme of complete exposure and vulnerability of all creation before God was common in Jewish theology of the era.[17]

---

16. Ibid.
17. Lane, *Hebrews* 1–8, 103.

Summary. The author suggests the possibility that some among the original hearers of Hebrews were at Kadesh (Num. 14:32–35). They were hanging between entrance to the rest of God and turning back to a spiritual desert marked by disobedience and punishment. They are now confronted with a moment of decision. The word of God to them will either be a word of promise, the acceptance of which will mean their entrance to God's rest, or a word of punishment, which will be fulfilled by their falling in a spiritual desert. Some of the hearers are marked by a casual attitude in their evaluation of the word of salvation and their estimation of the consequences of its rejection (cf. 2:1–4). The author wishes to impress on them the real opportunity that lies before those who will take God at his word and in obedience move forward to lay hold of his promise of rest.

Based on insights gained from Genesis 2 this rest consists of resting from one's own work as God did from his work on the seventh day. This, however, does not mean a cessation of effort but rather an obedient, active dependence on God. The powerful language of 4:12–13, by contrast, reminds the listeners that God is not casual in assessing their spiritual condition. Rather, his word cuts deeply to the darkest corners of the inner life and lays bare spiritual realities that one might wish to keep hidden.

THE TASK OF interpretation can resemble engaging in a game, with only a partial understanding of the rules, or attempting to read a foreign language armed only with an elementary vocabulary. In both situations the participant feels awkward and strains to "fill in the gaps" so as not to play the fool. Hebrews 4:1–13, with its discussion of God's rest into which believers enter, confronts the interpreter with such a challenge especially because of the ambiguity of the "rest" motif.

We have noted the author's definition of "rest" as "ceasing from one's own works." Further, we have suggested that entering the rest probably constitutes both a present reality and a future, yet-to-be consummated event. Nevertheless, as we approach the task of application, we must ask what exactly the author wanted his hearers to do. How were they (and how are we) to respond to this exhortation in concrete terms? The author calls for action. What specific actions carried out in our contemporary contexts will fulfill his call? Here lies our focal challenge as we move to consider the contemporary significance of this text.

How should we proceed? As we move toward application of Hebrews 4:1–13, a reminder illustrated well by the passage under consideration may prove helpful. Sound application of a text must take into consideration a complex of factors, especially when dealing with a text that seems ambiguous. Some of the avenues that we turn down may prove to be dead ends. Nevertheless, part of the processes of interpretation and application involves thinking through numerous possibilities, embracing some (or aspects of some), and jettisoning others.

Let me suggest that we take a three-step approach to clarifying where we need to turn in our applications of this section. (1) We need to move toward the big picture of the author's message in this passage by *understanding his interpretive processes*. These processes provide a framework for what he wishes to say. If we as interpreters fail to analyze the structure of the writer's logic, we have yet to grasp key aspects of meaning in the passage.

(2) We need to pull together the various strands of meaning gathered in our microstudy of the text and *make sure we are interpreting the "rest" and other concepts in the passage in light of the context*. This step involves analyzing different interpretations in light of how they fit the bigger theological framework of this passage. What interpretations pull the various strands together into a cogent understanding of the passage? If we approach the study and teaching of a text like Hebrews 4:1–13 atomistically, focusing only on a word or phrase at a time and never assessing the roles these play in the author's larger purpose of the section, we run the danger of presenting a fragmented application based on fragmented thinking. We become like a woodland traveler whose view of a particular tree or trees obscures the forest.

Words like "rest," "faith," or "works" lend themselves to eisegetical interpretations (i.e., reading information into our interpretation from sources other than the text), based more on our theological preunderstanding than on an investigation of these words in context. Thus, we must work from the specifics of the text to the whole and back to a consideration of the specifics. We must be able to answer the question, "What conceptual role does this word or phrase play in the unit as a whole?" If we cannot answer that question reasonably, we have yet to arrive at a starting point for application. We may not leave our study of the text only having analyzed words and phrases; we must continue the process until we have a basic understanding of the author's message as a whole.

(3) We must *draw possible parallels to modern cultures*, remaining sensitive to both genuine correspondences and inappropriate applications. Just as we move from the details to the larger unit and then back to the details of the text, we must move back and forth between the world of the text and our modern contexts, reflecting on the possible implications of the former for the latter. This movement, which has a dual look at the text and our contexts, has been described as a "spiral" of interpretation. Grant R. Osborne comments:

A "spiral" ... is not a closed circle but rather an open-ended movement from the horizon of the text to the horizon of the reader. I am not going round and round a closed circle that can never detect the true meaning but am spiralling nearer and nearer to the text's intended meaning as I refine my hypotheses and allow the text to continue to challenge and correct those alternative interpretations, then to guide my delineation of its significance for my situation today. The sacred author's intended meaning is the critical starting-point but not an end in itself. The task of hermeneutics must begin with exegesis but is not complete until one notes the contextualization of that meaning for today.[18]

Therefore, our application, which we present in the "Contemporary Significance" section, must be grounded in a sound and emerging understanding of the text as a whole and in reflection on the implications of the text for today.

The author's interpretive processes. In the past some scholars accused Hebrews of a reckless and fantastic method of interpretation, in which insights were pulled from thin air. More recently, however, students of Hebrews have pointed out the care with which the author approaches his treatment of the Old Testament text.[19] This care manifests itself starkly in Hebrews 4 by the author's use of two rabbinic approaches to interpretation: verbal analogy and an emphasis on the plain meaning of specific words.

We have already encountered the author's use of verbal analogy in 1:5–14.[20] The basic presupposition behind this technique holds the existence of a consistency and continuity in God's revelation of truth. Various passages having "verbal analogy" (i.e., words in common) may be considered in light of one another because God has used specific terminology to communicate specific truths to his people.

In the case of Hebrews 4 the author understands Genesis 2, because of its reference to "rest," to make a contribution to the interpretation of Psalm 95. The pentateuchal passage helps to "fill in the gaps" for this first-century exegete, providing a basic definition of rest lacking in the psalm. That Genesis 2 speaks of God's rest on the seventh day suggests to our author that this rest into which the desert generation did not enter was the same as that of the Genesis passage since in the psalm God calls it "my rest." The nature of

---

18. See Grant R. Osborne, *The Hermeneutical Spiral: A Comprehensive Introduction to Biblical Interpretation* (Downers Grove, Ill.: InterVarsity, 1991), 5–6.

19. See G. B. Caird, "The Exegetical Method of the Epistle to the Hebrews," *CJT* 5 (1959): 44–51.

20. See above, p. 67.

this rest, then, consists of ceasing from one's own works as God did from his (Heb. 4:10). The entering of the rest by God's people, therefore, involves obedience (4:11) and faith (4:1–3), two concepts closely aligned in the author's thought (cf. 3:18–19), which constitute the ceasing from one's own efforts or counsels and the embracing of God's will.

The author of Hebrews also approaches the Old Testament with a "literalist" interpretation, based on the plain meaning of specific words. "Literal" interpretations are referred to rather negatively in modern culture, but the principle as adhered to in ancient biblical study signified a deep respect for the text. On this aspect of early Jewish hermeneutics Richard Longenecker comments:

> It need not be argued at any length that Judaism often took the words of the Old Testament quite literally. Rabbinic literature contains a number of examples of where the Scriptures were understood in a straightforward fashion, resulting in the plain, simple and natural meaning of the text being applied to the lives of people—particularly in the application of deuteronomic legislation. Frequently, in fact, the interpretation is woodenly literal as, for example, the teaching of the School of Shammai that "in the evening all should recline when they recite [the Shema], but in the morning they should stand up, for it is written, 'And when thou liest down and when thou risest up.'" The School of Hillel is recorded as countering this by insisting, "they may recite it every one in his own way, for it is written, 'And when thou walkest by the way.'"[21]

This literalist care with which our author handles the Old Testament may be seen in the logic of 4:6–9. For him the "Today" of Psalm 95 speaks of a time of opportunity, which, spoken as it was through David, existed for the people of God who lived long after entrance into the land of Canaan had been accomplished. Psalm 95, as a word of warning, includes an implication for those who fail to heed it: They, like the disobedient Israelites in the desert, will not be allowed to enter God's rest. This implication further means that the rest still exists and may be attained by God's people. As found in Genesis 2:2 this rest has to do with ceasing from one's own works. Thus, the author arrives at these conclusions by carrying out specific interpretive processes common to his day.

What does insight into these processes offer us as we move toward application? An understanding of each of these methods of argumentation brings

---

21. Longenecker, *Biblical Exegesis in the Apostolic Period*, 28.

into sharper focus the author's own interpretation of various concepts in the passage. These concepts are utilized within a framework established by the processes described above. Therefore, as the interpreter understands the role of each in that framework, the meaning of each concept as it supports the author's purposes becomes more clear. Apart from an understanding of his reasoning, the specific meanings he wishes to communicate may be obscured.

Interpreting the "rest" in light of the context. To grasp what the author intends to communicate concerning God's promised rest is fundamental to interpreting and applying this passage. As mentioned in the "Original Meaning," the exact nature of the "rest" as a present or future reality remains somewhat veiled. Thus application of this text offers a rigorous challenge.

Perhaps we should begin with three cautions concerning interpretation and application of these verses. (1) One may be tempted to avoid an application of this text since a passage that is this "theologically oriented" does not lend itself as easily to application as, for example, 1 Corinthians 13 or a teaching from the Sermon on the Mount (Matt. 5–7). Yet, notice that this passage concludes a major section of exhortation! It may take more effort to work through to an application, but God's people should be challenged to respond to this text.

(2) One might mistakenly preach the text as offering mere physical rest. One can imagine the passage being used to proclaim God's concern for our physical well-being. Certainly we must not make a strict demarcation between physical, emotional, and spiritual fatigue when considering the promise of rest here. The first hearers may have experienced great physical and emotional tiredness as a result of the persecution they were facing. However, the promise of Hebrews 4 offers so much more than mere physical and emotional renewal. The land of rest to which the author calls the hearers has more to do with a spiritual state of right relationship with and blessing from God. This promise does have vast implications for physical and emotional well-being, but the beginning place must be with one's spiritual condition. An appropriate application, therefore, might start with the issue of physical fatigue, but only as a launching point to address the root problem of spiritual dysfunctionality.

(3) Hebrews 4:1–13 should not be used to preach a literal "Sabbath observance," in which one ceases from one's own physical labor on a given day of the week. The preacher who uses Hebrews 4 to promote the cessation of work on Sunday, for example, is misinterpreting and misapplying the text. Although the author does emphasize the gathering together of Christians as vital (e.g., 10:25), the imagery in Hebrews 4 relates more broadly to a spiritual state in which one draws near to God. Speaking of the spiritual principle of the Sabbath Augustine writes:

It is also for this reason, that of all the ten commandments, that which related to the Sabbath was the only one in which the thing commanded was typical [i.e., figurative]; the bodily rest enjoined being a type which we have received as a means of our instruction, but not as a duty binding also upon us. For while in the Sabbath a figure is presented of the spiritual rest, of which it is said in the Psalm, "Be still, and know that I am God," and unto which men are invited by the Lord Himself in the words, "Come unto Me, all ye that labour and are heavy laden, and I will give you rest. Take My yoke upon you, and learn from Me; for I am meek and lowly in heart: so shall ye find rest unto your souls"; as to all the things enjoined in the other commandments, we are to yield to them an obedience in which there is nothing typical. For we have been taught literally not to worship idols; and the precepts enjoining us not to take God's name in vain, to honour our father and mother, not to commit adultery, or kill, or steal, or bear false witness, or covet our neighbour's wife, or covet anything that is our neighbour's, are all devoid of typical or mystical meaning, and are to be literally observed. But we are not commanded to observe the day of the Sabbath literally, in resting from bodily labour, as it is observed by the Jews.... From this we may reasonably conclude, that all those things which are figuratively set forth in Scripture, are powerful in stimulating that love by which we tend towards rest; since the only figurative or typical precept in the Decalogue is the one in which that rest is commended to us, which is desired everywhere, but is found sure and sacred in God alone.[22]

With these cautions in mind, we must now ask what the text reveals about this promised rest and how these points might lead to appropriate application of this passage. (1) *It is a rest that the hearers must fear missing.* Those in the community who treat the word of salvation lightly have something to fear. The author confronts them with the possibility of missing out on God's promised rest. Fear of this prospect constitutes far more than a simple caution against missing out on a potentially gratifying experience (as in "Oh, I am afraid I might miss the party"). Rather, a healthy respect for the power and judgment of God, detailed in 3:7–19, underlies the exhortation to "fear" (NIV, "be careful") in 4:1. In other words, it is due to their lack of fear (i.e., respect) toward God that people need to fear negative consequences of their spiritual condition.

---

22. Augustine, *Book II. Of Replies to Questions of Januarius*, in *The Confession and Letters of St. Augustine, With a Sketch of His Life and Work*, vol. 1 in A Select Library of the Nicene and Post-Nicene Fathers of the Christian Church, ed. Philip Schaff (Grand Rapids: Eerdmans, 1979), 310.

Many readers of this commentary are familiar with the broader biblical concept of the fear of God.[23] A danger of drifting off a sound theological path exists when dealing with this motif, and this danger applies to one side of the road as well as the other. On the one hand, some church traditions may emphasize the "fear of God" in a way that obscures the grace, love, and promises of God. In the present context the fear of missing the promised rest might be used to spiritually bludgeon a group of hearers. The red-faced preacher, who week after week reminds his church members that God— appalled and angry at human shortcomings—sits enthroned in judgment above the heavens, yet never moves decisively to a thorough explication of grace and promise, fails to preach a balanced gospel.

On the other hand, in many corners of the church today a too-familiar approach to God has obscured the awesomeness and otherness of his character, exalting the concept of promise to the point of obscuring spiritual accountability. As witnessed in Hebrews 4, God's word of promise comes in the context of accountability. In both Old and New Testaments, to be addressed by God's voice caused the hearer to tremble. This holy awe of God may be seen, for example, in Jonathan Edwards' works, the most famous of which is his sermon "Sinners in the Hands of An Angry God." An application faithful to the passage under consideration must take seriously the interrelationship of the warnings and promises inherent in the author's message.

The gospel challenges us to embrace the grace and love of God in light of the holiness and justice of God. In fact, the latter characteristics enhance our understanding of the former. We must reflect on our preaching and teaching to ascertain whether we hold these aspects in a proper and balanced perspective. Thus, application of 4:1–13 must build on the passage's emphases on God's word as both warning and promise to those who have yet to enter his rest.

(2) *It is a rest that some in the community are in danger of rejecting because they have not combined faith with obedience to God's word.* The implications of this caution must be highlighted in our application as we consider who in our contemporary contexts should be objects of the concern expressed in Hebrews 4. Those of the ancient faith community with whom the preacher is most concerned *seem* to have fallen short of a true faith response to the message of the good news; they have not truly believed (4:1–3). They are active, but their activity suggests they may not have engaged faith to this point. The author has in mind those who are falling away from the Christian movement and, thus, are not taking advantage of the work of God in Christ. In so doing they manifest

---

23. See J. D. Douglas, "Fear," in *New Bible Dictionary*, 2d ed., ed. J. D. Douglas (Downers Grove, Ill.: InterVarsity, 1982), 373–74.

that they have not ceased truly from their own works, taken the true path of faith, and entered into the Sabbath rest found in Christ's atoning sacrifice.

Thus the first line of application of the passage may be for those who are aligned with the community of faith but whose lives call into question whether the life of faith truly has been embarked upon. This brings us to a third point.

(3) *It is a rest that consists of ceasing from one's own works.* This proposition in 4:10 parallels the concept of joining faith to the hearing of the good news (4:2). In the context this would seem to point to a life of faith and obedience, in which one has turned from trust in one's own desert ways and counsels and turned to embrace the good news and will of God. It is a rest, therefore, that involves action in the form of active obedience to God. In our application of the passage we must not think this rest involves a spiritual passivity that sits around waiting for God to act. God has acted, and we must act in response to his actions.

The relationship between faith and works has constituted a focal discussion for Christian theology from the earliest decades of the church. One emphasis in Paul concerns those who wanted to add deeds of righteousness to the grace of God, suggesting that faith must be accompanied by works in order for salvation to be accessed (e.g., Rom. 4:1–5:12; Gal. 2:16–19; Eph. 2:8–10). Paul stresses that faith alone, apart from works, brings salvation.[24]

James, on the other hand, deals with those who called themselves believers but had no works that manifested that reality (James 2:14–26). For James works do not earn salvation but are an expression of genuine faith. Thus Abraham offered his son Isaac as an expression of faith and was justified (2:21–23). Hebrews parallels James somewhat in this concern, since for its author a lack of obedience shows a lack of true faith (Heb. 3:12, 18–19; 4:2, 11). Yet, Hebrews also contains an element of Pauline conceptions of faith as trust in God, expressed in the ceasing from one's own works (4:10).[25] Thus Hebrews represents somewhat a cross-section of early Christian concerns related to the relationship between faith and works.

In Hebrews one finds neither "faith" in the modern sense of a "leap in the dark," nor the health-and-wealth emphasis on "pinning God down" to a cer-

---

24. The past twenty-five years have witnessed a so-called "new perspective" in Paul, which suggests that the Jews of Paul's day were wholly "grace oriented" rather than "works oriented." For an overview of the discussion and a cogent and balanced argument for the Reformation interpretation of Paul's doctrine of grace, see Frank Thielman, *Paul and the Law: A Contextual Approach* (Downers Grove, Ill.: InterVarsity, 1994).

25. Recently some scholars have been more open to associating Hebrews with a Pauline circle of influence. See J. C. McCullough, "Hebrews in Recent Scholarship," *IBS* 16 (April 1994): 67; Hurst, *The Epistle to the Hebrews*, 123–24.

tain response by use of the Scriptures. (a) As to the former, faith relates to the unseen (e.g., Heb. 11:1), yet consists of an obedient response to God's revelation. Instead of a leap into the dark, there is a step into the light. We know where to move because God has revealed truth to us. Nevertheless, he and our future remain unseen, and thus our steps must be steps of trust in the unseen Revealer. (b) As to the latter, Hebrews' reverence for God does not allow the presumption often evidenced in the health-and-wealth doctrine of faith. Hebrews emphasizes faith as important to obtaining the promises of God, yet these promises relate to greater realities of Christian existence rather than material possessions or physical health.

(4) *The rest may be entered now and will be consummated at the end of the age.* The author's challenge to the community stems from his understanding of salvation, which involves both events of inauguration and consummation, as well as a process in between. Some in the community "seem" to have fallen short of the rest (4:1) because they have ceased participation in the process of being aligned with the community of confession and faith. This position of faithlessness demonstrates that, as with the desert generation, hearing of the gospel has not truly been joined to faith. True believers live out faith, resting in God until the final rest is reached. In other words, true believers have already entered into God's rest through belief, but they will experience the consummation of that rest only as they endure to the end.

THE NEED FOR **a land of rest**. Modern cultures are often characterized by frenetic activity. The fast-paced, problem-prone, project-oriented existence many of us live resists the spiritual life, pushing away recognition of God's voice with its invitation to rest. We face endless "To Do" lists for work, home, family, and other organizations, and these add a weight to our souls, from which we find little respite even in a good night's sleep. It seems all we can do to keep up the pace. In Lewis Carroll's *Through the Looking Glass* the author comments on this aspect of modern society through the character of the Red Queen, who says to Alice, "Now here, you see, it takes all the running you can do, to keep in the same place. If you want to get somewhere else, you must run at least twice as fast as that!"

As a result, in the crush and rush of weeks that flash before our eyes we sacrifice the important for the urgent, the personal for the professional, the private for the public image needed to keep our opportunities to do more and more. Such frenzied activity perhaps manifests a deeper spiritual emptiness, which prompts us to be ever striving for something of eternal value to fill the void, a "promised land" of inner milk and honey. In other words, we long for true rest that goes deeper than skin, muscle, and bone.

At the same time, there are those of another life orientation who find fatigue a daily companion. These are those out of work, the poor, or the sick who know only a life of monotony and boredom. You can see the lethargy in their pace, mirroring the weight hanging on their inner lives. They witness to the fact that true rest—the kind that reaches down to the depths of a person—cannot simply be found in being dismissed from constant labor. These, too, long for rest, a rest from a life of inactivity and meaninglessness, and they desperately need the replenishment brought only by the Spirit of God.

Although physical or emotional fatigue may be a problem—certainly these are universal companions for humanity—the promise of Hebrews 4 confronts the reader with a spiritual condition of being "out of place" in God's order. To lack God's promised rest means to be spiritually stranded, stuck in the desert between the slavery of Egypt and the promise of Canaan. The rest of Hebrews 4 speaks of a promised position in which one is rightly related to God and partaking of his blessings.

Spiritual wandering and its resulting fatigue are not new problems. Jesus, the new Joshua who leads God's people successfully into the land of promised rest (4:8), once said, "Come to me, all you who are weary and burdened, and I will give you rest. Take my yoke upon you and learn from me, for I am gentle and humble in heart, and you will find rest for your souls. For my yoke is easy and my burden is light" (Matt. 11:28–30). As he looks out on a desert-wandering humanity, his solution is "Come to *me*." Not, "Come to a set of teachings" (although Jesus does call us to that as well); not, "Come to church" (although Jesus does call us to a community of faith); not, "Come to your psychologist" (although God can use gifted counselors); not, "Come to a vacation" (although an evaluation of our tendencies to be workaholics and a reassessment of our life priorities may be in order). No. Rather, he says, "Come to me."

Jesus offers the ultimate source for true rest, for true rest is found only in a right relationship with the person of God. The rest is *his* rest, for *his* people, found by obeying *his* Word. In the wake of a culture leaving the fragmented, fragile, and fatigued in its wake, the church has the phenomenal opportunity of pointing people to the ultimate land of promise and spiritual well-being.

In her article "Keeping Sabbath: Reviving a Christian Practice,"[26] Dorothy C. Bass points out that Sabbath commandments in the Old Testament are

---

26. *The Christian Century* 114 (January 1–8, 1997): 12–16.

grounded in two activities of God: creation and exodus. In the book of Exodus God's people are given the gift of joining him in the rest established as a creation ordinance. By their pattern of work and rest they exhibit the image of God. Thus to find God's rest means to fulfill our place as human beings in the created order.

If we wander in the desert and lack the promised rest, the problem is a dysfunctional relationship to God; all who are not in right relationship with God need the promised rest found in Christ's "Day of Atonement" sacrifice. This need, therefore, extends to many who may not seem fatigued physically or emotionally. They may even seem energetic and purposeful in their wanderings. Nevertheless, as Augustine noted long ago, rest comes to realization only as wanderers find rest in God. True rest, which involves ceasing from one's own work as God did at creation and entering God's promised blessing of forgiveness, cannot be had by slaves or desert wanderers. Rather, true rest is found in rightly relating to God through faith and obedience to his Word. Only by joining him in his creation rest and humbling ourselves in light of his Day of Atonement sacrifice can we experience the Sabbath celebration reserved for God's people.

Therefore, as a first-level application of Hebrews 4 we must reflect on our spiritual condition. I must ask myself whether my lack of attention to the needs of my spirit has led to a condition of perpetual spiritual fatigue, a falling short of the promises of God. What is the state of my relationship with God? Have I entered into relationship with him, and am I living out obedience to his voice? The failure to participate in God's promised rest in Hebrews 4 most prominently relates to disobedience. Therefore, Hebrews 4 invites us first of all to spiritual reflection concerning our relationship to God.

Challenging the churched. In his book *Inside the Mind of Unchurched Harry and Mary*, Lee Strobel tells of a thirty-one-year-old mother of two, who after attending two services where the gospel was presented said, "I've just realized I've been playing religion all my life. I'm active at church, I'm on committees, I've heard about the Crucifixion so much since I was a child that I've been numb to it. And I realized today that I don't have a relationship with Christ."[27] Similarly, in the church I attend is a young lady who has been with the church since its founding four years ago. She and her family have participated in worship events, joined in small group activities, and carried out a variety of ministries to others. Yet, this fall Becky realized she had yet to make a faith commitment to Christ. Her decision, neither impromptu nor emotional, was prompted by a slowly growing awareness of her spiritual condition. She was baptized as a profession of her new covenant commitment to Christ.

---

27. Lee Strobel, *Inside the Mind of Unchurched Harry and Mary: How to Reach Friends and Family Who Avoid God and the Church* (Grand Rapids: Zondervan, 1993), 118.

There are certainly many others who connect with the church but never seem to get beyond the association and activities to a real faith relationship with God. In their case the gospel is heard without being heard with spiritual ears; it is acknowledged without being assimilated; it remains a matter of the head never making it to the heart.

The churched need to be reminded of the nature of real faith, for some of them may have never experienced it. The author of Hebrews states that those he is concerned about have failed to combine hearing of the gospel with real faith (4:2). In his *Christian Theology* Alistar McGrath discusses three main points concerning faith that flow from Martin Luther's doctrine of justification.[28] (1) Rather than being purely historical, faith has a personal reference. Simply to give cognitive assent to the historical facts surrounding the gospel cannot put a person into right relationship with God. Faith must be understood as having relevance for us personally.

(2) Faith has to do with trust in the promises of God. This trust, much more than merely believing (as in "I trust you are telling me the truth"), consists of an active reliance on the object of faith. Luther used the image of a ship. It is one thing to believe a ship can make it across a storm-tossed sea and quite another to entrust oneself to the ship by stepping into it for the voyage. Faith is an active commitment. Hebrews speaks of this commitment in terms of obedient response to the Word of God.

(3) Faith unites the believer to Christ in a covenant relationship. The essence of Christianity focuses not on an abstract collection of church doctrines or a list of activities, but rather in a personal relationship with Christ. To know Christ is to be a Christian of true faith.

A number of years ago Mother Teresa was approached by a brother in the order who complained that the rules of his superior were getting in the way of his ministry to lepers. He lamented, "My vocation is to work for lepers." To this Mother Teresa replied gently, "Brother your vocation is not to work for lepers, your vocation is to belong to Jesus."[29] This is the essence of real Christianity. All else relates to and flows from this relationship.

Cultivating a reverence for God and a respect for his discerning Word. Those who have yet to come to real faith in Christ, who may be associated with the church in some way but continue to treat the gospel lightly, need to come to grips with what it means to have awe for God and the power of his Word. Thus, our communities of faith need to be places of real worship, reverence, and radical openness to that Word. When those who are "play-

---

28. Alistar McGrath, *Christian Theology: An Introduction* (Cambridge, Mass.: Blackwell, 1994), 384–85.

29. Charles Colson, *Loving God* (Grand Rapids: Zondervan, 1983), 126.

ing church," stranded between Egypt and Canaan, truly enter into his presence and are confronted with his holiness, they will have their flippant, shallow "churchianity" stripped away and, like Isaiah in the shadow of King Uzziah's death (Isa. 6:1–13), will find themselves naked before his striking presence, crying out that they are indeed ruined and dirty.

Donald W. McCullough, in his book *The Trivialization of God*, writes of a vapid Christianity approached without due reverence for God:

> Visit a church on Sunday morning—almost any will do—and you will likely find a congregation comfortably relating to a deity who fits nicely within precise doctrinal positions, or who lends almighty support to social crusades, or who conforms to individual spiritual experiences. But you will not likely find much awe or sense of mystery. The only sweaty palms will be those of the preacher unsure whether the sermon will go over; the only shaking knees will be those of the soloist about to sing the offertory.
>
> ... reverence and awe have often been replaced by a yawn of familiarity. The consuming fire has been domesticated into a candle flame, adding a bit of religious atmosphere, perhaps, but no heat, no blinding light, no power for purification.
>
> When the true story gets told, whether in the partial light of historical perspective or in the perfect light of eternity, it may well be revealed that the worst sin of the church at the end of the twentieth century has been the trivialization of God.[30]

How then do we come to grips with the awesomeness of God? One way is by living lives consistently open to the hearing and practice of his Word. This openness stands as the antithesis of a hardened heart (3:8), the way we know God's ways (3:10), the entrance to and experience of God's promised rest (3:18, 4: 6, 11), and the path of true faith (4:2). This "living and active" Word reaches to the depths of our existence and lays bare who we really are before the all-seeing God. This does not mean that God needs our interaction with his Word to see our innermost thoughts and the conditions of our souls. No. Our confrontation by the Word brings us in touch with the truth of God's perceptiveness. God sees us inside-out. The question is whether we realize it and, by his grace, join him in investigating our true spiritual conditions.

We tend to think of great faith in terms of following God in the accomplishing of great deeds in the world or of overcoming great obstacles. Yet, true faith must begin with a face-to-face experience with God, by which we journey to the inner recesses of our own hearts.

---

30. Donald W. McCullough, *The Trivialization of God: The Dangerous Illusion of a Manageable Deity* (Colorado Springs, Colo.: NavPress, 1995), 13.

The forging of a real-world faith means not only that one follows Christ into the Heavenlies to meet God, but that one follows Christ into the corridors of one's inner space in order to develop the spirit of Christlikeness. And Christlikeness in the inner life means an advancing knowledge of one's inner self and a growing ability to master it.[31]

The great sword of the Spirit, the Word of God, serves as our guide in following Christ through the inner corridors of the heart. This confrontation by God's living, piercing Word begins and must be a trademark of the true life of faith.

How then might we live our lives open to the Word of God? The father of German Pietism, Philip Jakob Spener, wrote *Pia Desideria* ("Pious Longings") in 1675. In this work Spener vied for greater attention to be given to the "hearing" of Scripture by those in the churches of his day. His words fit well a great need in the contemporary church:

Thought should be given to the more extensive use of the Word of God among us. We know that by nature we have no good in us. If there is to be any good in us, it must be brought about by God. To this end the Word of God is the powerful means, since faith must be enkindled through the gospel, and the law provides the rules for good works and many wonderful impulses to attain them. The more at home the Word of God is among us, the more we shall bring about faith and its fruits.

It may appear that the Word of God has sufficiently free course among us inasmuch as at various places (as in this city [Frankfurt am Main]) there is daily or frequent preaching from the pulpit. When we reflect further on the matter, however, we shall find that with respect to this first proposal, more is needed.[32]

Having acknowledged the important place of preaching in the life of the congregation, Spener goes on to encourage the public and private readings of the Scriptures, as well as the gathering together of believers in what would be the precursor to modern home, Bible-discussion groups.

Modern Christians have a number of "advantages" over those of Spener's Germany. In the latter half of the twentieth century, evangelical Christianity experienced a boom in the publishing of materials related to Bible study. Lexical aids, background tools, concordances, a host of excellent commen-

---

31. Gordon MacDonald, *Forging a Real-World Faith* (Nashville: Oliver Nelson, 1989), 119.

32. P. J. Spener, *Pia Desideria*, ed. and trans. T. G. Tappert (Philadelphia: Fortress, 1964), 87–88.

taries, and even computer programs have proliferated. Yet many congregations (and even their pastors!) could be considered resource rich and Bible poor. We trumpet the need for detailed consideration of the Scriptures but find little time in the crush of our over-extended schedules.

I have found personally that my ongoing spiritual well-being relates to a number of factors, none more basic than consistent, meaningful time in prayer and interaction with God's Word. We will consider prayer further in a later section, but I would like to mention several ways we should be opening our lives to the Word.

(1) With Spener I suggest that exegetical preaching and the reading of Scripture are foundational for the community of faith. I must challenge myself on a regular basis to think through application of what I am hearing preached or read, writing down notes and meditating on how I might assimilate the truths expressed in the coming days. My family and I are beginning a process in which we discuss one or two central truths from our weekend worship experience and meditate on those truths for the first half of the week. In the last half of the week we begin preparing our hearts for worship on the coming weekend. In seeking to apply Hebrews 4:12–13 I must ask myself whether I am truly *hearing* the Word preached in such a way that I am opening myself to obedient action and, therefore, life change.

(2) With Spener I affirm the need for private reading as well as small-group reading and discussion of the Bible. As I read the Scriptures on a daily basis and participate with others in biblically based discussion, I begin to get a better grasp on the broad sweep of Scripture. Spener suggested that for individual Christians to depend on preaching alone would be to neglect large portions of Scripture and fall out of touch with an overview of God's counsel. Therefore, great encouragement in the faith comes by setting aside a few minutes at some point in the day to read several chapters of the Bible systematically.

(3) Many modern Christians need to evaluate their time management and commit to consistent, personal Bible study. The Word of God is a gift that should be cherished with detailed attention. Personal study educates, stimulates right thinking, challenges to holy living, and encourages needy hearts. Thinking about the Word of God is (and should be) a community-conditioned activity. As individuals grow in biblical literacy the community is strengthened. Without personal Bible study, both the spiritual life of the individual and the community suffer.

(4) Flowing from hearing, reading, and studying the Scriptures should be a process of memorization and meditation. Most Christians are familiar with the psalmist's confession, "Your word I have hidden in my heart that I might not sin against you" (Ps. 119:11). Jesus clearly modeled these practices

in his own life and ministry (e.g., Matt. 4:1–11). Memorization and meditation were vital in the biblical world since the cost of manuscripts was exorbitant. Yet, the practice is no less needed in modern culture even though many families have multiple copies of the Bible in a wide variety of translations. A Bible at hand does not necessarily mean an incorporation of biblical truth into one's life. Memorization of and meditation on passages that have been studied in their original contexts can be great aids in spiritual growth and vitality.[33]

These modes of interacting with God's Word take time and discipline. If you are out of the habit of engaging the Bible meaningfully, you might begin by setting aside forty-five minutes or an hour a day to do basic study and memorization. Treat that time as nonnegotiable and choose a time during which you are least likely to be interrupted (e.g., early in the morning). Work at consistency rather than great volume. For example, you might start by memorizing one verse per week. Also, such a commitment to Bible study and memorization is bolstered if you have a friend that will encourage you and with whom you can share insights from your study. Such interaction with Scripture is costly, but you can be assured that the investment of consistently opening your life to God's Word will pay great dividends.

Further, when we reflect on those who are struggling with Christian commitment, as were those addressed by the author in Hebrews 4, we could do them no better service than living lives before them that are consistently transformed by the Word. As we engage them through authentic living, exegetical preaching, and discussion of the Bible, the spiritually border-lined come into contact with the active, powerful Word, which can penetrate the hardest of hearts and open the darkest of souls to the gaze of God. Then perhaps God's Word will become to them a word of promised rest by which they will find an eternal place of belonging.

---

33. For a helpful approach to Scripture memory see Lavonne Masters, *Memorize and Meditate* (Nashville: Thomas Nelson, 1991). On meditation see Richard J. Foster, *Celebration of Discipline: The Path to Spiritual Growth* (New York: Harper & Row, 1978), 13–29.

Hebrews 4:14–16

ᴡ

THEREFORE, SINCE WE have a great high priest who has gone through the heavens, Jesus the Son of God, let us hold firmly to the faith we profess. ¹⁵For we do not have a high priest who is unable to sympathize with our weaknesses, but we have one who has been tempted in every way, just as we are—yet was without sin. ¹⁶Let us then approach the throne of grace with confidence, so that we may receive mercy and find grace to help us in our time of need.

THESE VERSES STAND at a particularly important crossroad in the book. A number of thematic paths down which the author has already traveled lead to this way-station, such as Jesus as Son, the importance of faith, and the sin factor. Yet, this passage also serves as a departure point for a consideration of Christ's high priesthood, a vitally important theological motif that extends with vigor all the way to 10:25.¹ Although these three verses may seem brief and somewhat unadorned, they serve as a crystallization of Hebrews' main message, a snapshot of the sermon. Thus this passage offers an opportunity to rise momentarily above the complex twists and turns of the discourse and view the larger scope of the author's intention.

It is difficult to overstate the importance of 4:14–16 in understanding the organization of the book. This passage serves both as a conclusion to the exhortation running from 3:1 to 4:16 and as an opening for the great central exposition on the high priesthood of Christ. Thus it has been labeled an "overlapping transition."²

The passage coheres around three conceptually intertwined components, two of which are the exhortations to "hold firmly to the faith" and "approach the throne." The third, the author's reflection on Jesus' high priesthood, serves as the basis for these exhortations. It is because Jesus is our high priest that we can hold firmly to the faith and approach the throne of grace with confidence. The structure of the passage may be depicted as follows:

---

1. On the parallel relationship of 4:14–16 to 10:19–25 see above, pp. 28–29.

2. Guthrie, *The Structure of Hebrews*, 102–4. For the place of this passage in this book see above, p. 28.

basis for exhortation 1: Therefore, since we have a great high priest who has gone through the heavens, Jesus the Son of God,

EXHORTATION 1: *let us hold firmly to the faith we profess.*

expansion of basis for exhortation 1 and basis for exhortation 2: For we do not have a high priest who is unable to sympathize with our weaknesses, but we have one who has been tempted in every way, just as we—yet was without sin.

EXHORTATION 2: *Let us then approach the throne of grace with confidence,*

motivation related to exhortation 2: so that we may receive mercy and find grace to help us in our time of need.

Hold Firmly to the Faith (4:14–15)

IN THE OLD covenant the position of high priest was preeminent; he oversaw the ritual worship of God and functioned as the main representative between the nation and Yahweh. The Old Testament refers to him variously as "the priest" (Ex. 31:10), "the anointed priest" (Lev. 4:3), "the chief priest" (2 Chron. 26:20), and the "high priest" (2 Kings 12:10). This final designation occurs only at Numbers 35:25–32 in the Pentateuch and once in Joshua (20:6). The high priesthood was hereditary (Ex. 29:29–30; Lev. 16:32), a fact to which the author of Hebrews gives extensive attention (Heb. 7:11–28), and normally for life (Num. 18:7; 25:11–13; 35:25, 28; Neh. 12:10–11). Although the high priest shared a number of duties with the other priests, he alone entered the Most Holy Place on the annual Day of Atonement (Lev. 16:1–25).[3]

The theme of Jesus' high priesthood occupies the author's attention from 4:14 to 10:25 (with the exception of the strategically placed exhortation of 5:11–6:20). For him our high priest is "great" for a number of reasons that are explained in chapters 5–10. Because he has been tempted he can sympathize with us (4:15), but, unlike the earthly priests, he is entirely without sin (5:1–3; 7:26–28). He has been appointed by an oath from God (5:4–10; 6:17–20; 7:15–22), which assures his priesthood is eternal (7:16–25). Jesus' atonement offering has been made in the context of a new (and thus superior) covenant (8:7–13). Moreover, it was presented in the heavenly tabernacle rather than the earthly (8:2; 9:1–28), used superior blood (9:1–28), and, unlike the old covenant offering, only had to be made once for all time (10:1–18).

---

3. See Chris Church, "High Priest," in *Holman Bible Dictionary*, ed. Trent C. Butler (Nashville: Holman Bible Publishers, 1991), 645–48.

The present passage (4:14–16) focuses in part on the ministry of Jesus in which he entered the heavenly Most Holy Place to present his superior offering (cf. 8:2; 9:11, 23–24). Furthermore, the title "Son of God" (4:14) echoes a major theme of the book's first two chapters, where the exaltation and incarnation of the Son are displayed. In 4:14 the title rings a triumphant note, drawing especially on his exaltation ("having gone through the heavens"). That the Son, our high priest, has passed through the heavens provides a firm basis for the exhortation that follows.

The author encourages his hearers with the words "let us hold firmly to the faith we profess" (v. 14). The verb *krateo*, rendered here "let us hold firmly," is used forty-seven times in the New Testament. This word can refer to the grasping of a person, such as when Jesus grasped the hand of a sick person (Mark 1:31; 9:27), the women grabbed hold of the resurrected Jesus (Matt. 28:9), or the lame man clung to Peter and John (Acts 3:11). In Hebrews 4:14, however, the word refers to commitment—a use found, for example, in Mark 7:3–4, where the Pharisees are said to "observe" the traditions of the fathers. Similarly, Christians are challenged to "hold to the teachings" they have been given (2 Thess. 2:15), while the heretic in Colossians 2:19 has "lost connection with" (more correctly, "does not hold to") the Head. By contrast, those in the church at Pergamum "remain true" to Jesus' name (Rev. 2:13), and the churches of Thyatira and Philadelphia are challenged to remain doctrinally pure, holding fast to their commitments to the Lord (2:25; 3:11).[4] The author of Hebrews, therefore, is calling the recipients of this sermon to remain committed to Jesus, holding to their public confession of him as the Son of God.[5] Endurance in this commitment finds its basis in the follower's relationship to Christ as a heavenly high priest.

The author elaborates on Jesus' high priesthood in verse 15. We have a high priest who, because of his experience of temptation, can sympathize with our weaknesses. Thus, rather than being far removed from our human experience, the powerful, now-exalted Son has been in the thick of it. The word translated "weaknesses" (*astheneia*) can refer to sickness, physical weakness, general weakness related to being in the flesh, or moral weakness.[6] Here the context associates the weakness with a propensity to sin (cf. 5:2–3). Not that Jesus shared in our experience of sin—the author makes it clear he did not—but he did share in our experience of being tempted, a difficult aspect of life that too often leads to sin.

---

4. P. von Osten-Saken, "κρατέω," *ENDT*, 2:314–15.

5. In Hebrews *krateo* and its synonym, *katecho*, are variously used to encourage holding to hope (6:18; 10:23), confidence (3:6, 14; 4:16), and the confession of faith (here and at 10:23). See Ellingworth, *The Epistle to the Hebrews*, 267.

6. Attridge, *The Epistle to the Hebrews*, 140.

In this passage, therefore, the word "sympathize" does not necessitate a sharing of another's exact experience, but, as in 10:34—where the hearers are said to have sympathized with prisoners (though not being prisoners themselves)—the word connotes being "compassionate to the point of helping."[7] Our high priest does not stand aloof but cares for us in our human state of weakness.

Draw Near to God (4:16)

FOLLOWING THE DESCRIPTION of Jesus as a compassionate high priest in 4:15, the author gives a second exhortation: "Let us then approach the throne of grace." The exhortation flows naturally from verses 14–15 as shown by the conjunction *oun* ("therefore"; NIV, "then"). Jesus' compassionate disposition invites us to intimacy with God and makes that intimacy possible.

The exhortation "let us approach" translates a present tense form of the verb, indicating that drawing near to God constitutes an ongoing aspect of the Christian's relationship with God: "let us constantly approach." Under the old covenant the only person allowed into God's presence was the high priest, who entered the Most Holy Place once a year on the Day of Atonement. Under that covenant the high-priestly offering on that day won forgiveness for the people. Yet they were still locked out of the presence of Yahweh.[8] But under Jesus' high priesthood, the people of God find a new and happy situation. They themselves may enter the very presence of God on a continual basis, and can do so with "confidence"—a word that can also be translated as "bold frankness,"[9] which in both Hellenistic Judaism and early Christian usage is related especially to the believer's approach to God in prayer.[10]

Christians, therefore, should draw near to God with unabashed openness since God alone is the true source of mercy and grace. Because of these provisions we can expect God will "help us in our time of need." Literally this phrase reads that mercy and grace result in "timely aid." The author may have in mind the trial of persecution being faced by the community, a trial that was tempting them to reject God's mercy in Christ. The author assures them that if they remain faithful to their confession and approach God through Jesus' high-priestly work, God will come through with help in a timely fashion.

---

7. Spicq, *Theological Lexicon of the New Testament*, 3:320.
8. Lane, *Hebrews 1–8*, 115.
9. Ibid.
10. Attridge, *Epistle to the Hebrews*, 111–12.

THE LANGUAGE OF high priesthood. With Hebrews 4:14–16 we move into a section of the book highly dependent on religious language from the Old Testament. For modern readers—especially those whose association with church and church culture is limited—the concepts of high priesthood, faith, temptation, sin, the throne of grace, and mercy may seem obscure at best. One can imagine a secular, hard-edged businesswoman sitting in on a church service in which this passage is being preached. She might stare ahead glassy-eyed as the minister delights in the intricacies of old covenant worship; she might be awed at his obvious education or cringe at her own stark ignorance; and she might not come back—if he does not help her see the phenomenal relevance of this text for her life, work, and relationships. No one likes to attend parties where people use only "insider" language. I am not vying for the "dumbing down" of theology but rather the translation of theological language in a way that communicates.

In the next pew imagine a long-time church member, who lapses into a catatonic state any time the preacher crosses the canonical line, moving from New to Old Testament literature. There are Christians who have been in church all their lives and have yet to dig below the surface language and ritual to marvel at the God who works out relationships with frail human beings. They have heard the words so many times and too often been bored to tears with shallow explanations. With such parishioners we may face a greater challenge than with the secular seeker. They must be blasted out of their stupor and urged to recognize that while they may know the terms, they have never come to grips with the truth or with God himself! Thus, in bridging the gap between the original meaning of the text and its contemporary significance, we confront the challenge of exploring the meaning of religious language and probing its reflection of truths about our relationship to God.

For some not familiar with Old Testament literature the image conjured by the designation "high priest" might be that of a mythical figure with staff in hand, clothed with long robes and adorned with an aura of mystic light (e.g., a pagan high priest). The "high priest" for them presides over imperceptible religious rituals and stands apart from normal society. The concept, therefore, represents the head figure of some strange religion.

For Christians who have been in church a while, the title "high priest" points to the Old Testament context. They may remember vaguely that the high priest was dressed with special clothing such as the blue robe, the ephod, and the breastplate (Ex. 28:4–39; 39:1–31; Lev. 8:7–9). If especially knowledgeable, our hypothetical Christian might even remember the Urim and Thummim, sacred lots used to discern God's will (Ex. 28:29–30; Num. 27:21). This image of the high priest portrays a religious figure who represents the people before God. He serves as the go-between in a highly formal, ritualistic worship setting. In this picture God remains closed off from the common person, hidden from view behind a primitive veil.

For Hebrews, however, Jesus' high priesthood represents above all else open access to God. Building on the Old Testament concept, the author of Hebrews makes much of the uniqueness and superiority of the Son's high priestly role. Rather than one who stands between God and humanity, Jesus takes us to God, ripping away the moral and ritualistic obstacles that prevented our free entrance to his presence. He not only has passed through the heavens, but he also has paved the way for us to join him in that adventure (e.g., 2:10; 6:20; 10:19–20). Thus, when we communicate the high-priest concept, we must emphasize its signification of a "means of free access to God."

Jesus, a sympathetic high priest. Our high priest has made our approach to God possible by approaching us. He can sympathize with our weaknesses, offering compassion and help, because he has shared in an important aspect of what it means to be human, having been tempted "in every way, just as we are." We must ask, "What does this mean?" before we can ask, "What does this mean for us?"

We live in a modern world full of modern tools of sin. There are sins related to weapons, for example, that did not exist in the ancient world. We can sin by shooting another person in cold blood, blowing them up with a bomb, or devastating their health through chemical warfare. Was Jesus tempted to do these acts? Is that what the author meant when he wrote that Jesus was "tempted in every way"? We can steal from someone else by ripping off an insurance company, by cheating on our income taxes, or by embezzling funds through electronic bank fraud. Was Jesus tempted to do these sins? Pornography can be had in printed form, on cable television, in an R-rated movie, or over the Internet. Was Jesus tempted in these ways? Of course not; these things did not exist in the Palestine of the first century.

Although the *expressions* or *tools* of sin have changed in the past two millennia, sin's essential nature remains immutable: hatred, murder, greed, dishonesty, lust. These stalk our human path and "crouch at the door" (Gen. 4:6–7), awaiting any and every opportunity. Certainly the author of Hebrews has in mind the gambit of such spiritual plagues. An interesting question presents itself, however: "If we affirm that Jesus Christ is God-incarnate, how is it possible that his temptations were genuine?"[11] (cf. James 1:13). The

---

11. Bernard Ramm, *An Evangelical Christology: Ecumenic and Historic* (Nashville: Thomas Nelson, 1985), 80.

answer must be found in the paradox of Jesus' unique nature as the God-man. One way of expressing this paradox is to insist that as human, Jesus felt the full force of temptation, and the temptations he faced were real, inviting him to sin (they would not be temptations otherwise). However, as God he would not and did not sin.[12] This position allows us to affirm wholeheartedly Jesus as fully God and fully human.

Given the context, however, the author of Hebrews probably has one particular temptation uppermost in his thoughts: the temptation to break with one's commitments under severe suffering. In 2:18, a verse that foreshadows the one under consideration,[13] the author writes, "Because he himself suffered when he was tempted." In a related passage (5:7–8), a text that might be called "Hebrews' Gethsemane account," he adds: "Although he was a son, he learned obedience from what he suffered." For Jesus the ultimate temptation—and the one to which his response would have vast implications for the rest of humanity—was the temptation to try to get around his persecution unto death and to turn his back on God's will, which was leading him to a Roman cross. Commenting on the temptation account in Matthew and Luke's Gospels, Philip Yancey writes,

> As I reflect on Jesus' temptations . . . I realize they centered on his reason for coming to earth, his "style" of working. Satan was, in effect, dangling before Jesus a speeded-up way of accomplishing his mission. He could win over the crowds by creating food on demand and then take control of the kingdoms of the world, all the while *protecting himself from danger* [italics mine].[14]

For the listeners the point of Hebrews 4:15 could not have been more relevant. Jesus can sympathize with their temptation to turn and run in the face of persecution. He felt the same urge—but declined it. He can thus help them face the challenge (cf. 12:2–3), and he can help us. Consequently, on the basis of the Son's sympathetic high priesthood the author challenges the hearers of all Christian centuries to take action in two ways: to "hold firmly to the faith" and to "approach the throne of grace." The former speaks to our need for stability in the world, the latter to our need for access to resources beyond this world in order to gain that stability.

In 4:14 the concept of a "profession of faith" (or a "confession," as other translations render the term) must be understood as far more than just a verbal affirmation of truth. Broadly in religious culture, the concept of *confession*

---

12. See Erickson, *Christian Theology*, 720.
13. On the structural relationship between 2:17–18 and 4:14–16 see above, p. 111.
14. Yancey, *The Jesus I Never Knew* (Grand Rapids: Zondervan, 1995), 74.

speaks of admitting a wrong that has been done. A *profession of faith* may be thought of as the act of standing before a congregation to indicate one's initial commitment to Christ. Perhaps the author has in mind past public commitments made by his hearers. However, to hold to one's profession means to live out one's belief through a lifestyle of commitment. One cannot say, "I believe it is true, but because of the circumstances my commitments lie elsewhere." A Christian profession involves commitment of one's life, not just a phrase on one's tongue. To carry out such a commitment, however, demands resources beyond the Christian individual.

Approaching the throne. The image of "approaching the throne" carries at least two messages in the present context. (1) It communicates an act of prayerful worship. The "approach" draws on the Old Testament backdrop of the high priest's movement into the Most Holy Place. For Jews and Christians of the ancient world this image of approaching God had developed especially into a symbol for prayer. The throne image relates closely in that it represents the power and authority of God. To those of us who do not live in monarchies or in countries in which a king or queen still functions as a figurehead, the throne imagery seems archaic. (2) Yet, it is such a universal image we can grasp it with little effort. The one on the throne has more capacity to help us than anyone else. He holds both the authority and capability we need for our present concerns, and we can be assured his help will be timely.

Thus 4:14–16, focused as it is on the sympathetic high priesthood of Jesus, challenges us to remain true to our Christian commitment and to seek God in prayer for his help in the face of persecution.

HOLDING FIRMLY TO the faith. We live in an "age of reason," where many seem to think the most reasonable course in any given situation is to "look out for Number One." Thus, all reason leads to self-preservation. Thomas Paine wrote, "It is necessary to the happiness of man that he be mentally faithful to himself. Infidelity does not consist in believing, or in disbelieving; it consists in professing to believe what he does not believe."[15] In the same spirit, actress Shirley MacLaine states:

> The only sustaining love involvement is with yourself. . . . When you look back on your life and try to figure out where you've been and where you're going, when you look at your work, your love affairs,

---

15. Thomas Paine, *The Age of Reason*, pt. 1.

your marriages, your children, your pain, your happiness—when you examine all that closely, what you really find out is that the only person you really go to bed with is yourself.... [16]

Of course Paine has a point. Hypocrisy should be rejected, and mental health in part depends on an integration of our inner beliefs with our outward professions. Yet, this orientation to self-actualization proves above all else a poor position from which to live life and an impossible one from which to live an authentic Christian life.

We can be thankful that the church through the ages has been blessed with powerful examples of those who have stood against such a perspective. These heroes of the faith would reject the view of "self-actualization" as the ultimate goal of life. They would certainly renounce the primary view of the church as a "self-help" center where we get physically fit, emotionally supported, spiritually spoon-fed, intellectually stimulated, socially situated, and fiscally informed (although these may occur as a by-product of our church involvement); and they would call into question Christians who show a predominant self-centeredness in their Christianity.

We must ask ourselves whether our faith is God-centered or self-centered. Are we willing to pay a price for our association with Christ? Is our commitment to someone other than ourselves? Or do we hold that commitment only as long as church "ministers to us," questioning the "reasonableness" of staying when conflicts within or without threaten our sense of personal well-being?

How different the picture when we consider Martin Luther's stand at the Diet of Worms on April 18, 1521! Luther, that great leader of the Protestant Reformation, was summoned by Charles V, the Holy Roman Emperor, in an effort to reconcile Luther and the official church. When asked to recant his teachings the Reformer responded, "I cannot and will not recant anything, for to go against conscience is neither right nor safe. Here I stand, I can do no other, so help me God. Amen." Luther held fast to the faith he professed. He was able to do so because of a deep conviction concerning the lordship and high priesthood of the Son of God, who alone had paid for all his sins, removing the need for an earthly priest as go-between.

Run the historical footage ahead a little more than four centuries to World War II. Dietrich Bonhoeffer—German theologian, pastor, seminary professor, and participant in the Resistance movement—had been imprisoned by the Nazis for his role in the latter. In the final days of the war, Bonhoeffer and his fellow prisoners had experienced a strange mixture of hope and panic as

---

16. Shirley MacLaine, *Washington Post* interview, 1977.

they heard the Allied guns on the horizon. Moved from place to place in advance of the American and British forces, the little group of prisoners was finally brought to a schoolhouse in Schönberg.

Time finally ran out for Bonhoeffer. An interrogator from Berlin named Huppenkothen arrived with orders for Bonhoeffer's immediate trial and execution. On Sunday the theologian was entreated by his fellow prisoners, among them Roman Catholics and even a Communist from Russia, to hold a worship service. He gave an exposition on "By his wounds we are healed" (Isa. 53:5), and "Praise be to the God and Father of our Lord Jesus Christ! In his great mercy he has given us new birth into a living hope through the resurrection of Jesus Christ from the dead" (1 Peter 1:3). The sermon touched the others deeply. Following this message Bonhoeffer was called out of his cell and transported to Flossenberg, where he was interrogated, tried, and condemned. The next morning between five and six o'clock, Bonhoeffer, stripped naked beneath the scaffold, knelt to pray one last time in a woodland spring.[17] In his final morning meditation to reach the outside world, the professor wrote:

> The key to everything is the "in him." All that we may rightly expect from God, and ask him for, is to be found in Jesus Christ. The God of Jesus Christ has nothing to do with what God, as we imagine him, could do and ought to do. If we are to learn what God promises, and what he fulfills, we must persevere in quiet meditation on the life, sayings, deeds, sufferings, and death of Jesus. It is certain that we may always live close to God and in the light of his presence, and that such living is an entirely new life for us; that nothing is then impossible for us, because all things are possible with God; that no earthly power can touch us without his will, and that danger and distress can only drive us closer to him.[18]

Bonhoeffer embodied the principles inherent in Hebrews 4:14–16: Perseverance depends on one's relationship to Jesus, the Son of God. He lived that truth to the very end and left an enduring picture of true Christian faith and stability.

For us, therefore, these verses offer a message of hope and help—as well as a challenge—for our present difficulties that fight against our perseverance in the faith. Some reading this commentary may be facing a high degree of persecution, even death, but most are likely threatened by less dramatic

---

17. Mary Bosanquet, *The Life and Death of Dietrich Bonhoeffer* (New York: Harper & Row, 1968), 277–78.

18. Ibid., 263.

opponents. For instance, you may have a boss that pokes fun at the faith, a former friend who seeks to humiliate you publicly because of your Christian commitment, or a non-Christian spouse who makes your life miserable. Such struggles are both real and threatening.

If we find our grip on the faith "slipping," ourselves plagued with "conflicts on the outside, fears within," as Paul once said (2 Cor. 7:5), we must examine our view of Jesus. Do we have a clear picture of him and his high priesthood on our behalf? As seen in the examples of the Luthers and Bonhoeffers throughout the Christian centuries, resolve flows from a depth of conviction and a commitment of life and heart. Once we find such conviction, we will live lives of integrity, our outward actions matching our inner beliefs and our commitments of the past being lived out in the present and into the future.

The approach. As seen in Luther's plea for God's help and Bonhoeffer's fervent prayer in the final seconds of his earthly life, drawing near to God plays a vital role in perseverance in the faith. God offers us help in the face of our needs, and he has given prayer as a means to communicate those needs to him. Not that he does not know them! But prayer is a relational dynamic by which we actively approach God. We get off dead center, reach out beyond ourselves, and look to him in our time of need; and—mystery of mysteries—our seeking of his presence is as much desired by God as it is needed by us. He invites with, "Call to me and I will answer you and tell you great and unsearchable things you do not know" (Jer. 33:3), and he promises, "You will seek me and find me when you seek me with all your heart" (29:13).

The fact of the matter is, however, that we, along with our mother Eve and father Adam, shrink from that awesome Presence; we find it much more natural to drift or run away from God than to draw near to him. Thus, we leave the church or tune out the preacher, return to old, sinful patterns of life, or simply stop meeting with God for prayer and Bible study. In this fallen world the "gravitational" pull downward of the world, the flesh, and the devil at times make a move toward God seem the most unnatural action in the world.

Writer and naturalist Annie Dillard tells of a cold Christmas Eve when she, then a young girl, and her family had come home from a late dinner out. Ginger ale and a plate of cookies sat on a special table. Dillard had taken off her winter coat and was warming herself on the heat register. Suddenly the front door opened and a person entered whom Dillard never wanted to meet— Santa Claus! The family called to her, "Look who's here! Look who's here!" Little Annie ran upstairs. She explains that she feared Santa Claus as "an old man whom you never saw, but who nevertheless saw you. He knew when you'd been bad or good! And I had been bad." Santa stood in the doorway, ringing the bell and shouting "Merry Christmas! Merry Christmas!" Annie never came down.

Dillard found out later that this Santa was really a "rigged-up" Miss White, the old lady who lived across the street. Miss White constantly reached out to young Annie, giving her cookies, teaching her finger painting, and generally instructing her about the things of the world. Annie liked Miss White; but one day, six months after the Santa incident, she ran from Miss White again. The lesson of the day involved a magnifying glass. The older lady focused a pinpoint of sunlight on Dillard's palm to let her feel the heat. The little girl was burned by accident. She ripped her hand away and dashed home crying. Miss White called after her, trying to explain, but to no avail.

Reflecting on how these experiences paralleled her relationship with God Dillard writes,

> Even now I wonder: if I meet God, will he take and hold my bare hand in his, and focus his eye on my palm, and kindle that spot and let me burn?
>
> But no. It is I who misunderstood everything and let everybody down. Miss White, God, I am sorry I ran from you. I am still running, running from that knowledge, that eye, that love from which there is no refuge. For you meant only love, and love, and I felt only fear, and pain. So once in Israel love came to us incarnate, stood in the doorway between two worlds, and we were all afraid.[19]

Like Dillard's Miss White, God calls out after us, trying to explain. He invites us out of our want into his supply, out of our spiritual cold into the warmth of his holy fire, out of our fear into trust and love. Yet we like half-starved, rain-soaked strays run from our source of true help. We fear the throne as a throne of judgment but doubt it as a throne of grace.

No, it is not natural to draw near to God; it is supernatural, and he has called us to himself away from the natural pulls and thoughts of the world. His invitation and promises still stand. Our part is to respond to his call and approach the throne. Our sympathetic high priest has experienced the temptation to bolt and run. He has been with us in our humanness and invites us to be with him at the throne of grace. Therefore, we may approach with unabashed boldness. Let us make that approach today, for we will surely find timely help for whatever we need.

---

19. Annie Dillard, *Teaching a Stone to Talk* (New York: HarperPerennial, 1992), 139–41.

Hebrews 5:1–10

EVERY HIGH PRIEST is selected from among men and is appointed to represent them in matters related to God, to offer gifts and sacrifices for sins. [2]He is able to deal gently with those who are ignorant and are going astray, since he himself is subject to weakness. [3]This is why he has to offer sacrifices for his own sins, as well as for the sins of the people.

[4]No one takes this honor upon himself; he must be called by God, just as Aaron was. [5]So Christ also did not take upon himself the glory of becoming a high priest. But God said to him,

"You are my Son;
today I have become your Father."

[6]And he says in another place,

"You are a priest forever,
in the order of Melchizedek."

[7]During the days of Jesus' life on earth, he offered up prayers and petitions with loud cries and tears to the one who could save him from death, and he was heard because of his reverent submission. [8]Although he was a son, he learned obedience from what he suffered [9]and, once made perfect, he became the source of eternal salvation for all who obey him [10]and was designated by God to be high priest in the order of Melchizedek.

THE MAIN BODY of the great discourse on Jesus' high priesthood (5:1–10:18) can be divided into two movements.[1] The first addresses the Son's appointment as high priest according to the order of Melchizedek (5:1–7:28) and is bracketed by an *inclusio*, a parallel statement marking the beginning and end of the section:

---

1. See the discussion of Hebrews' structure above, pp. 27–31.

Hebrews 5:1–3	Hebrews 7:27–28
[1]Every **high priest** is selected from among men and is **appointed** to represent them in matters related to God, **to offer** gifts and **sacrifices for sins**. [2]He is able to deal gently with those who are ignorant and are going astray, since he himself is **subject to weakness**. [3]This is why he has **to offer sacrifices for his own sins, as well as for the sins of the people**.	[27]Unlike the other high priests, he does not need **to offer sacrifices day after day, first for his own sins, and then for the sins of the people**. He sacrificed for **their sins** once for all when he **offered** himself. [28]For the law **appoints** as **high priests men** who are **weak**; but the oath, which came after the law, **appointed** the Son, who has been made perfect forever.

If we bracket the exhortation running from 5:11–6:20, the exposition in 5:1–7:28 may be divided into three subparts. The passage under consideration, 5:1–10, provides an introduction on the topic of Christ's appointment as a Melchizedekan high priest. Hebrews 7:1–10 continues with a discussion on the superiority of Melchizedek to the old covenant priesthood, and 7:11–28 concludes with proclamation of Christ, our Melchizedekan priest, as superior to the Levitical priesthood. Hebrews 5:1–10, therefore, introduces the reader to a discussion of the Son's appointment as a high priest according to the order of Melchizedek.

This present passage also may be divided into three clearly defined movements. Verses 1–4 are axiomatic in that they draw on universally understood (within a biblical framework) principles related to the office of high priest. As such they do not address Jesus' priesthood but rather the office of high priest as designed under the old covenant. The last of these principles shows that one becomes a high priest by God's appointment. As the next step in the discussion, verses 5–6 proclaim that Christ has been appointed a priest by God via the quotation of Psalm 110:4. The unit concludes with a powerful treatment on what might be called the "path of appointment" that the Son had to walk in order to qualify for being designated high priest by God—a path of obedience to suffering death.

Universal Principles of High Priesthood (5:1–4)

THE AUTHOR OUTLINES four main principles related to the office of high priest as described in the Old Testament:

1. The high priest originates from among people (v. 1).
2. The role of the high priest is to represent people in matters related to God, especially through offering gifts and sacrifices (vv. 1–2).

3. The high priest's weakness enables him to deal gently with people, and he is required to offer sacrifices for himself as well as for the people (vv. 2–3).
4. God is the One who confers the office of high priest by appointment (vv. 1, 4).

When the author states "every high priest"(v. 1), he begins to lay the groundwork for an argument that spans all the way to 10:18 (with the exception of 5:11–6:20), arguing for the superiority of Christ's high priesthood on the basis of commonly understood truths from the Old Testament concerning the office of high priest. Thus he points out that the role, the duty, and especially the appointment of the high priest are all governed by divine standards. In essence he asserts: "This is how the office of high priest works according to the Scriptures."

(1) The high priest has a solidarity with people because he is taken "from among" them. This statement perhaps alludes to Exodus 28:1: "Have Aaron your brother brought to you *from among* the Israelites." The Old Testament principle has to do with both the identity of the high priest with the people (the emphasis here) and the distinction made between the priests and the people—the priests have a special role to fill and, therefore, are called out to be distinct. Both the identity and the distinctiveness are important to that role.

With 5:1 the author, therefore, continues a theme treated extensively in 2:10–18: The Son came down "among humanity" to accomplish something on our behalf. Hebrews 2 ends with a statement of Christ's identity with people as their high priest (2:17–18). In 4:14–16 the author rejoins this motif with his treatment of Christ's sympathy for those being tempted. He now expounds on the topic, beginning with the universality of the principle: Priests come from among humanity.

(2) The high priest represents people "in matters related to God," especially in the offering of "gifts and sacrifices." According to the Old Testament, the high priest shares in the general responsibilities performed by all the priests, including leading in worship by participation in various offerings (Ex. 29:1–46; Lev. 1–6). However, the high priest alone offers the sacrifices on the Day of Atonement (Lev. 16:1–25), when he takes two goats and a ram from among the Israelites (16:5). After casting lots for the goats, the high priest slaughters one of the goats as a sin offering "for the people" (16:15), and the other goat is brought forth alive from the tent. The high priest lays his hands on the head of the "scapegoat," confessing all the sins of the people before the Lord, then sends the goat away into the desert (16:20–22). By carrying out this part of God's instructions for the Day of Atonement, the

high priest acts before God as a representative on behalf of the people, making atonement for their sins.

(3) The next principle relates to another important aspect of the Day of Atonement: The high priest must offer a special sacrifice for himself and his household before he can offer the goat sacrifices on behalf of the people. In this regard the Old Testament reads: "Aaron shall bring the bull for his own sin offering to make atonement for himself and his household, and he is to slaughter the bull for his own sin offering" (Lev. 16:11). This necessity stems from the priest's being "subject to weakness" (Heb. 5:2). The word translated "subject to" (*perikeimai*) means "to be surrounded" by something. For example, in Mark 9:42 and Luke 17:2 the word speaks of a millstone being "tied around" the scandal-maker's neck, and later in Hebrews the author crafts an effective word picture, using *perikeimai* to describe the great cloud of witnesses that "surrounds" the Christian community (Heb. 12:1). So here the priest finds himself closed in by his own weakness, obligated to offer sacrifices for his own sins.

This malady, however, has redemptive value in that it enables him "to deal gently with those who are ignorant and going astray" (v. 2). Those who deal with sinners can err in one of several extremes: bearing a Stoic indifference to the sin, manifesting a mushy sentimentality that plays down its significance, or expressing anger born of exasperation. What is needed is the highly valuable quality of forbearance, which deals with sin seriously and the sinner patiently.[2] This quality encourages openness on the part of the people toward their high priest.

F. F. Bruce suggests the phrase "those who are ignorant and going astray" should be taken as a hendiadys, meaning "those who go astray through ignorance." It was for just this type of person—the person who, because of human moral weakness, has unintentionally wandered off the path of right living—that God designed the old covenant sin offerings. The defiant sinner, however, blasphemes God and thus finds no such provision (Num. 15:29–30).[3]

(4) The author of Hebrews next proclaims that the office of high priest is not one for which a person can enlist; God himself confers the honor by appointment (e.g., Ex. 28:1; Lev. 8:1; Num. 16:5). In other words, the position of high priest derives from divine rather than human authority. God initiated the role of high priest, and any high priest thereafter must be called by God to be considered the authentic and authoritative representative for the people before God.

---

2. Bruce, *Epistle to the Hebrews*, 120; Westcott, *The Epistle to the Hebrews*, 119.
3. Bruce, *Epistle to the Hebrews*, 120–21.

The Appointment of Christ as High Priest (5:5–6)

THE WRITER OF Hebrews now turns from the universal principles related to the old covenant high priesthood to their specific manifestation in Christ. Just as Aaron was called by God (Heb. 5:4), so Christ himself did not "take upon himself the glory" but was appointed to the position. The author of Hebrews uses the verb "give glory" (*doxazo*) only here. Elsewhere in the book, however, he employs the cognate noun *doxa* ("glory") to speak of the Son being the "radiance of God's glory" (1:3),[4] "crowned ... with glory" (2:7, 9), "worthy of greater honor [glory] than Moses" (3:3), and the one to whom should be ascribed "glory for ever and ever" (13:21). In each instance the glory comes to Christ from another party or parties; he never garners glory for himself. In 5:5–6 the author focuses on the glory bestowed by God the Father on the occasion of the Son's appointment to high priesthood, finding evidence for this honor in Psalm 110:4.

Once again the author draws on the rabbinic technique of "verbal analogy" to set up his argument, coupling Psalm 2:7 and 110:4 by virtue of their common elements.[5] Both psalms contain a pronouncement by God in the second person ("You are ..."). Consequently, the ancient exegete finds in these two passages a declaration made by God to Jesus. Yet, if Hebrews 5:5–6 deals with Christ's appointment to the office of high priest, why does the author feel compelled to return to Psalm 2:7, a text quoted four chapters earlier at Hebrews 1:5? By reiterating Psalm 2:7 here the author shows that the exalted and incarnate Son (the twin themes of Hebrews 1–2) is the same one who has been appointed by God to a new and unique high priesthood. The writer, therefore, links the concepts of sonship and priesthood in his Christology.[6]

The Path to Appointment (5:7–10)

RATHER THAN JESUS' appointment to high priesthood being conferred simply by virtue of his relationship to God, the path to appointment was one of suffering, obedience, and endurance. This motif of suffering as the prerequisite to exaltation agrees with the writer's theology elsewhere (e.g., 2:9)[7] and is expressed here with stark, compelling images.

The phrase "during the days of Jesus' life on earth" makes an overt reference to Jesus' incarnation in general, but the rest of verses 7–8 hints at a spe-

---

4. See the discussion of the word rendered "radiance" above, pp. 47–48.
5. See the discussion of "verbal analogy" above, p. 67.
6. See Attridge, *The Epistle to the Hebrews*, 145–47.
7. See above, p. 100.

cific event—Jesus' agonizing surrender to the Father's will in the Garden of Gethsemane (Matt. 26:36–46; Mark 14:32–42; Luke 22:40–46). Although some commentators have found fault with linking this passage to the Gospel garden accounts,[8] others have understood "the one who could save him from death" as a clear allusion to Jesus' request for the cup of suffering to pass him by.[9] While the outcome of Gethsemane may suggest that God did not "hear" that prayer in the sense of exempting Christ from the cross experience, God did "hear" it, affirming the righteousness of his Son's reverent submission through the resurrection.[10]

The "cries and tears" (v. 7), although not part of the Gethsemane accounts, probably stem from one or more "prayers of the righteous sufferer" found in the Psalms.[11] It may be best to understand the author's words in Hebrews 5:7–8 as offering reflection on Jesus' experience in Gethsemane (a critical point of climax in the Passion) in light of early Christian appropriation of "righteous-sufferer" psalm material. Both the psalms of righteous suffering and the Gethsemane accounts portray "reverent submission" (v. 7). This phrase renders the Greek word *eulabeia*, which can also be translated "fear (in the sense of reverence) of God, piety." The Father attended to the Son's cries because of Jesus' posture of complete abandonment to the Father's will.

Up to this point in the book the author has placed great emphasis on the Son's exalted status, emphasizing his superiority in part on the basis of his unique relationship to God the Father (1:1–2, 5; 3:1–6). This filial relationship, however, did not make the path to appointment an easy one. The structure of the passage—"Although he was a son, he learned ..."—expresses what grammarians label a "contraexpectation," or what one might call a "sweet surprise."[12] In other words, the dynamics in the situation are not what you would expect. Unlike an ancient prince, on whom positions were

---

8. See the discussion by Attridge, *Epistle to the Hebrews*, 148–49.

9. E.g., Hugh Montefiore, *A Commentary on the Epistle to the Hebrews* (New York: Harper, 1964), 97–98; Kistemaker, *Hebrews*, 136; Bruce, *Epistle to the Hebrews*, 127; Moffat, 65–67; Hughes, *A Commentary on the Epistle to the Hebrews*, 182–86, who states, "The occasion intended is beyond doubt that of Christ's agony in the Garden of Gethsemane."

10. See Hagner, *Hebrews*, 81.

11. E.g., August Strobel, "Die Psalmengrundlage der Gethsemane-Parallele Hbr. 5,7ff.," *ZNW* 45 (1954): 252–66. Strobel suggests Psalm 116 forms the basis for Hebrews 5:7–8. That psalm states in part, "I love the LORD, for he heard my voice; he heard my cry for mercy. ... The cords of death entangled me, the anguish of the grave came upon me; I was overcome by trouble and sorrow. ... You, O LORD, have delivered my soul from death, my eyes from tears, my feet from stumbling." Psalm 22, a psalm the early church understood as referring to the Gethsemane experience, offers another viable backdrop, placing great emphasis on the "cry" of the righteous sufferer.

12. I am indebted to my friend J. Scott Duvall for this designation.

bestowed by lineage, this divine Son was called to walk a path of obedience through suffering.

When the author says that Christ "learned obedience" and was "made perfect," he is not suggesting that the Son had been disobedient and flawed (cf. 4:15). Rather, Jesus' call involved walking obediently all the way to the end of a path to which the Father had appointed him. That he "learned obedience" means that the Son arrived "at a new stage of experience," having passed through the school of suffering.[13] Perfection refers to the Son's having "graduated" from that school, accomplishing the mission and making it to the end of that path of passion.

Hebrews 5:9–10 proclaims the happy result of the Son's reaching this perfection: He became "the source of eternal salvation." The affirmation links the perfection process closely to the cross, where our great high priest offered up himself as the sacrifice for sin. For the author of Hebrews it is the blood of Christ shed in his suffering death that opens the door to salvation.

Salvation comes, however, to those who "obey" him. With the exception of its use at Acts 12:13, the verb *hypakouo* always means "to obey" in the sense of submitting one's will, understanding, conduct, or allegiance to the will of another.[14] Just as Jesus "learned obedience" in his earthly suffering, he calls people to respond in obedience to his will. Just as Jesus persevered, reverently bending his will to that of the Father in spite of extreme suffering, so Christians are called to total abandonment to the divine will; this call does not change with the onslaught of persecution.

This unit concludes with the preacher's reiterating that as a result of the Son's suffering, he has been appointed by God to fill the position of high priest according to "the order of Melchizedek." This final statement plays an important role as a transition to the discussion of Melchizedek beginning in earnest at 7:1.[15]

Bridging Contexts

WHEN THE STUDENT of Hebrews sits down to interpret 5:1–10 for the modern church, the unique position and the importance of the passage in the book must be kept in mind. The author situated this passage to accomplish a specific task, and if one passes it over quickly, the intended impact might be lost. These ten strategic verses, sandwiched as they are between broad sweeps of exhortation, demand quick

---

13. Hagner, *Hebrews*, 82.
14. Spicq, *Theological Lexicon of the New Testament*, 1:446–50.
15. See below, p. 252.

changes in the reader's orientation from the author's challenge to his listeners (3:1–4:16) to his exposition on the person of Christ (5:1–10) and back again to direct challenge (5:11–6:20).

The dynamic of reading through this portion of Hebrews resembles driving through a city and being forced to follow a map closely in order to make turn after quick turn to arrive at the desired destination. In keeping on track with those quick turns one tends to miss the scenery. Therefore, the process of interpretation demands that we slow down long enough to reflect on the "why" and the "how" underlying this text, and this deliberate deceleration must be accomplished on at least two levels. (1) We must begin by considering the dynamics related to the whole, specifically the structure and the purpose of the passage. (2) We must then turn to analyze the proclamations and interpretive pitfalls of each of the unit's three distinct parts.

Structure and purpose. The passage before us forms a well-organized whole that starts with universal principles concerning the old covenant office of high priest (5:1–4) and moves to a specific manifestation of those principles in the new high priest, Christ (5:5–10). The structure of the author's exposition may be depicted as follows:[16]

A The old office of high priest (v. 1)
   B The sacrifice offered by the high priest (v. 1)
      C The weakness of the high priest (vv. 2–3)
         D The appointment of the high priest (v. 4)
         D' The appointment of Christ, the new priest (vv. 5–6)
      C' The suffering of the new priest (vv. 7–8)
   B' The sacrificial provision of the new priest (v. 9)
A' The new office of high priest (v. 10)

This type of structure is called a *chiasmus* and was used by the ancients for both rhetorical effect and mnemonic purposes.

Rhetorically the passage flows smoothly from the general statements on high priesthood in verse 1, to the pinnacle statements on appointment in verses 4–6, to the general statement on Christ's priesthood in verse 10. This orderly presentation pleases the ear as the discourse moves logically from step to step. As a memory device the original hearers would have been able to grasp the section's main points since the author's teachings on the old covenant priesthood and his teachings on the priesthood of Christ mirror one another, the correspondences knitting the passage together around the theme of appointment. Thus, rather than forming a fragmented collection of ran-

---

16. The following is based roughly on Lane, *Hebrews 1–8*, 111.

dom thoughts, Hebrews 5:1–10 offers a carefully crafted reflection on the nature of Jesus' call by God the Father.

The introduction in verse 1, the conclusion in verse 10, and pinnacle of the chiasmus (vv. 4–6) all focus the passage on the theme of appointment. As such the passage admirably accomplishes its role as an introduction to Christ's Melchizedekan appointment. The author does not intend this section, as an introduction, to raise all the pertinent issues related to the high priesthood of the Son; he carries out that task in the following chapters. Rather, the unit serves to provide the broad sweep of his priestly ministry, grounding his high-priestly Christology in the Old Testament. Furthermore, the writer rivets the hearers' attention on a new and vital subject in his sermon, capturing their attention with his well-crafted parallels and gripping word pictures.

This introduction, in other words, shifts attention to the new topic of high priesthood, anchors the topic as applied to Christ in divine decree, and reflects on it eloquently in light of both Psalms material and Gospel narrative—quite an accomplishment in only ten verses!

Reading the Old Testament with the author of Hebrews. Each of the passage's three movements confront the interpreter with both hermeneutical pitfalls and possibilities for further understanding of Hebrews. The first movement (5:1–4), which deals with the old covenant office of high priest, may seem fairly straightforward at first glance. Yet these verses once again raise the issue of how the author reads his Scriptures. A danger lies in making the assumption that the way he reads the Old Testament corresponds exactly with the way we read the Old Testament. Our paradigms of Old Testament interpretation, therefore, must be considered in light of the author's own intention at this point in Hebrews.

For example, I have seen some preachers or teachers take Old Testament material and identify allegorical parallels between the minutia of the law and new covenant realities. Each small detail of the tabernacle, for instance, is understood as an allusion to greater Christian realities. The various items of the high priest's clothing represent various aspects of Christian character. A preacher reading Hebrews 5:1–4 might be tempted to import information from the Old Testament passages behind this text in ways that would be inappropriate hermeneutically and distract from the author's real purpose.

We must keep in mind a basic principle held by the original preacher of this passage: There exist both continuities and discontinuities between the old and the new covenants. The older realities are vitally important, being both authoritative and informative. As this passage clearly points out, however, there are dynamics in which the new does not continue the pattern of the old. Jesus has not sinned and does not need to offer sacrifice for his own sins (cf. 5:3).

What, then, does the author intend to communicate in verses 1–4? He proclaims that an authoritative and authentic high priest must both identify with and be distinct from those to whom he ministers. His identity lies in his humanity. In the case of the old covenant priest, that humanity manifested itself in his being cornered by sin. Sin for this priest was inevitable and, therefore, had to be atoned for. This solidarity with other human beings, however, enabled him to understand and show sympathy for the plight of God's people.

As important as such solidarity was for the high priest's role, his distinction from God's people was equally important. The high priest had been appointed by God to represent the people through the offering of gifts and sacrifices. No one else in the community could carry out that task on the Day of Atonement. There were no "pinch hitters." That God himself appointed a special person to the duty bears witness to the gravity of this responsibility. Therefore, the writer to the Hebrews uses 5:1–4 to prepare the way for a discussion of both Christ's identity with human sufferers and the distinct honor of his divine appointment.

Power moves. When we come to the quotations of Psalm 2:7 and 110:4, the critical interpretive step is to ask why the two are juxtaposed here—that is, to move below the surface statements of these Old Testament passages to their underlying intention. After reading these quotations one might be tempted to respond, "OK, Jesus is a son and Jesus is a high priest." Yet, there is much more here than basic information. The author ties the two texts together through verbal analogy[17] to build what might be called an authority base, that is, a basis for why the readers should respond to Jesus. The first two chapters of Hebrews turn at critical points on the issue of authority. For example, the effectiveness of the "argument from lesser to greater" in Hebrews 2:1–4 depends on the authority of the Son established in 1:5–14.[18]

As he introduces the book's great central section on Jesus' superior priesthood and offering (5:1–10:18), the author must begin by establishing the authority of Christ in a different vein, redirecting the argument toward the concept of Jesus' position and sacrifice as means of true relationship to God. To do that, he builds on the authority established in chapters 1–2 by again quoting Psalm 2:7. His new topic of high priesthood, therefore, is infused with "authority" from the beginning. All that he will say about the high priesthood of Christ in the coming chapters flows from divine mandate. This is not just wrangling about obscure theological concepts. Rather, what the author wishes to say about Christ's appointment to the position of high priest derives from the heart of God, a fact witnessed to by the authority of God's decree.

---

17. On the use of this rabbinic technique in Hebrews see above, pp. 25, 67.
18. See above, pp. 84–85.

Thus the author has a great deal vested in this part of Hebrews, and his quotation of two Old Testament passages goes far beyond mere religious instruction. Underlying the presentation of these two messianic psalms is the author's goal of motivating his hearers to perseverance with nothing less than the authority of God himself. It is time for them and for us to sit up and take notice, to take this sermon seriously.

Was Jesus not already perfect? In my class on Hebrews, Exam 1 has this question (I am sure I at least have my students' attention at this point in the commentary!):

> *A junior-high student in your midweek Bible study comes to you and pleads, "Hebrews 5:9 says that Jesus 'learned obedience' and 'became perfect.' Does that mean that Jesus was not perfect before that? Does it mean that Jesus had not been obedient to God before that?" You notice a tear slowly making its way down her cheek. But you have had this class and exclaim, "Don't cry, little girl! That's not what this passage means. It means:....."*

The hypothetical girl's question poses significant interpretive issues for us. The passage can be taken out of context and hijacked to support the position that Jesus' identity with us extends to his having actually shared our moral imperfection, a state, some reason, necessary for Christ's ministry to humanity.[19] This perspective fits the old saw, "You cannot really speak to people about the moral problem of overdrinking unless you yourself have been a drunk." Yet the early Christians witnessed extensively to the sinlessness of Christ.[20]

We must grasp the significance of the terms *perfect* and *obedience* in this passage and see how they fit with the broader biblical concept of the "righteous sufferer." Rather than conveying the idea of overcoming a moral deficiency, the aorist passive participle *teleiotheis* (translated as "once made perfect" by the NIV) communicates the concept of "finishing" or "completing." By making it all the way to the end of his Passion, Jesus was made "complete" in the sense of being able to fulfill his role as our high priest. He finished the course. He drank the full measure of the experience that was needed in order to come before the throne with a sacrifice with which our sins would be addressed. Moreover, that he "learned obedience" means that the Son said "yes" to the Father's will in an extreme situation that he had not yet encountered.

There are at least three levels on which the action of Jesus portrayed in verses 7–8 offers us help. (1) Jesus' perseverance has made him a fit high priest, for which I owe him praise and obedience (vv. 8–9). His appointment

---

19. See Buchanan, *To the Hebrews*, 130.
20. See Heb. 4:15; also John 7:18; 8:46; 14:30; 2 Cor. 5:21; 1 Peter 1:19; 2:22; 3:18; 1 John 3:5, 7.

and consequent role of high priest make him distinct from me in relation to God and the rest of humanity. (2) As a "righteous sufferer" Jesus can identify with me in my suffering for the kingdom of God. He has felt pain; he has known the anguish of a gut-wrenching temptation to break and run at real danger (4:15). (3) Because of his perseverance through extreme suffering, Jesus offers a fitting example for us of what it means to relinquish control of our lives, deferring to the will of God.

WHAT MOTIVATES ME in my pursuit of God? The area of human behavioral science, that is, investigation into why humans do what they do, makes for fascinating study. Are we molded by social context or physiology? Do extrinsic or intrinsic dynamics pull the levers that drive our lives? In other words, what makes us tick? What makes us take one course of action and not another?

The world of advertising has a great deal at stake in being able to read human behavior—about $100,000,000,000 worth per year in the United States; that's more than the rest of the world combined. I think a good portion of that comes to my home in the form of junk mail! One phone company has been sending me checks, trying to get me to switch from another. I am told I need a new shampoo, a different make of car, the latest brand of jeans, and a strange-name cologne (does anyone understand those commercials?); evidently most banks in the United States have a card with a better interest rate than the one I now carry. What feels good, looks sharp, or works well motivates us.

In this social context of glitz and video clips, divine decree seems terribly out of place. It would be beastly hard to sell the concept on the open market (e.g., in a book), unless, of course we were making decrees about the divine. In his little essay "God in the Dock," C. S. Lewis wrote:

> The ancient man approached God (or even the gods) as the accused person approaches his judge. For the modern man the roles are reversed. He is the judge: God is in the dock. He is quite a kindly judge: if God should have a reasonable defense for being the god who permits war, poverty and disease, he is ready to listen to it. The trial may even end in God's acquittal. But the important thing is that Man is on the Bench and God in the dock.[21]

---

21. C. S. Lewis, "God in the Dock," in *God in the Dock: Essays on Theology and Ethics,* ed. Walter Hooper (Grand Rapids: Eerdmans, 1970), 244.

This does not represent the worldview of Hebrews. According to our author, divine decree should mean something to us; it should constitute *the* motive for action in our lives. We must sit up and take notice of what God has said and its implications for our lives. Specifically, we should recognize that Jesus' role as a representative on behalf of people has been made distinct by divine decree. Just as the high priest of the old covenant was appointed as a special representative before God on behalf of people, so Jesus plays a unique role in our relationship with God. He is both Authority and Answer to our deepest need—the need for a healthy relationship with God.

As an appropriate application of Hebrews 5:1–10, therefore, we might begin by reflecting on our current motivations for engaging in Christ-following. Why are you doing what you are doing? Why am I? Is the fact that God has appointed Jesus to a position of honor in which we are called to "obey" him significant for us as motivation for continuing in our commitment? Or are we more moved (as is evident by our actions and decisions) by the call of our world's system of values (even in our pursuit of Christianity)? Danger lies in embracing the world's value system, for she is a mother who often eats her young.

Jesus' prayer of relinquishment and ours. My wife and I currently are in the throes of parenting a preschooler, an exciting (we love parenting), frustrating (some moments we do not like parenting), and awe-filled responsibility. The "struggle of the will" certainly comprises a prominent theme at this stage of the parent-child relationship. The attempt to strike the balance between authoritarian parenting (forcefully denying the healthy growth of the child's will by completely subsuming it under the will of the parent) and permissive parenting (subjugating healthy processes and relationships in the family to the will of an immature child) is a full-time job. Teaching the child that one does not always get what one desires proves vital for healthy family life. The child must learn to surrender willfulness as a normal part of maturation in relation to others. Thus relinquishment may not be "natural"—any of us falls prey to our own self-centeredness when left to natural pulls and processes—but it is vital to a fulfilling and joyful life. I am happy to say that our daughter is learning the art and gives us great joy.

Just as a child must learn to relinquish willfulness if the natural processes of maturation are to take place, so we as spiritual children of God must learn to submit our wills to the will of the Father as we move on in the faith. Richard Foster, in his book *Prayer: Finding the Heart's True Home*, begins the chapter on "The Prayer of Relinquishment" with an analogy between human and spiritual development:

> As we are learning to pray we discover an interesting progression. In the beginning our will is in struggle with God's will. We beg. We

pout. We demand. We expect God to perform like a magician or shower us with blessings like Father Christmas. We major in instant solutions and manipulative prayers.

As difficult as this time of struggle is, we must never despise it or try to avoid it. It is an essential part of our growing and deepening in things spiritual. To be sure, it is an inferior stage, but only in the sense that a child is at an inferior stage to that of an adult. The adult can reason better and carry heavier loads because both brain and brawn are more fully developed, but the child is doing exactly what we would expect at that age. So it is in the life of the spirit.

In time, however, we begin to enter into a grace-filled releasing of our will and a flowing into the will of the Father. It is the Prayer of Relinquishment that moves us from the struggling to the releasing.[22]

Thankfully, we have the supreme example of relinquishment in the person of Jesus. The picture of Jesus in the Garden of Gethsemane I remember most from my childhood has the Lord kneeling serenely beside a great boulder, hands folded and body bathed in the warmth of the Father's light. That is not the picture I get as I read the Gospels, nor is it the scene described in Hebrews 5:7–8. Agony. Turmoil. Struggle. All emotions with which we can identify. There in Gethsemane we see Jesus' inner fight to bow before the Father all the way to the end of the path on which his feet had been placed. The Son was not feeling peaceful and warm emotions as he contemplated the gruesome fate of a Roman cross. His reflections were pain-racked.

Only to a certain extent can we empathize with Jesus. He alone could bear that particular moment, that responsibility. Yet we must empathize with him as much as we can. We too know how difficult surrender comes. Realizing the pressure of our will vis-à-vis God's will, we should stop and praise Jesus for his surrender and praise God for such a high priest, who can in turn empathize with those who are suffering for the sake of righteousness.

Furthermore, we should follow Jesus' example of completely relinquishing our wills to the will of the Father. What is the problem with that spiritual-sounding directive? We want to walk with God in the Garden of Eden ("God bless my life! Let me know you."), never having entered the Garden of Gethsemane. Yet the two gardens are a package tour with a specific itinerary. In reality the tour lasts a lifetime as we move from the one to the other. Andrew Murray writes:

The Spirit teaches me to yield my will entirely to the will of the Father. He opens my ear to wait in great gentleness and teachableness of soul

---

22. Richard Foster, *Prayer: Finding the Heart's True Home* (New York: HarperCollins, 1992), 47.

for what the Father has day by day to speak and to teach. He discovers to me how union with God's will is union with God Himself; how entire surrender to God's will is the Father's claim, the Son's example, and the true blessedness of the soul.[23]

This daily process of learning to relinquish my will to the will of God demands a maturation that moves me beyond the limitations of emotions. I must be able to say "yes" to the heavenly Father and his ways in the face of emotion-twisting pulls and poundings by the world. H. A. Hodges writes, "By our steady adherence to God when the affections [i.e., emotions] are dried up, and nothing is left but the naked will clinging blindly to him, the soul is purged of self-regard and trained in pure love."[24] May we be so trained.

> O Lord, how do I let go when I'm so unsure of things? I'm unsure of your will, and I'm unsure of myself.... That really isn't the problem at all, is it? The truth of the matter is I hate the very idea of letting go. I really want to be in control. No, I *need* to be in control. That's it, isn't it? I'm afraid to give up control, afraid of what might happen. Heal my fear, Lord.
>
> How good of you to reveal my blind spots even in the midst of my stumbling attempts to pray. Thank you!
>
> But now what do I do? How do I give up control? Jesus, please, teach me your way of relinquishment.[25]

---

23. Andrew Murray, as quoted in Foster, *Prayer: Finding the Heart's True Home*, 47.

24. H. A. Hodges, as quoted in Lorenzo Scupoli, *Unseen Warfare* (London: Faber and Faber, 1952), 31–32.

25. Foster, *Prayer: Finding the Heart's True Home*, 56.

Hebrews 5:11–6:3

W E HAVE MUCH to say about this, but it is hard to explain because you are slow to learn. ¹²In fact, though by this time you ought to be teachers, you need someone to teach you the elementary truths of God's word all over again. You need milk, not solid food! ¹³Anyone who lives on milk, being still an infant, is not acquainted with the teaching about righteousness. ¹⁴But solid food is for the mature, who by constant use have trained themselves to distinguish good from evil.

⁶:¹Therefore let us leave the elementary teachings about Christ and go on to maturity, not laying again the foundation of repentance from acts that lead to death, and of faith in God, ²instruction about baptisms, the laying on of hands, the resurrection of the dead, and eternal judgment. ³And God permitting, we will do so.

IF YOU HAVE ever been in a conversation that suddenly switched topics, you know that a sudden change can rivet the hearer's attention; one has to listen carefully to grasp the new topic and adjust to the conversation's new direction. In public oratory such a shift in theme can be used powerfully as a rhetorical tool. Such is the author's intention in Hebrews 5:11–6:3. Having begun his discourse on Christ's appointment as a superior high priest,[1] the author suddenly breaks off the topic and turns to confront his audience directly with the problem of their spiritual immaturity. The writer follows with a blistering warning against falling away from Christ (6:4–8), which in turn is followed by an expression of encouragement and confidence in the hearers' commitment (6:9–12). This balanced section of exhortation can be diagrammed as shown on the following page.

Thus the author both confronts and comforts as he warns this church concerning the dangers of falling away from Christ.

As the first piece in this puzzle, 5:11–6:3 focuses attention on the issue of spiritual immaturity. In 5:11–14 the author offers a bald assessment of his hearers' current condition. They exhibit a dullness as learners of God's truth,

---

1. See an explanation of the structure of 5:1–7:28 above, pp. 185–86.

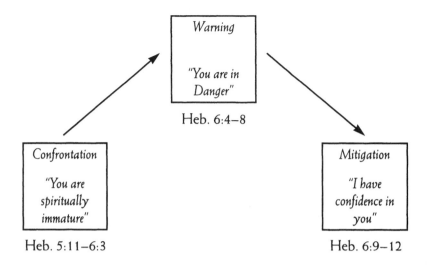

Exhortation in Hebrews 5:11–6:3

even though they have been engaged in the Christian walk long enough now to be teachers of others. The preacher likens them to infants still at a mother's breast, who cannot handle more substantive fare. Then in 6:1–3 he exhorts them to move on in the faith, progressing beyond the elementary teachings about Christ.

The Author Confronts the Hearers (5:11–14)

THE OPENING STATEMENT, rendered "We have much to say about this" by the NIV, refers to the author's declaration in verse 10 concerning the appointment of Christ as a "high priest in the order of Melchizedek." Indeed, the author does say a great deal about Christ's Melchizedekan high priesthood when he returns to this topic in chapter 7. This theme "is hard to explain," not because the motif itself resists explication, but because those being confronted have become spiritually hard of hearing.

The author articulates the slowness of learning of his readers with the words *nothroi … tais akoais.* In the ancient world the first of these words (*nothros*) could mean "sluggish, dull, dimwit, negligent, lazy." It was used in extrabiblical literature, for example, of a slave with ears "stopped up" by laziness, who was thus not obedient instantly to the call of his master. In the sphere of athletics, the word could designate a competitor who was out of shape, lazy, and sluggish. In a Christian inscription from Eumeneia a man who had used his own resources to build a tomb for his sisters calls his older brother, Amianos, "negligent," since it was he who had the responsibility to carry out the task and failed to do so. In other words, *nothros* connotes culpable negligence or sluggishness in some aspect of life. Moreover, that the recipients of this letter are lazy "in hearing" (*akoais*) points to their inattention to the public proclamation of biblical teachings. This passage, therefore, calls to mind the author's previous exhortation in 2:1 to "pay more careful attention ... to what we have heard."

However, our preacher finds the hearers' condition especially egregious in light of their long-term involvement in the church. By now they "ought to be teachers," but instead need someone else to teach them. The content of the needed instruction is described as "the elementary truths [*stoicheia*] of God's word." The phrase in Greek may be translated woodenly as "the basic principles of the beginning of the words of God." *Stoicheia*, as used in the broader literature of the era, sometimes had strongly metaphysical overtones, referring to spiritual beings of the universe. Here, however, it refers clearly to the elementary teachings of the Christian faith. Thus, this word's use in 5:12 is more in line with those places in ancient literature where it refers to the elements of the alphabet or the most basic aspects of education.[2] In line with this interpretation the NEB translates this phrase "the ABC of God's oracles."

Two other parts of verse 12 suggest that the author has in mind basic teachings, perhaps offered at the beginning of one's Christian commitment. (1) He states that the hearers need these basic lessons "again" (*palin*), a word that in context points to a time in the past in which they all did receive the instruction. The author seems to assume that they were all exposed at one time to such teaching. (2) The woodenly translated phrase (see previous paragraph) contains the word "beginning" (*arche*). This word adds emphasis to the rudimentary nature of these teachings.

This delineation of different levels in the educational process and the use of "milk" and "solid food" as metaphors for basic over against advanced teachings were common in the ancient world and apparently were brought over into the pedagogical language of the early church (e.g., 1 Cor. 3:1–2; 1 Peter 2:2).[3] So when the author exclaims, "You need milk, not solid food" (Heb. 5:12), he is describing in no uncertain terms a level of immaturity among his readers. Spiritually they are acting like babies still suckling at a mother's breast, unconcerned with the rich, hearty foods of the adults' table.

Consequently, the addressees of Hebrews are "not acquainted with the teaching about righteousness" (5:13). What the author has in mind by "teaching about righteousness" has been interpreted variously by scholars as "right speech," "moral teachings," "general teachings of Christianity," or "the theo-

---

2. Attridge, *The Epistle to the Hebrews*, 158.
3. Bruce, *Epistle to the Hebrews*, 135.

logical instructions on Christ as the believer's righteousness."[4] The "teaching about righteousness," however, may refer to advanced theological instruction that stresses the cost and responsibilities of discipleship. Lane points to uses of this phrase in the second century that place it in the context of Christian suffering under persecution. Polycarp taught, for example, that to obey fully the word of righteousness one must be willing to endure the severest mistreatment.[5] Lane comments:

> If this is the proper linguistic context for interpreting v 13, it suggests that what was involved in the regression of the community was a failure in moral character rather than in keen theological insight. The expression ... acknowledges a basic moral weakness aggravated by the fear of violent death (cf. 2:14–15). If the community had begun to avoid contact with outsiders because they were unprepared for martyrdom, a social setting is established for the rebuke of v 12, for the reference to the sharpening of one's faculties in the arena of moral decision in v 14, and for the prospect of crucifying the Son of God again and exposing him to public shame in 6:6.[6]

Because of the context and the author's emphases here, the moral failure in the face of persecution must be understood as stemming from a lack of response to theological instruction (cf. 2:1–4). These milk drinkers are in a perilous situation because they have neither an understanding nor an inclination toward deeper matters of the faith by which one understands the importance and means of perseverance. The writer's statement that they need again to be taught the basics shows how far they have regressed in the way of right Christian response to theological truth.

"The mature" (v. 14), on the other hand, are able to handle "solid food" (i.e., the advanced teachings of the faith), such as the author's exposition on Christ's priesthood, which will follow in chapters 7–10. Their adeptness at digesting such instructions stems from a spiritual condition consisting of certain spiritual abilities. The word translated incorrectly as "constant use" (*hexis*) by the NIV has been widely misinterpreted to mean "practice" or "exercise." The word, rather, connotes a "state" or "condition."[7] The mature are those who, because of a mature spiritual condition, possess trained faculties that enable discernment of good and evil. In other words, they know how to

---

4. See the discussion in Lane, *Hebrews 1–8*, 137–38.

5. See Polycarp's Letter to the Philippians 8:1–9:1.

6. Lane, *Hebrews 1–8*, 138.

7. John A. L. Lee, "Hebrews 5:14 and 'ΕΞΙΣ: A History of Misunderstanding," *NovT* 39 (1997): 151–76.

make the right choices when confronted with critical decisions. The author wishes to challenge his hearers with this image of maturity that they might wade with him into the deeper waters of the following chapters. His hope is that they will repent of their spiritual immaturity, grasp hold of the deeper matters of the faith, and, ultimately, endure in the face of persecution.

Moving on to Maturity (6:1–3)

HAVING ASSESSED THE spiritual condition of his listeners in 5:11–14, the author moves on to challenge them to correct their present course and move on to maturity. He expresses the challenge both positively (v. 1a) and negatively (vv. 1b–2), concluding with a statement of resolve (v. 3). As Bruce notes, the opening words of this unit are not quite what one would expect. The author has just used strong metaphors to describe their immaturity and consequent inability to handle advanced teaching. We might have expected him to acquiesce to their infantile appetites (e.g., "So we must begin where we are"; cf. 1 Cor. 3:2). If they needed to be taught the elementary principles of the faith again, should he not do so? Instead, the preacher pushes them toward an "adult table" fit for mature appetites. The "therefore" of verse 1 demonstrates his determination to move his readers on from their present state of immaturity. They are not responding to their circumstances as spiritual grown-ups, *therefore*, it is time to move from the children's to the adults' menu, leaving behind fundamental teachings.[8]

Throughout his exhortations to this community the author uses the plural pronouns "we" and "us," thus including himself in the action that must be taken by those in the community: "Let us leave...." The switch back and forth between the second person plural "you," the first person "I," and the first person plural "we" was common to the style of preaching found in the Greek-speaking Jewish synagogues of the period.[9] Moreover, the verb rendered "go on" is passive. Hughes suggests it means, "Let us be carried on," implying that it is not up to the preacher to bear the community forward, but rather God, who will move both the author and the community forward together in the process of maturation.[10]

This move forward, however, begins by leaving something behind. When the author suggests they "leave" the elementary truths of the faith, he does not see these Christian principles as dispensable. Indeed, they are no more dispensable than are letters of the alphabet for moving children beyond the first steps of education. Rather, the fundamental truths of the faith are pre-

---

8. Bruce, *Epistle to the Hebrews*, 138.
9. Thyen, *Der Stil des jüdisch-hellenistischen Homilie*, 17.
10. Hughes, *A Commentary on the Epistle to the Hebrews*, 194.

supposed in the continued trek toward maturity. The admonition of 6:1 has to do with the listeners' indifference to weightier matters of Christ-following and their consequent need to move to a new level of commitment.

The six "foundational" tenets listed in 6:1b–2 all find parallels within Judaism and its basic practices of religion. As proposed by Hagner, "this may suggest that the readers were attempting somehow to remain within Judaism by emphasizing items held in common between Judaism and Christianity. They may have been trying to survive with a minimal Christianity in order to avoid alienating their Jewish friends or relatives."[11] Moreover, commentators have noticed that the six fall into three groups: (1) "repentance from acts that lead to death, and of faith in God"; (2) "instruction about baptisms, the laying on of hands"; and (3) "the resurrection of the dead, and eternal judgment." Yet, it may be best to interpret the word "instruction" as in apposition to "foundation."[12] When read in this manner, teachings "about baptisms, the laying on of hands, resurrection of the dead, and eternal judgment" fill out the content of the foundation of repentance and faith. If this interpretation is correct, the structure of the passage may be depicted as follows:

not laying again	*the foundation of repentance and faith*
	=
instruction about	baptisms
	laying on of hands
	resurrection
	eternal judgment

The "repentance from dead works" and "faith toward God" (NRSV) constitute a summing up of the initial step of Christian commitment. The former refers to the turning away from acts of immorality committed by those apart from God (cf. Rom. 6:21), and the latter the basic orientation for those who have turned to God in belief and obedience.

Although the "baptisms" has been understood by many commentators to refer to specifically Christian baptism, the plural makes this interpretation problematic. It may be that the word refers instead to the internal spiritual cleansing from sins found in the new covenant, which was associated with the outward rite of baptism. Or the author may be referring to repeated ceremonial washings as found in expressions of first-century Judaism.

The "laying on of hands" was also a practice associated with the beginning of Christian commitment, specifically having to do with the coming of the Holy Spirit or anointing for ministry.

---

11. Hagner, *Hebrews*, 87.
12. Bruce, *Epistle to the Hebrews*, 138–39; Lane, *Hebrews 1–8*, 140.

If these two "instructions" have to do with the beginning stages of Christian commitment, "resurrection of the dead" and "eternal judgment" provide theological cornerstones related to the end of the age.

The author sums up the admonition to move on from these basic teachings by expressing his confidence in the move forward. "God permitting," he writes in verse 3, "we will do so." This statement at once expresses the author's confidence in the hearers, which he will reiterate at 6:9–10, and his own submission to God's will.[13] Although such expressions of piety were common to rabbinic Judaism, they were also used broadly in classical Greek literature.[14]

WHILE AT A local video store not long ago, I was browsing the "New Releases" section when the box of one video caught my eye. The movie, an updated version of *Pinnochio*, sported a catchy, 3-D cover that changed pictures as I walked past. At first the picture of Pinnochio was that of a wooden marionette held by its maker. As my angle of vision changed, however, the puppet transformed into a human boy, the actor who played the role in the movie. Both pictures were on the cover of the box, but my position determined which I saw at a given moment.

Because much preaching we hear presents the Bible in the form of propositions, we tend to look for the "point 1, point 2, point 3" instruction, which an author wishes to communicate through the text. However, some passages are of another nature, reflecting a *situation* of the author, or the hearers, or a third party. Such passages have inherent principles that often are of great significance for Christian living. Yet, these principles come by way of observing examples or situations—by looking at the text from a different angle. We can ask, for instance, what a particular text reflects about the author's approach to a difficult situation or what the circumstance reflects about life in the early church.

Hebrews 5:11–6:3 is such a passage. The language, although rich in imagery and nuance, is fairly straightforward. What can we glean from this text, then, that might be applicable for modern believers seeking to live as faithful Christians in today's world? What truths are inherent in the author's example or his listeners' situation?

Rhetorical impact. We must first understand that the writer crafts this passage for rhetorical impact. Some might misunderstand this break in the dis-

---

13. Cf. 1 Cor. 16:7; James 4:15.
14. Ellingworth, *The Epistle to the Hebrews*, 317.

course on "Appointment" [15] to suggest an awkwardness on the part of the writer. They ask, "Why does the author start a topic and then, almost immediately, leave it for another topic, which will in turn be followed by the original topic? It does not make sense!" Others might misunderstand the break as having to do with the ignorance of the audience based on the author's words: "It is hard to explain because you are slow to learn" (5:11). These interpreters understand the ancient preacher to be talking down his nose to his congregants.

However, this breaking off from the discourse on "Appointment," rather than reflecting the preacher's ineptitude or a lack in the congregation's learning skills, provides us with another glimpse at his admirable skill in oratory. That he inserts 5:11–6:20 just after an introduction to the heart of his sermon demonstrates this exhortation's importance. In effect, he wishes to make sure he has their attention before entering into a lengthy but vital exposition on the high priesthood and heavenly offering of Jesus. As the ancient preacher John Chrysostom suggested long ago, following this blistering, though mitigated, rebuke, the hearers' ears would have been turned vigorously toward the speaker when he resumed his discussion of Melchizedek at 7:1.[16]

With 5:11–6:3 the author begins by confronting the congregation with their spiritual condition. Having used both the positive and negative examples of others,[17] he now gets down to addressing their conduct. Thus, he fittingly confronts them with the chief concern on his mind—their spiritual condition—at a key point in the book. This rhetorical approach speaks more to the author's packaging of principles than to the principles themselves.

The social situation. Let us take a step back for a moment and observe the social situation reflected in the text. What is going on here? Is the author, a spiritual leader for the congregation being addressed, acting in an authoritarian manner, emotionally bludgeoning his listeners because of their failures? Is he angry or talking down to them as a spiritual superior to mere children? His words do seem harsh at points. However, the broader context of Hebrews projects an image far from that of an irate prelate attempting to intimidate his flock into submission. Rather, he must be understood as a pastor whose confrontation in 5:11–6:3 flows from a wellspring of Christian love and concern.

This passage suggests to us that loving, well-thought-out confrontation comprises an important aspect of Christian community. Such admonition

---

15. See above, pp. 185–86.

16. Chrysostom, "ʹOMIΛIA IBʹ," in J.-P. Mingne, ed., *Patrologia Graeca* (Paris, 1862), 63:423.

17. E.g., Heb. 3:1–6 and 3:7–19.

must be well-timed, must be offered with the right motives (the author obviously wants them to change for their own spiritual well-being rather than for his reputation or benefit), and must be offered both with encouragement (he will quickly turn to mitigation at 6:9) and with specific suggestions for action.

Early church life. By looking at the passage from another angle we learn something important about life among the earliest Christian congregations: education in Christian teachings was seen as vital and seems to have been carried out systematically. The author, by mentioning the "elementary truths of God's word" in 5:12 and providing a list of those truths in 6:1–2, opens a window for us on life in ancient Christian communities. The term "elementary" (i.e., basic principles) itself indicates both a distinction between levels of instruction and a time at which those instructions were given—at the beginning of one's Christian commitment. When the author uses the metaphor of infant feeding vis-à-vis adult diet, he again indicates an expectation that there should be a normal growth process in healthy Christian development. He also points to the "food" of which one should be partaking as a Christian—the words of God. The author indicates the outcome—discernment of the distinction between good and evil—that demonstrates growth to maturity has taken place.

The parallels with the modern church are obvious. Rather than being culture-bound, spiritual life and growth are universal needs of Christian experience. The development of believers, therefore, calls for a process by which they move from a state of immaturity to maturity, grounded in faithful teaching of God's Word. How, then, do we accomplish that goal in our congregations? The question should prompt reflection on appropriate applications of Hebrews 5:11–6:3. The author provides us with a list of the elementary Christian teachings he has in mind: "repentance from acts that lead to death, and of faith in God, instruction about baptisms [notice the plural!], the laying on of hands, the resurrection of the dead, and eternal judgment."

How does your church do with this list? Is the list comprehensive? Do we have to cover all the topics on the list to apply the passage or be faithful to early Christian teaching? How do we move people along the path of Christian growth? How do we equip them to move from those feeding as babies on the Word to those feeding others? How much of the process depends on the church leadership and how much of it turns on each member's willingness to be taught? These are the kinds of questions that must be answered as we move to application.

LOVING CONFRONTATION. SUE was a young lady in our singles group. One day she approached me—I was serving as head of the Singles' Council at the time—and requested we talk privately for a few minutes. Being a single, young man I was thrilled at the opportunity; but our talk had nothing to do with council business or romance. Sue started by thanking me for the job I was doing in leading the group and said she deeply respected my walk with the Lord. Then she said, "I want to share with you what seems to be a weakness in your life. You are so busy and move so fast from one project or person to another you often lose eye-contact with people. By being distracted, failing to maintain eye-contact and looking away from a person, you communicate that that person and what they are saying are not important to you at that moment."

Sue went on to give examples, showing that the problem, rather than an isolated incident, had a pattern. She also told me about a godly missionary she had known while serving overseas in a journeyman program. This man, with the weight of his vast mission responsibilities on his shoulders, had never failed to stop and listen intensely when Sue needed to talk. He had given her "the gift of his presence."

Sue's rebuke was painful but much needed. That encounter, which happened over a decade ago, has made a lasting impression on me. To this day if I am in conversation with a person and my attention begins to falter, Sue's exhortation comes to mind. I challenge myself, "Focus, George. Give your full attention." I still struggle with that focus, but that sister in Christ, who risked being misunderstood and becoming the object of my defensiveness, has by her truth-telling had an impact on the way I relate to others.

We understand that in the physical realm health sometimes comes via painful experiences. In the summer of 1980 while at a college retreat I contracted a staph infection under my right arm. I will spare you the details, but when my doctor saw the boil produced by the infection he gasped. I was immediately put in the hospital on an IV; the wound was drained and packed with gauze. When the doctor removed that gauze two days later I felt my arm was being ripped off. To say the experience was painful puts it lightly. I had to make myself vulnerable by raising my arm and allowing the doctor to work on me. The doctor had to be willing to give focused attention to the need and even inflict a bit of pain. Yet, as a result of the process, healing was able to take place.

Truth-telling confrontation has been a fairly consistent dynamic in my life. Sometimes I have been on the receiving end and sometimes on the giving. Most situations that loom in my memory involved a concerned friend addressing a problem in my life. I look back on those times when a brother or sister in Christ lovingly called a flaw to my attention as some of the most beneficial for my own development as a person. Never comfortable. Almost always profitable.

The Apostles' Creed, a concise summary of Christian teachings used especially in the Western church, says, "I believe in ... the communion of the saints."[18] What does it mean for us to live in communion rather than pseudo-community? Among other important relational practices, we must learn to speak and hear the truth in love (Eph. 4:15) if we are to have true unity and growth toward maturity. That is, we must commit to lives that rightly demonstrate the transformation brought about by Christ. Right theology must work its way out in our individual lives, and when this process is thwarted by sin, the sin must be confronted. Unfortunately the easiest course often is to "keep the peace" by keeping quiet. However, as Bill Hybels notes,

> When people submerge their true feelings in order to preserve harmony, they undermine the integrity of a relationship. They buy peace on the surface, but underneath there are hurt feelings, troubling questions, and hidden hostilities just waiting to erupt. It's a costly price to pay for a cheap peace, and it inevitably leads to inauthentic relationships.[19]

The church must be a "dangerous" place of vulnerability, where love demands more than the guarding of personal ego and truth looms larger than peace. Yes, pain plays a part in this indispensable activity of authenticity. Yet, this pain can be remarkably productive.

As demonstrated in Hebrews 5:11–6:3, this principle of loving confrontation must be a mode of operation at times between one who proclaims the Word of God and those under his or her charge. All bodies of believers need to progress in the faith and in the advancement of the kingdom, and most people need to be challenged from time to time to get back in step with biblical principles. The word that summons believers to evaluate their lives and move on in the pursuit of holiness must be a consistent word from those who preach the Word.

In those situations where the congregation perceives the pastor as "their employee," where the power brokers of the church place biblical principles in a secondary or tertiary position, this duty can be especially difficult. Many a pastor has been called before the church board to be told he is being too

---

18. The phrase was not part of the version used by the Eastern church. See McGrath, *The Christian Theology Reader*, 7–8.

19. Bill Hybels, *Honest to God: Becoming an Authentic Christian* (Grand Rapids: Zondervan, 1990), 53.

negative in his preaching; that people won't come to the church if he continues to give them such a hard time; that maybe God is leading him someplace else. But godly confrontation grounded in biblical principles goes with the territory. We must love, educate, and encourage. In a healthy church and in authentic relationships within the church, confrontation is inevitable. The pain and awkwardness accompanying such loving confrontation are not easy for anyone to experience. But "no-talk" rules, if allowed to prevail, will lead to spiritual demise, turning a community of faith into a mere crowd held together by formalities.

What, then, are guidelines for truth-telling? Let me suggest three gleaned from our author's example in Hebrews 5:11–6:3. (1) The confrontation must be given with the right motive (i.e., to restore those confronted to spiritual health) and in a context of love and encouragement. The one offering the rebuke must go through self-examination to see whether he or she is seeking to minister in the situation out of a broken heart and for the betterment of those being confronted. We must ask whether we seek to build up or tear down, that is, whether we want the other person(s) to walk away renewed or we are simply out to get emotional revenge for our own hurt feelings.

(2) The confrontation must be well thought out and well timed. Off-the-cuff comments offered at an ill-timed moment can be more damaging than helpful. Therefore, we do well to write out our thoughts and pray through them, reflecting on them in light of Scripture. The author's words in 5:11– 6:3 were artistically crafted and, thus, the product of much thought. That he waits until this point in the book—after laying both theological and hortatory groundwork in the first four chapters—speaks volumes. In building his sermon he waits patiently for the right moment to confront the listeners boldly with their problem.

(3) Finally, the person offering the rebuke should also offer specific suggestions for action when appropriate.

Spiritual formation and the modern church. The concept of "discipleship" has undergone a phenomenal transformation in the church over the past two decades. Until the late 1970s and early 1980s discipleship programs were unheard of in many churches. Yet today the expression is used broadly to communicate the concept of spiritual development.

Much of the form associated with the contemporary, grassroots concept of discipleship can be traced back to a California truck driver named Dawson Trotman, who in the late 1920s felt the need for growth in his own spiritual life. Trotman began to apply "spiritual disciplines" to facilitate that growth. These included daily time in the Bible, Scripture memory, regular times of prayer, and evangelism. Others noticed the spiritual growth in Trotman and asked him for help in their own spiritual lives. In 1933, Trotman founded the Navigators, the motto of which became "to know Christ and to make Him known." The Navigators' ministry has expanded and become diverse since the days of Trotman. Yet at its heart the ministry has continued to trumpet the need for personal devotion, Bible study, prayer, and personal evangelism. Any person who has benefited from their church's emphasis on having a "quiet time" or "Scripture memory" is an inheritor of sorts of the Navigators' influence on contemporary church life.

The established church has not always embraced the concept of discipleship as envisioned by Trotman. Prior to the early 1980s many leaders in established churches rejected any concept they perceived as originating in parachurch groups, including small-group Bible studies in homes and emphasis on "one-on-one" discipleship. Robert Coleman's little book *The Master Plan of Evangelism*, published by Revell in 1963, became read widely in the late 1970s and early 1980s, softening church leaders to the concept of discipleship as popularly conceived in the parachurch movements. Also, young adults who had experienced the impact of parachurch ministries like the Navigators and Campus Crusade began to filter back into established churches and brought with them emphases on devotional life and personal evangelism. Thus, pastors were able to witness firsthand the positive effect discipleship ministries had had on their members.

The broad success of the evangelical presses and evangelical periodicals like *Christianity Today* and *Moody Monthly*, which included emphases on the spiritual disciplines, added to the concept's popularization.[20] Many denominations began to produce discipleship materials for their churches. By the late 1980s discipleship had become a catchword of contemporary evangelical culture. In addition, various branches of the academic world had, in the 1970s and early 1980s, begun to give serious attention to spiritual formation as well.[21] Some works, such as Richard Foster's *Celebration of Discipline*, offered what Elton Trueblood has called an "intellectual integrity" to discussions on the practice of spirituality in Evangelicalism.[22]

The benefits of our contemporary stress on discipleship, as popularly conceived, lie in the accentuation of personal holiness, Bible study, memorization of Scripture, personal times of prayer, and proclamation of the gospel. We as Christians are to be people of God's Word, people of prayer, and peo-

---

20. One professor told me in 1985 that a publisher wanted anything with "discipleship" in the title, suggesting it was the hot topic of the decade.

21. For example, Gordon S. Wakefield, ed., *The Westminster Dictionary of Christian Spirituality* (Philadelphia: Westminster, 1983); John Garvey, *Modern Spirituality: An Anthology* (Springfield, Ill.: Templegate, 1985); Cheslyn Jones et al., eds., *The Study of Spirituality* (Oxford: Oxford Univ. Press, 1986).

22. Richard J. Foster, *Celebration of Discipline*, vii.

ple seeking to build the kingdom in a variety of ways through personal ministry, including evangelism. These are nonnegotiable as I read the Scriptures and perhaps have fueled the movement in the modern church toward an energetic endorsement of this modern conception of discipleship.

But with the concept's popularity we need to scrutinize our understanding of spiritual formation in light of biblical teaching and become cognizant of several potential problems with discipleship as popularly conceived. For example, the demarcation in the minds of some between "normal Christians" and "real disciples" leads to an inappropriate view of the Christian life. The term "disciple" (*mathetes*), which occurs 261 times in the New Testament, was used broadly to refer to all who belonged to the church.[23] All Christians are disciples, not just those who have gone through spiritual growth training, and spiritual growth is an expectation of all Christ-followers. When in the Great Commission (Matt. 28:19–20) Jesus said, "Go and make disciples," he meant, "Go and introduce people to me through the proclamation of the gospel." The participial clause that follows, "teaching them to obey everything I have commanded you," is applicable to every convert to Christianity, not just to a spiritual elite. Hebrews does, however, make a distinction between those who are spiritually mature and those who are spiritually immature, and such a designation can be helpful.

Another caution has to do with a "disciplines" orientation that measures spirituality by the execution of certain practices. In this orientation one is considered spiritual if one has a daily quiet time, memorizes Scripture, attends Bible study or church, and witnesses to the lost at least once per week. I do not mean to negate the significance of any of these activities, but they must not be seen as *the* measures of true Christianity lest we produce "human doings" rather than "human beings." The picture we get of dynamic Christianity from the New Testament is that of a balance between practices of devotion, such as those listed above, and care for others, corporate worship and ministry, and theological/biblical education.

This final point, education in biblical truth, brings us to the main concern of Hebrews 5:11–6:3. C. S. Lewis, addressing the importance of theology for Christian life and practice, has written, "We have to be continually reminded of what we believe";[24] and Dorothy Sayers adds:

In ordinary times we get along surprisingly well, on the whole, without ever discovering what our faith really is. If, now and again, this remote and academic problem is so unmannerly as to thrust its way into

---

23. P. Nepper-Christensen, "μαθητής; μαθητεύω," in *Exegetical Dictionary of the New Testament*, 2:374.

24. C. S. Lewis, *Mere Christianity*, 124.

our minds, there are plenty of things we can do to drive the intruder away. We can get the car out or go to a party or to the cinema or read a detective story or have a row with a district council or write a letter to the papers about … Shakespeare's use of nautical metaphor. Thus we build up a defense mechanism against self-questioning because, to tell the truth, we are very much afraid of ourselves.[25]

Sayers goes on to explain that pushing off theological reflection can only last so long. Life itself has a way of forcing us to deal with theology—that is, what we believe—sooner or later. The difficult experiences of life raise important questions about God and what he is up to. We especially must be focused in the deeper matters of the faith if we are to withstand the fire of persecution. Those who are shallow theologically manifest that superficiality in the face of strong challenges that oppose continued commitment to Christ.

This is not to say that one needs a graduate-school theological education in order to live the Christian life. Rather, the New Testament pattern is to educate God's people in the tenets of the faith from the beginning of Christian experience, providing them with the basic theological nurturing they will need for this earthly trip and maturing them through ongoing feeding on God's Word. All who are Christ-followers need systematic teaching of biblical truth, both at the beginning of our spiritual formation and along the way as we grow to maturity. I say it again: We need theology. Mark Shaw, in his creative little book *Doing Theology with Huck and Jim: Parables for Understanding Doctrine*, begins with the two title characters climbing aboard their raft, embarking on a life free of restraint. Having listed all the aspects of their lives they would not miss, the dialogue continues:

> After a time Huck spoke up. "What'd you bring for food? I'm hungry."
> Jim unwrapped his bedroll. His worldly wealth was contained in it. Immediately it was all laid out in full view. There was a hat and some fruit, a pair of socks, a rabbit's foot and a book. Jim tossed Huck a piece of fruit.
> "What'd you bring a book for?" asked Huck with a tone of irritation.
> "T' read," said Jim, rolling up the blanket again. "What else a book good for?"
> "Didn't think you could read," Huck said and then wished he hadn't.
> "I can read," Jim responded with intense seriousness, gazing into the night.
> "What kinda book is it?" Huck asked.
> "Book 'bout theology," Jim said, his voice trailing away.

---

25. Sayers, *The Whimsical Christian*, 29.

"Theology! I hate theology almost as much as I hate schools and rules," Huck said, and emphasized the point by spitting into the river. "What good is a theology book on a trip like this?"

Jim was silent for a long time before he answered. "Trip like this is long. Lotta things gonna happen. Might come in handy."[26]

Might come in handy, indeed. We make decisions in life based on our thought processes. Our beliefs, therefore, affect the way we live, the relationships we keep, and the commitments we make or break. Rather than being relegated to the ivory towers of theological education, theology must be taught and "bought" in the nitty-gritty highways and byways of grassroots Christian community. If we are deep in the faith and nurtured on biblical truth, we are better prepared to make the right decisions as we walk the Christian life—decisions in line with perseverance.

The process of theological education, therefore, must not be left up to our church leaders. Leaders cannot force theology down our throats if we are determined to side with Huck in his evaluation of biblical teachings. We have to be fed willingly. The question comes, then, whether we are taking advantage of the biblical truth being afforded us and advancing in the faith by going deeper in the Word? For Hebrews this constitutes a hallmark of Christian growth and should, for all of us, be one measure of true Christian "discipleship."

---

26. Mark Shaw, *Doing Theology with Huck and Jim: Parables for Understanding Doctrine* (Downers Grove, Ill.: InterVarsity, 1993), 9–10.

Hebrews 6:4–12

IT IS IMPOSSIBLE for those who have once been enlightened, who have tasted the heavenly gift, who have shared in the Holy Spirit, ⁵who have tasted the goodness of the word of God and the powers of the coming age, ⁶if they fall away, to be brought back to repentance, because to their loss they are crucifying the Son of God all over again and subjecting him to public disgrace.

⁷Land that drinks in the rain often falling on it and that produces a crop useful to those for whom it is farmed receives the blessing of God. ⁸But land that produces thorns and thistles is worthless and is in danger of being cursed. In the end it will be burned.

⁹Even though we speak like this, dear friends, we are confident of better things in your case—things that accompany salvation. ¹⁰God is not unjust; he will not forget your work and the love you have shown him as you have helped his people and continue to help them. ¹¹We want each of you to show this same diligence to the very end, in order to make your hope sure. ¹²We do not want you to become lazy, but to imitate those who through faith and patience inherit what has been promised.

IT IS NO EXAGGERATION to designate the passage we now consider as one of the most controversial in the book of Hebrews—indeed, one of the most disputed in the entire New Testament. It would not be surprising, therefore, if some readers of this commentary have come first to this spot in the volume to see where I stand on the issue of apostasy! This theological issue, although only one component among the concerns of Hebrews, does constitute a matter of the gravest concern and a matter at the heart of the author's intention for the book.

The two passages grouped in this section of the commentary (6:4–8 and 6:9–12) offer two sides of a balanced approach to exhortation: stern warning and mitigation, or softening, of the warning. In 6:4–8 the writer presents a well-crafted and harsh caution meant to put fear into the hearts of those drifting from the faith. Verses 9–12 then express the author's confidence that those in his audience do not fit the description just provided. This word of encour-

agement ends with twin exhortations: "show … diligence" and "do not …
become lazy" (vv. 11–12). In crafting an exhortation composed of both warning and mitigation, the author presents a symmetry in the rhetoric of this portion of his sermon. We begin, therefore, by looking at the structure and details
of 6:4–8 and 6:9–12 respectively, then move (in the Bridging Contexts section)
to consider the various interpretations of these passages offered by scholars.

A Harsh Word of Warning (6:4–8)

AT A NUMBER of points in Hebrews the author presents a compact, highly stylized treatment of an issue by stringing together participle clauses,[1] an approach
he uses in 6:4–8. The first three verses of this unit cohere around the central
assertion, "It is impossible for those … to be brought back to repentance." The
two main parts of this declaration (lit., "impossible the ones …" [v. 4] and "again
to renew to repentance" [v. 6]) are separated from each other by five intervening clauses. Such a separation of closely related elements was done at times
for rhetorical effect (i.e., by their isolation from one another they stand out
more clearly).[2] The structure of the passage may be depicted as follows:

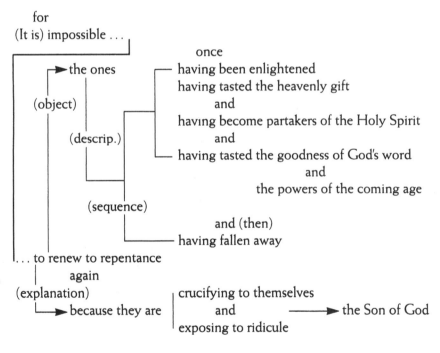

for
(It is) impossible …
the ones
(object)
(descrip.)
(sequence)
… to renew to repentance
again
(explanation)
because they are

once
having been enlightened
having tasted the heavenly gift
and
having become partakers of the Holy Spirit
and
having tasted the goodness of God's word
and
the powers of the coming age

and (then)
having fallen away

crucifying to themselves
and   the Son of God
exposing to ridicule

---

1. E.g., Hebrews 1:1–4.

2. F. Blass and A. Debrunner, *A Greek Grammar of the New Testament and Other Early Christian
Literature*, trans. and rev. by Robert W. Funk (Chicago: Univ. of Chicago Press, 1961), 249.

The author places the term translated "impossible" (*adynaton*) first in the passage for emphasis.[3] He uses this word at three other points in Hebrews, proclaiming it is "impossible for God to lie" (6:18), "impossible for the blood of bulls and goats to take away sins" (10:4), and "impossible to please God" apart from faith (11:6). The term clearly means that something cannot happen. That those under discussion "have once been enlightened" (*photizo*) probably refers to their initial exposure to the gospel or early instruction in Christian doctrine.[4] The only other use of *photizo* in Hebrews occurs at 10:32, where the author encourages his hearers with, "Remember those earlier days after you had received the light. . . ."

Although some have taken the word translated "tasted" (*geusamenous*, from *geuomai*) to mean "to have tried but not fully partaken of,"[5] this interpretation must be ruled out on consideration of its usage elsewhere.[6] Others have understood the act of tasting to refer literally to partaking of the Eucharist. However, little in the context commends such an interpretation. The word is used metaphorically, as at 2:9, where Christ is said to have "tasted" death for every person. Thus the verb *geuomai* means "to experience something."

What these people have experienced is "the heavenly gift." In Acts the "gift" refers to the Holy Spirit (Acts 2:38; 8:20; 10:45; 11:17), but here the author seems to make a distinction between this gift and the Holy Spirit. In Pauline usage the word refers more generally to the blessings of God surrounding salvation (e.g., Rom. 5:15, 17; 2 Cor. 9:15; Eph. 3:7; 4:7), and several commentators have found that interpretation most attractive in the present context.[7]

Ancient authors could use the word "partakers" (*metochos*; NIV, "who shared in") with reference either to a normal companion or to an associate in a legal or moral context. It can function as a synonym for *koinonos* ("partner," "sharer"), referring, for example, to a partner in business. We move closer to the meaning here when we understand the *metachoi* as those who share in spiritual realities. The word has been used several times in the previous chapters. It

---

3. On words being moved forward in a Greek sentence for emphasis, see ibid., 248.

4. See John 1:9; 1 Cor. 4:5; Eph. 1:18; 3:9; 2 Tim. 1:10. Some commentators have pointed to a second-century use of the word to refer to baptism, but Lane and Attridge are correct to point rather to illumination that comes through the preaching of the gospel as the meaning here. See Lane, *Hebrews 1–8*, 141; Attridge, *Epistle to the Hebrews*, 169.

5. E.g., Westcott, who states, "the enjoyment as here described . . . is only partial and inchoative. To feast, to live upon the fullness of the divine blessing belongs to another order" (see Westcott, *Epistle to the Hebrews*, 148).

6. Hughes, *A Commentary on the Epistle to the Hebrews*, 209; Delitzsch, *Commentary on the Epistle to the Hebrews*, 284.

7. E.g., Attridge, *Epistle to the Hebrews*, 170; Hughes, *Commentary on the Epistle to the Hebrews*, 209.

occurs in the quote of Psalm 45:6–7 at Hebrews 1:9, meaning "companions"; it probably has the same sense as 3:1, 14, where the hearers are called respectively (lit.) "companions of a heavenly calling" and "companions of Christ." A use later in the book (12:8) says that all true children of God are "sharers" of discipline. A cognate verb (*metecho*) appears in participial form at 5:13, referring to partaking of milk (i.e., basic teachings), and points to metaphorical uses of the word for eating and instruction.[8] Thus the word has a broad semantic range and generally seems to mean "to have a close association with" or "participate in." Thus, here those who have fallen away are said to have been "companions of" or "sharers of" the Holy Spirit.

Furthermore, these people "have tasted the goodness of the word of God and the powers of the coming age." The Word of God and his power are closely linked (e.g., 1:2–3; 2:3–4; 3:7–19; 4:12–13), and the language here is reminiscent of those who fell in the desert through lack of faith[9] even though they had heard God's voice and seen his mighty acts (3:7–11). The verb "tasted," as in verse 4, refers to something experienced. Consequently, those being used as a bad example in 6:4–6 in some way have experienced God's good Word and power.

At the climax of this string of participles comes the clause "if they fall away" (v. 6). Rather than reading the clause as conditional with the NIV, however, it might be better to understand it as the culminating experience in a sequence of experiences: "(who) have been enlightened, tasted the heavenly gift, become partakers of the Holy Spirit, have tasted the goodness of God's word and the powers of the coming age and *then* have fallen away. . . ." The verb "to fall away" (*parapipto*) can mean simply to "go astray," but the harshness of the descriptions that follow ("crucifying the Son of God" and "subjecting him to public disgrace") demand that it be understood in terms of a serious sin—that of rejecting Christ.[10]

The author finally rounds off the main verbal idea in this long sentence, informing the readers of what is "impossible": It is impossible for those who have fallen away "to be brought back to repentance." He uses the Greek words *palin* ("again") coupled with the infinitive *anakainizo* ("to renew"; NIV, "be brought back"), suggesting that those who had fallen away had repented previously. In other words, those who have fallen away cannot be brought back again to a true repentance. This thought has caused a great deal of anxiety among those who read the book of Hebrews. What does it mean?

---

8. Spicq, *Theological Lexicon of the New Testament*, 2:480–81; Wisdom 16:3; 1 Cor. 9:10; Sirach 51:28.

9. Note the correspondence with "faith in God" in 6:1.

10. Ellingworth, *Epistle to the Hebrews*, 322.

The assertion here must be considered in light of the broader context of Hebrews. In 6:1 the author has identified "repentance" as foundational in Christian teaching. In the view of the author of Hebrews true repentance can be experienced only in the shadow of Christ's sacrifice, since there exists no other valid sacrifice for sin (10:18, 26). In the Jewish literature of the day, repentance was God's gift, and Hebrews has taken that thought as specifically incarnated in the person and work of the Son of God. Repentance in 6:4–6 is "impossible" because there is nowhere else to go for repentance once one has rejected Christ. The apostate in effect has turned his or her back on the only means available for forgiveness before God.[11]

The writer now provides an explanation in the form of two parallel present-tense form participles: "to their loss they are crucifying the Son of God all over again and subjecting him to public disgrace." The switch to the present tense is significant since the author has used the aorist tense to this point in the passage. These present participles may indicate that the actions under consideration are actions in progress. Furthermore, the acts of "crucifying" and "subjecting ... to disgrace" should be understood as modifying the infinitive "to be brought back." The participles may be interpreted either as causal ("because they . . .") or temporal ("while they . . ."). In either case the effect is the same: Repentance has been (and is) ruled out because the fallen ones are rejecting Christ. If the incompleteness of these actions is stressed, however, Hebrews 6:4–6 does not negate the possibility of the fallen reversing course in the future (i.e., "as long as they are crucifying the Son of God and subjecting him to public disgrace").[12]

The language of crucifixion and public shaming is both potent and ironic. Instead of being blessed by accepting the forgiveness found in the crucified Christ, the ones who have fallen away identify with those who used the cross as an ultimate expression of rejection. Instead of being shamed in the eyes of the world by identification with the Son, "bearing the disgrace he bore" (13:13), the apostates stand with those before the cross who cast insults, disparaging Christ's claims as the true Messiah:

---

11. Lane, *Hebrews 1–8*, 142.

12. In my opinion Bruce, Hagner, and others rule out this possibility too quickly without providing sufficient reasons for doing so. The interpretation that the impossibility of repentance relates to the apostates' rejection of Christ, the only source of true forgiveness, leaves open the possibility that a turning back to Christ would effect repentance. In any case, the switch to the present-tense form for these participles, although possibly a stylistic device (i.e., to add variety to the style of writing), might suggest that the current state of apostasy *could* be abandoned in favor of true Christian repentance. See Bruce, *Epistle to the Hebrews*, 149; Hagner, *Hebrews*, 95.

Those who passed by hurled insults at him, shaking their heads and saying, "You who are going to destroy the temple and build it in three days, save yourself! Come down from the cross, if you are the Son of God!"

In the same way the chief priests, the teachers of the law and the elders mocked him. "He saved others," they said, "but he can't save himself! He's the King of Israel! Let him come down now from the cross, and we will believe in him. He trusts in God. Let God rescue him now if he wants him, for he said, 'I am the Son of God.'" In the same way the robbers who were crucified with him also heaped insults on him. (Matt. 27:39–44)

The author continues with common agricultural imagery,[13] illustrating the contrast between those who come to a good end in relation to God over against those who do not end well. Verse 7 portrays fruitfulness, which well describes the hearers in whom the author expresses confidence in verses 9–10. On the other hand, verse 8 illustrates the unfruitful persons just used as an object of warning in verses 4–6.

The vast majority of people reading this commentary probably are urbanites who spend little, if any, effort in raising crops for food or livelihood. The feel of dirt between your fingers, the anticipation of planting seeds or a young vine, and the joy of harvest might be aspects of a hobby but for most do not fall into the category of life necessities. Yet for most people of the ancient world, agriculture comprised a much more important aspect of life. There existed no frozen food or canned vegetable sections at a grocery store.[14] A bad crop had implications both for the farmer and his family and for those who depended on his supply of food in the markets.

In 6:7–8 the author describes twin experiences familiar to those from an agricultural context. On the one hand, seeds have been planted in the earth, rain falls on the land, crops are produced, and the farmers who planted the seeds envision an eventual harvest. This is a picture of God's blessing. On the other hand, we have a picture of disappointment and frustration. The seeds have been planted, rain falls in abundance on the land, but instead of the hoped-for crop, worthless "thorns and thistles" are produced. Rather than evidencing the blessing of God, such land is "near to a curse" (pers. trans.; cf. Gen. 3:17–18), suggesting inevitable devastation.[15] The farmer's only recourse is to burn off the area.

---

13. On the uses of this type of imagery in the Old Testament, rabbinic literature, classic literature, and the Gospels see Attridge, *Epistle to the Hebrew*, 172; Delitzsch, *Commentary on the Epistle to the Hebrews*, 1:294–95.

14. See J. A. Thompson, *Handbook of Life in Bible Times* (Downers Grove, Ill.: InterVarsity, 1986), 125.

15. The NIV translation at this point with "in danger of being cursed" is unfortunate. What is in view is that the land is on its way to destruction. See Attridge, *Epistle to the Hebrews*, 173.

An Encouraging Word (6:9–12)

WITH VERSE 9 the author changes tones abruptly. The harsh warning of 6:4–8 is now softened considerably by an expression of confidence in the listeners: "Even though we speak like this, dear friends, we are confident of better things in your case. . . ." This is the only place in the book he addresses his hearers as "dear friends" (*agapetoi*), a name of endearment perhaps meant to reaffirm his relationship with them as members of Christ's community.

The verb translated "we are confident" (*peitho*), used in the passive as here, means "to be confident, trust, be certain, be sure." [16] Although this word can express a mere opinion, it most often communicates a strong or absolute conviction (e.g., Phil. 1:6). Therefore, having become persuaded of their genuine commitment to Christ, the author communicates a personal conviction, based on his observations, that his readers share in "better things . . . that accompany salvation." The "better" (*kreisson*) motif figures prominently in Hebrews' wider discourse—see, for example, 1:4; 7:19, 22; 8:6; 9:23; 12:24, which speak of Christ's superior person and ministry. Yet here, as at 10:34, the word describes the hearers' experience. Their experience is "better" than that of the apostates described in 6:4–8, primarily because it relates in some manner to salvation. [17] The word translated "salvation" (*soteria*) has a strong orientation to the future for Hebrews (e.g., 1:14; 5:9; 9:28). The author suggests that, rather than a cursed outcome, genuine followers of Christ are on a path that will end in the consummation of their salvation.

What is the basis of the writer's confidence in these people? Their faith has been lived out in "work"; they have and are manifesting a "love" for God expressed through ministry to his people. The New Testament often speaks of God's judgment in relation to one's works (e.g., Rom. 2:6–7; 1 Cor. 3:13–15), and a right relationship with God expresses itself in substantive ministry to the saints (e.g., James 2:15–16; 1 John 3:16–20). Thus the author's description of his hearers points to a genuineness of personal relationship to God. God, as just, remembers their work and love and affirms their relationship to him.

Verse 11, however, again bears witness to a basic, though often neglected, dynamic in this author's sermon—the uncertainty that surrounds any evaluation of another person's status before God apart from continued manifestations of God's grace. [18] In other words, if the outward manifestations of genuineness dealt with in 6:9–10 cease, confidence in that genuineness evaporates.

---

16. Used in this way the word is popular in the LXX and Philo. See Spicq, *Theological Lexicon of the New Testament*, 3:75–76.

17. The common Greek idiom *echo* + an object means "pertaining to." See Attridge, *Epistle to the Hebrews*, 174.

18. See above, p. 136.

Therefore, this first-century preacher encourages his congregation to continue to exhibit "the same diligence" shown in their work and love to this point. The word rendered "diligence" (*spoude*) means "eagerness, effort, haste" and suggests the state of being meaningfully engaged in something. Such diligence leads to a hope characterized by conviction or assurance. What is called for, moreover, is a perseverance by which the hearers will remain engaged in the work and love of God, thus possessing a confident hope until the end of their earthly journeys.

By contrast, the author does not want his readers to lapse into laziness, but rather "to imitate those who through faith and patience inherit what has been promised." His desire that they emulate great people of faith manifests itself not only through this exhortation, but also through his use of positive examples, such as Abraham in the verses that follow (6:13–15), the Lord Jesus (3:1–2; 12:1–2), and the great host of the faithful in Hebrews 11.

SPECIAL DIFFICULTIES IN interpreting this passage. Both the diversity of interpretations and intensity surrounding discussions on Hebrews 6:4–12 have at their root at least two important factors that we do well to keep in mind as we move toward application of this controversial text.

(1) The language of the passage is notoriously ambiguous. At several points the terminology used *describes* certain phenomena without *defining* exactly what the author has in mind. Although I have attempted to do a credible job of shedding light on ambiguous phrases (such as "once been enlightened," "tasted the heavenly gift," and "shared in the Holy Spirit"), the problem remains that the author lists these without defining them. What does seem certain, given the evidence, is that the description in 6:4–6 fits those who have taken initial steps in associating with the Christian community. Whether this means they have been changed by the power of God into "new creatures," as some commentators suggest, or in some way have manifested certain phenomena normally associated with the new life but never giving evidence that a true life-change has taken place, forms the central question in debates on the passage.

(2) Since a "presuppositionless hermeneutic" is impossible, every interpreter comes to the text with preconceived ideas on the theological issues addressed. In other words, we all carry certain theological baggage into the task of interpretation. This baggage has been picked up over a long period of time and consists of our life experiences and the influence of interpretive communities to which we belong. This does not make objectivity impossible—just difficult to

achieve, especially when the stakes are so high. After all, the nature of salvation and perseverance are focal concepts to our understanding of the Christian life. Some who come to the text may belong to an interpretive community in which a "wrong interpretation" (from that community's perspective) carries with it vast professional and personal consequences. Therefore, to "bracket" our theological presuppositions when seeking to encounter such a text in a fresh way demands a resolute commitment to truth-seeking.

Several reminders. In light of these difficulties, therefore, we need to remember several important hermeneutical guidelines that might help to steer us through our discussion. (1) We must keep in mind that the genre of this passage is exhortation. Of course, theology underlies the author's hortatory material in Hebrews, but the primary purpose of 6:4–12 is to *motivate to action* rather than to offer theological instruction. This may be why the author does not stop to define his terms. Thus, when we approach a text like 6:4–8 for theological instruction, we come at the text with a purpose that was at least secondary in the author's mind.

I do not mean to suggest, of course, that the author has ceased thinking theologically in his exhortation sections, just that his theology is presupposed and is now in the service of exhortation. This does not make the theological questions we raise any less important, but it does force us to ask: "In what way did the author intend this particular passage to challenge his hearers to change their attitudes and actions?" and "What are the dynamics here that could be misinterpreted if we do not keep the 'hortatory factor' in view?"

(2) Also related to the issue of genre, we must recognize 6:7–8 as a widely used wisdom form found in both biblical and extrabiblical literature,[19] which depicts the blessing associated with fruitfulness over against the curse associated with barrenness.[20] As such, we should be careful of associating specific theological constructs with the images of "rain," "crops," "thorns," and even being "burned." The material here is meant to be metaphorical or analogous to spiritual realities without directly making reference to those realities. For example, even though it is true that the author uses "fire" as an image of judgment elsewhere in Hebrews (10:27; 12:29) and it certainly alludes to judgment here, to draw too narrow a theological conclusion from the image of burning in 6:8 (such as its being a reference to hell) is to neglect the wisdom form of the author's illustration.[21] The image of burning, rather, presents

---

19. Attridge, *Epistle to the Hebrews*, 172.

20. For uses elsewhere in Scripture, see Isa. 5:1–6; 28:23–29; Ezek. 19:10–14; Matt. 3:10; 7:19; John 15:6.

21. Contra Scot McKnight, who states, "The image of being cursed by, with its close association with fire, can only adequately be explained as an allusion to Gehenna or hell,

a general picture of destruction without defining the specific nature of that destruction.

(3) We must be careful about jumping from a possible word meaning to a theological conclusion when the author himself has not defined specifically the word in question. For example, I have suggested that the word "tasted" in 6:4–5 means "to experience something." Specifically in this passage, those under consideration have "tasted the heavenly gift" and "the goodness of the word of God and the powers of the coming age." The word does not mean "to sample" or "eat without fully digesting," as some have suggested. However, even when we say that the expression means to experience something, we have not defined the nature of that experience and must be careful about drawing theological conclusions from that word. For example, the desert wanderers— the author's paradigm for those who fall away from God—could be said to have fully experienced God's Word and power (Heb. 3:7–9, 16–19), yet faith was not in the mix of that experience. When we consider the pronouncement that the apostates had experienced the blessings surrounding salvation (if that is the meaning of "heavenly gift"), what does that mean? How did they experience those blessings? The writer of Hebrews does not say.

Furthermore, what does it mean to be a *metochos*, a "companion of" or "sharer in" the Holy Spirit? It may refer to someone who has been converted and thus been indwelt by the Spirit. Yet it could also mean one who has interacted with the Holy Spirit, in the sense of experiencing the Spirit's convicting presence, without being converted. F. F. Bruce, for instance, draws attention to the experience of Simon Magus in Acts 8. This miracle-worker had associated himself initially with the Christian movement, having hands laid on him in an act associated with the Spirit, yet was pronounced by Peter to be still in the bondage of sin.[22]

I do not mean to suggest that we must remain agnostic about the author's meaning in this passage. I will present and defend my own position on the message of 6:4–8 below. However, its ambiguity calls for caution. Whether we come from a tradition that affirms "perseverance of the saints" or one that holds apostasy as possible for true believers, we tend to seize on those word meanings that seem to support our position. Integrity demands that we consider carefully as much data as possible when attempting to arrive at an interpretation and open ourselves to the arguments of others who have grappled with this text.

---

an allusion to God's punishment and retributive justice." See Scot McKnight, "The Warning Passages of Hebrews: A Formal Analysis and Theological Conclusions," *TrinJ* 13 NS (1992): 35.

22. Bruce, *Epistle to the Hebrews*, 146–47.

Interpretations. Several years ago while attending a professional meeting in San Francisco, two friends and I went for an outing to a popular shopping district in the city. These friends are known authors and teach New Testament at prominent evangelical institutions. As we traveled across the city, we met yet another New Testament professor, a popular writer and speaker, who joined us on a crowded trolley. Somehow we began discussing the warning passages in Hebrews. There, packed like sardines in a mixed crowd of shoppers, tourists, and business people, we carried on an energetic debate about the situation described by Hebrews 6:4–8. Two in our party defended an Arminian position (i.e., that a true Christian can lose salvation). One proclaimed those described in 6:4–8 as real Christians who had not lost salvation but were under judgment as the people of God. The fourth member of the debate suggested that the "fallen" were never true believers in the first place.

The scene was somewhat comical. Here were four New Testament professors arguing over the intricacies of Greek grammar and word meanings, surrounded by a crowd silently staring straight ahead with blank faces but forced to listen to our theological wrangling. The picture illustrates that scholars are anything but of uniform opinion when it comes to the warnings of Hebrews, and many laypeople do not share our enthusiasm for the debate!

Therefore, let us consider the various positions scholars have set forth on Hebrews 6:4–8.[23] (1) The *hypothetical view* suggests that the author crafts this harsh warning for rhetorical impact, to blast the hearers out of their spiritual slumber, but that the state described cannot really happen. The passage, therefore, is read: "If there were those who fell away, which cannot really happen, then it would be impossible to renew them to repentance." In favor of this view, the author exhibits fine rhetorical skills and knows how to motivate his listeners through eloquent oratory. However, the problem with this position stems from the harshness and repetition of severe warnings in the book (e.g., 2:1–4; 3:6, 14; 4:12–13; 10:26–31, 39; 12:25–29). The author

---

23. For an overview of these different positions and the arguments that attend them, see McKnight, "The Warning Passages of Hebrews," 23–25; Robert H. Gundry, *Survey of the New Testament*, 3d ed. (Grand Rapids: Zondervan, 1994), 428–29; J. K. Solari, "The Problem of *Metanoia* in the Epistle to the Hebrews" (Ph.D. diss.; Washington, D.C.: Catholic University of America, 1970), 1–7; I. H. Marshall, *Kept by the Power of God: A Study of Perseverance and Falling Away* (Minneapolis: Bethany, 1969), 140–47; J. C. McCullough, "The Impossibility of a Second Repentance in Hebrews," *Biblical Theology* 20 (1974): 1–7; T. K. Oberholtzer, "The Thorn-Infested Ground in Hebrews 6:4–12," *BibSac* 145 (1988): 319–27; R. Nicole, "Some Comments on Hebrews 6:4–6 and the Doctrine of Perseverance of God With the Saints," in *Current Issues in Biblical and Patristic Interpretation*, ed. G. F. Hawthorne (Grand Rapids: Eerdmans, 1975), 355–64; V. Verbrugge, "Towards a New Interpretation of Hebrews 6:4–6," *CTJ* 15 (1980): 61–73.

appears to be concerned deeply that there are those associated with the community who indeed could fall away from God. His warnings to them speak of harsh, impending judgment for those who do not heed these exhortations, and the judgments are presented as real, not hypothetical.

(2) The *pre-conversion Jew view* states that those addressed are Jews who have associated somewhat with the Christian community but have yet to make a commitment to Christ. There can be no doubt that the audience had a rich background in Jewish thought and worship.[24] Yet, given the many and overt references to those being challenged as, for example, "holy brothers" (3:1), a part of Christ's house (3:6), Christ's companions (3:14), and those who have made a profession (4:14), this position does not seem tenable. Furthermore, in the immediate passage the language seems to point to those who in some way have been associated with Christian practice and belief.

(3) The *covenant community view*, set forth by Verlyn Verbrugge, suggests that the "Vineyard Song" of Isaiah 5:1–7 forms the backdrop of Hebrews 6:4–6 and that the author has in mind God's rejection of a whole community rather than individuals.[25] In this passage the Lord sings of a fertile vineyard on a hillside, well prepared and planted with high quality vines. Yet, this vineyard yields only bad fruit. The Lord's judgment consists of destroying the vineyard, breaking down its wall, making it a waste area, allowing the weeds to grow up, and refusing it rain. This illustration composes a judgment against the people of Israel and Judah (Isa. 5:7). In line with this Old Testament passage, which proclaims a devastating warning against the covenant people of God, Verbrugge proposes that the threatened rejection of the community in Hebrews does not equal the rejection of every individual. Yet, the author of Hebrews seems to make distinctions between different groups and individuals within this Christian community. In 4:1 he states, "let us be careful that *none of you* be found to have fallen short" (emphasis added). In 6:4–12 he makes a distinction between those who have fallen away (6:4–6) and the hearers of whom he expresses confidence.

(4) A fourth view might be called *the true believer under judgment view*. This position holds that those threatened by the judgment of God indeed are true believers and do face severe judgment by God but cannot lose their salvation. This position focuses on the desert wanderers as the author's primary paradigm for those who fall. The logic goes this way: "The Old Testament fallen were the people of God and were judged by him on the basis of his

---

24. See above, pp. 19–20.

25. V. Verbrugge, "Towards a New Interpretation of Hebrews 6:4–6," 61–73. The link between 6:4–6 and 6:7–8 is the Greek word *gar* ("for") at the beginning of verse 7 (omitted in NIV).

covenant with them. However, they did not lose their relationship with God but rather the earthly reward of entering the promised land." The position, moreover, takes seriously the language of 6:4–8 and other passages in the book that seem to suggest the fallen have been associated with the Christian movement. Hebrews 10:30 states, "The Lord will judge *his people.*"

The problem here, however, comes when we consider verses such as 3:6, 14, in which the author expresses concern over his friends if they do not hold on to their courage and hope. They seem to have "fallen short" of a commitment that combines faith with hearing the gospel (4:1–2). Furthermore, 10:26–31 describes the fallen as "enemies of God" (v. 27); they are those for whom there no longer exists a sacrifice and whose end is destruction (10:26–29, 39). In 6:9, moreover, the author contrasts the hearers, those from whom he expects better things associated with salvation, with the fallen of 6:4–6. The inference may be drawn that those of 6:4–6 have no part in the things related to salvation. It seems to me that the warnings simply are too harsh and specific to tone them down to a loss of reward rather than a loss of salvation.

(5) Another view has been called the *phenomenological true believer view.* This interpretation holds that those under consideration must be judged as having been true, regenerate believers, who have now lost their relationship with Christ and can no longer anticipate salvation upon Christ's return. This interpretation rests on the "phenomena" surrounding "Christian experience" detailed by the author of Hebrews in 6:4–8 and other passages in the book. One of the more exegetically oriented defenses of this position comes from Scot McKnight.[26]

McKnight's approach has several strengths. (a) He seeks to offer a systematic analysis of all the hortatory material in the book, thus drawing conclusions from a number of passages in concert rather than depending on isolated data from one particular passage. (b) His detailed exegetical work, at points, unveils the sloppy thinking of others in regard to word meanings and grammar. (c) McKnight places emphasis on the concept of inaugurated eschatology, an important theological construct in Hebrews.[27] Inaugurated eschatology understands salvation as a process involving conversion, development, and consummation at the coming of Christ. McKnight is correct in his suggestion that Hebrews places a great deal of emphasis on the "future orientation" of salvation.[28]

---

26. See his article "The Warning Passages of Hebrews: A Formal Analysis and Theological Conclusions." See also I. H. Marshall, *Kept by the Power of God: A Study of Perseverance and Falling Away*, 140–47.

27. Although I disagree with him concerning the exact nature of inaugurated eschatology. See above p. 136.

28. See above, p. 222.

However, I disagree with McKnight's analysis of the warnings in Hebrews on two major issues (as well as several minor points), which in the end have vast implications for our understanding of apostasy in Hebrews. (1) McKnight holds that one can have present dimensions of salvation and "lose ... faith."[29] In other words, one can have a true relationship with Christ and then, through a lack of perseverance, can lose that relationship. Yet, Hebrews is concerned about those whose association with the Christian community *appears* to be inauthentic because of a lack of perseverance: "We are his house, if we hold on ..."(3:6); "we have come to share in Christ if we hold firmly till the end ..." (3:14). At 4:1–2 the author expresses concern about those who seem to have "fallen short" of the promised rest, who have yet to combine true faith with their hearing of the gospel.[30] It must be remembered that faith for Hebrews equals obedience to the will of God.

Thus for Hebrews, and for New Testament theology generally, true relationship with God results in a lifestyle of obedience to God. If that obedience is absent, that person's relationship with God is questionable. So in Hebrews 6:7–8 the part of the illustration analogous to the apostate depicts barren land that, in spite of the blessings of God, has failed to produce fruit. By contrast, those who are truly being made holy have evidence of salvation (6:9), have been perfected for all time (10:14), have come to Mount Zion, where the spirits of righteous men have been made perfect (12:22–24), and will experience the consummation of salvation at the end (9:28). Salvation has a continuity from present to future and manifests a life of perseverance and obedience to God. If the present involves true salvation, that salvation will be consummated at the end. If at the end one has failed to persevere, then the former public association with the Christian community is manifested to have been illegitimate. This does not mean that the apostates were knowingly fraudulent, just that they had not truly been changed by God's power.

(2) McKnight's analysis does not consider adequately the author's confessed lack of omniscience. He states, "This view also contends vigorously that there is no evidence in Hebrews that the readers are perceived by the author to be either fakes or unregenerate. Rather, the author treats them as believers and identifies himself so closely with them that division into true and false believers is impossible." True. Yet, this statement misses a vitally important dynamic evident in Hebrews: Although the author addresses the community as a whole as believers, he hints at his own lack of omniscience—some may not be true believers even though by association they appear to be (3:6 ,14; 4:1–2; 6:11).[31]

---

29. McKnight, "The Warning Passages of Hebrews," 58.

30. On the rest as both a present reality and future promise for believers see above, pp. 151–52, 161–64.

31. See above, pp. 135–36.

McKnight's argument rests in part on the assumption that the author presents everyone under his teaching as a true Christian. The evidence seems to suggest, rather, that he knew some may not have been covenant people of Christ.

(6) This then brings us to a sixth position, the one proposed in this commentary, which might be labeled *the phenomenological unbeliever* view. The stance has been a favorite of those with a Calvinistic orientation and proposes that the "fallen" in Hebrews may have seemed to be genuine Christians as they participated in the community of believers, but in fact, by their rejection of Christ, have shown themselves to lack genuine faith. The danger heralded in the warnings, therefore, is real, constituting eternal judgment, and those being addressed could commit the sin.

There are at least two stringent challenges to this position that should be mentioned. (a) In the passage under consideration, especially 6:4–6, the author does use language that can be interpreted as referring to Christians. The phenomenological unbeliever view holds that the ambiguous language here suggests a participation in the things of God associated with entrance to the Christian community—they look from outward appearances like Christians—but that those under consideration have not experienced true faith. They may have been instructed in the basics of the faith (6:4), heard the Word of God and seen his power (6:5), experienced the convicting influence of the Holy Spirit (6:4), experienced the blessings associated with God's salvific activity (6:4), and even repented publicly (6:6); but they have not borne fruit (6:7–8) and, therefore, do not manifest the "better things" associated with salvation (6:9–10).[32]

(b) Hebrews 10:29 reads, "How much more severely do you think a man deserves to be punished who has trampled the Son of God under foot, who has treated as an unholy thing the blood of the covenant that sanctified him, and who has insulted the Spirit of grace?" Under this position the Greek phrase *en hō hagiasthē*, translated normally with "by which he is sanctified," must be understood as impersonal: "by which one is sanctified" (since an apostate, in this view, could not be said to have been sanctified). Grammatically, this impersonal translation is perfectly feasible. Moreover, it avoids an apparent conflict with 10:14, which suggests that sanctification is an ongoing process and true believers have been perfected forever by the sacrifice of Christ.

It seems to me that the two factors discussed above under an analysis of McKnight's work have been neglected for the most part among proponents of the phenomenological unbeliever view. (1) The temporal framework of our author's eschatology consists of both the "now" and the "not yet." Christ is

---

32. For a defense of this position see especially the argument by Bruce, *The Epistle to the Hebrews*, 144–49.

Lord now, for instance, but the full realization of his Lordship will come at the end of time (2:5–9). This orientation must be kept in mind for his soteriology as well. The continuum between present salvation and future salvation is a "package deal" in a sense. Both are important; yet you cannot have one without the other. As stated above, what this means is that if one comes to the end and does not have a relationship with Christ because of a lack of perseverance, that relationship never was really there in the first place. This is analogous to the statement in 1 John 2:19 that "they went out from us, but they did not really belong to us."

(2) Most discussions of the warnings in Hebrews have greatly neglected the "omniscience" factor. The author admits his lack of knowledge concerning the spiritual state of all those in this community of hearers. That spiritual state, moreover, can only be discerned in light of ongoing fruitfulness and perseverance.

Summary and conclusions. In this Bridging Contexts section we have noted certain difficulties in interpreting Hebrews 6:4–8, including the ambiguity of the author's language in the passage and our own presuppositions as we come to the task of interpretation. Further, we have delineated important hermeneutical considerations, such as the dynamics of genre in this portion of Scripture and the danger of jumping from possible lexical meanings to theological constructs. It goes without saying that the discussion of various interpretations of 6:4–8 falls short of offering a thorough explanation of each since our treatment is meant to provide a mere starting point for those considering the issue. However, in trying to be fair to the various positions, I have pointed to both strengths and weaknesses of each.

Having finished our discussion (for now), a passage like 6:4–12 tends to leave us somewhat fragmented in the Christian community. As we move toward discussion of this text's application today, therefore, we should note the principles from this text upon which we might be able to agree. (1) We must emphasize that those who fall away from God, cutting off their association with the Christian community and rejecting Christ, are in deep trouble and under the judgment of God. The nature of this judgment will differ according to one's interpretation; however, the warning here looms dark against the bright backdrop of Christian teaching on perseverance and fruitfulness. Those who fall away from God have reason for fear. Therefore, it is incumbent on all those who minister in the context of the church to be responsible in issuing warnings in this regard. Those who fall away from the faith must not be allowed to slip calmly into the night. They should be confronted with the spiritual peril associated with their actions. It is mandatory, therefore, that every professed believer take these words of harsh caution to heart, examining their lives "to make [their] hope sure" (6:11).

(2) Although the terms here will be applied according to one's interpretation of the passage, participation in the Christian community does not necessarily equal salvation. Just because a person starts well in his or her association with the church, we cannot afford to assume that finishing well will follow automatically; this places a great deal of responsibility both on us as individual Christians and on us as church leaders. As individuals we must rest in the grace and justice of God (6:10) even while we "show diligence to the very end" (6:11). As church leaders we are called to care for those who come into the church for spiritual nourishment and protection.

(3) True spirituality cannot be evaluated apart from fruitful faithfulness in the Christian life. Everywhere in the New Testament this principle stands out. Jesus admonished the disciples, "By their fruit you will recognize them" (Matt. 7:16). Paul proclaimed, "For we are God's workmanship, created in Christ Jesus to do good works, which God prepared in advance for us to do" (Eph. 2:10). James reminds us that a workless faith is suspect (James 2:14), and John warns that true relationship with God manifests itself in love of God and humankind (1 John 4:7–8, 20). In Hebrews 6:7–8 the wisdom saying depicts the dichotomy of a blessed fruitfulness over against a cursed barrenness. This does not mean that our works maintain our relationship with God, but rather that true relationship with God will manifest itself in our works. This "works as a result of salvation" orientation also points to the nature of Christian ministry as an occupation of all believers rather than a chosen few. As the author infers in 6:10, a hallmark of true Christianity is ministry to others. Therefore all true Christians engage in helping others.

A THIRTY-SOMETHING BUSINESSWOMAN prays a prayer after her friend shares the gospel over tea and cake. Yet, she begins to drift from the church and Christianity after two months of sporadic involvement, disillusioned with the church's teaching about topics such as giving, Satan, judgment, and the church's stance on certain social issues. A prominent black pastor leaves his church to become a Muslim, stating that Islam has become the real impetus for social change in the American black community. A young woman of the Third World faces terrible persecution from family and the government as a result of her conversion to Christianity. Under pressure she finally recants, returning to her former religion. A child goes through confirmation class at twelve years of age and seemingly is committed to Christ in the teen years but falls away as an adult, adopting an eclectic mix of New Age spirituality, philosophy, and naturalism.

Such scenarios are all too common in the church today. Anyone engaged in Christian ministry has certainly struggled with the pain and confusion of seeing those who have come into the church suddenly turn and walk away as if their professions of Christ were meaningless. Some of us have family members who, to our horror, have renounced the gospel, shaming the crucified Lord. Others, perhaps, are walking now alongside a person who has drifted dangerously close to the chasm of apostasy. How are we to respond? To those who have fallen or are close to falling away we should offer strong warnings in line with Hebrews 6:4–8. For those who have come into the church, joining our communities of faith, we should offer strong nurture in doctrine and relationships. For any of us who have struggled to throw off spiritual mediocrity and maintain passion about Christian commitment, we should offer encouragement, pointing to God's applause of our works in ministering to the saints.

The rhetorical power of a negative example. I have a confession to make. I used to drive through train crossings—when the barriers were down and the red signal lights were flashing. I developed the habit when I first lived in Fort Worth, Texas, a city crisscrossed with railroad tracks. My trek across town would be irritatingly interrupted when the black and white striped bars lowered in my path and the red lights gave a flashing, dinging caution that a train was on its way. I noticed, however, that often the train was distant, slowly making its way toward me; its ominous whistle cried a warning that seemed somehow irrelevant for me at the moment. Thus I would maneuver around the bar blocking my side of the road and be on my merry way.

This irresponsible practice came to an end with two confrontations. My wife-to-be, Pat, made known to me in no uncertain terms that this behavior was unacceptable. Pat has always had a healthy fear of trains. Further, in a period of about six months I read in the newspaper of numerous fatal auto accidents at train crossings. Photos of the mangled cars or trucks whose drivers had no time to spare for such a signal accompanied the articles. They now, simply, had no time. The red flashing lights and bars of the crossing became more meaningful to me when coupled with a personal admonition and dark images of those who had transgressed the barriers.

The use of strong "warning signals" in conjunction with negative examples has a long tradition in the new covenant community, dating back to Jesus' prophecy concerning those who say "Lord, Lord" (Matt. 7:22) and, later, Paul's words concerning the desert wanderers, whose bodies were scattered over the desert, in 1 Corinthians 10:6–12:

> Now these things occurred as examples to keep us from setting our hearts on evil things as they did. Do not be idolaters, as some of

them were. . . . We should not commit sexual immorality, as some of them did—and in one day twenty-three thousand of them died. We should not test the Lord, as some of them did—and were killed by snakes. And do not grumble, as some of them did—and were killed by the destroying angel.

These things happened to them as examples and were written down as warnings for us, on whom the fulfillment of the ages has come. So if you think you are standing firm, be careful that you don't fall!

Jesus, Paul, and other new covenant preachers through the ages have flashed the lights and brought down the bars against a destructive transgressing of the barriers, often pointing to those whose outcome has been devastation.

The use of negative examples points to an element with which our modern church cultures seem uneasy—fear.[33] As Charles Colson points out, "Fear of the Lord would not rank particularly high on the list of modern church growth strategies." Yet, as Colson notes, a healthy fear proved integral to the expansion of the church:

> We can feel that awe pulsating through the pages of Acts. The sense of worship and reverence, the conviction that Christ had risen and would return, the vibrant, absolute joy of their faith. It was a faith based on a series of heart-stopping paradoxes: God become man. Life out of death. And intimate glorious worship of the Lord they loved with holy fear.
>
> So filled were they with this awe that they could face a hostile world with holy abandon. Nothing else mattered, not even their lives.
>
> For the church in the West to come alive, it needs to resolve its identity crisis, to stand on truth, to renew its vision . . . and, more than anything else, it needs to recover the fear of the Lord. Only that will give us the holy abandon that will cause us to be the church no matter what the culture around us says or does. The fear of the Lord is the beginning. . . . [34]

Thus, a healthy perspective on life involves a certain amount of healthy fear; examples about those who have failed, used as warnings, can play an important role in developing healthy, spiritual fear. We do well, therefore, in our preaching and in our living to hold up before ourselves and others examples of those who have fallen away from God, such as those described in Hebrews 6:4–8. We should not shy away from such a passage but rather

---

33. See the treatment of "fear" in relation to Heb. 4:12–13 above, pp. 155–56.
34. Charles Colson with Ellen Santilli Vaughn, *The Body* (Dallas: Word, 1992), 383–84.

utilize it to the encouragement of modern-day church people. It can help us to flash the lights, bring down the barriers, and display pictures of wreckage against a coming tragedy.

Regeneration in contrast to participation. Regeneration is a mystery. "Conversion," suggests theologian Millard Erickson, "refers to the response of the human being to God's offer of salvation and approach to man. Regeneration is the other side of conversion. It is God's doing. It is God's transformation of individual believers, his giving new spiritual vitality and direction to their lives when they accept Christ."[35] Thus, it has to do with the action of the invisible God on a person's invisible spirit.

Furthermore, regeneration relates to the first stage of our salvation. As pointed out by J. I. Packer, salvation in the New Testament has a past, present, and future tense. In the past we have been saved from the penalty of sin; presently we are being saved from the power of sin—its rule over us has been broken; in the future we will be saved from the presence of sin.[36] Regeneration has to do with that first stage, in which we were transformed by the power of God, being made new creatures (2 Cor. 5:17) who now have peace with God because of our introduction by faith into God's grace (Rom. 5:1–2).

As an invisible action by the invisible God on a person's invisible spirit, the *act* of regeneration—that change of one's spirit into something new—has never been witnessed by a third party. We see the results. We witness what seems to be a powerful, spiritual surrender or a quiet dawning of gospel-understanding that leads to a refreshing newness. The change in perspective, the altering of character, and the gradual transformation of lifestyle point to a deeper reality, a regenerate condition of the heart. Yet, our scope of understanding, our perception of reality is limited greatly, often skewed. Only God knows the human heart perfectly. We must base our judgments on the outward manifestations of heart conditions rather than the conditions themselves.

What does all this have to do with Hebrews 6:4–12? As we deal with others in the church, our application of this passage relates to how we respond to the outward manifestations of imperceptible conditions of the human heart. Neither can we bring about regeneration (our part is to bear witness to the God of the gospel) nor perceive whether regeneration has taken place. It is entirely possible that some who come into the church and begin participating in what seems to be the life of faith have yet to experience regeneration. They manifest what seem to be spiritual realities and perhaps have even repented publicly. We must be careful, however, not to equate participation with spiritual transformation. If one has truly been transformed, it will

---

35. Erickson, *Christian Theology*, 942.

36. J. I. Packer, *Rediscovering Holiness* (Ann Arbor, Mich.: Vine Books, 1992), 46–47.

be manifest over a long span of time. We must take the "long look" at a person's life, final judgments being reserved for the end of the race.

Our part is to encourage others in the life of faith, doing everything possible to affirm their involvement in the Christian community and their growth in the things of God. This is what the author of Hebrews attempts in 6:4–12. He is doing what he knows to do, as skillfully as he knows how to do it, to prevent more of those in the community from falling away.

From our human standpoint, it may be helpful to ask why people do not stay engaged in our churches once they have joined and what we can do about it. We might write off their drifting away to a lack of commitment or a cliché: "It just wasn't meant to be." As the Christian community, however, we have responsibilities to those in our midst. So, beyond giving warnings concerning those who fall away, what *can* we do to help young converts stay with their commitments?

In their article "Closing the Evangelistic Back Door," Win and Charles Arn suggest the process by which people come to a Christian decision is a crucial determining factor. Among their findings I emphasize two. (1) New church members are more likely to drop out if they were introduced to Christianity through a manipulative process. Among those surveyed, "87 percent of those now *in*active came to their point of decision through a church member who used manipulative monologue."[37] This is contrasted with the 70 percent of those still active in the church who came to Christ as a result of nonmanipulative dialogue. In her book *Out of the Salt Shaker*, Rebecca Manley Pippert tells of an encounter that illustrates the latter process:

> At the University of California, Berkeley campus, I met a co-ed one afternoon in Sproul Plaza. Our conversation moved to whether we believed in God. It was an easy, almost casual talk. I began telling her about Jesus and she seemed interested. But as I became more enthusiastic about what it meant to be a Christian, she seemed to withdraw emotionally. Still I kept on talking about Jesus—for want of knowing what else to do. But even though my mouth kept moving, I was very aware that I was turning her off. So there I was, having a private conversation with myself, trying to figure out how to stop, while I could hear myself talking to her about Christ.
>
> Suddenly I realized how ridiculous all this was, so I said, "Look, I feel really bad. I *am* very excited about who God is and what he's done in my life. But I hate it when people push 'religion' on me. So if I'm coming on too strong will you just tell me?"

---

37. Win Arn and Charles Arn, "Closing the Evangelistic Back Door," *Leadership Journal* 5, no. 2 (Spring 1984): 26.

She looked at me in disbelief. "I can't believe you just said that. I mean, I cannot *believe* you honestly said that," she answered.

"Why?" I asked.

"Well, I never knew Christians were aware that we hate being recipients of a running monologue," she answered.[38]

Writing of the need for sensitive hearing in the process of evangelism, Earl Palmer notes:

> Evangelists who ignore the person's journey are missing something important. Or, we make the mistake of listening once—then freezing people in that state of rebellion. They may have spoken more outrageously than they believe; they may have only been trying to shock us; or they may have moved on from their first rejection of Christ. We must keep hearing the clues and moving along as they move.[39]

In other words, we must enter into sincere dialogue with those to whom we witness, listening to their objections, feelings, and questions. It makes sense that those who have had ample opportunity to consider the claims of Christ, asking questions and weighing the implications of Christ-following, would be better prepared to make solid, long-term commitments. This means that we must examine our methods of evangelism and evangelism training in our churches. Programs like *Evangelism Explosion* can be used effectively to train lay people to share the gospel clearly. Yet when mishandled, such a program can become a manipulative tool that places the focus on instant results rather than long-term relationships.

This is not to suggest that "invitations" at the end of a church service or challenging a hearer to accept the gospel after an initial hearing is wrong—God uses a variety of means to draw people to himself. The emphasis here rests on a mindset oriented to building healthy, long-term relationships with unbelievers. Thus, we must evaluate how we use such tools in our churches, reminding ourselves and others to proclaim the gospel both boldly and sensitively, allowing a person to experience the "music of the Gospel," as Joe Aldrich puts it.[40] As they witness the beauty of Christ's message in our lives and words, they are called to respond to that message.

(2) Dropouts are more likely to result from a process that neglects long-term development in the faith after a person has converted. Thus, those

---

38. Rebecca Manley Pippert, *Out of the Salt Shaker and Into the World: Evangelism as a Way of Life* (Downers Grove, Ill.: InterVarsity, 1979), 24–25.

39. Earl Palmer, "Evangelism Takes Time," *Leadership Journal* 5, no. 2 (Spring 1984): 23.

40. Joseph C. Aldrich, *Life-Style Evangelism: Crossing Traditional Boundaries to Reach the Unbelieving World* (Portland, Ore.: Multnomah, 1978), 20.

churches that see a person's engagement with the Christian community in the evangelism process and their initial entry into that community as the first steps in faith development are more likely to integrate meaningfully those who make commitments.[41] This calls us to a well-crafted program of educating and assimilating those who come into the church.

The applause of heaven. We all need encouragement. One of the great Christian hopes is that of the encouraging prospect of being told "Well done, good and faithful servant" at the end of our earthly travels. Speaking of our "homecoming" Max Lucado writes:

> You may not have noticed it, but you are closer to home than ever before. Each moment is a step taken. Each breath is a page turned. Each day is a mile marked, a mountain climbed. You are closer to home than you've ever been.
>
> Before you know it, your appointed arrival time will come; you'll descend the ramp and enter the City. You'll see faces that are waiting for you. You'll hear your name spoken by those who love you. And, maybe, just maybe—in the back, behind the crowds—the One who would rather die than live without you will remove his pierced hands from his heavenly robe and . . . applaud.[42]

This great hope the author of Hebrews expounds especially in chapters 11–13. Yet, 6:10 reminds us that God notices and applauds our work of ministry *now*—there exists a "now-and-not-yet" tension in God's affirmation of his covenant people. God, as just, remembers our works of the past and present, which means he values the ministry in which we are involved. He applauds our efforts as viable expressions of true relationship with him. Thus we should draw strong encouragement as we reflect on our past and present ministries to God's people. We can say to ourselves, "My hope in the Lord is well placed. God has and continues to work in and through my life." We can also encourage others as we witness God's ongoing work in and through their lives.

Ministry to the saints, therefore, represents a hallmark of real Christianity. This being the case, all Christians are expected to minister. In large, shadowed corners of the church, we still suffer from the false dichotomy between the "ministers" and the laity. Yet,

> all Christians without exception are called to ministry, indeed to spend their lives in ministry. Ministry is not the privilege of a small elite, but

41. See Calvin C. Ratz, "The Velcro Church," *Leadership Journal* 11, no. 4 (Fall 1990): 38.
42. Max Lucado, *The Applause of Heaven* (Dallas: Word, 1990), 189–90.

of all the disciples of Jesus. You will have noticed that I did not say that all Christians are called to *the* ministry, but to ministry, *diakonia*, service. We do a great disservice to the Christian cause whenever we refer to the pastorate as "the ministry." For by our use of the definite article we give the impression that the pastorate is the only ministry there is, much as medieval churchmen regarded the priesthood as the only (or at least the most "spiritual") vocation there is.[43]

The broad ministry by the whole body of Christ works not only to build the body through the orchestrated utilization of our various gifts. It also effects in each member of the body our own personal edification and encouragement in the faith, as we each see God's hand at work through our hands in the work. In short, ministry serves as a source of hope.

In 1834 Isaac D'Israeli stated, "It is a wretched taste to be gratified with mediocrity when the excellent lies before us."[44] As Christ-followers we are challenged to reject lives of lazy mediocrity, in which neither we nor others can witness the powerful ministry of God's Spirit in and through us. Lazy Christians who display paralyzing passivity in regard to ministry have treated the wine of the gospel, given to bring joy and fullness of life to ourselves and others, as if it were water. Insipid, ineffectual Christians bear witness to little and are those about whom little can be borne witness. Let us, therefore, show diligence "to the very end," giving ourselves and others a source for encouragement and living in a joyful awareness of heaven's applause.

---

43. John R. W. Stott, *The Contemporary Christian: Applying God's Word to Today's World* (Downers Grove, Ill.: InterVarsity, 1992), 140.

44. As quoted in Chuck Swindoll, *Living Above the Level of Mediocrity: A Commitment to Excellence* (Waco, Tex.: Word, 1987), 11.

Hebrews 6:13–20

WHEN GOD MADE his promise to Abraham, since there was no one greater for him to swear by, he swore by himself, [14]saying, "I will surely bless you and give you many descendants." [15]And so after waiting patiently, Abraham received what was promised.

[16]Men swear by someone greater than themselves, and the oath confirms what is said and puts an end to all argument. [17]Because God wanted to make the unchanging nature of his purpose very clear to the heirs of what was promised, he confirmed it with an oath. [18]God did this so that, by two unchangeable things in which it is impossible for God to lie, we who have fled to take hold of the hope offered to us may be greatly encouraged. [19]We have this hope as an anchor for the soul, firm and secure. It enters the inner sanctuary behind the curtain, [20]where Jesus, who went before us, has entered on our behalf. He has become a high priest forever, in the order of Melchizedek.

Original Meaning

IF YOU HAVE ever taken a detour, you know that once on the alternate route, it can be beastly difficult to get back on the main road. We pointed out that at 5:11 the author of Hebrews departs strategically for a time from the topic of Christ's appointment as high priest in order to warn the hearers concerning their spiritual immaturity.[1] He offers an assessment of their condition (5:11–6:3), presents a harsh warning (6:4–8), and then mitigates that warning with encouragement based on their involvement in ministry (6:9–12). With 6:13–20 the author both builds on his exhortation begun at 5:11 and begins a move back toward his discussion of Christ's superior priestly ministry. The section serves as an "on-ramp" of sorts that works to make a smooth transition from the strategically placed exhortation of 5:11–6:12 back to the exposition on Jesus' Melchizedek-like appointment as high priest.[2]

---

1. See above, pp. 200–206.

2. On the unit at 6:13–20 as a special form of transition, see Guthrie, *The Structure of Hebrews*, 110–11.

The Example of Abraham (6:13–15)

FOR THOSE ORIENTED to the Jewish Scriptures the author could have chosen no greater example of faithful perseverance than father Abraham. Especially apropos, the moment at which Abraham offered his cherished son, Isaac, at Moriah (Gen. 22:1–18) forms the backdrop of the discussion at Hebrews 6:13–15. Abraham, caught in a crisis charged with yearnings for his son and even greater yearnings to obey God, believed that the promises of God would not fail (11:17–19). Consequently, he stayed the course of sacrifice through intense, prolonged testing and became a paradigmatic receptor of God's covenant promise. Our preacher to the Hebrews uses the heroic figure of Abraham, therefore, as an especially apt illustration to encourage a community struggling with perseverance under trial.

In the Old Testament narrative (Gen. 22:15–18) God's response to the faithfulness of Abraham goes as follows:

> The angel of the LORD called to Abraham from heaven a second time and said, "I swear by myself, declares the LORD, that because you have done this and have not withheld your son, your only son, I will surely bless you and make your descendants as numerous as the stars in the sky and as the sand on the seashore. Your descendants will take possession of the cities of their enemies, and through your offspring all nations on earth will be blessed, because you have obeyed me."

This passage has two components on which the author concentrates. (1) The Lord's declaration "I swear by myself" constitutes the main concern in the immediate passage and leads nicely back to a discussion of Psalm 110:4 in chapter 7, that psalm also speaking of God's oath. (2) God's pledge to bless Abraham and give him numerous descendants forms the heart of the covenant promises and corresponds directly to Abraham's sacrifice of Isaac, the progenitor of that guaranteed host. That Abraham, "after waiting patiently ... received what was promised" made him a fitting model for sluggish Christ-followers in need of refocusing attention on the promised rewards attending perseverance (Heb. 6:12).

The Finality of Oaths (6:16–18)

THE DISCUSSION CONTINUES in verse 16 with a truism peppered with legal terminology of the ancient Mediterranean world.[3] Oaths given and received in human courts have two characteristics. (1) They require an appeal to one higher in status than the oath-giver. This action lends the witness a credibility

---

3. Attridge, *The Epistle to the Hebrews*, 180.

grounded in the worth or integrity of another. (2) Witnesses swear an oath given in court in order to bring about a "confirmation" (*bebaiosis*) or to provide a legal guarantee of a testimony's truthfulness,[4] thus strengthening the case being presented. Once a witness swears in this manner, such an affidavit leaves no room for further legal disputation since an oath may be taken as establishing the truthfulness of a given position.

If truthfulness can be confirmed in such a manner in human courts of law, it is even more assured when God himself swears an oath. The NIV translation of verse 17 begins with "Because God wanted to make the unchanging nature of his purpose very clear to the heirs of what was promised. . . ." This translation could be understood as suggesting that God takes his cue from a human system of oath giving—which is not the case. Rather, the author merely draws an analogy. In both cases, human and divine, oaths point to a confirmation of truth.

God's reason in giving the oath is twofold. (1) It shows the "unchanging nature of his purpose" in granting to the heirs their promised inheritance (v. 17). Again the author utilizes legal terminology to drive home his point. The word *epideiknymi*, translated by the NIV as "make clear," normally conveys the sense of "show." Used in a legal context as here, however, the word carries the special nuance "to give proof."[5] In other words, God gives proof by his sworn affidavit that his will is immutable or "unchanging" (*ametatheton*), a word appearing in wills and contracts of the ancient world to speak of terms or conditions that could not be annulled.[6] So the heirs need not worry that the terms of God's promised inheritance are going to change.

(2) God intends that his heirs, "who have fled to take hold of the hope offered to us," might find strong (*ischyran*), or powerful, encouragement from his oath-making (v. 18). That we have "fled to take hold of [grasp] the hope" means that we have turned from our former lives of sin and despair and to Christ for salvation, stability, and security.[7] The foundation for our encouragement, moreover, rests in the character of God, who cannot lie.

What, then, are we to make of the "two unchangeable things" of which 6:18 speaks? Remember that in 5:1–10 the author launches his section on Christ's appointment as high priest with a quote of Psalm 110:4. I believe this

---

4. Lane, *Hebrews* 1–8, 149. The author of Hebrews uses the adjectival cognate of this noun at 2:2 and 9:17, both in the context of legal discussions. The use of the cognate verb at 2:3 also has legal overtones. In broader Christian literature this word group serves to speak of the early Christian message as offering permanence and stability for the faith of believers. See A. Fuchs, "βεβαίωσις," *EDNT*, 1:210–11.

5. Lane, *Hebrews* 1–8, 149.

6. Ibid.

7. See Hughes, *A Commentary on the Epistle to the Hebrews*, 234.

verse is on the author's mind at 6:18 as he moves back to his discussion of Melchizedek (7:1–10) and Jesus' Melchizedekan high priesthood (7:11–28) in the next chapter. Notice the two components in God's oath given in this Christological psalm, which forms the basis for 7:11–28:

The Lord has sworn and will not change his mind:
    "You are a priest forever,
in the order of Melchizedek."

The first component, "You are a priest forever," composes the author's argument in 7:15–28 on the eternality of Christ's priesthood. The second component garners his attention in 7:11–14, where the Levitical decree that priests come from Aaron's tribe is shown to be set aside in the case of Christ. Rather, God's Son, who was from the tribe of Judah, comes to office by way of another order—the order of Melchizedek. These, then, are the "two unchangeable things in which it is impossible for God to lie" (6:18)—that Jesus is of the order of Melchizedek and that he has been declared by God as an eternal high priest. These truths offer powerful encouragement to the heirs of God's promise because they are grounded in the person and work of the eternal Christ.

The Encouragement of a Firm Hope (6:19–20)

THE AUTHOR EXPOUNDS the stability of Christian hope in 6:19–20, calling it "an anchor for the soul, firm and secure." The word "anchor" (*ankyra*), used three times in Acts 27 of a literal anchor, here represents the idea of stability. Such a metaphorical use of this nautical image occurs broadly in ancient literature; authors such as Plato, Plutarch, and Lucian write of various institutions or faculties that give life steadiness.[8] For example, Plutarch, a philosopher born in Greece some fifteen years after the resurrection of Christ, criticizes the incontinence of those at the mercy of their own passions. Extolling the virtue of reason, the philosopher quotes a piece of poetry—"The spirit yields and can resist no more, like an anchor-hook in sand amid the surge"—suggesting that a person who gives in to life's urges, in defiance of reason, has no more stability than the hook of an anchor lodged only in loose sand.[9] Philo, on the other hand, calls virtue a stabilizing factor by using the image of being firmly anchored in a safe spot.[10]

Correspondingly, our author here says our hope, as an anchor for the soul, is both "firm" (or "safe") and "secure." The latter word (*bebaios*) speaks of

---

8. Ellingworth, *The Epistle to the Hebrews*, 346.
9. Plutarch, *Moralia*, 446A.
10. Philo, *De Sacrificiis Abelis et Caini*, 90.

that which is "reliable, well-founded, or confirmed." It is a cognate adjective of the noun *bebaiosis* (translated in NIV as "confirms") in verse 16, which there refers in a legal sense to the confirmation of a testimony. Thus, our hope as an anchor offers both safety and a reliable basis for living.

When the author notes that this hope enters the "inner sanctuary behind the curtain" (v. 19), he refers to the Most Holy Place, that most sacred of space in the tabernacle, which was identified as the place of God's presence. Under the old covenant only the high priest could go behind the curtain separating the outer part of the Holy Place from the inner, and then only once a year on the Day of Atonement. This barrier keeping the broader people of God from entering into the presence of God, however, has been torn away in the new covenant—we all now may enter by following Jesus. The security of our souls rests firmly in the eternal, high-priestly work of Christ, by which he has entered into God's presence on our behalf and made a way for us to follow.[11] Our stability of soul thus stems from all the power and provisions to be found as we stand before the face of God.

 **A PRIMARY POINT, two implications, and three assumptions.** By its nature Hebrews 6:13–20 makes a smooth transition between the exhortation of 5:11–6:12 and the material of chapter 7. In doing so, the author focuses especially on one primary point: that *God's oath-making provides believers with a superior basis for stability in life.* Notice the prevalence of the concepts "oath," "promise," "swear," and "heir" in the present section. These concepts revolve around the affirmation of God's faithfulness to fulfill what he has pledged.

The passage's transitional purpose works as follows. The exhortation of 5:11–6:12 places the spotlight on *human* actions and responsibility. In 5:11–6:3 the writer points to the readers' lack of growth and need to move on in the faith. In 6:4–8 the apostates' rejection of Christ and consequent peril serves as a harsh example, the author emphasizing their lack of fruitfulness. In 6:9–12 the encouragement found in the listeners' own past fruitfulness plays a nice counterpoint to the warning of 6:4–8, yet keeps primary focus on human response to God. To be sure, the action of God underlies the whole of 5:11–6:12, but the author places the emphasis on human responsibility in responding to the works of God.

---

11. For a more extensive treatment of the tabernacle and the worship with which it was associated, see below, pp. 297–300.

All of this may lead to our feeling somewhat insecure. The reader of this commentary may have ended our treatment of 6:4–12 asking, "Then is it all up to me? Where is the provision of God in all of this?" The author of Hebrews, while wishing to emphasize the seriousness of our responsibility in responding properly to the gospel, does not intend to leave us feeling insecure.

Beginning with 6:13 the discussion turns back with full force toward God's provision of a superior basis for Christian perseverance. This general theme serves as the author's guiding principle through 10:18, in his focus on Christ's appointment as an eternal high priest in 7:1–28 and on his superior, heavenly sacrifice for sin in 8:3–10:18. In the first of these main sections the argument rests on God's oath in Psalm 110:4: "The LORD has sworn and will not change his mind: 'You are a priest forever in the order of Melchizedek.'" Hebrews 6:13–20 moves the sermon quickly from an emphasis on human responsibility (5:11–6:12) to a consideration of God's promises (i.e., "oath") and two implications of those promises for believers. (1) One implication is that *promises by their nature demand patience* (6:14–15), since the fulfillment of a promise seldom follows on the heels of the promise itself. (2) Also, *promises provide us with a superior basis for hope* (6:18–19) because we can rest in God's assurance of a better tomorrow.

Beneath the surface of the author's treatment of God's oaths lie three assumptions. The first two are as follows: (1) God is eternal, being ever present to fulfill what has been promised; and (2) God is omnipotent, having the ability to fulfill what has been promised. The Christian finds hope in the Lord's promises because, while all of life shifts beneath our feet, God remains the one true source of lasting stability. Thus we reject the assertion of Heraclitus, an ancient Greek philosopher, who said, "Change alone is unchanging." We know better; for we know the one who is the same yesterday, today, and forever (13:8). No power exists that can shake the fulfillment of God's oaths concerning his children (Rom. 8:35–39).

(3) The final assumption has to do with the integrity of God. Because of his integrity, when God makes an oath he can be trusted to fulfill what he has promised. Not only is he powerful and eternal, but he is also of unquestionable character. As Numbers 23:19 says, "God is not a man, that he should lie, nor a son of man, that he should change his mind. Does he speak and then not act? Does he promise and not fulfill?" The implied answer to each of these rhetorical questions is a resounding "no!"

Two problems. The author's treatment of God's oath-making in 6:13–20, however, raises what may be perceived as two problems. (1) In verse 16 the writer uses human testimony in a court of law as an illustration of oath-giving. By following with God's use of oath in verse 17 he almost seems to present God as following the pattern of a human, legal system—a system that we know to be less than fail-proof because of human nature. Yet, we must begin with where the author does in verse 13 regarding a primary *difference* between God's oath and the act of swearing in a human court. Whereas "men swear by someone greater than themselves" (v 16), God has no one greater by whom he can swear (v. 13).

The argument at this point is one "from lesser to greater,"[12] although this preacher begins here with the greater assumption, moves to the lesser assumption, and then back to the greater. His reasoning is as follows. (1) When God made his promise to Abraham, he swore by himself. (2) Humans participate in a legal system in which assurances are made and truth is verified. (3) Much more assurance may be had with reference to oaths made by God since he is so great (i.e., trustworthy) that no one greater could be found by whom he would swear. The passage, thus, presents us with the absolute trustworthiness of God's promises. Thus the author, rather than presenting God as imitating a human system of oath-making, uses that human system as a basis of comparison.

(2) This, however, raises a second issue: Why would God resort to oath-giving at all,[13] especially in light of Jesus' words concerning oaths in Matthew 5:34–37:

> But I tell you, Do not swear at all: either by heaven, for it is God's throne; or by the earth, for it is his footstool; or by Jerusalem, for it is the city of the Great King. And do not swear by your head, for you cannot make even one hair white or black. Simply let your "Yes" be "Yes," and your "No," "No"; anything beyond this comes from the evil one.

It should be remembered, first of all, that Jesus' words from the Sermon on the Mount are oriented to the frailty of the human condition. The swearing of oaths was a prevalent practice in the first century, and Jesus addresses the use of oaths as a means of compensating for one's lack of integrity. Disciples of the kingdom should be such persons of integrity that their words alone, unadorned with exclamatory oaths, should suffice as reflections of the truth.[14] In Hebrews, however, the orientation is different. The focus here is on the purposes and character of God as he meets the needs of people. Rather than needing oaths to shore up the veracity of his words, God employs oaths to provide assurance and encouragement to his people (Heb. 6:18). In other words, the reason for God's oaths is found in our need, not his.

Two pitfalls. We must also reflect on two possible pitfalls situated along the path toward application of this passage. (1) God's promises must not be

---

12. See the discussion on 2:1–4 above, pp. 84–85.

13. P. E. Hughes, *A Commentary on the Epistle to the Hebrews*, 229–30.

14. David S. Dockery and David E. Garland, *Seeking the Kingdom: The Sermon on the Mount Made Practical for Today* (Wheaton, Ill.: Harold Shaw, 1992), 60–61.

employed in an attempt to coerce him. In "health-and-wealth" preaching the reasoning too often goes as follows. "Does not God's Word say that he will give you whatever you ask in Jesus' name?" The congregation answers, "Yes!" The preacher then asks, "Is God true to his Word?!" Again the congregation shouts, "Yes!" Then the speaker concludes with an inference: "If God doesn't fulfill this promise to you (e.g., give you a house, a car, healing, etc.), then God is a liar, and we know that God is not a liar!" So if God said it and you step out in faith on what God said, then God must come through.

This line of reasoning, which attempts to back God in a corner by using his Word, runs dangerously close to Satan's temptation of Jesus in Matthew 4:5–7. Pointing to Psalm 91:11–12, the tempter reasoned with Jesus, "Here is a passage of Scripture that promises God will not let you get hurt [an interesting thought in light of the cross awaiting at the end of Jesus' ministry!]. Jesus, why don't you step out on God's truthfulness by throwing yourself off the pinnacle of the temple? God will have to come through based on his Word." Jesus responded that testing God is inappropriate. Our part is to submit to his will, not to attempt to dictate our will to him using his promises for support.

(2) We must not confuse true Christian hope with what the world often calls "hope." In a letter to Thomas More, English poet Lord Byron wrote, "But what is Hope? Nothing but the paint on the face of Existence; the least touch of truth rubs it off, and then we see what a hollow-cheeked harlot we have got hold of."[15] This speaks to hope as a form of wishful thinking. In the words of playwright Jean Kerr, "Hope is the feeling you have that the feeling you have isn't permanent."[16] This insipid, earth-bound emotion falls far short of Christian hope, which is grounded in revelation, encouraged by the Spirit's work in us, and cognizant of future realities. True hope, moreover, produces purity (1 John 3:3), patience (Rom. 8:25), fulfillment (5:4–5), joy (12:12), and stability (Col. 1:23). When compared to God's work through the old covenant, the new covenant hope is "better" (Heb. 7:19), providing for the Christ-follower something worthy of public confession (3:6; 10:23).

OUR NEED FOR hope. We live in a world that is a place of great despair for many. Like the widow of Zarephath, to whom God sent the prophet Elijah (1 Kings 17:8–16), people find their resources—their "bread and oil," the basic elements of life—almost spent, and

---

15. "Letter, 28 Oct. 1815," to the poet Thomas More (published in *Byron's Letters and Journals*, vol. 4, ed. by Leslie Marchand [Cambridge, Mass.: Harvard Univ. Press, 1975]).

16. Jean Kerr, in the play *Finishing Touches*, act III.

they are prepared to give up altogether. These resources may be economic, emotional, relational, or spiritual, but the lack thereof brings on a hopelessness leading to despair.

Dr. Armand Nicholi Jr., a professor of psychiatry at Harvard Medical School and editor of *The Harvard Guide to Psychiatry*, notes the rampant increase in depression in contemporary American society, some eleven million patients currently needing treatment and over 250,000 attempting to take their own lives each year. Dr. Nicholi suggests that relational dynamics, both on a personal and international level, which make up the basic nature of life, have remained constant over time. "How then," the professor asks, "do we explain the explosive increase in depression and hopelessness within our society as we enter the twenty-first century A.D.?" Pointing to the undercutting of spiritual resources in the past few decades, Dr. Nicholi states:

> Historians and social scientists tell us that we have fewer spiritual resources to draw from than at any time in Western cultural history. Some say that our culture has forsaken its spiritual roots, that we live in an overtly secular society without even the pretense of spiritual values. Many young people today feel that their cultures fail to provide answers to questions of purpose and meaning and destiny. We fail, they feel, to provide some reason for hope. The consequence is that we are now in a cultural crisis and living in what is being called "The Age of Despair." We hear of our "spiritual vacuum" and our "crisis of meaning."[17]

If the naturalists are correct that the sum of life is found in the "nasty here and now" and the phrase "dust to dust" sums up our origins and our destinies, then life seems both meaningless and hopeless. Yet, to this age of despair the book of Hebrews brings another perspective. God says that life is *more* than what can be seen immediately, and he offers us a wealth of spiritual resources to be found in relation to Jesus Christ. Those spiritual resources are accessed as we trust God's Word and build our lives on it. His "oaths" help us to see beyond our limitations to his limitless power and provisions. Encouragement comes from knowing we play a part in a life both full of meaning and lasting. Thus our current circumstances can never adequately define who we are or what we are about. This quality of hope breeds hope. As Paul states, "May the God of hope fill you with all joy and peace as you trust in him, so that you may overflow with hope by the power of the Holy Spirit" (Rom. 15:13). This Age of Angst asks, "Is there more?" The Christian conviction rings out: "Yes, and so we dare to hope."

---

17. Armand Nicholi Jr., "Hope in a Secular Age," in *Finding God at Harvard: Spiritual Journeys of Thinking Christians*, ed. Kelly Monroe (Grand Rapids: Zondervan, 1996), 112–13.

Longing for security. Much of modern Western life revolves around building some semblance of security into our lives. A home that provides shelter and protection from destructive elements in both nature and society. Insurance that safeguards against unforeseen tragedies. Bank accounts that assure the resources of tomorrow will prove sufficient for our needs. Relationships that give us comfort. Yet, in the back of our minds we realize that all of these could be gone in a moment. An illness. A business failure. A car wreck. Life is fragile, and we long and reach for a security that stretches beyond the dark possibilities crouched just around life's next corner. We are like the arachnid of Walt Whitman's "A Noiseless Patient Spider."

A noiseless patient spider,
I mark'd where on a little promontory it stood isolated,
Mark'd how to explore the vacant vast surrounding,
It launch'd forth filament, filament, filament, out of itself,
Ever unreeling them, ever tirelessly speeding them.

And you O my soul where you stand,
Surrounded, detached, in measureless oceans of space,
Ceaselessly musing, venturing, throwing,
    seeking the spheres to connect them,
Till the bridge you will need be form'd, till the ductile anchor hold, .
Till the grossamer thread you fling catch somewhere, O my soul.

Whitman's poignant reminder shows our souls are ever attempting to anchor our lives, to catch hold of something outside ourselves that will transform our detached existence to a state of stability.

Yet in flinging our threads, our aim too often is off, hitting water droplets and dust balls on the surface of reality, elements that themselves will soon evaporate or be swept away. Money, homes, positions, and even people are transitory. Such can provide no lasting stability in life. Thus Hebrews invites us to a security anchored in eternal realities found in the "inner sanctuary behind the curtain" (6:19), where a truth-telling God encourages us by giving oaths. His promises offer the only true surety for the future. All other sources of stability give but promissory notes that may or may not be fulfilled, depending on the character, resources, or future of the issuer. Our God, however, is a God of integrity, of endless resources, and of a never-ending future and, as such, offers us a superior basis for stability in life. An old hymn says it well.

How firm a foundation, you saints of the Lord
Is laid for your faith in his excellent word.
What more can he say than to you he has said,
To you who for refuge to Jesus has fled.

God's waiting room. Patience is one of the most difficult Christian virtues to grasp in our hurry-up, Type A, charge-ahead culture. Yet, "after waiting patiently, Abraham received what was promised." After waiting patiently!

> We live in an instant credit, get-everything-now economy. We eat add-water-and-mix foods or drive by fast-food outlets which poke our palates with immediate delicacies ranging from burgers and burritos to fried chicken and fish 'n' chips. All of this trains us to want what we want now on the basis of something that requires little or nothing of us. We don't grow trees in our yards, we buy them potted and several years advanced in their growth—or move to another house where they're already grown. Waiting is not in style, and patience has never been a forte of the flesh. . . .
>
> If God weren't growing sons and daughters, things would not take nearly as long. But since He is more interested in our growth than He is in our getting, waiting becomes a very essential and useful means toward that end. He doesn't traffic in add-water-and-mix saints. . . .[18]

God has a purpose for putting us in his waiting room. Abraham had to wait two and a half decades to see the birth of his promised son. You and I often must wait for God's help in matters related to family, finances, health, or direction for the future. A seemingly protracted pause in God's manifest activity on our behalf must especially be difficult for those undergoing persecution for the faith. Yet God is at work. He works character in you and me even when—sometimes, especially when—we cannot see him at work in our circumstances. If no word of help and hope existed, we might give way to despair. Yet, the promises of God help us to see future realities and draw encouragement from them.

We only experience such encouragement, we only grow in this dimension of Christian faith, as we sit in the waiting room. It can be a habitation of tension, frustration, and anxiety; but it also can be a place of unique peace and a work in which the spirit is deepened. Our posture toward God during times of waiting can make all the difference in the effect of such an experience on us. C. H. Spurgeon once wrote:

> [Waiting] is one of the postures which a Christian soldier learns not without years of teaching. Marching and quick-marching are much easier to God's warriors than standing still. There are hours of perplexity when the most willing spirit, anxiously desirous to serve the Lord, knows not what part to take. Then what shall it do? Vex itself

---

18. Jack Hayford, *Moments With Majesty* (Portland, Ore.: Multnomah, 1990), 214–15.

by despair? Fly back in cowardice, turn to the right hand in fear, or rush forward in presumption? No, but simply wait. Wait in prayer, however. Call upon God, and spread the case before Him; tell Him your difficulty, and plead His promise of aid. . . . But wait in faith. Express your unstaggering confidence in Him; for unfaithful, untrusting waiting, is but an insult to the Lord. Believe that if He keep you tarrying even till midnight, yet He will come at the right time; the vision shall come and shall not tarry. Wait in quiet patience, not rebelling because you are under the affliction, but blessing your God for it. Never murmur against the second cause, as the children of Israel did against Moses; never wish you could go back to the world again, but accept the case as it is, and put it as it stands, simply and with your whole heart, without any self-will, into the hand of your covenant God, saying, "Now, Lord, not my will, but Thine be done. I know not what to do; I am brought to extremities, but I will wait until Thou shalt cleave the floods, or drive back my foes. I will wait, if Thou keep me many a day, for my heart is fixed upon Thee alone, O God, and my spirit waiteth for Thee in the full conviction that Thou wilt yet be my joy and my salvation, my refuge and my strong tower."[19]

I WILL wait God even in this dark season, You will remain FAITHFUL as You have in the past. 2/27/08

Spurgeon's words reflect the spirit of Psalm 33:20–22, which reads:

We wait in hope for the LORD;
    he is our help and our shield.
In him our hearts rejoice,
    for we trust in his holy name.
May your unfailing love rest upon us, O LORD,
    even as we put our hope in you.

---

19. Charles H. Spurgeon, *Morning and Evening Daily Readings*, in *God's Treasury of Virtues* (Tulsa, Okla.: Honor Books, 1995), 174–75.

Hebrews 7:1–10

THIS MELCHIZEDEK WAS king of Salem and priest of God Most High. He met Abraham returning from the defeat of the kings and blessed him, ²and Abraham gave him a tenth of everything. First, his name means "king of righteousness"; then also, "king of Salem" means "king of peace." ³Without father or mother, without genealogy, without beginning of days or end of life, like the Son of God he remains a priest forever.

⁴Just think how great he was: Even the patriarch Abraham gave him a tenth of the plunder! ⁵Now the law requires the descendants of Levi who become priests to collect a tenth from the people—that is, their brothers—even though their brothers are descended from Abraham. ⁶This man, however, did not trace his descent from Levi, yet he collected a tenth from Abraham and blessed him who had the promises. ⁷And without doubt the lesser person is blessed by the greater. ⁸In the one case, the tenth is collected by men who die; but in the other case, by him who is declared to be living. ⁹One might even say that Levi, who collects the tenth, paid the tenth through Abraham, ¹⁰because when Melchizedek met Abraham, Levi was still in the body of his ancestor.

Original Meaning

EARLIER THE AUTHOR of Hebrews notified his hearers that he had a great deal to tell them about Melchizedek (5:11); he now gets to that didactic task in full earnest. He designs this unit of material as the groundwork for the following unit concerning the superiority of Christ's Melchizedekan priesthood (7:11–28). But he first must draw the connection between Christ and Melchizedek a bit more firmly, which he does with an exposition of Genesis 14:17–20, the only Old Testament narrative we have on the enigmatic priest.

The author must further demonstrate clearly that Melchizedek's priesthood is superior to the Levitical priesthood prescribed in the Mosaic law. He proposes this superiority on two primary bases—one that he also finds in the Genesis narrative and the other developed from a consideration of Genesis 14 in light of Psalm 110:4. (1) The superiority of Melchizedek's priesthood rests on *what he received from Abraham*, namely, a tenth of the patriarch's plunder won in battle when he retrieved Lot and the other captives from Sodom and Gomorrah. In proclaiming the preeminence of this priesthood by virtue of Abraham's tithe, he also notes the blessing Melchizedek gave to Abraham. This blessing, rather than demonstrating Melchizedek's superiority, was given by virtue of that superiority, as will be discussed below. (2) The author presents Melchizedek as superior on the basis of the *eternal* nature of his priesthood.

An Exposition on Melchizedek (7:1–3)

IN HEBREWS 7:1–3 the writer to the Hebrews briefly expounds Genesis 14:17–20, demonstrating typological connections between Melchizedek and the Son of God. His interpretation of the passage has a compact style with which he quickly highlights certain key points that strengthen the association between these two figures suggested by Psalm 110:4.

Verses 1–2a provide a concise summary statement of the Genesis passage. Melchizedek was a priest-king of the city Salem, who met Abraham as he returned from routing certain invading kings. In the Old Testament narrative four kings from the east (Kedorlaomer king of Elam, Tidal king of Goiim, Amraphel king of Shinar, and Arioch king of Ellasar) marched on a confederation of five kings from Sodom, Gomorrah, Admah, Zeboiim, and Bela. The armies of the latter were defeated in a valley called Siddim and their cities plundered. Lot, Abraham's nephew, was among the captives taken from Sodom, a fact brought to the attention of the patriarch by a servant who had escaped the battle. Abraham pursued the invaders to Dan, where he staged a night-time attack, putting the enemies to flight and recovering their booty. After his return home both the king of Sodom and Melchizedek, priest of God Most High, met Abraham. The author of Hebrews focuses on Abraham's encounter with the latter, in which Abraham gave a tithe and received a blessing.

The author of Hebrews points out that Melchizedek's name means "king of righteousness," alluding to the Hebrew words *melek* (which means "king") and *sedeq* (which is commonly rendered "righteousness"[1]). He further interprets "Salem," the city over which Melchizedek ruled as king, to mean "peace," associating the name with the Hebrew *šalom*. Thus, the author reasons, he is "king of peace." These concepts of righteousness and peace are appropriate for one who prefigures the Messiah, who would make righteousness and peace possible for the people of God.[2]

The writer finds what the Old Testament narrative does *not* say especially relevant for his argument. Following a common exegetical practice known

---

1. Bruce, *Epistle to the Hebrews*, 158.
2. Ibid., 159; cf. Rom. 5:1.

as "argument from silence," the author capitalizes on Genesis 14's lack of any reference to Melchizedek's ancestry, birth, or death. His point is not that Melchizedek exists as some form of supernatural being. Rather, he focuses on the details of what the narrative does and does not say, anticipating a stark contrast between Melchizedek's priesthood and the Levitical priesthood, which he will develop later in the chapter. Since the Genesis text says nothing of this priest's genealogy, birth, or death, his priesthood has neither the qualifications nor the parameters one finds concerning the Levitical priesthood in the law of Moses. The Levites were priests by virtue of heritage and ceased from the office upon death. Scripture places no such limitations on Melchizedek's priesthood. For the author of Hebrews, therefore, the Genesis narrative confirms what is clearly stated in Psalm 110:4—a priesthood according to the order of Melchizedek lasts forever.[3]

The Greatness of Melchizedek (7:4–10)

THE WORD *THEOREO*, used fifty-eight times in the New Testament, commonly means "to view" or "to watch" something; here it refers rather to perception. Thus the NIV translates the word "just think." The author calls his hearers to grasp the greatness of Melchizedek as indicated by the Old Testament narrative. He develops his claim for the enigmatic priest's eminence in one primary direction. Both a responsibility and honor held by Levi's descendants was the collection of the tithe (Num. 18:21–32), which they received as their inheritance from the Lord. This set them apart as unique among the children of Israel.

As the author of Hebrews points out, however, the Genesis passage has Abraham, the father of those who would become the Levites, giving a tithe to the priest Melchizedek, who, obviously, was not of the tribe of Levi (7:5–6). Thus the Levites, who were still "in the body of [their] ancestor" Abraham, in a sense paid a tenth to Melchizedek (7:9–10)! The author again brings in the eternality of Melchizedek's priesthood when he says, "In the one case, the tenth is collected by men who die; but in the other case, by him who is declared to be living" (7:8). That father Abraham (and the Levites in his body) gave a tithe to this priest shows his deference to him and respect for his unique service on behalf of God Most High.

By virtue of his greater position, Melchizedek in turn blessed Abraham. When the author states, "And without a doubt the lesser person is blessed by the greater," he is not giving a maxim that assumes only superiors give blessings. Not only do subordinates give blessings throughout the Old Testa-

---

3. Lane, *Hebrews 1–8*, 165–67.

ment,[4] but in Genesis 14:17–20 Melchizedek blesses God immediately after he blesses Abraham! No. Our author, based on his broader argument concerning the tithe and the eternality of Melchizedek's priesthood, parenthetically proclaims (rather than argues for) the superiority of Melchizedek in connection with the blessing offered by him. Melchizedek's superiority to the Levites primarily rests on his having received a tenth of the spoils from Abraham and the fact that Scripture gives no indication of his death.

HEBREWS 7:1–10 PRESENTS the modern expositor with one of the more fascinating pieces of interpretation found in the New Testament. The logic inherent in the author's argument is both rigorous and, perhaps, a bit perplexing for those unfamiliar with his conventions. What are we to make of his treatment of Melchizedek? How can we appropriate this text, which deals with an obscure priest mentioned in only a few Old Testament verses, into contemporary applications?

Hebrews' use (not abuse) of the Old Testament. In the not-too-distant past the exegetical methodology of Hebrews was most often associated with the allegorical exegesis of Philo of Alexandria, a first-century Jewish interpreter. Allegorical interpretation, later affiliated with the "Alexandrian School" of the early church fathers, probes for deeper or mystical senses in a text not readily apparent from the normal meanings of the words themselves. For those who saw Hebrews in this vein, the author fancifully drew meanings from Old Testament passages based on broad semantic associations. Thus, the meaning of a text was not to be found in the apparent meanings of the words used in association with literary context, historical background, and so forth. Rather, allegorical interpretation holds there are hidden or spiritual meanings in the text in addition to the literal sense.

More recently, however, a number of writers have recognized sharp differences between Hebrews and Philo. As indicated in the author's treatment of Genesis 14:17–20, Hebrews shows great interest in Old Testament contexts and the meanings of specific words. What governs his interpretation of this text is typology, not allegory. Before we consider his use of typology, however, we must focus on two related, but important, principles behind his hermeneutics.

(1) The author, as he does throughout Hebrews, uses "verbal analogy" in his interpretations detailed in Hebrews 7.[5] That is, he interprets the

---

4. Attridge, *The Epistle to the Hebrews*, 196.

5. On the uses of verbal analogy in Hebrews see above, pp. 25, 67.

Melchizedek passage found in Genesis 14 alongside Psalm 110:4, the only other Old Testament text to mention the priest from Salem. This principle, "Scripture interprets Scripture," has continued as a hallmark of valid exegesis throughout the history of the church down to the present day. Indeed, we utilize concordances to check linguistic parallels to terms we find in a text under consideration, at times for the purpose of clarifying word meanings or concepts.

I believe this principle of Scripture interpreting Scripture is vital for understanding the author's "argument from silence" (Heb. 7:1–3)—an approach to biblical interpretation that would be graded down in many modern hermeneutics classes![6] Yet, the author does not play fast and loose with his text at this point. Rather, he seeks to expound what an Old Testament author clearly indicates. Let me explain.

The author of Hebrews interprets the Melchizedek narrative of Genesis 14:17–20 in light of that which the psalmist declares in Psalm 110:4: "You are a priest *forever* in the order of Melchizedek" (italics mine). Thus, with use of the words translated "forever" (*eis ton aiona*), Scripture associates eternality with a Melchizedekan-type priesthood—a fact the writer of Hebrews expounds extensively in the rest of chapter 7. When our author reads the Genesis passage in this light, the lack of reference to Melchizedek's heritage and death makes sense. The enigmatic priest-king has an eternal quality to his priesthood. Thus, the author of Hebrews interprets Genesis 14:17–20 contextually rather than grasping facts from thin air, but the context, in this case, is the broader context of Scripture.[7]

(2) The author of Hebrews interprets his Old Testament Christologically. Speaking of the Christological hermeneutic woven through the fabric of the New Testament, David S. Dockery writes:

> The renewal of the preaching of Jesus after his crucifixion carried with it a statement concerning his own person and function, and reception of the message involved acknowledgment of Jesus as the exalted Lord and allegiance to him. This greatly influenced the church's reading of its Scriptures, the Old Testament, and had literary consequences

---

6. On the interesting question concerning whether we as moderns can or should imitate the exegetical methods of writers of the New Testament, see, for example, Moisés Silva, "The New Testament Use of the Old Testament: Text Form and Authority," in *Scripture and Truth*, ed. D. A. Carson and John D. Woodbridge (Grand Rapids: Baker, 1992), 147–65; G. K. Beale, ed., *The Right Doctrine From the Wrong Texts?: Essays on the Use of the Old Testament in the New* (Grand Rapids: Baker, 1994), especially the final two essays, opposing articles by Richard N. Longenecker and Beale.

7. See G. K. Beale, "Did Jesus and His Followers Preach the Right Doctrine From the Wrong Texts?: An Examination of the Presuppositions of Jesus' and the Apostles' Exegetical Method," in *The Right Doctrine From the Wrong Texts?* 401.

---

for the development of the New Testament. By reading the Old Testament in this fashion, the church preserved the christological approach that it learned from Jesus.[8]

That Jesus' own methods of interpreting the Old Testament in light of himself laid the foundation for apostolic hermeneutics was suggested by C. H. Dodd earlier this century.[9] Offering a summary of Jesus' interpretations in this regard and drawing his conclusions from the Synoptics, R. T. France writes:

> He uses persons in the Old Testament as types of himself (David, Solomon, Elijah, Elisha, Isaiah, Jonah) or of John the Baptist (Elijah); he refers to Old Testament institutions as types of himself and his work (the priesthood and the covenant); he sees in the experiences of Israel foreshadowings of his own; he finds the hopes of Israel fulfilled in himself and his disciples, and sees his disciples as assuming the status of Israel; in deliverance by God he sees a type of the gathering of men into his church, while the disasters of Israel are foreshadowings of the imminent punishment of those who reject him, whose unbelief is prefigured in that of the wicked in Israel and even, in two instances, in the arrogance of the Gentile nations.[10]

France's summary brings us to the topic of typology and locates the typological interpretation of Genesis 14 found in Hebrews 7 within the mainstream of early Christian hermeneutics. The word "typology" comes from the Greek term *typos*, which can mean "pattern, prefiguration, model, impression, foreshadowing." Typological interpretation involves identifying preordained connections between events, persons, things, or institutions in the span of salvation history. This identification of significant connections between Melchizedek and Jesus constitutes the interpretive strategy of Hebrews 7. For Hebrews the priest Melchizedek foreshadows the heavenly high priest, Christ. Melchizedek is not the Son of God but is "like the Son of God" in that he "remains a priest forever" (7:3) in the perspective of Scripture. This drawing of prefigured connections between Melchizedek and Christ constitutes the main program of Hebrews 7:1–10.

An interpretive pitfall. At least one word of caution is in order at this point. We need to reflect on typological interpretation in the New Testament and *our ability or inability* to practice the same. Among evangelical New

---

8. David S. Dockery, *Biblical Interpretation Then and Now: Contemporary Hermeneutics in the Light of the Early Church* (Grand Rapids: Baker, 1992), 34.

9. C. H. Dodd, *According to the Scriptures: The Substructure of New Testament Theology* (London: Nisbet, 1952), 126–27.

10. R. T. France, *Jesus and the Old Testament: His Application of Old Testament Passages to Himself and His Message* (London: Tyndale, 1971), 75.

Testament scholars the debate goes on as to where exactly the lines should be drawn. Klyne Snodgrass strikes a somewhat delicate balance on the issue of our appropriation of New Testament exegetical practices:

> With great fear of possible abuse ... I would not want to argue that the apostles could be creative because of their context, but that we are confined to more mundane methods. In terms of approaching the text, whether Old Testament or New Testament, we must be guided by the author's intention. We do also, however, read the Scriptures in light of the person and work of Christ. We must resist superimposing Christian theology on Old Testament texts and should feel no compulsion to give every Old Testament text, or even most of them, a christological conclusion. But we will have failed if we do not ask how Old Testament texts function in the whole context of Scripture. Without allegorizing the Old Testament, we must seek to understand God's overall purpose with his people....
>
> Specifically, I have become convinced that the concept of correspondence in history is particularly valuable to interpretation. We have not completed the interpretive task until we have determined how a text does or does not correspond with Jesus' ministry or the ministry of the church. The writers of the New Testament seem to have looked for patterns of God's working in the Hebrew Scriptures, in the life of Jesus, and in their own experience. Our reading of the Scriptures should do no less. Noting such patterns is a far cry from the abusive interpretation of allegorizing.[11]

The practice of recognizing correspondences rests in part on the belief that God acts consistently in accordance with his character and purposes and that Scripture reflects accurately a unified and interrelated "message" through its many sub-messages. The danger comes when our identification of true historical correspondences lapses into an allegorizing that reads hidden messages into the text. With the author of Hebrews we must take the text itself seriously and inquire concerning the author's intended meanings (to work within hermeneutical boundaries) as well as how those meanings might relate to later revelation.

Applying a "servant" text. Hebrews 7:1–10 does not serve as an exegetical or homiletic end in itself. Rather, by its explication of Melchizedek's superior priesthood, it serves the purpose of laying a foundation for the

---

11. Klyne Snodgrass, "The Use of the Old Testament in the New," in *New Testament Criticism and Interpretation*, ed. David Alan Black and David S. Dockery (Grand Rapids: Zondervan, 1991), 427.

author's main point that *Jesus'* priesthood is greater than that of the Levitical priests of the Old Testament. Thus we might call this first section of chapter 7 a "servant" text in that it prepares for a "punch line" to be offered later. This makes it no less significant, and we still must ask how this text is to be applied responsibly.

At least three directions come to mind in thinking about moving toward application. (1) The first has to do with our attitudes toward the Old Testament. God, as a God who works in corresponding ways in history, has revealed truth about himself and his relationship to people in the Old Testament as well as the New. We must remember that the old covenant materials were the Bible for the early church. They cherished the Old Testament as God's revelation, and so must we.

(2) Study of the interpretation of Scripture found in Hebrews 7 offers us an opportunity to reflect on models of interpretation. We live in a postmodern era, in which all interpretive strategies find an equal place at the table of public discussion. In postmodernity often what is more important is what a reader reads into a written text and how he or she responds to it rather than what the author may have originally meant. How should we as Christians respond to this? What can be learned from the author of Hebrews that can be applied in our own Bible study? What parameters are presupposed in his approach to Genesis 14:17–20, and how might his parameters relate to us?

(3) Finally, however one assesses his hermeneutics, the author's approach is both studied and intellectually rigorous. He systematically dissects and interprets Genesis 14:17–20 and utilizes his interpretation as a foundation stone in a broader, logical argument. This "intellectual" approach serves his pastoral purpose of challenging his hearers to endure in the Christian life. As a professor at a university, this text reminds me of the importance of rigorous study in service to Christ and the importance of keeping that service in view as one attempts rigorous study. Within a Christian context, the dichotomy between the life of the mind and the life of the heart is a false dichotomy. Our choice should not be between the heart and the head, and Hebrews invites us to integrate the two. This passage in Hebrews challenges us to reflect on that integration.

OUR ATTITUDES TOWARD the Old Testament. Take a moment and consider your own perspectives on the Old Testament. What part does it play in your thoughts about the Christian life? What role does it play in the Bible studies you attend? In the preaching at your church? For Jesus and his first followers, what we refer to as the "Old

Testament" comprised their written Scriptures. When Jesus went to synagogue on the Sabbath, the attendant would take a scroll of Isaiah or Deuteronomy, for example, from a box and hand it to the teacher for the day, who would then expound the Scriptures.

The New Testament itself is permeated with quotes from the Old Testament because, for the first Christians, that Old Testament was the powerful Word of God, "sharper than any two-edged sword" (Heb. 4:12). The preaching among the earliest Christians was based on the new covenant teachings about and from Christ, *anchored in the Old Testament Scriptures.* It is easy for that fact to be eclipsed in the full-orbed revelation of Christ found in the written Scriptures we now call the "New Testament." Some among us may even fall into the category of "practical Marcionites," who think of the Old as outdated by the New.[12]

> According to the common generalization, the New Testament is the source of all that is good, kind, and loving, embodied most of all in the person of Jesus Christ who reveals the friendly face of God. As the story goes, however, the Old Testament is at best a mixed bag. The occasional flash of brilliance may lighten the path of the believer, but on the whole, the angry, the vindictive, the bloodthirsty, is far more prominent.
>
> Now I suspect that there is at least a grain of truth in this common view of the two parts of our Christian Bible. At least I have never heard a Christian contrast the beauty and attractiveness of the Old Testament with the horrors of the New. No, Christians have always found refuge in the New Testament when the problems of the Old Testament have threatened to engulf them. In fact, some Christians even go so far as to claim with emphasis that they are *New Testament* Christians for whom the Old Testament is no longer authoritative.
>
> Even if the problems with the Old Testament should stem from some monumental misunderstanding, the fact that such a misunderstanding is so common is something we must reckon with.[13]

One way of reckoning with such misunderstanding is to reflect on the integral—indeed foundational—place the Old Testament has in Hebrews in communicating the author's Christology (as here in 7:1–10) and, more broadly, in dealing with Christian obedience and endurance. As the early church embraced

---

12. We will soon deal with the question of the old covenant being superseded by the new. See below, pp. 283–86.

13. Alden Thompson, *Who's Afraid of the Old Testament God?* (Grand Rapids: Zondervan, 1989), 13–14.

and was nourished by the Old Testament, so should we own it for ourselves and grow from its influence. Yes, we read it in light of Christ and the new covenant. This is inevitable. Yet, we also should read it as powerful, meaningful revelation from God in its own right, not as a secondary part of the canon.

Whose interpretive model? Several years ago I happened upon a talk show as I was changing the television channel. The subject matter and participants caught my attention immediately. A group of homosexuals were debating a group of fundamentalist Christians over the appropriateness of a homosexual lifestyle. The fundamentalists, contrary to stereotype, were both thoughtful and respectful, and they did a fairly good job of explaining the biblical basis for their belief that homosexuality is wrong. They took several texts from both Testaments and spoke of context and word meanings. In response to their use of Scripture, the show's host interjected, "Yes, but that's just your interpretation"; this comment, rather than a discussion of homosexuality, is my reason for introducing the story.

We live in what has been labeled a *postmodern* culture. Since the constituents of that culture often elevate the "right" to one's own interpretation above the idea of there being any correct interpretation, the concept of truth sits in the wings, never being invited on stage for discussion. The comment "That's just your interpretation" becomes the ultimate trump card in any debate.

Nevertheless, from the perspective of a biblical worldview Christian theology, rightly understood, "does not offer us a theology of speculation and exploration. It offers us a theology of revelation and salvation."[14] We may ever be growing in our grasp of that revelation—we must live as lifelong learners—but there are truths we can grasp, and detailed study of the Scriptures provides one way of growing in our understanding of truth. So what are elements of a proper model of biblical interpretation? Let me mention three seen in Hebrews 7:1–10.

(1) We must take the specifics of a scriptural passage seriously. Commentaries, such as the one you hold in your hands, deal with dynamics such as context, structure, and word meanings, belying a conviction that the author's original intent and, even more significantly, God's intent expressed through the author matter a great deal. The author of Hebrews depends on insight into context and word meanings for his interpretation of the Genesis Melchizedek passage. Hebrews' approach to studying this passage in terms of detailed analysis suggests the appropriateness of my attempt, as one within a Christian tradition, at writing on the details of a biblical text and your

---

14. Harry Blamires, *Recovering the Christian Mind: Meeting the Challenge of Secularism* (Downers Grove, Ill.: InterVarsity, 1988), 16.

attempt to understand what I am writing. We have precedent for detailed study of the Word as a profitable endeavor for Christians.

(2) We should interpret Scripture in light of Scripture. God has spoken "to our forefathers through the prophets at many times and in various ways" (1:1), but he has always been the one speaking and has never contradicted himself. Thus, we must read and study Scripture in light of the broader context of Scripture. This can give us greater insight into the truths of the Bible and can keep us from grave error.

(3) We should read and study our Bibles Christologically. As stated by Klyne Snodgrass in the quote earlier in this chapter, "We must resist superimposing Christian theology on Old Testament texts and should feel no compulsion to give every Old Testament text, or even most of them, a christological conclusion." Yet for the Christian, Christ is the ultimate point of reference for biblical truth—indeed, all truth. This Christological hermeneutic is an approach

> by which we seek to move beyond historical criticism to the christological, as opposed to the existential, significance of the text. The text's christological meaning can in fact be shown to carry tremendous import for human existence. I believe that I am here being true to the intent of the scriptural authors themselves and even more to the Spirit who guided them, since they frequently made an effort to relate their revelatory insights to the future acts of cosmic deliverance wrought by the God of Israel (in the case of the Old Testament) or to God's self-revelation in Jesus Christ (in the case of the New Testament). This approach ... seeks to supplement the historical-critical method by theological exegesis in which the innermost intentions of the author are related to the center and culmination of sacred history mirrored in the Bible, namely, the advent of Jesus Christ. It is believed that the fragmentary insights of both Old and New Testament writers are fulfilled in God's dramatic incursion into human history which we see in the incarnation and atoning sacrifice of Jesus Christ, in his life, death, and resurrection.[15]

When we approach Scripture in this way, we do so in the hermeneutical spirit and with the convictions manifested in the exegesis of the Bible found in Hebrews 7. Christ becomes the ultimate "north star," by which we can get our bearings in the constellation of old and new covenant writings.

---

15. Donald G. Bloesch, "A Christological Hermeneutic: Crisis and Conflict in Hermeneutics," in *The Use of the Bible in Theology: Evangelical Options*, ed. R. K. Johnson (Atlanta, Ga.: John Knox, 1985), 78–84.

Being a thinking Christian. John Stott tells of two women at the local supermarket who stopped to chat. One asked the other, "What's the matter with you? You look so worried." The friend responded, "I am. I keep thinking about the world situation." "Well," the first said, "you want to take things more philosophically, and stop thinking!"[16]

I am sure my colleagues in philosophy would take offense at the thought that more philosophy means less thought! However, this humorous dialogue reflects the attitude some have toward the Christian faith. The reasoning goes, "Christianity is a religion of the heart, the emotions; don't kill it by being so cerebral!" Although some of us in academia need to be reminded that Christianity deals extensively with matters of the heart (and our degrees on the wall and critical analyses in our heads do not excuse us from reckoning with those matters!), it is entirely appropriate that we stress our corporate call to "love the Lord your God . . . with all your mind" (Mark 12:30).

In *Pensées* Blaise Pascal wrote, "Man is obviously made for thinking. Therein lies all his dignity and his merit; and his whole duty is to think as he ought." Right thinking *can* lead to right feeling, right acting, right outcomes— although it does not necessarily do so. Without right thinking, however, we are in danger of having a zeal for God that is not in accordance with knowledge (Rom. 10:2). In a holistic approach to Christian faith heart and head, co-lovers of God, dance. If evangelicalism truly constitutes the future of Christianity, as Alistar McGrath suggests, it will be because head and heart both are valued and encouraged.[17] If we neglect the life of the mind, "our pagan culture is going to overwhelm us."[18]

In Hebrews 7 the author is thinking critically and inviting us to think with him. His arguments are logical and well crafted, drawing us into analysis of the Old Testament material. You cannot deal with Hebrews 7 in terms of the heart alone. The head must come into play or one's reading of the text is awash. He is leading us somewhere with this logic of his. We are moving once again toward a call to total engagement in the life of Christ. Heart, mind, emotions, and strength all will be called upon shortly. Nevertheless, we must begin here, with rationales for why we must act a certain way. Here we, with the author of Hebrews, begin by loving God with our minds.

---

16. John Stott, *The Contemporary Christian: Applying God's Word to Today's World* (Downers Grove, Ill.: InterVarsity, 1992), 114.

17. Alistar McGrath, "Why Evangelicalism is the Future of Protestantism," *Christianity Today* 39 (June 19, 1995): 22.

18. "Standing on the Promises," an interview in *Christianity Today* 40 (Sept. 16, 1996) with Carl F. H. Henry and Kenneth Kantzer, p. 35.

Hebrews 7:11–28

I F PERFECTION COULD have been attained through the Levitical priesthood (for on the basis of it the law was given to
the people), why was there still need for another priest to
come—one in the order of Melchizedek, not in the order of
Aaron? ¹²For when there is a change of the priesthood, there
must also be a change of the law. ¹³He of whom these things
are said belonged to a different tribe, and no one from that
tribe has ever served at the altar. ¹⁴For it is clear that our Lord
descended from Judah, and in regard to that tribe Moses said
nothing about priests. ¹⁵And what we have said is even more
clear if another priest like Melchizedek appears, ¹⁶one who has
become a priest not on the basis of a regulation as to his
ancestry but on the basis of the power of an indestructible
life. ¹⁷For it is declared:

> "You are a priest forever,
> in the order of Melchizedek."

¹⁸The former regulation is set aside because it was weak
and useless ¹⁹(for the law made nothing perfect), and a better
hope is introduced, by which we draw near to God.

²⁰And it was not without an oath! Others became priests
without any oath, ²¹but he became a priest with an oath when
God said to him:

> "The Lord has sworn
> and will not change his mind:
> 'You are a priest forever.'"

²²Because of this oath, Jesus has become the guarantee of a
better covenant.

²³Now there have been many of those priests, since death
prevented them from continuing in office; ²⁴but because Jesus
lives forever, he has a permanent priesthood. ²⁵Therefore he is
able to save completely those who come to God through him,
because he always lives to intercede for them.

²⁶Such a high priest meets our need—one who is holy,
blameless, pure, set apart from sinners, exalted above the
heavens. ²⁷Unlike the other high priests, he does not need to

offer sacrifices day after day, first for his own sins, and then for the sins of the people. He sacrificed for their sins once for all when he offered himself. ²⁸For the law appoints as high priests men who are weak; but the oath, which came after the law, appointed the Son, who has been made perfect forever.

 THE CRAFTER OF this sermon we call Hebrews now presents the culmination on his treatment of "The Appointment of the Son as a Superior High Priest." He first provided an introduction on the subject (5:1–10), then demonstrated the superiority of Melchizedek over the Levitical priests (7:1–10). Now, bringing Psalm 110:4 to the fore once again, he argues for the superiority of Jesus, our Melchizedekan priest (7:11–28).

In 7:11–28 the author argues for the superiority of Jesus as an appointed high priest on several bases. (1) With the appointment of Jesus to high priesthood (Ps. 110:4), the old regulations for worship, centered in the old covenant priests, have been ushered out and a better hope has been brought in (Heb. 7:11–19). (2) That his Melchizedekan priesthood was established by an oath from God shows its superiority, since by virtue of that oath Jesus has become the guarantee of a better covenant (7:20–22). (3) Jesus' eternal nature means that he, unlike the former, mortal priests, holds his office perpetually and thus offers help forever to those who draw near to God through him (7:23–25). The author of Hebrews summarizes and brings to climax his whole argument on Christ's appointment as high priest in the final three verses (7:26–28).

The Rules Have Changed (7:11–19)

AS A SKILLED preacher the author begins his comparison of Jesus' priesthood with that of the old covenant priests indirectly, using a conditional clause and a rhetorical question: "If perfection could have been attained through the Levitical priesthood . . . why was there still need for another priest to come—one in the order of Melchizedek, not in the order of Aaron?" With the conditional clause he assumes the impossibility of perfection having been brought about through the old order of priests. The word "perfection" (*teleiosis*) here, as elsewhere in Hebrews, does not mean "without flaws," but has to do with "arriving at a desired end" or "reaching a goal."[1] That "desired end" refers to the type of relationship established between God and his people under the new covenant.

---

1. Ellingworth, *The Epistle to the Hebrews*, 371.

As a rhetorical question the second half of verse 11 in reality makes a strong *assertion* concerning the need for a new order of priesthood. This assertion in the form of a question proclaims, "Since God's ultimate goal of establishing an eternal relationship between himself and people could not be attained through the Levitical priesthood, there was still a need for a priesthood to arrive that could bring that perfection." He takes this idea from Psalm 110:4, a text written years after the law was given. Since God gave an oath concerning a new order of priesthood, the old order must have fallen short of his final aim. This does not mean the Levitical system was completely ineffective, but that it was intended to foreshadow something better.[2]

The parenthetical statement, "for on the basis of it the law was given to the people," seemingly makes reference to the Levitical priesthood. The statement might better be translated "for concerning it the law was given to the people." The Old Testament people of God had received regulations related to the ministry of the Levitical priests through the law. Specifically, for example, the law required a priest to be a descendant of Levi.[3] Yet, as Psalm 110:4 shows, a priest of a new order has come. In verse 12, therefore, the author explains that a change to a Melchizedekan priesthood heralds a change in the law of genealogical descent.

Thus, the change in God's requirements concerning the office of priest may be seen most clearly from the fact that Jesus, the one appointed to high priesthood by God's oath of Psalm 110:4, does not meet the requirement of genealogical descent established under the law (Heb. 7:13–14). His tribe, the tribe of Judah, never served at the altar of God under the old covenant because that covenant's regulations made no provision for any tribe other than that of Levi.

The phrase "and what we have said" at the beginning of verse 15 refers back to the assertion of verse 12 that God has changed the rules for priesthood. This change in the law "is even more clear" because a priest like Melchizedek has appeared. In Jesus one understands clearly that this new high priest has been appointed not on the basis of ancestry, since he was from the tribe of Judah, but on the basis of his immortality, the author seizing on the term "forever" in Psalm 110:4 (Heb. 7:16–17).

The argument continues in verses 18–19 by providing the reason for Jesus' having been appointed by God as a new type of priest: "The former regulation is set aside because it was weak and useless." The words "weak" (*asthenes*) and "useless" (*anopheles*) both speak of ineffectiveness. The old covenant regulation concerning the priestly office simply could not and did not bring

---

2. Moisés Silva, "Perfection and Eschatology in Hebrews," *WTJ* 39 (1976): 68.
3. Lane, *Hebrews 1–8*, 174.

about God's ultimate relational aim for his people (v. 11). Consequently, with the appointment of Jesus to priesthood, God introduces a "better hope" (i.e., a means to achieve God's desired aim for relationship with his people), since we are offered a perpetual basis for drawing "near to God" (v. 19).

The Power of a Divine Oath (7:20–22)

HOW WAS THIS new order of priesthood established? The author answers this implied question with a negative statement: "It was not without an oath!" The "others" of verse 20 refers to the old covenant priests, who became priests by genealogical descent—a completely different means of appointment than that seen in the case of the exalted Son. The writer to the Hebrews sees clearly that God, in Psalm 110:4, used an oath in his Son's case: "The Lord has sworn. . . ." This psalm also proclaims confidently that the Lord "will not change his mind" and has promised to the Son that his priesthood will last "forever." Because of the unequivocal nature of God's oath, all danger of some change in the future has been wiped away.

Thus, Jesus has become the "guarantee" of a better covenant. The word "guarantee" (*engyos*), which can also be translated "guarantor," was not used normally in the ancient world to discuss covenants or testaments but was a common legal image. The word referred to a person who guaranteed the position or endeavors of someone else while putting him- or herself at risk. In the present context the author pictures Jesus as the one who guarantees God's covenant promises. The hearers, as new covenant people, have a covenant that is "better" because, by virtue of God's oath, Jesus, the mediator of that covenant (cf. 8:6), holds an unalterable position.[4] Our hope, therefore, rests on the most secure of terms.

The Permanent Priest (7:23–25)

WITH VERSES 23–24 the author introduces yet another stark contrast between Jesus and the old covenant priests. The Levitical priests' numbers through the centuries were great since, as mortals, any given priest's tenure in office was limited by death. Thus the mortality of its members may be seen as an inherent weakness in the old covenant priesthood, and this weakness requires the genealogical aspect of priestly appointment under the old covenant. Since this weakness does not apply to Christ, neither does the genealogical requirement, and, therefore, his office will not be ceded to a subsequent generation.

The author richly expresses this thought with the adjective *aparabatos* ("permanent," v. 24). This word, used only here in the New Testament and

---

4. Attridge, *Epistle to the Hebrews*, 208.

rarely elsewhere, was applied in legal contexts in the ancient world to mean "inviolable" or something not to be transgressed. "Permanent" represents a meaning widely attested in ancient literature. The first-century writer Plutarch, for example, used the word to describe the constancy of the sun's course through the sky.[5] Thus, Jesus' priesthood may be characterized as "unchangeable," since he will hold the office forever.

Consequently, Jesus is able to "save completely those who come to God through him." That is, since Christ's priesthood lasts forever, there are no limitations on the mediation he offers between us and God. His priestly ministry brings a complete salvation in that it not only offers temporary deliverance from sin, but perfects those who come to God through him for all time (10:1–3). As Hughes notes, we could not hope to draw near eternally to the eternal God through a dead priest.[6] In Jesus we have a priest who provides salvation for us perpetually and completely.

Moreover, in his office of high priest the Son makes continuous intercession on our behalf. The confession of the exalted Christ's intercession for his followers finds expression elsewhere in the New Testament. In Romans 8:31–34 Paul writes these comforting words:

> What, then, shall we say in response to this? If God is for us, who can be against us? He who did not spare his own Son, but gave him up for us all—how will he not also, along with him, graciously give us all things? Who will bring any charge against those whom God has chosen? It is God who justifies. Who is he that condemns? Christ Jesus, who died—more than that, who was raised to life—is at the right hand of God and is also interceding for us.[7]

Furthermore, while on earth the Son of God prayed for his disciples (e.g., Luke 22:32; John 17), giving help to them in their weakness. It seems that in the broader context of Hebrews, one aspect of Christ's intercessory ministry is prayer for believers struggling with temptation, perhaps specifically the temptation to deny the faith under persecution.[8]

---

5. *De Defectu Oracurlorum* 3. Spicq poses a derivative meaning based on context, translating the word as "nontransferable," a rendering suggested by others in the history of interpretation (Spicq, *Theological Lexicon of the New Testament*, 1:144). However, Lane judiciously cautions against this translation since this meaning for the word is unknown to ancient literature, as Spicq himself admits. See Lane, *Hebrews 1–8*, 175–76, note u.

6. Hughes, *A Commentary on the Epistle to the Hebrews*, 269.

7. F. F. Bruce also points to the fourth Servant Song in Isaiah, where the exalted Servant of the Lord is said to make "intercession for the transgressors" (Isa. 53:12). See Bruce, *The Epistle to the Hebrews*, 174.

8. See the discussion of Hebrews 4:16 above, p. 176.

A Summary and Transition (7:26–28)

IN THE FINAL verses of chapter 7 the author sums up the discussion started at 5:1. One can easily note the parallel ideas between 5:1–3 and 7:26–28.[9] The author begins 7:26–28 with a statement concerning our high priest's *character and status* (v. 26). The descriptions "holy, blameless, pure, set apart from sinners" all emphasize the Son's sinless character in contrast to the sinfulness of the earthly priests. Unlike them he has no need to offer a sacrifice *for* himself but, rather, has offered the sacrifice *of* himself.

Furthermore, whereas the ministry of the earthly high priest extended only to the tabernacle's Most Holy Place, Jesus' high-priestly ministry reaches into heaven, where he sits at the pinnacle of the universe, the right hand of God. This "heaven" motif is transitional, the author developing it extensively in 8:1–6 and 9:11–28.

The summary of 7:26–28 also anticipates the focal theme of 10:1–18: *The finality of the Son's sacrifice.* Unlike earthly priests, who must offer sacrifices day after day, this high priest's sacrifice has been made once for all time.

Finally, the author reiterates the contrasting *means of appointment* seen in the old and new orders of priesthood and the *nature* of the old priests over against that of the new high priest. The old priests were appointed by virtue of the law but were weak (i.e., sinful, 5:2; mortal, 7:23), but the Son was appointed by virtue of God's oath and has been "made perfect forever."[10]

 UNDERSTAND THE INTERPLAY of dominant and subordinate themes. Recently my wife, Pat, and I took our son, Joshua, to the Memphis Zoo. Upon entering we were given a graphic map that laid out for us how to get to various exhibits. We passed through "Cat Country," where large and small felines lounged in replicas of natural habitat. We visited "Primate Canyon" and saw monkeys swinging from branch to branch and large gorillas resting on "nests" high above the ground. This year the zoo featured an enclosed butterfly exhibit, in which hundreds of butterflies flitted freely among sweet-smelling flowers and trees. Chrysalis boxes held dozens of pupae, several of which opened before our eyes, revealing the beautiful outcome of metamorphosis. We also visited other exhibits, such as the Reptile House (not Pat's favorite), the Tropical Bird House, and the Seal Amphitheater.

---

9. These two passages form an *inclusio*, a literary device based on distant parallelism meant to mark the beginning and ending of a section. See above, p. 186.

10. On the perfection of the Son see above, p. 191.

At each exhibit primary species of animals held the focus of attention. Yet constant reminders of the larger context of the zoo were everywhere. Signs as we left one exhibit pointed back to those we had already visited or ahead to those on down the path. A tee shirt advertising the butterfly exhibit could be seen in Cat Country. Also, sounds from other parts of the zoo were ever present as a monkey screeched or a lion roared.

At every turn in Hebrews the author makes extensive use of transitional material. He reiterates themes from earlier in the book and anticipates those to which he will give attention later. As we walk through Hebrews, therefore, each section has dominant themes, like the various exhibits at the zoo, and subdominant themes, which function as pointers backward and forward in the author's line of reasoning. In 7:11–28, for example, the author mentions the weakness of the Levitical priests, an echo of 5:1–3.[11] He also mentions the "better covenant," the heavenly realm, and the finality of Christ's sacrifice, all of which he develops in detail later in the book.

Therefore, an important aspect of applying 7:11–28 might be to focus on the dominant themes, allowing subordinate themes to hold our focus where appropriate elsewhere in the book.[12] This does not mean we neglect the subthemes—their relation to the dominant themes must be brought into the discussion at some point—but we must not miss the author's main points for each section of the book. This also will force us to a balanced approach in teaching or preaching Hebrews, rather than seizing on topics about which we may be especially passionate. If we major on the dominant themes in each section, we will cover the author's primary concerns and do so in an equal-handed manner.

Two themes seem predominate in Hebrews 7:11–28. (1) The first addresses the shift from regulations surrounding the old covenant priesthood to the Melchizedekan order of priesthood realized in Jesus. (2) The other one, which flows from the first, addresses the relational implications of the "better covenant" (7:22) offered us in the exalted Son of God. These interrelated subjects must garner our focus as we move toward application.

Why the argument concerning the old covenant priests? For most of us involved in contemporary Christianity, holding too high a view of the Levitical priesthood does not constitute one of our greater temptations. Therefore, the author's protracted, detailed argument on the superiority of Jesus' priesthood when compared to that of the old covenant priests may seem somewhat irrelevant. "Give us practical help for living," or "talk to us about *real* temp-

---

11. When in 7:18 the author mentions "weakness," he speaks of the regulations of the old covenant.

12. See the discussion above, pp. 112–13.

tations faced in the modern world," we might say. Even for those immersed in Christian theology, the old covenant priests' inferior status when compared to Christ may be relegated to the realm of foregone conclusions. One might respond with a ho-hum attitude, "Why of course Jesus is greater than the priests of the old covenant; that's obvious!" Yet, the author had his reasons for going to great lengths with this discussion, and it is our part to discern both why he did so and the implications for us.

The author of Hebrews wishes to articulate and magnify Jesus' high priesthood, which he does in two steps. The first step considers the Son's *appointment* as high priest (5:1–10; 7:1–28). The heavenly, once-for-all *offering* of this high priest is addressed in a second step (8:3–10:18). The old covenant priests serve as a reference point in the discussion on appointment to the office of priest. The author of Hebrews shows the strength and durability of Jesus' priesthood by contrasting it with that of the old covenant priests. Ultimately the author wishes to demonstrate conclusively what Jesus has to offer the readers of this document by virtue of those characteristics that make him superior to the Levitical priests. The "hope" he offers and the "covenant" he guarantees are "better" because he, in nature, status, and work, is better.

However, the choice between the old covenant system and the new covenant system is not a choice between bad and good. Progression may be seen in the relationship between Jesus and the Levitical priests. God has not started over—he has brought perfection, in the sense of arriving at a desired goal, to that which was anticipated but unachievable in the Levitical priesthood. The role of the old covenant priestly regulations was a good role— that of facilitating worship during the time prior to Messiah (9:8, 23) and of foreshadowing Messiah's own priestly work. This role, while important for its era, has now been swallowed up in the "better," new covenant regulations and hope established by God's oath concerning his Son: "You are a priest forever" (7:18–19).

This passage, therefore, is not about two paradigms of authority. The author never argues against the Old Testament Scriptures, since they are as much an authority for him as they were for Jewish rabbis of his day, although our author reads them in light of Christian teaching.[13] Hebrews 7:11–28 really confronts us with two paradigms *of relating to God*, one that has anticipated but has now been replaced by the other, because by nature it was unable to arrive at God's ultimate aim. So the question posed by this passage is, "Who provides a superior basis for relating to God?" Thus, our application of the passage must address the question of religious paradigms and, especially, paradigms of worship, since the writer has two main points he wishes

---

13. See the discussion above on Hebrews 7:1–10, pp. 259–61.

to communicate: (1) With the appointment of Jesus as high priest, the paradigm for worship of God has shifted, and (2) the new paradigm must be embraced as better than the old one.

The move to relational theology. In seeking to bridge the gap between the first-century message and our application of that message, we already have discussed one of the author's main themes in 7:11–28: In Jesus' appointment as high priest we have a new and superior paradigm for approaching God. Yet the author has more in mind than merely arguing a theoretical point. He wants his hearers to grasp the implications of this paradigm shift for their relationships with God through Christ. Thus, to address application of this passage adequately, one must move to a consideration of the relational side of theology— its implications for worship and endurance in Christian obedience.

For example, we might ask how the "perfection" arrived at in Christ's appointment relates to our needs today. Some might point out that Christians are not perfect and the expressions of Christianity through the ages are far from perfect. Yet this perfection of which the author speaks connotes a "desired goal" born in the heart of God and accomplished by his Son. So how does this desired goal relate to us?

Furthermore, in what way might we draw encouragement from Jesus' being the "guarantee" of the better covenant? What does it mean that the Son is able to save us "completely," and how specifically might we be encouraged by the fact that he intercedes for us? In other words, how can the appointment of the Son as high priest answer our deepest needs and strengthen our relationship with God?

CHRISTIANITY AS PARADIGM shift. In 1962 American philosopher and historian of science Thomas Kuhn published *The Structure of Scientific Revolutions*, a work that sent shock waves through modern academia and provided modern culture with the concept of "paradigm shift."[14] Kuhn suggested basically that scientific investigation and knowledge depend on social structures. Analyzing the Copernican revolution he showed that in subsequent eras "normal science" has been carried out based on a paradigm, or way of viewing reality, that dominates thinking. "Revolutionary science," on the other hand, shifts the paradigm, bringing in a truly new way of viewing reality.

Kuhn's concept of "paradigm shift" has been applied to many (some suggest far too many) disciplines and arenas since his work appeared, including

---

14. Thomas S. Kuhn, *The Structure of Scientific Revolutions* (2d ed., Chicago: Univ. of Chicago Press, 1970).

areas such as education and business. The revolution from mechanical to digital systems in watch-making provides a classic illustration. Earlier in the twentieth century, the Swiss dominated the watch industry. Then, one of their own engineers invented a new way of making watches, based on digital technology. But executives of the Swiss watch industry failed to realize the potential of the new technology, dismissing it as a passing fad. The new approach to watch-making was snatched up by the Japanese, who took a firm hold on the market. The shift of market share to the East has resulted in economic devastation for the Swiss industry. Why the collapse of the Swiss watch-making empire? Its leaders were not able to shift paradigms. The "truth" of digital technology was foreign to those executives with the power of making decisions since they had lived for so long within a mindset of "Swiss superiority" in watches. They simply could not envision change.

Taylor Brancy writes, "Truth requires a maximum effort to see through the eyes of strangers, foreigners, and enemies."[15] In religion too it is important to be able to move out of the grasp of a specific paradigm when convinced of the truth of the new paradigm—even when the truth comes via a perceived enemy. We see this clearly in Paul's Damascus Road experience (Acts 9:1–19), which depicts well both the trauma and fulfillment of a paradigm shift. Paul embodied what in varying degrees was the experience of the earliest Christians, who were Jewish and oriented to the Old Testament law. Their paradigm shift to a Christ-centered interpretation of those Scriptures did not constitute a break, but rather a fulfillment. God was doing something "new," but in continuity with that which was "old." Nevertheless, the paradigm had shifted.

Sholem Asch presents a fictional conversation between Mary, the mother of Jesus, and another son, Jacob. The story portrays Jacob's struggle with Jesus' identity and Mary's insight to the fact that God alone can shift one's paradigm of religious knowledge in Yeshua's direction:

> Jacob, her second son, was coming slowly toward her on the garden path. He walked with difficulty, like a man newly crippled.
>
> "I know not who my brother is," he said, coming close, "and I cannot judge how far his rights extend. I know only that God will justify him in his doings. But we, we have nothing in our hands but the guide rope of the Law. And he who cuts this rope, whoever he may be, cuts off our path to God."
>
> "My son, my son," said Miriam passionately, "pray God that He plant a new spirit in you, that you may see the new path to the Lord

---

15. As quoted in Monroe, *Finding God at Harvard*, 172.

which your brother lays out for the poor and simple. Without God's help you shall never see your brother's light, for what he does is not done according to the laws of men but in accordance with the will of God."

Jacob's sunken eyes opened wide as he stared at his mother. He dropped his head shamefully and stammered out in a choked voice:

"*Ema*, Mother, who is Yeshua?"

Miriam laid her hand on his arm.

"It is not for me to reveal the mysteries of God. When the time is ripe it shall be known to you, my son."[16]

For the first believers, what warranted a shift from rabbinic or other forms of first-century Judaism to Christianity? "But when the time had fully come, God sent his Son, born of a woman, born under law ..." (Gal. 4:4). The appearance of God's Son—revelation of God's will in Christ—demanded the paradigm change. This paradigm shift did not mean a change in God, a view known as "process theology," but the progression of God's revelation.[17] In light of the new revelation in Christ, the reading of the old covenant Scriptures changed, associations changed, and individual lives changed.

So we may ask two millennia later, "What does this have to do with us?" and "How do we know that God will not radically shift the paradigm again?" (1) On the first question, we may answer in at least two directions, the first having to do with evangelism and the second Christian discipleship. (a) Christian evangelism, in essence, constitutes calling those outside the faith to shift paradigms to a Christian worldview.[18] Whether they realize it or not, those with whom we share the gospel are working under paradigms they hold to be true. This fact calls for us to pray that God might enlighten their hearts with the truth of Christ and for us to be patient as God reveals himself to them. The truth of the gospel may be clear to us, but for those outside the faith, who are operating under a different paradigm, the message of Christ seems foreign.

(b) As Christ's disciples we should monitor our own clarity of thought concerning the basic truths of the Christian faith. Are we holding faithfully to

16. Sholem Asch, *Mary* (New York: Carroll and Graf, 1985), 302–3.

17. On various models attempting to describe progressive revelation see Dockery, *Biblical Interpretation Then and Now*, 18. See also the statements of F. F. Bruce concerning how progressive revelation relates to "canonical exegesis" in F. F. Bruce, *The Canon of Scripture* (Downers Grove, Ill.: InterVarsity, 1988), 296.

18. See, for example, the chapter entitled "A Clash of Worldviews" in Alistar McGrath, *Intellectuals Don't Need God and Other Modern Myths: Building Bridges to Faith Through Apologetics* (Grand Rapids: Zondervan, 1993), 144–86.

the "paradigm," or are we moving away from it?[19] This is what the author meant when in 2:1 he wrote, "We must pay more careful attention, therefore, to what we have heard, so that we do not drift away."[20] At 7:11–28 the author helps his readers "pay more careful attention . . . to what [they] have heard" by, perhaps, expanding their understanding of Christ's superiority over another, older understanding of relationship with God. He attempts to "firm up" their confidence in the Christian paradigm.

(2) "Yet how," one might ask, "do you know God has not radically shifted, or will not shift, the paradigm again?" After all, Islam claims to own the culmination of God's revelation, as does Mormonism and other religions. These present much different pictures of Christ than that painted by the book of Hebrews. Modern, liberal Christianity, based on the advancement in human knowledge, presents various understandings of the Christian religion, and its view of Jesus is far removed from the exalted Savior of Hebrews 7.

In answer, remember that in chapter 7 Hebrews proclaims the eternality of the Son's high priesthood. Thus, in the view of Hebrews, this order—this paradigm, if you will—by its very nature will not change. God's new covenant way of relating to people, therefore, will never be altered. Thus religions such as Islam and Mormonism amount to *contradictions* of Hebrews 7 rather than progressive revelations, since they suggest a different view of Christ than one finds in Hebrews and the rest of the New Testament. Consequently, Hebrews' view of reality, grounded in the eternal high priesthood of the Son of God, offers us lasting stability for life.

Relational theology. In our ministry at Union University my wife and I have the privilege to mentor young men and women in a variety of life circumstances, one of these being engagement for marriage. Premarital counseling gives both joy and satisfaction—joy because we are able to help these young people think through the various aspects of healthy relationships, and satisfaction for me personally, because I am reminded time and again that I am not the only male who started marriage fundamentally ignorant of my wife's real needs!

For example, when in our first year of wedded "blisters" Pat was distraught over some matter, I was happy to provide her with the three reasons why she need not feel as she did. I quickly learned that my wife did not need my sermons in such moments, but rather my ear, my shoulder, my care. As we have matured in our understanding of each other, I have learned to speak more

---

19. Of course we may change our interpretations of certain aspects of Christianity upon further study and spiritual growth, but here I refer to the foundational tenets of what traditionally has been recognized as "orthodox Christianity."

20. See the discussion above, pp. 83–84.

sensitively and appropriately and have learned how words work in conjunction with healthy actions. When relationships are what they should be, they blend a give and take of words and behaviors given in timely fashion and with proper motives. These help build into a relationship the security and significance for which we all long.

God is a God of relationships, who has spoken and acted to bring about and foster our relationships with him. It is no exaggeration to characterize his book, the Bible, as one long, interconnected network of texts about relationships. In the Scriptures we find love and hate, joy and grief, hope and despair, all in the context of interpersonal associations. From Adam and Eve to David and Jonathan to James and John to Paul and Barnabas to the author of Hebrews and his congregation, the Bible recounts lives set in the ever-present context of relationships. And behind all the lives looms the Life, the Story, the great Lover, who from before time has envisioned and worked for a relationship with you and me.

In Hebrews 7 God has given us powerful words meant for a relational end. This discourse detailing the superiority of Jesus' high priesthood is far more than a theoretical treatise. It expresses relational theology, as all true theology is in essence.[21] (1) Notice that God has brought about the means for establishing a lasting relationship with us—the "perfection" of verse 11, the "better hope . . . by which we draw near to God" of verse 19, and the "better covenant" of verse 22. Thus he is the initiator in the relationship.

(2) God has paid a price to give us security in that relationship, Jesus being the "guarantor," who assures us of the covenant promises of God as the high priest who has been appointed to office "forever."

(3) God has expressed his commitment to meet our deepest needs for forgiveness, holiness, and future deliverance, Jesus being the Savior who is able to "save completely those who come to God through him" (v. 25).

(4) Finally, God maintains his relationship with us by the work of his Son as intercessor, a ministry he started in his incarnation and continues in his exaltation. God has gone and continues to go to great lengths to relate to us his love in words and actions. His aim has always been nothing less than a healthy relationship. May we relate to him in a healthy manner this day.

---

21. Stanley J. Grenz, *Theology for the Community of God* (Nashville: Broadman and Holman, 1994), 101–2.

Hebrews 8:1–13

THE POINT OF what we are saying is this: We do have such a high priest, who sat down at the right hand of the throne of the Majesty in heaven, ²and who serves in the sanctuary, the true tabernacle set up by the Lord, not by man.

³Every high priest is appointed to offer both gifts and sacrifices, and so it was necessary for this one also to have something to offer. ⁴If he were on earth, he would not be a priest, for there are already men who offer the gifts prescribed by the law. ⁵They serve at a sanctuary that is a copy and shadow of what is in heaven. This is why Moses was warned when he was about to build the tabernacle: "See to it that you make everything according to the pattern shown you on the mountain." ⁶But the ministry Jesus has received is as superior to theirs as the covenant of which he is mediator is superior to the old one, and it is founded on better promises.

⁷For if there had been nothing wrong with that first covenant, no place would have been sought for another. ⁸But God found fault with the people and said:

> "The time is coming, declares the Lord,
>   when I will make a new covenant
> with the house of Israel
>   and with the house of Judah.
> ⁹It will not be like the covenant
>   I made with their forefathers
> when I took them by the hand
>   to lead them out of Egypt,
> because they did not remain faithful to my covenant,
>   and I turned away from them,
>   declares the Lord.
> ¹⁰This is the covenant I will make with the house of Israel
>   after that time, declares the Lord.
> I will put my laws in their minds
>   and write them on their hearts.
> I will be their God,
>   and they will be my people.

¹¹No longer will a man teach his neighbor,
  or a man his brother, saying, 'Know the Lord,'
because they will all know me,
  from the least of them to the greatest.
¹²For I will forgive their wickedness
  and will remember their sins no more."

¹³By calling this covenant "new," he has made the first one
obsolete; and what is obsolete and aging will soon disappear.

A GOOD PREACHER knows when to sum up where the sermon has been and where it is going. Such a moment in the address allows the hearers to get their bearings and continue to track with the speaker. The first two verses of this section present us with a well-crafted but simple use of this oratorical device and offer us an opportunity to take stock of where we are in the book. The structure of the great central section of Hebrews may be depicted as follows:

Opening: We Have a High Priest ... (4:14–16)
A. The Appointment of the Son as a Superior High Priest (5:1–7:28)
   1. Introduction: The Son Taken From Among Humans and Appointed According to the Order of Melchizedek (5:1–10)
   [An Exhortation for the Hearers (5:11–6:20)]
   2. The Superiority of Melchizedek (7:1–10)
   3. The Superiority of Our Eternal, Melchizedekan High Priest (7:11–28)
ab. **Transition: We Have Such a High Priest, Who Is a Minister in Heaven (8:1–2)**
B. The Superior Offering of the Appointed High Priest (8:3–10:18)
   1. Introduction: The More Excellent Ministry of the Heavenly High Priest (8:3–6)
   2. The Superiority of the New Covenant (8:7–13)
   3. The Superiority of the New Covenant Offering (9:1–10:18)
Closing: We Have a Great Priest Who Takes Us Into Heaven ... (10:19–25)

Notice that 4:14–16 and 10:19–25 form a "bracket" (*inclusio*) around this part of the book, marking its beginning and ending. Also recognize the correspondences between A1 and B1, A2 and B2, and A3 and B3. In both A and B sections the writer to the Hebrews gives an introduction, follows it by arguing for the superiority of a figure or institution mentioned in the Old Testament, and concludes with vying for the superiority of Christ's high-priestly ministry. Hebrews 8:1–2 stands at the mid-point of this whole discussion.

An Important Transition (8:1–2)

THESE TWO VERSES, therefore, make an effective transition because they point back to the writer's discourse on the Son's appointment while at the same time anticipating the primary themes of the coming discourse on the heavenly high priest's superior service. Verse 1 begins by recapitulating the main theme of the previous section, proclaiming, "The point of what we are saying is this: We do have such a high priest. . . ." The word *kephalaion* can mean "summary" or "main point," and the NIV's choice of the latter sense suits the context. The author, rather than summarizing the material just covered, focuses it in the phrase "such a high priest."[1]

This high priest the writer identifies as he "who sat down at the right hand of the throne of the Majesty in heaven" (v. 1b). In 5:1–7:28, Psalm 110:4 garnered the lion's share of attention as a priesthood in the order of Melchizedek held center stage. Now the author reintroduces Psalm 110:1, a verse already alluded to at Hebrews 1:3 and quoted at 1:13. Our high priest, who has been appointed to this position by an oath from God (Ps. 110:4), has also "sat down at the right hand of the throne of the Majesty."

The wording of the allusion in our present passage, specifically the little phrase "in heaven," serves the author's purpose by mentioning a main motif of the following material: the location of the Son's ministry in heaven. This position makes it superior to the earthbound priesthood of the old covenant. In contrast to that mortal ministry, the one who sits at the right hand serves in the heavenly tabernacle built by the hand of the Lord rather than by human beings. Although some commentators have interpreted "sanctuary" and "true tabernacle" to refer to two parts of the heavenly place of worship (e.g., the Holy Place and the Most Holy Place), the NIV rightly understands the two references as a hendiadys referring to the same place—the place where our high priest ministers in the presence of his Father.[2]

Introduction on Christ's Superior, High-Priestly Ministry (8:3–6)

AT 5:1, THE opening verse on Christ's appointment to high priesthood,[3] the writer of Hebrews stated, "Every high priest is selected from among men and is appointed to represent them in matters related to God, to offer gifts and sacrifices for sins." Now with 8:3, the start of the section addressing the Son's superior offering, he reiterates the thought expressed by 5:1. Here, however, he places emphasis on the required need of an offering: "Every

---

1. Attridge, *The Epistle to the Hebrews*, 217.
2. See the excellent discussion by Hughes, *A Commentary on the Epistle to the Hebrews*, 288–89.
3. See above, pp. 185–87.

high priest is appointed to offer both gifts and sacrifices, and so it was necessary for this one also to have something to offer." These two verses (5:1 and 8:3) form parallel introductions to the author's sections on the "appointment" and the "superior offering" respectively.[4]

In 8:4—5 our writer continues to smooth his transition from the previous chapter by noting points of contrast between the Levitical priests and the exalted Son; yet the focus here rests on a differentiation between the two locales of their ministries, that is, the heavenly and earthly realms. In establishing this contrast the author notes again that the high priest according to the order of Melchizedek does not fit with the priests of the old covenant. Their system was earthly, and their offerings were presented in accordance with the law (v. 4). Furthermore, the tabernacle at which they served was but a copy, or shadow, of the true place of worship in heaven (v. 5).

This assertion finds support from the book of Exodus, where the Lord told Moses, "See to it that you make everything according to the pattern shown you on the mountain" (8:5; cf. Ex. 25:40). The old covenant tabernacle, sanctioned as it was by God, can only be seen as an imperfect copy of the real thing, since human beings constructed it. That it constitutes a "shadow" suggests the earthly sanctuary mimics enough of the original to point God's people to greater, heavenly realities. Nevertheless, since it is an earthly structure, it belongs to a realm that is passing away.[5] Since the old covenant priests were limited in their effectiveness by their mortality (cf. 7:11—28), the old covenant place of worship must be seen ultimately as an ineffectual copy of the heavenly reality. Consequently, "the ministry Jesus has received is superior to theirs" (8:6), and this superiority of his ministry as mediator corresponds to the superiority of the new covenant over the old. The writer of Hebrews now demonstrates that the new covenant "is founded on better promises" through his quotation of Jeremiah 31:31—34.

The Superiority of the New Covenant (8:7–13)

THE CONCEPT OF the new covenant occurs elsewhere in the New Testament (Luke 22:20; 1 Cor. 11:25; 2 Cor. 3:6), but nowhere with such extensive explication as in Hebrews. In Hebrews 9–10 the author associates the new covenant with cultic ideas of priesthood and sacrifice by seizing on the forgiveness of sins announced in Jeremiah 31:34 (e.g., Heb. 9:14–15; 10:15–18).

---

4. Guthrie, *The Structure of Hebrews*, 104—5.

5. Lane, *Hebrews 1—8*, 206—7. Lane rightly notes that although the language used by the author here might be confused for Platonic dualism, the similarities are merely verbal. The author's orientation, rather, is eschatological, drawing temporal contrasts between the past and present eras.

However, in the passage under consideration, the author focuses on the *inadequacy* of the old covenant, a concept presented as intrinsic to Jeremiah 31. In Hebrews 8:7 the author reasons, "For if there had been nothing wrong with the first covenant, no place would have been sought for another." The logic is simple: The announcement of a new covenant proves that something had gone wrong with the first.

The word *amemptos*, translated here as "nothing wrong," means "blameless." Luke uses this word, for example, to describe Zechariah and Elizabeth's observance of the Lord's commands and regulations (Luke 1:6); Paul uses it similarly to speak of his own faultless observance of the law (Phil. 3:6).[6] The difference in Hebrews 8:7, of course, is that the author refers to an institution rather than a person. The first covenant came up short, missing the mark, perhaps by its inability to deliver the fullness of relationship God ultimately desired with humanity. The author has already made clear that this was due in part to the inadequacy of the old covenant priesthood with which the older arrangement was intertwined (7:11–28; 8:3–6).

The wording of verse 8 demands some consideration because of a textual variant in the Greek. The NIV translation reads, "But God found fault with the people." We might render the text more literally as "for faulting them [*autous*] he says. . . ." The word "them" occurs here in the accusative case and has been taken by some commentators, as well as the NIV translators, to refer to those under the old covenant of whom Jeremiah 31 speaks. However, a textual variant has the "them" in the dative case (*autois*). If this reading is the better one—and it has much early manuscript support—there are two options. It can be understood to modify the participle "finding fault" and to refer to the people. However, *autois* can also be taken to modify the verb "says." In this interpretation the clause reads, "for finding fault [with the old covenant] he says to them . . . ," and this reading seems to flow more naturally from verse 7, which implies that the first covenant was flawed, and fits as well with the author's concluding comment in 8:13.[7] The discussion emphasizes the defective nature of the old covenant.

The quote of Jeremiah 31:31–34 (Heb. 8:8–12) has three parts. (1) The Lord promises a time when he will make a new covenant with the people of God (v. 8). (2) Following from the word "new," this promise is qualified negatively, in that this covenant would *not* be like the Sinai covenant. The reason for this change of arrangements is also given: Those led out of Egypt did

---

6. Phil. 2:15 and 1 Thess. 3:13 both use the word to encourage Christians in their manner of life.

7. See Lane, *Hebrews 1–8*, 202, notes; Hughes, *A Commentary on the Epistle to the Hebrews*, 298–99, note 19. Cf. also NIV text note on 8:8.

not remain faithful to God's covenant (v. 9). (3) Finally, the details of the new covenant are described positively. The laws of God will be placed on the minds and hearts of God's people, the relationship between God and his followers will be firmly established (v. 10), and everyone within the covenant will know the Lord (v. 11), because God will forgive their sins (v. 12). The emphasis on relationship and the internal quality of the effect on God's people is unmistakable. The new covenant, in essence, establishes a relationship with God. In that relationship the laws of God are internalized and the forgiveness of sins is foundational.

After such a long quote—indeed, the longest quote in the New Testament—one would expect extensive commentary. However, the author surprises with a brief comment on one word from Jeremiah: the word "new" (*kainos*). His approach here demonstrates use of a common rabbinic procedure that involved drawing out the implications of a text. Hebrews 8:13 contains the inference. Since God referred to the second covenant as "new," he relegates the first covenant to a status of "obsolete." These two covenants are not intended to coexist, but the second replaces the first, as suggested in the quote from Jeremiah.

The verb translated "made . . . obsolete" (perfect tense of *palaioo*) connotes becoming old in the sense of losing its usefulness. In Luke 12:33 the Evangelist quotes Jesus as saying, "Provide purses for yourselves that will not wear out [from *palaioo*], a treasure in heaven that will not be exhausted. . . ." In Hebrews 1:11, the word occurs in the quote of Psalm 102:26, which reads, "They will all wear out [from *palaioo*] like a garment." Thus here in Hebrews 8:13 the writer speaks of the old covenant as having gotten beyond its time of usefulness. When he states that "what is obsolete and aging will soon disappear," he speaks of the first covenant's complete demise as inevitable.[8]

AT FIRST GLANCE Hebrews 8:1–13 may seem to present us with a fairly cut-and-dried exposition of the Old Testament, more suitable for the theology classroom than the hard concrete and hot asphalt of real-world Christian living. However, this text offers a unique opportunity to reflect on several issues of paramount importance to those who wish to live our faith authentically in our local and global communities.

---

8. Bruce correctly cautions that these words do not necessarily mean that the Jerusalem temple complex was still intact at the time Hebrews was written. Yet if that system of worship was still functioning, as it would be if our date for Hebrews in the early 60s is correct (see above, pp. 22–23), the author could be reading Jeremiah as pointing to the system's

The relationship between two religions. In Hebrews 7–10 two understandings of God's dealings with his people intersect, collide, meld, or display a succession—depending on one's interpretation—and the comparison of the two takes a singularly concise and lucid form in chapter 8: the old covenant vis-à-vis the new, and the priesthood of the tabernacle over against the priestly, heavenly Messiah. There can be no doubt that the author of Hebrews intended the comparison. Again and again he employs the term "better" to describe God's revelation in Christ in contradistinction to the old covenant. If many commentators are correct, the author expressly utilizes the contrasts in order to bolster the commitment of Christians whose resolve was waning, who were tempted to return from the upstart, persecuted Christian community to the stable, long-standing traditions of Judaism proper.[9] These believers were a minority society within society, and that minority status had its pressures from which some wished to escape.

This, of course, is not the struggle for most reading this commentary. Currently the Jewish population in the United States has dropped to 2 percent of the total and continues to decrease. The problem of maintaining Jewish culture and the distinctiveness of the Jewish religion has become a weighty issue for Jews in America.[10] The call to embrace the Jewish religion may be an issue faced by one considering an interfaith marriage or a Christian struggling under minority status in modern-day Israel, but, for the most part, the tables have turned, so that the forces of change pull the other way. For many believers the "allure" of traditional Judaism is simply a nonissue. This may be why this middle section of Hebrews falls flat for some modern-day Christ-followers. The inferior status of the old covenant has become an axiom. When that approach to God is placed in a contest with Christianity, we perceive it as a batting competition between a little-leaguer and Babe Ruth, or a running match between a middle-aged jogger and Carl Lewis. Who can get excited about that?

At least two problems are inherent to this attitude. (1) This perspective belies a devaluation of what God did in the old covenant religion. How could God's interaction with his people, his provision for a covenant with them, be seen as less than magnificent, even if it was provisional? Although his sermon is polemical, calling for an increased appreciation for new covenant doctrine, the author of Hebrews does not mean to suggest that

---

ultimate demise. This would place him in the same line of thought expressed by both Jesus and Stephen, who had predicted the fall of the temple (Mark 13:2; John 2:19; Acts 6:14). See Bruce, *The Epistle to the Hebrews*, 195–96.

9. See the discussion in the introduction above, pp. 21–22.

10. See, for example, Elliott Abrams, *Faith or Fear: How Jews Can Survive in a Christian America* (New York: Free Press, 1997).

the old covenant activity of God was base or useless; he is no Marcionite. The Old Testament revelation was, after all, a form of God's speaking to humanity (1:1–2) and, for the author, a primary source of authority. No, it is the moon in relationship to the new covenant sun. In the darkness of the Old Testament era it shone brightly, giving insight to the holy, loving God of the universe; but this true, older light has now been eclipsed by the full intensity of revelation in God's Son.

One way of more greatly valuing what God has done in his Son is to begin by reflecting on the tremendous importance of what God did in the old covenant. Remember, the original hearers of Hebrews probably were drawn in some way to the desirability of the Judaism of their day, and it is in that light they are addressed in Hebrews concerning the much greater value of the new covenant in Christ. We miss the intended *impact* of Hebrews 8 if we fail to grasp the value of traditional Judaism.

(2) In the comfort of our Christian communities, insulated by long-worn customs and closely networked relationships, we can lapse into an unhealthy form of triumphalism, which does not play well with those of the Jewish faith, with those of other religions, or with those who hold to a pluralistic worldview. Our haughty celebration of Christian superiority damages our witness to those who intuitively sense the contradiction between a prideful spirit and the humility preached by Christ. How should we relate, therefore, to those of the Jewish faith? At least two cautions demand attention as we seek to apply ourselves to that question.

(a) We need to remember that the supersessionism described in Hebrews 8 has been misused at times to justify anti-Semitism, a cancer long-lived in the church and chillingly crystallized in Nazi Germany:

> Historians now recognize the importance of an anti-Semitism that long preceded Adolf Hitler and that was to considerable degree rooted in Christian doctrine and church practice. Centuries ago, having pushed the Jews beyond the boundaries of moral obligation, this Christian anti-Semitism prepared the ground for the more radical Nazi Jew-hatred that produced the Holocaust. Moreover, during the Holocaust itself this legacy of contempt for Jews was a crucial impediment to appropriate Christian behavior in occupied Europe. When the Nazis set to work annihilating Jews, they found a deep reservoir of scorn for Jews on which to draw in seeking collaborators in stifling action, or even sympathy, on behalf of their prey.[11]

---

11. David P. Gushee, *The Righteous Gentiles of the Holocaust: A Christian Interpretation* (Minneapolis: Fortress, 1994), 14.

The majority of those responsible for the Holocaust were associated with the Christian faith—having been baptized, instructed in the Christian way of life, and married in the church. Many Jewish survivor-victims of camps like Auschwitz and Dachau remembered with bitterness that their jailers celebrated Christmas and Easter.[12] Thankfully this does not paint the whole picture. As detailed by David Gushee in his excellent book, *The Righteous Gentiles of the Holocaust*, there were Gentile rescuers motivated by their Christian faith to help the Jews. However, their numbers were too few to stem the tide of the murder of six million of Abraham's descendants. The fact that Christian doctrine could be misused to such evil ends should give us cause to reflect deeply on the way we interpret and apply passages like Hebrews 8.

(b) There has been a growing tendency in some circles to misjudge the New Testament itself as anti-Jewish.[13] For example, Samuel Sandmel has commented, "The New Testament is a repository for hostility to Jews and Judaism. Many, if perhaps even most, Christians are completely free of anti-Semitism, yet Christian scripture is permeated by it."[14] A more judicious and exegetically sound approach, however, understands early Christianity as one of several movements within Judaism in an intramural struggle vying for the hearts and minds of first-century Jews. The Jews of Qumran, the followers of the rabbis, the Sadducees, the Zealots, and other groups formed anything but a monolithic culture. The polemic one finds in the New Testament occurs in these various branches of first-century Judaism, each group presenting itself as the future of Judaism.[15]

We must remember that Jesus, his first followers, all the apostles, all the writers of the New Testament except Luke, and all Christians in the first years of the church were Jewish. When God introduced the concept that his new covenant was intended to include the Gentiles, it scandalized the first Christians as well as those holding to more traditional forms of Judaism (Acts 10:1–11:3; 15:1–2; 22:17–22). Hebrews, as we have seen, is permeated by the Jewish Scriptures and replete with examples of rabbinic forms of exegesis.[16] Christianity is not a Gentile religion but a Jewish religion that has grafted in the Gentiles. It is polemical; but rather than being anti-Semitic, it

---

12. Ibid.

13. See S. Sandmel, *Anti-Semitism in the New Testament?* (Philadelphia: Fortress, 1978); J. T. Sanders, *The Jews in Luke-Acts* (Philadelphia: Fortress, 1987).

14. Sandmel, *Anti-Semitism in the New Testament?* 160.

15. See the collection of essays in Craig A. Evans and Donald Hagner, eds., *Anti-Semitism and Early Christianity: Issues of Polemic and Faith* (Minneapolis: Fortress, 1993).

16. See above, pp. 24–25; Robert W. Wall and William L. Lane, "Polemic in Hebrews and the Catholic Epistles," in *Anti-Semitism and Early Christianity*, ed. Craig A. Evans and Donald A. Hagner, 166–85.

is thoroughly Semitic, arguing for a specific interpretation of the history of God's work among the Jewish people, and through them, the broader world. Any charge of anti-Semitism, while understandable (given the faulty interpretations of the New Testament propagated by some Christians through the centuries), has failed to study adequately the historical context in which the New Testament literature developed.

The nature of the new covenant. I teach New Testament survey classes every year and am surprised consistently at many students' inability to explain concisely the essence of Christianity. Those with a history of church involvement may use descriptions such as "saved," "born again," "confirmed," "I belong to the church," or "I have a relationship with God," but the thinking about what those references mean often comes across as mushy. Those with little church orientation misconstrue Christianity as essentially having to do with certain external practices, such as going to church, being moral, and being nice—all vitally important to the practice of Christianity but off the mark as adequate explanations of Christian faith. One of the most gratifying experiences for me as a teacher occurs when I receive a note from a former student who writes, "I finally understood the basic message of the New Testament for the first time."

In Hebrews 8 we have a synopsis of the new covenant in prophetic form. Since the new covenant *is* true Christianity, this passage, although not exhaustive, sums up the essence of what it means to be a Christian. Thus as we move toward application, we do well to ask how our reflection on this passage might inform our thinking about the Christian faith and our explanation of that faith to others.

Let us consider what the new covenant is. It is, as expressed above, grounded in Judaism (8:10). Consequently, any adequate understanding of Christianity must grasp its Jewish roots and the implication of those roots for Christian belief. It is about the internalization of religion, not merely the external practice of religion (8:10). God's laws are written on the minds and hearts of true Christians. As such, transformation and intrinsic motivation form powerful, foundational elements of Christian life and living. The new covenant is about relationship with God (8:10–11), not merely service for God. Finally, the forgiveness of sins forms the basis for this new covenant relationship (8:12).

Any conception of Christianity, therefore, that neglects the idea of sin and forgiveness has departed from the understanding of covenant expressed in Hebrews 8 via the prophet Jeremiah. So the new covenant, in essence, has to do with a relationship with God established by the forgiveness of sins, lived out by the internalization of God's laws, and conceptually set against the backdrop of God's working through the people of Israel.

We should also pause to reflect on misconceptions about Christianity that could flow from a misuse of this passage. (1) Christianity is not about the rejection of the Jewish people. When Jeremiah writes of those led out of Egypt, "I turned away from them" (8:9), he expresses the Lord's disapproval of a specific group that had been disobedient, not the Jewish people as a whole. Note that the new covenant was prophesied as for "the house of Israel" (8:10).

(2) The new covenant does not mean that Christians need not give attention to external practices such as morality, kindness, and church attendance. Hebrews 8 cannot be used to suggest that believers should just "follow their hearts" in attempting to discern proper behavior. For example, the author of Hebrews later challenges his hearers to love fellow believers in tangible terms, to be sexually pure, and to reject greed (13:1–6). Believers are encouraged to perform "good deeds" (10:24; 13:16), with which God is well pleased.

(3) Closely related to the second caution, when Jeremiah proclaims that God forgives the wickedness of those under the new covenant and remembers their sins no more, this neither implies that true Christians cease from sin completely nor provides us with a license to sin. Elsewhere the author encourage us to "throw off . . . the sin that so easily entangles us" (12:1) and warns that a flippant attitude toward sin brings about imminent judgment (10:26–27). Moreover, that those under the new covenant "know the Lord" does not remove our need to grow in our relationship with God, since growth is a hallmark of true Christian faith (e.g., 5:11–6:3).

This understanding of Christianity in terms of covenant not only has implications for how we think about our faith but also for how we express our faith to others. Hebrews seeks to clarify Christianity for its audience in the hope of bringing about a decision. As we move to application, therefore, we should consider how the concept of covenant might be used to call people to a decision for Christ.

THE MARGINALIZATION OF **Judaism.** One night recently I listened to an interesting television interview, conducted by John McLaughlin, with a prominent Christian leader and a specialist on Jewish culture in America. At one point in this congenial conversation the specialist, himself a Jew, noted with a smile that it "drives Jewish people crazy" when evangelical Christians suggest their religion has displaced Judaism. How, then, do we relate meaningfully to those who feel our religion, by definition, marginalizes their own? Let me suggest three important elements and, along the way, comment on appropriate applications of Hebrews 8.

(1) *We must reject all forms of anti-Semitism and language that can be understood as anti-Semitic.* Anti-Semitism is contrary to the most basic tenets of Christian doctrine. This rejection of anti-Semitism includes threads of hatred of Jews in older works of theology. For example, Martin Luther stands as one of my greatest heroes of the faith. Yet, toward the end of his life my beloved Luther (and I use the term "beloved" sincerely), that great Reformer, who institutionally and theologically changed the course of church history, demonstrated profound blind spots. Read his words from a work entitled, *On the Jews and Their Lies*:

> God has struck [the Jews] with "madness and blindness and confusion of mind." So we are even at fault in not avenging all this innocent blood of our Lord and of the Christians which they shed for three hundred years after the destruction of Jerusalem, and the blood of the children they have shed since then (which still shines forth from their eyes and their skin). We are at fault in not slaying them. Rather we allow them to live freely in our midst despite all their murdering, cursing, blaspheming, lying, and defaming. . . .[17]

Luther continues by suggesting that Christians set fire to synagogues or schools (and bury whatever will not burn), raze their houses, take their prayer books and Talmudic writings, threaten the lives of their rabbis who continue to teach, ban them from the highways, and confiscate their money.[18] The Nazis later republished these grievous comments in support of their cause, and this should remind us of the imperfection of even our greatest theological heroes. As one friend noted, "It makes me wonder what corrupting blind spots we have today."

This rejection of anti-Semitism also should jettison stereotypes drawn from culture (e.g., the "miserly Jew") and language that can be misunderstood as anti-Jewish. As an example of the latter, the Gospel of John uses the designation "Jews" over sixty times, often with negative overtones when referring to the religious leaders who opposed Jesus (John 5:16–18). However, at times the word refers to the Jewish people as a whole, as when Jesus himself is included in the reference (4:22) or mention is made of "the feast of the Jews" (e.g., 5:1).

In the Fourth Gospel, one sees clearly the distinction between the Jewish people in general and the religious leaders in opposition to Jesus. In John 19:38, for example, Joseph of Arimathea, a Jew and religious leader himself

---

17. Martin Luther, *On the Jews and Their Lies*, in *Luther's Works*, vol. 47, ed. Franklin Sherman (Philadelphia: Fortress, 1971), 267.
18. Ibid., 268–70.

(Mark 15:43; Luke 23:50), is said to be a disciple of Jesus secretly, "for fear of the Jews." Was Joseph afraid of himself? No. Based on principles of sound interpretation we must read the designation "the Jews" in John most often as "religious leaders who opposed Jesus" in order to be true to what John meant to communicate. Thus, when we read to a congregation, "The Jews persecuted and sought to kill Jesus" (John 5:16–18), we must interpret the meaning for the hearers lest they think of the statement as a wholesale condemnation of Jewish people.

(2) *We must think clearly about what we believe as Christians and proclaim the gospel boldly.* Christian statesman John Stott has suggested:

> One of the tragedies of the contemporary church is that, just when the world seems to be ready to listen, the church often seems to have little or nothing to say. For the church itself is confused; it shares in the current bewilderment, instead of addressing it. The church is insecure; it is uncertain of its identity, mission and message. It stammers and stutters, when it should be proclaiming the gospel with boldness. Indeed, the major reason for its diminishing influence in the West is its diminishing faith.[19]

Reflection on Christianity vis-à-vis Judaism has taken at least two directions in modern theological circles. (a) There are those who believe Christian theology must be redefined since, they suggest, "traditional orthodoxy" is inherently anti-Semitic. This has led one scholar, on the basis of Hebrews' supersessionist theology, to suggest:

> The author's positive purpose was commendable, to contend that the grace of God through Jesus Christ is freely and utterly available to all sinners, and that the word of this grace is a sure and certain word on which we can rely. But we see two things clearly: the author's constructive thesis *calls for the dismantling of the negative, supersessionist framework in which it was cast lest the very grace it proclaims as radically free be conditional after all;* and its displacement theology was to have a long and tragic history.[20]

In other words, the author of Hebrews meant well but mishandled his message by using a negative message about Jewish religion.

(b) The other direction, represented by many evangelicals, suggests both that we should nurture a deep respect for the Jewish people as people, hon-

---

19. Stott, *The Contemporary Christian*, 183.
20. Clark M. Williamson, *A Guest in the House of Israel: Post-Holocaust Church Theology* (Louisville, Ky.: Westminster/John Knox, 1993), 110 (italics mine).

oring their role in history and biblical revelation, and that we should hold to an exegetically based interpretation of the New Testament. My understanding is that there are those in the Jewish community who do not want us to throw over our convictions but simply wish to be treated with integrity and respect. What might our doctrinal convictions look like, based on an exegesis of relevant New Testament passages?

(i) As we have already suggested in this commentary, there is continuity between the old covenant community and the new covenant age. In Luke 1:67–79 Zechariah points to the fulfillment of the old covenant in Christ. Paul can insist that God's promises of the old covenant still stand for the Jews (Rom. 9:6) and that God has not rejected his people (11:1). He even proclaims that "all Israel will be saved" (11:24–26). God has entrusted the Jewish people with his revelation in the Scriptures (i.e., what we refer to as the Old Testament).

(ii) However, we must take the discontinuity between the covenants seriously. From the New Testament perspective—and this is unmistakably affirmed in Hebrews 8—Christ is at the center of the purposes of God. All the promises of God are answered "yes" in him (2 Cor. 1:20). The election of Israel was ultimately to find its fulfillment in the person of Christ (Gal. 3:16), as do all the great themes of the Old Testament.

It follows, then, that God's people in both Testaments must be seen in light of Christ.[21] All who reject Christ, Jew or Gentile, are under God's judgment. For Jewish people specifically, they forfeit their membership in the "true Israel" (Rom. 9:6–7; cf. John 8:39–44). Paul says that the Jewish people will be saved (Rom. 11:25–26) and that they are "loved on account of the patriarchs," from the standpoint of God's choice (11:28). He means here that the salvation offered in Christ is promised first to them, if they will accept it, and then to the Gentiles. Their history with God is the foundation, but not the total picture of the ultimate Israel, which is not limited to one race but to all who are spiritually oriented in Christ.

I realize that the above will be unacceptable to many and that it represents a traditional (some will say naïve), supersessionist theology. However, I reject the notion that it implies a hatred or disrespect for the Jewish people—attitudes that I personally deplore. It is possible to love others and treat them with dignity even if we disagree with them. Such respect does not mean we must cease from our religious convictions and conversations with others who are open to such conversations. On the contrary, I believe we must share the gospel boldly to be true to the message of the New Testament; but respect does mean that we will conduct those conversations sensitively

---

21. See S. Motyer, "The New Israel," *EDT*, 571–72.

and "with grace" (cf. Col. 4:5–6), listening as well as sharing our own perspectives. Some may characterize my position as displaying "religious intolerance," but:

> religious tolerance is not always a sign of good will. It can be a sign of careless, perhaps hypocritical religious indifference of the most high-handed philosophic relativism. It can also be a mask behind which to hide down right malice. During the Nazi era, for example, arguments for Christian openness to other perspectives were used by German Christians in an attempt to neuter the church's protest against the neopaganism of Hitler and his minions. The Confessing Church in Germany found in [John 10] a theological basis to stand against Hitler. There are times in which the only way to keep alive the non-vindictive, nonjudgmental, self-sacrificing witness of Jesus Christ is to stand with rude dogmatism on the rock that is Jesus Christ, condemning all compromise as the work of the Antichrist.[22]

Commenting on Christianity in first-century Asia, W. M. Ramsay noted that an "easy-going Christianity," devoid of firm convictions and open to all religious positions as equally valid, "could never have survived; only the most convinced, resolute, almost bigoted adherence to the most uncompromising interpretation of its own principles could have given the Christians the courage and self-reliance that were needed. For them to hesitate or to doubt was to be lost."[23] Pluralism was as pervasive in the first century as it is in the present one. If those win the day who wish for a revision of Christianity as a "nondogmatic" religion, able to "fit in" with the plethora of religious systems offered modern humankind, then Christianity—that of the stripe proclaimed by Hebrews—will surely be lost. Thankfully, there are many who refuse to surrender that brand of Christianity and find in it their motivation for love, compassion, and respect for people of whatever religious conviction.

(3) *We must hold our doctrinal convictions with an uncompromising commitment to a holistic, biblical morality.* Our proclamation of the gospel will never be heard apart from lives and communities that reflect a resolute involvement in authentic, moral living. Jesus challenged his followers: "Let your light shine before men, that they may see your good deeds and praise your Father in heaven" (Matt. 5:16). He did not come to abolish the Law or the Prophets

---

22. Ronald Goetz in "Exclusivistic Universality," as quoted in *Christianity Today* (May 20, 1996): 54. It is interesting that the Gospel of John, a book some scholars consider to be anti-Semitic, was a primary source of religious conviction that motivated Gentile rescuers during the Holocaust.

23. W. M. Ramsay, *The Letters to the Seven Churches*, updated edition, ed. Mark Wilson (Peabody, Mass.: Hendrickson, 1994), 220.

but to fulfill them; thus he praised those who kept the commandments (5:17–20). Jesus moved the orientation of moral living from mere outward actions to the internal condition of the human heart (5:21–48), telling believers to "be perfect" as the "heavenly Father is perfect" (5:48).

One way Paul speaks of moral or righteous living is in terms of a person's "walk." Believers are to walk in newness of life (Rom. 6:4), walk in love (14:15; Eph. 5:2), walk in good works (Eph. 2:10), and walk according to the Spirit rather than the sinful nature (Rom. 8:4; Gal. 5:16). There must be a distinct difference between the Christ-follower and people of the world, who live immoral lives (Eph. 2:1–2; 5:8). Believers are not to walk as the unwise, giving place to sexual sins, lust, evil desires, greed, anger, malice, slander, and lying, for example (Col. 3:5–10). John continues this motif by condemning a walk in darkness (1 John 1:6–7) and hatred of one's brother (2:11) and by declaring that the person who claims to have a relationship with Christ ought to walk as he walked (2:6).

When non-Christians witness anger, greed, hatred, prejudice, dissension, lack of integrity, insensitivity, unconcern for the disadvantaged, and other such attitudes in those who wear the label "Christian," our claim that the laws of God have been written on our hearts and minds (Heb. 8:10) does not ring true. A truly transformed life, on the other hand, can be a powerful witness to the veracity of the Christian message.

One obstacle in challenging ourselves to live morally comes from our preconceived notions about morality, which are particular to our various segments of modern Christianity. Half a century ago Dorothy Sayers lamented "the strangely restricted interpretation on such words as *virtue, purity,* and *morality*" in her era, observing: "There are a great many people now living in the world who firmly believe that Christian morals as distinct from purely secular morality, consist in three things and three things only: Sunday observance, not getting intoxicated, and not practicing—well, in fact, not practicing immorality."[24]

In our day some churches have reinterpreted certain exhortations against extramarital sex as outdated, culturally bound commands of another century, while lifting high the standard of social responsibility to the poor and oppressed. More conservative churches may cry out against sins of sexual perversion and substance abuse, though neglecting a strong emphasis on racial injustice and care for the socially disadvantaged. In our American consumer culture one hears little (from the theological right or left) about the sins of gluttony and personal greed. They simply do not play well, even though they each have a place in biblical morality. We have what biblical scholars

---

24. Sayers, *The Whimsical Christian,* 152.

call a "canon within a canon," taking a smorgasbord approach to what we deem "moral" or "immoral." Yet if we claim to reflect the message of the Bible, is it not obligatory for us to take the whole of it seriously, even those parts not on the list of chief concerns in our immediate culture? To fail in such consistency will be to play the hypocrite in the eyes of those whom we wish to hear our message.

The externalization of Christianity. There seems to be an incessant pressure toward what might be called "the externalization of Christianity," in which the moral dimension of the faith becomes defined wholly in terms of external activities, neglecting dynamics of the inner life. "The contrast," writes Richard Foster, "between God's way of doing things and our way is never more acute than in this area of human change and transformation. We focus on specific actions; God focuses on us. We work from the outside in; God works from the inside out. We try; God transforms."[25]

The externals are vitally important; they may serve as markers of inner realities; yet, as Foster notes, they should be out-workings of those inner, spiritual realities, the laws written on the mind and heart. When the whole of Christianity becomes defined in terms of conformity to certain external associations or actions, we drift from the emphasis placed on the internal realities of kingdom thinking and living. We move from a consciousness of transformation to an attempt to orient our lives in various moral occupations.

Some Christians judge a person's spirituality by their associations (e.g., what church they attend, to what political party they belong, or who they hold as close friends), their practices (e.g., their devotional habits, the way they dress, the entertainment they enjoy), or their passions (e.g., whether they share our concern for certain ministries or messages). Such judgments brush dangerously close to a legalism that runs contrary to the spirit of the gospel. Legalism takes one's own associations, practices, and passions—perhaps true applications or expressions of biblical morality—and makes them normative for everyone else in the body of Christ. Life in the Spirit, on the other hand, places an emphasis both on clear biblical commands as well as on biblical principles and seeks to live out a broad-based morality revealed in Scripture under the leadership and power of the Holy Spirit.

The externalization of Christianity also takes place outside the body of Christ. Many in broader culture try to redefine our religion for us in terms foreign to the new covenant described in Hebrews 8. But Christianity cannot be conceptualized as merely a social association, a set of rules that may be incorporated into a pluralistic, global scheme of morality, a psychologi-

---

25. Richard J. Foster and James Bryan Smith, eds., *Devotional Classics: Selected Readings for Individuals and Groups* (New York: HarperCollins, 1993), 11.

cal pathology of guilt or gratification, or a mystical experience similar to those of other religions. No, biblical Christianity as described in Hebrews 8 must be understood minimally as involving the forgiveness of sins, a transformation of the inner life in accordance with the laws of God, and an intimate relationship with the living God. Certainly more can be said of Christianity, and the New Testament provides us with extensive development of these motifs. However, any definition of Christianity that neglects these realities must be considered suspect.

What do they hear? This brings us to a third point of application for Hebrews 8: How do we explain the gospel to those outside the faith? One night in Fort Worth, Texas, a little over a decade ago, I went to a party at a friend's house and found those in attendance to be a delightful mix of Christians and non-Christians. I fell into a conversation with a young, single lady named Jill, who described herself as "Jewish by birth" and "atheist by religion." We began to discuss movies we had seen, and Jill brought up *The Exorcist*, qualifying her appreciation for such horror films with, "But of course, I don't believe in spirits." To this comment I replied, "Jill, do you understand why you don't believe in spirits?" Looking puzzled, she said, "Well, I don't believe in spirits because they don't exist"; to which I responded, "If they did exist, you could not see them, so how do you know?"

This led to a lively discussion of naturalism, which in turn led to a discussion of my worldview, Christianity. As I explained my understanding of the faith, I said at one point, "Jesus Christ wants a relationship with you." Up to this point we were having a good conversation, but when I made that comment, I could tell Jill had a problem with it. I said to her, "That didn't communicate, did it?" She agreed it did not. As we talked further I realized that for my friend—a young single quite involved in the party scene—the idea of "a relationship" with someone carried sexual overtones. At that point I backed up and came at my explanation from another angle.

In her book *Out of the Salt Shaker*, Rebecca Pippert challenges us to translate our Christian "God talk" into words understandable to the uninitiated. In using good, biblical terms like "born again," "grace," and "redemption," and phrases from Christian culture such as "a personal relationship with Jesus" and "asking Jesus to come into your heart," we can inadvertently confuse our hearers and obscure the message.[26] This does not mean that we should refrain from using biblical language, but that we should translate, explain, or illustrate concepts with which our hearers might not be familiar.

The concept of *covenant* can be a confusing term for those not familiar with biblical lingo, but I have found it a valuable tool for communicating the mes-

---

26. Pippert, *Out of the Salt Shaker*, 130–32.

sage of the gospel. Most people in our world understand the concept of a meaningful, binding agreement. When I speak about *covenant* to my New Testament classes, I use several analogies. For example, I tell the students about when my wife and I bought our home. In a lawyer's office we sat across from the woman from whom we bought the house. The lawyer was to our right, at the end of the table, and led us through a host of forms that would make our "agreement" binding. We agreed to certain terms, such as how much we would pay, and the seller agreed to certain terms, such as when we could occupy the house. Both parties signed forms sealing the agreement.

The concept of "a meaningful agreement" also can apply to relationships, such as a wedding. When my wife and I got married, we said vows expressing our lasting commitment to each other. At the appropriate point in the service the minister asked, "Do you, George, take Pat this day to be your wife? Do you turn from a life of singleness to hold to her and her alone as your life partner and closest friend?" I responded, "I do." After the same had been repeated with Pat, he continued, "Then will you, George, serve Pat, putting her needs before your own? Will you make the choices necessary to nurture your love for her? Will you be faithful to her and stay pure in your relationship with her? Will you, by God's help, love her in such a way that she will continue to grow in her relationship with her heavenly Father . . . ?" I answered, "I will." These questions were also put to Pat, and she too affirmed her commitments. We then exchanged rings as symbols of our covenant.

When we speak of God and a person's relationship with him, analogies break down sooner or later; yet such analogies may prove helpful as a beginning point for a non-Christian struggling with certain theological ambiguities. Using Hebrews 8 we can explain that God offers us a "meaningful agreement" with himself—that he agrees to be our God and to allow us to know him. God agrees, furthermore, to transform us in our hearts and minds, providing us with intrinsic motivation for doing his will. Finally, he commits to forgive our wickedness and forget our sins. This "meaningful agreement" is the gospel in a nutshell.

Hebrews 8 does not speak directly of our response to God's offer of covenant by repentance and faith.[27] However, this passage, with its quotation of Jeremiah 31:31–34, provides an excellent beginning point for sharing the good news that God wants us to be in a committed relationship with him; and it is this relationship that forms both the foundation and essence of a superior way of living.

---

27. On the theology of conversion see Grenz, *Theology for the Community of God*, 528–62.

Hebrews 9:1–10

NOW THE FIRST covenant had regulations for worship and also an earthly sanctuary. ²A tabernacle was set up. In its first room were the lampstand, the table and the consecrated bread; this was called the Holy Place. ³Behind the second curtain was a room called the Most Holy Place, ⁴which had the golden altar of incense and the gold-covered ark of the covenant. This ark contained the gold jar of manna, Aaron's staff that had budded, and the stone tablets of the covenant. ⁵Above the ark were the cherubim of the Glory, overshadowing the atonement cover. But we cannot discuss these things in detail now.

⁶When everything had been arranged like this, the priests entered regularly into the outer room to carry on their ministry. ⁷But only the high priest entered the inner room, and that only once a year, and never without blood, which he offered for himself and for the sins the people had committed in ignorance. ⁸The Holy Spirit was showing by this that the way into the Most Holy Place had not yet been disclosed as long as the first tabernacle was still standing. ⁹This is an illustration for the present time, indicating that the gifts and sacrifices being offered were not able to clear the conscience of the worshiper. ¹⁰They are only a matter of food and drink and various ceremonial washings—external regulations applying until the time of the new order.

WITH CHAPTER 8 the author of Hebrews launched into a vigorous discussion of Christ's superior ministry by giving a brief introduction to the Lord's heavenly tabernacle (8:5) and sacrifice (8:3) and, especially, by demonstrating the scriptural basis for holding that the new covenant has displaced the old (8:6–13). In 9:1–10:18 the author explicates in detail the specific ways in which the Son's sacrifice for sins can be shown to be "better" than the sacrifices offered by the old covenant priests, bringing his discussion of Christ's superior high priesthood to a resounding climax.[1]

---

1. On the structure of this entire section of Hebrews see above, p. 278.

Specifically, the author argues for the superiority of Christ's offering on three bases. (1) The *place* of the offering was in heaven rather than on earth (9:11, 23–25; 10:12–13). (2) The *blood* of the offering was Christ's own blood rather than the blood of animals (9:12–28). (3) The offering of the heavenly high priest, unlike the continuous sacrifices of the old covenant priests, was *eternal*, having been made once for all (9:25–26; 10:1–18).

Rather than immediately getting to these Christological arguments, however, the author begins this extensive treatment of Christ's superior offering by describing the worship regulations and tabernacle of the old covenant (9:1–10). After a brief introduction to these topics in verse 1, the passage develops in two movements, the first dealing with the earthly sanctuary (vv. 2–5) and the second with the old covenant's guidelines for worship, including the significance of these guidelines in light of the new era (vv. 6–10). In these two movements, moreover, the hearers are introduced to the (earthly) place of sacrifice (vv. 2–5), the blood of the sacrifice (v. 7), and the perpetual nature of offerings under the old covenant (vv. 6–7)—themes to be developed later as they are placed in contrast to the superior sacrifice of Christ.

Introduction to the Passage and a Description of the Tabernacle (9:1–5)

HAVING ARGUED FOR the superiority of the new covenant in 8:7–13, the writer now presents a brief description of the sacrificial worship as executed under the first covenant. Most of the ten New Testament uses of the word translated "regulations" (*dikaioma*) refer to a "legal statute," "commandment," or "requirement,"[2] as is the case in 9:1.[3] The author of Hebrews has in view requirements "for worship," specifically the Mosaic commands concerning how priestly ministry was to be conducted. His introduction also mentions the structure in which this ministry was performed, the "earthly sanctuary." "Earthly" keeps the contrast between the old covenant tabernacle and the "heavenly" place of Christ's sacrifice in the foreground. These two themes, the requirements of priestly ministry and the structure for the performance of that ministry, are now explained in inverse order.[4]

---

2. K. Kertelge, "δικαίωμα," *EDNT*, 334–35; Spicq, *Theological Lexicon of the New Testament*, 1:343–45.

3. The word occurs only here and in 9:10 in Hebrews, forming an *inclusio* of 9:1–10 (see Attridge [who follows Albert Vanhoye], *Epistle to the Hebrews*, 231). On the use of inclusions in Hebrews see above, p. 71.

4. The inverting of themes (chiasmus) is a stylistic device used extensively by the author of Hebrews.

In describing the old covenant worship structure, the author spotlights the tabernacle of Exodus[5] rather than the temple of his own era, thus keeping with his characteristic practice of drawing his material from the Scriptures. The description found in 9:2–5 moves from the outer room of the worship tent to the inner. In the first room, called the "Holy Place" (*Hagia*), "the lampstand" and "the table" on which the priests placed the "consecrated bread" could be found. The lampstand was made of pure gold, having six flowered branches extending from its sides, three to a side. Seven lamps also were made to sit on the stand, and the stand was placed on the south side of the Holy Place (Ex. 25:31–40; 26:35). The table, made of acacia wood and overlaid with gold, held the Bread of the Presence (25:23–30). This piece of furniture was situated on the north side of the outer room (26:35).

The "second curtain" (9:3) separated the outer room of the sanctuary from the room the author calls the "Holies of Holies" (lit. trans. of *Hagia Hagion*), an emphatic superlative the NIV translates appropriately as "the Most Holy Place."[6] Verses 4–5 then present us with two elements peripheral to the author's main point, but somewhat problematic nonetheless. (1) The golden altar of incense was located in the inner room of the sanctuary with the ark of the covenant. However, both in the Pentateuch and in the ancient history of interpretation the exact location of this altar is ambiguous.[7] Westcott makes the important observation that the altar of incense is closely associated with the ark in numerous Old Testament passages, the former providing a means of approach to the latter.[8] In any case, the author of Hebrews clearly follows a tradition emphasizing the placement of the altar within the Most Holy Place.

(2) The ark of the covenant, a chest made of acacia wood and overlaid with gold (Ex. 25:10–16), was the most important element of the tabernacle, for above its cover, between the cherubim, God met with Moses (25:22). In all ancient literature, Hebrews alone says that in addition to the stone tablets, the jar of manna and Aaron's staff were placed in the chest. The Old Testament suggests these objects were located in the Most Holy Place in front of the ark (e.g., 16:32–34; Num. 17:10–11). Hebrews may follow a strand of rabbinic tradition that presupposed that elements were later placed inside the ark, along with the tablets.[9]

The author ends his description of the tabernacle tersely with the statement, "But we cannot discuss these things in detail now," indicating a reticence

---

5. See Ex. 25:1–31:11; 36:2–39:43; 40:1–38. See Attridge, *Epistle to the Hebrews*, 232.
6. Lane, *Hebrews 9–13*, 220.
7. For a discussion of various interpretations see Attridge, *Epistle to the Hebrews*, 234–35.
8. Westcott, *The Epistle to the Hebrews*, 247.
9. Lane, *Hebrews 9–13*, 221.

to get sidetracked on matters outside his current focus. Rather, he wishes to move to the more significant issue of how this structure provided a context for the priests' ministry.

Regulations for Worship (9:6–10)

CORRESPONDING TO HIS structural discussion, which relates in order the set-up of the "first" and "second" rooms of the tabernacle, the author now explains briefly the ministry performed in each part. He again begins with the outer or first room and shows this to be the domain of the priests, who entered this chamber for their service. In context, the little phrase *dia pantos*, rendered by the NIV as "regularly," probably refers to the priests' ongoing duty of either changing the Bread of the Presence (Lev. 24:8) or the lighting of the lamps on the lampstand (Ex. 27:20–21).[10] The emphasis here, however, rests on the daily performance of their service rather than what that service entailed, and on the location of that ministry in the Holy Place.

In contrast to the daily ministry of the priests in the first room of the sanctuary, the high priest was the only ministrant to enter the Most Holy Place, doing so only once a year on the Day of Atonement. This important sacrifice involved the offering of a bull's blood for his own sins and the sins of his household, and the blood of a goat for the sins of the people. In both cases the blood was sprinkled on the ark cover and in front of it (Lev. 16:6–17). Especially relevant to the larger discussion of Hebrews, this atonement offering was for the cleansing of the Most Holy Place because of the "uncleanness and rebellion of the Israelites" (16:16). Here for the first time the author mentions "blood" in a cultic context. In the material that follows, he repeatedly draws attention to sacrificial blood as imperative for drawing near to God.[11]

The writer now turns to a lesson that the Holy Spirit wishes to teach through these old covenant regulations (v. 8): During the old covenant era there existed no means of entrance into the presence of God. That way had not been disclosed "as long as the first tabernacle was still standing." Up to this point in the chapter the word *protos* ("first") and the phrase *prote skene* ("first tent") have been used with reference to the outer room of the tabernacle (the Holy Place), where the priests performed their ministry (9:2, 6). This should also be the interpretation of the phrase translated by the NIV as

---

10. For other possibilities see Ellingworth, *The Epistle to the Hebrews*, 433. Ellingworth's suggestion that the author might have in mind the twice-daily sacrifices of Ex. 29:38–43 or the burning of incense of 30:7–8 seems less likely because the altar for offerings was outside the tent. As we have seen, the author locates the altar of incense within the inner room.

11. Lane, *Hebrews 9–13*, 222–23.

"first tabernacle" in verse 8. The Holy Place portrays a barrier space separating the people of God from the presence of God.

Verse 9 begins with a relative clause (lit., "which is an illustration for the present time"), the antecedent of which has been debated much. Does the "illustration for the present time" refer to the entire old system of worship or to the front room of the tabernacle just mentioned at the end of verse 8? The latter interpretation offers a more consistent reading of the passage. The "present time" mentioned in verse 9 does not mean the time present to our author and his hearers, but rather the time concurrent with the old covenant system of worship.[12] The outer room of the tabernacle, therefore, illustrates the whole era managed by the older covenant. It was a time in which the general populace could not draw near to God because provision had yet to be made for their consciences to be cleansed.

The word *syneidesis* ("conscience"), used rarely prior to 200 B.C., is found in writers of the first century such as Plutarch, Philo, and Josephus, as well as in the New Testament. The word denotes either personal intuition (i.e., a knowledge of something) or, more specifically, the moral awareness of good or evil (cf. Heb. 9:9, 14; 10:2, 22; 13:18).[13] The problem under the old covenant consisted of the sacrificial system's inability to resolve one's awareness of personal guilt. Thus, the outer room of the tabernacle illustrated the inner, spiritual condition of the people. Ultimately the conscience, not a material, earthly space, keeps a person from intimacy with God. Consequently, more than external regulations that dealt with practices regarding food, drink, and certain washings would be required to make entrance to the presence of God possible. These rituals simply were provisional, given until the new covenant system could be established.

WE HAVE AS our task in this commentary to bring the ancient text's original meaning over to contemporary significance by "bridging" the two contexts. Yet, the passage before us deals with an institution the author considers passé. So one might reasonably ask, "How do you apply a text that describes something as no longer applicable for a Christian?" Let me answer the question from two vantage points, the first having to do with the use of basic guidelines for interpretation and the second with how to draw truths from the text, even though the institution described in the text may not be directly applicable to the modern reader.

---

12. See Attridge, *Epistle to the Hebrews*, 241.
13. Spicq, *Theological Lexicon of the New Testament*, 3:332–36.

Discerning the meaning and purpose of the text. Let us again recall a basic goal of biblical interpretation: to grasp the author's purpose for the text in light of the text's meaning. Hebrews 9:1–10 fits into a larger homiletic complex being developed by the author. He wants this unit to function purposefully in paving the way for exposition and application later in the book. With his description of the old covenant worship, he sets up an effective contrast of themes, describing the old covenant system of worship in order that it might highlight, by contrast, the new method of approaching God established by the work of Christ. In order for us to grasp this contrast, we must first understand the old covenant system.

One problem for our interpretation and, therefore, our application of this passage concerns the ambiguity of several terms and phrases. For example, in 9:8 the author writes, "the way into the Most Holy Place had not yet been disclosed as long as the *first tabernacle [prote skene]* was still standing" (lit., "is having existence"). As noted above, the NIV's translation should be rejected as faulty at this point. Our interpretation of the phrase as "first room" pinpoints the Holy Place as the barrier of separation with which the author is concerned.

Moreover, the phrase "the present time" in verse 9 is also beset with ambiguity and has led to interpretations unprofitable for the author's designed purpose for this text. The phrase does not refer to the author's own day, for he understands himself and his community to participate in the new covenant era, the time of the Messiah. Rather, "the present time" refers to the time of the old covenant system. Thus the outer room of the tabernacle represents that era. The new era of Christ focuses in the inner room, the place of the presence of God.

Another guideline as we deal with the author's description of Old Testament tabernacle and worship concerns the distinction between descriptive details and primary concerns. We already have pointed out that three main themes occupy the reader's attention from this point in Hebrews all the way to 10:18: the *place* of Christ's offering was in heaven rather than on earth, the *blood* of the offering was Christ's own blood rather than that of animals, and Christ's offering was *eternal*, having been made once for all. These three themes may be noted as we read 9:1–10 in light of the discussion that follows.

In the author's own interpretation of the old covenant tabernacle's significance (9:8–10), he demonstrates its inability to win a person access to God. This "access" motif encapsulates all three main themes of the section. Jesus entered the presence of God in heaven to win our access, his blood provided a superior basis for that access by cleansing us from sin, and his offering was "once for all," access being indefinitely opened to us in the future.

However, in 9:1–10 the author gives us more than just these three main points. We are told of the lampstand, the table, and the altar of incense. In seeking to apply this passage we must understand these elements as "trappings" or "context" for the main issues the writer wishes to address. A creative preacher might be tempted to delve into allegorical significance of each of these items in the process of elaborating these verses. For example, one might claim that the light of God's lamp represents truth and the table represents God's provision. Although colorful, such elaboration strays from the author's own purposes for this text. He himself saw no need to give further attention to such details (v. 5).

Gleaning truths from the text. A second general approach to applying a passage on Old Testament information involves asking what the text indicates about God, his nature, and his relationship with people. If God acts consistently in accordance with his nature, then his interaction with the old covenant worshipers reveals theological truth, even though the particular system of old covenant worship is no longer applicable to us.

We see at least three primary truths in this text, all having to do with the nature and activity of God. (1) *God desires people to approach him.* The old covenant system of worship may seem formal and rigid. It certainly would not be deemed a "cutting-edge" model of worship for contemporary culture! But look beyond the ritualistic orientation of that system to its significance. The path of the priests from the outer court to the inner sanctuary paints a picture of movement toward God. The regulations provided a means of drawing near. In the Old Testament language of holiness and punishments we can miss the main point—God was at work, working out means for his people to live in intimacy with him. Therefore, our application can reflect on God's desire for intimacy with us, his creatures.

(2) *God is particular about how people approach him.* Not only does God desire that people approach him, but the Old Testament regulations for worship suggest that God has in mind specific requirements for our drawing near. Unless we conceive of God as a petty deity who hands out regulations on a whim, we must ask, "Why such detail?" In the Pentateuch the commands concerning all aspects of Israel's life, including its acts of worship, strike the reader both for their comprehensive scope and for their minute parts. In moving to application, therefore, we should ask ourselves concerning the implications of this insight for contemporary worship of God. Are there universals presupposed in the picture of worship we find in Hebrews 9:1–10? If so, what are they? This leads us to a third principle.

(3) *In addition to the presence of God, treated in (1) above, the details of worship surrounding the priestly ministry of the tabernacle focus on the holiness of God and the sinfulness of people.* The Bible reveals two basic aspects of God's holiness. (a) The

holiness of God means that God is unique.[14] For example, Exodus 15:11 (part of Moses' song of victory following the Red Sea crossing) states, "Who among the gods is like you, O LORD? Who is like you—majestic in holiness, awesome in glory, working wonders?" The Hebrew word for "holy" basically means to be "marked off, withdrawn from common and ordinary use." Thus the tabernacle celebrates the otherness or uniqueness of God by having him separated from the common person.

(b) The other aspect of God's holiness has to do with his moral purity and goodness. His character is completely untainted by evil, since he, as holy, can do no wrong. Habakkuk 1:13 says of God, "Your eyes are too pure to look on evil; you cannot tolerate wrong." As his people, moreover, we are called to excellence of moral character: "I am the LORD your God; consecrate yourselves and be holy, because I am holy" (Lev. 11:44).[15] This command to holiness may seem unrealistic from the perspective of an "I'm only human" theology, but as C. S. Lewis notes in *Mere Christianity*, Jesus' appropriation of this passage in his teaching (Matt. 5:48) was intended as a concrete moral directive, not a religious, pipe-dream:

> He never talked vague, idealistic gas. When He said, "Be perfect," He meant it. He meant that we must go in for the full treatment. It is hard; but the sort of compromise we are all hankering after is harder— in fact, it is impossible. It may be hard for an egg to turn into a bird: it would be a jolly sight harder for it to learn to fly while remaining an egg. We are like eggs at present. And you cannot go on indefinitely being just an ordinary, decent egg. We must be hatched or go bad.[16]

Thus, for humans generally, our sinfulness, which fights against holiness, constitutes a problem in our relationship with God, and it is a problem that must be grappled with under the new covenant as well as the old.

In biblical revelation the holiness of God and the sinfulness of people are universal truths. Neither has God changed nor have people been able to throw off their sinfulness. Thus, as we seek to apply 9:1–10, we should give attention to these themes as relevant for contemporary Christian living. How do we respond to a God who witnesses that he is holy and that we should be holy? For that matter, how do we think about holiness or sin? How do these concepts relate to our contemporary worship of God?

---

14. Erickson, *Christian Theology*, 284–85.
15. Ibid.
16. C. S. Lewis, *Mere Christianity*, (New York: Macmillan, 1952), 154–55.

THE PARENTAL BURDEN of God. Reflecting on "the burden of God" as our creator, author Calvin Miller presents a delightful, allegorical retelling of the old Italian tale *Pinocchio*, which he entitles "Penteuchio." In Miller's story, Japheth ben Levi, a rabbi in sixteenth-century Germany, cries out to God for a son. "God," the old rabbi says, "is it right that you should have made yourself a whole world of children and that my wife, Esther, and I should be condemned to live alone? Your children are as the sands of the sea, but we have no inheritance at all. Furthermore, your family is not well behaved.... If you give us a son, I promise you that my boy will turn out no worse than some of yours have." God reminds the old man that he had also created an ungrateful rabbi or two and that rabbis should not sass God.

In the end God grants Japheth's request and instructs him to carve a marionette out of a table leg; but he warns the man, "When you create children, you put your whole reputation on the line. Make ugly children and you're sure to take a lot of heat." As Japheth carves Penteuchio, the wooden boy's eyes snap open and he begins to talk; but his response to Japheth is far from what the old rabbi desires. From the first, even before he has hands or feet, the marionette acts so rebelliously that his maker stuffs a sock in his mouth and puts him in the corner. God, with a gentle smile, laughs at Japheth's frustration and asks, "How can your little boy have so many socks and no feet as yet?"

The rabbi continues to carve and quotes the Pentateuch to his would-be boy—and he grows to love Penteuchio deeply. Upon finishing the marionette, the wooden lad wreaks such havoc on his maker that Japheth gags him, ties him up completely, and places him under a huge stone in a chest. The rabbi weeps, longing to set his wooden son free. Finally, the boy promises to act honorably if liberated. Briefly, after being released, Penteuchio calls Japheth "Father," wrapping his small arms around the man's neck. They dance together around the room. Then suddenly the marionette grabs a burning log from the fireplace, throws it into the kindling box, and dashes off into the night. For the rest of his life, the wizened, old rabbi talks to God about the burden of making children and setting them free. It seems some would rather run into the night than live in harmony with their maker.[17]

The picture of God we get from the tabernacle commands described in Hebrews 9:1–10 may strike us as rather flat—he is the commanding God of ritualistic detail. But a more accurate reading of the forms and formalities of

---

17. Calvin Miller, *An Owner's Manual For the Unfinished Soul* (Wheaton, Ill.: Harold Shaw, 1997), 15–24.

priestly worship shows us the love of a Creator whose children have run into the night and cannot find their way home on their own. The tabernacle worship centers around, and calls us to, movement toward God, a movement in which we celebrate his presence, living in awe of his majestic holiness. Since God placed the tabernacle at the center of Israel's existence, his presence in the midst of his people would seem to be at the center of God's plan.

Moreover, mortal movement to the inner chambers comes by God's design, not by ours. The Israelites were in Egyptian captivity, their request amounting to a loud, "Let us out of here!" They were seeking to get out and would never have thought of "moving into the Presence," fearing as they did the closeness of God. No, the passage of the high priest, as the representative of the people, into the Most Holy Place was God's idea, not ours. We should celebrate this desire for intimacy on God's part. What if he had been satisfied to let us wander in the night, never knowing that path into the tabernacle, never knowing our way home?

Furthermore, God does not leave us to make a way into his presence. He gives specific instructions, for he is holy and we are sinful. There can be no digging a tunnel underneath the walls of the Most Holy Place, no barging in to demand our right to see God, no philosophizing about the "social constructs of religious knowledge," or no musings on "pluralism in modern religious thought" that can win us entrance. This was God's idea; it's his tent and he makes the rules. We must come in by the path of a high priest or not come in at all.

Holiness and wholeness. The term *holiness* has several uses in contemporary culture, few of them positive in the minds of the general populus. The image of a distant god, untouchable by real human concerns and frailties, or a "holier-than-thou" person who reeks with judgmental attitudes both are too common. Also, "Holiness" is used as a title in a Catholic context, as in "His Holiness." Yet when we speak of a person as being holy, the connotations normally have to do with a committed abstinence from most of what people call necessities—food, sex, drink, fun. Further, holiness may be seen as having to do with repetitive religious practices that seemingly are irrelevant for the fast pace of contemporary life. Some moderns would look at a passage like Hebrews 9:1–10 and yawn at the sheer monotony.

Yet monotony may be a sign of vibrant, pulsating existence that revels in a place, time, and practice of what is right and beautiful.

A child kicks its legs rhythmically through excess, not absence, of life. Because children have abounding vitality, because they are in spirit fierce and free, therefore they want things repeated and unchanged. They always say, "Do it again," and the grown-up person does it again until he is nearly dead. For grown-up people are not strong enough to exult in monotony. But perhaps God is strong enough.... It is possible that God says every morning, "Do it again," to the sun; and every evening, "Do it again," to the moon. It may not be automatic necessity that makes all daisies alike: it may be that God makes every daisy separately, but has never got tired of making them. It may be that He has the eternal appetite of infancy; for we have sinned and grown old, and our Father is younger than we.[18]

The turn of the seasons, the beating of a heart, the revolutions of the earth, the year-to-year march through the decades of a committed marriage—all are signs of life that can never be labeled "dull." God seems to like rhythms, and we must join him in the rhythm of holiness: drawing near, living in a "monotonous" submission to his will. Jesus reflected perfectly this type of holiness, a wholeness of life centered on the perfect and beautiful will of God.

From Jesus we see that holiness does not mean placidity or suppression of emotions. For example, Scott Peck notes that Jesus was constantly frustrated.[19] We can add that he also became angry, wept, and jumped up and down with excitement. In a new covenant context, holiness must not mean a separation from sinners. That was the Pharisees' program, not Jesus'.[20] Holiness does not mean a denial of all that is earthly, walking with one's head "in the clouds." Jesus was earthy. He spoke of practical aspects of everyday life. His hands were certainly callused and, at times, dirty. If the Incarnation had happened in our century rather than the first, perhaps he would be more comfortable wearing blue jeans than stained glass.

Yet when we look at Jesus, we see that holiness does mean a wholeness involving separation from sin and submission to the will of the Father.

> Genuine holiness is genuine Christ-likeness, and genuine Christ-likeness is genuine humanness—the only genuine humanness there is. Love in the service of God and others, humility and meekness under the divine hand, integrity of behavior expressing integration of character, wisdom with faithfulness, boldness with prayerfulness, sorrow at people's sins, joy at the Father's goodness, and single-mindedness in seeking to please the Father morning, noon, and night, were all qualities seen in Christ, the perfect man.[21]

---

18. G. K. Chesterton, *Orthodoxy* (New York: Doubleday, 1959; repr. 1990), 60.
19. Scott M. Peck, *Further Along the Road Less Traveled* (New York: Simon & Schuster, 1993), 160.
20. Yancey, *The Jesus I Never Knew*, 258–59.
21. J. I. Packer, *Rediscovering Holiness* (Ann Arbor, Mich.: Servant, 1992), 28.

Of course, it is these twin issues of sin and submission that pose difficulty. We like neither to admit the former nor to perform the latter. We would rather reconfigure our sins and our lack of submission as weaknesses ("I am not very good at that"), mistakes ("I didn't mean to do that"), social outcomes ("Because of my background I really cannot help that"), relational difficulties ("It really is her fault, you know"), or nonissues ("Sin? What sin?"). We would like for God, the Bible, and preachers to get up-to-date and call sin by some other name.

But our nature does not change—and our needs do not change—with such mind games. Our consciences still are not cleansed, and God does not change his requirements for holiness. "Much of our difficulty," writes A. W. Tozer, "stems from our unwillingness to take God as He is and adjust our lives accordingly. We insist upon trying to modify Him and bring Him nearer to our own image."[22] If we have gotten comfortable with sin, why can't he? What a tragedy that would be! For God can bring wonder and wholeness to our lives only if the sight-skewing, humanity-sapping power of sin is broken.

> It is when we face ourselves and face Christ, that we are lost in wonder, love and praise. We need to rediscover the almost lost discipline of self-examination; and then a re-awakened sense of sin will beget a re-awakened sense of wonder.
>
> Perhaps then God will no longer have to say, "Is it nothing to you, all you who pass by?"[23]

God does not want people who pass by but those who enter. There, in the true Holy Place, we will find the living Presence; we will find true wholeness; we will find true beauty and rightness, the true humanity for which we have longed all our lives; we will find God.

---

22. A. W. Tozer, *The Pursuit of God* (Harrisburg, Pa.: Christian Publications, 1982), 101.
23. Andrew Murray, *Daily Celebration*, as quoted in *Christianity Today* 38 (August 15, 1994): 40.

Hebrews 9:11–28

WHEN CHRIST CAME as high priest of the good things that are already here, he went through the greater and more perfect tabernacle that is not man-made, that is to say, not a part of this creation. ¹²He did not enter by means of the blood of goats and calves; but he entered the Most Holy Place once for all by his own blood, having obtained eternal redemption. ¹³The blood of goats and bulls and the ashes of a heifer sprinkled on those who are ceremonially unclean sanctify them so that they are outwardly clean. ¹⁴How much more, then, will the blood of Christ, who through the eternal Spirit offered himself unblemished to God, cleanse our consciences from acts that lead to death, so that we may serve the living God!

¹⁵For this reason Christ is the mediator of a new covenant, that those who are called may receive the promised eternal inheritance—now that he has died as a ransom to set them free from the sins committed under the first covenant.

¹⁶In the case of a will, it is necessary to prove the death of the one who made it, ¹⁷because a will is in force only when somebody has died; it never takes effect while the one who made it is living. ¹⁸This is why even the first covenant was not put into effect without blood. ¹⁹When Moses had proclaimed every commandment of the law to all the people, he took the blood of calves, together with water, scarlet wool and branches of hyssop, and sprinkled the scroll and all the people. ²⁰He said, "This is the blood of the covenant, which God has commanded you to keep." ²¹In the same way, he sprinkled with the blood both the tabernacle and everything used in its ceremonies. ²²In fact, the law requires that nearly everything be cleansed with blood, and without the shedding of blood there is no forgiveness.

²³It was necessary, then, for the copies of the heavenly things to be purified with these sacrifices, but the heavenly things themselves with better sacrifices than these. ²⁴For Christ did not enter a man-made sanctuary that was only a copy of the true one; he entered heaven itself, now to appear for us in God's presence. ²⁵Nor did he enter heaven to offer himself

again and again, the way the high priest enters the Most Holy Place every year with blood that is not his own. [26]Then Christ would have had to suffer many times since the creation of the world. But now he has appeared once for all at the end of the ages to do away with sin by the sacrifice of himself. [27]Just as man is destined to die once, and after that to face judgment, [28]so Christ was sacrificed once to take away the sins of many people; and he will appear a second time, not to bear sin, but to bring salvation to those who are waiting for him.

WITH 9:11 THE author embarks on his Christological arguments concerning the superiority of the Son's offering for sin. As is his custom, he provides a brief introduction to these arguments (9:11–12) and follows that up by their more extensive explication (9:13–28). The writer demonstrates three bases on which Christ's covenant offering for sin is superior to the priestly sacrifices of the old covenant: (1) The *blood* of the offering was Christ's own blood (9:13–22); (2) the *place* of the offering was in heaven rather than in the earthly tabernacle (9:23–24); (3) the offering was *eternal* (9:25–28).

Furthermore, 9:11–28 speaks of three different "appearances" of Christ, presented in chronological order. Alluding to his sacrifice for sins, the author speaks of the Son's "past" appearance, at which he obtained our redemption (9:11). In 9:24 he remarks that Christ, in his role as high priest, now appears in God's presence on our behalf (9:24). Finally, Christ will appear at the end of the age (a "second time" in relation to this creation) to bring final salvation to those who await his coming (9:28). In these three affirmations Hebrews presents the work of Christ as past, present, and future.

Introduction (9:11–12)

THE AUTHOR BEGINS with a temporal clause: "when Christ came as high priest of the good things that are already here." The designation "Christ" appears at the beginning of the Greek sentence, making it emphatic, and carries the force of a title.[1] The significance of the Messiah's appearance is that he comes as a high priest of "good things that are already here." The Greek phraseology continues to build a stark contrast between the old and new covenant systems. The "good things" are all those blessings associated with the new

---

1. Ellingworth, *The Epistle to the Hebrews*, 448.

covenant (8:6), blessings that have now been ushered in by Christ's establishment of that better agreement.

The writer has two prominent Old Testament images in mind as he walks us through this part of his argument: the high priest's Day of Atonement sacrifice, and the sacrifice made by Moses to inaugurate the Sinai covenant. Christ's death on the cross incorporates and fulfills the meaning of both. At present he stays with his high priest motif and proclaims that as the earthly high priest passed through the outer to the inner room of the sanctuary, so Christ "went through the greater and more perfect tabernacle that is not man-made."

Mention of the "greater and more perfect tabernacle" has given rise to various expressions of creative exegesis. Some commentators have understood this tabernacle to be the Lord's incarnate body, pointing to those references where the Lord referred to his body as a "temple" (e.g., John 2:19–22). Others, including Westcott and Bruce, have suggested the tabernacle of Hebrews 9:11 refers to the church, the people of God, as the place of our high priest's ministry. A third view considers our high priest's passage through the "greater and more perfect tabernacle" to refer to a cosmic passage, the outer chamber of the heavens. However, Hughes is correct when he suggests that all three interpretations have missed specific indicators offered by our author.[2] What he has in mind is simply Christ's passage into the very presence of God in heaven (8:1). The accuracy of this reading may be seen in a parallel text (9:24), where he writes, "For Christ did not enter a man-made sanctuary that was only a copy of the true one; he entered heaven itself, now to appear for us in God's presence."

This high priest did not enter the presence of God "by means of the blood of goats and calves," but "by his own blood," shed in sacrifice. The author means no crass materialism here, as if the exalted Lord took his physical blood into heaven, similar to how the old covenant high priest took the blood of animals into the Most Holy Place. Christ's entrance with his own blood means his sacrificial death on the cross, which established his mediatorial relationship between us and the Father, after he "obtained our eternal redemption." The word "redemption" can also be translated "liberation" or "deliverance." The Jews expected the Messiah to deliver Israel from their enemies.[3] The deliverance brought by the heavenly high priest, however, involves deliverance from sin's penalty and is eternal in nature, Christ having "entered the [true] Most Holy Place once for all."

---

2. See Hughes' presentation of these various interpretations and his cogent reply in *A Commentary on the Epistle to the Hebrews*, 283–90.

3. Spicq, *Theological Lexicon of the New Testament*, 2:423–29. See Psalm 109:9, in which the concepts of redemption and covenant are associated, and Luke 24:21.

The Superior Blood of Christ (9:13–22)

THE OLD COVENANT high priest offered the most important sacrifices of Israel's year on the Day of Atonement (Lev. 16:1–25). As noted in our treatment of Hebrews 5:1–3, the high priest first offered a special sacrifice for himself and his household and then presented the sacrifice on behalf of the people. Having cast lots for the two goats taken from among the Israelites, he slaughtered one of the goats as a sin offering "for the people" (Lev. 16:15) and brought forth the other goat alive from the tent. The high priest then laid hands on the head of the "scapegoat," confessing all the sins of the people before the Lord, and sent it away into the desert (16:20–22). God instructed Aaron to take the blood of both the bull and the sacrificed goat "behind the curtain" so that the blood of each might be sprinkled on the atonement cover (16:15–16). Our writer refers to these rituals in Hebrews 9:13.

In addition to "the blood of goats and calves," the writer of Hebrews mentions a third sacrifice not associated with the Day of Atonement. Here alone in the New Testament does an author refer to the "ashes of a heifer." In Numbers 19:1–21 God commanded the Israelites to bring Moses and Aaron a red heifer, perfect in body and never having been under a yoke. The heifer was taken outside the camp and slaughtered, its blood sprinkled seven times toward the front of the Tent of Meeting. Then the animal was burned and its ashes collected for later use. When needed for ceremonial cleansing, the ashes were mixed with water and the mixture was sprinkled on the unclean person. The tabernacle also had to be sprinkled when an Israelite had touched a dead body, thus defiling the worship center.

For the author of Hebrews these sacrifices were external oblations that dealt with external defilement. They were able to clean worshipers temporarily so that they might have ceremonial purity in relation to the old covenant system. But these offerings fade in contrast to the offering made by Christ (9:14).

In reality verses 13–14 form one long sentence, with verse 13 presenting a conditional clause that can be translated: "if [or since] the blood of goats . . . sanctify them so that they are outwardly clean." Verse 14, as the follow-up "then" clause, presents a theological capsule of the efficacious sacrifice of Christ: "How much more, then, will the blood of Christ . . . cleanse our consciences. . . ." These two verses form an "argument from lesser to greater," which reasons: "If something is true in a lesser situation, it is true to an even greater degree in a greater situation."[4] Here the sacrifice of animals constitutes the lesser circumstance and the offering of the blood of Christ the greater.

---

4. See above, pp. 25, 84–85.

Christ, as the great high priest, is said to have made his offering of himself "through the eternal Spirit" and "unblemished to God." The first of these phrases is ambiguous, presenting a challenge to interpreters. Some commentators, including Attridge, Hughes, and Westcott, understand the "spirit" here to refer to the spiritual nature of Christ's sacrifice or, more specifically, to Christ's own spirit.[5] Others, however, including Lane, Hagner, Bruce, and Ellingworth, take "eternal Spirit" as a reference to the Holy Spirit, who anointed our high priest for every aspect of his ministry, including his sacrificial death.[6]

The interpretation of the second phrase, "unblemished to God," is more certain. The author alludes to the Old Testament requirements for sacrifice under the first covenant, in which God gave the requirement that a sacrificial animal be "without blemish or defect" (Lev. 14:10). In relation to Christ this does not refer to a lack of physical imperfections; rather, it refers to his spiritual and moral flawlessness (1 Peter 1:19). Because of his perfection, his sacrifice of himself is able to "cleanse our consciences from acts that lead to death."[7] With consciences cleansed from deeds that are spiritually lethal, we are set free rightly to "serve the living God."

With verse 15 the discussion shifts from a treatment of Christ's sacrifice vis-à-vis the sacrifices offered within old covenant worship to the inauguration of a covenant through sacrifice. Two focal truths emerge from a consideration of this important verse. (1) Christ is the "mediator" (*mesites*) of the new covenant. The word *mesites* occurs especially in literature of the Hellenistic period, often with legal connotations. It referred, for example, to an arbiter in a political dispute or to a peacemaker in a business conflict. It also functioned as a synonym for *engyos* (7:22), meaning the "guarantor" of an oath. Philo speaks of angels and Moses as intermediaries between God and people;[8] this religious meaning for the word is also evident in its six New Testament occurrences (Gal. 3:19–20; 1 Tim. 2:5; Heb. 8:6; 9:15; 12:24).[9] Christ as mediator of the new covenant has stood between God and people and accomplished the bringing of the two parties together in this agreement (1 Tim. 2:5). The result for the new people of God is that they receive the eternal inheritance.

(2) This mediatorial relationship was established by Christ's death, in which he served as a ransom to liberate people from sins. The word ren-

---

5. Attridge, *Epistle to the Hebrews*, 251; Hughes, *A Commentary on the Epistle to the Hebrews*, 359; Westcott, *The Epistle to the Hebrews*, 261–62.

6. Lane, *Hebrews 9–13*, 240; Bruce, *The Epistle to the Hebrews*, 216–17; Hagner, *Hebrews*, 139–40; Ellingworth, *The Epistle to the Hebrews*, 456–57.

7. On the "conscience" see above, p. 300.

8. *Dreams* 1:142–43; *Moses* 2:1.66.

9. Spicq, *Theological Lexicon of the New Testament*, 2:465–68.

---

dered by the NIV as "ransom" (*apolytrosis*) is rare outside the New Testament; it occurs especially in Paul's writings, where the word refers to God's redemptive act on behalf of his people to set them free from the ravages of sin. Christ, by death, has liberated us, establishing a means by which we might be forgiven for our transgressions (Rom. 3:24; 1 Cor. 1:30). This constitutes a blessing of the new covenant, in which the sins of God's people are remembered "no more" (Heb. 8:12).

Regarding 9:16–17, two main lines of interpretation have been followed among commentators. (1) The first suggests the author crafts a play on words, in which the word normally translated "covenant" in Hebrews (*diatheke*), following from the reference to "inheritance" in verse 15, should be understood as meaning "will" or "testament."[10] This view has as its cornerstone the reference to the ratifier's death in verses 16–17, suggesting that covenants are not established by the death of those who make them. Rather, wills go into effect only when the one who made the will dies.

(2) The other position, the one adopted in this commentary and taken up most rigorously by Westcott and Lane, points out that the interpretation of *diatheke* as "will" in verses 16–17 is out of step with the immediate discussion. In context the author focuses on the old covenant sacrifices (vv. 12–14) and the establishment of the old covenant through sacrifice (vv. 18–22).[11] These explain the reference to the ratifier's death as symbolically realized in the death of the sacrificial victim. By this interpretation, verses 16–17 proclaim simply that someone (represented by the sacrificial victim) had to die in order for the covenant to be established. As Lane points out, these verses

> explain why Christ had to die in order to become the priestly mediator of a new covenant. The ratification of a covenant required the presentation of sacrificial blood (cf. v. 18). Such blood is obtained only by means of death. Christ's death was the means of providing the blood of the new covenant. His sacrificial death ratified or "made legally valid" the new covenant promised in Jer. 31:31–34.[12]

This reading of Hebrews 9:16–17 in terms of sacrifice squares perfectly with what follows in verses 18–22, which relate Moses' inauguration of the Sinai covenant with sacrificial blood (Ex. 24:3–8). The focus of the author's interest may be seen in verse 18, where he points out that the first covenant was inaugurated with the shedding of blood. In verses 19–21 the details of

---

10. See the NIV; Attridge, *Epistle to the Hebrews*, 255–56; Bruce, *Epistle to the Hebrews*, 221–24; Hughes, *A Commentary on the Epistle to the Hebrews*, 368–73.
11. Westcott, *Epistle to the Hebrews*, 265–66; Lane, *Hebrews 9–13*, 242–43.
12. Lane, *Hebrews 9–13*, 243.

this Old Testament event are summarized. Having informed the people of the Lord's words concerning the law (Ex. 24:3, 7), Moses took the blood of the calves sacrificed as fellowship offerings and sprinkled it on the people, proclaiming, "This is the blood of the covenant that the LORD has made with you in accordance with all these words" (24:8).[13] Hebrews alone among ancient references to this event states Moses also sprinkled the book of the covenant.

The author's assertion that the tabernacle and ceremonial vessels were also sprinkled with blood is problematic at first blush, since the Exodus passage does not include this fact. However, our writer, on the principle of verbal analogy,[14] may be considering the Exodus text in concert with one or two others that refer to sprinkling—the Day of Atonement ritual of Leviticus 16 and, perhaps, the red heifer ceremony of Numbers 19, both already alluded to in Hebrews 9:12–13. In the red heifer passage Eleazar the priest was instructed to take some of the heifer's blood on his finger and sprinkle it seven times in the direction of the Tent of Meeting (Num. 19:4).[15] Similarly, in the Day of Atonement ceremony the high priest took some of the blood from the bull and goat, sprinkling it on and in front of the atonement cover seven times. He was to sprinkle the blood on the Tent of Meeting and on the altar in the same manner (Lev. 16:14–19).

This use of blood in cleansing the various aspects of tabernacle worship demonstrates the truth stated in Hebrews 9:22: "The law requires that nearly everything be cleansed with blood, and without the shedding of blood there is no forgiveness." The Day of Atonement ritual especially focused on the use of blood for atonement from sin.

The Heavenly Tabernacle (9:23–24)

THE FIRST PART of 9:23 continues a comment on the old covenant system of worship. The law required that the various elements of the earthly tabernacle be purified with the blood from animal sacrifices. However, it may strike the reader as odd that it was necessary for the heavenly things to be purified at all. How could something in the heavenly realm be considered defiled?[16]

---

13. The elements of water, scarlet wool, and branches of hyssop are not found in the Exodus text, but the use of these in ceremonial sprinkling seem to have been common (see Ex. 12:22; Lev. 14:4–7, 51–52; Num. 19:6, 18). See Lane, *Hebrews 9–13*, 244; Hughes, *Commentary on the Epistle to the Hebrews*, 375–76.

14. See above, pp. 25, 67.

15. Later in Num. 19:17–19 the tent and all the furnishings and the people who were in the tent when it was defiled are sprinkled with the water of purification.

16. For the various interpretations of this text see Hughes, *A Commentary on the Epistle to the Hebrews*, 379–81.

The answer rests squarely in the Old Testament texts to which the author has already been alluding. In the instructions for the Day of Atonement (Lev. 16), the high priest was to take the blood from the goat presented as a sin offering for the people and sprinkle it on and in front of the atonement cover (16:15). The text continues:

> In this way he will make atonement for the Most Holy Place because of *the uncleanness and rebellion of the Israelites*, whatever their sins have been. He is to do the same for the Tent of Meeting, which is among them *in the midst of their uncleanness*. No one is to be in the Tent of Meeting from the time Aaron goes in to make atonement in the Most Holy Place until he comes out, having made atonement for himself, his household and the whole community of Israel.
>
> Then he shall come out to the altar that is before the LORD and make atonement for it. He shall take some of the bull's blood and some of the goat's blood and put it on all the horns of the altar. He shall sprinkle some of the blood on it with his finger seven times *to cleanse it and to consecrate it from the uncleanness of the Israelites*. (16:16–19; italics mine)

In other words, the need for purification of the tabernacle had to do with its association with a sinful people. This holy space was made fit for continued interaction between God and his people by sacrifices that addressed the problem of sin. Correspondingly, the heavenly tabernacle, the author's conception of the place of God's presence (9:24), was made accessible to the new covenant people of God by Christ's sacrificial death. The "heavenly things" are purified in conjunction with the purification of God's people. Rather than carrying out his high-priestly, Day-of-Atonement ministry in the earthly copy of the true tabernacle, Christ entered heaven to bring his sacrifice before God on our behalf (9:24). That his appearance before God was "for us" marks his act as distinct from the earthly high priest, who also had to offer a sacrifice for himself (5:1–3; 7:27–28). The author emphasizes this act as Christ's paving the way for God's people to enter his presence (10:19–22).[17]

The Once-for-All Offering (9:25–28)

FURTHERMORE, UNLIKE THE earthly ritual in which the high priest entered the Most Holy Place annually with "blood that is not his own" (i.e., the blood of animals), this Day of Atonement sacrifice, made by the heavenly

---

17. Attridge makes the important observation that the Day of Atonement analogy breaks down at this point. Our author says nothing of Christ sprinkling the blood in the heavenly realm since he does not wish to speak of the heavenly offering as separate from his death on the cross; they are one and the same. See Attridge, *Epistle to the Hebrews*, 263.

priest, was eternally effective, never having to be repeated (9:25). The author explains the importance of this insight. If Christ's sacrifice of himself was an annual event, as was the Day of Atonement sacrifice under the first covenant, he would have had to suffer over and over again since the time of creation; but, of course, this is not the case. Human beings by nature die once (9:27), and Christ, as human, could die only one time.

Consequently, he has appeared "once for all" to do away with sin completely by sacrificing himself in death. His sacrifice, because of its superior quality, is able to reach back to the time of creation and forward to the time of consummation of the ages, fully cleansing the people of God. The Messiah's first appearance, therefore, marks the beginning of the messianic age, the "end of the ages," in which he effects redemption for God's people. Accordingly, whereas normally a human being faces judgment following death, Christ's sacrifice of himself will be followed by a second appearance in this earthly realm. Whereas the first coming was for the purpose of dealing with sin through his sacrificial death, the second coming will be to bring salvation—complete deliverance from this fallen, sinful world and its effects—to those who are anticipating his return (9:28).

As WE SEEK to bring this text into our contemporary contexts we must address simultaneously at least two main issues. (1) Several challenges exist regarding the communication of certain truths or motifs from our passage to contemporary contexts. These challenges are both conceptual (namely, that moderns tend to think of "sacrifice" and "heaven" as primitive concepts) and attitudinal (many in contemporary society questioning the existence of sin and the need for forgiveness).

(2) Once again we must move beneath the surface, cultic-worship language of the Scriptures and pinpoint the significance of the affirmations found in 9:11–28. What does the author wish for us to understand about the sacrifice of Christ? One of our tasks in this regard must be the identification of certain false moves interpreters have made in handling this text so that we do not fall to the same errors. Specifically, we focus here on the concepts of Christ's blood and the location of his offering in the heavenly tabernacle "not made with hands." Since the author presents his full-blown treatment on the finality of Christ's sacrifice in 10:1–18, we reserve discussion of that motif for the next section of the commentary.

The challenge posed by popular conceptions of morality. One of the critical challenges facing the expositor who wishes to communicate Hebrews 9:11–28 to a modern audience stems from a cultural shift from concern either with biblical morality or with the idea of a "macro-morality" (i.e., a universal moral standard), to various popular conceptions of morality. Stated another way, many of our contemporaries have a loosely arranged mental construct that they think of as "morality" (i.e., "concepts of right and wrong"). This construct may be made up of teachings from parents, professors, friends, movies, television, commentaries, novels, self-help books, or experiences.

In other words, the contemporary person sets the standards of morality, picking and choosing ideas that will be included in the moral system. Popular choices might include, "tolerance is right, exclusivity is wrong"; "free choice is right, restrictions are wrong"; "helping others is right, harming others is wrong"; and the list goes on. Wrong takes the form of "not being true to oneself," "not being inclusive," or, perhaps, the obvious acts of harm or violence against others; but the lines are fuzzy at best. Since most of us are not likely to label our own tendencies as "sin"—an unpopular word anyway in our culture—the need for "forgiveness" may be considered outdated. It would not be unusual for us to hear someone say, "Basically I consider myself a good person," or, "She is a very moral person," which may have a variety of meanings, depending on one's system of morality.

In fact, our culture increasingly places the emphasis on being "good" to others as well as good to ourselves. When a person sees the whole of morality in terms of whether or not one is "doing good"—certainly an admirable pursuit in itself—this may dull our sense of need for forgiveness of what the Bible terms *sin*. In his classic *Mere Christianity*, C. S. Lewis writes:

> Christianity tells people to repent and promises them forgiveness. It therefore has nothing (as far as I know) to say to people who do not know they have done anything to repent of and who do not feel they need any forgiveness. It is after you have realized that there is a real Moral Law, and a Power behind the law, and that you have broken the law and put yourself wrong with that Power—it is after all this, and not a moment sooner, that Christianity begins to talk.[18]

My point is that we must communicate a biblical view of morality as a replacement for the popular view that many have, if we want Christianity (and esp. Heb. 9:11–28) to speak to them.

Even so, contemporary conceptions of morality present us with a great challenge. As Blaise Pascal reminds us in *Pensées*, "There are only two kinds of men: the righteous who think they are sinners and the sinners who think they are righteous."[19] Many of our society have become like the Pharisee of

---

18. C. S. Lewis, *Mere Christianity*, rev. and enlarged ed. (New York: Walker, 1987), 45–46.

19. Blaise Pascal, *The Provincial Letters, Pensées, Scientific Treatises*, trans. W. F. Trotter, in *Great Books of the Western World*, vol. 33 (Chicago: Encyclopedia Britannica, 1952), 265.

Luke 18, who focused on his own goodness. Their version, however, might go as follows: "God, I thank you that I am not like the *really* bad people I see on the news every night!"

The concept of "blood." This brings us to a second challenge in communicating the truth of our passage. The concept of sacrifice, the shedding of blood to satisfy a requirement made by God, seems horribly primitive and dark to many moderns. Think for a moment about "the shedding of blood" and its associations in most modern cultures of the world. The image conjures pictures of violence, murder, and war—not exactly positive, life-affirming images. Moreover, there exists a great concern for being humane to animals. We spend thousands of dollars to save a pair of whales stranded in an ice field and, at the end of certain movies, read the disclaimer, "No animal in this film was harmed." How, then, can we communicate the sacrificial slaughter of animals and the new covenant sacrifice of Christ himself to a congregation inundated with cultural messages that seem to contradict these motifs at their core?

We must return to the question of significance. Why are these images in the biblical record? What does God wish to communicate through them? (1) At least since the time of B. F. Westcott commentators have been misinterpreting the "blood" motif in the New Testament as signifying "life."[20] For example, in his commentary on John's Gospel, Westcott states,

> Thus, in accordance with the typical teaching of the Levitical ordinances, the Blood of Christ represents Christ's life (1) as rendered in free self-sacrifice to God for men, and (2) as brought into perfect fellowship with God, having been set free by death. The Blood of Christ is, as shed, the Life of Christ given for men, and as applied, the Life of Christ now given to men, the Life which is the spring of their life (John xii. 24).... The Blood always includes the thought of the life preserved and active beyond death.[21]

Along this same line Westcott comments on Hebrews 9:18–22: "By the use of the words 'not without blood' the writer of the Epistle suggests the two ideas of atonement and quickening by the impartment of a new life which have already connected with Christ's work."[22] Thus, the concept of "blood" communicates the idea of life being imparted. This idea that the death of the sacrificial victim means that life has been released can also be found in the works of scholars such as Vincent Taylor and C. H. Dodd.[23]

---

20. See especially the study by Alan M. Stibbs, *The Meaning of the Word "Blood" in Scripture* (Leicester, Eng.: Theological Students' Fellowship, reprint, 1978).

21. B. F. Westcott, *The Epistles of St. John* (1883), 34–37.

22. Westcott, *Epistle to the Hebrews*, 266.

23. For a history of interpretation see Stibbs, *The Meaning of the Word "Blood" in Scripture*, 3–9.

Yet, the biblical evidence points strongly in another direction. References to sacrificial blood in Scripture point to the death of the victim, not the bestowal of life. Specifically in Hebrews, when the author mentions the shedding of Christ's blood, he speaks of the Lord's sacrificial death on the cross. It is his sacrificial death, not the communication of life, that cleanses us (9:14); it is his death that brings freedom (9:15) and inaugurates the new covenant (9:16–18). The analogy throughout Hebrews 9 between Christ's death and that of animals makes this interpretation more sure. Through their deaths the animals were not imparting life, but giving their lives for the purpose of cleansing sin and reconciling people to God. In other words, the blood motif represents death in Scripture, and when alluding to Christ, connotes his sacrificial death on the cross, by which he "expiated our sins, propitiated our Maker, turned God's 'no' to us into a 'yes,' and so saved us."[24]

"Death" and modern society. This fact raises a third challenge related to Hebrews 9, closely related to the concept of sacrifice. John Stott notes the modern objection to the relevance of a person long dead. He humorously parallels the modern questioning how a figure from ancient history can have relevance for us to a passage from Mark Twain's *The Adventures of Huckleberry Finn*. Huck responds to the widow Douglas' recount of the Moses story:

> I was in a sweat to find out all about him; but by and by she let it out that Moses had been dead a considerable long time; so then I didn't care no more about him; because I don't take no stock in dead people.[25]

Many people in contemporary society avoid the topic of death at all costs. In a context in which naturalism governs the worldview, death represents termination, the end of one's existence, the ultimate enemy. However, the concept of Christ's sacrificial death, given on behalf of people, may give us a connection with modern audiences that does not seem apparent at first thought. Christ sacrificially accomplished something for us which we were at a loss to accomplish for ourselves. This reiterates one theme on the rise in American culture—that of volunteerism, the giving of oneself on behalf of another. On the verge of the third millenium some ninety-three million adults ages eighteen and up have served as volunteers, giving on average 4.2 hours per week, 85 percent of whom worked on some serious social problem.[26] Is

---

24. James I. Packer, "What Did the Cross Achieve? The Logic of Penal Substitution," *Tyn-Bul* 25 (1974): 21–22.

25. Mark Twain, *The Adventures of Huckleberry Finn* (1884; Pan, 1968), 202, as cited in Stott, *The Contemporary Christian*, 16.

26. "Fifty Ways to Make a Difference," *Ladies' Home Journal* (May 1997), 142.

this not what Christ has done for us? Moreover, it was a "volunteer service" rendered at the greatest personal expense and for a greater cause.

The point here is not to attempt to remove the cross from its "stumbling block status" or to water down the doctrine of penal substitution. That a violent death two millennia ago can somehow transform modern individuals will continue to be mocked in many quarters. Rather, we are looking for contact points for communication, and the concept of volunteerism may provide such a connection.

Heaven and pop culture. How we and our contemporaries think of heaven presents a fourth challenge to communication, and here too we have much cultural baggage to overcome. Asked for their ideas about heaven, many moderns either deny its existence or present a shallow portrait based on pop mythology. The picture probably includes clouds or a mist across the floor, everyone having become an angel, each with a harp to play and, perhaps, gold trimmings. Movies such as the classic *It's a Wonderful Life*, one of this writer's favorites, have perpetuated such pop myths.

Admittedly, the New Testament's own portrayals of heaven are minimal, for the authors attempt to describe the indescribable. But all this modern poppycock of clouds and harps is dull at best and horribly misleading at worst. "Clouds," for instance, are associated by the New Testament with the interchange between the heavenly realm and the earthly.[27] In focusing on clouds and harps, we set our sights on the rocks—not even the rocks but the dirt particles—at the foot of the mountain as if they were the mountain itself. Such fixations stunt biblical thinking about heaven, which by New Testament accounts is so much *more.* "More what?" we ask. More of God's good gifts (referred to as our "inheritance" in Hebrews) and of God himself.

Specifically, in heaven we will know fully the presence of God, and this brings us to the point of the author's references to heaven in Hebrews 9. Heaven is ultimately the place of God's presence fully known and experienced. When Jesus died on the cross, God the Father was present since God is omnipresent. Yet Hebrews notes that Jesus "entered heaven itself, now to appear for us in God's presence" (9:24). So heaven is the place into which we follow our great high priest, Jesus, drawing near to God, entering into his presence. Thus heaven can be experienced now because of the high-priestly sacrifice of Christ, which has won us entrance into the presence of God, and will be experienced fully at the end of the age. One point of application, therefore, might reflect on how we as believers think about heaven and its relation to the Christian life.

---

27. See Matt. 17:5; Luke 21:27; Acts 1:9; Rev. 10:1; 11:12; 14:14–16.

TRIVIALIZING THE CROSS. The cross of Christ, once respected, if not reverenced, as a significant religious symbol, has undergone a transmutation. For example, on a Holy Week cover of *The New Yorker* magazine, a bunny rabbit—arms outstretched, head bowed, legs together in an obvious caricature of crucifixion—portrays "Theology of a Tax Cut."[28] Such adaptations of the cross to make a political statement or to define the perverted, quasi-religious image of pop-stars such as Madonna obscure the crucifixion's significance. In the mind of the general public the cross amounts to mere jewelry that can be had with or without "the 'little man' on it."[29]

There are at least two reasons for this metamorphosis of the cross. (1) With vast segments of the population, the Christian religion as popularly perceived has become a too-familiar, empty fixture of the culture. With the passage of time, images related to Christianity—such as the church building, the minister, the cross (images that once represented significant referents)—have vaporized into faint echoes of their real counterparts: true bodies of believers, committed men of God, a symbol of ultimate, atoning sacrifice.

(2) The concept of sacrifice, especially blood sacrifice, has been deemed such a primitive idea as to be completely irreconcilable to modern thinking. John Stott writes:

> The gospel contains some features so alien to modern thought that it will always appear "folly" to intellectuals, however hard we strive (and rightly) to show that it is "true and reasonable." The cross will always constitute an assault on human self-righteousness and a challenge to human self-indulgence. Its "scandal" (stumbling-block) simply cannot be removed. Indeed, the church speaks most authentically to the world not when it makes its shameful little prudential compromises, but when it refuses to do so; not when it has become indistinguishable from the world, but when its distinctive light shines most brightly.
>
> Thus Christian people, who live under the authority of God's revelation, however anxious they are to communicate it to others, manifest a sturdy independence of mind and spirit.[30]

In her article, "After the Gang, What?" Evelyn Lewis Perera tells of an experience that illustrates Stott's point. When her younger sister, Vee, first professed Christ to her, she said, "I mean, I have realized that Jesus really is

---

28. April 17, 1995.
29. Wendy Murray Zoba, "Trivializing the Cross," *Christianity Today* (June 19, 1995), 17.
30. Stott, *The Contemporary Christian*, 26–27.

exactly who he says he is, that he really died for my sins and rose again, and I have decided to entrust my whole life to him." Evelyn and her friend Barbara sat stunned. Having excused themselves, they agreed to make a united front to talk Vee out of her new perspective, but this did not work. When they tried to speak to her of art, music, poetry, and novels, which they assumed stood in contradistinction to Christianity, Vee further informed them of the faith of Bach, Michelangelo, T. S. Eliot, and Blaise Pascal. Then Evelyn informed Vee "that according to Buckminster Fuller, Competitive Man would soon evolve into Cooperative Man, and then human behavior would improve, without Jesus and 'all that blood. . . .'" In the end Evelyn came to understand the significance of "all that blood" and devoted herself to the crucified and risen Christ.[31]

We must retake this ground from the culture; we must take back our image of the cross and the sacrifice it represents. Why? Because the world must hear, and we must hear in a fresh way every day, that God loved us enough to experience voluntarily the death of his Son on our behalf. Christ volunteered to meet a need for us that we could not meet for ourselves. This is the giving God of grace and his Son, the Cosmic Volunteer. Therefore, we must not abandon the concept of the blood of Christ, for it lies at the heart of our redemption.

At the same time, we must interpret and communicate the significance of the blood for our modern audiences scandalized by the "primitive sacrifice" concept. This image itself is strong meat, perhaps too strong for those without the Spirit or for those recently acquainted with him. We must help them see the significance of the blood as both an aspect of and, in New Testament theology, a representation of Christ's death.

We must also help contemporary people see that they need help. The problem with popular conceptions of morality stems from their inability to "cleanse the conscience," as Hebrews 9 puts it. The expositor, therefore, must point out the biblical picture of God's holiness and his terms of establishing a relationship with us, his fallen creatures. God does not grade on a curve, and the point is neither to have our good deeds outweigh our bad nor simply to keep from doing the "very bad" sins (however one might define those). The question, as the Bible defines it, is whether we are set apart from the tyranny and consequences of wrongdoing. Any person, except the most deluded, would admit that they do wrong at times, and this opens for us an opportunity for communicating a biblical view of morality. It also calls us to praise a God who would work out a means for our forgiveness and cleansing.

---

31. Evelyn Lewis Perera, "After the Gang, What?" in *Finding God at Harvard: Spiritual Journeys of Christian Thinkers*, ed. Kelly Monroe (Grand Rapids: Zondervan, 1996), 51–52.

The limited but important view. Ernest Hemingway, in a 1925 letter to F. Scott Fitzgerald, wrote of his view of heaven:

> To me heaven would be a big bull ring with me holding two barrera seats and a trout stream outside that no one else was allowed to fish in and two lovely houses in the town; one where I would have my wife and children and be monogamous and love them truly and well and the other where I would have my nine beautiful mistresses on nine different floors.[32]

But this conception of heaven, admittedly stemming from wishful thinking rather than theological reflection, is more in line with C. S. Lewis's portrayal of hell in *The Great Divorce*. In this fictionalized musing Lewis dramatizes a hell in which the inhabitants move further and further away from others because of utter selfishness, a selfishness that produces incessant quarreling. Those who have been in hell the longest live millions of miles from anyone else, lost in self-centered isolation.[33]

Some may think of Hemmingway's thoughts on heaven as too broad. But his selfish view of heaven, centered as it is on his pleasures alone, is not too broad but too narrow. Heaven, the real heaven, is a place in which the focus of attention reaches outward and rests on God. All our greatest desires and pleasures will be realized beyond our wildest hopes and dreams—"no eye has seen, no ear has heard, no mind has conceived" (2 Cor. 2:9)—because they will be realized in him, the Limitless One. If this sounds rather dull to us, it shows how little we know of him.

But heaven, a clear view of that for which we are to long, eludes us dreadfully in our earthly sojourn. In *Murder at the Cathedral* T. S. Eliot wrote, "I have had a tremor of bliss, a wink of heaven, a whisper. . . ." W. Arnot suggests:

> Throughout the whole circumference of the earth, a dead wall, very near and very thick, obstructs the view. Here and there, on a Sunday or another season of seriousness, a slit is left open in its side. Heaven might be seen through these slits, but the eye that is habitually set for earthly things cannot, during such momentary glimpses, adjust itself to higher things. Unless you pause and look steadfastly, you will see neither clouds nor sunshine through these openings, nor the distant sky. The soul has looked on the world so long, and the world's picture

---

32. In *Ernest Hemingway: Selected Letters*, 1981.
33. C. S. Lewis, *The Great Divorce* (New York: Macmillan, 1946), 18–19. Lewis makes clear that he intends this book to be taken as pure fiction, presenting no real speculations about the afterworld (see pp. 7–8).

is so firmly fixed in its eye, that when the soul is turned for a moment toward heaven, it feels only a quiver of inarticulate light and retains no distinct impression of the things that are unseen and eternal.[34]

Nevertheless, this heaven, as both present place and ultimate destination, is to be a matter of important focus for Christian pilgrims. As the locus of God's fully known presence, it is the point of Christ's work. He has died for us and redeemed us to bring us *here*. This is where we belong. This is the realm of our ultimate hopes and desires. This is our dwelling place now and then—now in spirit and then in resurrected fullness.

---

34. As quoted in *Images of Heaven: Reflections on Glory* (Wheaton, Ill.: Harold Shaw, 1996), 29.

Hebrews 10:1-18

THE LAW IS only a shadow of the good things that are coming—not the realities themselves. For this reason it can never, by the same sacrifices repeated endlessly year after year, make perfect those who draw near to worship. ²If it could, would they not have stopped being offered? For the worshipers would have been cleansed once for all, and would no longer have felt guilty for their sins. ³But those sacrifices are an annual reminder of sins, ⁴because it is impossible for the blood of bulls and goats to take away sins.

⁵Therefore, when Christ came into the world, he said:

> "Sacrifice and offering you did not desire,
>   but a body you prepared for me;
> ⁶with burnt offerings and sin offerings
>   you were not pleased.
> ⁷Then I said, 'Here I am—it is written about me
>   in the scroll—
>   I have come to do your will, O God.'"

⁸First he said, "Sacrifices and offerings, burnt offerings and sin offerings you did not desire, nor were you pleased with them" (although the law required them to be made). ⁹Then he said, "Here I am, I have come to do your will." He sets aside the first to establish the second. ¹⁰And by that will, we have been made holy through the sacrifice of the body of Jesus Christ once for all.

¹¹Day after day every priest stands and performs his religious duties; again and again he offers the same sacrifices, which can never take away sins. ¹²But when this priest had offered for all time one sacrifice for sins, he sat down at the right hand of God. ¹³Since that time he waits for his enemies to be made his footstool, ¹⁴because by one sacrifice he has made perfect forever those who are being made holy.

¹⁵The Holy Spirit also testifies to us about this. First he says:

> ¹⁶"This is the covenant I will make with them
>   after that time, says the Lord.
> I will put my laws in their hearts,
>   and I will write them on their minds."

¹⁷Then he adds:

"Their sins and lawless acts
I will remember no more."

¹⁸And where these have been forgiven, there is no longer any
sacrifice for sin.

WE NOW COME to the culmination of the author's
discussion on Jesus, the Son of God, as our high
priest. Previously he has argued that the Son is
superior to the angels (1:5–14) but for a time
came to earth, a position "lower than the angels," in order to identify with
human beings and suffer on our behalf (2:10–18). By virtue of his identity
with humanity and his suffering, the Son was appointed by God as a high
priest superior to the Levitical priests of the old covenant (5:1–11; 7:1–28).
As a superior priest, he also presents to God a superior offering—one that
relates to a better covenant (8:3–13), has its locus in the heavenly realm,
involves the death (i.e., "blood") of Christ rather than mere animals, and has
been made once for all (9:11–28).

This final point the writer now drives home and elaborates in 10:1–18,
all the while incorporating truths from his entire Christological discourse. The
Son as exalted above the angels, the incarnate, suffering One who identifies
with humanity, the great appointed high priest, and the offerer of a superior
sacrifice—all find expression here in a theological crescendo.

The Limited Abilities of the Law (10:1–4)

THE AUTHOR HAS already made the point that the old covenant tabernacle
was a "shadow" of greater, heavenly realities (8:5);[1] he now applies the same
description to the law itself, specifically as it relates to the sacrificial system.
As with the old covenant tabernacle, the law's sacrificial system can only be
seen as an imperfect copy of what God ultimately had in mind, since it contained elements that had a degree of ineffectiveness. That it constitutes a
"shadow" suggests that the earthly system mimics enough of the original to
point God's people to greater, heavenly realities. Nevertheless, by its perpetual need for new sacrifices, it demonstrates its inadequacy.

What concerns the author most is the law's inability to "make perfect
those who draw near to worship" God (v. 1). The "perfection" he has in mind

---

1. See the discussion above, p. 280.

does not involve a "lack of flaws" but, rather, a state of right relationship with God, in which the worshipers are once and for all cleansed from sin and delivered from a nagging sense of guilt.[2] The fact that the old covenant system could not deliver in this regard, as demonstrated by offerings made year after year, shows the need for a better system.

The law's sacrificial system, rather than delivering worshipers from guilt, actually has the effect of reminding them of their sinfulness and, thus, their constant separation from God (v. 3). Why is this the case under the older covenant? Because the sacrifices of that system—"the blood of bulls and goats"[3]—do not have the ability to remove sins (v. 4). The author already has made the point that the old sacrifices could "sanctify" or "purify" (9:13, 23) people, but here, significantly, he uses "take away" or "remove" (*aphaireo*), a word used with reference to sin only one other place in the New Testament. At Romans 11:26–27 Paul quotes the prophet Isaiah saying, "The deliverer will come from Zion; he will turn godlessness away from Jacob. And this is my covenant with them when I take away [a form of *aphaireo*] their sins."[4]

In Hebrews 10:4, as in the Romans passage, the idea of "removing" sin speaks of the burden sin placed on the worshiper's conscience being lifted in a decisive, perpetually effective cleansing, which establishes one's status before God.[5] This is what the old covenant sacrifices were unable to do, which is why sin remained a separator, a perennial, detrimental force disallowing a permanently right relationship between God and his people.

The Superior Sacrifice of Christ (10:5–10)

THANKFULLY, CHRIST CAME into the world to set things right, and the author supports this assertion by quoting Psalm 40:7–9. The use of the conjunction "therefore" (*dio*) in 10:5 shows the coordination of thought between what has come before and what now follows, the inability of the law's sacrificial system being set in stark contrast to the ministry of Christ. That Christ "came into the world" could be used in Jewish contexts to refer simply to someone's birth, but here, as elsewhere in the New Testament, the author uses the clause to refer to the Incarnation (e.g., John 1:9; 6:14; 11:27).[6]

The author takes the psalm quotation itself from the Greek translation of the Old Testament, as is his practice. This text has two primary components in which he shows special interest: (1) God's dissatisfaction with the old

---

2. See above, p. 300.
3. Heb. 9:12–14.
4. Paul's quote is probably a conflation of Isaiah 59:20–21 and 27:9.
5. Lane, *Hebrews 9–13*, 261–62.
6. Attridge, *Epistle to the Hebrews*, 273.

covenant sacrificial offerings and (2) the willing obedience of the speaker, whom our author understands to be Christ. Furthermore, Hebrews 10:8–9 demonstrates that the order in which these components are found in the psalm is also important. In 10:8 the writer remarks, "First he said, 'Sacrifices and offerings, burnt offerings and sin offerings you did not desire, nor were you pleased with them.'" Parenthetically he explains that the sacrifices of the old system were, for some reason, unsatisfactory even though God had prescribed them in the law. This motif is a common one in the Old Testament (e.g., 1 Sam. 15:22; Ps. 50:8–10; Isa. 1:10–13; Jer. 7:21–24; Hos. 6:6), pointing to heartfelt devotion as an essential component of true worship. The practice of ritualistic sacrifice apart from a sincere commitment to God's will falls short of the divine intention for the sacrificial system.

In 10:9 the author continues, "Then he said, 'Here I am, I have come to do your will.'" The "then," taken from Psalm 40:7, indicates to the writer a temporal sequence within the psalm. In other words, the accomplishing of God's will by Christ now has supplanted the use of animal sacrifices, as indicated by his comment, "He sets aside the first to establish the second" (Heb. 10:9). The writer concludes his interpretation of the Old Testament passage by introducing the term *body* (10:10), taken from the first verse of the Psalm text. It was by God's will, expressed in the sacrifice of the body of Jesus Christ once for all, that believers have been made holy.

Christ's Priestly Activity Contrasted With That of the Levitical Priests (10:11–14)

THE ARGUMENT NOW turns again to the finality of Christ's sacrifice (cf. 9:25–28) and sets forth several contrasts between the high-priestly service of Christ and that of the old covenant priests. In 10:11 we find four elements that the author understands to characterize the older sacrificial service. (1) The sacrifices under the law were presented daily; (2) the priests stood when rendering their service; (3) multiple sacrifices were offered again and again; and (4) those sacrifices, regardless of how many times they were offered, never could "take away sins."[7] In 10:12–14 the writer to the Hebrews demonstrates that by contrast Christ's sacrifice has the following characteristics: (1) It was offered "for all time"; (2) it culminated in Christ sitting down at the right hand of God (v. 12); (3) it involved one sacrifice (vv. 12, 14); and (4) it accomplished perfection of those for whom the sacrifice was offered (v. 14).

In 10:12 the author, by allusion, reintroduces Psalm 110:1, the most commonly cited Old Testament passage in the New Testament. The writer of

---

7. The verb translated "take away" here is the aorist infinitive form of *periaireo*, a word used only here in the New Testament to refer to the removal of sin.

Hebrews already has pointed to this particular verse of Psalm 110 three times at key turning points in his sermon (1:3; 1:13; 8:1).[8] He now employs it to demonstrate the decisive, final nature of the Son's sacrifice. Psalm 110:1 proclaims that the exalted Christ has taken his seat of authority until his enemies are made a footstool for his feet; for Hebrews this truth demonstrates that the Son's sacrifice was completely satisfactory, never having to be repeated. In other words, he will remain seated until his second appearing (9:28), since no further sacrificial work needs to be accomplished. His task is finished until the final subjugation of his enemies is at hand.

In verse 14 our author expresses concisely the effect of Christ's work on new covenant people: " ... by one sacrifice he has made perfect forever those who are being made holy." The word translated "has made perfect" (a perfect tense of *teleioo*) serves as the clause's main verb and connotes a past action with present results. The word speaks of new covenant people as having been made whole or complete. Christ has suited us for relationship with the Father.[9]

The reference to God's people, the object of this act of perfecting, is communicated with the present passive participle *hagiazomenous*, translated with "who are being made holy." This reference could be taken as a remark on the ongoing process of sanctification for the believer.[10] However, the concept of "being made holy" in Hebrews refers to cleansing from sin (2:11; 9:13–14; 10:10; 10:29; 13:12), a deed accomplished preeminently by the sacrifice of Christ. Thus with F. F. Bruce we read the present tense form of this participle as "timeless," speaking of the cleansing of God's people from sin.[11] Our cleansing by the sacrifice of Christ (10:10) is the means by which we are made "perfect"—wholly adequate for a relationship with God.

A Reflection on the Finality of Christ's Sacrifice in Light of the New Covenant (10:15–18)

BY THE WAY the author introduces the quote of Psalm 40:7–9 at Hebrews 10:5, he clearly understands Christ as the speaker of that portion of Old Testament text. Now in 10:15, he introduces a Scripture passage once again by pointing to the Holy Spirit as its author (cf. 3:7; 9:8).[12] That is, the Spirit "also testifies" to the hearers via the Scripture text. The word "also" alludes to the quotation of Psalm 40:7–9 in Hebrews 10:5–7 and the commentary of 10:8–14, wherein

---

8. Guthrie, *The Structure of Hebrews*, 123.

9. On the use of this word elsewhere in Hebrews see above, e.g., 108, 191.

10. E.g., Attridge, *Epistle to the Hebrews*, 280–81.

11. Bruce, *Epistle to the Hebrews*, 247.

12. That God, Christ, and the Holy Spirit are considered the originators of Scripture implies an implicit Trinitarianism in the author's theology.

Jesus Christ proclaimed the ineffectiveness of the old covenant system and the forgiveness of sins. Moreover, Psalm 110:1 indicates the finality of the Son's sacrifice (Heb. 10:11–14). In a similar manner, the Spirit also proclaims[13] the need for a new covenant and the decisive forgiveness of sins.

In support of this last assertion, the author employs a loose rendering of two portions from Jeremiah 31:31–34, the focal text quoted in full near the beginning of his discourse on Christ's superior sacrifice (8:8–12). The first section, related in 10:16, focuses on the description of the new covenant as an agreement of transformation by which God's laws will be written on the hearts and minds of his people. Thus, the new covenant provides a means for the process of sanctification (cf. 10:14). In 10:17 the writer to the Hebrews then highlights the forgiveness of sins offered under the new covenant. That God "will remember no more" the sins of his people demonstrates that this covenant involves a superior sacrifice for sins by which those sins are dealt with fully. As the author points out in 10:18, this kind of forgiveness means that all future sacrifices for sin have been rendered obsolete.

Summary. In Hebrews 10 the author begins with a problem, the limited ability of the law to deal with sins. The repetitious nature of the Levitical sacrificial system demonstrates that the sacrifices presented under that system were unable to take away sin and, therefore, left a burdened conscience. The answer to this problem came in the person of Christ, our great high priest. As seen in Psalm 40:7–9, Christ's sacrifice of his own body was God's way of fulfilling the divine will with regard to making his people holy. Furthermore, Psalm 110:1 implies the finality of that sacrifice, since our great priest has sat down at the right hand of God. No further sacrificial service is required of Christ because, by his one sacrifice, he has perfected for all time those in the process of being made holy. These proclamations fit perfectly with the prophesy of Jeremiah 31:33–34, which speaks of the transformation of God's people and God's decisive forgiveness of their sins.

Bridging Contexts

IN ATTEMPTING TO bring this passage out of the ancient world and into our own, we must remember, first of all, both the purpose and the importance of this particular section of Hebrews. As to its purpose, the author wishes to crystallize for his hearers the effectiveness and finality of Christ's sacrifice. The hearers are in danger of turning their

---

13. Also used to introduce an Old Testament passage at 7:17, the verb translated "testify," as employed in this context, simply means to proclaim the truth of something.

backs on their Christian commitment; but the author reminds them, in no uncertain terms, that in so doing they walk away from God's provision by which people may have a cleansed conscience and a healthy, permanent relationship with him. In the new covenant alone can one find a means for decisive forgiveness from sin and, thus, right relationship with God. The Scripture bears witness specifically that the old covenant system is shown up as defunct by the ministry of Jesus.

The structural location of 10:1–18 indicates this text's importance, for it culminates the author's entire expositional treatment of Christ's person and work in this passage.[14] Therefore, we must resist the temptation to move past this section too quickly. The "forgiveness of sins," heralded in the author's treatment of the Lord's sacrifice, is, of course, one of our most basic Christian doctrines. The fact that it is basic may lull us into brushing past it on our journey as if we have already covered this ground, whereas the author intends it to be a permanent place of firm grounding, a source of soul-anchoring stability. Here is where all his Christological work has led us. We have arrived back at the throne at the right hand of God (1:3; 10:12), the place at which we started Hebrews, the most stable place in this or any universe. Here we find a culminating expression of the person and work of our great high priest, Jesus Christ.

The main point. Perhaps more than any other place in Hebrews, 10:1–18 presents clearly the Christian gospel and, therefore, calls us to think clearly about that message and its implications for Christian living. The primary elements of Hebrews' message of forgiveness are as follows: (1) *We have a problem with sin*, even if we are ritualistically religious. Rituals cannot place us in right relationship with God and cleanse our consciences from guilt.

(2) *The problem of sin has been dealt with in the person and work of Jesus Christ*. This is the focal truth of "God's will," as 10:10 puts it. God willed to make us holy by the sacrifice of his son, Jesus Christ.

(3) *Christ's work is decisive, a final reckoning with sin by which participants in the new covenant are made perfect forever.* There exists no longer a need to work out a way to God. It is finished. The forgiveness one experiences under the new covenant has a finality to end all groping for the means, or the path, to God. The path lies before us, as firm and rock-solid as any reality, and more so than all earthly ones. This is truth on which one may build a life. This is why the author has led us here. The fluctuations in human existence may seem eased by running away from the difficulties of Christian commitment; yet, it is at the heart of Christian truth, the essence of the gospel, that a person can find real stability in life.

---

14. For an overview of the structure of Hebrews see above, pp. 39–40.

Here we find answers to our inadequacies as we learn that it is not up to us to work out our ultimate purpose in this life. Here we find a solution for our nagging, debilitating guilt, that incessant accuser who whispers what we already know in our ear. Here, even in our journeying through this life, we find a place of permanence, a place of stability in which we will always be "home," for we find our rest in the presence of God himself. Our application of this text must speak to these implications of gospel truth for the Christian life.

Are you "guilty"? At the same time, this passage contains several interpretive pitfalls into which an expositor might stumble. Speaking of the old sacrificial system in 10:2, the author addresses that system's inability to cleanse worshipers permanently. If the sacrifices of animals could have cleansed them once for all, he reasons, then the worshipers "would no longer have felt guilty for their sins." The interpreter might infer from these statements that under the new covenant system, since the sacrifice of Christ can cleanse completely and permanently, Christians no longer "feel guilty" about sins. Yet, this assumption presents us with a serious pastoral and theological problem.

Imagine a woman sitting in church on Sunday morning, listening to the preacher's sermon. She has been brooding all morning because of an event the night before. Last evening her husband came home late from work, even though they were to have guests for supper, and she needed help with their three children. He did not call to tell her he was detained at work, and by the time he walked through the door she was in a rage. Her anger expressed itself both in profanity and hurtful comments about his inadequacy as a husband. After a miserable evening with their guests, her husband attempted to ask forgiveness and discuss the situation. She would have none of it. In fact, this morning as they dressed for church, she still would not speak to him.

Now she sits in church and the Spirit of God has begun to work on her heart. She begins to think of those New Testament passages that speak of not sinning through anger and not using unwholesome language in one's speech. Her conscience has begun to bother her—she is "feeling guilty." Yet, as the preacher goes on with his sermon, he comes to Hebrews 10:2 in his NIV text. Drawing implications from the text, he explains that under the new covenant a believer should no longer feel guilty. Given her state of heart and mind, she is confused by that pronouncement. What should she do? Since Christians are not supposed "to feel guilty," should she see her feelings as an attack of the evil one and say to herself, "There must not be anything to this"? Should she question whether she is indeed a true Christian? Or is it the Spirit of God who prompts her, as God's child, to deal with her actions of the night before?

The clause from 10:2 translated by the NIV as "have felt guilty for their sins" may be rendered as "have a consciousness of sins." As detailed in our treatment of Hebrews 9, the word "conscience" (*syneidesis*) means either personal intuition (i.e., a knowledge of something) or, more specifically, the moral awareness of good or evil.[15] Hebrews proclaims that believers now, through the work of Christ, have a clean conscience before God—we are no longer separated from him by our sins, since Christ has taken them out of the way. What can be inferred from 10:2 is that sin no longer looms in front of the Tent of Meeting, barring our way to God. We no longer have a consciousness of sin as a factor determining our standing before God. We have been forgiven completely and finally.

In this sense the term "guilt" or "guilty" may not be the best way to refer to a Christian from the standpoint of New Testament theology. The New Testament almost never speaks of a Christian as "guilty."[16] We are not guilty before God since we have been justified by the work of Christ. Of justification Millard Erickson writes:

> In the New Testament, justification is the declarative act of God by which, *on the basis of the sufficiency of Christ's atoning death,* he pronounces believers to have fulfilled all of the requirements of the law which pertain to them. Justification is a forensic act imputing the righteousness of Christ to the believer; it is not an actual infusing of holiness into the individual. It is a matter of declaring the person righteous, as a judge does in acquitting the accused.[17]

Hebrews' concept of the "cleansed conscience" closely relates to this theological tenet (cf. Heb. 9:9, 14; 10:2, 22).

Nevertheless, Christians still sin,[18] as may be seen in the few New Testament passages that call for believers to repent (2 Cor. 7:9–10; 12:21; 2 Tim. 2:25; Rev. 2:5, 16; 3:3, 19) or confess their sins (James 5:16; 1 John 1:9). Also, the Lord's Prayer, which emphasizes asking for forgiveness, may certainly be considered still relevant for the believer (Matt. 6:7–15). When believers sin, however, they are not cut off from relationship with God, since God's new covenant commitment of forgiveness through Christ still stands. However, the sin committed is one for which Christ had to die as sacrifice. While the evil done does not separate us from God, its cost and its incongruity with Christ's work of sanctification in us (Heb. 10:14) still rightly burden our hearts.

---

15. Spicq, *Theological Lexicon of the New Testament*, 3:332–36; see above, p. 300.

16. One possible exception is 1 Cor. 11:27, which speaks of those who take the Lord's Supper in an unworthy manner and thus are "guilty of sinning against the body and blood of the Lord." See also James 2:10.

17. Erickson, *Christian Theology*, 956.

18. This is contrary to the "perfectionist view," which suggests Christians can live entirely above sin. See Erickson, *Christian Theology*, 971–74.

This brings us back to the lady in church. She should feel burdened by her sin and confess it to the Lord and her husband (the husband needs to confess his insensitivity as well). Her burden, however, should not, in and of itself, cause her to question her relationship with God, if she has committed herself to a new covenant relationship with God. In this sense, her subjective feeling of guilt should be addressed by the fact that objectively, before God, she is not guilty because of Christ's sacrifice. Finally, the preacher in this case study should clarify the passage under consideration, interpreting rightly what lies behind Hebrews' proclamations concerning the "cleansed conscience."

Perfect people? A second interpretive pitfall is closely related to the pitfall of misunderstanding "guilt" in Hebrews and stems from a failure to interpret terms in context. We have seen the concept of *perfection* from time to time in Hebrews,[19] and the possible misunderstandings of the term warrant a closer look at 10:1 and 14. The first speaks of the law's inability to make worshipers perfect; the second turns this dismal pronouncement on its head, stating that by his sacrifice Christ has accomplished this very feat: "because by one sacrifice he has made perfect forever those who are being made holy."

Now if we read this statement with our usual definition of "perfect" in mind, we likely will be either shocked or confused. Christians know they are not "perfect" in the sense of "no faults or failings." Yet, the term *perfect*, as used in Hebrews, carries the sense of "complete, whole, adequate, having arrived at a desired end." Insofar as Christ has perfected us for all time, it means that by his sacrifice he has made us completely adequate for a relationship with God by consecrating us.[20] We have arrived at the end that God desired to accomplish via his Son's death on the cross. His work to put us in right relationship with himself has been made complete.

A forgetful God? A third hermeneutical misstep involves the quote of Jeremiah 31:34 in Hebrews 10:17. Through the prophet God says, "Their sins and lawless acts I will remember no more." This statement should not be taken, with crass literalism, to mean that God literally cannot remember the sins we commit (recall that this text covers the sins of our past, present, and future). God is *omniscient*, all-knowing. The words "I will remember no more" are a concise summary of Jeremiah's statement: "For I will forgive their wickedness and will remember their sins no more." Notice the parallelism. The verbal concepts "forgive" and "remember no more" parallel each other, as do the objects "wickedness" and "sins." Just as these latter words convey the same basic idea of wrongdoing, so also the verbal concepts both speak of forgiveness. The parallelism is used for style and emphasis, but communicates one truth—that God forgives sins.

---

19. E.g., 2:10; 5:9; 7:11,19, 28; 9:9.
20. Lane, *Hebrews 9–13*, 267–68.

One of my favorite writers, Max Lucado, provides an example of this misstep:

> I was thanking the Father today for his mercy. I began listing the sins he'd forgiven. One by one I thanked God for forgiving my stumbles and tumbles. My motives were pure and my heart was thankful, but my understanding of God was wrong. It was when I used the word *remember* that it hit me.
>
> "Remember the time I . . ." I was about to thank God for another act of mercy. But I stopped. Something was wrong. The word *remember* seemed displaced. It was an off-key note in a sonata, a misspelled word in a poem. It was a baseball game in December. It didn't fit. "Does he remember?"
>
> Then *I* remembered. I remembered his words. "And I will remember their sins no more."
>
> Wow! Now, *that* is a remarkable promise.
>
> God doesn't just forgive, he forgets. He erases the board. He destroys the evidence. He burns the micro-film. He clears the computer.
>
> He doesn't remember my mistakes.[21]

Unfortunately, Lucado has missed the point. When the Scripture says to us that God "forgets" our sins, what it means is that God "forgives" us completely, stamping our sins as having been dealt with.

THE ACCOMPLISHMENT. MY father, to whom, along with my mother, I have dedicated this commentary, has been one of my greatest encouragers in life. I remember my father, again and again as I grew up, boosting the flagging confidence of a sometimes awkward boy with, "You can do anything you put your mind to." This statement, of course, spoke of work-ethic values—determination, perseverance, confidence, preparation, willingness—sweat-stained values that have marked my life and for which I am grateful. My father was saying to me, "If you will work hard for your dreams, you can accomplish much." And he was right. He and the authors of Proverbs would feel at home discussing life over homegrown vegetables and hearth-fire stew.

Nevertheless, life has a hard edge of reality to it. We are forced to face our limitations sooner or later. We fail, sometimes repeatedly. Some tasks or

---

21. Max Lucado, *God Came Near: Chronicles of the Christ* (Portland, Ore.: Multnomah, 1987), 101.

goals in life stay beyond our reach, no matter how much we "put our minds to" them. I will never run a four-minute mile. I cannot speak all the languages of the world. I even have a hard time killing all the grass in my garden. At times I do not even do well those things of which I am quite capable. In a pastoral ministries class in seminary my colleagues and I were taught that the first, foundational confession of the minister should be, "We are but dust" (actually, I think the first should be, "God is God"!).

Of course such limitations have been with us from the beginning. I now am the father of a two- and a five-year-old, the younger a girl, the older an energetic boy. Anna cannot yet clean herself, much less her clothes. She has just started to walk but cannot walk a great distance. She is utterly dependent on her parents for food, shelter, and a host of other basics. Joshua cannot mow the yard, although he sometimes rides the mower with me. He cannot throw a baseball like a big-leaguer—yet. He has just started to read and write but cannot do multiplication. These kids are wonderfully limited, wonderfully dependent.

Naturally they will outgrow most of these limitations, just as their parents and grandparents have. But there is at least one limitation they will not outgrow on their own, a limitation with which their parents, their parents' parents, and all their ancestors to time immemorial have not been able to handle by force of human will. That limitation, of course, has to do with sin. We simply cannot overcome sin or turn back its consequences, and neither can they. No one can—except God.

Most religions involve some form of human "doing" for God—"sacrificing" something to win favor with the Almighty. At the heart of Christianity stands the core truth that God has done something for us, through the sacrifice of his Son, that we could never do for ourselves. He has taken our sins out of the way, forgiven us completely, and relates to us, intimately and eternally.

An analogy to how we should respond to God's graciousness is set in Brazil. A woman named Dona Nusa lay in her casket, killed in a car accident the day before. Her son Cesar, her daughter, other relatives, and a young woman named Carmelita stood near by. Tall and dark, Carmelita was dressed this day in simple clothing. The young woman, from the interior of Brazil, had been adopted into Dona Nusa's family more than two decades earlier. At that time she was seven years old and an orphan, the product of a prostitute and an unnamed father. Moved by compassion, Dona Nusa intervened, taking little Carmelita into her family.

When almost everyone else had left the funeral chapel, Carmelita stayed behind, weeping quietly at the side of the casket. Earnestly, tenderly, she leaned over the coffin of her adopted mother, caressing it gently. She voiced her good bye with "*Obrigada, obrigada*" ("Thank you, thank you"). Dona Nusa had reached out and given Carmelita a life that the little orphan had no ability to craft for herself.[22] Pure graciousness.

We should weep; for God has given us the freedom, the forgiveness, the life, which we could not win for ourselves. Our tears are not tears of separation but tears of homecoming; not tears of death but tears of life; not tears of a past but tears falling on a bedrock of hope for the future. Our sins have been taken away and we, through the accomplishment of another, have been brought to the Father and incorporated into his family forever. This is the gospel.

Freedom from guilt. While in graduate school I worked residential construction for a while. One young man, also a seminary student, started to work for my boss at the same time I did, and we became friends. As we came to know one another, my friend confided in me about the difficulties he was having at home. He and his wife had been married for about a year, but they were struggling emotionally and had no physical relationship. It seems she had had a sexual encounter prior to meeting him and now lived in the dark, debilitating shadow of that immoral act. Her guilt weighed on her to the point of breaking her emotional stability and almost breaking her marriage.

All of us have a past, a few black secrets we would not want broadcast to our friends and associates. A sexual sin. A lie. A cheat at school or work. An act of pure meanness. Sins of attitude and action that are hard to forget. Our enemy, the Accuser, loves to lead these shades of the past into our consciences, pricking our hearts and damaging our minds with darts dripping of guilt. Yet, if we are new covenant people, we are, in fact, not guilty before God. Our wrong action of the past has been consumed in Christ's right work of sacrifice. Yes, we should confess and repent as we sin—Christ paid a great price for each sin we commit, and each must be taken seriously lest we be stunted in our spiritual progress. But then each sin should be left behind, for the deal has been closed, God has turned away from our unrighteous deeds and turned toward us.

I have wondered often what Simon Peter experienced upon meeting Jesus for the first time after the resurrection—for the first time after *the denials.* How hard it must have been to carry that past into the presence of Christ. Elizabeth Barrett Browning writes beautifully of the event, with its strained mix of overwhelming joy and grief:

> The Savior looked on Peter. Ay, no word,
> No gesture of reproach: the heavens serene,
> Though heavy with armed justice, did not lean
> Their thunders that way: the forsaken Lord
> *Looked* only on the traitor. None record

---

22. Lucado, *God Came Near,* 155–57.

What that look was, none guess; for those who have seen
Wronged lovers loving through a death-pang keen,
Or pale-cheeked martyrs smiling to a sword,
Have missed Jehovah at the judgment-call.
And Peter, from the height of blasphemy—
"I never knew this man"—did quail and fall,
As knowing straight *that* God, and turn'd free,
And went out speechless from the face of all,
And filled the silence, weeping bitterly.

I think that look on Christ might seem to say,
'Thou Peter! Art thou, then, a common stone
Which I at last must break my heart upon,
For all God's charge to His high angels may
Guard my foot better? Did I yesterday
Wash *thy* feet, my beloved, that they should run
Quick to deny me 'neath the morning sun?
And do thy kisses, like the rest, betray?
The cock crows coldly, Go, and manifest
A late contrition, but no bootless fear;
For, when thy final need is dreariest,
Thou shalt not be denied, as I am here:
My voice to God and angels shall attest,
'Because *I know* this man, let him be clear.'"[23]

"Let him be clear." The same has been said to us. We like Bunyan's Christian have, in reality, come to the cross and had our burden of guilt cut from off our backs and rolled into the tomb. There is but one resurrection—and later another—with which each of us has to do. Let guilt lie.

Assurance of salvation. We live in a world of people and things that are less than completely dependable. It seems at times that we cannot be sure of anything. The dishwasher breaks. The copier at work needs to be repaired—again! The car has yet another problem that breaks the budget for the month. Things simply do not always work; they are visible evidences that this world and its elements are "pass[ing] away" (1 John 2:17). People too disappoint. A friend hurts you with an unguarded remark. A spouse fails to do that errand that you had been assured would get done "today." The repairman doesn't show up when he promised. The boss doesn't come through with the raise.

---

23. Elizabeth Barrett Browning, "The Look" and "The Meaning of the Look," in *The Country of the Risen, An Anthology of Christian Poetry*, comp. Merle Meeter (Grand Rapids: Baker, 1978), 300.

And to make it worse, we cannot even depend fully on ourselves. The "new year's resolution" has become a cliché joke because no one expects anyone really to follow through. For the Christian such shortfalls are especially egregious when related to sin. We bludgeon ourselves with our lack of consistency in the ways of God. The lingering habit that sucks our spiritual vitality like a leech can lead to a crisis of faith as we face our own blaring weaknesses. We may ask, "If I cannot get myself together better than this, am I really a Christian?"

What gives assurance? As a professor at a Christian, liberal arts university, I have students who struggle with that question. Most often the query arises from a relentless battle with some unholy act or lifestyle. It is beastly difficult to live with a strong sense that Christ has broken the power and penalty of sin in you if sin seems to win the day, almost every day. And so they come seeking assurance.

Rather than pointing them back to a conversion or confirmation experience of the past,[24] I ask the following two questions: (1) *Are you committed to a relationship with God through the work of Jesus Christ, depending on his sacrificial death alone for the forgiveness of your sins?* We go through the gospel in detail to make sure they understand its message, and I stress the *comprehensive nature* and *decisiveness* of Christ's sacrifice for sins. His work on behalf of new covenant people covers all our sins, past and future, and covers them completely and for all time. No sin is too great or too long in duration for Christ to forgive.[25] Our stumbling does not negate the work of Christ.

(2) If the person is committed to a relationship with God through trust in Jesus (I trust them to be genuine in this confession since I cannot look into their hearts), then I ask a second question: *Is there any sin in your life that is causing you to doubt your salvation?* Quite often this is also answered in the affirmative. If so, we discuss the dynamics of spiritual development and ways to deal with temptation (such as prayer, Bible study and memorization, staying out of situations conducive for falling into the sin, and meaningful involvement in the church and in the lives of fellow believers). I end by challenging my brother or sister in Christ to persevere in trusting the sufficiency of Christ's work and to endure in the fight against sin.

The process described above has seemed to help many since it directs one's attention anew to the decisive work of Christ as our only true basis for assurance. "He has made perfect forever those who are being made holy" (10:14).

---

24. See above, pp. 141–43.

25. The one sin that will not be forgiven is the "blasphemy against the Spirit" (Matt. 12:31). For comment on this sin see D. A. Carson, "Matthew," *EBC*, 8:290–92.

Hebrews 10:19–25

THEREFORE, BROTHERS, SINCE we have confidence to enter the Most Holy Place by the blood of Jesus, [20]by a new and living way opened for us through the curtain, that is, his body, [21]and since we have a great priest over the house of God, [22]let us draw near to God with a sincere heart in full assurance of faith, having our hearts sprinkled to cleanse us from a guilty conscience and having our bodies washed with pure water. [23]Let us hold unswervingly to the hope we profess, for he who promised is faithful. [24]And let us consider how we may spur one another on toward love and good deeds. [25]Let us not give up meeting together, as some are in the habit of doing, but let us encourage one another— and all the more as you see the Day approaching.

THE PREVIOUS UNIT of Hebrews served to culminate our author's lengthy exposition on the person and work of Christ. The present unit functions both as the capstone of that exposition and a transition point leading into the great, rolling exhortation that takes us to the end of the book. The writer sums up the theological truths that have occupied him, for the most part, since 4:14, including the Son's appointment as high priest and his high-priestly offering. He crafts this passage around three focal exhortations: "Let us draw near to God" (10:22); "Let us hold unswervingly to the hope we profess" (10:23); and "Let us consider how we may spur one another on toward love and good deeds" (10:24). In this way, he uses the exposition concerning Christ as the foundation for motivating his hearers to action, while at the same time accomplishing a smooth changeover to the hortatory material in 10:26 and following.[1]

Hebrews 10:19–25 contains an important "marker" that indicates the author has come to the end of a major movement in his argument. This passage forms the close of an *inclusio* that opened at 4:14–16.[2] As depicted in the figure below, these verses have no fewer than eight verbal parallels with

---

1. On 10:19–25 as a transition with "overlapping constituents," see Guthrie, *Structure of Hebrews*, 102–4.

2. As noted above, p. 71, an *inclusio* is a literary device by which an author marks the beginning and ending of a section by verbal parallels.

4:14–16, the two passages clearly marking off the beginning and ending of the discourse on Christ's appointment and work as high priest.

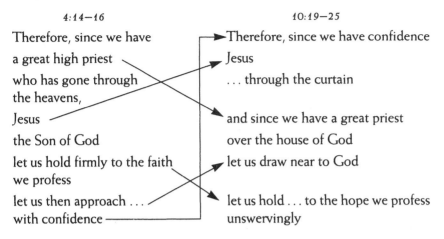

4:14–16	10:19–25
Therefore, since we have	Therefore, since we have confidence
a great high priest	Jesus
who has gone through the heavens,	... through the curtain
Jesus	and since we have a great priest
the Son of God	over the house of God
let us hold firmly to the faith we profess	let us draw near to God
let us then approach ... with confidence	let us hold ... to the hope we profess unswervingly

Let Us Draw Near to God (10:19–22)

THE FIRST EXHORTATION, echoing 4:16, challenges the hearers with "let us draw near to God."[3] Once again the old covenant worship and, especially, the role of the high priest under that system form the appropriate conceptual grid for understanding the author's words. Whereas this exhortation to "draw near" concludes the series of exhortations at 4:14–16, it initiates the series in 10:19–25. In the latter text the author addresses the *bases*[4] for the exhortation, the *manner* in which the action is to be carried out, and the *means* by which one may draw near to God:

> **basis for exhortations:** Therefore, brothers, since we have confidence to enter the Most Holy Place by the blood of Jesus, by a new and living way opened for us through the curtain, that is, his body
> **2nd basis for the exhortations:** and since we have a great priest over the house of God,

EXHORTATION 1: LET US DRAW NEAR TO GOD

> **manner:** with a sincere heart
> **2nd manner:** in full assurance of faith
> > **means:** having our hearts sprinkled to cleanse us from a guilty conscience
> > **2nd means:** and having our bodies washed with pure water

---

3. On the exhortation, "Let us draw near to God," see the discussion at Heb. 4:16, p. 176.

4. The two bases are related grammatically to the exhortation to "draw near" but conceptually extend also to the other two exhortations in 10:19–25.

(1) The author begins with two bases for his exhortation. (a) The first one states, "since we have confidence to enter the Most Holy Place by the blood of Jesus, by a new and living way opened for us through the curtain, that is, his body. . . ." As in 4:16, the approach to God is characterized by "confidence," but in 10:19 the hearers' possession of that confidence is assumed.[5] The word "confidence" (*parresia*), a rare word in Greek literature, has to do with free and open expression or conduct[6] and, in an ancient Jewish context, relates especially to approaching God in prayer.[7] This is a "reasoned confidence"[8] or boldness with which a believer approaches God, the worshiper being emboldened by the work of Christ. Just as the older covenant high priest was able to enter the earthly Most Holy Place by the blood of animals, the blood (i.e., death)[9] of Jesus has won us confident entrance to the Divine Presence.

Our entrance, moreover, is "by a new and living way." The path is "new" in that it departs from the perennial, ritual requirements as detailed under the old covenant system and also in that it constitutes a way first walked by Christ "through the heavens" (4:14). Yet the word translated as "new" (*prospha-ton*) can also carry the meaning "previously unavailable," which seems to fit the broader context nicely (9:8). Jesus has opened a path for us, a path unknown and inaccessible to people before the completion of his high-priestly work. Moreover, this way is "living" because we walk it in association with our resurrected Lord. The "way" into God's presence, therefore, is no longer characterized by death but by following the path of the Living One,[10] who has opened, or inaugurated, a route for us "through the curtain."

"The curtain," an allusion to the veil separating the outer and inner rooms of the tabernacle, ultimately points to a greater (i.e., "heavenly") reality—the spiritual barrier through which one must pass in order to enter the presence of God. Closed to any but the high priest under the old covenant system, this passage has now been opened to God's people by Christ's sacrifice. The author further draws an analogy, which has been the source of much discussion among commentators, between this curtain and the "body" of Christ. The best interpretations take the phrase "his body" to refer to Jesus' sacrificial death.[11] The whole phrase, then, reiterates a main assertion concerning

---

5. The author uses the term *echontes*, an adverbial participle of cause appropriately translated by the NIV with "since we have."

6. Spicq, *Theological Lexicon of the New Testament*, 3:56–62.

7. Attridge, *Epistle to the Hebrews*, 111–12. Also, see above, p. 176.

8. Spicq, *Theological Lexicon of the New Testament*, 3:61–62.

9. See above, pp. 318–19.

10. Hughes, *A Commentary on the Epistle to the Hebrews*, 406–7.

11. Attridge, *Epistle to the Hebrews*, 287; Lane, *Hebrews 9–13*, 284.

the effect of that death: The new covenant priest's sacrifice has made possible our entrance to God's presence. As the old covenant priest had to pass through the veil, the new covenant people of God enter his presence via the sacrificial death of Christ.

(b) The other basis for the exhortation to "draw near" (10:21) also restates elements of earlier thoughts in Hebrews. The clause "since we have a great priest" mirrors the "since we have a great high priest" of 4:14 and carries the full force of the intervening discourse on the appointment (5:1–10; 7:1–28) and offering (8:3–10:18) of our heavenly high priest. Because of his person and work, our priest is "over the house of God," a reference reverberating from the writer's earlier discussion in 3:1–6, which sets forth a comparison of Moses and Christ as leaders of God's people. Christ's superior offering has established him as the one who by his work has brought into existence and has responsibility for a new people intimately related to God.[12]

(2) The writer goes on to present two thoughts concerning the manner with which we are to draw near to God. (a) We must come "with a sincere heart" (10:22). In the Scriptures the heart often represents the inner life of a person, which may involve one's thoughts, will, emotions, or character. Thus it is significant that the new covenant, with which our author has been greatly occupied, involves the writing of God's laws on the human heart (8:10). As the reservoir of inner resources (e.g., Prov. 4:23), the heart determines outward behavior. God sees the motivations and commitments of the human heart and requires that the worshiper's heart be in the right condition. Thus, we must come with a "true" (*alethine*) heart, the word connoting the idea of being "real, genuine, loyal." Therefore, if we are to draw near to God, we must do so with hearts genuinely committed to him.

(b) This genuine commitment is closely associated in this passage with a second thought on how we are to approach God: "in full assurance [*plerophoria*] of faith" (cf. 6:11), a phrase that can also be translated "conviction" or "certainty of faith." *Plerophoria* describes the clear-headed confidence and stability generated in true believers as a result of Christ's work on their behalf.[13] To many in modern culture the concepts of "faith" and "full assurance" seem contradictory since faith, especially in the context of religion, communicates a blind leap. Yet in the biblical literature, faith suggests a firm trust placed in God, who has shown himself faithful in his dealings with his people.[14]

(3) The discussion now follows with the means by which the heart is prepared and, consequently, the believer receives confidence to draw near to

---

12. See above, pp. 126–28.
13. Lane, *Hebrews 9–13*, 286.
14. See the discussion below on Heb. 11:1–40, pp. 387–90.

God. The two concepts of "hearts sprinkled" and "bodies washed" must be understood against the backdrop of the old covenant purification rituals. The author alludes to the ceremonies for the establishment of the covenant and the purification under that covenant for one who would approach God.

Commentators have been too quick to find in "having our bodies washed" a reference to Christian baptism;[15] who can deny that the phrase *may* have been intended to draw such a connection? Yet the author gives no overt signals that he has the Christian rite in mind. What we do have in Hebrews are uses of the washing imagery in connection with the purification rites found in the Pentateuch (e.g., Heb. 9:13). Thus, the writer continues his use of Old Testament imagery to communicate that the work of Christ has prepared believers to enter the presence of God. To suggest any more moves the interpreter into the realm of speculation.

Let Us Hold to Our Hope (10:23)

THE AUTHOR NOW encourages his hearers with the verb *katecho*, which the NIV translates with "let us hold" (the same verb used in 3:6, 14 and a synonym of *krateo*, used in 4:14). The writer's use of the present tense in 10:23 perhaps emphasizes the hearers' call to "hold on" as an ongoing call. An ancient author variously used the word to mean "hold to, keep, detain, retain, contain, occupy, or possess." In extrabiblical sources students could be said to "retain" a body of teaching, which calls to mind early Christian exhortations to hold onto the traditions of the faith (e.g., 1 Cor. 11:2; 15:2).[16] The author of Hebrews uses *katecho* to speak of keeping a tight grip on the Christian faith, keeping it from slipping away.

At 10:23, the writer intensifies the concept of "holding on" with the adverb *akline*, which the NIV renders as "unswervingly." This rich word literally means "that which does not bend" or "that which is straight," which communicates the concept of stability or immutability. It could be used, for example, of a lasting friendship, or of one not being moved from a given perspective or judgment.[17] Philo employs the word to speak of God's immutability—creatures are fickle, vacillating back and forth between various directions and positions, but God does not change his will or his ways.[18] Thus in 10:23 the believer is challenged to hold onto the Christian hope, which the author so clearly has depicted as grounded in the person and work of Christ, without being moved by changing circumstances.

---

15. E.g., Moffatt, *Epistle to the Hebrews*, 144–45.
16. Spicq, *Theological Lexicon of the New Testament*, 2:288.
17. Ibid., 1:59.
18. Philo, *Allegorical Interpretation*, 2.83.

Let us Encourage One Another (10:24–25)

THE FINAL EXHORTATION of this passage calls this community of Christ-followers to a life of mutual encouragement. Christians have a high calling to care for one another and stimulate one another spiritually and morally. The word translated "let us consider" (*katanoeo*), the main verb around which verses 24–25 revolve, occurs just fourteen times in the New Testament; it means to "notice, consider, pay attention to, look closely at."[19] Believers are to rivet their attention on the need for conscious activities of encouragement among those in the Christian community.

The author expresses this need with the word *paroxysmos*, which could be used negatively to connote a strong emotion of irritation (e.g., Acts 15:39) but here communicates positively stimulation or motivation. Believers are to motivate one another to love expressed in good works,[20] by which the community has been characterized in the past (Heb. 6:10). The need to be challenged to a love actively expressed is ever present in a Christian ethic (e.g., Gal. 5:13; 1 Thess. 1:3; Rev. 2:19) and a cornerstone of authentic Christian community.

The author explains the context for stimulation toward love and good works in verse 25, using contrasting expressions that mark out what the hearers must not and must do. What they must not do is stop meeting together on a regular basis. The participle *enkataleipontes* carries the idea of "abandonment" or "forsaking" someone or something. This is the word that translates Jesus' cry of dereliction from the cross (Matt. 27:46): "My God, my God, why have you forsaken me?" Apparently some in the community were abandoning their gathering together for worship. God would never forsake them (Heb. 13:5), but some of those who had been associated with the Christian community were forsaking him (6:4–8; 10:26–31) and his people. They may have been discouraged from Christian gatherings by the threat of persecution, by the delay of the Parousia, by continued connections with the Jewish synagogue, or by mere apathy.[21]

Whatever the reason, the author sees their discontinuance of common fellowship and worship as fatal for perseverance in the faith. Encouragement cannot take place in isolation. Thus, what they must do is gather for mutual encouragement (cf. 3:13). Christians are to display a deep care and concern

---

19. Balz and Schneider, *EDNT*, 2:265. See, e.g., Matt. 7:3; Luke 12:24; 20:23; Acts 27:39; Rom. 4:19; James 1:23–24.

20. Ellingworth is probably correct that the pairing of love and good works "is a virtual hendiadys, since the good works are the direct expression of love." See Ellingworth, *The Epistle to the Hebrews*, 527.

21. Lane, *Hebrews 9–13*, 290; Bruce, *Epistle to the Hebrews*, 257–58.

for one another, expressed not only through positive support and reassurance, but also through reproof and warning. Both consolation and encouragement to spiritual alertness are to be given in light of the great "Day" of Christ's coming. Believers must remind one another that we live from day to day in anticipation of that Day at the end of the age.

Bridging Contexts

WE HAVE SEEN these topics before. When I was first asked to do this commentary and grasped the three-step process with which each passage was to be addressed, one of my first reactions had to do with the challenge of application in the great central section of Hebrews (4:14–10:25). In this section the author weaves a "tapestry" of certain prominent theological themes, and this reiteration of common motifs presents the expositor wishing to draw application with an exciting and sometimes daunting task. How does one deal faithfully with the material without repeating the same themes time and again in the task of preaching or teaching the text?

We should remember that repetition is a good teacher. Those whom we teach or to whom we preach need to hear important doctrinal truths repeated. At the same time, however, we must guard our own hearts and minds so that we do not slip into a "been there—done that" attitude. We must remember that each section of the book of Hebrews has a unique role to play, and we must ask, "What specifically does the author wish to accomplish by his material in this section?" and, "What does this mean for our application?"

One role of this passage. As to its roles, we have already noted that 10:19–25 echoes 4:14–16, forming the close of an *inclusio* that marks the great central section of the book. Nevertheless, 10:19–25 does more than restate 4:14–16; when compared to that text, it demonstrates a development of ideas *based on the intervening discussion of Christ's superior ministry.* In a sense, the author has more theological material built into his exhortation at this point, material manufactured in his carefully developed arguments on Christ's person and work.

For example, note how in 4:14 the author asserts that Jesus "has gone through the heavens," and in 6:20 that Jesus has gone before us, entering behind the curtain on our behalf. By contrast, the emphasis in 10:19–20 is *our* entrance into the Most Holy Place, an entrance made possible by the sacrifice of Christ. Also, in 4:16 we are challenged to "approach the throne of grace with confidence"; but the same imperative in 10:22 is accompanied by a strong statement both of the *manner* in which and *means* by which we may draw near to God. Both the manner and means have been explicated in the author's previous treatment of Christ's sacrifice for sins. Finally, whereas the hearers are challenged to draw near with confidence in 4:16, the possession of that confidence is assumed in 10:19 (i.e., *echontes* = "having"), based on the author's Christological exposition in the previous chapters.

Thus the theological content developed so carefully in 5:1–10:18 has a noticeable impact on 10:19–25. This once again emphasizes for a contemporary audience the important, foundational role theology must have in relation to application. Therefore, our applications of the passage will flow from the theological messages woven throughout Hebrews, especially those focusing on the impact of Christ's death.

Grammatical structure and a second role of the passage. As important as theology is to this passage, we must also recognize the text's organization around three imperatives: the challenge to draw near to God, to hold unswervingly to our hope, and to encourage one another. Grammatically, the rest of the material in this passage functions to support these three exhortations.[22] These commands demonstrate a second important role of this text: The author wishes his hearers to put their Christian profession into action. In fact, 10:19–25 serves as an introduction to the exhortation material running from here to the end of the book.

With 10:19–25, therefore, the author of Hebrews once again demonstrates the important connection between the truths concerning Christ and the implications of those truths for the Christian life. Theologizing alone is not sufficient for a holistic vision of the Christian life. We are called to action. Therefore, the author gives us clear statements of what we should do to put our faith into action. We too are called to (1) draw near to God, seeking intimacy with him, (2) to hold unswervingly to our hope, and (3) to encourage one another consistently—all on the basis of a sound and vibrant Christology. Our Christianity, in order to be in line with the author's view of the Christian life, must be both doctrinally grounded and energetically acted upon. To neglect doctrine robs our practice of its motivation and means. To neglect acting upon our faith truncates God's twin goals for us of our maturation and perseverance.

Missteps to avoid. As with other passages in Hebrews, this one has a few hermeneutical stumbling blocks we should mention before moving on to application. (1) For example, when the author calls us to "draw near to God," he has an activity in mind that transcends time and place. Most have probably seen movies in which a character goes to a church building to ask God

---

22. The one exception here is the second part of 10:23, "for he who promised is faithful," which is grammatically independent. Semantically, however, this assertion supports the exhortation to hold onto the hope.

for something special. The physical structure is treated as "holy," a place where "God lives." We must remember that in terms of New Testament theology, God lives in us, his people (1 Cor. 3:16). Consequently, we should not think of "drawing near to God" as an activity limited to a church worship service, although that should be one important place in which we draw near. No, we should cultivate lives in which we practice the daily presence of God through prayer and the reading of his Word. To yearn to know him means that we will set aside planned times of fellowship with God and pray continually in the midst of demands of each day (1 Thess. 5:17).

(2) It is my opinion that commentators have rushed too quickly to reading baptismal imagery in the references to "sprinkling" and the washing of our bodies "with pure water." The author here gives no indication that he is doing other than continuing to draw on important images found in the old covenant system. Such sprinkling and washing are pictures the author uses to point to the greater and more perfect cleansing from sins found in the sacrifice of Christ. One can argue that the words at this point would certainly raise thoughts of Christian baptism, but there is no firm indication of that. The danger is that one might too closely associate the physical waters of baptism with the cleansing of sins. Rather, the images of sprinkling and washing here are figurative symbols of the effect of Christ's sacrifice. Any other suggestion is based on pure speculation rather than on any indication supplied in the text.

(3) Another caution is in order with regard to the author's challenge to "not give up meeting together." This exhortation has been used at times to exhort church members to attend every meeting offered by the church during the week: Sunday School, Sunday morning worship, evening worship, visitation on Monday night, prayer meeting Wednesday night, Bible study Friday noon; all are held up as part of the standard for "let us not give up meeting together."

The principle behind this part of the author's challenge, however, has to do with consistent involvement in the life of the church rather than frenetic activity in all the programs of the church. We as Christian leaders must not burden people with a guilt trip if they are not at the church five nights a week. The question is whether they are meaningfully engaged in the life of the body on a weekly basis. Are they involved in worship? Are they being educated through preaching and teaching of God's Word? Are they ministering, exercising their spiritual gifts? Are they experiencing Christian fellowship? We should teach these aspects of healthy Christian living and allow the Holy Spirit to show them how these are to be lived out consistently.

FOR WHAT DO we yearn? The call to be God's person is often given in terms of right belief coupled with right personal desires and actions—to live "from the head" and "from the heart," to believe and to yearn for the right things. In the *Shema* (Deut. 6:4–5), the focal text for the life of a Jewish person, we see this kind of call: "Hear, O Israel, the LORD our God, the LORD is one [right belief]. Love the LORD your God with all your heart and with all your soul and with all your strength [right desire and action]." The command to love and serve with all the heart and soul is repeated in 11:13, with an accompanying promise of blessing if the directive is followed, and again in 13:3, suggesting the Israelites' devotion would be tested. One finds this call to love God from the heart's wellspring peppered throughout the Old Testament (e.g., Ps. 27:8, Jer. 29:13–14a). God calls us to draw near and then directs the call to our hearts.

Yet we have a problem, perhaps the focal challenge of life, for our hearts are not always what or where they should be. We go seeking to find our hearts and are led to treasure troves hidden in dark caverns shunned by God (Matt. 6:21). We find there hearts in need of cleansing (Ps. 51:10) and surgery (Deut. 30:6), which are deceitful (Jer. 17:9). We yearn for the wrong things in life, things that crowd out God's voice and love for him (Mark 4:19). I must ask myself daily, "For what am I yearning today? To what are my energies and efforts being drawn?" Am I, like Moses, drawing near to God in a "face-to-face" intimacy, crying out to God, "Teach me your ways so that I may know you and continue to find favor with you" (cf. Ex. 33:11, 13)? Or am I like Solomon, whose heart was divided as he turned after other gods (1 Kings 11:1–6)?

To come to God, to draw near to him, must be done with a "sincere heart," one that has been sprinkled clean from a guilty conscience. This cleansing is only possible if one has a right understanding, a right belief in who Jesus is and in what he has accomplished on our behalf. Even for those who have new covenant hearts, to persevere in this drawing near we must keep right thinking in place and yearning hearts engaged in the pursuit of God. A. W. Tozer writes:

> To have found God and still to pursue Him is the soul's paradox of love, scorned indeed by the too-easily-satisfied religionist, but justified in happy experience by the children of the burning heart. St. Bernard stated this holy paradox in a musical quatrain that will be instantly understood by every worshipping soul: "We taste Thee, O Thou Living Bread, and long to feast upon Thee still: we drink of Thee, the Fountainhead and thirst our souls from Thee to fill."

> Come near to the holy men and women of the past and you will soon feel the heat of their desire after God. They mourned for Him, they prayed and wrestled and sought for Him day and night, in season and out, and when they had found Him the finding was all the sweeter for the long seeking. [23]

Some may object that an emphasis on feeling "the heat of" desire opens the way for emotionalism. But we should ask ourselves regarding the alternatives. Are we suggesting that we should be emotionless? Are not emotions God's gift and a part of our humanness? If the answer to the first question is "no" and the answer to the second is "yes," what is worth being emotional about if not our relationship with God? Our commitment to God is not based on or grounded in emotion, but it must surely engage our emotions sooner or later.

There is another difficulty. "Day and night, in season and out." We may ask, "Who has time for that any more?" Such seeking, such drawing near to God may seem archaic, conjuring pictures of medieval monks. How does one fit God into a day planner? How does one seek God in the rush and crush of corporate (or even small-town) America? If we are to draw near to God, our yearnings must be cultivated in the right direction because, if they are not, our culture will consume us, siphoning off our energies, our desires.

> In an incisive article called "Fast Folk," which appeared in ... *Harpers*, Louis T. Grant dissects an article published earlier in *Woman's Day* in which the life-style of one working mother is praised and presented as a model of sorts. Listen to this woman's life. She rushes from home to work in the morning, eating yogurt in the car for breakfast; has lunch at the spa where she works out; leaves child care to her husband, who also has a managerial position forty miles the other side of home; pilots a small plane in her leisure time for pleasure; teaches on the side a class at a local women's college; leaves the kids with Grandma; leaves the kids with sitters; leaves the kids.... Grant likens this life-style, which he calls "fast folk," to keeping up with the gerbils. In his immensely perceptive piece, he illustrates the shallowness of relationships in a fast-folk family. There's no time in such a family for one another, for intimacy, for communication, for listening. That's for slowpokes. [24]

---

23. A. W. Tozer, *The Pursuit of God*, as quoted in Bob Benson, Sr. and Michael W. Benson, *Disciplines for the Inner Life* (Nashville: Thomas Nelson, 1989), 55.

24. Dolores Curran, *Traits of a Healthy Family* (Minneapolis: Winston, 1983), 117–18.

We can add that such a lifestyle also leaves little place for intimacy, for communication, for listening to God. It takes time to keep our lives focused on the right things. We are called to draw near to God on the basis of the completed work of Christ. Will we heed that call today, or will our hearts be yearning for other things? "Let us draw near with a sincere heart. . . ."

To what am I committed? Little Martin Rowe lived on a farm with his family in rural Georgia. When he was six years old, Martin was riding the tractor with his father when the massive machine turned over. The little boy was hurt so badly that he lost the use of one of his arms and suffered damage to the other. While in the hospital, the family incurred a $32,000 debt. One day he heard his mother and father talking outside the hospital room door, his mother weeping and wondering how they were going to pay off such a large amount of money. When they came into the room Martin informed his mom that he was going to pay off the bill himself. She responded as you and I would, thanking him for his concern, but knowing silently that such a goal was fantasy for a child.

But when Martin Rowe got out of the hospital, he began to pick up bottles along the side of the road every day after school, redeeming the bottles for cash. After several months he had collected $400 and brought that to his mother (may my children be so industrious some day!). About that time, Martin learned that aluminum cans could be redeemed and began collecting those as well. The Reynolds Aluminum Company heard of the little boy's endeavor and put him in touch with the Bear Archery Company in Gainesville, Florida; the two companies began donating their scrap aluminum to this young man. Every day after school for five years Martin continued to pick up cans after school, and at eleven years of age walked into the hospital and paid off his $32,000 debt.

Martin's story is amazing because a little boy, motivated by his great love for his parents, seized on a goal and, having put his feet on the path to attain that goal, stayed on it "unswervingly" until its end. He was tenacious because he had a worthy, though formidable, task that called him away from other distractions. He lived a long-term "obedience" to his calling and was rewarded in the end.

It takes resolve to live a "long obedience" to the call of God. To "hold unswervingly to the hope we profess" demands a mature response to the obstacles and oppositions built into the warp and woof of a fallen world rebelling against God. To "hold unswervingly" demands a choice to be faithful, but our hope is well-grounded in the faithfulness of God. "If God is for us, who can be against us? He who did not spare his own Son, but gave him up for us all—how will he not also, along with him, graciously give us all things?" (Rom. 8:31b–32). Indeed!

Here rests our ultimate basis for perseverance. Ultimately we do not have the resources within ourselves to stay with the goal God has set before us. We must choose. We must tighten down our resolve. We must hold. But at the end of the day, we must rest in the goodness, the resolve, and the faithfulness of God, who has promised an inheritance to his children. We hold on even as he holds us and takes us all the way to the end of the path.

With whom will I walk? Our associations in life make a tremendous difference, for good or for ill, in our outlook and endeavors. Peers can wield heavy influence on our actions, our goals, and, yes, our perseverance in given tasks and treks. Thus, for the believer who wishes to hold to the Christian hope, the community of the saints is vital, offering the needed mix of accountability and encouragement. As different parts of the human body need the resources and abilities supplied by the other parts, so those in the body of Christ cannot exist apart from the rest of the body. Our identity in Christ is a "corporate identity," in which we are individuals meaningfully related to the whole. Neither are we self-made nor self-maintained; we need others.

It is said that the giant redwood trees of the Western United States have a relatively shallow root system. Their enormous weight is supported, in part, by the interlocking of a tree's roots with those of the other trees around it. As Christians we need "interlocking roots" with other believers in the church to withstand the enormous weight of life. We need others spurring us "on toward love and good deeds" in a world so bent on self-centeredness and self-gratification. Speaking of the importance of spiritual friends, Tilden Edwards writes:

> Unless we are particularly heroic or saintly persons, each of us needs a relationship with at least one other person who also seeks and trusts the simple way, the Simple Presence. Such a "spiritual friend" can be enormously supportive to us, and we to them.... You feel a little less alone, a little less tempted to fall mindlessly into complicating traps. Someone else is there who knows whether or not you are trying to pay attention to the simple way; that brings a kind of accountability that is important. When someone else knows and cares, then we pay that much more attention to what we are doing.[25]

And Thomas R. Kelly asserts of Christian community:

> We know that these souls are with us, lifting their lives and ours continuously to God and opening themselves, with us, in steady and humble obedience to Him. It is as if the boundaries of our self were enlarged,

---

25. Tilden H. Edwards, as quoted in Bob Benson and Michael W. Benson, *Disciplines for the Inner Life* (Nashville: Thomas Nelson, 1989), 138.

as if we were within them and as if they were within us. Their strength, given to them by God, becomes our strength, and our joy, given to us by God, becomes their joy.[26]

This spiritual community can take at least two forms. (1) The foundational assembly is that of a local body of believers, meeting together regularly for fellowship around the Word and worship of God. The person who asserts that God can be known, worshiped, and followed "out in nature" apart from the church knows little of Scripture, church history, or true Christian experience. Thus, we are called to gather together regularly for encouragement and accountability. We must not forsake this aspect of the Christian life.

(2) The other form that Christian fellowship can take is that of spiritual friendships, friendships that transcend the boundaries of individual local churches. Most Christian gatherings of the first century were in house churches, which existed in a network reaching throughout a given city. Therefore, we may find meaningful fellowship with like-minded believers outside our immediate church group. Bible study fellowships, accountability groups, and times over coffee or tea should be encouraged as long as they are doctrinally sound and do not detract from one's commitment to the local church. Such groups can be wonderfully enriching and supporting for the Christ-follower. These relationships can enhance our sense of community with the broader body of Christ as we seek to live each day in light of the great Day of Christ's return.

Therefore, as I begin to seek to apply Hebrews 10:24–25, I might ask myself: "To whom in the body of Christ am I giving encouragement this day or this week by my presence, my actions, and my words? Am I receiving encouragement by remaining faithful to my association with the body of Christ?" Such reflection, when followed with action, serves as a foundation stone for healthy Christian living.

---

26. Thomas R. Kelly, as quoted in Benson and Benson, *Disciplines for the Inner Life*, 142.

Hebrews 10:26–39

IF WE DELIBERATELY keep on sinning after we have received the knowledge of the truth, no sacrifice for sins is left, ²⁷but only a fearful expectation of judgment and of raging fire that will consume the enemies of God. ²⁸Anyone who rejected the law of Moses died without mercy on the testimony of two or three witnesses. ²⁹How much more severely do you think a man deserves to be punished who has trampled the Son of God under foot, who has treated as an unholy thing the blood of the covenant that sanctified him, and who has insulted the Spirit of grace? ³⁰For we know him who said, "It is mine to avenge; I will repay," and again, "The Lord will judge his people." ³¹It is a dreadful thing to fall into the hands of the living God.

³²Remember those earlier days after you had received the light, when you stood your ground in a great contest in the face of suffering. ³³Sometimes you were publicly exposed to insult and persecution; at other times you stood side by side with those who were so treated. ³⁴You sympathized with those in prison and joyfully accepted the confiscation of your property, because you knew that you yourselves had better and lasting possessions.

³⁵So do not throw away your confidence; it will be richly rewarded. ³⁶You need to persevere so that when you have done the will of God, you will receive what he has promised. ³⁷For in just a very little while,

"He who is coming will come and will not delay.
³⁸   But my righteous one will live by faith.
And if he shrinks back,
    I will not be pleased with him."

³⁹But we are not of those who shrink back and are destroyed, but of those who believe and are saved.

THE AUTHOR OF Hebrews utilizes a masterful mix of warnings, promised rewards, and human examples in encouraging his hearers to persevere in the Christian faith. In 10:26–39 he employs all three to good effect, balancing the harsh warning (10:26–31)—arguably the harshest in the book—with a gentler reminder of past success (10:32–34), then rounding out the whole by calling this struggling community back to a life lived in light of the Parousia (10:35–39). The passage follows roughly the same pattern as 6:4–20: severe warning (6:4–8), softening of the warning by a reminder of the community's past ministries (6:9–12), and an encouragement to take seriously the promises of God (6:13–20). Here again, therefore, we see the tension in the book between the dreadful dangers of rejecting the Word of God over against the glorious promises for those who endure to the end under the authority of that Word.

A Harsh Word of Warning (10:26–31)

AS F. F. Bruce notes, commenting especially on the phrase "deliberately keep on sinning," "this passage was destined to have repercussions in Christian history beyond what our author could have foreseen,"[1] insofar as interpreters have struggled with the issue of "post-baptismal sin." Whatever one's interpretation of this deliberate sin (10:24), the additional proclamations concerning "raging fire," consumption of the enemies of God, and a punishment more severe than death have put fear into many hearts—and rightly so! A living God is not one with whom we can trifle. Yet, what problem is being addressed?

The word placed first in the Greek text, a position marking it as important to the author, is the word translated as "deliberately" (*hekousios*). This adverb communicates the idea of willing participation in an action, something done with a clear mind and firm step, and is important to our interpretation of the passage. What the author has in mind is a deliberate, sinful lifestyle of high-handed rebellion against the gospel. If a person keeps on sinning in this way after receiving a knowledge of the gospel's truth, no sacrifice for this kind of sin remains.

The distinction between those who sin in ignorance, wandering off the path (5:2), and those who radically rebel against the Word of God may be seen in Numbers 15:27–31, where the latter course is said to be blasphemy.[2] So in Hebrews 10:26 those whom the author has in mind demonstrate a continuity between the time before hearing the gospel and after, continuing

---

1. Bruce, *Epistle to the Hebrews*, 261.
2. Hughes, *A Commentary on the Epistle to the Hebrews*, 419.

a lifestyle of rejecting God's Word. For those persons there exists no sacrifice for their sins. In 10:1–18 the author has already made clear that the sacrifice offered by Christ has rendered all others obsolete. Where, then, can one go other than to Christ for an efficacious sacrifice? Once he and his provision have been rejected, there is nowhere else to turn.

What does remain is anything but pleasant. The writer mentions "a fearful expectation of judgment" and "of raging fire," images that continue to play off old covenant imagery and also communicate eschatological realities. The concept of *fear* in the biblical literature often describes a human response to the awesomeness and power of God. Here in Hebrews 10 the expectation of certain judgment is said to be "fearful." Much more than a mere feeling, this expectation has to do with an awareness of an impending event—God's reckoning with the sinners' defiant rebellion against his grace.[3]

The author describes the nature of that judgment by alluding to Isaiah 26:11. The context of that Old Testament passage is suggestive since it depicts a contrast between the righteous, who walk in the ways of God and long for his presence, and the wicked, who go on doing evil in spite of God's grace toward them. The former look forward to the judgments of God on the earth; the latter belong to the ranks of God's enemies, for whom the fire is reserved.

In 10:28–29 the writer of Hebrews crafts an "argument from lesser to greater," much like that found in 2:1–4.[4] In such an argument the ancient preacher first presents an assertion the hearers will recognize as undeniably valid: "Anyone who rejected the law of Moses died without mercy on the testimony of two or three witnesses" (10:28), alluding most directly to Deuteronomy 17:2–7. This passage from the Pentateuch proclaims that those who violate the covenant by turning away from the Lord's commands and worshiping other gods must be put to death. That the punishment is to be carried out "without mercy" introduces an additional element from Deuteronomy 13:8.[5] The author of Hebrews wishes to remind the hearers of the extreme penalty for rejection of God's revealed will under the old covenant. This, however, he presents as the *lesser* of two important situations, the greater situation being delineated in Hebrews 10:29.

That greater situation, of course, is the rejection of the new covenant high priest and his offering—see the words "how much more" at the beginning of verse 29. Those who have turned away from the work of grace accomplished in God's Son are faced with a more serious situation than the apostates of the

3. Ellingworth, *The Epistle to the Hebrews*, 534–35.
4. See above, pp. 84–85.
5. Lane, *Hebrews 9–13*, 293.

old covenant era. The new covenant is better than that covenant (8:3–13), the new covenant priest greater than the priests of old (7:1–28), and the new covenant sacrifice superior in every way to old covenant sacrifices (9:11–10:18). Therefore, it is logical that those who reject the superior workings of God through his Son deserve even greater punishment than those who rebelled under an older revelation. Inherent to the argument is the assumption that those who have heard the message of the gospel have had a greater opportunity and greater resources for a response of obedience (2:3–4).

The rebellion of those who have turned away from the gospel is depicted in terms of three actions graphically expressed. (1) They have "trampled the Son of God under foot." The metaphor of "trampling on" someone was used in both classical literature and the Greek Old Testament as an image of utter disdain.[6] Thus, those who have rejected the gospel have shown the lowest form of contempt not only for a set of teachings but for the very person of God's Son.

(2) The rebels have "treated as an unholy thing the blood of the covenant." The word translated "unholy" by the NIV (*koinos*) can mean "common, defiled, unclean." In the context of the Levitical purity laws it especially referred to that which was unfit or ceremonially impure (e.g., Mark 7:2, 5; Acts 10:28). Under the old covenant great emphasis was placed on the fitness of the sacrifices used to atone for sins, and the author of Hebrews has gone to great lengths to demonstrate that Christ's own blood was superior to that used under the older system (Heb. 9:13–14, 23–25). Therefore, for the apostates to reject his sacrifice constitutes their declaration that it is unfit as a sacrifice for their sins. Based on broader contextual concerns we translate the phrase "that sanctified him" as "by which one is sanctified,"[7] suggesting that those in this condition in reality have not been sanctified by Christ. Those who truly have been sanctified by the offering of the Son of God have been perfected for all time (10:14).

(3) Finally, those rejecting Christ and his sacrifice have "insulted the Spirit of grace" or caused him outrage. During Jesus' earthly ministry those who rejected his work and words suggested that his power originated with Satan rather than the Holy Spirit of God (Mark 3:22–30). Correspondingly, those who turn away from the gospel and the Spirit's gentle promptings toward its reception have blasphemed, denying the gospel's true origin and importance. They have committed a sin with eternal implications.[8]

---

6. Attridge, *The Epistle to the Hebrews*, 294. See, e.g., Plato, *Leges*, 4 (714a); Ps. 56:2–3; Dan. 8:10; Zech. 12:3.

7. See the discussion above, pp. 230–31.

8. Hughes, *A Commentary on the Epistle to the Hebrews*, 423–24.

In 10:30 the author reinforces his assertion concerning the seriousness of the situation by quoting two brief portions of the Song of Moses in Deuteronomy 32. This song, sung by Moses at the end of his life, eloquently delivered a warning to the people of Israel by depicting God's judgment toward a faithless people who had turned their backs on his covenant. In spite of all he had done for them, they had abandoned him. God's response to them was scathing judgment. The relevance for the audience of Hebrews could not be more striking.

The author's quotations comprise two parts of Deuteronomy 32:35–36, which reads:

> It is mine to avenge; I will repay.
>> In due time their foot will slip;
> their day of disaster is near
>> and their doom rushes upon them.
> The LORD will judge his people
>> and have compassion on his servants
> when he sees their strength is gone
>> and no one is left, slave or free.

Both portions quoted by Hebrews—"It is mine to avenge, I will repay," and "The LORD will judge his people"—emphasize that God himself takes responsibility for judging those who have spurned the gospel and deserted the community of faith.[9]

The author tersely concludes with, "It is a dreadful thing to fall into the hands of the living God" (v. 31). The word translated "dreadful" (*phoberon*) communicates the idea of terror and, for emphasis, is placed first in the Greek sentence. To "fall into the hands" of God speaks both of God's awesome power and of the helplessness of the recipients of judgment. There exists no means of escape for those who have rejected the grace of the Living One (4:12–13).

Remember the Past (10:32–34)

IT IS INTERESTING that at one point in the Song of Moses, two portions of which the author has just quoted, the great leader exhorts the Israelites to "remember the days of old" (Deut. 32:7). For the author of Hebrews now encourages his listeners to "remember." Whereas Moses' song focused on

---

9. Lane, *Hebrews 9–13*, 295. Lane points out that the Song of Moses was used both in the liturgy of the Diaspora synagogue as well as the early church. Therefore, the community addressed by Hebrews was likely familiar with the broader Old Testament context of these quotations.

remembering God's past deeds, Hebrews 10:32–34 uses the hearers' own past commitment as a basis for hearty encouragement. The author challenges them to "remember those earlier days after you had received the light," pinpointing the time frame at their experience of receiving the gospel.[10] The assertion that they "stood [their] ground in a great contest in the face of suffering" speaks of a time of great, perhaps unusual, trial. The word *athlesis* ("contest") connotes not just a challenge but a difficult struggle. Both Lane and Bruce have suggested the expulsion from Rome under Claudius in A.D. 49 as a possible identification of this experience, and the evidence provided in these verses matches the circumstances we know from that time.

Specifically, the believers had endured at least four forms of ill treatment. (1) They had faced public ridicule and persecution. The verb rendered "publicly exposed" (*theatrizo*) originally meant "to bring up on the stage," but as the language developed it took on the figurative meaning of "to make a public spectacle of."[11] They had been made an item of derision in public both by "insult and persecution," that is, both by verbal and physical abuse.

(2) Moreover, even when they had not been the objects of such abuse, they had felt the pain of identification with those who were so treated.

(3) This solidarity extended from the public square to the prison cell, as the listeners "sympathized" (*sympatheo*) with those incarcerated (v. 34). This verb communicates the idea of being "affected by the same suffering, the same impressions, the same emotions as another" person. It is compassion put in action by one rendering aid to someone in dire straights (cf. 13:3).[12]

(4) Finally, the believers "joyfully accepted the confiscation" of their property. If the eviction from Rome in A.D. 49 is the social setting behind the author's reminder, the confiscation of property attending such an eviction would be in mind here. At various times in the first century the Jews were publicly abused as a group, and after being evicted from their homes they witnessed widespread looting of their properties and possessions.

A key to the author's use of his hearers' past stance as a present example is the attitude of "joy" attendant on these circumstances. This manner in which they accepted the theft of their properties describes a spiritual condition by which one sees and celebrates greater realities than those immediately observable. The hearers had joy in the midst of their persecution because they knew that "better and lasting possessions" were promised them by virtue of their identification with the Lord and his church.

---

10. Bruce, *Epistle to the Hebrews*, 267.
11. Lane, *Hebrews 9–13*, 299.
12. Spicq, *Theological Lexicon of the New Testament*, 3:319–20.

Encouragement to Persevere (10:35–39)

FOLLOWING FROM THIS reminder of their former boldness in the face of severe persecution, the author exhorts his hearers to stay that course: "So do not throw away your confidence." The word "confidence" (*parresia*) can mean "openness, boldness, confidence"; often, as here, it has overtones of something done in public.[13] The author, therefore, is encouraging the believers not to retreat from a pattern of public identification with the body of Christ (10:25), reminding them that such identification will be rewarded richly. This reward, however, comes to those who accomplish God's will by persevering in their public confession (10:36).

The quotation found in 10:37–38 brings together parts of two Old Testament texts (Isa. 26:20–21 and Hab. 2:3–4) and focuses on a contrast between the righteous who live by faith and the wicked. The two passages probably were brought together by virtue of their common reference to "the coming."[14] In the Isaiah passage it is the Lord who is coming to punish the wicked; in Habakkuk it is the revelation of judgment that will come both to reward the person who lives by faith and to deal with the unrighteous.

The Isaiah text carries with it strong overtones of the end of time, since it speaks both of resurrection and comprehensive judgment,[15] and thus has been adopted by our author to speak of Christ's second coming. The Habakkuk passage also lends itself for application to that eschatological event, since it speaks of "the end." Originally, that prophecy concerned the destruction of Israel at the hands of the Chaldeans. The Lord instructs the prophet to write the revelation on tablets and assures him that though the fulfillment lingers, it will surely come at the appointed time. Habakkuk then follows with a contrast between the wicked person, who has a crooked soul, and the righteous, who lives by faith (Hab. 2:4).

The author of Hebrews applies these conflated Old Testament texts to his hearers' situation. The concept of "waiting" for an impending time of reward and punishment fits the tension of their circumstances precisely. They struggle (as do we) to remain faithful in a time prior to the Lord's coming. The decision before them is clear. They can choose the route of faith and be rewarded by the Lord at his coming, or they can "shrink back" and face the Lord's displeasure and destruction (v. 39a). The author ends this section with a confident assertion that he and his community belong to those who have

---

13. E.g., John 7:4; Col. 2:15; the word also occurs in 10:19; see comments above, p. 342.

14. On the use of "verbal analogy" as an interpretation tool in early Christianity, see above, pp. 25, 67.

15. Attridge, *The Epistle to the Hebrews*, 301.

chosen the former path (v. 39b), for they walk the way of faith as "those who believe and are saved," more literally, those "of faith resulting in the preservation [or salvation] of the soul" (cf. 4:1–3).

IN SOME WAYS it is easy to identify both the "timely" and the "timeless" in Hebrews 10:26–39. The passage speaks volumes about the hearers' immediate, critical situation. The threat of some members apostatizing from the community comes through clearly in the author's rigorous warning of 10:26–31. We have at least a hint of why they might have been turning their backs on Christianity, for in 10:32–34 the author speaks of severe, public persecution that had been faced in the past. His use of that time of persecution for instruction probably indicates something about their present difficulty.

Although some have been leaving, these believers on the whole have been faithful witnesses to Christ and maintained solidarity with one another. Hebrews 10:32–34 provides one of the writer's most clear descriptions of those to whom he preaches—a portrait seized from a time of great faithfulness in the face of suffering. That he can use them as an example for themselves indicates that many in this church have come far in the faith and need to hold onto their progress. Thus, the author indirectly depicts a Christian fellowship made up of many who have been Christians for a long time and have paid a great price for that commitment, but a fellowship in which some are growing weary and are abandoning the faith altogether. Both his warning and encouragement must have been timely at the book's first reading.

However, the timeless nature of the text also jumps out and presents itself. When in all of Christian history have believers not needed both warnings and encouragement? When have we not needed the challenge to live in light of eternity, as seen in 10:35–39? The principle has been with us from the beginning: "Therefore keep watch, because you do not know on what day your Lord will come" (Matt. 24:42). He is coming and will find both the righteous living by faith and those who shrink back and, therefore, are ashamed at his coming (cf. 1 John 2:28).

We have, of course, dealt with warnings and encouragements earlier in Hebrews,[16] but these dynamics and their respective roles in Christian preaching are richly multifaceted. Therefore, we are challenged to tease out principles that to this point in the commentary have been treated but lightly. I will treat three of them in this section.

---

16. See, e.g., 2:1–4; 3:1–18; 6:4–12.

Christians must think clearly about authority structures upon which they base their beliefs and actions. When we speak of "authority structures," we mean those dynamic contexts or forces in our lives that in reality determine the decisions we make. As depicted in the illustration below, these authority structures may be either divine or human in orientation and either internal or external. For example, most Christians would probably place the Holy Spirit in quadrant A since the Spirit is a divine authority who dwells within a believer (Rom. 8:9).

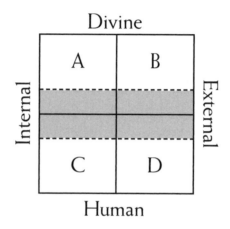

Authority Structures

In quadrant B we would place the Scriptures since the Bible is external to us but authoritative to us nonetheless. As John Stott states, "Scripture then is 'God's word written,' his self-disclosure in speech and writing, the product of his revelation, inspiration and providence."[17] True, we acknowledge the Bible must be rightly interpreted and applied, and many who have held up the authority of the Bible have done so, in reality, in service to their own prejudices and traditions. But the mishandling of the Bible diminishes none of its authority.

This brings us to a third quadrant, quadrant D, for there exist many external human authorities that clamor for our conformity. For example, we might list government, parents, a document (e.g., the "Constitution of the United States"), a pastor or elder board, cultural norms, cultural perspectives, or traditions (either religious or secular). Some would argue that several of these (namely, government, parents, and church leaders) reside somewhere in the gray area between divine and human authority since these are sanctioned by God for leadership in the world. The authorities of this quadrant need not

---

17. Stott, *The Contemporary Christian*, 210.

carry the label "authority" in order to be so functionally. For example, a cultural perspective holds no official position but may, in reality, be determinative for decisions an individual makes; it functions as an authority for that person.

Finally, quadrant C draws our attention to internal human authorities. For example, many people live out of their emotions as the primary driving force for their lives. For most the conscience constitutes another important internal authority. It may be argued that the conscience might be pushed up toward the area of divine authority, since it is an aspect of human nature by God's design (Rom. 2:14–15).

It is this writer's perspective that we must seek to live our lives from the top of this grid down. In other words, all human authorities must be considered in light of divine authority. We must hear and obey the Word of God as illumined by the Spirit of God. This word must determine the way we relate to both the external and internal human authorities calling for our attention. The rub, of course, comes with our determination of whether or not we truly are hearing God's Word and discerning the true prompting of the Spirit. We all face the danger of reading our own cultures, experiences, and traditions into our interpretations of Scripture to such an extent that the voice of God is effectively drowned out of consideration. When the authority grid is inverted so that either consciously or unconsciously the Word and Spirit are relegated to a back-seat position, our lives are driven primarily by what is human. Thus we are no longer living from a standpoint of authentic Christianity.

For example, some so exalt the status of their denominational traditions that they will entertain no further discussion in light of further biblical study. Others in our culture are so saturated with pop notions about God that they have dismissed biblical teachings that contradict such notions. The "judgment of God," for instance, in some corners has been completely eradicated in the presence of a one-sided proclamation of the "love of God." Moreover, the very existence of God has been dismissed by those who suggest that a naturalistic worldview gives adequate explanation for human and material existence. These are examples of external human authorities being given precedent over divine authority.

I remember painfully an occasion at which I was attempting to arbitrate a divisive situation in a church. The pastor was being attacked unfairly by a subgroup within the church, which, by the way, had a history of dismissing pastors after a brief term of service. At one point in the conversation with a certain individual I reminded him that the Scriptures teach believers to be reconciled to one another. I pointed out that the pastor, who had done no moral wrong, had gone to great lengths to be reconciled with the factional group. I asked the man what it would take for him to be reconciled to the pastor.

He responded bitterly, "I will not be reconciled to him!" I inquired, "Even though you understand that Scripture teaches that you must?" "That's right," he replied. This man provides us with an excellent example of one who has placed his emotions—an internal, human "authority"—in a place of preeminence over the Scriptures.

My point is this: Unless one comes to grips with the primacy of divine authority for life thoughts and life choices, scriptural warnings, such as the one found in Hebrews 10:26–31, are meaningless. Such warnings only make sense within a certain matrix of authority. Therefore, it may be that we will need a "pre-step" to preaching the warning texts of Hebrews, which will include a discussion of authority structures in life.

Christians must think clearly about the nature of spiritual development or nondevelopment. Hebrews 10:26–39 in part presents us with a picture of community development on the one hand and nondevelopment on the other. We receive a snapshot of those who have progressed in the faith to the point of taking a public stand with the persecuted church. At the end of the day the author is confident that many in this beleaguered church will not "shrink back" but will persevere to the end. Evidently, however, some associated with the community have failed to develop at all, calling into question the reality of their commitment, or have stagnated spiritually. The forces of this fallen world ever pull the Christian downward, grabbing at spiritual shirttails in order to hold him or her back from true Christian growth.

Our author knows that progress in the Christian life does not just happen; it is the product of an ongoing life of choices made in light of God's will—in light of warnings, promises, and examples that help us perceive God's will more fully. Yet, as shown in this text, either we move ahead in a way that is perceived or, perhaps, unperceived, or we stagnate spiritually. Therefore, the Christian life calls for deep reflection and volition. Evelyn Underhill writes:

> However busy we may be, however mature and efficient we may seem, that growth, if we are real Christians, must go on. Even the greatest spiritual teachers, such as St. Paul and St. Augustine, could never afford to relax the tension of their own spiritual lives; they never seem to stand still, are never afraid of conflict and change. Their souls too were growing entities, with a potential capacity for love, adoration and creative service: in other words, for holiness, the achievement of the stature of Christ. A saint is simply a human being whose soul has thus grown up to its full stature, by full and generous response to its environment, God.[18]

---

18. Evelyn Underhill, *The House of the Soul and Concerning the Inner Life*, as quoted in Benson and Benson, *Disciplines for the Inner Life*, 346–47.

Nevertheless, we need to understand that growth is seasonal. As I write these words, I am experiencing one of my favorite times of the year. The sugar maple outside my bedroom window in recent days has transformed to an almost iridescent yellow. My perennials are bowing down to the ground for sleep, and the grass, thankfully, has stopped its persistent plea for attention. These all will awake with new leaves, new development, new "life" in a few months; but for now they are content to be what they are in this special season.

In a similar manner we experience the ebb and flow, the rotation of seasons, in the Christian life. Some periods seem as vibrant as spring; the presence of God is as real to us as the presence of a spouse or friend in the next room. Other periods seem more dormant, the signs of life having been removed from our perception for the time being, leaving us to make right choices, to think right thoughts, in the midst of a spiritual dryness. Both kinds of times play an important part in the big picture of Christian development. One writer has put it this way:

> I am always reminded that the experience which may be mine at a particular moment may be an experience in which things are stopping. Or it may be an experience in which things are just beginning. It is important that I know which process is taking place. An intimate part of growing into life is the development of a sensitiveness, an apprehension of process in its totality, that I may be enabled to know the character of the event with which I am dealing. Then I will not act in the house of death unnaturally by not accepting it. All of this is to say that there is inherent in life and brooding over life of man the creative mind and the spirit of the living God.[19]

The danger comes when a dry or seemingly dormant season dominates our lives for months or years on end. When this happens we should ask if the perceived dry spell is a normal part of development, because of a crisis in life or the product of our own wrong choices. A time of crisis, such as that being faced by the original addressees of Hebrews, may catch us at a point in life in which our spiritual resources are running low. Such a time may serve as a wake-up call that shakes us to our senses.

Thus, in applying Hebrews 10:26–39 we should ask ourselves where we, or those to whom we speak, are at this moment. What is called for concerning progress in the faith? Warning? A reminder of the past? A promise of future reward? All three? Yes, perhaps all three on a somewhat consistent

19. Howard Thurman, *The Growing Edge*, as quoted in Benson and Benson, *Disciplines for the Inner Life*, 346.

basis; for we are people in tension, needing to move on in a world that wants to hold us back. At any given point, however, the various applications of this passage will be needed by some in any given Christian community. We must keep before us the grace of God in the face of God's wrath, godly examples, and God's promises. These will take us through various stages in the Christian life, hopefully building more and more consistency as time goes on. There is grace for struggle; his warnings, promises, reminders, examples, and the community of faith itself are expressions of that grace.

Christians must be willing to identify publicly with Christ and his body. Notice how much this passage has to do with public identification with or disassociation from Christ and his covenant people. The broader context suggests that those who "trampled the Son of God under foot" did so by publicly renouncing Christ or at least by quitting the community (6:6; 10:25). The positive example offered by those in the church involved their open association with Christ as they themselves were persecuted, and with others in the covenant as those brothers and sisters faced persecution. The author does not want them, therefore, to throw away their public boldness (i.e., "confidence," v. 35) or to "shrink back." Rather, they must by faith stand forward in face of the current crisis.

Christ's call to discipleship has always been one that involves a great cost, for association with Jesus inevitably leads down the path of persecution (John 15:20; 2 Tim. 3:12). People outside the faith do not appreciate our devotion to Christ, and conflict arises as they realize we are not committed ultimately to them or to their views of life. This relational conflict, moreover, may be played out in the living room or the town square, but it does not occur in a closet. There comes a time when we must be willing to be counted with Christ or against him. There is no middle ground; we all must choose one side or the other.

Therefore, our application of Hebrews 10:26–39 may include probing into how we identify or fail to identify with Christ and his church today. What price are we willing to pay for our association? In what ways might we stand forth with Christ in the public contexts of our work, business, government, friendships, or family relationships? What is the difference between associating with an organized local church and the body of Christ invisible? Might there be times when we will be called to stand against an institution with "church" in its title in order to more fully identify with Christ? These are just a few of the questions we should ask as we seek to apply the text.

NOT A TAME **God.** One of C. S. Lewis's favorite comments on Aslan, that great beast, the figure of Christ in the Narnia Chronicles, is, "He is not a tame lion." The deep growl, the severe mercy; the uncompromising, firm-but-smiling gaze. When Aslan speaks no one in the story can question who is in charge. When the lion speaks, one not only gets the sense, but one knows that nothing more need be said. This is really the way things are and not only will they not be changed, indeed they cannot—we have bumped up against a greater reality than ourselves and our particular perspective. He is Lord and he does what he wills. He calls children from another world when and to where he desires. He vanquishes foes in his own good time. No one can ever think of sitting in judgment on *him.* To think of controlling him would be preposterous. The lightning is too powerful to be bottled, the mountain too furious to be captured in a video tape. There is a wildness in his nature and he will not be muzzled.

The "god" to which our culture invites us, with whom our culture is comfortable, is more like the simple and simplistic donkey in the stable of *The Last Battle.* Hidden away in a dark barn, he appears only for a few seconds in the night by the light of a dim fire. Many are fooled, but the donkey is a poor substitute for a real lion. He waddles when he walks; he does not roar; he has an old, dead covering that gives him a hint of lion-likeness. But when the real thing shows, all that is ripped away. When Aslan comes, no one can stand against him.

Nongods and dead gods and donkey gods are no threat, but a Living God is another matter altogether. The Living God has cosmic-sized, power-laden hands and is dreadful indeed. He will not be tamed by our postmodern repulsion for Truth, nor by our aversion to the concept of judgment. We must adjust ourselves to him or face the consequences. The great foolishness of walking away from his gospel, judging Christ as insufficient, lies in this: He has no greater means for dealing with sin. This sacrifice, this work on the cross, is the best work for dealing with our sins, and all other means are by nature inferior. We should fear our lack of grasping that reality; only real lions are dangerous, and donkeys can do us no harm. He is the Living God and it is a dreadful thing to fall into his hands as an enemy.

Calling to ourselves from the past. I am not sure why, but I have always liked time-travel stories (if you are not into science fiction, please bear with me for a moment). A popular movie, *Back to the Future*, tells of a boy named Marty, who, by a friend's time-travel invention (a car), is zapped back in time. The boy's visit to the past has a profound impact on the future as he interacts with his parents (then teenagers) and their peers. He even saves the life of his friend, the inventor, by giving him a message in the past, a note warning him that terrorists will eventually kill him.

Our past can also affect our present and future as we speak to ourselves from the past, as we "remember those earlier days" of our commitment to Christ. Perhaps there was a time when we as individuals stood in the face of severe trial. We should own and build memorials for the remembrance of those past times, using them for our own encouragement to endurance. If we as individuals have had no such experience, we can benefit from the example of our broader community of faith, looking to a time in the past at which they sacrificed greatly. Is there in the location where your church meets, a place for people to remember the past boldness of your faith community, perhaps through photographs or written documents? Are there times during which your church celebrates those past stances publicly? How are you creating an organizational memory that can help people stand firm in their commitment to Christ in the present?

If our local church has had no such experience (which is unlikely), we can benefit from the example of those in the broader body of Christ, perhaps by weaving through our preaching or teaching accounts of the public stands made by those in various arenas of church history. We as the church should call to ourselves from the past, challenging ourselves to endure in our public identification with Christ.

Identifying with Christ and his church. William Faulkner, in his book *Intruders in the Dust*,[20] graphically depicts the racial prejudice of a small Mississippi town in the pre-civil rights South. The story has two main characters, whose lives become intertwined as the plot develops. Both chance and crisis throw Charles Mallison, a twelve-year-old white boy at the beginning of the story and a sixteen-year-old at its end, into an unwelcome relationship with Lucas Beauchamp, a black man who refuses to bow to the accepted social "position" to which he is assigned by virtue of his ancestry.

While hunting rabbits twelve-year-old Charles falls off a footlog into an icy creek. After crawling out of the water he looks up to find Lucas Beauchamp, with an ax on his shoulder, wearing a sheep-lined coat and a broad felt hat like Charles' grandfather used to wear. The boy now experiences a series of cultural role reversals in the story. He is told what to do by this man and obeys, following him to the Beauchamp house. Charles strips naked by the fire, wraps himself in the "negro" blanket and eats the "negro" food. Being indebted to Lucas, the boy tries to pay him for helping him (indeed, after throwing the seventy cents to the floor, Charles commands Lucas with a heated "Pick it up!"). But Lucas "beats" him, refusing to take the money and instructing the two black boys present to return the money.

---

20. William Faulkner, *Intruders in the Dust* (New York: Random House, 1948).

Later Charles tries again to repay and cleanse his conscience from debasing "not merely his manhood but his whole race." He sends a dress to Molly, Lucas's wife; but Lucas "beats" him again, sending in return a gallon of fresh homemade sorghum molasses by the hand of a white boy riding a mule. So Charles remains indebted to Lucas Beauchamp.

Four years later Lucas is accused of murdering a white man, Vinson Gowrie, from a family of "brawlers, and farmers and fox-hunters and stock- and timber-traders who would not even be the last anywhere to let one of its number be killed by anyone . . ." and faces the threat of being lynched by a mob. Charles, under direction from his uncle, goes to the jail to take Lucas some tobacco, and their encounter at this point is the part of the story I am most interested in at this moment. There in the jail Lucas asks the now-sixteen-year-old Charles to go out and dig up the body of the dead man. He asks him, in effect, to risk his life to help one of a different, perceived-as-inferior race. He asks him to join with the minority and risk severe persecution.

Charles realizes that he is no longer held by the plate of collard greens and the warm fire. He is held by the thought that Lucas is reaching out to him in hope that he "would hear the mute unhoping urgency of the eyes." When Lucas approaches the bars of the cell and takes hold of those bars, Charles looks down and sees his "own hands holding to two of the bars, the two pairs of hands, the black ones and the white ones, grasping the bars while they faced one another above them." And the boy agrees to join in Lucas's cause.

We as followers of Christ are called to identify with a spiritual, minority "race"—believers of every race, nationality, and church affiliation—even at great cost to ourselves. We are called to take a stand for Christ publicly and to stand with those who are being persecuted for the Christian message. We face moments of "grasping the bars" with those hurt by enemies of the truth found in Jesus, moments at which we must decide to be counted with "confidence," a public boldness that chooses the difficult path of identification. The only other option is to "shrink back" from that identification.

Back in what has been called his "born-again Christian phase" Bob Dylan, a pop music icon, made a public profession of faith in Christ with songs like "You've Gotta Serve Somebody." Yet, now Dylan begins to get uneasy when asked about that era of his life:

> It's not tangible to me. . . . I don't think I'm tangible to myself. I mean, I think one thing today and I think another thing tomorrow. I change during the course of a day. I wake and I'm one person, and when I go to sleep I know for certain I'm somebody else. I don't know *who* I am most of the time. It doesn't even matter to me. . . .

... Here's the thing with me and the religious thing. This is the flat-out truth: I find the religiosity and philosophy in the music. I don't find it anywhere else ... I don't adhere to rabbis, preachers, evangelists, all of that. I've learned more from the songs than I've learned from any of this kind of entity. The songs are my lexicon. I believe the songs.[21]

He seems to have shrunk back from identification with Christ, preferring instead to identify with the songs. Ironically, the cover of *Newsweek* in which the article appears carries a large picture of Dylan's face and the proclamation, "Dylan Lives."

---

21. David Gates, "Dylan Revisited," *Newsweek* (October 6, 1997), 64.

Hebrews 11:1-40

NOW FAITH IS being sure of what we hope for and certain of what we do not see. ²This is what the ancients were commended for.

³By faith we understand that the universe was formed at God's command, so that what is seen was not made out of what was visible.

⁴By faith Abel offered God a better sacrifice than Cain did. By faith he was commended as a righteous man, when God spoke well of his offerings. And by faith he still speaks, even though he is dead.

⁵By faith Enoch was taken from this life, so that he did not experience death; he could not be found, because God had taken him away. For before he was taken, he was commended as one who pleased God. ⁶And without faith it is impossible to please God, because anyone who comes to him must believe that he exists and that he rewards those who earnestly seek him.

⁷By faith Noah, when warned about things not yet seen, in holy fear built an ark to save his family. By his faith he condemned the world and became heir of the righteousness that comes by faith.

⁸By faith Abraham, when called to go to a place he would later receive as his inheritance, obeyed and went, even though he did not know where he was going. ⁹By faith he made his home in the promised land like a stranger in a foreign country; he lived in tents, as did Isaac and Jacob, who were heirs with him of the same promise. ¹⁰For he was looking forward to the city with foundations, whose architect and builder is God.

¹¹By faith Abraham, even though he was past age—and Sarah herself was barren—was enabled to become a father because he considered him faithful who had made the promise. ¹²And so from this one man, and he as good as dead, came descendants as numerous as the stars in the sky and as countless as the sand on the seashore.

¹³All these people were still living by faith when they died. They did not receive the things promised; they only saw them and welcomed them from a distance. And they admitted that they were aliens and strangers on earth. ¹⁴People who say

such things show that they are looking for a country of their own. [15]If they had been thinking of the country they had left, they would have had opportunity to return. [16]Instead, they were longing for a better country—a heavenly one. Therefore God is not ashamed to be called their God, for he has prepared a city for them.

[17]By faith Abraham, when God tested him, offered Isaac as a sacrifice. He who had received the promises was about to sacrifice his one and only son, [18]even though God had said to him, "It is through Isaac that your offspring will be reckoned." [19]Abraham reasoned that God could raise the dead, and figuratively speaking, he did receive Isaac back from death.

[20]By faith Isaac blessed Jacob and Esau in regard to their future.

[21]By faith Jacob, when he was dying, blessed each of Joseph's sons, and worshiped as he leaned on the top of his staff.

[22]By faith Joseph, when his end was near, spoke about the exodus of the Israelites from Egypt and gave instructions about his bones.

[23]By faith Moses' parents hid him for three months after he was born, because they saw he was no ordinary child, and they were not afraid of the king's edict.

[24]By faith Moses, when he had grown up, refused to be known as the son of Pharaoh's daughter. [25]He chose to be mistreated along with the people of God rather than to enjoy the pleasures of sin for a short time. [26]He regarded disgrace for the sake of Christ as of greater value than the treasures of Egypt, because he was looking ahead to his reward. [27]By faith he left Egypt, not fearing the king's anger; he persevered because he saw him who is invisible. [28]By faith he kept the Passover and the sprinkling of blood, so that the destroyer of the firstborn would not touch the firstborn of Israel.

[29]By faith the people passed through the Red Sea as on dry land; but when the Egyptians tried to do so, they were drowned.

[30]By faith the walls of Jericho fell, after the people had marched around them for seven days.

[31]By faith the prostitute Rahab, because she welcomed the spies, was not killed with those who were disobedient.

[32]And what more shall I say? I do not have time to tell about Gideon, Barak, Samson, Jephthah, David, Samuel and

the prophets, ³³who through faith conquered kingdoms, administered justice, and gained what was promised; who shut the mouths of lions, ³⁴quenched the fury of the flames, and escaped the edge of the sword; whose weakness was turned to strength; and who became powerful in battle and routed foreign armies. ³⁵Women received back their dead, raised to life again. Others were tortured and refused to be released, so that they might gain a better resurrection. ³⁶Some faced jeers and flogging, while still others were chained and put in prison. ³⁷They were stoned; they were sawed in two; they were put to death by the sword. They went about in sheepskins and goatskins, destitute, persecuted and mistreated—³⁸the world was not worthy of them. They wandered in deserts and mountains, and in caves and holes in the ground.

³⁹These were all commended for their faith, yet none of them received what had been promised. ⁴⁰God had planned something better for us so that only together with us would they be made perfect.

HEBREWS 11, OFTEN referred to as the great "Hall of Faith," has become through the centuries one of the church's most-loved portions of Scripture. Poetic in its cadence, panoramic in its historical sweep, and imminently relevant in its challenge, this chapter calls the believer to faithful endurance by use of voluminous testimony from the lives of ancient saints. The whole of 11:1–40 may be divided as follows:

(1) Overture (11:1–3)
(2) Movement 1: First Examples of Faith (11:4–12)
(3) Interlude: A Faith of Pilgrims (11:13–16)
(4) Movement 2: More Examples of Faith (11:17–31)
(5) Crescendo and Conclusion (11:32–40)

In this passage the author challenges his hearers to live lives of faith according to the pattern seen in those who by faith were faithful to God in their earthly pilgrimages.

Two literary devices give form to the writer's challenge in Hebrews 11. (1) He uses the phrase "by faith" (*pistei*) repeatedly, reiterating the phrase over and over again, driving it into the hearers' consciences like a poignant, monotonous melody. Through this literary tool the author focuses attention on the centrality of a life of faith for the people of God.

(2) The author follows the form of an "example list," a rhetorical tool used by ancient authors to challenge hearers to action.[1] This device worked by impressing the audience with the extensive evidence that the desired course of action is indeed the best one to take. In the case of Hebrews 11 the author, through his list of biblical examples, provides strong support for his contention that God's people must be people of faith—even in the face of disheartening difficulties. The general pattern followed with each example throughout chapter 11 is as follows:

    (a) The word *pistei* ("by faith")
    (b) the name of the person who by his or her own faith or the faith of another is being used as an example
    (c) the action or event by which faith is expressed
    (d) the positive outcome

Sometimes the positive outcome is omitted, as in each of the examples at 11:20–22; at other times the author includes a concession (e.g., "even though" at 11:11) or a rationale for the act of faith (e.g., 11:10, 19, 23, 26).

Overture (11:1–3)

THE WRITER OF Hebrews begins his example list with a two-part definition of faith: "Now faith is being sure of what we hope for and certain of what we do not see." The word *hypostasis*, translated by the NIV as a participle ("being sure"), is in fact a noun, which was used variously to communicate the idea of substance, firmness, confidence, a collection of documents establishing ownership, a guarantee, or a proof.[2] It probably should be understood in 11:1, as in 3:14, in the sense of a "firm, solid confidence"[3] or a "calm courage" with reference to things hoped for. Thus, we can translate this part of the verse: "Now faith is the resolute confidence. . . ."[4] The examples that follow demonstrate a posture of firm confidence in the promises of God even though the believers had not yet received the fulfillment of those promises (11:39).

This interpretation stands in parallel with the assertion in the second half of the verse: "and certain of what we do not see."[5] The word *elenchos*, used here, means a

---

1. Michael R. Cosby, "The Rhetorical Composition of Hebrews 11," *JBL* 107 (1988): 250–70.

2. Spicq, *Theological Lexicon of the New Testament*, 3:421.

3. See Lenski, *The Epistle to the Hebrews*, 373.

4. Some have suggested the alternate translation "title deed" or "guarantee," but F. F. Bruce is correct to express caution in the face of a lack of contextual evidence (*Epistle to the Hebrews*, 277).

5. The verse does not contain a conjunction "and" (*kai*), perhaps lending support to the interpretation that the first and second halves of the verse are parallel thoughts.

conviction [that] is not a static emotion of complacency but something lively and active, not just a state of immovable dogmatism but of a vital certainty which impels the believer to stretch out his hand, as it were, and lay hold of those realities on which his hope is fixed and which, though unseen, are already his in Christ.[6]

Some realities are unseen because they belong to the spiritual realm and some because they lie in the future, when that realm will break into the earthly sphere.[7] In either case, the person of faith lives out a bold confidence in God's greater realities.

It was by a life lived in this bold confidence, this firm assurance in what was not immediately observable, that the Old Testament saints "were commended" by God (v. 2). In other words, not only did they bear witness to God, he bore witness to them, affirming their lives of faith.

This principle of faith grasping the reality of the invisible may be seen in the believer's confession that God created the world (v. 3). The author states what would have been a foundational point of theology for his community, namely, that God brought the visible, created order into being by his word and out of nothing. The author of Hebrews probably has in mind the creation song of Genesis 1, in which the creative word of God called forth the various aspects of creation.[8] Faith is what looks at that created order and has a firm and resolute confidence in the God to whom it bears witness, who, though unseen, has provided a foundation for such a confidence through his mighty acts.

Movement 1: First Examples of Faith (11:4–12)

THE WRITER NOW follows, in sequence, great examples of faithfulness from Genesis, beginning with Abel and progressing to an initial discussion of Abraham's faith. In each example the emphasis lies both on an act accomplished by faith and the right spiritual posture of the exemplar.

By faith Abel presented God with a sacrifice superior to that of Cain (v. 4). The account of this action in Genesis 4:4 does not provide us with details as to why Abel's offering was pleasing to God and Cain's was not, but we are given hints. Abel's sacrifice consisted of "fat portions from some of the firstborn of his flock," which may speak to his giving the best of what he had. Notice that the Genesis text reports "the LORD looked in favor *on Abel* and his offering," while he rejected Cain and his offering. Cain had not done

---

6. Hughes, *A Commentary on the Epistle to the Hebrews*, 440–41.

7. Bruce, *Epistle to the Hebrews*, 277, fn. 11.

8. Ibid., 279.

what was right (4:7), revealing that *he himself* was not right spiritually. His brother Abel, by contrast, was "a righteous man" (according to Heb. 11:4), the author tying Abel's example back to the Old Testament quotation found in 10:37–38, which states, "But my righteous one will live by faith." Consequently, he was "commended" by God[9] and still today "speaks" even though he has been dead for a long time. His attitude and action were such that his example of faithfulness continues among people of faith.[10] Thus Hebrews emphasizes this vital link between internal attitudes and external actions.

The emphasis in the Enoch example (11:5–6) rests even more squarely on the importance of one's spiritual posture. This faithful believer, according to Hebrews' interpretation of the Old Testament text, was taken out of this world by God without experiencing death (Gen. 5:24). Why? Because in his life he was "commended as one who pleased God"; that is, he brought God pleasure. This observation reflects a conviction inherent to the Genesis text, which tells us that Enoch "walked with God." Most significantly, however, the author still has in mind the quotation of Habakkuk 2:3–4 (Heb. 10:37–38), which speaks of God's lack of pleasure toward one who shrinks back from commitment. By contrast, Enoch was resolute in his commitment, thus bringing God pleasure.

Although the Old Testament text does not mention Enoch's faith, our author can assume that he exemplifies such a stance towards God, based on that Habakkuk quote. "Without faith," he goes on to tell us in 11:6, "it is impossible to please God, because anyone who comes to him must believe that he exists and that he rewards those who earnestly seek him." In other words, the life of faith may be said to have at least three components. (1) It involves a life of coming to God and seeking him earnestly. This point is in keeping with the author's challenge to approach or draw near to God (4:16; 10:22). Thus God's people are called to live lives of radical openness to and in conversation with God.

(2) This life of faith involves believing that God exists. It is absurd to think that a person can sincerely come to God in prayer without a firm confidence in his existence. A foundational belief in God supports further acts of faith in which the believer comes to God for help.

(3) This life of faith involves confidence that God will reward those who exercise such faith. The acts of persons expressing confidence in the living

---

9. In biblical literature God is the witness par excellence since he has the ability to look at a person's heart (Jer. 42:5). His testimony is certain (Ps. 19:8) and greater than that of people (1 John 5:9). See Spicq, *Theological Lexicon of the New Testament*, 2:447.

10. Attridge, *Epistle to the Hebrews*, 317. Attridge points to a quote from Philo, *Quod deterius potiori insidiari soleat*, 48: "[Abel] is alive with the happy life in God. To this the declaration of Scripture shall be our witness, where Abel is found quite manifestly using his 'voice' and 'crying out' the wrongs which he has suffered."

God do not go unnoticed or unrewarded. God, by his nature and in accordance with his promises, rewards those who act in faith toward him.

Rounding off his account of exemplars prior to Abraham, the author introduces Noah (Gen. 6:1–9:17), the first to act in faith based on a message from God. Noah acted on the divine warning in regard to a flood that was not yet seen and did so "in holy fear" (a form of the verb *eulabeomai*, meaning that he paid close and reverent attention to God's instruction). Accordingly, Noah built an ark to save his family and, correspondingly, condemned the world. His building of the ark both bore witness to the unseen God and his Word and constituted a stark, prophetic rebuke to that godless generation.[11] Their unbelief stands in bold relief to Noah's faith stance toward God. As one who lived by faith, or confident boldness, with regard to God's Word, he became an heir of righteousness.

The author now moves to an extensive treatment of the greatest example of faith in the Old Testament, Abraham the patriarch. Verses 8–12 focus on two foundational events from the great exemplar's life as evidencing his faith. (1) Abraham obediently followed God's call to move to a place with which he was unfamiliar (see Gen. 12:1–9). Abram's father, Terah, originally had taken his son Abram and his family from Ur of the Chaldeans and settled in Haran, intending to go to Canaan (Gen. 11:31). In Haran Abram received the word of the Lord (12:1–3):

Leave your country, your people and your father's household and go to the land I will show you.

I will make you into a great nation
  and I will bless you;
I will make your name great,
  and you will be a blessing.
I will bless those who bless you,
  and whoever curses you I will curse;
and all peoples on earth
  will be blessed through you.

Abraham demonstrates his faith by obeying God, even though he was completely unfamiliar with the land to which he was going. This thought continues the motif that faith consists of acting with reference to the unseen. It is important to note that the promise that his descendants would inherit the land did not come until Abraham was already in Canaan, and the promise would not be realized by Abraham himself but by his offspring. Thus, he did not go to the land to possess it but to live out an act of obedience to God.

---

11. Lane, *Hebrews 9–13*, 339–40.

Also, his mode of living in Canaan—dwelling in tents—served as a symbol of his commitment not to settle into the earthly cities of the Canaanites, but to seek a more permanent city built by God.

(2) Abraham was enabled to become a father because he believed God (see Gen. 18:10–15; 21:1–7).[12] Faith, moving beyond the normal boundaries of possibility, works miracles. Abraham, an old man, and Sarah, his wife, well past the age of being able to conceive, became parents, trusting in the faithfulness of God. Again the emphasis here challenges the hearers to take their eyes off the obvious—in this case the inability of old people to become pregnant—and to focus on the faithful God of integrity, who keeps his promises.

In verse 11 the writer alludes to Genesis 15:6: "Abram believed the LORD, and he credited it to him as righteousness." The happy result, in accordance with the promise of God (Gen. 15:5), is recorded in Hebrews 11:12: "And so from this one man, and he as good as dead, came descendants as numerous as the stars in the sky and as countless as the sand on the seashore." Out of nothing comes a multitude too numerous to count.

Interlude (11:13–16)

THE AUTHOR NOW pauses in his person-by-person account of the faithful to tease out certain implications he wishes his hearers to recognize. The interlude is both didactic (the principles here are highly instructional for their current crisis) and rhetorical (the author, ever the skilled orator, interrupts his rapid-fire list to heighten his audience's attention). The "all these" of 11:13 almost certainly refers to Abraham and his family and does not include Abel, Enoch, and Noah, since the travel motif found in verses 13–16 fits best the patriarch and his company. Enoch for sure cannot be included since the author has already noted that he did not see death (11:5), which means he was not among those "living by faith *when they died*." Rather, the focus continues on Abraham, his wife, and his son Isaac.

That "they did not receive the things promised; they only saw them and welcomed them from a distance" alludes to the content of God's promises to Abraham in Genesis 12:2–3; 15:5; 17:1–8. The possession of the land, the multitude of descendants (including those who would be kings), and the blessing of the nations all would be fulfilled in a time after Abraham and his immediate family passed from the scene.

Yet to what does the author refer when he says, "And they admitted that they were aliens and strangers on earth"? In the Old Testament narratives the

---

12. For a discussion as to whether Sarah should be understood grammatically as the subject of v. 11 see Hughes, *A Commentary on the Epistle to the Hebrews*, 471–76.

patriarchs and their descendants refer to themselves as "aliens and strangers" in the land (e.g., 1 Chron. 29:15; cf. Gen. 23:4; Ps. 39:12). Both in Jewish theology during the New Testament era and in the New Testament itself, this concept developed to emphasize the disparaging of earthly desires and the longing for a heavenly home.[13] For example 1 Peter 2:11 reads, "Dear friends, I urge you, as aliens and strangers in the world, to abstain from sinful desires, which war against your soul." In Hebrews 11:13–16 the author likewise wishes to emphasize that the patriarchs' faith relationship to God was their preeminent commitment, not the obtaining of an earthly, secure place of residence. They died in a state of trust, never having seen their descendants' reception of the land. Thus, the true object of their deepest desire was God himself and God's city. Consequently, "God is not ashamed to be called their God."

The message to the original hearers must not be missed, for their circumstance must be seen as analogous to that of the patriarchs. Perhaps their current experience of persecution has highlighted the alien nature of their earthly existence. They cannot perceive the fulfillment of God's promises to them; all they can see is the difficulty of their present crisis. The writer's point is that this is normal for people of faith. The promises of God must be embraced even though their fulfillment lies in the future. Life must be lived in our challenging, terrestrial cities in light of a better, heavenly country that will be experienced in the future. God is not ashamed of identifying with those who live in this way.

Movement 2: More Examples of Faith (11:17–31)

HEBREWS 11:17–19 CONTINUES the author's exposition on Abraham, offering a third major event exemplifying this father's faith. Abraham, in a test by God, "offered Isaac as a sacrifice." As an interpreter of Old Testament material in the tradition of the rabbis, the author of Hebrews draws out implications of Genesis 22:1–8, a brief narrative that had come to carry great significance in Jewish interpretation by the time of our book's writing.[14] This is the example par excellence of a magnanimous act of faith, born as it was of an excruciating decision placed before the patriarch by God. The crux of Abraham's crisis is the seeming contradiction between the promises of God, which were to be fulfilled through his heir, Isaac (Heb. 11:18), and the command of God to sacrifice that heir (11:17). Thus Abraham was forced into a radical posture of trusting God. Our author's logical deduction is that "Abraham reasoned that God could raise the dead" (11:19)—the only way that both the promises and the command could be fulfilled.

---

13. Ellingworth, *The Epistle to the Hebrews*, 594.
14. Attridge, *The Epistle to the Hebrews*, 333–34.

The author of Hebrews moves rapid-fire through the next three generations in his example list, using his formulaic pattern cited above (11:20–22).
By faith Isaac offered a blessing to Jacob and Esau (Gen. 27:27–40). By faith
Jacob continued the pattern, blessing the sons of Joseph, Ephraim and Man-
asseh (48:8–22). By faith Joseph himself spoke about the exodus from Egypt
and provided instructions as to what should be done with his bones (50:24–
25). In each of these events death confronted the person of faith, who spoke
of things that were as yet unseen.

Moses has been presented already as a stellar example of faithfulness in
3:1–6. In that passage the author uses the lawgiver as a picture of "servant
faithfulness," who fulfilled his duty to God as leader of the Israelites. The
author focused on the greatness of Moses to highlight the even greater status of Jesus as God's faithful Son. Moses was specially venerated by Greek-
speaking Jews of the first century as one who was unusually close to God. In
certain expressions of Jewish tradition he was considered to be the greatest
person in history.[15] Therefore, it is not surprising that in his example list
(11:23–28) the writer gives sustained attention to Moses.

The author's treatment of Moses actually begins with the faith expressed
by Moses' parents (the emphasis in the Hebrew text is on Moses' mother)
when he was a baby: "By faith Moses' parents hid him for three months after
he was born, because they saw he was no ordinary child, and they were not
afraid of the king's edict." This synopsis recounts the narrative of Exodus 2:1–
4. Two points of the retelling are significant. (1) In describing the child Moses,
the author of Hebrews follows the LXX in using the word *asteion*, a word meaning "beautiful, attractive." The only other New Testament text to use the word
is Acts 7:20, where we are told that Moses was "beautiful before God." This
probably communicates a superior quality about the child. Thus, the NIV
translates Hebrews 11:23 with the phrase "no ordinary child." The writer,
therefore, depicts the parents as having spiritual insight into his significance.[16]

(2) As a result of this insight they directly disregarded the king's command
to drown the boy in the Nile (Ex. 1:22). The author of Hebrews states that "they
were not afraid of the king's edict," deducing this fact from their action of hid-
ing the child. This lack of fear does not speak to the parents' not having the
negative emotions we generally associate with fear, but rather suggests a firm
boldness in which they refused to shrink before the hostility of Pharaoh.

Moses himself also exhibited such boldness, and the writer to the Hebrews
points out three events from the lawgiver's life that illustrate his faith. (1)

---

15. Mary Rose D'Angelo, *Moses in the Letter to the Hebrews*, SBLDS 4 (Missoula: Scholars,
1979), 91–131.

16. Hagner, *Hebrews*, 202.

Moses chose to identify with God's people rather than with the godless (11:24–26). The author already has made much of the virtue of standing with those under duress because of their commitment to God (e.g., 10:32–34). Moses chose his biological family over his adoptive family at great personal cost: loss of wealth, relinquishment of status, and intense mistreatment. The author explains that he "regarded disgrace for the sake of Christ as of greater value than the treasures of Egypt." The NIV's "disgrace for the sake of Christ" (lit., "disgrace of Christ") renders the genitive *tou Christou* in terms of the "benefit" or "advantage" for Christ. Yet, the sense of this phrase may be understood more accurately as "the disgrace experienced by Christ." P. E. Hughes comments:

> [This disgrace] was not simply the reproach accepted by identifying himself with the people of God but, more precisely, the reproach of the coming Messiah with whom he was united by faith. Hence (as Stephen reminded his accusers) his assurance to the Israelites: "God will raise up for you a prophet from your brethren as he raised me up" (Acts 7:37); and hence, also, the rebuke of Jesus Christ to his adversaries: "If you believed Moses, you would believe me, for he wrote of me" (John 5:46).[17]

Thus Moses experienced the same kind of reproach experienced later by Christ—rejection faced by a prophet standing on the side of God, proclaiming the word of the Lord in boldness against an ungodly generation.

(2) By faith Moses left Egypt and persevered in the mission given him by God (11:27). This verse seems to discount Exodus 2:14, which says that Moses was afraid concerning the consequences of his act of killing the Egyptian. But the author of Hebrews wishes to emphasize the boldness of Moses' actions rather than his negative emotion of dread. He made a decision to leave Egypt, and that step the writer understands as a step of faith. In line with his larger emphasis on endurance (e.g., 10:32, 36; 12:1–3, 7), the author notes that Moses persevered because he paid attention to the unseen God rather than to a visible king.

(3) By faith Moses led the Israelites in the observance of the Passover ordinance (11:28). The mention of "the sprinkling of blood" calls to mind the author's earlier references to Christ's sacrifice as paralleling the old covenant sacrificial rituals (9:12–14, 18–22). Here, however, he specifically has in mind the smearing of blood on the Israelites' door posts to avoid the death angel's work. This act was an act of faith since Moses led the Israelites in obedience to God's command with regard to an as-yet-unseen event.

---

17. Hughes, *Commentary on the Epistle to the Hebrews*, 496–97.

The author rounds out his primary example list with three other events from the life of God's covenant people. In 11:29 he mentions briefly the crossing of the Red Sea (see Ex. 13:17–14:31). The confession that they passed through the body of water "by faith" does much to illustrate the emphasis the author puts on acts of obedience carried out in light of God's command. This group of people, according to the Old Testament narrative, in general was marked by timidity, complaining, and a *lack* of trust in God or his deliverance, as the author already has detailed in Hebrews 3:7–19. However, when God told them to "move on" (Ex. 14:15) they did so, and this constituted an act exemplifying faith.[18]

In obedience to another seemingly illogical command, the Israelites, under the command of Joshua, marched around the city of Jericho for seven days. Their obedience was rewarded with the walls falling down (11:30).

Finally, Rahab, in accordance with God's will, helped the spies who had come to investigate the land (Josh. 2:1–15). Her faith is expressed in her confession of 2:9 ("I know the LORD has given this land to you") and was rewarded with deliverance from death.

Crescendo and Conclusion (11:32–40)

THE AUTHOR REALIZES that time constraints do not permit him to continue a detailed account of old covenant men and women of faith.[19] So, with the rhetorical "and what more shall I say?" he turns a corner, finishing the section with what one commentator calls a "sledge-hammer style"[20] summary of Old Testament and, perhaps, intertestamental acts of faith.

The writer begins his summary with six figures spanning the era of the judges through the united monarchy, and to these adds the expansive "the prophets." Many commentators note that the six names are not listed in chronological order, since the author, rather, intends to provide random examples of valor in the face of great challenges.[21] Presumably he hoped to

---

18. Lane, *Hebrews 9–13*, 377–78.

19. The phrase translated "I do not have time to tell," found widely in both classical oratory and Philo, is highly stylistic. See Bruce, *Epistle to the Hebrews*, 320. The author of Hebrews does, in fact, go on to tell of those he has in mind but in a much more succinct fashion than his treatment thus far. I once heard a gifted preacher use this device. He proclaimed, "I don't have time to tell you about . . . ," then proceeded to give the audience a stirring account of all that he did not have time to preach on! The homiletical device was quite effective.

20. Lenski, *The Interpretation of the Epistle of Hebrews and of the Epistle of James*, 415, citing A. T. Robertson.

21. E.g., Ellingworth, *The Epistle to the Hebrews*, 623; Hughes, *A Commentary on the Epistle to the Hebrews*, 506. Samuel may be listed last of those named to place him in conjunction with "the prophets."

prompt his audience to think of memorable events behind these names. The list of mighty deeds that follows would call to mind a host of those who lived faithfully before God in a hostile world. This is the intention of an example list—to provide a sample of people and events that point to a much larger body of data that can be brought to bear on a given subject—and the author brings his list to a crescendo with enviable skill.

Gideon, of course, serves as a powerful example of faith, since he and his three hundred select men routed the massive Midianite army with torches and empty jars (Judg. 7:7–25). Barak, a military leader who served under Deborah, led Israel in a defeat of Sisera and the Canaanites (4:8–16). Samson, in spite of his vices, served as a great champion of the Israelites during a period of Philistine oppression (13:1–16:31), and Jephthah, in spite of his foolish, horrific vow, led in the defeat of the Amorites and Ammonites (10:6–12:7). Samuel serves as somewhat a bridge-figure between the time of the judges and the united monarchy,[22] with his great commitment and sensitivity to God's laying the foundation for the monarchy's golden years. David (the only king named), although having his own faults and grievous sins, lived a life of devotion to God, performing outstanding acts for God. Finally, the author of Hebrews mentions "the prophets," presenting a host of stellar figures who, by their words and deeds, lived for the unseen God in mostly hostile circumstances.

The passage now turns from the great "performers" of faith to their actions (11:33–38). They "through faith conquered kingdoms," especially calling to mind the period of the judges through the reign of King David. That they "administered justice" speaks of governmental administration and is an extension of their conquering. As God's servants they carried out his justice and righteousness to the people under their rule (e.g., 2 Sam. 8:15; 1 Kings 10:9).

These saints of old "gained what was promised," an affirmation that can be interpreted as their reception of the promises themselves or as their reception of the *fulfillment* of those promises. From the context it would seem that the emphasis lies on God's giving them promises, some of which were not fulfilled in the receptor's lifetime (cf. 11:39).[23] Nevertheless, the covenant promises to Abraham's children, such as the Promised Land and the promise of God's abiding presence with his people, are certainly in view. The author's twin points are that the promise-making God is faithful to his oaths, and that people of faith live in light of God's promises. With this confession the author echoes his earlier treatment of God's oaths in 6:13–20.

These great heroes of the faith, moreover, "shut the mouths of lions," an obvious reference to that great exemplar Daniel, of whom it was written,

---

22. Hughes, *A Commentary on the Epistle to the Hebrews*, 507.

23. Yet see, e.g., Josh. 21:43–45, which emphasizes the fulfillment of God's promises to his people.

"no wound was found on him, because he had trusted in his God" (Dan. 6:23). Daniel's associates, Shadrach, Meshach, and Abednego, who were cast into the furnace because of their stubborn refusal to serve false gods, "quenched the fury of the flames" (3:16–30). Several prophets, including Elijah, Elisha, and Jeremiah, "escaped the edge of the sword."

There were many others "whose weakness was turned to strength; and who became powerful in battle and routed foreign armies." One thinks, for example, of the boy David facing Goliath, or of Gideon, a most unimpressive figure of his day; nevertheless, God used both as instruments of power and victory. The author may also have in mind the Maccabees, who, during our author's time, were considered among the greatest of military heroes of history. Even death could not stop the work of God on behalf of his people, for women such as the poor widow of Zarephath and the woman of Shunem received their sons back from the dead by the hands of Elijah and Elisha respectively (1 Kings 17:17–24; 2 Kings 4:17–37).

In the middle of verse 35 the writer to the Hebrews shifts gears from more positive outcomes encountered by faith to faith expressed in the face of great hardship. Although some experienced resurrection, others expressed faith by embracing torture and death, refusing deliverance in light of a greater reward beyond the grave. F. F. Bruce, for example, points to the account of Eleazar of the Maccabean period, who chose death over disloyalty to God (2 Macc. 6:19, 28). He also refers to the story of a mother and her seven sons who spoke eloquently of the afterlife even while being tortured to death (2 Macc. 7:1–41; 4 Macc. 8:1–17:24).[24] It could have been said of many throughout the era of the prophets, the intertestamental period, and even the New Testament era that they "faced jeers and flogging while still others were chained and put in prison." The author has already stated these uncomfortable circumstances had occurred among those in the community to which he is writing (Heb. 10:32–34).

Still others "were stoned" (e.g., Jeremiah, according to tradition), "sawed in two" (the fate of Isaiah, according to tradition), or "put to death by the sword." When the author speaks of those who wore "sheepskins and goatskins," who were "destitute, persecuted and mistreated," wandering "in deserts and mountains, and in caves and holes in the ground" (11:37–38), he may be referring to prophets such as Elijah, Elisha, and Ezekiel, as suggested by Clement of Rome (1 Clement 17:1). But these words also describe the Jews persecuted under Antiochus IV Epiphanes during the Maccabean revolt.[25] By its rejection of such great figures of faith, the world condemned itself as unworthy of those who live for an eternal reward (11:38).

---

24. Bruce, *Epistle to the Hebrews*, 325–26.
25. Ibid., 329.

The author concludes his example list with a fitting epilogue (11:39–40), contrasting these great exemplars of faith, who were commended by God, with the new covenant community. The wording of verse 39 echoes that of 11:2, forming an *inclusio* that marks the beginning and ending of the passage.[26] When the author notes that the great heroes of faith "were commended by God," he means that God himself had borne witness to their faithfulness. They had faced a plethora of trials, tortures, and tests and, therefore, paralleled the challenging experiences of the recipients of this book, who, however, had yet to experience martyrdom (12:4). Moreover, by living out faith in the unseen God these men and women of history had established themselves as appropriate examples for the hearers, who were now being faced with choosing the path of faith or the alternative, the path of faithlessness.

The author's main point through his example list is that faith is the only right path for God's people. The heroes of faith demonstrate a resolute determination to live faithfully even though "none of them received what was promised." True, the author has mentioned that some indeed did receive certain promises (11:11, 33), but his point here is that they did not receive "the *definitive* fulfillment of God's promise," that is, the eternal inheritance known through the new covenant established by Christ.[27]

When the author says that "God had planned something better for us so that only together with us would they be made perfect" (v. 40), he means that historically these people of old did not experience the coming of Messiah and the new covenant. Yet now they are made "perfect," seeing that the great community of faith that had lived for God throughout history has been "brought to fulfillment" or "to a desired goal."[28] Their faith in God has been vindicated since God has broken into the world in the person of his Son, Jesus Christ. With us they now know the perfecting power of Christ's sacrifice and the eternal inheritance of the saints.

TO STAY WITH the step-by-step progression of thought in the first ten chapters of Hebrews one must remain focused, analytical, and persevering. We have followed an argument that has taken us from heaven to earth and back to heaven again in dealing with truths about God's Son, our great high priest. Furthermore, interwoven between sections

---

26. On the uses of *inclusio* in Hebrews see above, p. 71.
27. Lane, *Hebrews 9–13*, 392.
28. On the author's use of the concept of perfection see above, pp. 108, 191.

dealing with Christ's person and work, the author has challenged his readers relentlessly with promises and warnings, good examples and bad, words of encouragement and harsh rebuke. We have trekked through beautiful but imposing theological and homiletical terrain. Now, suddenly, we have come up over a rise to find Hebrews 11 stretched before us like a lovely, powerful, rolling river, winding its way across our path.

The beauty of the author's example list in chapter 11 draws us into a melodic and sweeping look at God's people down through the biblical ages. The change to a new ordering of material, one that is more narrative in approach, presents a pleasing shift of pace. However, we must not allow the change or its beauty to blind us to the author's intention for this chapter—he wishes to challenge his readers to bold living for God.

Thus far in our treatment of Hebrews 11, we have worked our way through the rather lengthy catalogue of examples. For all its length, the chapter really presents us with a simple message that must not be missed: *The life of faith is the only life that pleases God.* The author uses the phrase "by faith" repeatedly throughout the chapter, calling the hearers to the manner by which one must live for God. The whole point of his example list is to provide voluminous evidence that faith is the posture by which people live lives of purposeful impact by and for God. We are convinced, as the original hearers certainly must have been, that these great heroes of faith are merely representatives of a much larger host to whom God has offered commendation. Yet, it may take some doing to imagine their circumstances and accomplishment as applicable to us. This brings us to the first pitfall that must be addressed before we can apply the passage to our contemporary contexts.

Pitfall 1: "I'm no hero." As the author of Hebrews showcases spiritual luminaries marched before us across the stage of history, there exists a danger for us as contemporary readers. These people are different from us, we may reason. After all, *they are in the Bible.* So of course they were able to act nobly in relation to the unseen God and in response to a hostile world! We may see ourselves, by contrast, as much too normal, or worldly, or powerless to live extraordinary lives of faith.

But if this is our perspective we miss the whole point—this life of faith is normal for the people of God. This is "mere" Christianity, as C. S. Lewis put it. The author's whole program is to call struggling, sometimes bumbling Christians to live boldly by faith. He calls *us*—with all our habits and hangups, warts and worries—to action. We are called to step out of step with the world, hop up on the stage of history, and take our place in God's roll call of the faithful. Of course we are inadequate; but so have been all others who have evidenced the grace of God. It would not be grace otherwise.

There are our brothers and sisters around the world, in places like Saudi Arabia, China, and Cuba, who have long been thrust into lives of conflict in which faith is a necessary tool for survival. They are forced to discover their own spiritual fortitude, many living faithfully in light of eternity, in light of the unseen God and his kingdom. Those of us in the West often have lived, by contrast, in relative comfort with what is "seen." Why focus on the coming world when the present one seems so nice? But this state of affairs may be changing. Philip Yancey, in his potent book *What's So Amazing About Grace?* writes:

> The culture war is under way. Ironically, every year the church in the United States draws closer and closer to the situation faced by the New Testament church: an embattled minority living in a pluralistic, pagan society. Christians in places like Sri Lanka, Tibet, Sudan, and Saudi Arabia have faced open hostility from their governments for years. But in the United States, with a history so congenial to the faith, we don't like it.[29]

Thus Hebrews 11, a text highly relevant to any believer, may have increasing relevance even for those of us in parts of the world historically congenial to Christians. We must be ready, practicing faith in the little things of bank accounts and boardrooms, if we are to honor God with greater opportunities. In whatever our situation, we must hear God's call to join the ranks of faith examples.

Pitfall 2: Misconceptions of faith. Another of our challenges in applying this chapter to contemporary life is the work of getting past certain misconceptions of faith. Use of the term "faith" calls to mind different things for different people. Here I mention four misconceptions, the first two normally held in Christian circles, and the second two normally held in the broader culture. (1) There is faith as *faith in God's goodness to me.* This expression can be found in the "health-and-wealth" corners of Christendom as well as among other, idealistic Christians, who reason that a good God can only produce good things in lives lived in a good way. To these faith only has one aim, one fruit—a life of ease, blessing, and bounty. There is, of course, truth to the claim that God wishes to bless his children, but this vision of faith comes crashing down on the rocks of reality. Certainly God is the giver of good gifts (James 1:17), but those gifts sometimes come wrapped in odd packages (James 1:2–4).

(2) At times faith is misunderstood as summed up in a *faith-equals-creed* approach. The New Testament does refer to "the faith" as a set of beliefs (e.g., Gal. 1:23; 1 Tim. 4:1, 6; Jude 3), but generally the concept of faith

---

29. Philip Yancey, *What's So Amazing About Grace?* (Grand Rapids: Zondervan, 1997), 241.

denotes something much more dynamic and active—a life lived in a trust relationship with God. This active faith certainly rests on sound belief, but it cannot be summed up by "cognitive assent" (James 2:14–26). The stance of "faith-equals-creed" remains a danger for anyone who rightly places a great deal of emphasis on doctrine.

(3) Both those sympathetic and those hostile to religion can misunderstand faith as a *blind leap* into the unknown.[30] Many moderns, for example, misunderstand faith as the antithesis of scientific endeavor. They reason that a true scientist cannot be a person of faith, for scientists are people grounded in facts. Even those of the broader culture sympathetic to religious belief often see faith as a warm-hearted step into the black, cavernous hole of one's hopes or dreams. "You've just got to have faith" most often means, "You've just got to act contrary to all that you know to be true and trust that things are going to work out the way you want them to."

(4) Still others understand faith as *a life of reflective devotion* to any god one happens to follow. "She is a person of deep faith" may be applied to a follower of Buddha, Krishna, or Christ. Thus, faith is seen as fairly synonymous with spirituality. In contradistinction to the faith-equals-creed approach, this definition of faith suggests that a particular set of beliefs is in essence unimportant. What matters is a sincerity and, perhaps, a commitment that transforms the individual into a more purposeful, loving person.

But none of these approaches to faith—faith as God's goodness to me, faith as creed, faith as a blind leap, and faith as reflective devotion—does justice to the dynamic, challenging portrait of authentic Christian faith as presented in Hebrews 11. This picture, when carefully analyzed, eclipses the false visions of faith detailed above, showing them to be inadequate.

Faith as "defined" by Hebrews 11. As portrayed in the lives of God's faithful through the ages, (1) *faith involves confident action.* Most of the examples delineated in Hebrews 11 involve a person acting confidently in accordance with what God says. By faith Abel offered to God a superior sacrifice, Noah built an ark, Abraham obeyed by leaving familiar territory and later by offering Isaac, Isaac blessed his sons, and one of those sons blessed Isaac's great-grandsons, and on the list goes. The author spits out action words in rapid succession in verses 32–34: they conquered, administered, gained, shut, quenched, escaped, became powerful, and routed. Faith acts out a bold confidence.

(2) True faith is action *taken in response to the unseen God and his promises.* Faith, rather than merely static belief or cognitive assent, spurs one to act in accordance with God's truth. Its boldness, however, seems especially to do with

---

30. See the discussion above, pp. 164–65.

the fact that these great people of faith are backed up by the Unseen. They step forward with eyebrow-raising tenacity and confidence and with no perceptible reason for doing so. But God has spoken. God has manifested himself, and this is reason enough. Therefore, we too are called to an active, confident faith that finds its reason in the unseen God. If we have faith of another stripe, we need to reevaluate our "faith."

(3) *Faith involves God's working extraordinary miracles in the lives of ordinary people.* We call the example list of Hebrews 11 the "Hall of Faith" and think of these inductees as especially heroic. Yet if we stop and reflect for a moment, we realize that there is much about those on the list that was less than admirable. Noah, for example, got drunk and lay naked in his tent; Abraham lied about Sarah; Isaac lied about Rebekah; Jacob was a deceiver; Moses committed murder; the people of Israel were a bunch of ungrateful grumblers, Gideon a doubter, and David an adulterer. We may think that the author of Hebrews is stretching things a bit in holding these people up as exemplary if not for one thing— real faith must be expressed by real people, real pilgrims who have yet to reach the heavenly city. They are searching; they have not yet arrived. These are "heroes" not because they are perfect, but because they worked with God in his perfect work. Thus, we too are eligible for enlistment in the life of faith.

(4) *Faith works in a variety of situations.* It is striking that in the list of Hebrews 11 we do not have one healing, although support for that form of miracle can be found readily elsewhere in the New Testament. We have an offering, a transportation to heaven, the building of a boat, the moving of a family, the ability to have a child, obedience in offering that child back to God, the blessing of children, seeing into the future, defying an authority, the choosing of mistreatment above pleasure, the keeping of a religious ordinance, suffering persecution, and so on. Faith involves conquering in war, deliverance from animals and fire, and resurrection.

(5) Biblical faith *may have a variety of outcomes* as well. Notice that faith sometimes has an immediate, "positive" outcome, as when the children of Israel passed through the sea, the walls of Jericho fell, and widows received their dead back by resurrection. But we also find that faith can be rewarded with a "delayed" outcome or even a "negative" outcome. Abel still got murdered. Abraham had to wait for the son of the promise. Faith can also involve being tortured, mocked, beaten, destitute, stoned, put in prison, generally mistreated, and even mutilated. These do not fit easily into the "see all the wonderful things God wants to do in your life" gospel of modern, Western Christianity. Yet the picture is biblical. Our application of this passage must point out that faithful people sometimes do not see "results" in this life.

(6) However, *faith is rewarded by God.* One resounding point of Hebrews 11 is that God's pilgrims look beyond the immediate to grasp the significance

of the ultimate. Faith involves believing "that he rewards those who earnestly seek him." One primary reward stands out in this chapter—God's commendation (11:2, 39), his "well done" that every true believer longs to hear.

So what have we found characterizes biblical faith as depicted in Hebrews 11? What might be a definition? *Faith is confidence that results in action carried out in a variety of situations by ordinary people in response to the unseen God and his promises, with various earthly outcomes but always the ultimate outcome of God's commendation and reward.* In its essence biblical faith involves people orienting their lives to God and his values against the "perceived" realities and values espoused by the world. Just as faith was applicable in a wide variety of situations during the biblical era, so our applications might be quite varied.

Those of our brothers and sisters around the world who "by faith" are facing severe persecution and death are an example to the rest of us. But we too are called to the life of faith. This means that in family life, work, education, intellect, social life, and countless other contexts we are called to reject a posture of fear and to live our lives with bold confidence in the unseen God, his Word, and his ultimate reward. Thus the life of faith—true, biblical faith—works to integrate life, and we must focus on greater realities than those easily seen with the eye, touched by the hand, or bought with financial resources.

ON BECOMING ORDINARY "heroes." How would you and I live today if we believed absolutely that God existed and loved us completely and had a destination for us that made all the world pale by just one square foot of its turf? How would we live if we believed that God cared about our every action and every concern and wished to reward us magnanimously for our faith? How would you and I live in the face of opposition if we believed in God, really believed as if our whole lives depended on him and his? You say, "But I do; I do believe absolutely. I believe with all I am and all I have."

Then how would you live differently if you did not believe? Would there be much difference? This is a critical question. If all I am and have and do differs little from my unbelieving neighbor, then I have embraced his world and his values and fool myself by saying I am living for another world and kingdom values. My life must be radically different in what I embrace—the values of a heavenly kingdom. When I live "by faith," I then will be one to whom God can bear witness and one who bears witness to God in such a way that others will be stimulated to faith. My life will portray that "faith works!" Then I will be a "hero" in the best sense of the word, for I will live a life that helps others and honors Another. Then I will be extraordinary, having chosen a narrow path.

This is not the provenance of "super Christians," however. Do not check the "Not Applicable" box yet. As Christians we are extraordinary because of what God has done in the midst of and in spite of our spiritual dullness. Speaking of the humbling amateurishness of those with whom God works, author Annie Dillard writes:

> A high school stage play is more polished than this service we have been rehearsing since the year one. In two thousand years, we have not worked out the kinks. We positively glorify them. Week after week we witness the same miracle: that God is so mighty he can stifle his own laughter. Week after week, we witness the same miracle: that God, for reasons unfathomable, refrains from blowing our dancing bear act to smithereens. Week after week Christ washes the disciples' dirty feet, handles their very toes, and repeats, It is all right—believe it or not—to be people.[31]

Just a few pages later Dillard reflects on a tall Catholic priest in his sixties who, "when he knelt at the altar, and when he rose from kneeling, his knees cracked. It was a fine church music, this sound of his cracking knees."[32] So God makes his own sweet, often unappreciated music with second-hand, pawn-shop instruments cast off by the world. Only eternity will reveal their true worth, but at times even earth time gives glimpses.

Living boldly. A great and significant shift in the posture of Eastern European Christians happened during the 1970s. For years members of the underground church had met in secret, used code for communication, rarely talked on public telephones, and wrote pseudonymous essays for underground papers. Believers in Poland and Czechoslovakia decided that this posture of fear must change, so they began to live boldly, meeting openly, signing their names and addresses to articles, and handing out newspapers on street corners. They paid a price for their dissidence, such as time in jail, but they reaped a much greater reward as the infrastructure of communist ideology began to crumble before their eyes. A rag-tag group of peasants, poets, and clergy brought down a seemingly impregnable ideological fortress—by faith.[33]

In May 1990, the May Day Celebration was carried out in Red Square as dusk began to settle on the U.S.S.R. Myriads of troops and tanks filed through

---

31. Annie Dillard, *Teaching a Stone to Talk: Expeditions and Encounters* (New York: Harper & Row, 1982), 20.

32. Ibid., 28.

33. Yancey, *What's So Amazing About Grace?* 261–62.

the Square in an impressive, oppressive show of force as banners and pictures of Marx, Lenin, and Engels pointed to the sky. Communist leaders watched the scene from a seemingly unapproachable platform, as the common person was held back by barricades.

> Suddenly, eight men began pushing their way thorough the barricades. The police and the army tried to run over and stop them, but six of them got away and rushed between tanks to the front of the platform while Gorbachev looked down. One of them shouted, "Mikhail Sergeyevich, Christ has risen!" and lifted an 8-foot-high crucifix into the sky. And the crowd responded with a great swell, "Christ is risen, indeed!"[34]

A bold act. An act of faith. An act undertaken in light of the unseen but living God. The staunchest structures of the world have given way before God's pilgrims of faith.

We are challenged by our contemporaries around the world who have lived out such public, God-honoring displays of courage. Yet the life of faith, the life of bold confidence in God, is not only the call of those forced by oppression to stand or shrink before a hostile world. God's examples of this virtue may be found in all corners of the world and in a wide variety of circumstances.

John and Brenda Green, friends and fellow church members of mine, recently sat on their front lawn as they watched their house burn. Church people and pastors gathered around them, consoling them in their loss. John is a doctor. The home was beautiful, filled with beautiful things. As I arrived on the scene, the first thing Brenda said to me was, "George, pray for our neighbors. This is going to give us a great opportunity to witness to them." Later, as a helper aided in cleaning up the inside of the charred and smoke-smeared interior, she commented to Brenda on the devastating loss. Brenda replied with conviction, "All we lost were material things." For John and Brenda the kingdom and people are more important than their possessions.

Prior to the fire, a single mother from our church who has come far in her faith in the past year was living with them, a testimony to John and Brenda's priorities. That faith has sustained them thus far through a difficult chapter of their lives. Faith is seeing beyond the smoke-clouded, hard-nosed realities of this world to a greater and lasting reality. Helen Keller once noted, "I can see ... in what you call the dark, but which to me is golden. I can see a God-made world, not a man-made world."[35]

---

34. Charles Colson, "Can Society Survive Without Christianity?" *Veritas Vincit* (Fall 1997): 7.

35. As quoted in Karey Swan, *Hearth and Home: Recipes for Life* (Evergreen, Colo.: Singing Springs, 1997): 148.

By faith the director of an inner-city youth outreach program ministers to at-risk teens. By faith a missionary couple shares the gospel with Arab Muslims over a span of decades. By faith a businessman lives with integrity and openness about his relationship with Christ—and is fired by an unbelieving boss. By faith a money manager gives three-quarters of his income to the church's work, setting a financial cap on his family's standard of living. By faith a successful saleswoman leaves her job to enroll in seminary, believing that God has called her to the mission field. By faith a church decides to stay in a land-locked, downtown location, rather than moving to suburbia, believing God has not abandoned the residents of the downtown area. By faith these all live out their lives as if God "exists and . . . rewards those who earnestly seek him" (v. 6).

A "blind" and focused journey. My wife, Pat, and I just celebrated our ten-year anniversary. For our honeymoon ten years ago we were to fly into El Paso, Texas. From there we would drive up into the southern Rockies of New Mexico to my aunt's cabin. On the day of our flight, however, El Paso (yes, El Paso, Texas!) received a record twenty-two inches of snow—a real blizzard by West Texas standards. Being unable to land because of conditions, we were taken on to Phoenix (I had gotten food poisoning the day before at a five-star restaurant and was still suffering the effect, but that is another story).

Immediately upon touching down, however, the pilot informed us that the snowstorm had stopped. He told us to stay on the jet; we were going back to El Paso. Yet by the time we got back to El Paso the storm had cranked up its white fury again, and the pilot now told us we would be landing "in almost zero visibility." This was not comforting. The jet descended through a white, winter curtain that opened only at the last second, revealing the ghostly lights of the runway. We flew in on the instruments, and the ride was neither comfortable nor enjoyable. I do not like flying blind.

The Christian journey is a sure-but-blinded flight, brought home on the instruments of divine revelation. The blinding sin-rage and naturalistic wisdom of the age blow relentlessly against the windshield of our progress in the faith, but faith keeps a steady nose pointed to where God's Word indicates we have a promised destination. Just as the pilot in the storm had a bold though, perhaps, tension-filled confidence in his flight plan, so the Christian lives step by steady step on a path whose Maker and end are imperceptible to an earthbound eye.

I lie awake in bed some nights listening to the night noises that play around the rooms of my semirural home in Tennessee. My wife stirs comfortably next to me; the old oak beams crack in the cold; pipes pop; a log falls in the fireplace. Occasionally a pack of coyotes ventures to our side of the cornfield across the road, tossing its unsettling, surreal yelp-barks to the sky and down through our roof upon sleepy ears. Yet, there is a sound that brings great comfort to me as I lie awake. Our gas heating unit resides in the attic on the bedroom end of the house. Suddenly, as I strain to listen for a child's cough or an intruder's step, the gas burner ignites with a gentle "whoosh." Almost immediately the electric brain of the contraption clicks and begins to blow warmth throughout every cooling corner of our home. In the dead of winter I have become fairly adept at judging the temperature outside by the frequency with which the heater rumbles to life inside. The heater, mostly unseen, makes its presence ever known by surrounding my family with its radiance. Its presence rumbles in the background of my life, weaving a thread of comfort through night after dark night, as I lie awake and listen to my wife's gentle breathing.

During these nighttime awakenings, at this stage in my life, I am tempted to hear the call of various fears: the fear that something might happen to Pat or one of the children; fear that something might happen to me, preventing me from being there for my family; fear that I might not be able to follow through on a project (like this book!); fear of evil people who oppose the gospel; fear of something going wrong at work; fear of mid-life; and so on and so forth. There is much of which to be afraid in this dark and morbid world. One session of the evening news provides ample evidence that the world has much harm to offer us as people. These fears call me to shrink back from life and, at times, from the Lifegiver. As people of faith we must not answer this call.

Although the world is dark, the presence of God rumbles in the background, blowing evidence of his presence and blessings into its every corner. It is a comforting presence, a warming against the cold night of meaninglessness, hostile selfishness, and fear that otherwise would consume us. How cold the world would be if not for the unseen God. How comforted those who know the path of faith, who have submitted themselves to the beautiful work of God in their groping lives. There really is no other way to *live*.

Hebrews 12:1–17

THEREFORE, SINCE WE are surrounded by such a great cloud of witnesses, let us throw off everything that hinders and the sin that so easily entangles, and let us run with perseverance the race marked out for us. ²Let us fix our eyes on Jesus, the author and perfecter of our faith, who for the joy set before him endured the cross, scorning its shame, and sat down at the right hand of the throne of God. ³Consider him who endured such opposition from sinful men, so that you will not grow weary and lose heart.

⁴In your struggle against sin, you have not yet resisted to the point of shedding your blood. ⁵And you have forgotten that word of encouragement that addresses you as sons:

"My son, do not make light of the Lord's discipline,
and do not lose heart when he rebukes you,
⁶because the Lord disciplines those he loves,
and he punishes everyone he accepts as a son."

⁷Endure hardship as discipline; God is treating you as sons. For what son is not disciplined by his father? ⁸If you are not disciplined (and everyone undergoes discipline), then you are illegitimate children and not true sons. ⁹Moreover, we have all had human fathers who disciplined us and we respected them for it. How much more should we submit to the Father of our spirits and live! ¹⁰Our fathers disciplined us for a little while as they thought best; but God disciplines us for our good, that we may share in his holiness. ¹¹No discipline seems pleasant at the time, but painful. Later on, however, it produces a harvest of righteousness and peace for those who have been trained by it.

¹²Therefore, strengthen your feeble arms and weak knees. ¹³"Make level paths for your feet," so that the lame may not be disabled, but rather healed.

¹⁴Make every effort to live in peace with all men and to be holy; without holiness no one will see the Lord. ¹⁵See to it that no one misses the grace of God and that no bitter root grows up to cause trouble and defile many. ¹⁶See that no one is sexually immoral, or is godless like Esau, who for a single meal sold his inheritance rights as the oldest son. ¹⁷Afterward, as you know, when he wanted to inherit this blessing, he was rejected. He could bring about no change of mind, though he sought the blessing with tears.

IN HIS RHETORICAL toolbox the author of Hebrews has numerous apparatuses for communicating a power-packed message. Metaphor, analogy, and example all draw parallels between an earthly circumstance or event and a spiritual truth in order to elucidate that truth. In 12:1–17 the writer uses all three of these devices to good effect. In verses 1–2 he begins the chapter with the image of a race in order to exhort his hearers to "run with perseverance," laying aside impediments to endurance and keeping a focus on Jesus as the pacesetter. This metaphor of a race resumes briefly in verses 12–13, emphasizing especially the disciplined endurance required of a long-distance runner.

An analogy to another form of discipline, that offered by a parent, forms the core of 12:3–11, where the author expounds Proverbs 3:11–12. He uses this Old Testament text to weave a tight-knit argument why believers should embrace their hardships as an expression of God's love and acceptance. Just as an earthly parent uses what the child perceives to be unpleasant circumstances to bring about a desired end, so God, who deserves even more respect than an earthly parent, disciplines his true children to bring about holiness.

Finally, 12:14–17 hints at a critical problem among the addressees: the problem of disunity. The disunity here, moreover, seems to stem from friction caused by those abandoning Christian commitment. Since they have missed the grace of God, they have brought bitterness into the church, a defiling bitterness wreaking havoc on the community. By abandoning the hope of God's inheritance, these bitter persons are following the example of Esau, who afterwards "when he wanted to inherit this blessing . . . was rejected."

The theme of endurance works as the thread binding 12:1–17 together. In each use of figurative or illustrative material—a race, parental discipline, the foolish Esau—difficult experiences and the struggle of Christian perseverance form the backdrop. The image of the race and that of loving, parental discipline also reveal God as a great redeemer of pain and, therefore, as the God of hope for believers who find themselves in painful circumstances.

Running the Race (12:1–2)

THE WRITER OF Hebrews begins chapter 12 with the familiar race metaphor, presenting a forceful challenge for Christians to endure in a "marathon" commitment to Christ. The author crafts a logical transition between chapters 11 and 12 with the particle "therefore" (*toigaroun*[1]) and a reference to the "great

---

1. This word occurs elsewhere in the New Testament only at 1 Thess. 4:8 but was common in literature outside the New Testament.

cloud of witnesses," the exemplars of faith just recounted. With 12:1 he turns the spotlight on his own community of faith, using the first person plural "we" to challenge this community to recognize themselves as part of the great host called to live by faith. The basis for this exhortation has been laid well with the example list of chapter 11.

Authors of classical literature used the image of a "cloud" to describe a large group of people, and our writer employs this metaphor with an added emphasis, pointing back to the multitude of persons listed or alluded to in chapter 11 as "such a great cloud." In what sense, however, are the heroes of the faith surrounding the Christian community a "great cloud of witnesses"? Some, in light of the race imagery, have understood this confession to mean that the countless thousands of God's faithful throughout the ages now sit in the "stands" of eternity, observing Christians as they seek to live for Christ in the world. The word "witness" (*martys*) certainly can carry the meaning "spectator," as in 1 Timothy 6:12, and "surrounded" (*perikeimenon*) brings to mind the ancient amphitheater with its tiered rows of seats.

However, the author intends more from this image than to conjure the faithful of the ages as passive spectators. Rather, they are witnesses in the sense that they bear witness to the Christian community of God's faithfulness and of the effectiveness of faith.[2] God has given witness to them ("commended" in 11:2, 39 is from a related word, the verb *martyreo*), and they, as examples, bear witness to him before succeeding generations. In this way, the great cloud of faithful Christ-followers through history offer the community motivation in its current struggle to stay the course of commitment. As F. F. Bruce notes, "It is not so much they who look at us as we who look to them—for encouragement."[3]

The writer calls his hearers to "throw off everything that hinders and the sin that so easily entangles." An ancient writer could use the word *onkos* to mean "mass, weight, heaviness, bodily fat," or more positively, "fullness." In line with the sports imagery of verse 1, the word could refer to a runner stripping of burdensome clothing or losing excess bodily fat. For success one had to get rid of anything that would "hinder breathing or the free movement of the limbs."[4] So the Christ-follower must lay aside "everything that hinders" if the faith race is to be run triumphantly. More specifically, we are to get rid of the "entangling sin" (cf. NIV). The word *euperistatos* possibly refers to something that clings so closely that it impedes movement, but its meaning

---

2. See Lane, *Hebrews 9–13*, 407–8; Attridge, *Epistle to the Hebrews*, 354–55; Bruce, *Epistle to the Hebrews*, 333.

3. Bruce, *Epistle to the Hebrews*, 333.

4. Spicq, *Theological Lexicon of the New Testament*, 2:561–62.

is uncertain.[5] Those who prefer a translation in line with the NIV understand the term to derive from *periïstemi* ("to surround"). The author does not seem to have a specific sin in mind,[6] but rather understands any sin as hindering progress in the faith.

The main clause of 12:1–2a is translated with "let us run." This image of "running" emphasizes that Christ-followers have a course to complete or a goal to reach, and must exert effort if the Christian life is to be lived faithfully.[7] The author has in view, however, a marathon rather than a sprint, as seen in the phrase "with endurance." The effort called for, consequently, is a sustained effort that goes the distance, following through on one's commitment with dogged determination. This is how we must run "the race marked out for us."

Prokeimai, translated here as "marked out," can also be translated "lie before, lie in view, be at hand";[8] the author has already used the word at 6:18 to speak of the hope that has been "offered to" or "placed before" the believer. The picture evoked in 12:1 is that of runners looking down the track at the course they must run. They know where they must go and now must bring their training and commitment to bear on the task of running the race successfully. As runners see the path lying before them, so Christians see the path of the faith life stretch into the future.

Yet, thankfully, the path is not all the believer sees. We are called to "fix our eyes on Jesus, the author and perfecter of our faith" (12:2). Looking to a king or leader as a model, or to God for inspiration, was a common motif in various rhetorical literatures of the ancient world.[9] In the context of the "race," Jesus is the one who has run the path before us, and he offers the preeminent example of how the race is to be run. But he is more; that he is the "author and perfecter of our faith" sets him apart from all the examples enumerated in Hebrews 11.

The word translated "author" is rich with meaning and can communicate variously the idea of a champion, leader, forerunner, or initiator. The word has already been used in Hebrews in the context of Christ's bringing of sal-

---

5. The word does not occur anywhere else in the Greek Bible or secular Greek, and other Christian uses are dependent mostly on the passage under consideration. Consequently, interpreters struggle with the best way to translate the word in this context, suggesting variously, "easily besetting," "leading to distress," "easily avoided," "admired," "dangerous," "so easily entangles," and so forth. See Lane, *Hebrews 9–13*, 398–99 (note f), who discusses the difficulty thoroughly and opts for the strong variant *euperispaston*, which means "easily distracting."

6. Throughout Hebrews he has used "sin" in a general sense.

7. Ellingworth, *The Epistle to the Hebrews*, 639.

8. Balz and Schneider, eds., *Exegetical Dictionary of the New Testament*, 3:157.

9. Attridge, *Epistle to the Hebrews*, 356.

vation (2:10). These various nuances may overlap in the present context. Both the concepts of *forerunner* and *champion* fit the athletic imagery of the passage. Juxtaposed with the word translated "perfecter,"[10] however, it also may connote the idea of an *initiator*. That he perfected our faith means that the Lord accomplished fully what it would take for new covenant faith to be a reality. Donald Hagner comments:

> As perfecter of faith, he brings it to its intended goal. Thus, whether one talks about faith as a possibility or as the experience of fulfillment, all depends upon Jesus. For this reason, Christians must keep looking away from this world to him. He is not only the basis, means, and fulfillment of faith, but in his life he also exemplifies the same principle of faith that we saw in the paragons of chapter 11.[11]

Ultimately, Jesus accomplished the perfection of our faith by his sacrificial death on the cross. In keeping with the race imagery, he has cleared the path of faith so that we may run it. The way is open, and although hurdles exist, the roadblocks have been removed.

As Hagner notes, Jesus not only perfected faith but also provided the preeminent example of endurance because he looked beyond immediate, painful circumstances to the reward that was ahead. The verb *kataphroneo*, translated here as "scorning," means to treat someone or something as if he or it had little value. Paul uses the same word in Romans 2:4, where he speaks of "scorning" God's kindness. It also occurs in Jesus' proclamation that no one can serve two masters; rather, one will be loved and the other scorned (Matt. 6:24; Luke 16:13). That Jesus "scorned" the shame of the cross means that he treated it as insignificant or of little consequence.

The author's choice of words here is powerful. The cross was the lowest form of capital punishment in the Roman world, reserved for slaves and criminals and involving both torture and public humiliation. On the cross Jesus was treated as valueless, being mocked and ridiculed—in short, being "scorned" or "shamed." He, however, turned the experience inside out, "scorning the scorn," or in the author's words here, "scorning the shame"; the cross was insignificant compared to the joy set before our Lord. The end result of its shame was his exaltation to the right hand of God (Ps. 110:1). Thus, Christians are encouraged to look beyond their present difficulties to God's promised rewards.

---

10. See N. Clayton Croy, "A Note on Hebrews 12:2," *JBL* 114 (Spring 1995): 117–19.

11. Hagner, *Hebrews*, 212. The word translated "perfecter" (*teleiotes*) only occurs here in the Greek New Testament and does not occur outside of biblical literature prior to the New Testament era. The author, however, is fond of the word's cognates, especially the verb *teleioo*, and uses them throughout the book. See, e.g., 2:10; 5:9; 7:19, 28; 9:9; 10:1.

The Discipline of Children (12:3–13)

HEBREWS 12:3 IS transitional, leading into the author's exposition of Proverbs 3:11–12, a text that challenges the Christ-follower not to "lose heart" in the face of God's discipline. When the author says, "Consider him who endured such opposition from sinful men," he restates the need to focus on Jesus as he endured the cross (Heb. 12:2), but here he gives the reason: "so that you will not grow weary and lose heart." In this statement, the hearers' critical circumstance stands out clearly. They were facing persecution at the hands of unbelievers in a way that was causing emotional weariness. The word translated "lose heart" is a participle (*eklyomenoi*) and means "fainting" or "giving up." Thus they were experiencing a weariness of soul that was rendering them emotionally fatigued and was tempting them to quit the faith.

Consequently, a parallel exists between their situation and that of Jesus' cross—both were trials of suffering at the hands of sinful people. Because of this parallel, the persecuted community could draw strength from the positive outcome of Jesus' suffering. However, as 12:4 points out, those in this church, unlike Jesus, had yet to shed their blood in the struggle against sin. This verse implies that if Jesus endured through the pouring out of his life's blood, they could endure in the lesser persecution they were facing.[12]

In verses 5–6 the author quotes from the book of Proverbs. The emotional discouragement of his hearers prompts him to offer a gentle rebuke, "And you have forgotten that word of encouragement . . . ," which can as easily be read as a question, "Have you forgotten that word of encouragement . . . ?" Two points stand out in the way he introduces the quote. (1) The author places the subject of discipline in a positive framework as a topic for "encouragement" or "comfort" (*paraklesis*) because of the references to the Lord's love and acceptance in Proverbs 3:12 (Heb. 12:6). (2) The writer takes the references to the "son" in the proverb to be directly applicable to the Christian community. This use of the "sonship" motif mirrors the earlier treatment of believers as the "children of God" in 2:10–18.[13]

The Proverbs quotation itself falls into two movements, the first a twofold exhortation concerning the Lord's discipline/rebuke, and the second the rationale for adhering to the word of encouragement. The word *oligoreo*, translated "make light of," is a synonym of the word translated "scorning" in 12:2 and means to treat something as insignificant or of little value. Thus, the Lord's discipline or training is not to be looked down on as worthless. The proverb also encourages the reader not to "lose heart" (the same word as used at the end of v. 3) when the Lord "rebukes" (*elencho*).

---

12. The fact that those of this church had yet to die for the faith plays a crucial role in determining the date of Hebrews. On the question of the book's date see above, p. 22.

13. See above, pp. 108–10.

The rationale for taking the Lord's discipline seriously and taking courage when facing his rebuke has to do with his motive of love. The Lord does not discipline arbitrarily, but rather as an expression of genuine relationship. The word rendered by the NIV as "punishes" (*mastigoo*) is used in the context of parental discipline (cf. Prov. 19:25; Jer. 5:3; 6:7). This image is one of loving training given to amend actions and attitudes. Such training is only given to legitimate children, that is, to those whom the Lord "accepts" or "acknowledges" (*paradechomai*) as his own.

The author begins his exposition of the proverb with the exhortation, "Endure hardship as discipline."[14] Apart from its four occurrences here in Hebrews 12 (vv. 5, 7, 8, 11), the word translated "disicipline" (*paideia*) is found in the New Testament only at Ephesians 6:4 and 2 Timothy 3:16. The former verse speaks of a father training his children and the latter of Scripture as useful for "training in righteousness." The writer, therefore, makes his focal connection between this proverb and the situation of the hearers. They are to recognize in their current difficulties the Lord's hand lovingly training them in right character.

The exposition that follows occurs in three movements. Hebrews 12:7b–8 presents discipline as a validating mark of their relationship to God as Father. Next, in verse 9, the writer addresses the proper filial response to God's discipline. Finally, verses 10–11 deal with the productivity, or benefit, of the Father's loving discipline.[15]

(1) The original hearers of Hebrews could have interpreted the persecution they were facing as an indication of God's inattention. In verses 7b–8 the author of Hebrews asserts that nothing is further from the truth. Rather, the difficulties they face are actually a sign that they are true children of the Father. He asks, "What son is not disciplined by his father?" implying that discipline is a normal part of the parent-child relationship. On the contrary, he argues in verse 8, if a person does not experience discipline as a child, that lack of discipline is a mark of illegitimacy.

(2) How then should one respond to the Lord's discipline? In verse 9 the author uses an a fortiori argument or an "argument from lesser to greater"[16] to answer this question. Such an argument reasons that if something applies in a less important situation, it certainly applies in a more important situation. The less important situation in verse 9 has to do with discipline given by a human father. The author comments that human fathers are given respect in response to their discipline. Since this is the case, therefore, God deserves even

---

14. The verb can be read either as indicative or imperative, but the latter reading is called for, based on the hortatory context.

15. Lane, *Hebrews 9–13*, 421.

16. On this form of argument see above, p. 25.

more reverence. Indeed we should "submit" to him as "the Father of our spirits and live." The verb translated "submit" (*hypotasso*) is the same as used in 2:5–9 and means "to yield to, subordinate oneself to." In the present context, the author suggests that in the face of difficult circumstances, we should bow our wills to the will of the Father, since his will is the path that leads to life.

(3) In 12:10–11 the writer rounds out his exposition of the proverb by pointing out the benefits of divine discipline. "Our fathers" (i.e., our human fathers) did the best they could with discipline during the years of our childhood, but, the author implies, their perspective was limited. God, on the other hand, "disciplines us for our good" (*sympheron*, which means something done for the advantage of another). Specifically, his discipline is given "that we may share in his holiness." The whole context suggests that right parental discipline involves training or instructing in right living. So the discipline of God, when received in the right manner, trains the Christian in right character, purifying the heart.

The author admits (v. 11) that the experience of discipline is not pleasant but painful. However, the fruit of the discipline is worth the price of pain. Discipline from the Lord "produces a harvest of righteousness and peace for those who have been trained by it." Paul wrote the believers at Thessalonica that their sufferings, even while condemning their persecutors, showed the sufferers as worthy of the kingdom of God (2 Thess. 1:4–8).[17] Thus, suffering is a blessing that the Christian should consider a cause of joy because it has a positive outcome in one's character and relationship with God (James 1:2–4; 1 Peter 3:14; 4:14).

With verse 12 the author returns briefly to his earlier use of athletic imagery (vv. 1–2) and draws his material both from a passage in Isaiah and from yet another passage in Proverbs. The picture of "feeble arms and weak knees" portrays exhaustion, an echo of the spiritual and emotional fatigue with which the writer has already shown concern in 12:3, 5. Here, however, he uses a portion of a prophetic passage of encouragement that challenges the readers to hope in God's salvation and to look to his way of holiness (Isa. 35:3–8):

> Strengthen the feeble hands,
>> steady the knees that give way;
> say to those with fearful hearts,
>> "Be strong, do not fear;
> your God will come,
>> he will come with vengeance;
> with divine retribution
>> he will come to save you."

---

17. Bruce, *The Epistle to the Hebrews*, 345.

Then will the eyes of the blind be opened.
    and the ears of the deaf unstopped.
Then will the lame leap like a deer,
    and the mute tongue shout for joy.
Water will gush forth in the wilderness
    and streams in the desert.
The burning sand will become a pool,
    the thirsty ground bubbling springs.
In the haunts where the jackals once lay,
    grass and reeds and papyrus will grow.
And a highway will be there;
    it will be called the Way of Holiness.
The unclean will not journey on it;
    it will be for those who walk in that Way;
    wicked fools will not go about on it.

In other words, those who are discouraged because of their dire situation are called to hope in the coming, the justice, and the blessings of God (cf. Heb. 10:37). The strengthening of the arms and knees, therefore, is figurative of taking heart or hoping in the Lord; this message could not be more applicable to the original hearers of Hebrews, who were trudging along a path of persecution.

Hebrews 12:13 continues with a quote from Proverbs 4:26, which also concerns choosing of a right path: "Make level paths for your feet." The straight or level path is a common image in wisdom literature for God's way of right living, as is clear from Proverbs 4:25–27. In Hebrews 12:13 the author vies for his hearers to take courage in and choose the Lord's way of holiness so that their spiritual and emotional conditions might be strengthened.

The reference to "the lame" in 12:13 is another image of exhaustion or the crippling effect of spiritual discouragement. Running a race on an uneven path full of bumps and potholes is not only inconvenient but also dangerous, especially for a person who is not in good physical condition to begin with. In other words, if the hearers choose the wrong path, their spiritual condition will get worse. The verb *ektrepo* can be translated "turn aside, go astray," but the context supports the NIV's rendering "disabled."[18] In the ancient world the word was used in technical medical contexts to refer to dislocation.[19] Thus, the readers are called to follow the Lord's "level path" of holiness so that their current spiritual condition will result in healing rather than in a more serious spiritual condition.

---

18. For a different opinion see Hughes, *A Commentary on the Epistle to the Hebrews*, 535.
19. Attridge, *The Epistle to the Hebrews*, 365.

The Importance of Choosing Holiness (12:14–17)

THE EXHORTATIONS OF 12:14–17 may seem somewhat disjointed from 12:1–13, but these verses continue with two themes that are central to the first thirteen verses: spiritual struggle and the need for holiness. Verse 14 reads, "Make every effort to live in peace with all men and to be holy; without holiness no one will see the Lord." Believers are to "make every effort" or "strive for" two things: peace with others and holiness, the two being intertwined dynamics in the present context.

Holiness is expressed as vital for two relationships in life. (1) Holiness has a profound impact on our relationships with other people (Rom. 12:18), a thought the author will develop in the next verse; it is impossible to "live in peace" with others when we choose the unholy path. (2) The author makes it clear that holiness is indispensable for an authentic Christian life. The person who chooses to live an unholy life can be offered no assurance of "seeing the Lord." This probably refers to meeting the Lord joyfully upon his return (Heb. 9:28; 1 John 3:2).

Verse 15 begins with a participle the NIV translates with "see to it." Grammatically the word relates back to the main verb in verse 14, translated "make every effort," and can be rendered "seeing to it." Thus, Christians are to strive for peace and holiness in part by being mindful of certain spiritual dynamics in their community, such as three delineated in the author's continuing discussion (cf. 2:1; 3:12; 4:1). (1) They are to see to it that no one "misses the grace of God." The verb *hystereo* can mean "to lack, fall short of." The state of missing the grace of God is the same as that warned against in 4:1; 6:4–6; 10:26–31, namely, the state of rejecting the gospel and missing the forgiveness offered by virtue of Christ's sacrifice.[20]

(2) The believers are to see to it that "no bitter root grows up to cause trouble and defile many." Here the author alludes to Deuteronomy 29:18, which reads: "Make sure there is no man or woman, clan or tribe among you today whose heart turns away from the LORD our God to go and worship the gods of those nations; make sure there is no root among you that produces such bitter poison." The context of this Old Testament text is significant, since it deals with idolatry and apostasy from the covenant community. Those among Hebrews' original recipients who were jettisoning their confession of Christ were causing severe friction within the community, and relationships were breaking down.

The verb *miaino*, translated by the NIV as "defile," communicates the idea of contamination. It is used variously in the New Testament to speak of cer-

---

20. See esp. the discussion of 6:4–8 above, pp. 226–32.

emonial impurity (John 18:28), a person who lives in impurity or has a corrupt mind (Titus 1:15), and a person who is sexually immoral (Jude 8). In Hebrews 12:15 the author speaks of apostasy as introducing an insidious, spiritually corroding element into the church.

(3) The hearers are to see to it that no member of the church falls into the pattern of immoral Esau (12:16–17). That Esau was "sexually immoral" is somewhat problematic since the biblical text does not mention sexual promiscuity on his part. However, some strands of Jewish interpretation describe him as sexually suspect because of his marriage to the Hittites Judith and Basemath (Gen. 26:34), and our author may be picking up on this tradition.[21] The word *bebelos*, which the NIV renders "godless," speaks of something that is unholy, ungodly, or base. Hebrews describes Esau in this way because of his misplaced values that led to his unwise decision to give up his inheritance. For something as valueless as a meal—simply a means of gaining immediate gratification for physical hunger pangs—he foolishly gave up his rights as the firstborn, that is, the double portion of his father's inheritance.

The author of Hebrews goes on to allude to what happened later in the Genesis account, when Jacob stole Esau's blessing (Gen. 27:30–40). Having given up his inheritance and being rejected from receiving the blessing, Esau, weeping, pleaded with his father to reverse the situation, but the patriarch could not. The author of Hebrews wishes to drive home the point that only tears and rejection await those who sell out the inheritance that God promises to his children.

HEBREWS 12:1–17 OFFERS us a tapestry of rich images by which the author wishes to motivate his readers to endurance in the Christian life. Figurative language is meant to stimulate the imagination, inviting a reader to enter into the image and connect with the relevant material the image has to offer. The key in dealing with such images is to discern the connecting point between the image and the topic at hand.

Focusing on the "race." There are many ways, for example, in which the author of Hebrews does *not* intend the race imagery to be read. He certainly does not play up the idea of competition, as in "God wants you to beat the other fellow." Nor does he mean to emphasize here that God gives Christians the ability to overcome all obstacles.[22] One finds no hint of "the race belongs

---

21. Attridge, *The Epistle to the Hebrews*, 368–69.

22. The way, for instance, that many American athletes misuse Philippians 4:13, a text that has more to do with contentment in a variety of circumstances than with God-give ability to succeed.

to the strong," or "pace yourself—you will get farther," or "break out of the pack!" We must not read anachronistically our modern clichés of a race back into this text. Therefore, the preacher or teacher of this text needs to exercise restraint in the use of this image.

What the author means to emphasize by his use of the race motif can be seen clearly by a grammatical analysis of the structure of 12:1–2a. This structure is obscured by the NIV translation, which renders this text as a series of exhortations (i.e., with its repetition of "Let us . . ."). In the Greek, there is but one exhortation in the passage: "Let us run." As depicted in the following diagram, this focal verb is supported by a series of participles and prepositional phrases. The diagram maintains the order of the clauses as they occur in the Greek text and depicts the subordination of clauses and phrases by indenting them. Objects are marked by their location following an arrow. The diagram also translates the participles to show their subordination to the main verb.

> **since we are surrounded by such a great cloud of witnesses**
>
> throwing off ⎯⎯⎯▶ everything that hinders
> > and
> > the sin that so easily entangles
>
> through perseverance
>
> <u>**Let us run**</u> ⎯⎯⎯▶ the race marked out for us
>
> fixing our eyes on Jesus, the author and perfecter of our faith.

The examples of faith in Hebrews 11 provide a solid basis for the exhortation, and the author gives three elements that may be understood as the means (or, perhaps, manner) of running the race well. We are to run (1) throwing off all that hinders and sin, (2) by means of perseverance, and, especially, (3) fixing our eyes on Jesus. The author understandably gives the last of these, the focus on Jesus, the greatest attention, since he has dedicated much of his book to building the hearers' understanding of God's Son. It is Jesus who provides the ultimate basis for a Christian's perseverance.

Thus, the race image provides at least three primary concepts that overlap with the Christian life. (1) Some things in life must be rejected if we are to run effectively. (2) The Christian life, like a long-distance run, is difficult and, therefore, takes sustained effort. (3) If we are to live for God in a faithful manner, a healthy view of Christ and relationship with him are paramount. Consequently, our application of 12:1–2 should focus on these aspects of living the Christian life as a well-run "race." From the context, it seems that making right choices in the face of opposition to the Christian worldview and message is especially in view.

God's love and "parental discipline." The analogy of God's discipline through our trials with the discipline offered by an earthly parent provides us with an interesting hermeneutical exercise on several counts. (1) We live in a time when certain kinds of parental discipline, especially those involving pain, are viewed as unacceptable by many. It is not uncommon to hear a social commentator proclaim the emotional and psychological damage done to a child by any form of "negative" treatment, be it a "spanking" or a verbal rebuke. Now, we need not digress to a discussion of contemporary parenting theories. My point is that if we hold to a theory that disallows any form of pain or unpleasantness in the training of a child, we will have difficulty either in grasping or applying Hebrews 12:3–13, which assumes that parental discipline involves pain in some form (12:11).

These points on the human side of the analogy are inescapable: Parental discipline is mandatory for the well-being of the child, and it is painful for the child. On the other hand, if one has experienced abuse at the hands of a parent or injustice in the welding of discipline, it may be equally difficult to see discipline as a positive, loving aspect of the parent-child relationship.

(2) The focus on the "father-child" relationship in this passage returns us to the use of gender in dealing with such passages.[23] Many children in modern culture do not know their fathers, or if they do, the father is disengaged from any aspect of child training. For many the mother functions as the dominant figure in the home. For these, a surface reading of this text might be difficult to identify with.

What is needed as a first step, therefore, is to have a clear picture of the background behind the author's view of a father's discipline. In the cultural context behind Hebrews (both in Judaism and the broader Greco-Roman culture) the father was seen as having the ultimate responsibility for the training of a son (the language used here). Although a tutor might be responsible for the care and training of a boy after age six or seven, the ongoing role of the father was much more significant (cf. 1 Cor. 4:15). In a positive sense, the father's responsibility was to train his son in such a way that he was well prepared for adulthood. This training often involved correction and punishment, but the goal was to help the child develop character and wisdom.

This relationship, therefore, parallels any parent—mother or father—in modern culture who seeks to train a child—son or daughter—in areas of character development, since the responsibility for parental discipline in many modern contexts rests with either father or mother, or both. Furthermore, most modern cultures no longer demarcate between the training of a son and a daughter. Moreover, most parents acknowledge the need for some

---

23. See above, pp. 113–14.

form of discipline in the training of a child. Even if that discipline consists of disappointment over not getting one's way or painful consequences experienced because the child did not obey the parent's instructions, such experiences are inevitable in a child's development.

Therefore, we might do well to focus on this aspect of the author's message. God uses the difficulties we encounter as an aspect of training and moral development. They really are a gift that we might be all that he wants us to be. It does not take much reflection for us to recognize that much of our progress as persons comes through challenging or even painful experiences, whether they be in the realm of athletics, relationships, or other areas of skill development. So our author's point is that God can redeem the pain we experience in life, using it for our good.

This raises the question of theodicy, the query concerning how a good God can allow, and even use, evil, since it is likely that the difficulties the author of Hebrews has in mind in 12:3–13 stem from persecution at the hands of evil people (e.g., 12:3–4). We can respond that God's ability to redeem bad circumstances and turn them to good use is expressed throughout Scripture (e.g., 1 Sam. 16:14–16; Isa. 45:7; Jer. 4:6; Amos 3:6; Rom. 8:28). Christians are constantly encouraged to perceive their difficulties as a cause for celebration instead of sorrow (1 Thess. 5:16–18; James 1:2–4). This shows that God, never the source of evil, can turn evil "inside out," utilizing it for his greater purposes. No event bears witness to this truth more than the cross (Heb. 12:1–3).

What role for Hebrews 12:14–17? Several commentators have chosen to place verses 14–17 with what follows rather than the first thirteen verses of the chapter.[24] Indeed, the Greek text I am using at the moment (UBS[4]) and my copy of the NIV both place a break between 12:13 and 12:14. However, there are good reasons for understanding 12:14–17 as having a direct connection with 12:1–13. The emphasis on holiness and, especially, the continued focus on the role of a "son" testify that 12:14–17 is an important concluding statement on 12:1–13. In verses 1, 4, 10–11 the author speaks to turning from sin and growing in holiness, themes echoed in the references to holiness over against immorality in verses 14–17. Also, the author's focus on the role of a "son," a motif not addressed since 2:10–18, begins with 12:5 and continues through the exposition on Esau in 12:16–17.

---

24. E.g., Ellingworth, *The Epistle to the Hebrews*, 661; Lane, *Hebrews 9–13*, 431; Attridge, *The Epistle to the Hebrews*; 366. Lane and Attridge both point to the use of "the God of peace" in 13:20 as forming the closing "bracket" of an *inclusio* opened with the reference to "peace" in 12:14. However, the parallel is too weak to make a strong case for this position. Of more importance are the themes in 12:14–17 that provide a conclusion to primary themes of 12:1–13.

So, what is the point of the author's treatment of the "bitter root" and Esau in 12:14–17? Let's begin with the latter. Esau is a paradigm for a person who treats the honors of an heir lightly. He is the consummate fool because he threw away a precious privilege on a whim born of a physical appetite. The cravings of the moment outweighed the premier gifts of a lifetime.

It may seem to us that our author is unfair in his assessment of Esau, especially in relation to "the blessing." After all, Jacob tricked the poor fellow out of that blessing! The writer, however, wishes to leave a stark picture in our minds through his use of Esau, who represents someone who has missed out on the blessings attached to the position of an honored child. Because of his rejection of his right of inheritance in the first instance and his brother's trickery in the second, Esau could no longer be considered a legitimate bearer of those blessings. The author wants his hearers to avoid that foul position in relation to God the Father. They must not reject the honored status offered them as "legitimate children" because of momentary cravings (e.g., getting out from under the pressure of persecution).[25]

The image of the "bitter root" that defiles the community carries an underlying theme shared with the Esau exposition. The Old Testament context behind the image is critical if we are to grasp its significance. The image, derived from Deuteronomy 29:18, deals with those who have rejected the covenant and, therefore, have damaged the community of faith. Like Esau they have rejected something precious, and the outcome is most unpleasant. Whereas the focus of the Esau passage has to do with the personal implications of such a foolish decision, Hebrews 12:14–15 points to the devastating implications of rejection of the covenant for the community of faith. Thus, in seeking to apply 12:14–17, we must reflect on both personal and corporate losses when those within the church turn away from Christ.

Threads of unity in this section. Before moving on to our application of this passage, we should reflect for a moment on the "big picture" unifying this section of Hebrews 12. The author's treatment of each of the images used here witnesses to the difficulty of the Christian life. The race is portrayed as challenging, the discipline of God as unpleasant, and the dangers of the bitter root or the foolishness of Esau as to be avoided. This all adds up to a realistic picture of Christ-following as costly. Struggle goes with the call to be Christ's person in this world.

Consequently, the believer faces the constant need for endurance, wise choices, and perspective. "Hindrances" must be put off and discouraged hearts strengthened. Outward difficulties must be perceived as lovingly used by the

---

25. For a discussion of the theology of "falling away" from the Christian faith and my position in that regard see the discussion above, pp. 226–32.

Father for our good. The community of faith must be protected by the members' good choices to live peaceably and in holiness as they value the blessings as God's children. Hebrews 12:1–17 calls us to endure in the Christian life, following our preeminent example, the Lord Jesus himself (12:1–?).

RUNNING THE RACE. The Eighth Olympiad of modern times began on July 5, 1924, and was held in the city of Paris, France. Over forty-five countries were represented, and the stadium swelled to a crowd of 60,000 spectators. Among the competitors from Great Britain, Eric Liddell, a Scot with wings on his feet, had come under the shadow of controversy. As a Christian, Liddell held the conviction that he should not run on Sunday, which he considered the Sabbath. Months before the Olympic games Liddell informed Great Britain's Olympic committee that he would not be able to participate in the preliminary heat for the hundred-meter run. As the Olympics drew near, the criticism of Liddell's "fanaticism" increased, but he doggedly refused. As Harold Abrahams ran the hundred-meter preliminary, Eric Liddell preached to a congregation in the Scots Kirk in another part of Paris. Abrahams went on to win the final in that race and set a world record that would stand for fifty-six years.

On the following Tuesday, Liddell and Abrahams both qualified for a place in the two hundred-meter final, to be held on the following day. Eric became the first Scot ever to bring home a medal in that race, winning the bronze. No one from Great Britain had ever placed higher. Eric went on to compete in the four hundred-meter race, joining runners from Canada, United States, and a fellow Briton named Guy Butler in the final. Just prior to the race Liddell went down the line, shaking his competitors' hands in a ritual that he had made familiar over time. At the gun Eric bolted into a three-meter lead. As the race progressed, Fitch, the American, began to close in on the Scot, but Liddell increased his speed. As he crossed the finish line with a five-meter lead, his head cocked back and arms flailing the air, Eric brought home the gold medal. After an explosive roar from the British spectators, a hush finally fell over the crowd as they waited for the official time. The cheers erupted again as it was announced that Eric Liddell had set a new world record of 47.6 seconds.[26]

Eric Liddell was a sprinter as an Olympian, but the young believer from Scotland, just twenty-two years of age during the Eighth Olympiad, provides

---

26. Catherine Swift, "Olympic Gold," in *More Stories for the Heart*, ed. Alice Gray (Sisters, Ore.: Multnomah, 1997), 94–97. Liddell's story is told dramatically, if not completely accurately, in the powerful, award-winning film *Chariots of Fire*.

a powerful example of one who ran the Christian race with a marathoner's endurance. Based on his commitment to Christ,[27] he "threw off" the opinions of both the general public and the powerful, giving up the opportunity for glory in the hundred meters, a race for which he had trained for years. Liddell endured not only in the months prior to the Olympic games, but afterward embarked on a career as a missionary to China, where he died eventually in a Chinese prison. His life evidenced a long-term focus on Christ as his reference point. In all things he took his cues from the Lord Jesus, who was his example, sustainer, and guide. Because he had thrown off hindrances to his spiritual race and had chosen a path of perseverance, Liddell had a clear view of Christ and his call, and he abides as a strong example of the Christian life lived nobly.

As we look to those like Eric Liddell, who looked to Christ for how they should run the race of life, we should reflect on what we need to "throw off." There may be encumbrances that are not bad or sinful in and of themselves but should be evaluated in light of their effect on our running the race. Certain possessions, hobbies, patterns of life, or even people can occupy us in a way so as to cool our hearts to Christ.

Reading the newspaper or watching a television program, for example, may be minor considerations unless they distract us constantly from reflection on God's Word or reading edifying literature. An unmarried person may take great pleasure in the company of a new romance, but such a relationship must be weighed in light of its effect on one's Christian commitment. A sport such as golf might be a source of physical exercise and fellowship but can also cause a person to neglect his or her family. We should assess how we are responding to the pull of popularity, position, or place in our given life occupations—none necessarily bad inherently, but potentially stunting to spiritual development if they are out of line in what should be Christian priorities.

It goes without saying that all sins, including especially such sins as lust, greed, hatred, or pride, hamstring us in the contest and must be rejected over and again if we are to run well and run long. For to run with perseverance means that we will grow in a pattern of obedience to God's Word, day after day, year after year. It means that we will train to make the right choices, choosing the level path of righteousness. The premier sin to be jettisoned is the sin of abandoning Christian commitment altogether. We must strengthen our "feeble arms and week knees" if we are lagging in a rut of despair. This exercise is helped most by riveting "our eyes on Jesus," who has shown us what to scorn and what to hold as a cause of joy, and joy is set before us if we will persevere in the race.

---

27. One might differ with Liddell on his application of Sabbath principles to Sunday, but his conviction was held and applied as an expression of devotion. It is this devotion that is both praiseworthy and worthy of emulation.

Facing hardship from a biblical perspective. Most of us perhaps can remember an incident from our childhood in which we were disciplined and failed to grasp fully why it had to be so. On occasion our lack of understanding may have resulted from unfairness or poor communication on a parent's part. Yet I can remember clearly unpleasant, though loving, confrontations by my father, the significance of which later—sometimes much later—dawned on me. He had *very* good reasons for driving some lessons home with a painful tenacity. He loved me enough to move me toward greater maturity and responsibility, which normally were found outside of my childish, self-centered comfort zone.

Now I deal with my own children, a five- and a two-year-old, both of whom I love dearly. They struggle with understanding, at times, why certain negative consequences follow from unacceptable actions. As my youngest reaches to investigate a lamp plug poked into an electrical outlet, I pull her hand away with a firm "No, no, Anna!" Tears well up and her bottom lip pokes out in a heart-wrenching visage of dejection. She doesn't understand. When Joshua recently was too rough with Anna as they played, he lost the privilege of playing with her for the rest of the afternoon. He cried in disappointment—he loves his sister. He struggles to understand such situations. I discipline my children, often bringing tears of pain or disappointment. But I do this so that they might grow in wisdom and maturity.

Christians have never been entirely comfortable with hardship, which looks, feels, and smells like a "snake" but which Hebrews suggests is "fish," brought by the Lord for our spiritual nourishment. We simply do not like hardship's pain. Hebrews says this is normal. Yet pain and difficulty are part and parcel of living in a fallen world. As Oswald Chambers notes in his classic devotional guide, *My Utmost For His Highest*:

> We say that there ought to be no sorrow, but there *is* sorrow, and we have to receive ourselves in its fires. If we try and evade sorrow, refuse to lay our account with it, we are foolish. Sorrow is one of the biggest facts in life; it is no use saying sorrow ought not to be. Sin and sorrow and suffering *are*, and it is not for us to say that God has made a mistake in allowing them.[28]

In a now famous passage, C. S. Lewis notes the meaningfulness of pain: "God whispers to us in our pleasure, speaks in our conscience, but shouts in our pains: it is His megaphone to rouse a deaf world."[29]

---

28. Oswald Chambers, *My Utmost for His Highest: Selections for the Year* (New York: Dodd, Mead, and Company, 1935), 177.

29. C. S. Lewis, *The Problem of Pain* (London: 1940), 81.

We too in the Christian community can turn a deaf ear to this language of God, this pain language, or at best strain to hear God's message through our difficulties, especially when they come at the hands of unfair and hurtful people. We weep at our emotional loss, our bitter sense of rejection and being misunderstood. Our pain deafens us to God's music playing in the background, music that seeks to teach us to sing joyfully of what God can do *in* us, even while others seek to do harm *to* us. But we must ask him to discipline our ears to hear, to help us rouse ourselves to readiness for receiving what he wishes to teach us through our painful experiences. Speaking of enduring hardship, Thomas à Kempis, as if quoting Christ, writes:

> The better you prepare yourself to meet suffering, the more wisely will you act, and the greater will be your merit. You will bear all the more easily if your heart and mind is diligently prepared. Do not say, "I cannot endure such things from this person," or, "I will not tolerate these things: he has done me great injury, and accused me of things I never considered; from another person I might bear it, and regard it as something that must be endured." Such thoughts are foolish, for you ignore the merit of patience and Him who rewards it, and think only of the person who has injured you and the wrong you endure.
>
> You are not truly patient if you will only endure what you think fit, and only from those whom you like. A truly patient man does not consider by whom he is tried, whether by his superior, his equal, or his inferior; whether by a good and holy man, or by a perverse and wicked person. But however great or frequent the trial that besets him, and by whatever agency it comes, he accepts it gladly as from the hand of God, and counts it all gain.[30]

He "counts it all gain." Yes, this is easier said than done, but we are called to this perspective, called to make a choice to view our struggles from an angle that reveals God's loving hand. Thankfully, that love of God expresses itself in his working his perspective in us as we yield to him. It is in yielding our rights to ease and happiness that we find true joy; it is in yielding our poverty of spirit because of what we are tempted to give up that we find the riches and supply of his Spirit. It is by yielding our weakness that we find his strength. We can trust him, for he is the most loving Father. He will bring us home to himself through the fire and flood of our difficulties.

The root of bitterness. One of the tempter's most insidious weapons, self-centeredness, causes one to focus on one's own perspective, one's own

---

30. Thomas à Kempis, *The Imitation of Christ*, trans. Leo Sherley-Price (New York: Penguin, 1952), 117–18.

circumstances, and the implications of certain decisions for one's own life. In church life this issue demands more attention. When "bitter roots"—dynamics within the church introduced by those who have become disaffected with the fellowship—spring up, many are defiled, according to Hebrews. The fellowship suffers contamination. In the introduction to this commentary I started by sharing a fictitious story about Antonius Bardavid, a young Jewish participant in a house church of first-century Rome.[31] As Antonius struggles with estrangement from his family and verbal abuse at the hands of his employer, it is easy to perceive his cooling commitment to Christ as detrimental to him alone. At the end of the introduction I shared about two couples, Betty and Fred Johnson and Amanda and Tom Smith, members of Community Church, cared for by Pastor David.

In our individualistic Western culture we can forget the vast implications, the detrimental effects of Antonius, Betty, Fred, and Tom's apostasy on those around them. How would Antonius's leaving the house church change that church and those in it? What effect would Tom's apostasy have on those in Community Church who had witnessed his testimony, to whom he had ministered, and perhaps those whom he had led to Christ? How would Betty and Fred's children respond, their views of Christ altered forever by the immediate choices of their parents? How would Elder Joseph in Rome or Pastor David be affected? Certainly not toward encouragement, and maybe they would struggle with deep discouragement at a moment when another in the church desperately needed help. Apostasy defiles the community it touches. It must not be perceived solely as an individual choice with implications only for an individual. This is why it remains a community problem and responsibility (3:12–13; 10:24–25).

In a letter from the persecuted believers of Vienna and Lyons to the churches of Asia and Phrygia, dated A.D. 177, a description is given of the disheartening effect apostates had on those who were seeking to stand strong in the faith. The Christians of that area had been mocked, beaten, robbed, stoned, and imprisoned by unbelievers. Having confessed their faith publicly before the city rulers, many were held in prison to await the arrival of the governor, who upon examining them treated them cruelly. Having described the distinction of a Christian named Vettius, who, although young, was called "the Advocate of the Christians" because of his rigorous and bold defense of the church, the letter goes on to describe the distress caused by those who waffled in their commitment:

> But some appeared who were unprepared and untrained. They were still weak and unable to bear the tension of a great contest. Of these

---

31. See above, pp. 17–18.

about ten in number proved abortions; causing great grief and immeasurable sorrow amongst us and damping the ardor of the others who had not yet been arrested. For these, although they suffered every kind of cruelty, remained nevertheless in the company of the Witnesses and did not forsake them. Then all of us were greatly alarmed because of our uncertainty of their confession. We did not fear because of the tortures inflicted, but because we looked to the end and dreaded lest any one should fall away.[32]

The emotional grief and dread caused by the specter of apostasy in this ancient church should cause us to pause for reflection. How do we respond to the apostasy of those from within our churches? Is there an intensity of grief and dread over this problem? If not, why not? What is there in our theological or cultural makeup that tempts us to accept apostasy as of minimal importance? If you as an individual are struggling with following the example of Esau, treating God's promised inheritance as if it was of little consequence, have you stopped to consider the impact of that decision on those around you? Your close associates in the church? Those in your Bible study? Your spouse or closest friends? Your children? Your pastor? Please stop and consider the curse of being one who introduces a bitter root to the church of the living God! In doing so you not only affect yourself, but you also contaminate others in such a way that will mark your life and theirs forever.

---

32. "The Letter of the Churches of Vienna and Lyons to the Churches of Asia and Phrygia," *Christian History Institute's Pocket Classics* (Worcester, Pa.: Christian History Institute), 1–3.

Hebrews 12:18-29

YOU HAVE NOT come to a mountain that can be touched and that is burning with fire; to darkness, gloom and storm; [19]to a trumpet blast or to such a voice speaking words that those who heard it begged that no further word be spoken to them, [20]because they could not bear what was commanded: "If even an animal touches the mountain, it must be stoned." [21]The sight was so terrifying that Moses said, "I am trembling with fear."

[22]But you have come to Mount Zion, to the heavenly Jerusalem, the city of the living God. You have come to thousands upon thousands of angels in joyful assembly, [23]to the church of the firstborn, whose names are written in heaven. You have come to God, the judge of all men, to the spirits of righteous men made perfect, [24]to Jesus the mediator of a new covenant, and to the sprinkled blood that speaks a better word than the blood of Abel.

[25]See to it that you do not refuse him who speaks. If they did not escape when they refused him who warned them on earth, how much less will we, if we turn away from him who warns us from heaven? [26]At that time his voice shook the earth, but now he has promised, "Once more I will shake not only the earth but also the heavens." [27]The words "once more" indicate the removing of what can be shaken—that is, created things—so that what cannot be shaken may remain.

[28]Therefore, since we are receiving a kingdom that cannot be shaken, let us be thankful, and so worship God acceptably with reverence and awe, [29]for our "God is a consuming fire."

THE STRIKING, WELL-CRAFTED section of material running from Hebrews 12:18–29 consists of two primary movements. (1) The first is composed of rhythmic phrases detailing the terrors of Mount Sinai set over against the joys of Mount Zion (12:18–24). The emphatic "not" of verse 18 (*ou*), situated at the beginning of the sentence in Greek, finds its balance in the "but" (*alla*) at the beginning of verse 22.

As detailed in this passage, the two mountains represent the two covenants, highlighting the stark contrasts between the old and the new. As new covenant believers, the original believers addressed in Hebrews "have not come" to the old covenant mountain, Sinai—a place of fire, darkness, gloom, and storm; a place of the trumpet blast and of the voice of God as a voice of terrifying judgment. Rather, they "have come" to the new covenant mountain, Mount Zion. They are citizens of the heavenly Jerusalem and are in fellowship with thousands of celebrating angels, members of the church on earth, and those who have already died. Especially, they have come to Jesus, the mediator of the new covenant, whose blood speaks well for them.

(2) The other movement (12:25–29) is a warning that mirrors earlier warnings in the book (cf. 2:1–4; 10:26–31). The writer again uses an "argument from lesser to greater" to drive home his exhortation.[1] The theme of God "speaking," introduced as a focal point of 12:18–24, continues in 12:25–29. Those who rejected the voice from Mount Sinai did not escape God's judgment; consequently, those who now turn away from the heavenly warning certainly will not escape. The earth shook at Sinai, but that shaking will pale in comparison to the shaking promised in Haggai 2:6. The author interprets this Haggai passage to mean that the created order will be done away with, for in the coming judgment God will shake the cosmos, crumbling its very foundation. Therefore, the hearers should worship God reverently and give him thanks for their part in the unshakable kingdom.

Throughout Hebrews the author has addressed his readers as needing to move on, to progress, in some way. Thus, the concepts of *coming* or *drawing near* have played a significant role, especially as they relate to drawing near to God (e.g., 4:16; 7:25; 10:22; 11:6). The readers are to emulate those who sought a heavenly country (11:16) and are to follow Christ in the race marked out for them (12:1–2). In a sense they are a people who are "on the move" spiritually, hopefully moving in the right direction rather than drifting or falling away from God (2:1–2; 3:12; 6:6). A dramatic change of orientation takes place in 12:18–24, however, where the recipients are addressed as those who have arrived at a significant destination, though the author begins with a graphic description of a mountain to which his audience has *not* come.

The Old Covenant Mountain (12:18–21)

ALTHOUGH THE AUTHOR of Hebrews never mentions Sinai by name, he clearly has that mountain in view in his poetic comments in these verses. He draws his depiction of the desert wanderers' encounter of God at Mount Sinai from the books of Exodus and Deuteronomy (e.g., Ex. 19:16–22; 20:18–21; Deut.

---

1. On the use of an a fortiori argument see above, p. 25.

4:11–12; 5:23–27). In the Sinai encounter they came near to God in a solemn assembly to covenant with him (Deut. 4:10–14). But the experience was terrifying, and the author uses seven images from the Old Testament to drive home the event's terror:

(1) [the mountain] that can[not] be touched
(2) burning with fire
(3) darkness
(4) gloom
(5) storm
(6) a trumpet blast
(7) a voice speaking words

The word "mountain" does not occur in the Greek text of verse 18, but most commentators have understood the concept as implied in the phrase "that can be touched." This idea probably alludes to Exodus 19:12: "Put limits for the people around the mountain and tell them, 'Be careful that you do not go up the mountain or touch the foot of it. Whoever touches the mountain shall surely be put to death.'" The images of "fire," "darkness," and "storm" are also taken from the Old Testament (Ex. 19:16–19; Deut. 4:11; 5:22–23). Paired with the word translated "to darkness" (*gnopho*), the word translated "[to] gloom" (*zopho*) functions euphonically, offering a pleasing, corresponding pronunciation in Greek. These manifestations of God's presence at Sinai were visible, striking the eyes of the desert wanderers with awe.

The two remaining manifestations of God's presence were auditory. The "trumpet blast" pierced the air around Sinai on the morning of the third day in the people's encounter with God, growing louder and louder, causing the covenant makers to tremble with fear (Ex. 19:16, 19; 20:18). Concluding the list, the "voice speaking words" came out of the fire (Deut. 4:12). The people did not see God's form but only heard the words. In response, they begged that God would speak to them no further (Ex. 20:18–19; Deut. 5:23–27), thus rejecting his message to them. Hebrews 12:20 adds the explanation, "because they could not bear what was commanded: 'If even an animal touches the mountain, it must be stoned'" (Ex. 19:12–13). The people were aware of the boundaries God had placed between them and him and were terrified that the boundaries seemed to be dissolving under the weight of that terrible voice.

In Hebrews 12:21 the writer concludes by noting that even the mediator of that covenant, Moses, was overwhelmed by the experience—a fact not easily recognized in the passages to which the author up to this point has been alluding. Perhaps the best explanation is that the author is alluding to Deuteronomy 9:19a, where Moses says, "I feared the anger and wrath of the

LORD." Although the context of Deuteronomy 9 concerns the people's idolatry with the golden calf, there exist several touch points with the earlier theophany recounted in Deuteronomy 4. For example, both experiences occur at Sinai (9:8) and both concern the preeminent expression of covenant guidelines, the Ten Commandments (4:13; 9:9–11). Both contexts also involve the mountain burning with fire (9:15) and Moses' speaking with the Lord (9:19). If this reading of the reference in Hebrews 12:21 is correct, Moses' "trembling with fear" is a response to the intensity of God's red-hot wrath in face of the people's sin. In any case, verse 21 adds to the impression of Mount Sinai, the old covenant mountain, as a place of darkness and dread.

The New Covenant Mountain (12:22–24)

THANKFULLY, NEW COVENANT believers have not come to Mount Sinai, a mountain of terror and separation from God. Rather, they have come to Mount Zion, the dwelling place of God. The author balances his previous list of seven dynamics related to Mount Sinai with seven here:

(1) the heavenly Jerusalem, the city of the living God
(2) thousands upon thousands of angels in joyful assembly
(3) the church of the firstborn, whose names are written in heaven
(4) God, the judge of all people
(5) the spirits of the righteous made perfect
(6) Jesus, the mediator of a new covenant
(7) the sprinkled blood that speaks better than the blood of Abel

These images may be understood as creating a picture of the new covenant assembly in the heavenly Jerusalem, and the contrast with the Sinai encounter could not be more pronounced. William Lane comments:

> Every aspect of the vision provides encouragement for coming boldly into the presence of God (cf. 4:16). The atmosphere at Mount Zion is festive. The frightening visual imagery of blazing fire, darkness, and gloom fades before the reality of the city of the living God, heavenly Jerusalem. The cacophony of whirlwind, trumpet blast, and a sound of words is muted and replaced by the joyful praise of angels in a festal gathering. The trembling congregation of Israel, gathered solemnly at the base of the mountain, is superseded by the assembly of those whose names are permanently inscribed in the heavenly archives. An overwhelming impression of the unapproachability of God is eclipsed in the experience of full access to the presence of God and of Jesus, the mediator of the new covenant.[2]

---

2. Lane, *Hebrews 9–13*, 464–65.

Micro

The author's picture of the gathered assembly at Mount Zion, therefore, communicates exultation, warmth, openness, acceptance, and relationship, set off in bold relief against the dismal portrait of the Sinai assembly.

Mount Zion and the city of Jerusalem are so closely associated in the biblical literature that the two should be understood as conceptually syn onymous, representing the dwelling place of God.[3] Sometimes Zion is mentioned alone as God's residence (e.g., Ps. 2:6; 50:2; 110:2); but in other places Zion and Jerusalem are mentioned in poetic parallelism (e.g., Joel 2:32; Mic. 4:2), as at Amos 1:2: "The LORD roars from Zion and thunders from Jerusalem."[4] Thus the Greek word *kai* (often translated "and" but left untranslated by the NIV) between "Mount Zion" and "the city" may be read as adjunctive, meaning "even": "You have come to Mount Zion, even the city of the living God, the heavenly Jerusalem."[5]

Here, of course, as indicated by the adjective "heavenly" attached to "Jerusalem," the author has in mind the Zion and Jerusalem that are not of this creation (cf. Gal. 4:26). That God's true dwelling place, the place where he meets his new covenant people, is in the heavenly realm, forms a prominent aspect of the author's theological framework (e.g., 4:14–16; 6:19–20; 7:26–28; 8:1–2). This is the "heavenly city" of 11:16 and the "city that is to come" of 13:14.

The multitude of angels in God's presence exults "in joyful assembly" (*panegyris*), a noun only found here in the New Testament. In secular literature this word was used of parties or the celebratory atmosphere at the annual athletic competitions, such as the Olympics. In the LXX, it speaks of a multitudinous gathering to celebrate an occasion of joy or delight, often associated with a feast (e.g., Ezek. 46:11; Hos. 2:11; 9:5; Amos 5:21).[6] Thus, the word communicates a sense of excitement, revelry, and well-being.

The word *ekklesia*, translated "church" by the NIV, almost always refers in biblical literature to a gathering or assembly of God's people.[7] The author has already referred to the Son as "the firstborn" (1:6). However, the plural of this word in 12:23 and the reference to these "firstborn" as having their names "written in heaven" indicate that God's new covenant people are in view here. The idea that the righteous have their names inscribed in a heavenly

---

3. Bruce, *The Epistle to the Hebrews*, 356.

4. Westcott, *The Epistle to the Hebrews*, 413.

5. The NIV places "the heavenly Jerusalem" between "Mount Zion" and "the city of the living God"; the Greek reads literally here: "Mount Zion, and [even] the city of the living God, heavenly Jerusalem."

6. Spicq, *Theological Lexicon of the New Testament*, 3:4–8.

7. Ellingworth, *The Epistle to the Hebrews*, 679.

registry is common (e.g., Ex. 32:32; Ps. 69:29; Isa. 4:3; Dan. 12:1; Luke 10:20). The "firstborn," therefore, are those who share the inheritance of the Son, the Firstborn par excellence.[8]

Those addressed by Hebrews also have come "to God, the judge of all men," and "to the spirits of righteous men made perfect." The position of the word "judge," which precedes the word "God" in the Greek text, makes the former emphatic. Participants in the new covenant have come "to a judge, the God of all." That he is "the God of all" demonstrates his right to pass judgment, and in some forms of apocalyptic literature Mount Zion was understood as the mountain of God's eschatological judgment of the whole earth (4 Ezra 13:1–39).[9] The author probably has in mind a strong note of the vindication of God's righteous people, a prominent theme in portions of Scripture (e.g., Ps. 9:8; 58:11; 82:8; 94:2; 96:13; 119:84; Isa. 11:4; Jer. 22:16; Lam. 3:59). For example, Psalm 9:7–12 reads:

> The LORD reigns forever;
>> he has established his throne for judgment.
> He will judge the world in righteousness;
>> he will govern the peoples with justice.
> The LORD is a refuge for the oppressed,
>> a stronghold in times of trouble.
> Those who know your name will trust in you,
>> for you, LORD, have never forsaken those who seek you.
> Sing praises to the LORD, enthroned in Zion;
>> proclaim among the nations what he has done.
> For he who avenges blood remembers;
>> he does not ignore the cry of the afflicted.

In line with this motif of vindication, the new covenant people have not come to Mount Zion for God to pass judgment on them, but for him to vindicate them before their wicked persecutors.

In the next breath the writer hastens to point to "the spirits of righteous men [and women] made perfect" by God's divine grace. This phrase probably designates the godly who have already died, since the expression is a common idiom used thus in Jewish apocalyptic.[10] These have been "made perfect forever" by the sacrifice of Christ (10:14).

The author already has gone to great lengths to show Jesus as the mediator of the new covenant, whose sprinkled blood cleanses completely and for

---

8. Attridge, *The Epistle to the Hebrews*, 375.
9. Lane, *Hebrews 9–13*, 470.
10. Ibid.

all time from sin (8:7–13; 9:11–14; 10:15–18). But what does the author mean when he refers to the blood of Christ as speaking "a better word than the blood of Abel"? After Abel was killed by Cain, his blood "cried out" to God for judgment (Gen. 4:10). Abel's blood bore witness against Cain, indicating his guilt. Christ's blood, on the other hand, has won our forgiveness, "crying out" that people of the new covenant are no longer guilty, having been cleansed completely from sin.

A Final Warning (12:25–29)

BOTH 12:18–21, WHICH concerns the Old Testament approach to Mount Sinai, and 12:22–24, which expresses the blessings of the new covenant, involve speaking from God. The "word" (v. 24) of God has functioned as a focal motif for the author of Hebrews from the beginning of his book and now is expressed forcefully in a final, powerful warning. Thus, he begins with the somber exhortation, "See to it that you do not refuse him who speaks." The rest of the passage is built around the author's often-used technique, an "argument from lesser to greater."[11] The "lesser" situation in this passage is that of those in the desert, who, refusing to heed the message of God, were judged (cf. 3:7–19). That God "warned them on earth" is a reference to his manifestation at Mount Sinai.

The more significant, or "greater," situation that concerns the author relates to his hearers' receptivity to the voice of God from heaven. If those of the old covenant did not escape the wrath of God when they turned from his Word, the judgment on those who reject the message of salvation received in the new covenant era is even more certain (2:1–3). Describing the coming judgment, the author quotes Haggai 2:6, weaving an interpretation into his quotation. The Old Testament text reads, "Yet once more I will shake heaven and earth." The author of Hebrews reverses the words "heaven" and "earth" and includes the phrases "not only" and "but also" to bring out the significance of the text for his discussion.

The shaking of the earth he understands as a reference to the event of terror at Mount Sinai in the Old Testament, since that manifestation of God's presence is associated with the Sinai theophany (Ex. 19:18; Judg. 5:5; Ps. 68:8; 77:18). In other words, at the Sinai event God "shook the earth" but has promised a more extensive "shaking" for the future—a shaking that will include the heavens.

The writer then goes on to reason (v. 27): "The words 'once more' indicate the removing of what can be shaken—that is, created things—so that

---

11. See above, p. 25.

what cannot be shaken may remain." Thus, he interprets the shaking that God will do "once more" as the eschatological judgment to be visited on the earth at the end of the age, when the material universe will pass away (1 Cor. 7:31; 2 Peter 3:10, 12; Rev. 21:1). At that point only the kingdom of God will remain, the kingdoms of this world having been utterly destroyed.

Based on this insight, the author concludes the unit with 12:28–29. In verse 28 he challenges his hearers with, "Therefore, since we are receiving a kingdom that cannot be shaken, let us be thankful, and so worship God acceptably with reverence and awe. . . ." Their inheritance of an "unmovable" kingdom should inspire thanksgiving and reverent worship. On the other hand, those who, like Esau, reject such an inheritance, failing to be thankful and worship God appropriately, should be reminded that "God is a consuming fire" (a quote from Deut. 4:24).

ARE THOSE MOUNTAINS **far away?** Most moderns live in a "live-for-today" culture. A businessperson once quoted me the maxim, "Yesterday is a canceled check, tomorrow is just a promissory note; only today is cash." We may chafe against those who draw our attention to the distant past or the distant future, reasoning, "I have enough to worry about today." True, our Lord echoed that sentiment in Matthew 6:34: "Therefore do not worry about tomorrow, for tomorrow will worry about itself. Each day has enough trouble of its own." His concern, however, was to prevent people from becoming so preoccupied with meeting their own material needs that they are distracted from more vital, spiritual issues. His listeners were captivated by the need for clothing and food and forced to live hand to mouth and thread to tunic.

In a sense moderns are often so pressed by their schedules that the worry of tomorrow has been forced back into today. The rush and crush of these schedules have the same effect, however, of forcing spiritual considerations to a back burner. In our cultural context, therefore, the reality and relevance of the two mountains of Hebrews 12—one seemingly a fossil of the ancient past and the other a celestial image of another world—may be difficult to grasp. The looming, booming picture of Mount Sinai painted in 12:18–21 may seem more a caricature from some horror film than a real-life threat. The festive gathering of Mount Zion, with angels, spirits, and God in the heavenly city, may seem equally fantastic and far removed from the down-to-earth world of daily living.

Points of application related to the mountains. However, these two mountains, foreboding Mount Sinai and festive Mount Zion, could not be

more up to date. Pregnant with relevance for modern living, the two mountains must be understood as theological constructs, two ways of viewing
relationship with God, that are as meaningful today as when these words were
first written. *This is the most important foundational key to interpreting Hebrews 12:18–
24.* Although the author couches his words in spatial language ("you have not
come . . . but you have come"), he is not concerned with physical movement
and literal mountains. No, these mountains represent two covenants, and
the author is concerned with where his listeners are in relation to God.

There can be no doubt concerning which orientation is to be preferred.
The writer crafts the whole of 12:18–24 around the contrasts between the
two. Certainly there are connections or correspondences between the two
mountains. God's presence may be found on both summits, and God speaks.
Moreover, both mountains, which represent the covenants, have a mediator—the trembling Moses and the high priest Jesus. Nevertheless, the great
weight of Hebrews' imagery goes to building an unmistakable picture of
sheer contrasts.

The sense of *terror* at Sinai, a place of noise and macabre images, flashes like
lightning against a black storm cloud. The gloomy sights and the loud noises
are the stuff of nightmares. Understandably, the people at the foot of the
mountain want no part of it, begging that God will not speak anymore to
them. Even Moses trembles with fear. Note further that the images in verses
18–21 are highly *impersonal*. Here we have fire, storm, gloom, warning, and a
"disembodied" voice. Everything about this picture of Sinai says, "Stay away!
Don't come any closer!" The covenant, that meaningful agreement between
God and the Israelites, was ratified from a distance because of the unholiness
of the people. God resided in the gloom of his mountain, and the people
were not allowed even to touch its base. The emphasis, therefore, rests on *the
unworthiness* of the covenant assembly, on God's judgment of their sin.

By contrast, Mount Zion depicts utter *joy and excitement*. The gathering of
the angels, the assembly of the firstborn, and the spirits of those who have
gone on to be with the Lord resemble the revelry of a national holiday. To
what are we calling people when we call them to our form of religion? Is it
a place of dread, a place from which God seems remote and unapproachable?
Or are we calling people to joy? When was the last time in your church or
my church that someone from the outside could have mistaken what was taking place for a party because such joy and festivity permeated the event? I
am not suggesting that worship services should be raucous. But we should ask
whether joy, real joy, is a product of people's encounter with God through
our communities of faith.

Moreover, mark how utterly *personal and relational* the images of verses 22–
24 are! We have come to God our vindicator, angels, other believers, and our

Lord Jesus. In contrast to the Sinai portrait, everything about Zion says, "Come! Belong here! Be part of this community! There is no better place to be." Are we calling people to a religion that fosters healthy relationships with God and others? Do the ministries of our churches invite people to draw near to God and to our fellowships? Or do people find barriers surrounding our churches, be they cultural, traditional, or spiritual? How can we be living out authentically the community life of Mount Zion, a life that reverberates with the invitation, "Come and belong," when by our actions and attitudes we communicate, "Don't get too close—to us or our God!"?

The final note rings loudest for the author of Hebrews: Only on the new covenant mountain can one find holiness, forgiveness, and *grace*. We need not be in terror of God's voice here. Jesus' blood speaks a good word on our behalf, saying that the sacrifice for our sin has been offered once for all time. Relationship with God has been assured since the new covenant mediator came down off the mountain, lived among the people, and offered himself as the ultimate sacrifice. Do we communicate a strong message of *grace* through our actions, preaching, teaching, and ministries? Does Jesus' blood speak louder than the blood of Abel in our churches? Or have we elevated the condemning word over the word of forgiveness?

This does not just apply to those with whom we are attempting to share the gospel. Let's remember that the author of Hebrews uses this word of grace *as a key motivator for those who were struggling with perseverance*. Application of the passage, therefore, must consider the effects of grace on those who are struggling with drifting from the faith.[12]

Applying Hebrews 12:25–29. With the final passage in Hebrews 12, the writer has brought us back to several familiar themes. Once again he puts forward the Word of God as a reality with which one must reckon. The Word must be received or rejected; there is no middle ground. For those who reject the Word, there exists no escape from God's judgment. At the end a person either resides as a citizen of God's unshakable kingdom or perishes with the rest of the universe. The author uses these themes, packaged in his argument from lesser to greater, to end the material recorded in this chapter on a note of forceful warning. It may seem strange that such a harsh warning follows so closely on the heels of the beautifully poetic—almost ecstatic—vision of grace in 12:22–24. Would it not have been better to end the section on a positive note and leave it at that?

In answer we might reply that grace towers over judgment. Yet those who would play "fast and loose" with grace must be reminded that wrath

---

12. On this whole issue of grace and the church, see the book by Philip Yancey, *What's So Amazing About Grace?* (Grand Rapids: Zondervan, 1997).

still waits in the wings. God still sits in his seat as Judge. Thus, grace does not mean a universal message of "forgive and forget." God does not say to humanity, "Whatever you have done, come—and O yes, everything will really be OK even if you don't come, or even if you play at coming and then leave again!" No, grace must be received and enjoyed in the context of covenant. Those who reject the new covenant reject grace and embrace judgment.

The reason our author follows his picture of festive celebration (12:22–24) with a stern warning (12:25–29) has to do, once again, with the purpose of this book and the spiritual condition of the community. For some in the audience, the matter of their eternal destiny has yet to be discerned; their status has been called into question by their flirtation with apostasy. The warning, therefore, demonstrates that the preacher cannot give an unqualified message of grace to a community of people among whom are those considering abandoning the faith.[13]

The harsh admonition of 12:25–29, moreover, rivets attention on the consummation of the ages as a key motivator toward right decision. We are called to "live in light of eternity," weighing our decision regarding God's offer of grace in light of that decision's implications at the return of Christ (9:28; 10:37–39). The key question here concerns what we will invest in over the long term. Will we invest our lives in a lasting kingdom?

When I teach this passage to my students I use the following illustration. I ask the class to imagine that I have taken one of my son's marbles outside and found a mound of dirt. From that mound I take a handful of earth and, placing the marble in the middle, begin making a large dirt-clod. Once made, I leave it out in the sun to dry. I ask them to imagine that on the next day I go back to my dirt-clod, pick it up, and begin shaking it in my hands. As I shake the ball harder and harder, it begins to crumble; more and more pieces, large and small, disintegrate beneath the pressure. Finally, the dirt has completely fallen away to expose the marble, that unshakable, perfect sphere at the core of the clod.

In New Testament theology the seen and the unseen worlds may coexist at present, but the former has a point of termination. Those who belong to the new covenant inherit the kingdom of God, the essence of the unseen world, and thus invest their lives in that which is unshakable. By contrast, those who refuse that kingdom, investing their lives in the seen kingdoms of this age, will not escape the judgment of God. Therefore, the message of 12:25–29 invites us to live in light of eternal values, a life that should be characterized by thankfulness and appropriate worship of God (12:28–29).

---

13. In this regard see the discussion above, pp. 134–38.

To what are we calling people? I recently organized a banquet for the university and invited a
number of prominent laypersons from the surrounding area. As I talked to them on the tele-
phone, they wanted to know the nature of the meeting and, especially, what,
if anything, would be expected of them. Fair inquiries.

From the earliest days of the Christian movement, the "call to come" has
been a central aspect of the church's message. We need to think clearly about
that to which we are inviting people through our public and private proclamations. They have a right to know, and we have a responsibility to call
them to the right "mountain" from a biblical perspective. For the call has
had many different expressions throughout church history, some of which
have veered dangerously from the gospel of grace, joy, and relationship
reflected in Hebrews 12:22–24. At times the church has called people to war;
at other times the call has been to an inquisitor's rack. People have been
called to a political platform or to endorse a king or political regime.

Aberrant theology has formed the focus of the call at critical junctures
along the way of history, as has the desire for acceptance from secular
thought-crafters, who do not even believe in God. Out of a desire to reflect
clearly God's holiness, we can steer dangerously close to Sinai, not just as a
necessary way station but as a permanent, spiritual destination, preaching a
gospel of terror rather than a gospel of beauty. Do our sermons boom and
flash with the darkness of Sinai more than they sing and gather people to the
festiveness of Zion? This raises three questions.

(1) Are we calling people to grace? At the beginning of his book *What's
So Amazing About Grace*, author Philip Yancey tells of a personal encounter
that puts an exclamation point on this question:

> A prostitute came to me in wretched straits, homeless, sick, unable
> to buy food for her two-year-old daughter. Through sobs and tears, she
> told me she had been renting out her daughter—two years old!—to
> men interested in kinky sex. She made more renting out her daughter
> for an hour than she could earn on her own in a night. She had to do
> it, she said, to support her own drug habit. I could hardly bear hearing
> her sordid story. For one thing, it made me legally liable—I'm required
> to report cases of child abuse. I had no idea what to say to this woman.
>
> At last I asked if she had ever thought of going to a church for
> help. I will never forget the look of pure, naïve shock that crossed her
> face. "Church!" she cried. "Why would I ever go there? I was already
> feeling terrible about myself. They'd just make me feel worse."[14]

---

14. Yancey, *What's So Amazing About Grace?* 11.

Yancey goes on to reflect that people, the worst of people, always seemed to be drawn to Jesus rather than repelled by him. In fact, the drawing seemed to be in direct proportion to the depths to which the person had sunk. How is it possible for a church, which claims to be the body of Christ, to repel the type of people who were so drawn to Jesus himself?

In some branches of modern Christianity we seem to have latched onto the thought that the most important truth to which we can call the world is the holiness of God—a vitally important spiritual truth! As we see the moral fiber of our cultures decaying, unraveling before our eyes, we can become fixated on shouting against the decay lest we be lost in it. But if we are not careful, grace can get lost amid our shouts. We can, in effect, be perceived as dragging people to the foot of Mount Sinai, attempting to hold their heads back and forcing them to face the storm, feel the red-hot flash of lightning, and tremble at the weighty Voice. Most unholy people still do not like Sinai and will respond, "I don't want to listen to that voice anymore!" In short, if we bear a message of ungrace, they run the other way when they see us coming.

Although it is true that the path to Mount Zion brushes past Mount Sinai—the holiness of God *is* a foundational aspect of the message of true grace—Zion must loom large in our vision and the vision of Christianity that we communicate to others. It would be a shame if people never hear the music of the heavenly Jerusalem because the thunder of our Sinai drowns it out, if they never move past trembling Moses to meet Jesus, who stands with his outstretched hands.

(2) Are we calling people to relationship? In a recent letter to Dear Abby, an elderly couple who had retired and moved to Florida expressed a sad experience too frequent in modern Christianity. They had chosen to live in a small town because of its beauty and slow-paced lifestyle. Their primary attempt at building relationships had been to join a church, but the social network within that church had been such that after months of trying, reaching out to others for friendship, they gave up. The public messages and PR had proclaimed a hearty "come and belong," but their experience within that community proclaimed otherwise.

We must reflect on the ease or unease with which people assimilate into our churches. In the church to which I belong we struggle on the "unease" end of the scale, and the difficulty of meaningfully embracing people into the fellowship is a perennial issue. From my conversations with pastors I sense the problem is almost universal. What are the social, programmatic, cultural, and theological dynamics that hinder that assimilation? How can we build a community that reflects the unity, the festive gathering of Mount Zion? We *are* that community! We have already come to the new covenant mountain. How can we live that truth out? Correspondingly, is our preaching, teaching, and living of theology introducing people to the relational God of Zion or to the hidden God of Sinai? I realize, of course, that God is both. We must remember, however, that the author of Hebrews here presents us with two visions of people vis-à-vis God. Are those to whom we minister encouraged to draw near to or run away from God?

(3) Are we calling people to joy? In Joy Davidman's delightful little book *Smoke on the Mountain*, she reflects on the Sabbath by telling of a Martian anthropology student who has been sent to earth for an assignment. The student sweeps over the United States on a fine Sunday morning, writing furiously with his writing tentacle. In his report he notes that creatures of the third planet are obviously sun worshipers, this one day in seven set aside for religious observance. The sometimes loud and rowdy rituals are conducted in open air, drawing large crowds to arenas or bodies of water. Some of the religion's mystics address a holy ball—a solar symbol—by themselves or in groups of three or four with long clubs in open green fields. Others go down to the ocean, stripping almost naked and hurling themselves in ecstasy into the waves. When they are exhausted, they anoint their bodies with holy oils and lay flat on the ground, surrendering completely to the deity.

The Martian goes on to tell of a small group of unbelievers who have rejected sun worship. They dress soberly and gather behind closed doors in stained-glass buildings, obviously designed to keep the sunlight out. Their faces and gestures demonstrate none of the "almost orgiastic religious frenzy with which the sun worshipers pursue their devotions." In fact, they almost appear placid, "indicating minds blank of thought or emotion."

Reflecting then on contemporary Christian believers and their lack of sheer joy in their Christianity, Davidman asks:

> Was the Martian wildly wrong, or fantastically right?
> . . . So the unbelievers must go on with their games. But what of the believers? It is so easy for them to be tempted into joining the games, first now and then, later as a habit; finally, the uneasy sense of something forgotten on Sunday morning gradually fades away entirely, and faith in God perishes not by conviction but by disuse. Even many who do come to church come out of a dull sense of duty rather than a joyous sense of devotion—the life has gone out of their belief.[15]

Davidman is concerned with how joy has somehow been leeched from Sunday worship, yet her concern is more broadly relevant. Do we live joyfully in our covenant with God? From the picture of the Mount Zion festivities,

---

15. Joy Davidman, *Smoke on the Mountain: An Interpretation of the Ten Commandments* (Philadelphia: Westminster, 1954), 49–51.

especially seen in the angelic assembly, we are terribly out of place or out of step with eternity if we do not. Furthermore, if we do not live joyfully, reflecting the reality of the heavenly Jerusalem, how can we invite people to that reality? If our lives reflect the gloom of Sinai more than the excitement of Zion, we do the kingdom poor publicity. This does not mean, of course, that we always are thrilled with our situations, but are we *characterized* by joy? That is a key question. If we are not, then the reality of Zion is not invading our lives. Perhaps we need a clearer view of that mountain and must hear again the song of the angels and the message of the sprinkled blood.

An orientation to the future grace of God. Many Christians seem content to live with their lives oriented to past expressions of God's grace, such as a conversion experience, a time during which God manifested himself unusually through answered prayer, or a time of special spiritual vitality. But God's workings of grace and our need for faith must not be relegated to past experiences. We must hear God now and we need hope for the future, hope that finds energy in faith and accesses the grace of God for the needs of tomorrow. Thus, we must have a holistic interaction with the grace of God— one that rejoices in past experiences, interfaces with the Lord in the present, and trusts him with the future. On the interaction of God's past and future grace in the Christian life, John Piper notes:

> There is a sense in which gratitude and faith are interwoven joys that strengthen each other. As gratitude joyfully revels in the benefits of past grace, so faith joyfully relies on the benefits of future grace. Therefore when gratitude for God's past grace is strong, the message is sent that God is supremely trustworthy in the future because of what he has done in the past. In this way faith is strengthened by a lively gratitude for God's past trustworthiness.
>
> On the other hand, when faith in God's future grace is strong, the message is sent that this kind of God makes no mistakes, so that everything he has done in the past is part of a good plan and can be remembered with gratitude. In this way gratitude is strengthened by a lively faith in God's future grace.[16]

The person who claims an experience of past grace but senses no need for present interaction with the Lord or for future grace at the coming of Christ, may not be living biblical faith, and his or her relationship with Christ is suspect.[17] Faith in the grace of God means that I embrace Christ in all his biblical roles: as high priest and sacrifice for my sins, as intercessor, and as Lord of the universe, who in the future will "shake the heavens and the earth."

---

16. John Piper, *Future Grace* (Sisters, Ore.: Multnomah, 1995), 48–49.
17. In this regard see the discussion of Hebrews 3:1–19 above, pp. 124–97.

This is why the author of Hebrews can follow the portrait of new covenant relationship (12:22–24) with the harsh warning of 12:25–29. His warning reminds us that biblical grace links all the workings of God in our lives in a continuum. Those who grasp the gravity of God's future judgment of the world, living their lives in light of God's will and trusting God's grace for that moment, find that God's grace is working its way back into the present. Hope in that grace for the future has a powerful, transforming effect on the present (1 John 3:3).

Theologian Jürgen Moltmann has noted that Christian theologizing about the end of the world remains sterile unless that future event is allowed to exert an impact on present thought and action.[18] This is true Christian hope concerning the coming of Christ, a hope that not only comforts concerning the future but also transforms the present. If one truly grasps the reality of biblical eschatology—that heaven breaks into earth and will one day consummate that inbreaking—it changes everything. How I think and live will be changed in light of that transforming vision. That knowledge of the coming shaking of the world, *the* End, can cause me to evaluate in what I am investing my life. Thus the Christian lives *now* in light of the unseen *then*, when Christ will appear. The Christian lives for what will be stable eternally.

> This view separates what is real from what is unreal. What is real is what will last. Everything else, no matter how real it seems to us, is treated as insubstantial, hardly worth a snort. That is why Scripture can seem at times so blithely and irritatingly out of touch with reality, brushing past huge philosophical problems and personal agony. That is just how life is, when you are looking from the end. Perspective changes everything.[19]

This commitment to valuing that which is of eternal value was embodied in the five young missionaries who sought to reach out to a group of Indians in the rain forest of Ecuador in the late 1950s. Jim Elliot and his four companions had spent months planning the outreach to the Aucas, Stone-Age killers who had come to distrust any contact with the outside world. Yet the effort ended in a seeming tragedy. Just two days prior to the fateful day of their murders, Elliot and the others had met three of the Indians on the sandy beach that the missionaries used as an air strip. The meeting was friendly and heightened the hopes of those who had come to share the gospel.

---

18. Jürgen Moltmann, *Theology of Hope: On the Grounds and Implications of a Christian Eschatology* (London: SCM / New York: Harper & Row, 1968), 32–36.

19. Tim Stafford, "The Age to Come," *Christianity Today* (May 17, 1985): 32.

When they returned some forty-eight hours later, the missionaries waited expectantly for their newfound friends to arrive. But before 4:30 that afternoon these young ministers had given their lives, slain with spears by the men with whom they had hoped to share Christ. The world called it a nightmare—and it was tragic. Yet the cost of that terrible moment must be weighed ultimately on the scales of eternal values. Seven years prior, in 1949, Jim Elliot had penned a now-famous quote that puts the loss in perspective: "He is no fool who gives what he cannot keep to gain what he cannot lose."[20]

Hebrews challenges us to live in light of that which cannot be lost, the unshakable kingdom of God. We "gain what we cannot lose" by trusting in God's grace of the past, present, and future, heeding the Word of God, and living in reverent awe of him. May we be found living in light of eternity today.

---

20. E. Elliot, *Shadow of the Almighty* (San Francisco: Harper & Row, 1958), 15, 18–19.

Hebrews 13:1–25

KEEP ON LOVING each other as brothers. ²Do not forget to entertain strangers, for by so doing some people have entertained angels without knowing it. ³Remember those in prison as if you were their fellow prisoners, and those who are mistreated as if you yourselves were suffering.

⁴Marriage should be honored by all, and the marriage bed kept pure, for God will judge the adulterer and all the sexually immoral. ⁵Keep your lives free from the love of money and be content with what you have, because God has said,

> "Never will I leave you;
>   never will I forsake you."

⁶So we say with confidence,

> "The Lord is my helper; I will not be afraid.
>   What can man do to me?"

⁷Remember your leaders, who spoke the word of God to you. Consider the outcome of their way of life and imitate their faith. ⁸Jesus Christ is the same yesterday and today and forever.

⁹Do not be carried away by all kinds of strange teachings. It is good for our hearts to be strengthened by grace, not by ceremonial foods, which are of no value to those who eat them. ¹⁰We have an altar from which those who minister at the tabernacle have no right to eat. ¹¹The high priest carries the blood of animals into the Most Holy Place as a sin offering, but the bodies are burned outside the camp. ¹²And so Jesus also suffered outside the city gate to make the people holy through his own blood. ¹³Let us, then, go to him outside the camp, bearing the disgrace he bore. ¹⁴For here we do not have an enduring city, but we are looking for the city that is to come.

¹⁵Through Jesus, therefore, let us continually offer to God a sacrifice of praise—the fruit of lips that confess his name. ¹⁶And do not forget to do good and to share with others, for with such sacrifices God is pleased.

¹⁷Obey your leaders and submit to their authority. They keep watch over you as men who must give an account. Obey them so that their work will be a joy, not a burden, for that would be of no advantage to you.

¹⁸Pray for us. We are sure that we have a clear conscience and desire to live honorably in every way. ¹⁹I particularly urge you to pray so that I may be restored to you soon.

²⁰May the God of peace, who through the blood of the eternal covenant brought back from the dead our Lord Jesus, that great Shepherd of the sheep, ²¹equip you with everything good for doing his will, and may he work in us what is pleasing to him, through Jesus Christ, to whom be glory for ever and ever. Amen.

²²Brothers, I urge you to bear with my word of exhortation, for I have written you only a short letter.

²³I want you to know that our brother Timothy has been released. If he arrives soon, I will come with him to see you.

²⁴Greet all your leaders and all God's people. Those from Italy send you their greetings.

²⁵Grace be with you all.

Original Meaning

THE WRITER OF Hebrews concludes his work with a series of practical guidelines on how his hearers might serve God—how they might live out a persevering faith. The first five of these (13:1–6) provide general instructions that would have been familiar throughout the Christian churches. The remaining seven (13:7–19) revolve around the community's relationship with its leaders, ending with the author's personal appeal for prayer. The benediction of 13:20–21 was probably the ending to the original sermon, and the closing (vv. 22–25) an epistolary addendum added when the author sent the manuscript by courier.

Some scholars have questioned whether Hebrews 13 was part of the original work, but this view generally has been abandoned in light of detailed studies that demonstrate the integrity of this chapter with the rest of the book.[1] The author's use of vocabulary, the Old Testament, conceptual ties, patterns of argumentation, structural patterns, and literary style all point to this chapter as a strategically crafted final movement to this powerful sermon. Having put before his listeners a lucid Christology and a series of robust exhortations, the author now closes with sensible instructions for living out the Christian faith in the details of daily responsibilities.

---

1. For example, Floyd V. Filson, *"Yesterday": A Study of Hebrews in Light of Chapter 13*, Studies in Biblical Theology (Naperville, Ill.: Alec R. Allenson, 1967).

General Guidelines for Christian Living (13:1–6)

(1) *LOVE FELLOW CHRISTIANS* (13:1). The New Testament resounds with the command to love the "brothers," an idiom for fellow believers (e.g., Matt. 22:39; John 13:34; Rom. 13:8; 1 Cor. 13; 1 Peter 1:22; 1 John 2:10; 3:10; 4:7).[2] *Philadelphia*, a noun translated here "loving ... as brothers,"[3] was used commonly in early Christian ethical teaching (Rom. 12:10; 1 Thess. 4:9; 1 Peter 1:22; 2 Peter 1:7). Rather than speaking to a particular emotion, the emphasis in the New Testament focuses on the call to meet one another's needs. Thus, it may be that the author intends Hebrews 13:2–3 as application of this admonition in verse 1.[4] He has treated well the interwoven themes of God's "fatherhood," the Christians' status as "heirs," and Christ's role as the "first brother," who leads them to their inheritance (2:10–18; 12:3–17).[5] The concept of believers as united in a close spiritual family lays the foundation for practical exhortations to meet the needs of those in the family. Believers must live out love practically as an ever-present, foundational dynamic within the community.

(2) *Show hospitality* (13:2). The word rendered "entertain strangers" (*philoxenia*) connotes treating a person, perhaps a stranger, nobly and magnanimously in the context of one's home, joyfully seeking to bring that person refreshment.[6] In the ancient world it was expensive to stay overnight at an inn, and such establishments usually had poor reputations. Thus, an aspect of Jewish and early Christian piety, as well as etiquette in the broader Greco-Roman culture, involved taking people in for an evening. In the Christian context such admonitions to show hospitality have their foundation in the Old Testament and the teachings of Jesus.

The practice of hospitality is evident in the life of the early believers as witnessed in Acts and the New Testament letters.[7] The earliest Christians shared the mobility of the broader culture, and, therefore, many opportunities existed for them to practice hospitality toward traveling teachers, businesspersons, or refugees from persecution. The supreme paradigm for hospitality in early Jewish literature was the hospitality of Abraham, shown to his heavenly visitors (Gen. 18:2–15), which is probably alluded to in

---

2. Hughes, *A Commentary on the Epistle to the Hebrews*, 562.

3. The verse reads more literally, "Let brotherly love continue."

4. Hagner, *Hebrews*, 234; Lane, *Hebrews 9–13*, 511.

5. On the use of "gender specific" language here, specifically the use of a masculine designation for all Christians, male and female, see above, pp. 113–14.

6. Spicq, *Theological Lexicon of the New Testament*, 3:454–47; Lane, *Hebrews 9–13*, 511–12.

7. E.g., Gen. 19:13; 31:32; 2 Sam. 12:4; Isa. 58:7; Matt. 25:35; Luke 7:36–47; 10:34–37; Acts 21:4–17; Rom. 12:13; 1 Tim. 3:2; Titus 1:8; 1 Peter 4:9; see Ellingworth, *The Epistle to the Hebrews*, 694.

Hebrews 13:2: "for by so doing some people have entertained angels without knowing it."

(3) *Minister to those in prison and to those who are mistreated* (13:3). The community of faith addressed by Hebrews had demonstrated practical ministry to those in prison in the past (10:34), and they are called here to continue that practice. Prisoners were not treated well in the first century, often having to depend on friends and family even for the most basic necessities of life.[8] Christians could minister to fellow believers in prison, who were suffering for the sake of the gospel, either by offering consolation and gifts (Matt. 25:36; 2 Tim. 1:16) or by praying for them (Col. 4:18; Heb. 13:18–19). To "remember" (*mimneskomai*) means to keep present in one's thoughts, an idea strengthened by the adverbial phrase "as if you were their fellow prisoners." In other words, Christians are to keep their imprisoned friends constantly in mind as if they were right there looking at them.

Such concern should also be extended to those suffering mistreatment. Rather than a reference to the "body of Christ" as used in Paul's letters (e.g., 1 Cor. 12; Eph. 4:1–16), the clause at the end of verse 3 (lit., "as also those being in the body") is rendered appropriately by the NIV with "as if you yourselves were suffering." The thought here is "be concerned for those who are suffering as if every blow they receive puts a stripe across your own back."

(4) *Hold marriage as honorable and keep the sexual relationship pure* (13:4). Another motif common in early Christian ethical teaching was the need to keep the marriage relationship in proper perspective. The institution of marriage was assaulted from two sides in the ancient world. Some felt chastity in marriage was unreasonable. For example, in some corners of Greco-Roman culture men were expected to take mistresses as their confidants and sexual partners. Others felt marriage stunted spiritual devotion and thus held asceticism as the ideal. As the verse develops, it is clear that the former, rather than the latter, error is in view.

The word "honor" (*timios*) connotes "respect" or attributes "preciousness or value" to someone or something.[9] For example, *timios* can be used of valuable material possessions (e.g., 1 Cor. 3:12), a respected teacher (Acts 5:34), the promises of God (2 Peter 1:4), or even the blood of Christ (1 Peter 1:19). As used in Hebrews 13:4, the word suggests that marriage, rather than an arrangement to be treated lightly, should be esteemed as of great worth.

Correspondingly, the marriage bed (*koite*), used here as an idiom for the sexual relationship, is to be guarded or "kept pure." The defilement that the author has in mind is expressed in the explanatory "for God will judge the

---

8. Leon Morris, "Hebrews," 146.
9. Balz and Schneider, *EDNT*, 3:359.

adulterer and all the sexually immoral." The former word, "adulterers" (*moi-choi*), is more focused than the latter, referring specifically to those who betray their marriage vows. The latter, "the sexually immoral" (*pornoi*), refers to all those involved in sexual activity apart from the sanctity of the marriage relationship. Together the two words cover the gamut of illicit sexual behavior.[10] For those so involved in dishonoring marriage and defiling the marriage bed, the judgment of God awaits.

(5) *Be content with your financial status* (13:5). The sins of sexual impurity and covetousness are linked in several New Testament passages (e.g., 1 Cor. 5:10–11; Eph. 4:19; 1 Thess. 4:3–6), probably because their prohibitions are given side by side as the seventh and eighth of the Ten Commandments. Both the sexually immoral and those greedy for money pursue a myopic self-gratification that takes them outside the bounds of God's provision. Such greed amounts to accusing God of incompetence as a provider of one's most basic needs and, therefore, is incompatible with commitment to God himself (cf. Matt. 6:24). Consequently, Christians are exhorted to keep their lives "free from the love of money" and to "be content" with what they have.

Absence of the love of money (*aphilargyros*) was extolled in secular culture as a virtue because leaders would be incorruptible in the management of certain affairs, a thought that parallels a requirement for church leaders (1 Tim. 3:3).[11] Here, however, the author has in mind Christians in general and the struggle to keep money in perspective in daily life. For the one who is *aphilargyros*, money is simply a means of meeting needs rather than a driving motivation or preoccupation of life. Such a person is "content" (*arkoumenos*) with what God has given.

The basis for such contentment is God's promise of his ever-present help: "Never will I leave you; never will I forsake you." No Old Testament quotation perfectly corresponds to this quote in Greek, although several approach correspondence (e.g., Gen. 28:15; Deut. 31:6–8; Josh. 1:5), and various theories have been offered as to how the author was using his source material. Perhaps he conflated two Old Testament passages or used a Greek translation no longer in existence.[12] Nevertheless, the significance of the promise is clear: God keeps his covenant to provide for his people. Therefore, believers need not worry that their needs will go unmet.

Thus, the Christian can profess with confidence, "The Lord is my helper; I will not be afraid. What can man do to me?" (13:6). This response comes from Psalm 118:6–7 and asserts that the plans of the wicked will be thwarted

---

10. Bruce, *The Epistle to the Hebrews*, 373.

11. Spicq, *Theological Lexicon of the New Testament*, 1:245–46.

12. The latter is more likely since the exact quote as given here also occurs in Philo.

by the provisions of God. The backdrop for the author's use of this promise and for this human response placed on the lips of believers certainly involves the hearers' situation. If, as was the case in their past, they were being persecuted in part by being forced to give up property or material possessions (Heb. 10:32–34), this promise of God and the encouragement to make an appropriate response would be especially relevant.

Guidelines on Church Leadership and Doctrine (13:7–19)

THE BOUNDARIES OF the middle portion of Hebrews 13 are marked by the references to the community's leaders in verses 7 and 17. The exhortation to "remember your leaders" (v. 7) leads into a somewhat complex discussion of theology that hints at a significant struggle for this church and ends with a practical challenge to application (vv. 9–15). The exhortation to "obey your leaders" (v. 17) extends to the author's request that the church pray for him (vv. 18–19).[13]

In 13:7 the readers are exhorted to "remember your leaders." The present participle of the word *begeomai* was used in the broader Greco-Roman culture of state officials and in the LXX for religious, political, and military leaders.[14] Used in a Christian context for a church office, the word finds expression in ancient Christian documents especially related to the city of Rome.[15] Most interpreters suggest the author has in mind here church leaders who have already died;[16] the identifying relative clause, "who spoke the word of God to you," is understood as a technical reference to the preaching of the gospel in the founding of this church. Also, the word translated "outcome" (*ekbasis*) can refer to the sum total of one's accomplishment in life.[17] The author, therefore, exhorts his hearers to consider closely or scrutinize the fruit of their

---

13. Attridge, *The Epistle to the Hebrews*, 390–91.

14. E.g., Sirach 17:17; 33:19; 1 Macc. 9:30; 2 Macc. 14:16.

15. Specifically 1 Clement and The Shepherd of Hermas.

16. E.g., Hughes, *Commentary on the Epistle to the Hebrews*, 569; Westcott, *The Epistle to the Hebrews*, 436; Moffatt, *A Critical and Exegetical Commentary*, 230; Lane, *Hebrews 9–13*, 526–27; Attridge, *The Epistle to the Hebrews*, 391–92.

17. Hughes, *Commentary on the Epistle to the Hebrews*, 569. Although this interpretation has a great deal of strength and is, perhaps, preferred, the argument can be put forward that these were current leaders in the congregation for the following reasons. (1) The word "remember" (*mnemoneuo*) need not refer to a past event but can be used in the sense of "be mindful of." (2) The word for "leaders" in v. 7 is used for *current* leaders in v. 17. Both are present participles in form, the former in the genitive case, the latter in the dative case. (3) The note that the leaders "spoke the word of God to you," although probably referring to the original preaching of the gospel to the community, does not rule out current leaders, some of whom could have been involved in that activity. (4) The word translated "outcome" (*ekbasis*) could merely be used as a reference to the positive result of godly living on the part of the current leaders.

leaders' manner of living and imitate their faith. In other words, the leaders are placed in the same category of "heroic examples" as the paragons of biblical history (6:12–15; 11:1–40).

Hebrews 13:8 sets forth a beautiful proclamation of Christ's immutability: "Jesus Christ is the same yesterday and today and forever." The theological perspective behind this concise Christological formula has been developed well in the course of Hebrews. The author asserts the Son's role in creation (1:2, 10), certainly an aspect of "yesterday." Presently the Son sits in his exalted status as Lord of the universe, who intercedes for his people (1:3, 13; 7:26–28). The author has vigorously promulgated the perpetual nature of Christ's rule "for all time" into the eternal "tomorrow" (1:8a, 10–12):

> Your throne, O God, will last for ever and ever....
> ... the heavens are the work of your hands.
> They will perish, but you remain;
> they will all wear out like a garment.
> You will roll them up like a robe;
> like a garment they will be changed.
> But you remain the same,
> and your years will never end.

In the current context of Hebrews 13, the author has a specific reason for interjecting this confession concerning the Son's immutablity. The key lies in the phrase "who spoke the word of God to you" from verse 7. The proclamation of the gospel had played a significant role in the founding of this church. That event, now in the distant past, perhaps has faded in the minds of those who are struggling with the faith. With this Christological statement the author reminds his audience that the same Christ who was so real to their community in the beginning, as they were ministered to by their former leaders, presently sits in his exalted state and will rule perpetually. Although their circumstances and perspectives change, Jesus Christ and his gospel do not.

It is important, therefore, that the congregation guard against "all kinds of strange teachings," to which some were being drawn (13:9). These teachings evidently promised spiritual strengthening through ceremonial foods and apart from God's grace found in Christ. In first-century Judaism participants celebrated special cultic meals, particularly the fellowship meal, as a means of communicating the grace of God. These meals involved the blessing of God, thanks for his grace, and prayers of request. More broadly, Jewish meals were understood to give spiritual strength—strength for the heart—through the joy experienced at the table (Ps. 104:14–15). Every meal offered faithful Jews the opportunity to reflect on God's goodness and thus be nourished spiritually. It reminded them that the ultimate expression of thanks to God for redemption must be made via the thank offering and the fellowship meal at the altar in Jerusalem. Some Jews of Diaspora Judaism, moreover, celebrated special fellowship meals in an attempt to imitate the cultic meals of the temple.[18]

Some of the recipients of Hebrews are perhaps being drawn away from Christian fellowship and doctrine to theological expressions heralded within a community practicing Judaism. They are embracing aspects of Jewish community life and thought that are at odds with the gospel of grace through Jesus Christ. The author asserts that such ceremonial foods have no "value to those who eat them." They are not the true means of grace and spiritual strength. When he states, "We have an altar from which those who minister at the tabernacle have no right to eat" (v. 10), he reiterates the demarcation between those who participated in the old covenant religion and the members of the new covenant. Although it is not clear exactly what he has in mind regarding the Christian's "altar," this much is certain: The participants of the new covenant draw spiritual sustenance and life from a source unavailable to those of the tabernacle, and that source is the sacrifice of Christ.

Speaking of the offering on the Day of Atonement, Leviticus 16:27 reads, "The bull and the goat for the sin offerings, whose blood was brought into the Most Holy Place to make atonement, must be taken outside the camp; their hides, flesh and offal are to be burned up." This verse forms the backdrop of Hebrews 13:11–14, which reiterates the author's interpretation of Christ as the Day of Atonement sacrifice (9:11–14, 24–28; 10:1–4). With 13:12 the author draws two parallels between Jesus' sacrifice and that of Yom Kippur. (1) "Jesus also suffered outside the city gate." As the old covenant atonement sacrifices were taken outside the camp, so Jesus was taken outside the city of Jerusalem. (2) The purpose of Jesus' sacrifice was "to make the people holy." Jesus' high-priestly offering, however, was "through his own blood," one vital point in the author's extensive defense of that offering's superiority (9:11–28).[19]

Having reasserted the superiority of Jesus' sacrifice and thus the superiority of Christian doctrine, the author offers an application in 13:13–14: Believers must reject the tempting security of Judaism and be resolute in their identification with Christ. Throughout the book the author has encouraged his audience to go into ("enter") God's "rest" (4:11) or the heavenly Most Holy Place (4:14–16; 6:19–20; 10:22). Now, however, he challenges the hearers to "go out."[20] The "camp" represents the religion of Judaism, grounded in the tabernacle rituals of the old covenant.

---

18. For a lucid explanation of this interpretation of 13:9–10 see Lane, *Hebrews 9–13*, 533–35.

19. See above, pp. 311–12.

20. Attridge, *The Epistle to the Hebrews*, 398–99.

For the listeners to turn their backs on Judaism will mean rejection and "disgrace," such as that experienced by Christ. The motive for bearing this disgrace has to do with the eternal perspective offered at the end of chapter 12 (12:25–29). Judaism, a religion wed to the old covenant, is depicted as an aspect of the present world that will be shaken to pieces at Christ's return. By contrast, new covenant believers have "an enduring city," one "that is to come"—the heavenly Jerusalem (12:22). Thus, Christians should hold to their confession of Christ in the face of opposition because his sacrifice means lasting holiness and his "city" is one that will endure.

Although Christians should not participate in the Jewish cultic meals, they have their own appropriate "sacrifices" to offer (13:15–16). These offerings are to be made "through Jesus," since Christ, the mediator, has made it possible for believers to come before God in worship (9:9–14; 10:1–14). The writer details two spiritual sacrifices in 13:15–16. (1) He exhorts the readers to "continually offer to God a sacrifice of praise," which he explains as "the fruit of lips that confess his name." The words translating "sacrifice of praise" occur in the LXX of Leviticus 7:12 and speak of the highest form of peace offering under the old covenant.[21] This thank offering was voluntary and could only be made after the expiatory offerings had been presented and the worshiper was ritually clean; its primary purpose was to express gratitude to God.[22] However, the author's explanatory comment concerning the "fruit of lips" shows that he has in mind a metaphorical application of this language found in the Psalms, where the "sacrifice" is the prayer of thanks (e.g., Ps. 50:14, 23; 107:22; also 2 Chron. 29:31).

(2) The Christ-follower is also to offer a sacrifice of good deeds (13:16). Already having emphasized the necessity of good works in the form of ministry to others (e.g., 10:24; 13:1–3)—activities in which these believers had been engaged in the past (6:10; 10:34)—the author reminds them again to be faithful in this regard. The word translated "share with others" (*koinonia*) emphasizes a life in the covenant community, in which members meet the practical needs of one another. As the life of faith pleases God (11:6), so the sacrifices of praise and practical ministry give him pleasure.

With 13:17 the writer returns to the subject of the church's leadership, this time focusing clearly on current leaders. The members of the congregation have a responsibility to "obey" these leaders and to "submit to their authority." The verb translated "obey" (*peitho*) as used by ancient authors had various nuances. It could mean to "conform one's actions" (e.g., Gal. 5:7; James 3:3), but it could also connote the idea of "being persuaded by" or "putting one's

---

21. Westcott, *The Epistle to the Hebrews*, 445.
22. See W. A. VanGemeren, "Offerings and Sacrifices in Bible Times," in *EDT*, 791–92.

confidence in."[23] The further injunction to "submit to their authority" (*hypeiko*) means the listeners are to have "a readiness to comply" and may indicate a strained relationship between the leadership and some members of the Christian community.[24]

The admonitions to obey and submit probably relate to the leaders as deliverers of proper instruction, a focal role of early Christian elders (1 Thess. 5:12; 1 Tim. 5:17). Thus, these two commands involve yielding to and respecting the leaders as they give direction concerning right Christian doctrine. By guiding the church in doctrinal integrity the leaders "watch over" (*agrypneo*) the lives of those committed to their charge. This word, when used metaphorically, means to be spiritually alert or wide awake (see Mark 13:33; Luke 21:36; Eph. 6:18). The responsibility associated with such leadership is weighty, since the leaders must "give an account" of their instructional oversight (James 3:1).

Consequently, instead of working against them, the members of the congregation are to yield to their leaders so that their ministry may be carried out with "joy." The phrase "not a burden" can be translated as "not groaning." When members of the church fail to submit themselves to the leadership, the leaders end up working under an emotional burden that gives them a life filled with sighs. Such a condition is "of no advantage" to the congregation since ministry is diminished by undue emotional stress.

The author rounds out his series of admonitions with a personal request in 13:18–19. In saying "pray for us," he uses an "authorial plural," a stylistic device by which he refers to himself (cf. 5:11; 6:9).[25] The exhortation to pray is in the present tense and should be understood as durative: "Keep on praying." In saying, "We are sure that we have a clear conscience and desire to live honorably in every way," the writer commends himself to his hearers as one for whom they should pray as a good Christian leader (2 Cor. 1:11–12; 4:2). He specifically asks them to pray that he "may be restored" to them, indicating that he was a member of this church, who, for whatever reason, had been prevented from rejoining them.

Benediction and Closing (13:20–25)

THE AUTHOR OF Hebrews has given his readers a well-crafted exhortation for right Christian thinking and living. The stakes are high, for their spiritual con-

---

23. Spicq, *Theological Lexicon of the New Testament*, 3:74–77.

24. Lane, *Hebrews 9–13*, 554.

25. See Attridge, *The Epistle to the Hebrews*, 402; Bruce, *The Epistle to the Hebrews*, 386; against Lane, *Hebrews 9–13*, 556–57, who understands the "us/we" as referring to the author and leaders of the church as a group.

dition is at stake. We would expect, therefore, that his closing statements have been given much thought.

In the ancient world benedictions were important to an address, and in the Jewish context specifically a benediction was an aspect of worship.[26] They expressed a wish of well-being for the reader or hearer and often followed a general formula, such as our author's "may the God of peace," common in Paul's letters, and "to whom be glory for ever and ever. Amen" (13:20–21). However, a writer could craft a benediction to address specific needs of the audience or to express a summary of his main message. Thus, the author of Hebrews ends with a prayer containing the essential elements of his book. At the heart of his message is Christ's work of effecting the new covenant and God's work in us to do his will. The author wants believers to live out God's will in light of the work of Christ. Therefore, we come back to the foundational relationship between right thinking and right living.

The writer begins his closing in verse 22, urging the readers to bear with or "put up with" his "word of exhortation," a rather diffident request that is rhetorical in nature. The expression "word of exhortation" is probably a technical phrase referring to a sermon (cf. Acts 13:15, where Paul and companions are invited to give a "message of encouragement" in a synagogue service; the same expression is used in both places: *logos parakleseos*). This understanding is not diminished by the next statement: "for I have written you only a short letter." The Greek text does not contain the word "letter" and would be better translated, "I have written to you briefly." The author is referring to the writing down of his sermon. That he has written "briefly" is a literary convention of the day, a polite statement included at the end of a correspondence.[27]

The "Timothy" of verse 23 is commonly assumed to be Paul's missionary companion. If so, his "release" indicates an incarceration not mentioned in Acts or elsewhere in the New Testament. In any case, Timothy is a companion of the author and is known to this church. The author expects him to arrive soon and anticipates that they will travel together to see the recipients of Hebrews.

The book closes with a formal greeting and a final blessing (13:24–25). The author greets the leaders and the saints generally, using a common literary form of the day. He also sends greetings from those from Italy who are currently with him,—presumably the destination of the author's correspondence.[28] His closing blessing states simply, "Grace be with you all."

---

26. J. L. Wu, "Liturgical Elements," in *DLNT*, 660.
27. Lane, *Hebrews 9–13*, 568–69.
28. See above, p. 20.

IS THERE A **bridge?** The NIV Application Commentary series seeks to treat each text of the New Testament in a three-step process, addressing the original context, the contemporary significance, and dynamics by which the original and the contemporary concerns are bridged. One assumption behind this approach is that such a bridge is both possible and desirable. But that is not an assumption shared by all who interpret Scripture. Some scholars believe that the modern reader's presuppositions so skew interpretation that "objective" reading of any ancient text is impossible. To them, the author's original meaning is lost to modern Christians, so that we must make our own meaning; the text merely serves to stimulate responses from the interpreter's own framework. Others suggest that bridging from the message of the New Testament to the contemporary scene is not even desirable. They reason, 'The morality represented by these ancient texts belongs in a museum and is completely irrelevant for modern life."

Why do we believe that the prescriptions concerning hospitality, for instance, or sexual ethics, love of money, and church leaders should be followed today? Are these perhaps just throwbacks to a social structure that has long since passed from the scene, disintegrating in the light and heat of modern learning?

Perhaps the most graphic departure from these guidelines found in Hebrews 13 is in the area of sexuality. For many in modern culture the sanctity of the marriage bed is a nonissue. Adultery and sexual immorality are so widely accepted in the Western world as to barely raise a yawn, much less an outcry. In some circles the love of money is seen as a virtue rather than a vice, and in a democratic society, who wants to talk about submission to leaders or anyone else? For many in the modern world it does no good to say simply, "The Bible says so!" What reasons can we give that these should be brought across the bridge of interpretation as of contemporary significance?

(1) The early Christian movement was far from homogeneous culturally. That movement assimilated people of both Jewish and Greco-Roman cultures, spanned continents, and broke down barriers of race. The earliest Christian writers give us examples to follow as they taught Christian ethics concerning money, sexuality, family, and church structure across cultural lines. They bridged the gap between different contexts in their world. The technical term for lists such as the one found in Hebrews 13:1–6 is *paraenesis*, and scholars have noted that such lists occur throughout the New Testament. The parallels between these lists of ethical teachings indicate that the early Christians, following in the path of their Jewish heritage, shared a common understanding of how life should be lived from a Christian perspective.

(2) Early Christian teachers had a body of Scripture we call the Old Testament, parts of which were written more than a millennium prior to its use by the earliest Christ-followers. Certainly, many of the contemporaries of first-century believers would have considered the Ten Commandments outdated. The view that people of the first century generally were prudish is naïve from a historical perspective. Sexual immorality in a wide variety of forms was rampant. The prescriptions concerning the purity of the marriage bed in Hebrews 13:4, therefore, would have been considered absurd to many. Yet Jesus himself and the authors of the New Testament practiced interpretation and application of the "much-older" Testament, bridging the contexts between the messages found in their scrolls and their own world. Thus, we have a precedent for bridging the context between the world of an ancient body of literature and a later time period.

(3) The moral guidelines found in Hebrews 13 are grounded not in a person's existential sense of morality but in a covenant relationship with Jesus Christ, who is "the same yesterday and today and forever." The exhortations to love others by practicing hospitality and caring for their needs when oppressed are grounded in revelation from God. Commands concerning marriage fidelity and greed span the covenants because the holy God is God of both covenants, and his requirements concerning morality do not change. Furthermore, the warnings concerning the end of the age indicate that the new covenant will be in force until that time. Changes in the winds of social and cultural thought do not change God's covenant or his moral requirements.

Therefore, we suggest that the cultures of the ancient and modern world can be bridged through proper interpretation. Not only is it possible, but it is also mandatory from a Christian perspective. Our faith is grounded historically in God's revelation through his Son, Jesus Christ, and in the apostolic witness. To depart from the basic theological and ethical teachings of the New Testament, therefore, is an egregious error for those who call themselves Christians.

Across the bridge. One of the supreme challenges in teaching (or commenting!) through the book of Hebrews has to do with its theological orientation. Many moderns are so oriented to "daily practical application" that a theological treatise threatens to overwhelm them. As I have argued and attempted to demonstrate throughout the commentary, however, theology has a pervading relevance for daily life.

But as we come to Hebrews 13, we find a wealth of so-called "topics for practical application." We can identify with the essential importance and relevance of issues concerning marriage and sexuality, money, caring for the suffering, and leadership. Most of us probably struggle with one or more of those issues on a weekly if not daily basis. The difficulty here, however, involves narrowing the scope of our application. A book could be written on any of these topics. Potential pitfalls are legion. What is a commentator, preacher, or teacher to do?

If you have the time, a series of messages, lessons, or personal Bible studies would be in order. The topics here are as fresh and vital as any topics in your morning newspaper. Unfortunately, I share the author of Hebrews' time and space constraints ("And what more shall I say? I do not have time to tell about ... ," 11:32)! Therefore, let me suggest that we proceed as follows. The instructional part of Hebrews 13 divides into two primary movements: the practical instructions of verses 1–6 and the guidelines surrounding church leadership in verses 7–19. What primary issues lie at the heart of each of these passages? How can parts of the material here be used in an illustrative manner to address those primary issues?

Verses 1–6 demonstrate that true Christian commitment involves living out commitment to Christ in the nitty-gritty of daily living. Beds and bankrolls cannot be separated from theology. This is where the reality of our relationship with God is manifested. The dusty and crowded sidewalks, the kitchen tables, the lunchrooms and lounges, are the places where we must "confess his name" and "do good and ... share with others" (13:15–16) if we are to live authentically as believers. We must work out these principles in daily practice.

Verses 7–19, by contrast, concern Christian leaders and their role in leading the church through right doctrine. Just as the first six verses address Christian living "out in the world," the next thirteen address life "in the church." At least three issues are paramount here with regard to a leader's role. (1) Leaders are responsible for living in such a way that their lives are worthy of imitation. (2) They must lead the way in holding to right doctrine, which will lead to right identification with Christ and his church. (3) They are responsible for caring for those under their charge, and those under their charge are responsible for facilitating their leadership.

Notice the orientation of this passage, however. *These remarks are addressed to the church members in response to their leaders!* (1) Church members are to keep in mind the example of godly leaders, scrutinizing the outcome of their manner of life and imitating their faith. In our application, therefore, we must reflect on those in our church life whom we should be holding up as examples worthy of imitation.

(2) Church members are to respond to leadership by embracing right doctrine, valuing the Christian community and Christian thought more than the comfort and community offered by other groups that do not believe the gospel. Believers are to respect and yield to their leaders in this regard, being teachable when it comes to Christian instruction.

(3) Believers should offer to God "thank offerings" for the sacrifice of Christ and should perform practical ministry to one another in the community of faith. The impetus for such worship and work is the work of Christ, who has redeemed and leads the community.

(4) Finally, members of the church should reflect on the effects of their responses on the church's leadership. Does a relationship with you or me facilitate their difficult work or hinder it? This does not mean that members of a church are to give their leaders a "blank check" or uncritical deference in all situations. The leaders need accountability and members of the church must exercise spiritual gifts. However, when leaders are living within biblical guidelines and teaching faithfully the central tenets of the Christian faith (the focus here is on the sacrifice of Christ as the communication of God's grace), church members should seek to make the leaders' ministry a joy. Application, therefore, involves reflection on how this can be accomplished. When leaders are ministering faithfully and members of the church are following with right attitudes, it is to everyone's "advantage" (v. 17).

EVERYDAY CHRISTIANITY. ONE of the most insidious dynamics in the modern church involves the bifurcation of life into two spheres, the sacred and secular. The life of the spirit and the life of the street, meant to be integrated, instead are ripped apart and thrown in different directions. Where this aberrant vision of the Christian life prevails, "church language" has the hollow thud of wordy noise rather than the ring of authenticity.

> When Christ-following truth is no longer spoken in street language, when it is no longer directed at street life, and when it no longer challenges men and women to live as Christ-followers in those streets, there is no longer a chance for real-world faith. People are tamed, learning how to act with deftness inside the religious institutions. But they do not learn how to live faithfully in the real world.[29]

Real-world faith is replaced by a shallow substitute—a spiritual-looking, institutionalized religion that is completely irrelevant to everyday life. The vibrant, zesty fullness and realness of true Christianity is replaced by a tame spiritual vapidity that must be checked inside the door of the church lest it vaporize under the heat of the streets.

Conversely, it is through the devoted living for God in common aspects of life that the truth of the gospel is proclaimed in a thousand varied voices, and

---

29. MacDonald, *Forging a Real-World Faith*, 165.

the kingdom is built. In the common practices of financial management, date nights, cleaning dirty faces and dirty bottoms, integrity at work, care for the burdened or oppressed, and hospitality God finds pleasure, for these are worthy sacrifices when presented on an altar made holy by the blood of Christ.

For example, a healthy sexual relationship within marriage gives a platform for truth's proclamation to the world and a joyful dance of worship before God. In marriage pleasure and fidelity we shout against the inevitability of marital breakup and adultery proclaimed by the godless. Our healthy marriages trumpet the redemption of people from self-centeredness and destructive, immoral life patterns. The bed becomes a mini-church in which the two covenant members sacrificially and ecstatically meet one another's needs and offer their bodies as living sacrifices in worship before God. We should remind the world that God created the wonder and fireworks of sex long before the advent of the glossy, counterfeit sex-sellers of modern culture.

Nevertheless, our sexuality rumbles as thunder in our bones, a power both beautifully dynamic and horrifically damaging in its relational potential—both in relation to people and God. Author Mike Mason writes:

> Surely it was God's full intention for the physical joining together of a man and a woman to be one of the mountaintop experiences of life, one of those summit points of both physical and mystical rapture in which He Himself might overshadow His people in love, might come down among them and be most intimately and powerfully revealed. How horribly tragic, therefore, that it is here at this very point, here at this precious male-female encounter which ought to be overflowing with holiness, here that godless people have succeeded in descending to some of the most abysmal levels of human degradation.... Sex is sacred ground.... It is more conspicuously than anywhere else, the place where the angel and the animal in man meet face to face, and engage in mortal struggle.[30]

This mortal struggle is why we need to be reminded of guidelines such as those found in Hebrews 13:6. Good marriages and good sex do not just happen; they take thought and effort, both born of a selfless willingness to live for God in the details of life over a long period of time. It may also be that the intensity of the struggle increases proportionately the worth of this pleasing sacrifice.

Money is another area that tests the authenticity of our devotion to God. The heart that is too close to the back pocket is out of place and grows

---

30. Mike Mason, *The Mystery of Marriage: As Iron Sharpens Iron* (Portland: Multnomah, 1985), 150.

numb to the good gifts and provisions of God. Again, it provides an arena in which great spiritual vitality can be grown and demonstrated.

Corrie ten Boom recounts an event from her childhood that well illustrates the power of keeping money in perspective. The ten Boom family prayed one morning that God would send a customer that day to the family's shop to purchase a watch, the income from which would pay bills that had come due at the bank. During that day a customer with a large sum of cash came into the store. He picked out and paid for an expensive watch but, at the same time, complained about a Christian watchmaker, suggesting that the merchant had sold him a defective piece of merchandise. Casper, Corrie's father, asked the man if he could examine the watch that was not working properly. Only a minor repair was needed, which Casper made, assuring the customer that he had been sold a fine quality watch that would work well for him. He then gave the astounded gentleman his money back, and the man returned the watch for which he had just paid.

Little Corrie asked, "Papa, why did you do that? Aren't you worried about the bills you have due?" Her father responded, "There is blessed and unblessed money," explaining that God would not be pleased with the ruination of another believer's reputation. God would provide, he assured her. Just a few days later another man came into the shop and paid for the most expensive watch produced at that time. The purchase not only allowed the family to pay their bills, but also provided the funds for Corrie to receive training in Switzerland as a watchmaker for two years.[31]

C. S. Lewis once remarked, "He who has God and everything has no more than he who has God alone." The truth of this statement and freedom from the love of money can elude rich and poor alike. The poor struggle against the clinging, grasping demands of daily existence. An empty stomach, a lack of transportation or social advancement, and dire surroundings can cry out against God's promise of provision as a mockery. The rich, by contrast—and the vast majority of Christians in the Western world should be considered rich by the world's standards—experience the drowning out of God's promises by their super supply of material things. "Provision? Who needs provision?" Such questions are but a short step away from, "Who needs God?"

Along these lines James warns the poor and rich to think rightly. The poor should take joy in their exalted status as Christ's persons; the rich should focus on their low station as Christ's servants and on the temporality of life (James 1:9–11). We cannot be both lovers of money and lovers of God because these loves divide our allegiance, passions, and efforts in life (Matt. 6:24). Thus, if

---

31. As told in Stacy and Paula Rinehart, *Living in Light of Eternity: How to Base Your Life on What Really Matters* (Colorado Springs: Navpress, 1986), 103.

we are to be effective Christ-followers, productive members of his covenant community, we must keep ourselves "free from the love of money."

In areas such as marriage and money the worlds of the spirit and the street meet. Such meeting places either become dance floors on which we move to the music of his will or a stage of games on which we play at Christianity with dichotomized, hypocritical hearts. Everyday. Everyday. God wants us and wants us to want him in the nitty-gritty wonder, the plain and exalted dance of everyday.

Follow the leaders. Kent and Barbara Hughes tell of the wife of a close pastor friend, who relates a humorous nighttime encounter with her husband. One night she awoke to find her sleeping husband on elbows and knees at the foot of their bed. With his arms wrapped around some unseen object before him he was mumbling to himself. The startled wife asked, "George! What on earth are you doing?" "Shhh," the sleeping pastor answered. "I'm holding a pyramid of marbles together, and if I move, it's going to tumble down." A pyramid of marbles—an appropriate metaphor for a church leader's ministry![32]

In the years I have been involved in ministry, it has struck me how naïve some church members are about the realities of daily church leadership. Most pastors have heard with chagrin, "So, I know you preach on Sunday. What do you do the rest of the week?" One close friend of mine, a layperson in his church, suddenly found himself thrown into (over his head!) a critical leadership position because of the pastor's sudden departure from the church. The circumstances of that departure and the continuing needs of a young congregation made for late nights and weary days. My friend, who has been involved in church faithfully for many years, exclaimed, "I had no idea!!!" Most do not, unless they have been there.

Church leaders, especially those who serve as the "main minister" or "pastor," have difficult jobs. In many contexts they are expected to wear the multiple hats of social coordinator, superb orator (several times a week), sensitive and insightful counselor, administrator, motivator, teacher, evangelist, mender of relationships, "marryer," and "buryer"—all the while cultivating an exemplary personal, spiritual, and family life. The pressure to spend hours in study, hours in the community, hours in visiting prospects, hours in counseling, hours in training the staff, and hours in prayer all add up to unrealistic expectations on the part of the church. The effect can be overwhelming.

In 1925 the great theologian Karl Barth was offered the pastorate of a church in Neumunster near Zurich, Switzerland. Reflecting on his previous

---

32. R. Kent Hughes, *Liberating Ministry From the Success Syndrome* (Wheaton, Ill: Tyndale, 1987), 177.

pastorate he sighed, "I am troubled by the memory of how greatly, how yet more greatly, I failed finally as a pastor of Safenwil.... The prospect of having to teach children again, of having to take hold of all kinds of practical problems ... is really fearful to me."[33]

So what can you and I do in response to our church leaders? I would like for us to reflect on a number of questions in light of the principles found in Hebrews 13:7–17. (1) Church members are to keep in mind the example of godly leaders, scrutinizing the outcome of their manner of life and imitating their faith. Who are those leaders in your church life that you should be holding up as examples worthy of imitation? Have you of late thought carefully about the fruit of a great leader's life, using that scrutiny as a motivation in your own spiritual life? Do the expectations your church has of its pastor(s) facilitate a spiritual life that is worthy of imitation, or is the pastor so overwhelmed with responsibilities that there is little time to be with God in prayer and study?

(2) Church members are to respond to the leadership by embracing right doctrine, valuing the Christian community and thought more than the comfort and community offered by groups who do not believe the gospel. Are you respecting and yielding to your leaders in this regard, being teachable when it comes to Christian instruction? Are you struggling with the pull of social or religious groups outside the Christian community, and have you begun to drift from thinking clearly about Christ? Do you value the community of faith? What in your life demonstrates clearly that value? Do you value your leaders' seriousness about right doctrine? Do you encourage their theological training, their further education? Or do you fight against it? Do you cloud church discussions by downplaying the leaders' pleas for theological reflection?

(3) Believers should offer to God "thank offerings" for the sacrifice of Christ and should perform practical ministry to one another in the community of faith. The impetus for such worship and work is the work of Christ, who has redeemed and leads the community. Are you characterized by thankfulness to God, or are you a grumbler, constantly finding fault with people and processes in the church? Are you engaged in meeting the needs of others in the church on a weekly basis? Do you see your ministry as a sacrifice that pleases God?

(4) Members of the church should reflect on the effects of their responses on the church's leadership. Does their relationship with you facilitate the difficult work of your church leaders or hinder it? Are you a source of emotional refreshment or emotional fatigue? Does your pastor leave you with a

---

33. T. H. L. Parker, *Karl Barth* (Grand Rapids: Eerdmans, 1975), 49.

song on the lips or a groan in the heart? What might be a way you can show encouragement to your church leaders this week?

Church life is difficult. Relationships get strained because the church is full of real people. But when church leaders lead well, living lives worthy of imitation, and when church members follow their lead, the kingdom is built. God is pleased. This helps and benefits all.

Conclusion. So, dear reader of this commentary, we come to the end of Hebrews. Thank you for taking up this volume. Unless you are unusual, you have not read it from beginning to end—we do not normally interact with commentaries in that way! However, whatever your circumstance—whether you are doing personal study in Hebrews, have stopped by this wonderful New Testament book for a brief look at an isolated passage, or are engaged in leading others through a more detailed study—I pray that you will heed "the word of exhortation" that is Hebrews. May you grasp fully the message of the exalted Christ, who has died for our sins and lovingly embraces us in the new covenant. May you consider him, fixing your eyes on the author and perfecter of our faith. May you heed the warnings and exult in the promises of this book, following the good examples such as Abraham and Moses and avoiding the errors of the bad. May you receive an inheritance with the saints in the heavenly Jerusalem as we worship with the angels "in joyful assembly." In the words of Hebrews 13:20–21:

> May the God of peace, who through the blood of the eternal covenant brought back from the dead our Lord Jesus, that great Shepherd of the sheep, equip you with everything good for doing his will, and may he work in us what is pleasing to him, through Jesus Christ, to whom be glory for ever and ever. Amen.

Scripture Index

Genesis

1–2	151
1	375
2	152–53, 157, 159
2:2	149, 152, 160
3:1–7	146
3:17–18	221
4:4	375
4:6–7	178
4:7	376
4:10	422
5:24	376
6:1–9:17	377
9:5–6	92
11:31	377
12:1–9	377
12:1–3	28
12:2–3	378
12:4–7	28
14	257
14:17–20	252–53, 255–56, 259
15:5	378
15:6	378
17:1–8	378
18:2–15	435
18:10–15	378
19:1–22	70
19:13	435
21:1–18	241
22:1–8	379
22:15–18	241
23:4	379
26:34	405
27:27–40	380
27:30–40	405
28:15	437
31:32	435
48:8–22	380
50:24–25	380

Exodus

1:22	380
2:1–4	380
2:14	381
3:2–6	70
12:22	314
13:2, 15	69
13:17–14:31	382
14:15	382
14:19–20	70
16:7	48
16:32–34	298
19:12–13	418
19:16–22	417
19:16–19	418
19:18	418
20:18–21	417
20:18–19	418
22:19	92
22:29	69
24	49
24:3–8	313–14
24:8	314
25:1–31:11	298
25:10–16	298
25:22–30	298
25:31–40	298
25:40	280
26:35	298
27:20–21	299
28:1	187–88
28:4–39	177
28:29–30	178
29:1–46	187
29:29–30	174
29:38–43	299
30:7–8	299
31:10	174
32:32	421
33:11	145, 349
33:13	349
33:18	48
36:2–39	298
39:1–31	298
40:1–38	298

Leviticus

1–6	187
4:3	174
7:12	441
8:1	188
8:7–9	177
11:44	303
14:4–7	314
14:10	312
14:51–52	314
16	49, 314–15
16:1–25	174, 187, 311
16:5	187
16:6–17	299
16:11	188
16:14–19	314
16:15–16	311
16:15	187, 311, 315
16:16–19	315
16:20–22	187, 311
16:27	440
16:32	174
18:22	92
20:10–14	92
23:26–28, 32	154
24:8	299
27:26	69

Numbers

3:13	69
12:7	127
14:1–38	131
14:32–35	157
15:27–31	355
15:29–30	188
16:5	188
17:10–11	298

18:7	174	
18:21–32	254	
19	314	
19:1–2	311	
19:4	314	
19:6	314	
19:9	49	
19:17–19	314	
23:19	245	
25:11–13	174	
27:21	178	
35:16–21	92	
35:25–32	174	
35:25, 28	174	

Deuteronomy

4:10–14	418
4:11	418
4:13	419
4:24	423
5:22–27	418
6:4–5	349
9	131
9:7	131
9:8–11, 15	419
9:19	418–19
9:24	131
11:13	349
13:3	349
13:8	356
17:2–7	356
22:24	92
29:18	404, 409
30:6	349
31:6–8	437
32:3	49
32:7	358
32:8	97
32:35–36	358
32:43	67

Joshua

1:5	437
2:1–15	382
20:6	174
21:43–45	383

Judges

2:1–15	70

4:8–16	383
5:5	422
7:7–25	383
10:6–12:7	383
13:1–16:31	383

1 Samuel

15:22	328
16:14–16	408

2 Samuel

7:14	67–68
8:15	383
12:4	435
13:36–37	69

1 Kings

10:9	383
11:1–6	349
17:8–16	247
17:17–24	384
19:1–8	70

2 Kings

4:17–37	384
12:10	174

1 Chronicles

3:1	69
29:11	49
29:15	379

2 Chronicles

26:20	174
29:31	441

Nehemiah

12:10–11	174

Job

11:20	92
18:14	121
34:11	92
42:3–4	105

Psalms

2	75
2:6	420
2:7	47, 67–68, 71, 189, 194

2:8	47
8	100
8:4–6	71, 96–98, 106
8:6	99
9:7–12	421
9:8	421
19:1–6	81
19:8	376
22	190
22:1	109
22:7–8	109
22:16–18	109
22:22	109–10, 114, 116
27:8	349
33:20–22	251
39:12	379
40:7–9	327, 329, 330
40:7	328
44:23–26	103
45:6–7	67, 71, 219
50:2	420
50:8–10	328
50:14, 23	441
51:10	349
56:2–3	357
58:11	421
62:12	92
68:8	422
69:29	421
77:18	422
78:22, 32	131
82:8	421
91:11–12	247
94:2	421
95	138, 149, 152–53, 155, 159–60
95:7–11	125, 129, 131
95:7–8	130
95:7	155
95:11	152–53
96:13	421
97:7	67, 69, 76
102:25–27	67, 74
102:26	282
104:4	67–69, 76
104:14–15	439
106	131
107:22	441

109:9	310
110:1	49, 53, 67–68, 70–71, 77, 97–100, 279, 328–30, 399
110:2	189, 194, 241–42, 245, 252–54, 256, 265–67, 279, 420
116	190
118:6–7	437
119:11	171
119:84	421
145:3, 6	49

Proverbs

1:24–31	92
3:11–12	396, 400
3:12	400
3:21	84
4:23	343
4:25–27	403
4:26	403
19:25	401
24:12	92

Isaiah

1:10–13	328
4:3	421
5:1–6	224
6:1–13	169
8:14	109
8:17–18	109, 116
11:4	421
26:20–21	360
27:9	327
28:23–29	224
35:3–8	402
40:5	48
45:7	408
53:5	182
53:12	268
58:7	435
59:20–21	327

Jeremiah

4:6	408
5:3	401
6:7	401
7:21–24	328
11:11	92
17:9	349
22:16	421
29:13–14	349
29:13	183
31:31–34	280–81, 295, 313, 330
31:34	334
33:3	183
42:5	376

Lamentations

3:59	421

Ezekiel

7:3, 27	92
19:10–14	224
46:11	420

Daniel

3:16–30	384
6:23	384
8:10	357
10:20–21	97
12:1	97, 421
12:3	107

Hosea

2:11	420
6:6	328

Joel

2:32	420

Amos

1:2	420
3:6	408
5:21	420

Micah

4:2	420

Habbakuk

1:13	303
2:3–4	360, 376

Haggai

2:6	417, 422

Zechariah

5:4	92
12:3	357

Matthew

1:20–24	70
3:10	224
4:1–11	172
4:5–7	247
5:16	291
5:22	92
5:34–37	246
5:48	303
6:7–15	333
6:21	349
6:24	399, 437, 449
6:34	423
7:3	345
7:15–23	136
7:16	232
7:19	224
7:22–23	143
7:22	233
9:35	85
10:40	126
11:28–30	166
12:31	339
15:24	126
16:16	68
16:27	92
17:5	320
21:16	96
22:39	435
23:14	92
24:8–10	104
24:42	361
25:35	435
25:36	436
25:41–46	92
26:36–46	190
26:63	68
27:35	109
27:39–44	221
27:43	109
27:45–46	105
27:46	109, 345
28:9	175
28:19–20	213

Mark

1:9–11	68
1:15	85
1:31	175
3:22–30	357
4:19	349
7:2	357
7:3–4	175
7:5	357
8:29	68
9:27	175
9:37	126
9:42	188
11:24	103
12:30	263
13:2	283
13:9–13	104
13:33	442
14:32–42	190
15:43	289

Luke

1:1–4	89, 93
1:6	281
1:32	68
1:67–79	290
2:8–14	76
2:41–50	68
3:21–22	68
4:1–13	68
4:41	68
6:41	126
7:36–47	435
9:32	48
10:16	126
10:20	421
10:34–37	435
12:24	345
12:33	282
16:13	399
17:2	188
18	318
20:23	345
21:27	320
21:36	442
22:20	280
22:32	268
22:40–46	190

23:50	289
24:21	310

John

1:1	79
1:2	48
1:3	47
1:9	218, 327
1:13	113
1:14	48, 114
2:11	48
2:19–22	310
2:19	283
3:18	102
4:22	288
5:1	288
5:16–18	288–89
5:29	102
5:46	381
6:14	327
7:4	360
7:18	195
8:39–44	290
8:46	195
10	291
11:27	68, 327
12:24	318
12:31	102
13:34	435
14:30	195
15:6	224
15:20	366
17	268
17:5	48
18:28	405
19:23, 31–36	109
19:38	288
20:31	68

Acts

1:9	320
2:10	20
2:22–36	89
2:22	86
2:26	123
2:38	218
3:1–10	86
3:11	175

3:16	50
4:7, 10	50
4:23–31	68
5:29–42	104
5:34	436
6:14	283
7:20	380
7:37	381
7:38	84
8:20	218
9:1–19	273
9:20–22	68
10:1–11:3	285
10:28	357
10:45	218
11:17	218
12:7–11	70
12:13	191
13:14–15	24
13:15	443
13:32–34	69
13:33–34	68
14:3–11	86
15:1–2	285
15:39	345
16:18	50
17:22–31	79, 82
18:2	20
18:24–28	26
19:13–17	50
21:4–17	435
22:17–22	285
23:6	123
26:7	123
26:24–29	89
27	243
27:39	345

Romans

1:1	23
1:4	69
2:3	92
2:4	399
2:6–7	222
2:14–15	363
3:24	313
4:1–5:12	164
4:19	345

5:1–2	235	3:12	436	11:14	79
5:2	123	3:13–15	222	12:12	86
5:4–5	247	3:16	348	12:21	333
5:15, 17	218	4:5	218	13:5	135–36
6:1–4	142	4:15	407		
6:4	292	5:10–11	437	**Galatians**	
6:8–14	142	7:31	423	1:6–10	88
6:21	205	8:6	47	1:11–16	23
8:7	97	9:10	219	1:23	387
8:9	135, 362	10:1–11	133	2:16–19	164
8:17	48, 107, 135	10:6–12	233	2:20	123
8:23	136	11:2	128, 344	3:16	290
8:25	123, 247	11:25	280	3:19–20	312
8:28	105, 408	11:27	333	3:19	84
8:29–30	136	12	436	4:4	126, 274
8:29	69	13	435	4:26	420
8:31–34	268	15:1–8	89	5:2–5	8
8:31–32	351	15:1–6	93	5:5	123
8:35–39	245	15:2	128, 344	5:6	9
8:35–37	104	15:8	23	5:7	441
9:6	290	15:14–15, 17	93	5:13	345
9:6–7	290	15:19	123	5:16	292
9:25–29	67	15:20	122		
9:33	109	15:25–27	99, 104	**Ephesians**	
10:2	263	15:26	121	1:18	218
10:9–10	143	15:27–28	97	1:20–22	99
10:18–21	67	15:27	96	1:21	50
11:8–10	67	15:28	47, 97	1:22	96–97
11:22	135	15:43	107	2:1–2	292
11:25–26, 28	290	15:54–55, 57	123	2:8–10	164
11:26–27	327	15:56	111	2:10	232, 292
12:10	435	16:7	206	3:7	218
12:12	247	16:16	97	3:9	74, 218
12:13	435			4:1–16	436
13:1	97	**2 Corinthians**		4:7	218
13:8	435	1:11–12	442	4:15	210
14:15	292	1:20	290	4:19	437
15:13	248	1:22	136	5:2	292
15:19	86	2:9	323	5:3	107
		3:6	280	5:8	292
1 Corinthians		4:2	442	5:21, 24	97
1:17–29	62	4:8–12	104	6:4	401
1:23–24	107	5:5	136	6:5, 12	97
1:23	109	5:17	235	6:17	156
1:30	313	5:21	195	6:18	442
2:8	48	7:5	183	**Philippians**	
3:1–2	202	7:9–10	333	1:6	136, 222
3:2	204	9:15	218	1:29	105

2:5–11	55, 61	**1 Timothy**		1:10	47, 54, 439
2:6–7	114	2:5	312	1:11	282
2:6	48	2:10	107	1:13	47, 54, 57,
2:9	50	3:2	435		96–97, 100,
2:10–11	97	3:3	437		114, 279, 439
2:15	281	3.16	115	1:14	54, 107, 222
3:6	281	4:1, 6	387	2:1–4	20–21, 68, 72,
3:21	48, 97, 107	4:14	85		79–80, 97, 106,
4:13	405	5:17	442		125, 157, 194, 203,
		6:12	397		226, 356, 361, 417
Colossians				2:1–3	422
1:5	123	**2 Timothy**		2:1–2	127
1:15	48, 69	1:10	218	2:1	23, 202, 275, 404
1:16–17	74	1:16	436	2:2	54, 242
1:16	47	2:15–16	62	2:3–4	47, 151, 219, 357
1:18	69	2:25	333	2:3	23, 26–27, 242
1:22–23	135	3:12	366	2:5–9	28–29,
1:23	247	3:16	401		58, 71, 106,
1:24	105				125, 231, 402
1:27	107	**Titus**		2:5	47, 54, 69
2:15	360	1:2	123	2:7	54, 189
2:19	175	1:8	435	2:8–9	47, 74
2:20–23	116	1:15	405	2:9	54, 107, 189, 218
3:5–10	292	2:1	107	2:10–18	27–29, 96,
3:18	97	2:5, 9	97		98–99, 125,
3:25	92				132, 187, 326,
4:5–6	291	**Hebrews**			400, 408, 435
4:18	436	1:1–4	20, 28, 86, 217	2:10	65, 126, 132,
		1:1–3	27		178, 334, 399
1 Thessalonians		1:1–2	86, 190, 284	2:11	126, 329
1:3	345	1:2–3	156, 219	2:12	58, 126
3:13	281	1:2	68, 84, 439	2:14–15	65, 203
4:3–6	437	1:3	68, 71, 126, 189,	2:16	54
4:8	396		279, 329, 331, 439	2:17–18	126, 179, 187
4:9	435	1:4–2:18	27	2:17	134
4:13–14	122	1:4	134, 222	2:18	131, 179
4:13	123	1:5–2:18	28–29,	3:1–4:16	192
5:9	136		106, 125	3:1–4:13	27
5:12	442	1:5–14	28–29, 50, 57,	3:1–19	430
5:17	348		83, 97–98, 114,	3:1–18	361
5:16–18	408		125, 159, 194, 326	3:1–6	19, 21, 27, 58,
		1:5–7	54		190, 207, 343, 380
2 Thessalonians		1:5	47, 58, 189–90	3:1–2	223
1:4–8	402	1:6	57, 420	3:1	54, 80, 99, 112,
2:13–14	136	1:8	57, 439		173, 219, 227
2:14	48	1:9	114, 126, 219	3:3	54, 189
2:15	175	1:10–12	439	3:6	175, 226,
		1:10–11	58		227–29, 247, 344

3:7–4:2	21	5:3	111	7–10	283
3:7–19	27, 31, 84,	5:4–10	174	7:1–28	28–29, 245,
	149, 162, 207,	5:5	134		326, 343, 357
	219, 382, 422	5:7–10	107	7:1–10	29, 186, 243,
3:7–11	219	5:7–8	179		265, 271, 278
3:7–9	225	5:7	126	7:1	112, 191, 207
3:7	155, 329	5:8	69	7:7	50, 54
3:8, 10, 18	169	5:9	108, 134, 222,	7:11–28	29, 174,
3:12–13	414		334, 399		186, 243, 252,
3:12	164, 404, 417	5:11–6:20	174, 186–87,		278, 280–81
3:13	34, 59, 345		192, 278	7:11	334
3:14	175, 219,	5:11–6:12	244–45	7:15–22	174
	226–29, 344, 374	5:11–6:3	21–22,	7:16–25	174
3:16–19	225		240, 244, 287	7:17	330
3:18–19	160, 164	5:11	134, 240, 252, 442	7:19	50, 54, 128,
4:1–3	361	5:13	219		222, 247, 334, 399
4:1–2	27, 228–29	5:17–20	292	7:22	50, 54, 222, 312
4:1	136, 227, 404	5:21–48	292	7:26–28	174, 420, 439
4:3–11	21, 27	6:1–3	111	7:26	54
4:11	440	6:1	219–20	7:27–28	186, 315
4:12–13	21, 219,	6:2	92	7:28	334, 399
	226, 234, 358	6:4–20	355	8:1–6	269
4:12	260	6:4–12	361	8:1–2	29, 65, 420
4:14–10:25	28, 346	6:4–9	136	8:1	49, 54, 57, 310, 329
4:14–5:3	111	6:4–8	21, 38, 200,	8:2	174–75
4:14–16	28, 65,		222, 240, 244,	8:3–10:18	29, 154,
	126–27, 144,		345, 355		245, 271, 343
	278, 340–42,	6:4–6	404	8:3–13	326, 357
	346, 420, 440	6:4	37, 54	8:3–6	29
4:14	21, 54, 111–12,	6:6	203, 366, 417	8:3	296
	127–28, 135, 143,	6:9–20	21	8:5	54, 296
	149, 227, 342–44	6:9–12	200, 240, 355	8:6–13	296
4:15–16	65	6:9–10	206	8:6	50, 54, 222, 267,
4:15	117, 191, 195–96	6:9	54, 135, 208, 442		310, 312
4:16	111, 149, 268,	6:10	345, 441	8:7–13	29, 174,
	376, 417, 419	6:11	128, 136, 343		297, 422
5:1–10:18	194, 347	6:12–15	439	8:8–12	330
5:1–7:28	278–79	6:12	34, 54, 241	8:10	343
5:1–11	326	6:13–20	240, 355, 383	8:12	313
5:1–10	28–29, 242,	6:13–17	111	9	333
	265, 271,	6:13–15	223	9:1–10:18	29, 49, 65,
	278, 343	6:17–20	174		278, 296
5:1–7	227	6:17	54	9:1–28	174
5:1–3	174, 269–70,	6:18	128, 175,	9:2	299
	311, 315		218, 246, 398	9:5	420
5:1	111–12, 279–80	6:19–20	420, 440	9:8	271, 329, 342
5:2–3	175	6:19	23	9:9–14	441
5:2	188, 355	6:20	178, 346	9:9	333–34, 399

9:11–10:18	357	10:23	21, 127–28,	11:34	134
9:11–28	269, 326, 440		135, 143, 175, 247	11:35–12:3	22
9:11–14	422, 440	10:24–25	22, 414	11:35	50, 54
9:11	175, 297	10:24	287, 441	11:36–37	104
9:12–28	297	10:25	59, 111, 161,	11:39	104, 397
9:12–14	381		173–74, 366	11:40	50, 54
9:13–14	329, 357	10:26–31	22, 226, 228	12:1–3	107, 116,
9:13	49, 327, 344		345, 404, 417		127, 381
9:14–15	280	10:26–27	287	12:1–2	22, 59, 80, 99,
9:14	300, 333	10:26	220		223, 417
9:15	54	10:27	224	12:1	188, 287
9:17	242	10:28–31	92	12:2–3	179
9:18–22	381	10:29	108, 329	12:2	57
9:23–25	297, 357	10:30–31	38	12:3–17	435
9:23–24	54, 175	10:30	87, 228	12:3–13	22
9:23	50, 54, 222,	10:32–39	22–23	12:4	22, 385
	271, 327	10:32–34	22, 26, 381,	12:5–13	135
9:24–28	440		384, 438	12:7	22, 381
9:25–28	328	10:32	135, 218, 381	12:8	219
9:25–26	297	10:33	134	12:9	97
9:26–28	107	10:34	50, 54, 176,	12:12	31
9:28	102, 130, 136,		222, 436, 441	12:14–17	22
	222, 229, 329,	10:36	33, 381	12:17	22, 54
	404, 426	10:37–39	426	12:18–24	22
10:1–18	174, 269,	10:37–38	376	12:22–26	54
	297, 316, 356	10:37	403	12:22–24	65, 122, 126
10:1–14	441	10:39	226, 228		135, 229
10:1–4	440	11–13	238	12:22	54, 441
10:1	399	11	132, 397–99, 406	12:23	152
10:2	300	11:1–40	34, 343, 439	12:24	50, 54, 222, 312
10:4	218	11:1	165, 290	12:25–29	226, 441
10:5–11	49	11:2	397	12:25	84
10:10	108	11:3	48	12:26–29	22
10:11	49	11:6	218, 417, 441	12:27	126
10:12–13	297	11:7–8	54	12:28–29	15
10:12	57	11:7	134	12:28	152
10:14	108, 229,	11:12	54	12:29	224
	230, 357, 421	11:13	127	13:1–6	59, 287
10:15–18	280, 422	11:14–16	126	13:2	54
10:18	220, 245, 301	11:15–16	122	13:3	22, 359
10:19–25	29, 65, 126–	11:16	50, 54, 152,	13:5	345
	27, 173, 278		417, 420	13:7–24	26
10:19–22	315	11:17–19	241	13:7	21
10:19–20	154, 178	11:23	69	13:8	80, 245
10:19	360	11:24–26	290	13:9	22
10:22	152, 300, 333,	11:24	134	13:12–13	22
	376, 417, 440	11:32	23, 446	13:12	329
		11:33–34	104	13:13	22, 220

13:14	122, 152, 420	3:22	97, 99	2:5	333
13:15	127	4:9	435	2:12	156
13:16	22, 287	4:14	402	2:13	175
13:17	21	5:5	97	2:16	333
13:18–19	436			2:19	345
13:18	300	**2 Peter**		2:25	175
13:20	408	1:4	436	3:3	333
13:21	189	1:7	435	3:11	175
13:22	24	3:10, 12	423	3:19	333
13:24	20–21, 27, 135			4:11	74
		1 John		5:5	101
James		1:6–7	292	10:1	320
1:2–4	387, 402, 408	2:3	136	10:6	74
1:9–11	449	2:5–6, 19	136	11:12	320
1:13	178	2:6	292	14:10–11	92
1:17	387	2:10	435	14:14–16	320
1:23–24	345	2:11	292	19:15	156
2:10	333	2:17	338	20:14	110
2:14–26	136, 164, 388	2:19	231	21:1	423
2:14	232	2:28	361	21:4	104
2:15–16	222	3:2	404	22:12	101
2:21–23	164	3:3	247, 431		
3:1	442	3:5, 7	195	**Apocrypha**	
3:3	441	3:10	435		
4:15	206	3:16–20	222	*Wisdom*	
		4:1–6	8	16:3	219
1 Peter		4:1	79		
1:3	182	4:7–8	232	*1 Maccabees*	
1:19	195, 312, 436	4:7	435	9:30	438
1:22	435	4:20	232		
2:2	202	5:9	376	*2 Maccabees*	
2:8	109			6:19, 28	384
2:11	379	**Jude**		7:1–41	384
2:21	104	3	387	14:16	438
2:22	195	8	405		
3:1, 5	97			*Sirach*	
3:14	402	**Revelation**		17:17	438
3:18	195	1:5	69	33:19	438
		1:16	156	51:28	219

Subject Index

a fortiori argument, 84, 86, 246, 356, 417, 401; *see also* argument from lesser to greater
Aaron, 311
Abel, 376, 422
Abraham, 241, 250, 252, 254, 377–79
acceptance by God, 401
access to God, 301
accomplishments, 335
accountability, 91, 163, 209, 352
acting on God's word, 145
adultery, 437
agricultural imagery, 221
aliens and strangers, 379
allegory, 140
ambiguity of language, 223
anchor, 243
ancient rhetoric, 25
angelic powers, 97
angels, 19, 49, 69, 71, 72, 97, 417; as mediators, 84; modern view, 78
anti-Semitism, 284, 288
Apollinarianism, 115
apostasy, 20, 37, 229, 231, 404, 426; effect of, 414
application, 59
appointment of Christ as high priest, 127, 186, 265
argument from lesser to greater, 84, 86, 246, 356, 417, 401
argument from silence, 254
ark of the covenant, 298
asceticism, 116
ashes of red heifer, 311
assimilation into church, 146, 428
assurance of salvation, 141–42, 338, 404
authentic Christianity, 447
authentic relationships, 210
"author," Christ as 398
author's intent, 261

authority, 87, 197; crisis in, 77; of Christ, 49, 72; structures, 362
authorship of Hebrews, 23
autonomy, 89
awe of God, 169
awesomeness of God, 169

baptisms, 205
Barak, 383
basic Christian teachings, 201
being a thinking Christian, 263
benediction, 443
benefits of discipline, 402
"better than" motif, 54, 222, 271
bitterness, 18, 404, 409
blessing, 254, 405; of God, 221
blood, 299, 309, 311, 318–19, 381, 400; of Christ, 311–14, 357; of the covenant, 49, 357
boldness, 128, 392
Bonhoeffer, Dietrich, 181–82
Bread of the Presence, 298

Calvinist-Arminian debate, 37, 226–32
ceremonial meals, 440
challenge of communication, 32
chiasmus, 192
Christ, appointment as high priest, 127, 186, 189, 265; as "champion," 108; as King, 70; as perfecter of faith, 398; as Son, 68; blood of, 417; death, as fitting, 107; effect of death, 110, 315; immutability of, 439; obedience of, 195; perfection of, 195; person of, 47; priestly activity of, 328; sacrifice of, 164; sinlessness of, 195; solidarity with humans, 113; status of, 47; suffering of, 116; work of, 47
Christian community, 207, 352
Christian tradition, 94
Christians as holy, 126
Christological interpretation, 256, 262

Christology, 55, 116
church, 419–20; leadership, 441
Claudius, 17, 359
cleansing, 311
Clement of Rome, 21
cloud of witnesses, 397
coming of Christ, 431
commendation by God, 376, 390
commitment, 88–89
communion of the saints, 210
communism, 391–92
community, 345
"companions," 126
compassion, 359
conditional clauses, 134, 135–37
confidence, 128, 222, 342, 360; in God, 374
confrontation, 207, 209, 211
conscience, 300, 312, 333
considering Jesus, 126
context, importance of, 158
conversion, 235
"courage," 128
covenant, 271, 295, 313
Covenant Community view, 227
creation, 20, 47
cross of Christ, 321, 399
crucified Lord, 107
crucifixion, 220
cultural challenge to communication, 32
culture war, 387

Daniel, 384
darkness, 418
date of Hebrews, 22
David, 153, 383–84
Day of Atonement, 49, 154–55, 174, 176, 187, 244, 299, 315, 320–21, 315, 346, 440
day of Christ's return, 346
Dead Sea Scrolls, 68
"dear friends," 222
death, 319, 384; fear of, 120–21; victory over, 121–23
death angel, 381
defilement, 404
deity of Christ, 80

deliberate sin, 355
deliverance, 95
depression, 248
desert wanderers, 225
despair, 248
divine decree, 196
divine revelation, 46, 86
devotion, 328
devotional life, 145
difficulty of Christian living, 409
diligence, 223
discipleship, 211, 274
discipline, 400
discouragement, 18–19
disdain for Christ, 357
disgrace, 381, 441
disobedience, danger of, 133
dispelling of confusion, 99
divine oath, 267
Docetism, 115
drawing near to God, 176, 183–84, 267, 299, 305, 341, 349
drifting, 21, 84, 87
dynamic Monarchianism, 58

early church life, 208
education, early Christian, 208
eisegesis, 158
Elijah, 384
Elisha, 384
emotional fatigue, 400
encouragement, 18–19, 22, 130, 146, 238, 345, 353, 359
endurance, 351, 401, 405
enemies of God, 71, 73
"enlightened," 217–18
Enoch, 376
eros, 56
Esau, 405, 406
eternal judgment, 205
eternal offering, 309
evangelism, 237, 274
exaltation, 47, 49, 69, 279
example list, 374, 386
examples of faith, 374; use of, 132–33
excitement, 424
exhaustion, spiritual, 403
exhortation, 21, 27, 132, 224, 443

exposition, 28
externalization of Christianity, 293

facing of hardship, 412
faith, 222, 343, 373; and obedience, 146; and works, 164; as a "leap," 164; as a race, 397; definition of, 390; living by, 386
faithfulness, 125–29, 137, 361
falling away, 219
falling in the desert, 129
family, spiritual, 435
fear, 394; of death, 23, 111; of God, 163
fellowship, 345
fidelity in leadership, 132
filial faithfulness, 128
finality of Christ's sacrifice, 329
fire, 418
firstborn, 69, 419–20
fixing our eyes on Jesus, 398
focus on Jesus, 400
"forever," 266
forgiveness, 49, 280, 334, 337, 422, 425
forsaking God, 345
forsaking other Christians, 345
freedom from guilt, 337
fruitfulness, 221
future grace, 430

gender-specific language, 113
genealogical descent, 266–67
genre, 224
Gentiles, 20, 285
Gethsemane, 190
Gideon, 383
glory, 48, 189
Gnosticism, 115
God, as eternal, 245; as Judge, 426; as omnipotent, 245; faithfulness of, 244; his will, yielding to, 198; holiness of, 303; image of, 48; integrity of, 245; presence of, 320
good works, 345, 441
gospel, 336–37, 439; proclamation of, 289
grace, 386, 425, 427
"guarantee," 267
guilt, 332–33

hardship, 384
health and wealth gospel, 164–65, 247, 337, 387
hearing the gospel, 151
heart devotion, 343, 349
heaven, 49, 279–80, 309, 320, 323
heavenly calling, 126
heavenly Jerusalem, 417, 419–20, 441
Hebrews, as pastoral appeal, 37; authorship of, 23–27; background of, 19; date of, 22; main message of, 30; main themes of, 53; structure of, 27–30
heirs, 242
help from God, 437
heroes, 138, 386
high priest, 111, 174
high priesthood, 186; qualifications, 174
historicity of Christianity, 93
"hold on," 128
holding to faith, 130, 175, 344
holiness, 305, 306, 404, 425; of God, 427
Holy Place, 298
Holy Spirit, 362
honor, 436
hope, 238, 243, 247, 248, 271, 403, 431
hospitality, 435
house church, 18, 20
humanity of Christ, 118
humility, 284
hymn, 55
hypothetical view, 226

identification with Christ, 362
imitation, 446
immaturity, 204
"impossible," 217–18
inadequacy of old covenant, 281
inaugurated eschatology, 99, 101, 111, 228
incarnation, 47, 106–7, 113–15, 189, 327; reasons for, 110–11
inclusio, 185, 278
inheritance, 47, 313, 405
inner life, 145

insulting the Spirit, 357
intercession by Christ, 268
intermediary transition, 149
interpretation, 32, 157–58, 261
involvement in church life, 348
Isaac, 241, 379
Islam, 275

Jacob, 405; and Esau, 380
Jephthah, 383
Jesus, as apostle, 126; as example, 127;
    as high priest, 178; blood of, 425
Jewish worship, 19–20
Jewish people, 20, 285
Joshua, 382
joy, 399, 424, 429
Judaism, 284–85
judgment, 356, 358
justification, 333

Kadesh, 157

lampstand, 298
last days, 46
law, old covenant, 326
laying on of hands, 205
leaders, 21, 438–52
level paths, 403
Levites, 254
Levitical priests, 328
Levitical priesthood, 265
limitations, 35
listening to God's Word, 84
"literalist" interpretation, 160
"living and active," 156
losing heart, 400
love, 345
Luther, Martin, 288, 345, 435

marriage, 436, 448
martyrdom, 17
maturity, spiritual, 204
mediator, Christ as, 312
Melchizedek, 186, 243, 252, 254, 256
message of salvation, 84
Messiah, 17, 309
messianic psalms, 109
milk, spiritual, 202
ministry, 232, 238

ministry of the priests, 299
miracles, 389
misconceptions of faith, 387
missing God's grace, 404
money, love of, 449–50
morality, 291, 316–17
Mormonism, 275
Moses, 19, 125, 127, 311, 380–81, 418;
    as an example, 132
Most Holy Place, 176, 244, 299, 342
motivation, 345
mountain, 418–20

"name," 49–50
Navigators, the, 212
need for perseverance, 22
negative examples, 129, 234
Neoapollinarianism, 117
Nero, 22–23
New Age, 78
"new and living way," 342
new covenant, 280–81, 330, 417, 419–20
Noah, 377

oath-making, 246
oaths, 241–42
obedience, 132, 195, 229
obeying leaders, 441
occult, 77
offering for sin, 309
old covenant, 417
Old Testament, 19, 24, 73, 259–60,
    284; use of, 24–25, 193
original hearers, 19
outcome of faith, 389

pain, 408, 412
paradigm shifts, 273
parallelism, 56
parental discipline, 401, 407–8
"partakers," 217–18
Passover, 381
pastors, 21
patience, 250
peace, 404
peers, 352
people of God as a "house," 127

perfection, 108, 191, 195, 265–69, 271, 329, 334
persecution, 17–18, 88–99, 104, 359, 361, 400, 436
perseverance, 35, 224, 231, 241, 345, 352, 360
phenomenological true believer view, 228
phenomenological unbeliever view, 230
pilgrimage motif, 151
pluralism, 291
postmodernity, 261
pragmatism, 59
prayer, 176, 183, 197–98
preacher, 24
preaching, 61, 170–72, 361
preconversion Jew view, 227
presuppositions, 223
priesthood, 243
prison, 436
progressive revelation, 274
promises of God, 241
psalms of righteous sufferer, 190
pseudo-community, 210
public identification with the church, 360
punishment, 88, 91
purification, 49

rabbinic interpretation, 25, 159
race imagery, 397; 405–6
radiance, 48
Rahab, 382
ransom, 313
real faith, 168
rebellion, 355
Red Sea, 382
redemption, 309–10
regeneration, 235
regulations, 297
rhetorical questions, 185, 266
rejecting Christ, 219
rejection, 441
relational theology, 275
relationship with God, 424
relationships, 276
relevance of Hebrews, 35

religious tolerance, 291
relinquishment, 197–98
remembering the past, 358
renunciation of the gospel, 233
repentance, 205, 219–20, 235
repetition of themes, 346
rest, 149–72
resurrection, 205
return of Christ, 426
revelation, 20
rewards, 241, 376
rhetorical impact, 206
right hand, 49
Rome, 17–20
rule of Christ, 47

Sabbath, 154–55, 429
Sabbath rest, 162
sacrifice, 187, 357, 440
salvation, 191, 222, 224, 231, 309, 422
Samson, 383
Samuel, 383
sanctification, 333
sanctuary, earthly, 297
scandal of the cross, 321
scapegoat, 187, 311
science and faith, 80
scorning shame, 399
Scripture, 362; interpreting, 256; memory, 170–72; reading, 170–72; use of, 170
security, 249
self-actualization, 89
sermon, 34, 45, 443; form, 50; Hebrews as, 434; of first century, 24
servant faithfulness, 128
sex, 436
sexual immorality, 437
sexuality, 448
shadow, 280
shaking heaven and earth, 422
shame of the cross, 399
shaming Christ, 220
shift in genre, 131–32
sin, 307; as entangling, 397
Sinai, 310, 417, 424
sincere heart, 343
sinfulness, 303

slave, 18
solid food, 202
solidarity of Christ with humanity, 108
Sonship of Christ, 45–46, 50
Song of Moses, 358
sound interpretation, 34
spiral of interpretation, 158
spirituality, apathy in, 85; boundaries, 418; community, 353; development of, 208, 362; disciplines in, 211; drifting, 129; formation, 211; laziness, 223; lethargy, 201; nakedness, 156; reference points in, 78; struggle of, 404
sprinkled hearts, 344
sprinkling of blood, 314
stability in life, 243
standing before God, 333
standing with Christ, 368–69
storm, 418
strange teachings, 439
subjection to Christ, 98–99
submission, 97, 307, 441
submission to God, 402
suffering, 436
superiority of Christ's offering, 280, 297
supersessionism, 284, 289
sword imagery, 156
sympathy, 359
synagogue, 17, 19, 20, 24; services, 24

tabernacle, 299, 310
"tasted," 219, 255
temptation, 111
temptation of Jesus, 175, 178–79
thanks to God, 336–37
theological instruction, 203
theological language, 57; as analogical, 113

theology, 58; interpretation of, 59; relevance of, 445
thinking critically, 263
tithe, 253, 254
torture, 384
training in character, 401
transitions, 112, 149, 279
tribe of Judah, 266
Trinity, 76
triumphalism, 284
trivialization, of the cross, 321; of God, 169
true heart, 343
trumpet blast, 418
trusting God, 379
truth telling, 209
"two unchangeable things," 242
typology, 257

unanswered prayer, 102–6
unblemished, 312
unconverted church members, 167
unfruitfulness, 221

veil as barrier, 342
verbal analogy, 149, 159, 255
vindication, 421
volunteerism, 319

warning, 130, 217–18, 355, 422
warning passages, 225–26
way to God's presence, 342
"weak," 266
wholeness, 205
winning, 22
wisdom, 20
word of God, 48, 156, 422
word of salvation, 85, 93
world, 69
wrath of God, 422

Zion, 417, 419–20, 424

We want to hear from you. Please send your comments about this
book to us in care of zreview@zondervan.com. Thank you.

GRAND RAPIDS, MICHIGAN 49530 USA

ZONDERVAN.COM/
AUTHOR**TRACKER**